FREAKERY

FREAKERY

CULTURAL SPECTACLES OF THE EXTRAORDINARY BODY

EDITED BY

Rosemarie Garland Thomson

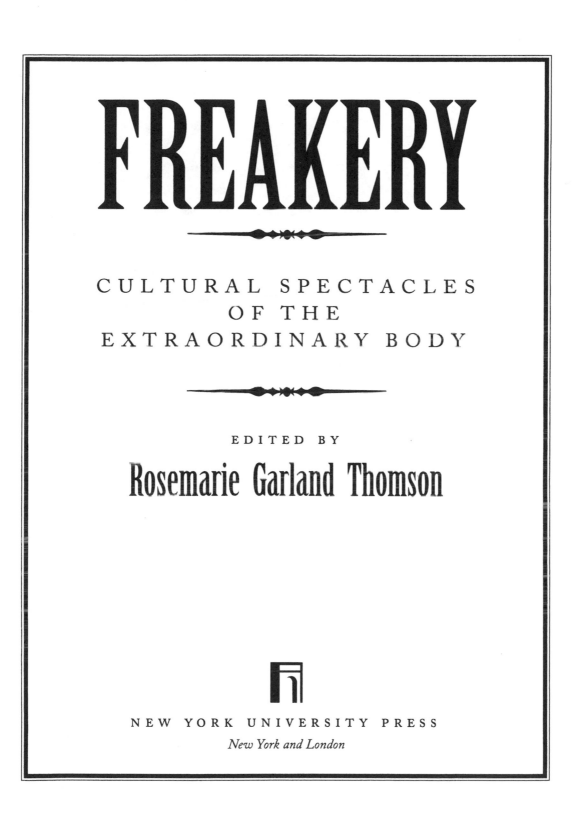

NEW YORK UNIVERSITY PRESS

New York and London

NEW YORK UNIVERSITY PRESS
New York and London

TEXT PERMISSIONS:
A version of chapter 2 originally appeared in *Social Semiotics* 1, no. 2 (1991): 22–38.
A version of chapter 3 originally appeared in *Actes de la recherche en sciences sociales,* September 1994.
A version of chapter 4 originally appeared in *Disability, Handicap and Society* 7 (1992): 53–71.
Lyrics to the song "Me Too" (Woods/Tobias/Sherman) reprinted by courtesy of The Hal Leonard Publishing Company, Shapiro, Bernstein and Co., Inc., Al Sherman Music, and the Songwriters Guild.
In chapter 18, program note in the Pacific Film Archives series "Received Images: A Reading of Disability in Cinema," University Art Museum and Pacific Film Archive *Calendar,* July 1990; University of California at Berkeley; © Regents of the University of California.

Library of Congress Cataloging-in-Publication Data
Freakery : cultural spectacles of the extraordinary body / edited by Rosemarie Garland Thomson.
p. cm.
Includes bibliographical references and index.
ISBN 0–8147–8217–5 (cl. : alk. paper).—ISBN 0–8147–8222–1 (pb. : alk. paper)
1. Abnormalities, Human—Social aspects. 2. Body, Human—Social aspects. 3. Sideshows—History. I. Thomson, Rosemarie Garland
GT6730.F74 1996
391'.6—dc20   96–10034
                    CIP

New York University Press books are printed on acid-free paper, and their binding materials are chosen for strength and durability.

Manufactured in the United States of America

10 9 8 7

TO THE MEMORY OF
IRVING KENNETH ZOLA

CONTENTS

ILLUSTRATIONS

FOREWORD

LESLIE A. FIEDLER

When, nearly two decades ago, I published my pioneering study of the way in which self-styled "normals" perceived certain of their physically anomalous fellow humans traditionally called "freaks," scarcely any of my academic colleagues responded positively. This did not, of course, surprise me, since my earlier books, beginning with *Love and Death in the American Novel,* had been similarly ignored or calumniated by more orthodox critics and scholars, who—whatever the reigning orthodoxy—found them wilfully, perversely heterodox. For all their heterodoxy, however, these earlier books dealt primarily with works which even the most orthodox considered "canonical"—or at least plausible candidates for eventual canonization.

But in *Freaks: Myths and Images of the Secret Self,* I dealt at considerable length with what the critical establishment still thought of as subliterature: comic books, rock music, circus sideshows, and carnival Ten-in-Ones. What interested me in such pop forms, as it also had in High Art, was not their message or their medium but their underlying myths, especially the Myth of the Stranger. In this study, I found that the archetypal outsider was figured not by the woman, the homosexual, the Jew, the Red Man, and the Black, as it often has been in classic American literature. Instead, I discovered that the strangely formed body has represented absolute Otherness in all times and places since human history began.

Though at the moment my book appeared, the demeaning colloquial epithets for all exploited "minorities" had become taboo, I insisted on calling the most exploited of my brothers and sisters not by a politely euphemistic name like "special people" or a presumably neutral scientific one like *"terata,"* but simply "freaks": a designation then considered in some quarters as offensive as "faggot" or "nigger" or "kike."

Yet what offended some of my colleagues even more was that I talked about the protagonists of "great books" like Captain Ahab or Hester Prynne and sleazy circus performers like JoJo the Dog Faced Boy or the Bearded Lady, as if they were of equal cultural import. This seemed to them not merely a lapse in good taste, but a flagrant betrayal of what they felt to be their essential professional function and mine: to defend the standards of High Culture, indeed, of civility itself, against the onslaught of the leveling and hopelessly vulgar culture of the marketplace.

This was first made clear to me when I tried out the thesis of my still unfinished book at Johns Hopkins before an audience of graduate students and their teachers, most of them at that point newly converted to poststructuralism. Even as I spoke I could feel their silent resentment; and as I walked out I could hear them murmuring to each other that this was where they had foreseen I would end up: not merely as a critic of pop literature, but a pop critic as well. Though a couple of maverick students in the audience actually followed me back to SUNY Buffalo, this only served to confirm the doubts of their mentors, as did the marketplace success of my book when it finally appeared.

Though *Freaks* never became, of course, a real bestseller, it initially sold many more copies than any other book I published, even my now-classic study, *Love and Death in the American Novel.* The initial attention *Freaks* garnered was in large part because of the way it was marketed by Simon and Schuster. For a while, everything seemed to be working out to our mutual profit and delight. To begin with, I was reviewed in periodicals which seldom if ever noticed the publication of any book written by a Ph.D. These included the *Daily News, Penthouse, Hustler,* and even *High Times,* whose readership was drawn largely from the drug-obsessed generation of the sixties, young men and women who though physiologically "normal," liked to refer to themselves as "freaks." The mention of my name in such places persuaded even my youngest and freakiest son (then just turning fifteen) that I existed not just in the Neverland of academia but in what was to him the only real world, the hyperspace of mass culture.

So, too, it persuaded the masters of the postprint media who presided over the large audience who never read the *New York Times Book Review,* but watched the *Phil Donahue Show,* the *Today Show,* the *Tomorrow Show,* the *Late, Late Show*—sometimes even the *Dick Cavett Show.* When I first began the book about freaks, they were starting to dominate the postprint media. The story of the "Elephant Man," for instance, was attracting record audiences in movie houses and on television, even as more grotesque variations from the human norm, in the guise of aliens from outer space, were achieving similar box-office success. Simon and Schuster, therefore, had no difficulty persuading the producers of talk shows to let me promote my book before their cameras. I ended up talking about the freak as stranger to this hypothetical mass audience on all of these shows.

To be sure, more often than not such appearances turned out to be comedies of errors. None of my hosts, it became clear, had actually read my book. Worst of all, was my experience with Phil Donahue, when I found myself confronted (with no previous warning on either side) by a pair of conjoined twins and cast somehow as their heartless exploiter. The live studio audience, at any rate, clearly perceived me as such, self-righteously reviling and insulting me until I withdrew into an uncustomary silence. As they really do say—"that's Show Biz'." But the alacrity with which I agreed to appear on these shows made me realize that I had been on some buried level yearning to try to reach the mass audience.

In the hope of doing so, I had from the start determined to make *Freaks*—unlike anything I had written before—an illustrated book: so profusely illustrated, in fact, as to provide an alternative kind of text, available to the majority audience who may be unaccustomed to reading words with ease or pleasure but has no trouble with images on the printed page or the screen. I was especially pleased, therefore, by a letter from a librarian in Philadelphia who told me about a group of eight- or ten-year-old inner city kids who kept returning to stare with baleful fascination at the quasi-obscene images on the new page of *Freaks* to which she flipped daily in a copy she had displayed under glass. So, too, I was even more delighted when I discovered that someone had optioned the book for a possible movie. After all, persistent memories of Tod Browning's elegantly crafted movie, *Freaks,* had first triggered in me the meditations which eventuated in the book of the same name.

I had, moreover, always dreamed that one or another of my works would be translated into the more universally comprehensible language of film. Two times at least, that dream seemed tantalizingly close to being realized, but each time (as is true, I gather, of almost all such enterprises) these projects fizzled out after many false starts and unfulfilled promises, as did the desired filming of *Freaks.* Clearly, if my dream of breaking through to a larger and more varied audience was to be realized, I had to seek it elsewhere.

By the time I realized this, such a new audience was seeking me. It consisted, improbably enough, of precisely the sort of medical professionals whose initial reaction to my book had been generally quite hostile. They had not only been annoyed because I, a self-confessed amateur, had entered a territory they considered their own. To make matters even worse, I had challenged their attempt to redefine as potentially curable medical challenges many deviations from the physiological norm that had traditionally been regarded as awesome mysteries. What vexed them most, however, seemed to have been my offhand observation that more "malformed" babies had been allowed to die by what they euphemistically call "removal of life supports from inviable terata" than had been killed by ritual exposure in ancient times.

Quite unexpectedly, however, these medical professionals now keep inviting me to participate in the conclaves where they gather to discuss the ethical ambiguity of certain of their procedures which, ultimately, they are willing to confess trouble them almost as much as they do critical humanists like me. "Bioethics" is what such soul-searching among professionals in the health sciences has come to be called. Aware now that they are the amateurs in the area of ethics, they appeal for help from philosophers, theologians, sociologists, anthropologists, as well as an occasional humanist like me. Since writing *Freaks* put me well on the way to becoming a bioethicist without quite knowing it, I accept their invitations without hesitation. Moreover, my first attempt to explore that subject further was an essay called "The Tyranny of the Normal," originally delivered as a talk to health professionals, and then published in *Which Babies Shall Live?,* a collection of essays addressed to such an audience.

These days, indeed, I prefer talking to and writing for that audience rather than my colleagues, who often eschew the traditional vocabulary of esthetics or ethics. Therefore, I—who for many years ventured outside the classroom mostly to speak at meetings of the Modern Language Association or the English Institute—am now more likely to address a World Congress of Theologians or a session of the United Nations inaugurating the Year of the Handicapped. Consequently, my next collection of essays deals chiefly with topics like gerontology, child abuse, and organ transplants, setting them in the context of such long-time best-selling mythic works as *Frankenstein, Dracula, Dr. Jekyll and Mr. Hyde,* and *The Island of Dr. Moreau,* in which our fears and fantasies about doctors are made manifest.

At long last, doctors seem ready to listen, as they were not when *Freaks* was published. But when the book first appeared, the people whom the medical profession seek both to demystify and "cure" responded sympathetically to my book. Early on, for instance, I began receiving mail from dwarfs and midgets, who are often the most militant and articulate of show freaks. Later, I heard from women, homosexuals and bisexuals, those similarly cast as archetypal outsiders, albeit for their gender or sexual preference rather than their physiology. Presumably people such as these invited me more recently to speak after the showing of a film about a bearded lesbian at a meeting held about "Queer Theory," a field that celebrates human deviance in all its manifold forms.

So after twenty years, my apology for freaks seems to be current once again. Though it had earlier been allowed to go out of print, *Freaks* was recently reissued by Anchor Books. Apparently confused about its content and genre, however, the editors catalogued it as sociology rather than criticism. No such doubts, though, seem to have troubled the makers of the two anthologies about freaks due to be published before the year is out. One, called *The Tyranny of the Normal*, contains my essay of that name, a long passage from *Freaks*, essays about congenital malformations, and a selection of fiction and verses in which such people appear. The other book is, of course, this very volume, *Freakery: Cultural Spectacles of the Extraordinary Body*.

Most of this Foreword consists of afterthoughts on my own *Freaks* and reflections on its subsequent fate, rather than comments on the essays in this volume that it presumably helped inspire and that extend its ideas. Nevertheless, I have read all of the chapters that comprise *Freakery* with profit and pleasure, learning much from those that ventured into areas I had not myself explored. Although I am, to be sure, deeply grateful for the respectful references to me and my work, I am surprised a little that the essays here so comfortably participate in the academic arena and are so grounded by the scholarly apparatus that I myself sought to avoid in my flight from the traditional limits of criticism and toward a mass audience. It seems that my deliberately unfashionable book has opened the way for an innovative yet mainstream volume on a once iconoclastic subject that is nevertheless published by a university press, suitable for classroom use, and appropriate to both an interdisciplinary academic audience as well as the general reader. Although this is not what I expected my renegade book on freaks to occasion, I am pleased to have contributed to making such studies of popular culture like *Freakery* not only possible but integral to cultural studies, the academic field of inquiry my earlier work helped authorize.

LESLIE A. FIEDLER
Buffalo, New York

PREFACE AND ACKNOWLEDGMENTS

"You need to read this," said Irv Zola—father of academic disability studies—as he pulled piles of books for me from his office shelves in his characteristically generous manner one day in 1989 at Brandeis University. As he pressed into my hand a copy of Robert Bogdan's new study, *Freak Show: Presenting Human Oddities for Amusement and Profit*, I recoiled with horror. The lurid cover photo of a midget standing on a platform and the garish red book jacket, emblazoned with "FREAK," repelled and stunned me. "Freak" disturbingly summarized the accusation I had secretly most dreaded my entire life. Having recently come out as a person with a disability, and feeling nervous about my new professional mission of weaving disability studies into literary and cultural criticism, I was still fairly thin-skinned about confronting the negative images of disability I had previously disclaimed. Flatly refusing to read the book, I nonetheless deferentially left Irv's office with it, depressed by the suspicion that I could not possibly expose myself by calling attention in my scholarly work to what seemed then the personal bogeyman I had spent my whole life trying to get everyone to ignore. It was two years before I could bring myself to read Bogdan's book.

I survived *Freak Show*, however. In fact, the book consolidated the direction of my scholarly work and galvanized my professional aims. The notion that someone with a very visible physical disability might "come out" perhaps seems oxymoronic to those for whom the cultural assumptions that structure the normal remain unquestioned. Indeed, pressures to deny, ignore, normalize, and remain silent about one's own disability are both compelling and seductive in a social order intolerant of deviations from the bodily standards enforced by a quotidian matrix of economic, social, and political forces. That I am now authoring studies on freaks and editing this collection no doubt witnesses my own personal and professional journey within an academic community that is beginning to both accommodate and recognize disability as a political issue, a social construction, an individual difference, and a category of inquiry. Nevertheless, what enabled my own coming out, as well as the more important accompanying scholarly work, was discovering that disability studies is an emergent academic discourse in the social sciences that can be interrogated and infused into recent trends taken in the humanities by cultural studies and literary criticism.

Freakery has been created in such a spirit. Although it does not explicitly declare itself as a study of disability, its purpose is to reveal the practices and cultural logic that construct certain corporeal variations as deviant and to denaturalize the generally assumed opposition between normal and abnormal bodies. The essays assembled here invoke a wide range of disciplinary approaches within cultural studies to argue collectively that the freak is a historical figure ritually fabricated from the raw material of bodily variations and appropriated in the service of shifting social ideologies. In short, we show the freak of nature to be a freak of culture.

I wish to acknowledge gratefully that my own understanding of freaks, expressed in both the introduction and the orchestration of this volume, arises from research generously supported by the National Endowment for the Humanities Fellowships for University Teachers, the College of Physicians of Philadelphia's Wood Institute Research Fellowship, the Massachusetts Historical Society's Andrew W. Mellon Research Fellowship, and the Howard University Faculty Research Program in the Social Sciences, Humanities, and Education. The contributors to this collection also greatly expanded my understanding of freaks and their cultural contexts. I am deeply indebted to all the contributors for the outstanding scholarship that made this volume possible, and I appreciate their cheerful enthusiasm. I also offer thanks to Michael Gilmore, Eric Lott, Lenny Cassuto, Bob Bogdan, David Gerber, and Leslie Fiedler, all of whom encouraged my interest in freakmaking as a legitimate subject of inquiry and some of whom read my work at various stages. I am grateful as well to Michael Dumas, Fred Dahlinger, Fred Pfening, and Bob Bogdan for their help with illustrations. Particular thanks are due to Niko Pfund, editor-in-chief at New York University Press, who initiated the collection, supported it efficiently and generously at every stage, and whose good humor and compelling interest in freaks persisted throughout the project. As always, I am grateful to Bob, Rob, Lena, and Cara Thomson for their support and patience.

Rosemarie Garland Thomson
Washington, D.C.

ONE

Introduction: From Wonder to Error—A Genealogy of Freak Discourse in Modernity

ROSEMARIE GARLAND THOMSON

People who are visually different have always provoked the imaginations of their fellow human beings. Those of us who have been known since antiquity as "monsters" and more recently as "freaks" defy the ordinary and mock the predictable, exciting both anxiety and speculation among our more banal brethren. History bears ample witness to this profound disquiet stirred in the human soul by bodies that stray from what is typical or predictable. Such troubled fascination with the different body has occasioned enduring cultural icons that range from the cyclopic Polyphemus and the gigantic Goliath to werewolves and the seven adorable little dwarfs. Perhaps even the founding Judeo-Christian myth that Adam's body contained Eve, drenched as it is by millennia of interpretation, derives from reports of the rare condition *fetus in fetu*, in which tumors encasing fetuses are embedded in the bodies of their living siblings.[1] The presence of the anomalous human body, at once familiar and alien, has unfolded as well within the collective cultural consciousness into fanciful hybrids such as centaurs, griffins, satyrs, minotaurs, sphinxes, mermaids, and cyclopses—all figures that are perhaps the mythical explanations for the startling bodies whose curious lineaments gesture toward other modes of being and confuse comforting distinctions between what is human and what is not. What seems clearest in all this, however, is that the extraordinary body is fundamental to the narratives by which we make sense of ourselves and our world.

By its very presence, the exceptional body seems to compel explanation, inspire representation, and incite regulation. The unexpected body fires rich, if anxious, narratives and practices that probe the contours and boundaries of what we take to be human. Stone Age cave drawings, for example, record monstrous births, while prehistoric gravesites evince elaborate ritual sacrifices of such bodies. Clay tablets at the Assyrian city of Nineveh describe in detail sixty-two of what we would now call congenital abnormalities, along with their prophetic meanings. Aristotle, Cicero, Pliny, Augustine, Bacon, and Montaigne account for such disruptions of the seemingly natural order in their interpretative schemata. For these fathers of Western thought, the differently formed body is most often evidence of God's design, divine wrath, or nature's abundance, but it is always an interpretive occasion.

Perpetually significant, the singular body has been alternately coveted, revered, and dreaded. Their rarity made exceptional bodies instrumental and lucrative to those who appropriated them, even in precapitalist societies. For example, Egyptian kings, Roman aristocrats, and European royalty kept dwarfs and fools as amusing pets. Cheap, popular "monster ballads" in Renaissance England detailed the corporeal particulars of anomalous bodies and uncovered their hidden lessons: a cleft palate cautioned against lewd talk; missing fingers warned against idleness. An anxious England even made bestiality a capital offense in 1534, lest the occasional, unsettling birth anomalies that suggested hybridity might burgeon uncontrolled as testimonies to some threatening cousinship between man and beast.[2] Tributes to Matthew Buchinger—who was virtually armless and legless, but nevertheless powdered and wigged—record that he dazzled eighteenth-century Europe with his conjuring, musical performances, calligraphic skills, and marksmanship with the pistol.[3] Learned gentlemen of the early Enlightenment collected relics of the increasingly secularized monstrous body in their eclectic cabinets of curiosities, along with an array of oddities such as sharks' teeth, fossils, and intricately carved cherrystones.[4] As scientific inquiry began to eclipse religious justification, the internal anatomy of exceptional bodies was exposed in the dissection theaters and represented in early medical treatises upon which reputations were built. The cabinet of curiosity commercialized into such equally diverse popular museums as P. T. Barnum's famous American Museum, all replete with their sensationalized, hyperbolic narratives.[5] The ancient practice of exhibiting anomalous bodies in taverns and on streetcorners consolidated in the nineteenth century into institutions such as American circus sideshows or London's Bartholemew Fair, where showmen and monster-mongers proliferated in response to a seemingly insatiable desire to gawk contemplatively at these marvelous phenomena.[6] In a definitive bifurcation from the popular, nineteenth-century science officially enunciated teratology as the study, classification, and manipulation of monstrous bodies. As scientific explanation eclipsed religious mystery to become the authoritative cultural narrative of modernity, the exceptional body began increasingly to be represented in clinical terms as pathology, and the monstrous body moved from the freak show stage into the medical theater. Thus, even though the discourses of the anomalous body comprise a series of successive reframings within a variety of registers over time, the uneasy human impulse to textualize, to contain, to explain our most unexpected corporeal manifestations to ourselves has remained constant.[7]

As this very brief recapitulation of the exceptional body's appropriations in Western culture implies, what we might call "freak discourse" can be seen as a single gauge registering a historical shift from the ancient to the modern era. Although extraordinary bodily forms have always been acknowledged as atypical, the cultural resonances accorded them arise from the historical and intellectual moments in which these bodies are embedded. Because such bodies are rare, unique, material, and confounding of cultural categories, they function as magnets to which culture secures its anxieties, questions, and needs at any given moment. Like the bodies of females and slaves, the monstrous body exists in societies to be exploited for someone else's purposes. Thus, singular bodies become politicized when culture maps its concerns upon them as meditations on individual as well as national values, identity, and direction. Under the extreme pressures of modernity, it would seem, the significances imposed upon such bodies intensified and the modes of representation proliferated in ways from which we can coax fresh cultural understandings.

As a way to introduce the chapters that comprise this volume, I want to suggest in rather broad strokes here how freak discourse is both imbricated in and reflective of our collective cultural transformation into modernity. The trajectory of historical change in the ways the anomalous body is framed within the cultural imagination—what I am calling here the freak discourse's genealogy—can be characterized simply as a movement from a narrative of the marvelous to a narrative of the deviant. As modernity develops in Western culture, freak discourse logs the change: the prodigious monster transforms into the pathological terata; what was once sought after as revelation becomes pursued as entertainment; what aroused awe now inspires horror; what was taken as a portent shifts to a site of progress. In brief, wonder becomes error.

Consider, for instance, the semantic distinctions applied to anomalous bodies over time. Never simply itself, the exceptional body betokens something else, becomes revelatory, sustains narrative, exists socially in a realm of hyper-representation. Indeed, the word *monster*—perhaps the earliest and most enduring name for the singular body—derives from the Latin *monstra*, meaning to warn, show, or sign, and which has given us the modern verb *demonstrate*. Monsters were taken as a showing forth of divine will from antiquity until the hand of God seemingly loosed its grip on the world. When the gods lapsed into silence, monsters became an index of Nature's fancy or—as they now appear in genetics and embryology—the Rosetta Stone that reveals the mechanics of life. As portents, monsters were the premier manifestation of a varied group of astonishing natural phenomena known as prodigies, marvels, or wonders. Under the sign of the miraculous, comets, earthquakes, six-legged calves, cyclopic pigs, and human monsters confirmed, repudiated, or revised what humanity imagined as the order of things. By challenging the boundaries of the human and the coherence of what seemed to be the natural world, monstrous bodies appeared as sublime, merging the terrible with the wonderful, equalizing repulsion with attraction.

Whether generating awe, delight, terror, or knowledge, the monstrous emerges from culture-bound expectations even as it violates them. Certainly the cultural relativity of what counts as monstrous is witnessed by the medieval Wonder Books, which imagined as monsters the alien races of distant geographies, particularly those of "The East."[8] In a similar genre, the French surgeon Ambroise Paré in 1573 conflated what we would today see as the normal, the deviant, and the fanciful in an illustrated treatise on monsters that catalogues together marvels such as conjoined twins, giraffes, hermaphrodites, sea devils, elephants, unicorns, comets, incubi, and Egyptian mermaids.[9] Paré's *Des Monstres et prodigies* straddles the seam between wonder and error, between marvelous and medicalized narratives of the anomalous body. Along with the traditional divinely driven explanations, Paré initiates a secular, clinical approach to monsters that runs parallel to and competes with religious interpretations, finally eclipsing them around the beginning of the twentieth century. This incipient scientific view, which depends upon the fantasy of objectivity and sees regularity rather than exceptionality as founding epistemology, imposes empiricism upon the narrative of wonder that had ranged relatively freely across earlier representations of monsters. By the seventeenth century this alternative humanistic, scientific discourse, which endorses the predictable, entwines itself with the idea of religious prodigies, casting extraordinary bodies as nature's benevolent whimsies, bestowed upon the world to delight man's curiosity and inspire his awe. This is not, however, the awe of divine warning, but rather an implication that the world exists increasingly not to glorify god but to please man, who is destined to be its master.

The notion of the monster as prodigy fades at this juncture, transfiguring singular bodies into *lusus naturae,* nature's sport or the freak of nature. As divine design disengages from the natural world in the human mind, the word *freak* emerges to express capricious variegation or sudden, erratic change. Milton's *Lycidas* seems to have initiated *freak* into English in 1637 to mean a fleck of color. By the seventeenth century *freak* broadens to mean whimsy or fancy. Not until 1847 does the word become synonymous with human corporeal anomaly. Thus, *wonder,* which enters the language as early as 700, separates from augury to become whimsy as Enlightenment thinking begins to rationalize the world. What was once ominous marvel now becomes gratuitous oddity as monsters shift into the category of *curiosities.*[10] Curiosity fuses inquisitiveness, acquisitiveness, and novelty to the ancient pursuit of the extraordinary body, shifting the ownership of such bodies from God to the scientist, whose *Wunderkammern,* or cabinets of curiosities, antedate modern museums. Simultaneous with the secularism that finds delight in nature's corporeal jokes arises the contrasting empiricism that creates the knowledge used to drive fancy from the world.

Consequently, at just the historical moment when the foreboding monster transforms into the whimsical freak, the Enlightenment logic Max Horkheimer and Theodor Adorno have termed "the disenchantment of the world" produces teratology, the science of monstrosity that eventually tames and rationalizes the wondrous freak.[11] Formally articulated in 1832 by the French zoologist Isidore Geoffroy Saint-Hilaire, teratology recasts the freak from astonishing corporeal extravagance into the pathological specimen of the terata. Mastered and demythologized by modernity, then, is the marvelously singular body whose terrible presence in the world quickened such cultural narratives as Genesis and the *Odyssey.* Domesticated within the laboratory and the textbook, what was once the prodigious monster, the fanciful freak, the strange and subtle curiosity of nature, has become today the abnormal, the intolerable. The exceptional body thus becomes what Arnold Davidson calls an "especially vicious normative violation," demanding genetic reconstruction, surgical normalization, therapeutic elimination, or relegation to pathological specimen.[12]

In response to the tensions of modernity, the ancient practice of interpreting extraordinary bodies not only shifted toward the secular and the rational, but it flourished as never before within the expanding marketplace, institutionalized under the banner of the freak show. Especially in Victorian America, the exhibition of freaks exploded into a public ritual that bonded a sundering polity together in the collective act of looking. In a turbulent era of social and material change, the spectacle of the extraordinary body stimulated curiosity, ignited speculation, provoked titillation, furnished novelty, filled coffers, confirmed commonality, and certified national identity. From the Jacksonian to the Progressive eras, Americans flocked to freak shows. With the older narrative of wonder still culturally tenable and the newer narrative of error ever more compelling, the mid-nineteenth to early twentieth centuries comprised a heightened, transitional moment for such ceremonial displays. Redolent with the older authority of the prodigious, infused with the fitfulness of the fanciful, and susceptible to the certainties of scientific positivism, the singular body on exhibit was ripe for reading.[13]

But before we probe further the ways the freak show entwines itself with the social, economic, political, and ideological structures of what was arguably America's most intense period of modernization, we should first explore the conventions of display that created Victorian America's celebrated freaks. The early itinerant monster-mongers who exhibited human oddities in taverns and the slightly more respectable performances in rented halls evolved in the mid-nineteenth century into institutionalized, permanent exhibitions of freaks in dime museums and later in circus sideshows, fairs, and amusement park midways. The apotheosis of museums, which both inaugurated and informed the myriad dime museums that followed, was P. T. Barnum's American Museum, which he purchased and revitalized in 1841. Later, Barnum shaped the circus into the three-ringed extravaganza, infusing it with vigor and freaks well into the twentieth century. Until the turn of the century, dime museums proliferated, offering spectacles of amusement parading as edification to all classes of Americans.[14] Human freaks were the central magnets of Barnum's showplace and all successive dime museums. In the museums' curio halls and lecture rooms as well as on the sideshows' stages and platforms gathered an astonishing array of corporeal wonders, from wild men of Borneo to fat ladies, living skeletons, Fiji princes, albinos, bearded women, Siamese twins, tattooed Circassians, armless and legless wonders, Chinese giants, cannibals, midget triplets, hermaphrodites, spotted boys, and much more. Augmenting the marvelous bodies were ancillary performers and curiosities such as ventriloquists, performing geese, mesmerists, beauty contestants, contortionists, sharpshooters, trained goats, frog eaters, sword-swallowers, tumbling monkeys, boa constrictors, canaries whistling "Yankee Doodle," and a "Nail King" who drove nails through boards with his teeth.[15] From the Prince of Wales and Henry James to families and the humblest immigrants, Americans gathered at this most democratizing institution to gaze raptly at the ineffable other who was both the focus and the creation of the freak show's hyperbolic conventions of display.[16]

The exaggerated, sensationalized discourse that is the freak show's essence ranged over the seemingly singular bodies that we would now call either "physically disabled" or "exotic ethnics," framing them and heightening their differences from viewers, who were rendered comfortably common and safely standard by the exchange. Freak discourse structured a cultural ritual that seized upon any deviation from the typical, embellishing and intensifying it to produce a human spectacle whose every somatic feature was laden with significance before the gaping spectator. An animal-skin wrap, a spear, and some grunting noises, for example, made a retarded black man into the Missing Link. Irregular pigmentation enhanced by a loincloth and some palm fronds produced the Leopard Boy. Feathers, blankets, and a seven-pound hammer turned an "ordinary nigger" into the Ironed-Skulled Prince.[17] Shaved heads, top-knots, and gaudy tunics render two microcephalics into the Aztec Children. Congenital anomalies and progressive or hereditary conditions yielded imaginative hybrids of the human and animal reminiscent of classical satyrs, centaurs, or minotaurs: the Turtle Boy, the Mule-Faced Woman, Serpentina, the Camel Girl, the Dog-Faced Boy, the Bear Woman, the Lobster Boy, the Lion Woman, the Alligator Man, and Sealo. Bodies whose forms appeared to transgress rigid social categories such as race, gender, and personhood were particularly good grist for the freak mill. Albino Africans with dreadlocks, double-genitaled hermaphrodites, bearded women, fat boys, half-people, the legless and/or armless, and con-joined twins violated the categorical boundaries that seem to order civilization and inform individuality. Such hybridity, along with excess and absence, are the threatening organizational principles that constituted freakdom. At once dangerous and alluring, this cultural space of seemingly infinite license is what the freak shows both amplified and contained with their conventions of display.

An interlocking set of stylized, highly embellished narratives fashioned unusual bodies into

1.1. Charles Tripp, the "Armless Wonder," demonstrates his ability to eat with his feet. Courtesy of Bogdan Collection, Syracuse, New York.

1.2. Lipstretching, often exoticized in circuses and freak shows, in an African tribe. Courtesy of the Circus World Museum, Baraboo, Wisconsin.

freaks within the formalized spaces of shows, museums, fairs, and circuses. The four entwined narrative forms that produced freaks were, first, the oral spiel—often called the "lecture"—that was delivered by the showman or "professor" who usually managed the exhibited person; second, the often fabricated or fantastic textual accounts—both long pamphlets and broadside or newspaper advertisements—of the freak's always extraordinary life and identity; third, the staging, which included costuming, choreography, performance, and the spatial relation to the audience; and fourth, drawings or photographs that disseminated an iterable, fixed, collectible visual image of staged freakishness that penetrated into the Victorian parlor and family album. For commercial ends, freak exhibits enlisted, then, the oral and visual senses as well as their technological prosthetics, the reproducible printed word and image, to bombard actual and potential audiences with the freaks that their conventions manufactured.

Although commercial hyperbole drove all these narrative modes, the linguistic genres themselves varied. The fabulous was shot through with the scientific; truth claims abutted the credulous; the mundane flanked the peculiar. One example is the sensationally embroidered printed biographies of the freak's life, accomplishments, and corporeal irregularities. According to one pamphlet, the pregnant mother of the hirsute Madame Howard, the Lion Woman, was attacked by lions that her brave father then slew. Similarly, the Lobster Boy's fate was determined when his pregnant mother allegedly fainted at the sight of her husband's exceptionally large catch of the day.[18] Tattooed white men were ostensibly captured and tortured by cannibals. Missing Links were discovered in the jungles of darkest Africa. The

1.3*a, b, c.* A common practice at freak shows was to juxtapose stark physical differences. Collection of Robert Gould Shaw, Harvard Theatre Collection, The Houghton Library.

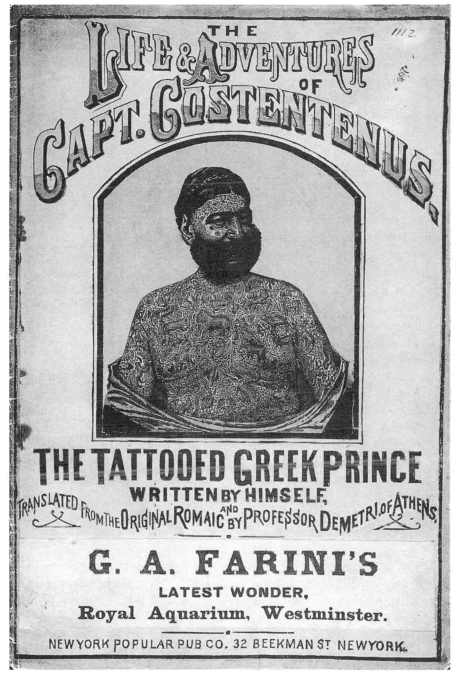

1.4. The cover of the life narrative of Captain Costentenus, "the Tattooed Greek Prince, Written by Himself and Translated from the Original Romaic by Professor Demetri of Athens." These exaggerated and frequently fraudulent pamphlets were often sold at freak shows. Courtesy of the Ron Becker Collection, Syracuse University Library, Department of Special Collections.

armless and legless performed on stage, with their alternative limbs, such ordinary tasks as violin playing, calligraphy, needlework, or taking tea, which were then detailed in inflated language that makes them remarkable even as it invites pity and admiration. Autographed souvenir cabinet photographs or the extremely popular *cartes d'visites* literally framed freaks by surrounding them with enhancing props like jungle backdrops or by juxtaposing giants with midgets, for instance, or fat men with human skeletons to intensify by contrast their bodily differences.[19] Presented along with the printed souvenirs were the oral narratives of the showman's pitch, the lecturer's yarn, and the "professor's" pseudo-authoritative accounts—all ornamented with the lurid and dramatized to the point of caricature. Respected medical doctors authenticated the exhibits by detailing their examinations in language at once clinical and reverent. Costuming enhanced the extraordinary quality of the freak's body, and staging established distance as well as literal hierarchies between the group of spectators and the lone spectacle on the elevated platform or in the sunken pit. Living skeletons wore leotards; fat or bearded ladies sported frills and jewels; hermaphrodites dressed in half-male and half-female outfits; Zulu warriors became alien by way of animal skins, spears, whoops, and jungle scenes. Conventionalized stage names created parodic juxtapositions as well. Midgets always had inflated titles from "high" society, such as Commodore Nutt, General Tom Thumb, Princess Wee-wee; fat ladies' names, such as Dolly Dimples, Captivatin' Liz, and Winsome Winnie, mocked feminine scripts. Taken together, these mediating narratives, as well as the cultural premise of irreducible corporeal difference upon which the freak show was founded, comprise the process David Hevey calls "enfreakment."[20]

Enfreakment emerges from cultural rituals that stylize, silence, differentiate, and distance the persons whose bodies the freak-hunters or showmen colonize and commercialize. Paradoxically, however, at the same time that enfreakment elaborately foregrounds specific bodily eccentricities, it also collapses all those differences into a "freakery," a single amorphous category of corporeal otherness. By constituting the freak as an icon of generalized embodied deviance, the exhibitions also simultaneously reinscribed gender, race, sexual aberrance, ethnicity, and disability as inextricable yet particular exclusionary systems legitimated by bodily variation—all represented by the single multivalent figure of the freak. Thus, what we assume to be a freak of nature was instead a freak of culture.[21]

The freak show made more than freaks: it fashioned as well the self-governed, iterable subject of democracy—the American cultural self. Parading at once as entertainment and education, the institutionalized social process of enfreakment united and validated the disparate throng positioned as viewers. A freak show's cultural work is to make the physical particularity of the freak into a hypervisible text against which the viewer's indistinguishable body fades into a seemingly neutral, tractable, and invulnerable instrument of the autonomous will, suitable to the uniform abstract citizenry democracy institutes. Yet the freaks' popularity—the strange blend of reverence and condescension audiences registered—suggests ambivalence toward such forfeiture of the bodily distinction that marked eminence in traditional societies. Bound together by their purchased assurance that they are not freaks, the fascinated onlookers perhaps longed in some sense to be extraordinary marvels instead of mundane, even banal, democrats in a confusing cultural moment. Nevertheless, the privileged state of disembodiment that the freak show conferred upon its spectators, however fraudulent, must have been seductive. It evidently was well worth the dime or quarter at a time when modernization rendered the meaning of bodily differences and vulnerabilities increasingly unstable and threatening.

The freak show's golden age occurred specifically within the productive context of nineteenth-century America's swift and chaotic modernization. That rich cultural matrix provided a conducive environment for the archaic custom of exhibiting and interpreting extraordinary bodies and alien cultures to thrive in the invigorated form of the freak show. But the very cultural and socioeconomic conditions that animated anew this ancient, almost anachronistic, practice composed the very context that at the same time rendered it obsolete, making the freak show today virtually synonymous with bad taste, a practice that has gone the way of public executions. In the escalating upheaval of modernization between about 1840 through 1940, what we now think of as the freak show flared like a comet and then vanished from view, re-emerging in almost unrecognizable forms in the late twentieth century.[22] Although it is impossible to disentangle or establish causality among the interlocking and mutually determining cultural phenomena that quickened and then quieted the freak show, let us nevertheless try roughly to uncouple the forces modernization brought to bear on the exhibition of the anomalous body.

Most fundamentally, modernization reconstituted the human body. Freak shows became ritual sites where the uncertain polity could anxiously contemplate the new parameters of embodiment that cultural transformations had wrought. The changes in production, labor, technology, and market relations that we loosely call industrialization redeployed and often literally reconfigured the body, perhaps turning America's collective eyes more attentively on the extraordinary body for explanation, validation, or simply comfort. Machine culture created new somatic geographies. For example, the decline of the apprentice system, the rise of the machine and the factory, as well as wage labor, put bodies on arbitrary schedules instead of allowing natural rhythms to govern activity. Rather than machines acting as prosthetics for the human body as they had in traditional cultures, the body under industrialization began to seem more like an extension of the machine, which threatened to replace the working body or at the least restructure its relation to labor. Efficiency, a concept rooted in the mechanical, ascended to prominence as a measurement of bodily value. Mechanized practices such as standardization, mass production, and interchangeable parts promoted sameness of form as a cultural value and made singularity in both products and bodies seem deviant. The professionalization of authority, wage labor, the logic of slavery and abolition, as well as the women's rights movement challenged the common citizen's sense of autonomy and mastery over his own body and others' bodies. Moreover, industrial accidents as well as the technologies and scale of the Civil War literally changed the shapes of human bodies on a dramatic new scale. Both sentimentalism and realism, the major representational modes of the freak show period, register in differing ways the concern with the place and meaning of the body. If this new body felt alien to the ordinary citizen, the freak's bizarre embodiment could assuage viewers' uneasiness either by functioning as a touchstone of anxious identification or as an assurance of their regularized normalcy.[23]

Modernization not only reimagined and reshaped the body, it relocated it as well. The new geography of labor changed the physical relationships between bodies, literally separating workers from owners, the skilled from the unskilled, men from women and children. Mental and manual work migrated apart. Transportation systems and new work patterns moved people from farms and familial contexts into cities as well as into anonymous social and labor hierarchies. Wage labor and urbanjzation created unstructured leisure time and forged situational, transient relationships, while change stimulated a taste for the novel. In addition to restless physical migrations, a surging marketplace both promised and threatened social mobility founded upon unstable incomes. All these dislocations created anonymity, forcing people to rely upon bodily appearance rather than kinship or local memberships as indices of identity and social position.[24] In addition, secularization deemphasized the condition of one's soul, while an intensifying market system spawned the anxious display of status, and technologies such as portraiture photography located identity in one's exterior image. Social upheavals such as immigration, emancipation, and feminism—along with discriminatory responses such as nativism, segregation, and eugenics—depended upon the logic of visual corporeal differences for their coherence and enactment. Consequently, the way the body looked and functioned became one's primary social resource as local contexts receded, support networks unraveled, and mobility dominated social life.

In this way, modernity effected a standardization of everyday life that saturated the entire social fabric, producing and reinforcing the concept of an unmarked, normative, leveled body as the dominant subject of democracy. Clocks, department stores, ready-made clothing, catalogues, advertising, and factory items sculpted the prosaic toward sameness, while increased literacy and the iterable nature of a burgeoning print culture fortified the impulse toward conformity. With its dependence on predictability, scientific discourse also reimagined the body, depreciating particularity while valorizing uniformity. Statistics quantified the body; evolution provided a new heritage; eugenics and teratology policed its boundaries; prosthetics normalized it; and asylums cordoned off deviance. Additionally, allopathic, professionalized medicine consolidated its dominance, casting as pathological all departures from the standard body. Finally, the notion of progress and the ideology of improvement—always a fraught consolation against the vagaries of contingency—implemented the ascendance of this new image of a malleable, regularized body whose attainment was both an individual and national obligation.[25]

Thus the iconography of social status transformed as the polity concerned itself with the subtleties of decoding bodies pressed toward the homogenous, even while the ideology of individualism called for distinction. In the midst of this communal quest for identity, the extravagantly marked, pliant figure of the freak quietly commanded the imaginations of practically everyone. During a confusing era, the freak body represented at once boundless liberty and appalling disorder, the former the promise and the latter the threat of democracy. The enterprising entrepreneur capitalized on all of this amid the prevailing culture of exhibition in which eager and puzzled citizens sought truth, meaning, edification, and distraction within a ceremonial cultural space that ritually fused the visual with the textual.

This standardization of life and body under modernity was accompanied by a tendency toward compartmentalization and stratification. As culture became more dynamic, complex, and literate with modernization, broad discourses tended to cleave into multiple, discrete discursive systems inflected by an elaborate system of social markers. Such differentiation created, for example, myriad branches of specialized knowledge and work, each located somewhere on the ladder of social status. In democratized nineteenth-century America, class distinctions solidified, bifurcating cultural discourses as well into high and low.[26] Swept along on this wave, freak show discourse, which from premodern times had been primarily iconographic—that is, of the show, whether religious or secular—began to be intersected by literate, scientific discourse and to fragment into an array of specialized discourses, some popular and some elite. With this dispersion of discourses, Victorian middle-class decorum's project of self-definition increasingly repudiated the popular freak show, while sentimentality recast awe into pity, and other forms of visual entertainment like theater—and, later, movies—proliferated. Thus the freak show itself—which although perpetually democratic, had always vexed respectability—came to rest irrevocably at the bottom of low culture. Indeed, the word "freak" was stigmatized enough by 1898 that the Barnum and Bailey Circus replaced it with the term "human curiosities" by 1903, supposedly in response to a group protest by the circus freak performers.[27]

Yet before the freak show broke off from respectable society around the turn of the century, it was a central element in our collective cultural project of representing the body. Although the earlier freak show, with its hybrid of old wonder narratives, commercialized show narratives, and clinical scientific narratives, seems today to have dissipated, it has instead dispersed and transformed. Freak discourse did not vanish with the shows, but proliferated into a variety of contemporary discourses that still allude to its premises. Before this dissemination, however, the exhibition of freaks was inextricably entwined with an array of now-discrete discourses that were then only beginning to differentiate from one another in the nineteenth century. Genetics, embryology, anatomy, teratology, and reconstructive surgery—the discrete, high scientific discourses that now pathologize the extraordinary body—were once closely linked with the showmen's display of the freak body. The equally elite discourses of anthropology and ethnology, as well as museum culture and taxidermy, were inseparable from the display of freaks in the early nineteenth century. The entertainment discourses of vaudeville, circuses, beauty pageants, zoos, horror films, rock celebrity culture, and Epcot Center have descended from the freak show, to which displays of these kinds were once fused.

I have suggested here that modernity moved the freak from the embodiment of wonder to the embodiment of error. This volume, however, documents that shift not as an exhaustion of the genre but rather as a dispersal of freak show discourse into an array of other representational modes, some of which—for example, the theater of surgery that normalizes the bodies of today's conjoined twins—may not be recognizable today at first glance. Focusing, though not exclusively, on the classic freak show's most intense manifestation in nineteenth- and twentieth-century America, the chapters assembled here center on particular aspects of freak show culture, scrutinizing the structures of meaning, sociopolitical context, and conventions of display that constitute the figure of the freak in modernity. Taken together, they demonstrate how the social ceremony of the freak show sits at the crossroads of all systematic discourses—race and gender, for example—that underpin sociopolitical subordination by representing difference as deviance. The volume thus comprises a wide-ranging, interdisciplinary conversation that charts the interconnections among a profusion of both muted and blatant discourses of the freakish body.

This volume extends and elaborates the investigation of freaks initiated in 1978 by Leslie Fiedler's literary critical study, *Freaks: Myths and Images of the Secret Self,* and continued in 1988 by Robert Bogdan's sociohistorical account, *Freak Show: Presenting Human Oddities for Amusement and Profit.* Fiedler probes the archetypical aspects of the freak, while Bogdan argues for the freak as a social construction. Representative of their respective decades and disciplines, both studies inform the essays here. The casting by cultural studies of a wider net of inquiry has brought freaks and their exhibition onto the academic deck, inviting the kinds of politicized and historicized interrogations collected here. Fiedler's foreword, Bogdan's essay (chapter 2 below), and this introduction launch the subsequent conversations that probe the resonances imposed upon the ritual spectacle of visible difference that is the freak.

The book's first section, "The Cultural Construction of Freaks," gathers three germinal perspectives that, along with Fiedler's foreword, comprise an introductory examination of the freak as a historical and cultural phenomenon. Bogdan historicizes the mediation of the freak's body by show conventions, emphasizing that the freak is essentially a fraudulent figure produced by modes of presentation that show business employs to construct freaks from people with disabilities or non-Western ethnicities. Summarizing the taxonomy of representation identified in his book, Bogdan details a variety of strategies, such as the "exotic" and the "aggrandized status" modes, that the shows use to promote freaks. By foregrounding the problem of exploitation, historian David A. Gerber shifts the focus of analysis from Bogdan's social constructionist narrative to a consideration of consent and free will on the part of the performers. Gerber advocates "remoralizing" the question of the freak show, suggesting that we see it *both* as a socially constructed form of entertainment *and* as a product of unequal social relations. Whereas Bogdan and Gerber focus on enfreakment strategies, Elizabeth Grosz probes the essential meaning of the freak body to its viewers. Exploring the effects of lived and represented corporeality on identity, philosopher Grosz posits that the freak imperils the very categories we rely on to classify humans. Focusing on hermaphrodites and conjoined twins, the two modes of freakishness whose embodiments are most ambiguous, Grosz concludes that such corporeal ambiguity is culturally intolerable and always subjected to surgical intervention because it questions the integrity of received images of the human self.

The second section, "Practices of Enfreakment," centers on strategies of mediation used to frame the freak as a spectacle appropriated for the showmen's or the viewers' purposes. Paul Semonin's chapter on monster exhibits in the marketplaces of early modern England glimpses the beginnings of the freak show's institutionalization. In accounting for the shows' enduring, cross-class appeal, Semonin challenges the assertion that monsters were viewed as either religious portents or scientific specimens by unearthing a popular folk discourse that interprets monsters as comic grotesques. Edward L. Schwarzschild examines next one of the earliest institutions of enfreakment in America as he shows how Charles Willson Peale colonized the spectacle of the dead body in his eighteenth-century Philadelphia museum. Peale's taxidermy, paintings, and plan to embalm Ben Franklin testify to his museum's attempt to make a freak show of death to achieve individual and national distinction by controlling human mortality. If P. T. Barnum's purchase in 1850 of Peale's failing enterprise supports Schwarzschild's imbrication of museum and freak discourses, Eric Fretz's essay on Barnum's orchestration of a theatrical self akin to that of his freaks cements the conjunction of museum and freak cultures in nineteenth-century America. Delineating the larger culture of exhibition in which freak shows and museums were embedded, Fretz demonstrates how Barnum's multiple autobiographies and other forms of self-presentation stylize a malleable figure that precisely parallels his fashioned freaks, leading us to ponder the relation between exploitation and agency in the freakmaking process. Ellen Hickey Grayson next examines the practice of psychological enfreakment, while continuing to chart correlations between museum and freak discourses, as she traces the interpretation of the laughing gas demonstrations that augmented revenues from the 1845–48 traveling exhibit of Rembrandt Peale's monumental temperance painting "The Court of Death." Grayson reveals that these laughing gas experiments by audience members shifted from subversive to reactionary, acting finally to reveal character and censure aberrant behavior so as to affirm bourgeois respectability. Finally, Ronald E. Ostman's chapter analyzing Farm Security Administration photographs taken between 1935 and 1942 explicates the role of photography in establishing the persuasion, veracity, and commercialism that supported human exhibitions during the waning freak show era. Ostman's re-created carnival spiels and his analyses of the dynamic among viewers, showmen, and workers revealed by the photographs suggests how much the shows had to strain for credibility in the twentieth century after they had been severed from the more respectable urban museum culture to which they were earlier united.

The third section, "Exhibiting Corporeal Freaks," places particular freak exhibits choreographed from people whom we would now term "disabled" into their sociohistorical contexts, analyzing the larger political meanings of these individual displays and revealing strong links between the shows and other seemingly unimplicated strands of cultural discourse. James W. Cook, Jr., begins by scrutinizing Barnum's long-running exhibition, "What is It?"—the remarkably pliant figure of indeterminate corporeal otherness upon whom audiences or showmen could project numerous geographical, racial, and cultural templates. By revealing Barnum's manipulation of "What is It?" as a "nondescript," Cook contests Fretz's claims in the previous section about freaks' agency, demonstrating that this particular exhibit literally embodied the era's deep conflicts over race. Nigel Rothfels extends Cook's linkage of race and freak discourse, adding to it an account of how scientific and freak discourses intersected in the framing of several exhibitions. Rothfels shows how the German scientific community used the bodies of Bartola and Maximo (the "Aztec Children"), the hirsute Krao, and a group of Fuegians—all of whom were cast as "missing links"—as sites on which to formulate and debate the two most important scientific theories of the nineteenth century: evolution and recapitulation. Focusing next on the famous performing twins Daisy and Violet Hilton, Allison Pingree examines not only how conjoined twins threaten notions of individual personhood, but also how gender politics were mapped onto the pair's attachment. Pingree shows that the popular representations of the twins cast their bond as a threatening substitute for marriage that is both exploited and contained by entertainment discourse. Lori Merish then probes the cultural spectacle of "cuteness" by establishing a genealogy between prodigious midgets such as Tom Thumb, whose wedding was one of the century's greatest mass spectacles, and the equally prodigious and cute Shirley Temple. Exploring as well the politics of cuteness in Toni Morrison's *The Bluest Eye* and Shirley's constant pairings with childlike blacks, Merish yokes the comic theatrical style of cute to both racial and gender politics.

The fourth section, "Exhibiting Cultural Freaks," demonstrates how exhibitions exoticized non-Westerners as physically deviant figures parallel to the freaks with disabilities. The concept of "ethnological show business" elaborated in Bernth Lindfors's chapter on the nineteenth-century British display of Africans—the famous Hottentot Venus, Zulu Warriors, and Bosjesmans—suggests the early fluidity between freak discourse and the nascent project of anthropology. Pointing to the irony that the British simultaneously abolished slavery and institutionalized imperialism, Lindfors reveals how cultural others become corporeal others in the context of exhibitions. Christopher Vaughan examines a similar incarnation during the United States' turn-of-the-century missionary imperialist era. Vaughan argues that the display of Philippine Igorots at the 1904 St. Louis World's Fair fed a public hunger for cultural difference that affirmed America's sense of cultural progress, of being "civilized" rather than "savage." Continuing to track the conjunctions of race, anthropology, and freakishness, Leonard Cassuto demonstrates how tattooing acts as a code for racial difference in Herman Melville's account of failed cultural tolerance, *Typee*. Cassuto investigates the ways in which freak discourse ultimately attempted to maintain a fiction of absolute racial distinction at a time when abolitionism was threatening such assertions. Focusing in the section's last chapter on the intersection of gender, race, and eroticism in the figure of the Circassian Beauty/Circassian Slave, Linda Frost shows how this Barnum freak figure served political ends as a representative of racial purity who was desired and enslaved by the dark, barbaric Turk.

The fifth section, "Textual Uses of Freaks," looks at some implementations of the freak figure in literature and film. Joan Hawkins unearths the disturbing ambivalence in Tod Browning's classic horror film, *Freaks*, noting at the same time the misogyny that dovetails with the troubling presentation of corporeal difference. Released in 1932 at the moment when freak shows became an unacceptable genre, the controversial film, according to Hawkins, simultaneously humanizes and dehumanizes the film's actual freak performers. Rachel Adams continues by scrutinizing Katharine Dunn's equally disturbing 1989 novel, *Geek Love*, which she argues vacillates between recognizing that freakishness is socially produced and at the same time validating bodily materiality as the familial history of the bizarre freak family at the novel's center. Adams introduces the troubling issue of the postmodern body's almost infinite mutability through surgery and technology, a theme that Shirley Peterson examines in her chapter on the enlistment of freakishness for a feminist agenda in Angela Carter's *Nights at the Circus* and Fay Weldon's *The Life and Loves of a She-Devil*. Peterson shows that the female protagonists, a hulking giantess and a winged aerialist, explore the transgressive potential of the unfeminine woman in patriarchal culture. In the section's final chapter, Brian Rosenberg surveys literary and film representations of freaks by detailing his experiences teaching a literature course on freaks—what he calls "a walk on the pedagogical wild side." Finding that human oddities are a persistent, if muted, presence in literature, Rosenberg explains how in the classroom freak discourse can encourage complex thinking and highlight significant social issues.

The last section, "Relocations of the Freak Show," enumerates several contemporary sites where culture reconfigures the freak show into currently acceptable forms that nevertheless replicate the earlier choreographies of embodied otherness. Andrea Stulman Dennett juxtaposes late-nineteenth-century dime museum freak shows and contemporary television talk shows, charting the similarities in structure and presentation between the two displays of ostensible human aberrance, the earlier physical and the later psychological. Moreover, Dennett argues that the one true remaining physical freak today is the fat person, a ridiculed stock talk show figure cut off from the sympathy that ostensibly rescues disabled people from such scorn. If Dennett suggests that technology informs postmodern freak shows, Jeffrey A. Weinstock confirms her point by demonstrating that science fiction films are the last frontier of freakdom in contemporary culture. Examining the uses of anomalous bodies in the film

Star Wars and the television series *Star Trek: The Next Generation,* Weinstock suggests that the extraterrestrial alien is a complex figure of disavowal and identification that validates an often narrow version of the human as superior. David L. Clark and Catherine Myser's analysis of a documentary film about the surgical separation of conjoined twins yokes together even more securely science, entertainment, and freak discourse in the postmodern era. Clark and Myser's interrogation of such separations ultimately questions the very idea that the body has a fixed, normative outline to which anyone's form can be restored. Cecile Lindsay moves next from surgical transformations to other forms of bodily plasticity as she demonstrates the parallels between the freak figure and the contemporary bodybuilder, a form of bodily production Adams commented upon in her chapter. Lindsay argues that bodybuilders, finding new categories to blur, perform themselves and become their own projects, thus potentially challenging the enforcement of cultural norms and embodying postmodern selfhood. Finally, David D. Yuan continues pondering the freak in postmodernity by seeing Michael Jackson as a postmodern celebrity freak who creates himself as a freakish figure of theatricalized transgression even while his audience creates him at the same time. Yuan enlists Jackson's reputed identification with Joseph Merrick, the "Elephant Man," as well as Jackson's manipulation of his own appearance and skin color to suggest that his refashioned body is part of a performance that challenges gender, sex, and racial boundaries in the manner of enfreakment.

This volume, then, enlists a wide array of scholarly perspectives that collectively illuminate a generally ignored arena of popular culture. These richly varied, often interconnected analyses uncover the practices and ideologies through which representation situates the body both in history and in the communal consciousness. What lingers here as a residue of these explorations is the poignant image of the freak, the person cordoned off from the rest of humanity by this embroidering, sensationalizing discourse that makes of his or her body not only a cultural spectacle but a token of the anxieties and aspirations of a society intent upon publicizing the freak's private body with its stares. My hope is that our collection will be an invitation to further discussions that aim ultimately at installing the humanity these discourses deny freaks.

NOTES

1. George M. Gould and Walter L. Pyle, *Anomalies and Curiosities of Medicine* (Philadelphia: W. B. Saunders, 1897), 199–200.

2. Keith Thomas, *Man and the Natural World* (New York: Pantheon, 1983), 135.

3. Ricky Jay, *Learned Pigs and Fireproof Women* (New York: Villard, 1986), 44–57.

4. Oliver Impey and Arthur MacGregor, eds., *The Origins of Museums* (Oxford: Clarendon, 1985), 4.

5. For discussions of Barnum, see Neil Harris, *Humbug: The Art of P. T. Barnum* (Boston: Little Brown, 1973); and A. H. Saxon, *P. T. Barnum: The Legend and the Man* (New York: New York University Press, 1989).

6. Richard D. Altick, *The Shows of London* (Cambridge: Belknap, 1978).

7. The history of monsters and freaks is found in Gould and Pyle, *Anomalies and Curiosities;* John Block Friedman, *The Monstrous Races in Medieval Art and Thought* (Cambridge: Harvard University Press, 1981); Mark V. Barrow, "A Brief History of Teratology," in *Problems of Birth Defects,* ed. T. V. N. Persaud (Baltimore: University Park Press, 1977), 18–28; Josef Warkany, "Congenital Malformations in the Past," in *Problems of Birth Defects,* ed. T. V. N. Persaud (Baltimore: University Park Press, 1977), 5–17; Dudley Wilson, *Signs and Portents: Monstrous Births from the Middle Ages to the Enlightenment* (London: Routledge, 1993); Charles J. S. Thompson, *The Mystery and Lore of Monsters* (New Hyde

Park: University Books, 1968); Kathryn Park and Lorraine Daston, "Unnatural Conceptions: The Study of Monsters in Sixteenth- and Seventeenth-Century France and England," *Past and Present: A Journal of Historical Studies* 92 (August 1981): 20–54; Yi-Fu Tuan, *Dominance and Affection: The Making of Pets* (New Haven: Yale University Press, 1984), chap. 13; Leslie Fiedler, *Freaks: Myths and Images of the Secret Self* (New York: Simon and Schuster, 1978); Robert Bogdan, *Freak Show: Presenting Human Oddities for Amusement and Profit* (Chicago: University of Chicago Press, 1988); Daniel P. Mannix, *Freaks: We Who Are Not as Others* (San Francisco: Re/Search Publications, 1990); and Frederick Drimmer, *Very Special People* (New York: Amjon, 1983).

8. Freidman, *Monstrous Races;* and Mary Bane Campbell, *The Witness and the Other World: Exotic European Travel Writing, 400–1600* (Ithaca, N.Y.: Cornell University Press, 1988).

9. Ambroise Paré, *On Monsters and Marvels,* trans. Janis L. Pallister (Chicago: University of Chicago Press, 1982).

10. All definitions are from the *Oxford English Dictionary,* 2d ed. (Oxford: Clarendon, 1991).

11. Max Horkheimer and Theodor W. Adorno, *Dialectic of Enlightenment,* trans. John Cumming (1944; reprint, London: Allen Lane, 1973), 3; see also Keith Thomas, *Religion and the Decline of Magic* (New York: Scribner's, 1971).

12. Arnold I. Davidson, "The Horror of Monsters," in *The Boundaries of Humanity: Humans, Animals, Machines,* ed. James J. Sheehan and Morton Sosna (Berkeley: University of California Press, 199), 51.

13. For a discussion of prodigies and religion in America, see Michael P. Winship, "Prodigies, Puritanism, and the Perils of Natural Philosophy: The Example of Cotton Mather," *William and Mary Quarterly,* 3d series, L1, no. 1 (January 1994): 92–105.

14. The words *muse* and *amusement* both descend from the related Old French and Old English words for staring, gaping, or being idle. *Museum* comes directly into English from the Latin.

15. George C. D. Odell, *Annals of the New York Stage* (1927–49; reprint, New York: AMS Press, 1970), 14:1888–91; and William G. FitzGerald, "Side-Shows," parts 1–4, *Strand Magazine,* March–June 1897, 321–28, 405–16, 521–28, 776–80.

16. Brooks McNamara, " 'A Congress of Wonders': The Rise and Fall of the Dime Museum," *Emerson Society Quarterly* 20, no. 3 (1974): 216–32; Marcello Truzzi, "Circus and Side Shows," in *American Popular Entertainment,* ed. Myron Matlaw (Westport, Conn.: Greenwood, 1979) 175–85; and James B. Twitchell, *Carnival Culture: The Trashing of Taste in America* (New York: Columbia University Press, 1992), 57–65.

17. FitzGerald, "Side-Shows," part 2, 409.

18. The theory of maternal impression as a source of congenital anomalies is discussed in Marie Hélène Huet, *Monstrous Imagination* (Cambridge: Harvard University Press, 1993).

19. Michael Mitchell, *Monsters of the Gilded Age: The Photographs of Charles Eisenmann* (Toronto: Gage, 1979).

20. David Hevey, *The Creatures That Time Forgot: Photography and Disability Imagery* (New York: Routledge, 1992), 53.

21. Susan Stewart, *On Longing: Narratives of the Miniature, the Gigantic, the Souvenir, the Collection* (Baltimore: Johns Hopkins University Press, 1984), 109.

22. Richard D. Brown, *Modernization: The Transformation of American Life, 1600–1865* (New York: Hill and Wang, 1976); and Bogdan, *Freak Show,* 2.

23. For a discussion of the body's historicity, see Thomas Laqueur, *Making Sex: Body and Gender from the Greeks to Freud* (Cambridge: Cambridge University Press, 1990); for a history of disability in America, see Deborah A. Stone, *The Disabled State* (Philadelphia: Temple University Press, 1984). For discussions of the body in modernity, see Mark Seltzer, *Bodies and Machines* (New York: Routledge, 1992); David S. Landes, *Revolution in Time: Clocks and the Making of the Modern World* (Cambridge: Belknap, 1983); and Richard Sennett, *The Fall of Public Man* (Cambridge: Cambridge University Press, 1974).

24. Karen Halttunen, *Confidence Men and Painted Women: A Study of Middle-Class Culture in America, 1830–1870* (New Haven: Yale University Press, 1982); and Sennett, *The Fall of Public Man.*

25. Paul Starr, *The Social Transformation of American Medicine* (New York: Basic Books, 1982); and

David Rothman, *The Discovery of the Asylum: Social Order and Disorder in the New Republic* (Boston: Little, Brown, 1971).

26. Lawrence W. Levine, *Highbrow/Lowbrow: The Emergence of Cultural Hierarchy in America* (Cambridge: Harvard University Press, 1988); and Stuart M. Blumin, *The Emergence of the Middle-Class: Social Experience in the City, 1760–1900* (Cambridge: Cambridge University Press, 1989).

27. Bruce A. McConachie, "Museum Theater and the Problem of Respectability for Mid-Century Urban Americans," in *The American Stage: Social and Economic Issues from the Colonial Period to the Present,* ed. Ron Engle and Tice L. Miller (New York: Cambridge University Press, 1993), 65–80; "The Uprising of the Freaks," *Barnum and Bailey Route Book,* 1897–1901, p. 21. John Lentz, in "The Revolt of the Freaks, *Bandwagon* Sept./Oct. 1977, p. 26–29, concludes that this revolt was a publicity stunt; nevertheless, its success demonstrates that the term *freak* was considered generally objectionable by the end of the century.

PART I

The Cultural Construction of Freaks

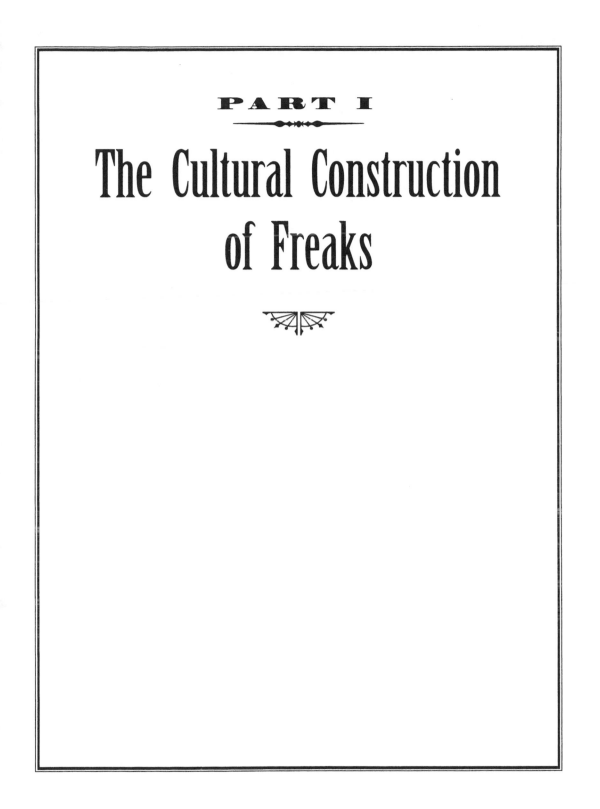

TWO

The Social Construction of Freaks

ROBERT BOGDAN

At the height of the freak show's popularity, people strolling in urban entertainment districts or down midways of circuses and carnivals heard the hardy voice of a freak show lecturer pitching to the crowd: "Step right up ... see the most astonishing aggregation of human marvels and monstrosities gathered together in one edifice" (Isman 1924). "Freak shows," the formally organized exhibition of people with alleged physical, mental, or behavioral difference at circuses, fairs, carnivals, and other amusement venues, was once an accepted, popular, and lucrative practice in the United States. There is no record of these shows being attacked as offensive until well into the twentieth century. Today, they are on the fringe of society, seen by many as crude, rude, and exploitive. The few remaining freak shows are only the seedy vestiges of a once gala practice.

This chapter introduces "freaks" as a social construction. The focus is the presentation (Goffman 1959) of human exhibits to the public for amusement and profit. The study of "freak shows" provides an exciting opportunity to develop understanding of past practices and changing conceptions of human variation. What strategies, techniques, and images did managers and exhibits use in promoting attractions? How did these presentations fit with the culture of the amusement world and with commonsense and scientific notions about human differences? What can we learn about current methods of retailing bodies from this sociological encounter with history?[1]

The years 1840 to 1940 witnessed the rise and fall of the freak show in the United States. By 1840 "human curiosities," who up to then traveled and were exhibited independently, were joining burgeoning amusement organizations (Wilmeth 1982). P. T. Barnum, the major figure in the nineteenth-century amusement business, took over the American Museum in New York City during the early 1840s, and this Disneyland of Victorian America featured "human curiosities." By 1940, economic hard times, technological and geographic changes, competition from other forms of entertainment, the medicalization of human differences, and changed public taste resulted in a serious decline in the number and popularity of freak shows, although they continued through the 1950s and 1960s, and vestiges exist even today.

THE SOCIAL CONSTRUCTION OF "FREAKS"

In the mid-1920s Jack Earl, a very tall University of Texas student, visited the Ringling Brothers circus sideshow. Clyde Ingles, manager, spotted Earl in the audience and approached the young man to ask him: "How would you like to be a Giant?" This story clarifies a point freak show personnel understood but those who have written about "freaks" often neglect: while being extremely tall is a matter of physiology, being a giant involves something more. Similarly, being a "freak," a "human oddity," or a "human curiosity" is not a personal matter, a physical condition that some people have (Goffman 1963). "Freak" is a way of thinking about and presenting people—a frame of mind and a set of practices.

What were the various kinds of human freaks? The few who have written about the sideshow, mainly popular historians, answer the question by concentrating on the physical characteristics of those exhibited (Drimmer 1973; Durant 1957; Fiedler 1978; and Mannix 1990). They organize the chapters of their books like medical textbooks. Headings include such topics as: "little people" (dwarfs and midgets), "giants," "hairy people," "human skele-tons," "armless and legless wonders," "pinheads," "fat people," "albinos," "Siamese twins," "people with extra limbs," "half men/half women," "people with skin disorders," "tattooed people," and "anatomical wonders."

People on the inside of the exhibiting business use the physiological categories as well, but they also distinguish among "born freaks," "made freaks," and "novelty acts" (Gresham 1948). According to this classification, "born freaks" are people who, at birth, had a physical anomaly that makes them unusual, such as Siamese twins and armless and legless people. "Made freaks" do something to themselves that makes them unusual enough for exhibit, such as adorning their bodies with tattoos. The "novelty act" has an unusual performance, such as swallowing swords or charming snakes. In addition to these three main types, sideshow people refer to "gaffed freaks"—the fakes, the phonies—such as the armless wonder who tucked his arms under a tight-fitting shirt, or the four-legged woman whose extra legs really belonged to a person hidden from the audience. When in public, freak show personnel showed disdain for the gaff; their competitors might try to get away with it but they would not. The "born freak" was publicly acknowledged as having esteem.

This is the standard typology as those in the business present it, and it has not changed over the last 120 years. In the abstract, the insiders' way of categorizing differentiates freak show exhibits from one another, but even they had difficulty applying it. Most exhibits were too complex to fit into this simple scheme, and the categories did not acknowledge the pervasive fraud and deception that were characteristic of the whole freak show enterprise. If taken at face value, the insiders' typology veils more than it reveals. It is of interest not because it clarifies the freak show or the exhibits, but because embodied in it are the commonsense notions of the amusement world.

THE WORLD OF AMUSEMENT: GRIFT, FRAUD, AND HUMBUG

The major venues for freak shows became distinct organizational forms in the nineteenth century, but the boundaries that separated them remained permeable. Showmen and "human curiosities" jumped back and forth from museums to carnivals to circuses, often playing the traveling shows in the warm months and permanent exhibition halls during the winter. They shared a sense of camaraderie and a perspective on life. They divided humanity into two categories, those who were "with it" (the insiders' phrase for being part of the amusement world) and those who were not. They developed a unique language, life style, insiders' secrets, and contempt for those who were outsiders. The "marks," "rubes," "suckers," or "yokels," as customers were contemptuously referred to, were targets for systematic shortchanging, rigged games of chance, establishment pickpockets, and a whole variety of grift,[2] fraud, and humbug (Sharpe 1970; Dadswell 1946; Inciardi and Petersen 1972). Although freak shows were often presented as educational or scientific exhibits, they were always first and foremost a for-profit activity, and within the climate of the amusement world, misrepresentation was an accepted practice.

Those exhibiting freaks learned, along with their medicine show colleagues, that packaging was as important as content. Using imagery and symbols managers and promoters knew the public would respond to, they created a public identity for the person that was being exhibited that would have the widest appeal, and thereby would collect the most dimes. To accomplish this they took citizens, some with abnormalities and others with none (except the desire to live the life of a trouper), and made freaks out of them.

In a strict sense of the word, every exhibit was a fraud. This is not to say that freaks were without physical, mental, and behavioral anomalies. Many had profound differences (severe disabilities in today's language), but, with very few exceptions, every person exhibited was misrepresented. Showmen fabricated freaks' backgrounds, the nature of their condition, the circumstances of their current lives, and other personal characteristics. The accurate story of the life and conditions of those being exhibited was replaced by purposeful distortion designed to market the exhibit, to produce a more appealing freak. In some cases, only a minor detail of the person's true identify was altered—the albino from Australia really came from New Jersey. In other cases the deception was merely exaggeration—inches added to the height of giants and subtracted from midgets. The gaffed freak was only the extreme of fakery.

Flagrant misrepresentation was part and parcel of the most famous as well as the minor exhibits. The Davis brothers were short and mentally retarded. One was born in New York, the other in England. Both grew up on a farm in Ohio. From 1852 until 1905 they achieved national fame as exhibits in dime museums, fairs, and in the circus sideshow as the Wild Men of Borneo, who were presented as having been, after a bloody struggle, captured by a ship's crew in the far-off Pacific and domesticated. The five-year-old, Connecticut-born Charles Stratton became the eleven-year-old, English-born Tom Thumb when Barnum began exhibiting him. Stratton later married, and although he and his spouse were infertile, they were exhibited with a baby that was presented as theirs (Saxon 1983). An additional Thumb, it was hoped, would stimulate business.

Show people would not classify Tom Thumb or the Wild Men of Borneo as gaffs. Telling of their view of genuineness, they referred to them as the "original" and "authentic" Tom Thumb and Wild Men of Borneo. Fabrications and misrepresentations were just part of the taken-for-granted hype of the freak show world. People who were "with it," by emphasizing the gaffed freak in their typology, and by publicly dwelling on this extreme form of fraud as being distasteful, glossed over the accepted widespread misrepresentation that was part and parcel of freak shows and the larger institution of which they were apart.

2.1. A mediator, such as this carnival talker, is a fixture of the freak show, which requires a figure of authority to negotiate the encounter between freak and audience. Courtesy of the Pfenig Collection, Columbus, Ohio.

PROMOTING THE SHOW

The organization and promotion of freak shows became standardized during the second half of the nineteenth century. One form of promotion was the exaggerated come-ons that were presented through newspaper advertisements, handbills, couriers, and posters. Shows were located in tents on midways at fairs and circuses, in buildings on busy city streets, and on board walks in amusement parks. The potential customers were part of the strolling crowds. A row of large canvas paintings of individual attractions called the "bannerline" appeared outside many shows, with depictions that outlandishly distorted what was inside.

Although written publicity and signs were used, the person who stood outside the entrance spieling to the crowd about the attractions inside was the key to the promotion. The job of the "talker" or "outside lecturer" was to get people to "step right up" and buy a ticket. The best of them were orators who had mastered the art of persuasion. Using exaggeration and falsification, they told passersby of the wonders that awaited within for the price of a thin dime. To help attract the crowd the talker often had a "bally"—one of the exhibits out front as a lure to move the customers closer. A scantily clad woman with a python around her neck or a colorfully dressed person with a blatant physical deformity would serve the purpose.

Inside, a series of platforms formed separate stages for each "human oddity." An "inside lecturer" would take over, going from attraction to attraction telling in fabricated detail "the life and true facts" behind each one. A few exhibits would just sit observing the observers, but most actively performed. The elastic skin man would stretch his epidermis, the wild man would look ferocious and pace up and down, and the armless woman might sign autographs with her feet. Some played musical instruments or sang and danced. Many lectured about themselves. Whatever they did, it had to correspond to the fabricated image that was created for them. It also had to be short because the inside lecturer had to keep the crowd moving to make space for the next batch of customers.

Nevertheless, they did not rush the audience and rob them of the opportunity to buy souvenirs from the "curiosities." Photographic portraits of each exhibit were available and would be inscribed with a personal message for an additional fee. Professional photographers took the pictures, and they carefully posed the attraction in their studios to promote the exhibits' staged identity (Mitchell 1979). Booklets containing the concocted "true life story and facts about the conditions" of each exhibit were also available. The popularity of these and other items afforded the freaks a convenient way to supplement their incomes, measure their own popularity, and break the boredom of the routine of the show.

STRATEGIES OF PROMOTING FREAKS

The pitches that freak show promoters used in selling tickets contained the same appeals other entrepreneurs employ in promoting cars, vacuum cleaners, or colleges for that matter. Show people presented exhibits as unique, or the best of their kind—the tallest, or the shortest, the only one, or one of a category never seen before. All were recommended by or associated with prestigious people and organizations—scientists, doctors, clergy, newspapers, and scientific organizations. People were told about the great popularity of the exhibits and of the need to act quickly so as not to miss the chance of a lifetime. Freak shows were heralded as morally uplifting and educational, not merely as frivolous amusement. The price was right as well, too much of a bargain to pass by—particularly if you believed the talker's description of the great time and expense involved in getting the exhibits from far-off lands and the high salaries some exhibits allegedly received. These ploys, many of which have become the clichés of the sales industry, were liberally injected in the promotion of exhibits.

In addition to these general appeals, there developed two specific modes of presenting freaks: the *exotic mode* and the *aggrandized status mode*.[3] These modes of presentation represent patterns of particular techniques, strategies, and styles that promoters and managers used to enhance the appeal of the exhibits. They provided the formulas for developing the fabrications that made up the "true life stories and facts regarding" the staged appearance, the pictures, and other aspects of the "freaks" promotion.

These modes of presentation provide an alternative to categorizing sideshow exhibits on the basis of physiological characteristics and help avoid the trap of seeing "freaks" as objective facts. These patterns reveal the implicit assumptions embodied in the freak show world by allowing the focus to be on the institution of exhibiting people and the perspective of those involved rather than on the bodies of those exhibited.

The Exotic Presentation

In the exotic mode, the person received an identity that appealed to people's interest in the culturally strange, the primitive, the bestial, the exotic (Alloula 1983; Said 1978; Karp and Lavine 1991; Banta and Hinsley 1986). For example, promoters told the audience the person on exhibit came from a mysterious part of the world—darkest Africa, the wilds of Borneo, a Turkish harem, an ancient Aztec kingdom. The geographic location of origin was most often the non-Western world, but occasionally American venues such as Native American villages or the wilds of the Far West qualified. The lecturer and the "true life story" booklet would tell of the person's origin, giving specific or purposefully erroneous and distorted information about the life and customs of the area of alleged origin and of the freaks place in that society. Tales of albinos, for example, contained descriptions of them either being worshipped or, more usually, being prepared for sacrifice. Sacrifices were curtailed by an explorer who saved the life of the albino by taking her or him from the tribe. Some stories were so elaborate they took thirty-five pages to tell.

Dressed to fit the story, the exhibit would behave consistently with the front. The "wild men" or "savages" might grunt or pace the stage, snarling and growling, letting off warrior screams. Dress might include a loincloth, a string of bones around the neck, and, in a few cases, chains allegedly protecting the audience from the beast before them. In the case of people from the Middle East or Asia, the presentation and the performance would be more subdued, with the freak acting out in exaggerated stereotypic ways the mannerisms and customs of its supposed country of origin. The freak presented in the exotic mode typically appeared in his or her photos with a painted backdrop depicting jungle scenes or exotic lands. Papier-mâché boulders, imitation tropical plants, and other touches of exotica added a three-dimensional flare to the set.

The exotic stories used in presenting exhibits maximized interest. In a period of intense world exploration and Western expansion, news events provided some of the scripts and descriptions for the presentation of freaks. Thus, when Stanley and Livingstone were lost in the "dark continent" and imperialist Britain was fighting those they were colonizing, the "savage African" was a popular motif (Lindfors 1983). Late in the nineteenth century and early in the twentieth, when the United States took the Philippines from Spain and was fighting the indigenous peoples, the Philippine backdrop was prominent. The scientific reports and travelogues of nineteenth and early twentieth century natural scientists were another important source of stories for the promotion of freaks. Pre- and post-Darwinian discussions about the place of human beings in the great order of things and the relationships of the various kinds of humans to each other and to baboons, chimps, and gorillas were in the air (Gould 1981, Jordan 1968, Gossett 1963). Pseudoscientific writing on classification and anthropological reports about the "races of man" provided the ideas for the decorations and the details of the presentation narratives in the exotic mode.

Natural scientists were involved more directly with freak shows. Showmen asked scientists to authenticate the origin and credibility, and the scientists' commentary appeared in newspapers and publicity pamphlets (Altick 1979). Some exhibits were presented to scientific societies for discussion and speculation. Showmen played up the science affiliation. They used the word "museum" in the title of many freak shows and referred to freak show lecturers as "professor" or "doctor." Linking freak exhibits with science made the attractions more interesting, more believable, and less frivolous to Puritanical anti-entertainment sentiments.

In the most flagrant distortion under the exotic mode, Americans citizens were misrepresented as non-Western foreigners—Ohio raised dwarfs were said to be from Borneo, a tall North Carolinian black from Dahomia. But the exotic mode was not just employed for native-born Americans. Many people who were exhibited as freaks actually were born in the countries promoters said they were from. In these cases, the distortion and misrepresentation came in the details of the stories and in the exaggeration of the exotic in the descriptions of the culture and the person exhibited. The odd, bizarre, erotic, and savage was highlighted (Rydell 1984). Favorite themes included cannibalism, human sacrifice, head hunting, polygamy, unusual dress, and food preferences that repelled Americans (eating dogs, rodents, and insects).

People with demonstrable physical differences (those who were very tall, very short, without arms and legs, conjoined, etc.) were brought from the Third World and exhibited within the exotic motif, emphasizing their anomalies plus their "strange ways." But many freaks who were brought from abroad had nothing "wrong" with them physically. Nevertheless, they were referred to as freaks by those in the business as well as by the press and the general public and often shared the freak show platform with people we would describe as having disabilities. What made them "freaks" was the racist presentations of them and their culture by promoters.

Aggrandized Status

The exotic mode emphasized how different and, in most cases, how inferior the persons on exhibit were. The aggrandized mode reversed that by laying claim to the superiority of the freak. Social position, achievements, talents, family, and physiology were fabricated, elevated, or exaggerated and then flaunted. Prestigious titles such as "Captain," "Major," "General," "Prince," "King," "Princess," and "Queen" aggrandized exhibits. Since Europe and England were admired by Americans as culturally superior, changing common-sounding names to those that suggested European or English birth, accompanied by a changed birthplace, was another technique of elevating status. Showmen sometimes told the public that the freak was highly educated, spoke many languages, and had aristocratic hobbies such as writing poetry or painting. In addition, having an audience with royalty or with the president of the United States was commonly flaunted or fabricated. This publicity claimed that the "human curiosity" was in the same social circle as the celebrities, not merely a scientific specimen. The aggrandized status mode also required dressing the part. Expensive jewelry, stylish clothes, top hats and tails, evening gowns, furs, and the acquisition of fine taste figured lavishly in some presentations. For others, merely being very clean and neat and respectably dressed was the aggrandizement. Another way to enhance the exhibited person was to boast of conventional but status-significant organizational affiliations and attainments. Membership and offices held in churches, the Masons, Eastern States, and the Daughters of the American Revolution were mentioned in lectures and pamphlets. Some of the "human curiosities" wore pins and displayed other symbols of their membership while on their platforms.

Performances in the aggrandized status mode were of two types. The first involved doing tasks that one might assume could not be done by a person with that particular disability. A person without legs, for example, might show how he walked with his arms. The emphasis was on how the person exhibited compensated for the disability. The second kind of performance was more standard show business. Freaks sang, danced, and played musical instruments,[4] emphasizing their conventional talents and accomplishments.

Boasting about the normalcy of the freak's spouse was another technique of the aggrandized presentation. Many of the photographic portraits of freaks sold at exhibits pose them with their families against a sitting room backdrop with stuffed chairs and other symbols of middle-class aspirations. "True life" booklets and the lecturers' descriptions sometimes dwelled on the exhibits' family roles and the spouses' and children's accomplishments. Presentation of freaks who were children stressed the normalcy of the parents and siblings, who sometimes were displayed with the freak.

Those displayed in the aggrandized mode tended to be presented as physically normal, or even superior, in all ways except for the particular anomaly that was their alleged reason for fame. In many presentations the exhibit was described as physically attractive and in no way distasteful to the audience. This was standard in the promoting of midgets.

The exotic mode of presentation borrowed its narratives from imperialistic excursions and natural science exploration. On occasion, medical doctors examined the specimen, but for the most part the freak was presented as belonging to the anthropologists or zoological and philosophical taxonomers. The scientific underpinnings of the aggrandized mode were provided by teratology, the study of human "monsters"—the word given to infants born with congenital abnormalities—as well as other medical specialties (Gould and Pyle 1986). The nineteenth century popularized the idea that human birth abnormalities were not the result of Satan or evil acts by the parents but were part of God's natural order, an order that could be understood by rational science. Doctor's testimonials and pronouncements, often appearing at length in the "true life booklets," were used as part of the presentations in the aggrandized status mode. These testimonials emphasized that the abnormality was a discrete condition, not an indictment of the integrity or morality of the exhibit or his or her parents. Because little was known about genetics and the endocrine system prior to the turn of the century, teratology was primarily a science of classification. The causes of the conditions were open for popular speculation, and theories of maternal impression dominated presentations as well as

2.2. Freakishness was often created from gender transgression, as in this image of a bearded lady, which replicates the traditional Victorian portrait of marriage. Collection of Robert Gould Shaw, Harvard Theatre Collection, The Houghton Library.

explanations.[5] With the rediscovery of Gregor Mendel, the rise of the eugenics movement, and advances in the understanding of the thyroid and pituitary glands, freaks appeared increasingly in newspaper articles describing them as "sick" and in the domain of doctors, not the public. This medical assault, accompanied by the eugenics movement (Reilly 1991, Ludmerer 1972), undermined the aggrandized mode in the first third of the twentieth century (Circus and Museum Freaks 1908).

CHARACTERISTICS OF PEOPLE AND MODES OF PRESENTATION

What factors determined which mode a would-be freak was cast into? To some extent, particular kinds of anomalies typed the person as being in one mode or the other. For example, people with microcephaly, a condition associated with mental retardation and characterized by a very small, pointed head, were typically presented in the exotic mode as "wild men," "missing links," or atavistic specimens of an extinct race. Hypopituitary dwarfs—commonly referred to as midgets—and who tend to be well proportioned and physically attractive, were cast within the aggrandized status mode. Achondroplastic dwarfs, whose head and limbs tend to be out of proportion to their trunks, appeared in the exotic mode. But the person's particular disability was not always the crucial factor. A very tall person, for example, might be presented in the exotic mode as a warrior from a lost civilization, for example, or in the aggrandized mode as a European prince.

Skin color was an important factor. Blacks tended to be cast as exotics, billed as missing links or as savages from Africa. White, native-born Americans were less likely to be exotics though some were said to be from the South Sea Islands or South American. Although the presentation and the characteristics of the person exhibited often were congruent, promoters were very creative with their tales. Whites became exotic with stories about being raised by, or tortured by, or living among non-Western people by virtue of having been captured, kidnapped, or washing ashore after surviving a shipwreck. Tattooing as a torture inflicted, supposedly by barbaric people, was the standard way of presenting Caucasian "human art galleries." Some of the most famous exhibits in the aggrandized status mode were carefully groomed and trained for exhibit. For example, Millie and Christine, black conjoined twins born in slavery, became the celebrated Victorian singing nightingales. P. T. Barnum carefully prepared Charles Stratton, a man born to a family of modest means, to hobnob with society's elite as General Tom Thumb.

COMPLEXITY IN THE MODES OF PRESENTATION

The exotic and aggrandized modes of presentation represent clear patterns, but they do not capture the entire range of freak images, nor do they suggest the complexity in the imagery of many exhibits. Especially in the mid-nineteenth century, the exotic and aggrandized modes were often enacted with the serious intent of getting the audience to believe the façade. With other exhibits, and increasingly toward the last decade of the nineteenth and into the twentieth centuries, the presentation was more whimsical, containing elements of farce, mockery, ridicule, and humor. While there are a few examples of exhibits being dressed as clowns and cast as fools, the direct presentation of exhibits in a humorous mode, separate from the exotic and aggrandized modes, never fully developed. Rather, comic and mocking elements were incorporated into the modes already discussed. Usually humor took the form of exaggeration. The fabrications, the appearance of the freak, and the overall presentation were so outlandish that both the talker and most in the audience shared a sense of the ridiculous. Perhaps the best examples of this were the "fat people" exhibits. Obese people were common in freak shows and were so popular that a few carnivals carried sideshows made up exclusively of extremely heavy people. "Congresses of Obesity" exhibited women dressed in dainty, frilly lace dresses and other trappings of stereotyped petite femininity and gave them names like "Babe Ruth," "Little Emma," and "Dollie Dimples." The lecturer would acknowledge his participation in the farce with asides, humor, and commentary. In some cases, hints of irony were subtle, allowing the showmen to play to the more worldly segment of the audience as a farce, while playing straight to the more naive. By presenting some exhibits on the borderline between farce and straight, showmen avoided some of the confrontations that might occur with members of the audience who wanted to expose the fraud. By playing this borderline skillfully, showmen could have the audience participate in the hoax much in the way adults participate in seeing Santa in the presence of children.

The exotic and aggrandized modes were not always mutually exclusive. Some freaks appeared in a mixed mode, borrowing elements from each and deriving interest as well as

2.3. A 1903 shot of the Barnum and Bailey Circus Sideshow Group, depicting forty-seven performers and illustrating the remarkable diversity of sideshow freakishness. Courtesy of the Circus World Museum, Baraboo, Wisconsin.

humor by juxtaposing incongruity. A famous example was Krao Farini, a hirsute female from Laos. In the 1880s, when she was still a child, she started her freak career as "Darwin's Missing Link," portrayed as halfway between human and monkey. Even though she remained "Darwin's Missing Link" throughout her career, as she entered her teens she began to be presented as a cultured, intelligent lady who spoke five languages. In the case of Krao, juxtaposing elements of the exotic mode with aggrandized status created novel incongruities that had an obvious public appeal given her long and successful career.

As Krao's case suggests, some exhibits changed modes over the course of their careers. It was common early in careers for managers to try different modes to see which seemed to appeal to the audience and fit the person behind the façade. The changing characteristics of the person and the changing tastes of society affected the mode's appreciation. Displays of the original Siamese twins, Chang and Eng, for example, first emphasized their cultural differences, exotic dress, and habits (Hunter 1964). In early publicity drawings, the twins appear in Asian dress and pigtails. Later in their careers, after they had been Westernized, they dressed American by wearing suits and ties, and the fact that they each were married and had large families was stressed. Many freaks moved from a straight, one-mode presentation to taking on elements of farce as they got older.

By the turn of the century humor and mockery became stronger element of the freak show. This is not to say that the unironic, straight exotic and aggrandized modes were completely absent. As late as the 1930s, Ringling Brothers, Barnum and Bailey Circus, the most prestigious and popular of the circuses, showed two separate groups of indigenous people, the "Ubangi Savages" and the "Burmese Giraffe Neck Women," as "educational and scientific attractions."

By the early twentieth century the audience was learning to view the freaks differently. People with disabilities started being viewed as sick—as having various genetic and endocrine disorders. As the public became knowledgeable about the people of the world, exotic hype lost its appeal. The razzle-dazzle died down and was replaced by a more staid presentation. The "talker" began using a microphone, and "true life booklets" became shorter and much less embellished. The carefully posed, professional quality photographic images of the freaks were replaced by poor quality postcards.

DISCUSSION

By seeing freak shows as a business and exhibits as presentations, we can begin to understand the manufacture and management of disability images for profit. Well into the twentieth century, such shows were an accepted part of American popular culture. As we have seen, the way exhibits were presented—the exotic mode that exploited the public's interest in the "races of man," and the aggrandized mode that capitalized on the public's status concerns—was not offensive to nineteenth- and early twentieth-century citizens. There are a few isolated examples of attractions promoted in a way designed to work on the sympathies and compassion of the audience for the plight of the freak, but they are rare. Pity as a mode or even as an element of presentation was nearly absent. If it had pleased audiences, promoters might have developed presentations emphasizing how difficult life was for the "handicapped" exhibits, told the crowds how unhappy they were, how the admission charge would help pay their expenses and relieve their suffering. But pity did not coincide with the world of amusement where people used their leisure time and spent their money to be entertained, not to confront human suffering.[6]

Pity as a mode of presenting people with physical, mental, and behavioral differences fit better the medicalized conception of human differences. While in the nineteenth century natural scientists, teratologists, and other doctors examined freaks, they were not patients. Professionals had not gained control over human deviation; people with physical and mental anomalies were still in the public domain. Into the twentieth century, the power of professions increased and the eugenics movement grew strong. People with physical and mental anomalies came under the control of professionals and many were secluded from the public. Their conditions were to be contained or treated behind closed doors. During the first three decades of the twentieth century, human differences were thought of as a threat to the "American Race." People with physical and mental differences became dangerous because they were alleged to have inferior genes that, if not controlled would weaken the breeding stock. They needed to be locked away and in other ways controlled to protect the gene pool. This was accompanied by the professionalization of organized charities and fund raising, the invention of the poster child. Pity combined with the medical model became the dominant mode of presenting human differences for money. It is through this lens that we look back on freak shows and find them distasteful.

This is not to suggest that the earlier imagery of the disabled promoted by the freak show enhanced the well-being of disabled people more than modern renderings. The exotic mode obviously presented people in ways that offend current taste and positive ideas of the capabilities of people with physical and mental differences. Steeped in racism, imperialism, and handicapism, this mode emphasized the inferiority of the "human curiosity." The negative imagery paralleled the visions of natural science at the time by casting the exhibits as specimens, as inferior and as contemptuous. The association of various human differences with danger, with subhumans, and with animals, was developed as well as perpetuated by these exhibits (not to mention its impact on images of racial minorities and non-Westerners).

At first glance the aggrandized mode seems positive. Exhibits were lauded for their achievements and for how, except for their particular physical anomaly, they were quite normal, even superior. The audience must have wondered why, if they were so competent, they made a living having others look at them. With the best circuses, dime museums, and amusement parks, salaries and living conditions were good. Some exhibits chose their careers because of the financial benefits and fame they brought. But for the majority, those who were exhibited in the second-rate establishments, life was marginal and precarious. Here the exhibits chose their way of life not because of what it offered, but because of what they got away from. With an urbanizing country, no social security, discrimination in employment, architectural barriers, and strained interpersonal relations, persons with anomalies found refuge in a world where there were others similarly situated. If they did not find fortune and fame, they found acceptance and more freedom than either custodial institutions or the mainstream might provide. Although to some extent the imagery of the aggrandized mode was positive, the mere presence of the exhibits as part of the amusement world, which itself was depraved in the public view, suggested that they belonged with their own kind and that they were not competent enough to prosper in the larger world.

CONCLUSION

To some the word "freak" is offensive. It was the preferred term in the amusement industry, even among the exhibits themselves, at least through the 1930s (Johnston 1933). Human exhibits were not offended by the term because they did not take the nouns people used to refer to them seriously. Their main concern was to make money. Any designation that facilitated profit was acceptable. As freaks sat on the platform, most looked down on the audience with contempt—not because they felt angry at being gawked at or at being called freaks, but simply because the amusement world looked down on "rubes" in general. Their contempt was that of insiders toward the uninitiated. For those in the amusement world the sucker who came to the show was on the outside, not the exhibit. I have not used the term "freak" to mean people who have certain physical conditions. "Freak" is a frame of mind, a set of practices, a way of thinking about and presenting people. It is not a person but the enactment of a tradition, the performance of a stylized presentation.

Whenever we study deviance we have to look at those in charge—whether self-appointed or officially—of telling us who deviants are and what they are like. Their versions of reality are presentations, people filtered through stories and world views. The concept of "freak" no longer sustains careers. Human differences are now framed in other modes and by different institutions. For sideshow participants, the world view was that of show business, and the images were fabricated to sell the person as an attraction. In the hands of professional organizations, the images created will be designed to reach the organization's aim most effectively. In the professions and human services, success often comes to be defined as survival and expansion, which is possible only with a proper cash flow though charitable contributions and public support. In the end, the freak show has much in common with human service agencies. The imagery may be different but the issue of the relation between presentation and profit is similar. The job of those who want to serve people seen as disabled or different is to get behind the scenes, to know them as they see themselves, not as they are presented. Presentations are artifacts of changing social institutions, organizational formations, and world views. To understand the presentations, to become dislodged from their hold on our reality, we have to trace their origins and understand their place in the world as it is presently constructed.

Notes

1. The chapter is based on a larger historical study of freak shows in the United States (see Bogdan, 1987, 1988, and 1993). Memoirs of show people, period newspapers, magazines, photographs, and various forms of circus, carnival, fair, and dime museum memorabilia made up the bulk of the data. Private correspondence and interviews with show personnel were also a source of information.

2. "Grift" is a circus and carnival term for "the crooked games, short change artists, cloths line robbers, merchandise boosters, pickpockets and all other types of skull duggery" (McKennon 1980).

3. Showmen did not use these phrases. Whether they consciously thought in terms of these concepts is not clear, but their actions suggest that such ideas were part of their perspective.

4. In the late nineteenth and early twentieth centuries troupes of midgets put on elaborate theatrical and musical performances (see Roth and Cromie 1980).

5. The theory held that pregnant women's babies could be influenced by the experiences, especially frightening experiences, the mother had. Thus, in one case, an African-American woman's delivery of a piebald child was attributed to her being frightened by a white horse while pregnant.

6. In non-freak show venues, sympathy and pity were at work. Charity and begging coexisted in the society at large with the freak show.

References

Alloula, M. 1983. *The Colonial Harem.* Minneapolis: University of Minnesota Press.

Altick, R. 1979. *Shows of London.* Cambridge: Belknap.

Banta, M. and C. Hinsley. 1986. *From Site to Sight.* Cambridge: Harvard University Press.

Bogdan, R. 1993. "In Defense of Freak Show." *Disability, Handicap and Society* 8, no. 1.

———. 1988. *Freak Show.* Chicago: University of Chicago Press.

———. 1987. "Exhibition of Mentally Retarded People for Amusement and Profit, 1850–1940." *American Journal of Mental Deficiency* 91.

Circus and Museum Freaks. 1908. *Scientific America Supplement,* April 4.

Dadswell, J. 1946. *Hey There, Sucker!* Boston: Bruce Humphries.

Drimmer, F. 1973. *Very Special People.* New York: Amjon.

Durant, A. 1957. *A Pictorial History of the American Circus.* New York: A. S. Barnes.

Fiedler, L. 1978. *Freaks.* New York: Simon and Schuster.

Goffman, E. 1963. *Stigma.* Englewood Cliffs, N.J.: Prentice-Hall.

———. 1959. *Presentation of Self in Everyday Life.* Garden City, N.Y.: Doubleday.

Gossett, T. 1963. *Race.* Dallas: Southern Methodist University Press.

Gould, G., and W. Pyle. 1896. *Anomalies and Curiosities of Medicine.* New York: Bell.

Gould, S. 1981. *The Mismeasure of Man.* New York: W. W. Norton.

Gresham, W. 1948. *Monster Midway.* New York: Rinehart.

Hunter, K. 1964. *Duet for Life.* New York: Coward-McCann.

Inciardi, J., and D. Petersen. 1972. "Gaff Joints and Shell Games." *Journal of Popular Culture* 6.

Isman, I. 1924. *Weber and Fields.* New York: Boni and Liveright.

Johnston, A. 1933. "Sideshow People III." *New Yorker,* April 28.

Jordan, W. 1968. *White over Black.* Chapel Hill: University of North Carolina Press.

Karp, I., and S. Lavine. 1991. *Exhibiting Cultures.* Washington, D.C.: Smithsonian Press.

Lindfors, B. 1983. "Circus Africans." *Journal of American Culture* 6, no. 2.

Ludmerer, K. 1972. *Genetics and American Society.* Baltimore: Johns Hopkins University Press.

Mannix, D. 1990. *Freaks.* San Francisco: RE/SEARCH Publications.

McKennon, J. 1980. *A Pictorial History of the American Carnival.* Sarasota, Fla.: Carnival Publishers.

Mitchell, M. 1979. *Monsters of the Gilded Age.* Toronto: Gage.

Reilly, P. 1991. *The Surgical Solution.* Baltimore: Johns Hopkins University Press.

Roth, H., and R. Cromie. 1980. *The Little People.* New York: Everest House.

Rydell, R. 1984. *All the World's a Fair.* Chicago: University of Chicago Press.

Said, E. 1978. *Orientalism.* New York: Vintage.

Saxon, A. 1983. *The Autobiography of Mrs. Tom Thumb.* Hamden, Conn.: Archon.

Sharpe, A. 1970. "Circus Grift." *Bandwagon* 14.

Wilmeth, D. 1982. *Variety Entertainment and Outdoor Amusements.* Westport, Conn.: Greenwood.

THREE

The "Careers" of People Exhibited in Freak Shows: The Problem of Volition and Valorization

DAVID A. GERBER

If an individual consents, by virtue of what appear to be acts of free choice, to being degraded, exploited, or oppressed, does that act of consent end the moral problem that his or her situation seems to constitute? In my own field of social history this question has been asked frequently in the analysis of a number of different social groups: proletarianized industrial workers, African-American slaves, and Victorian women are prominent examples. Contemporary feminists ask these same questions about women who choose to work as go-go dancers, mud wrestlers, and prostitutes, or women who choose to remain in abusive relationships.

I would like to pose this problem in the context of disabled people exhibited in freak shows. For centuries people with visible physical anomalies (broadly defined to include body deformities, disfigurements, deficiencies, and superfluities) have consented to display these anomalies, in public and for money. How are we to evaluate the quality of that consent—especially in light of the extent to which people with physical anomalies have experienced broad and abiding social oppression and marginalization? By what criteria can we judge that consent fictive or credible? Under any circumstance, should that consent necessarily have any weight at all in reaching a judgment about the morality of such a display? And once having come to terms with the issues posed by that act of consent, how do we measure the quality of the performance the act of display may be said to constitute?[1]

Take the prototypical case of an ultra-obese individual, whose performance consists of little more than wearing clothes that reveal her extreme weight, while being seated in an especially small chair that enhances the same impression, and allowing herself to be stared at by an audience. Say she nonetheless considers herself an actress. What are we to make of the gap between her evaluation of her "career" (that it is a worthwhile pursuit that enhances her status) and what her situation actually seems to be (that she is a human exhibit—"the fat lady"—exploited for possessing qualities that the audience regards as grotesque)? Our analytical goals aside, we must also ask by what right we question either the quality of her volition or the criteria she has adopted in valorizing her role.

I am prompted to ask these questions by the viewpoint advanced in Robert Bogdan's fascinating book, *Freak Show: Presenting Human Oddities for Amusement and Profit* (1988), and other writings. In this book Bogdan does us an important service by opening up for systematic discussion the history of Americans with physical anomalies, and by suggesting the commercial and cultural roots of one process by which physical differences might become endowed, under specific historical circumstances, with significant meanings. Other aspects of the book are, for me, troubling. Bogdan advances a social constructionist approach to the history of displaying people with physical anomalies that, in effect, serves to accept the morality of that display in the belief that: (1) "freak" is an invention or construct, not a person, so the display of such people is not an offense to humanity but, more or less, show business; (2) historically the freak show has constituted a legitimate performance, because it was consciously staged for commercial and artistic success; (3) the freak show ultimately was founded upon the willing participation of those displayed, the majority of whom were "active participants" in creating their presentations and found value and status in their roles as human exhibits; (4) we need to question our assumption that we have a legitimate claim to argue with and condemn the choices, such as participating in a freak show, of those who lived in other historical epochs, especially when they saw no moral issue in their activities; and (5) the freak show is a long-gone phenomenon, so it is useless to condemn it.[2]

In this chapter the phenomenon of the freak show provides the basis for appraising the issue of volition and valorization, both as a problem conceptualized in the abstract and as it presents itself in the limited instance of the display of people with physical anomalies. I seek to revitalize the issue of the moralization of the freak show by combining historical inquiry with exploration of the problem of uncoerced—that is, not forced by violence or the threat of violence—consent. I first examine the problem of choice and consent in social relations, and then engage principal assumptions of *Freak Show* and question, in the conceptual context of consent theory, the examples Bogdan develops. Finally, with reference to the same or to similar examples, I test those assumptions based on the sociohistorical situation and cultural representations, past and present, of some types of people frequently displayed. In this exercise I purposefully do not go much beyond Bogdan's own evidence in order to suggest that there are other ways—actually more complimentary to his approach than conflicting—to read the artifacts by which we have come to understand the freak show. We can, I believe, see the freak show as both a socially constructed phenomenon of commercial entertainment and a product of unequal social relations, oppression, and exploitation, but we cannot understand it exclusively in either way. Up to a point, social construction provides a powerful tool for dislodging assumptions about the naturalness of disability, but, as I will demonstrate, it cannot help us much to grasp to concrete social relations in which disability is embedded.

My purpose is largely to remoralize the question of the freak show, but my argument is less with the past than with a troubling aspect of Bogdan's book: his attempt to illustrate the social construction of disability seems based upon neutralizing the problem of exploitation. This is furthered by the testimonies of those human exhibits who found worth in their "careers" as freaks. Whereas Bogdan takes these people at their word when they claim to find value in the lives they led as freaks, I intend to interrogate these testimonies. Bogdan's goal is to empower disabled people by establishing their agency and removing them from the category of victims. As he has said, too many people wish, patronizingly, to speak for the disabled and not allow them their own voice. I do not believe, however, that it is disrespectful or condescending to assume an interrogatory stance. There is no higher mark of being taken seriously than to be admitted to the circle of participants in an argument about questions of importance. Before returning to this justification for my inquiry, I want to make clear my own ethical position as an investigator. I cannot claim to feel strongly that the issue animating my concern is exclusively whether, in a limited, technical sense, human exhibits actually freely chose to be in freak shows and found value in doing so. Beyond the question, "Is this choice voluntary?" or the surmise, "This choice is so bad, it could not be voluntary," another point asserts itself just as insistently in my mind: "This choice is so bad, I don't care if it is voluntary."[3] In short, I want to establish at the start that I do not approve of freak shows and thus find condemnation of them, past or present, a compelling purpose.

CHOICE AND CONSENT

At the heart of the problem must be our effort to understand both the nature of choice and the ways in which choice ultimately may or may not be said to inform acts of uncoerced consent. For this, it is useful to explore the historical and intellectual frameworks in which free-choice arguments have been conceived in Western discourse. Perhaps the most incisive recent exploration of these frameworks is the suggestively titled *Happy Slaves* (1989), an analysis of the problem of consent in social relations by Don Herzog, a political scientist. Moving considerably beyond the question of the "consent of the governed," Herzog defines consent theory in a general way that makes it a useful frame of reference for our inquiry. Consent theory is "any political, moral, legal, or social theory that casts society as a collection of free individuals, and thus seeks to explain or justify outcomes by appealing to their voluntary actions, especially choice and consent."[4]

As Herzog makes clear, consent theory predates the rise of capitalism and free-market economic thought, with which we usually associate its historical origins. It arose in sixteenth-century England as feudalism declined and the Protestant Reformation spread across Europe. For the first time in the history of the West, political, religious, and intellectual authorities concerned with the sources of social order found it necessary to imagine the bonding of people, who were now increasingly without masters and appeared to make their own choices in ever-broader areas of life, to society without the mediation of such traditional, authoritative institutions as manorial estates and without an all-encompassing ecclesiastical system. Far from being merely a mask for bourgeois privilege, Herzog contends, consent theory began as an attempt to map out the bases of a new world of social relations. Consent theorists posited axioms that would serve to explain the process by which societies composed of sovereign individuals might spontaneously achieve coherence and order without state coercion. Because we are still without masters, as that term is used to describe feudal social relations, consent theory remains a way of understanding the social relations of groups and individuals.[5]

As Herzog demonstrates, however, from its inception consent theory has been vulnerable to at least three criticisms. First, consent theorists have centered moral and political arguments on the choices of allegedly free individuals. The original act of choice was conceived by John Locke and others as a type of contract by which individuals gave consent to affiliate with society. The notion that somehow people enter into their relationship with society by an act of consent, and not by virtue of birth and circumstance, is hardly correct. Moreover, consent theory arose in a society in which most people—women, children, the indigent and impoverished—were only nominally free and actually had little, if any, choice in giving their consent to the social arrangements into which they were born. Even as an intellectual exercise for imagining the possibility of an orderly body politic, consent theory was really only relevant to understanding the social relationships of those middle- and upper-strata males who were allowed to exercise political rights and enjoyed legal and informal authority in social relationships. But even among these persons, the notion of a voluntary compact with society is not realistic. Choice and consent continue to be problematic precisely because of the role of circumstances, such as the accident of the social situation into which we are born, in our lives, and because we are not equal in power to influence the course of our lives or even to understand them. Thus, a second criticism of consent theory is that consent theorists typically have refused to consider the relevance of natural and social inequalities that limit our range of choices and ultimately frame our acts of consent. Third, consent theory resists the claim that society is an organism or seamless web of connected parts in favor of the fallacious notion that society is a collection of atomized, egoistic individuals. The latter viewpoint may make for tidy analytical work, but its understanding of human beings makes neither anthropological nor sociological sense. Society and culture exist as much as structures of relational and mental boundaries constraining individuals as they do as guides to libertarian possibilities. Choices are made within society and culture, not outside of them by sovereign individuals.[6]

Nonetheless consent theory does have serviceable dimensions. If historically contextualized and governed by psychologically realistic premises, the study of choice and consent may provide a baseline for analyzing social relations from the standpoint of individuals. Consent theory cannot, however, substitute for a theory of social relations, such as the minority group model that seeks to explain the social position of people with disabilities, but rather may serve only as a framework of questions to be addressed through the application of such a theory and the analysis of data. We shall see, in fact, that understanding choice and consent in the lives of the human exhibits appearing in freak shows may best be accomplished through use not of consent theory, but of a historically grounded minority group model.

Herzog outlines various conceptual strategies to help us generate just such a framework of questions. Situating the ethical position of the analyst is a logical place to begin. By what right do we sit in judgment of the choices of such people as the "fat lady" who displays herself for money? "By virtue of the necessity of understanding the world," or "In the service of learning," we may answer. Yet though such goals are admirable, riding roughshod over individuals in their pursuit is neither desirable nor right. Of course, the problem seems less acute when it is a question of dealing with the choices of individuals that directly or indirectly do harm to others. But what about cases in which individuals end up harming only themselves or sabotaging their own interests? Here one evidently runs the risk of condescension. Realism dictates, however, that we acknowledge that individuals often do make poor choices, even when, as is frequently not the case—especially with those who appeared in freak shows— they have everything going for them (i.e., they do not face the prospect of being unable to support themselves; they are not hurried; they have the right information; and they are not coerced by external sources). One simply has to adopt a hierarchy of priorities and goals in analyzing human behavior, and truth—in this case, acknowledging the imperfections and confusions of people in determining what is in their own interest (in the awkward Marxian formulation, the falseness of their consciousness)—has to take priority. This need not necessarily be done at the expense of respect or empathy. Indeed, it is just as easy to argue that one shows disrespect by refusing to extend the claims of truth-telling to an individual. In personal relations, moreover, we consider ourselves well served by friends who question our version of reality, especially when that version may prove harmful to us. Arguing with our sources may similarly be said to serve them well, even if it does so indirectly. Of course, many cases are not clear-cut examples of exposing the probability of harm to others or of self-sabotage. Among other things, such cases demand a microscopic examination of motivations as well as alternatives and outcomes. To this extent, it would seem that without seeking empathy—the illusive but necessary capacity to imagine oneself as another person in a particular set of circumstances—one cannot succeed, so the analysis has built into it some check against condescension.

Let us assume then that we do not ethically compromise ourselves by sitting in judgment of the choices made by the "fat lady" and others. The question then is, "How do we make sense of choice and consent? We can divide the problem into two issues, structured as questions and axiomatic responses, culled from Herzog's analysis.[7]

First, what are the significant preconditions for effective choice and consent?

1. One makes a free choice not only when one is uncoerced, but also when one has a significant range of meaningful choices. One must have freedom, in other words, to make choices from a number of options as well as freedom from the necessity of choosing only one course of action.
2. Such freedom is greatest in societies in which the social environment fosters the opportunity for individuals to play a number of different roles that do not excessively limit one's choices to take on other roles.
3. One must have occasions for choice—that is, times when one may exercise independent agency rather than have things done for one.
4. One must have the physical and mental capacity to make choices and carry out the course of action they suggest.
5. One must have information about the alternatives one needs to evaluate.
6. One must have sufficient time and physical and mental security to evaluate options.

Next, how do we interpret choices once they are made and understand the ways in which choice variously informs consent? The range of problems here is considerable, but among the most important considerations are the following cautions:

1. We cannot necessarily infer consciousness from behavior in appraising the motivations behind choice, and thus in taking the measure of consent. Apparently voluntary choices may be products of volition, but also of apathy, which leads to refusing to appraise all alternatives, or simply of a lack of alternatives.
2. Consent may not explain the condition of a person who appears to be content with a bad situation. She may not understand her situation, let alone how she came to it, or she may lack the motivation to change a situation she knows to be bad.
3. Choice, Herzog says, is like opening Pandora's box: "If you chose to open the box, does it follow that you've chosen each and every one of its contents?"[8] We need to remember, in other words, that there may be unintended and often undesired consequences from any course of action, which we would not choose if they were presented to us individually.

With these considerations in mind, we can proceed to examine the world of the freak show and those displayed within it, as they existed in the past and as Bogdan has presented them to us, paying particular attention to Bogdan's understanding of the volitional status of the freak show performer. We shall see that by the criteria just outlined, the freak show hardly emerges as a universe of free choices. Moreover, the complex acts by which those displayed may be said to have consented to their situation considerably strain our understandings of consent.

THE FREAK SHOW AND ITS INTERPRETERS

The display of people with physical anomalies has ancient roots. We have evidence that in pharaonic Egypt dwarfs lived in royal households, where they were employed to give comic relief to statesmen burdened by the responsibilities of office. Many royal courts in Europe between 1600 and 1800 employed dwarfs as court jesters or kept a complement of "fools," who either were developmentally disabled or feigned retardation for amusement.[9] During the Middle Ages and thereafter, people with deformities and mental disabilities were frequently displayed for money at village fairs on market days, and peasant parents are known to have toured the countryside displaying for money recently born infants with birth defects.[10] But the access of most people to such spectacles was random until the rise in the 1840s in the United States of the commercial freak show, which took form eventually either as an independent production or as a sideshow attached to a circus. The modern freak show was a response to the growing mass market for amusements generated by urbanization and economic growth. The New York City entrepreneur P. T. Barnum (1810–91) pioneered the modern exhibition of physically anomalous individuals at his American Museum, a popular, inexpensive pleasure palace. For the next century, in its various guises, the freak show remained a widely proliferated, popular, and highly conventionalized form of amusement in both Europe and North America. By 1950 because of a combination of the new, medicalized understandings of physical anomalies, the growth of concern for minority rights, and the rise of alternative forms of amusement such as television and the movies, the freak show had begun to decline. In the 1980s there were perhaps no more than five freak shows of the traditional sort left in the United States. A number of small productions continued displaying faked or crafted human oddities (contortionists, extensively tattooed men and women, etc.), but usually not people with physical anomalies.[11]

Today it is difficult to avoid responding to the existence of the traditional freak show from anything but a moral standpoint, reinforced perhaps by aesthetic condemnation. To us the freak show appears nothing but vulgarity and exploitation. A barbaric legacy of the past, we are well rid of it. So what is there left to discuss? Yet, as Bogdan informs us, recent interpreters of the freak show have disagreed sharply on how to understand its meanings. In the past two decades the display for amusement of people with physical anomalies has indeed been denounced as reprehensible and worthless.[12] But it has also been conceived as evidence of a basic human desire, springing from the intermingling of affection and the will to dominate, to make trained pets of humans, valuing them the more particularly if they are exotic or anomalous and trained to be passive and submissive.[13] The fascination with people who are physically different also has been attributed to a psychological propensity to conceive of people with bodily anomalies as "infrahuman," frightening but compelling throwbacks to our prehuman, animal origins.[14] It has also been claimed that such people are mirror images of what we fear we might become, if our inchoate but deep-seated anxieties about violations to the integrity of our bodies were somehow realized.[15] Finally, freak show performers have been conceived as battlers against adversity and oppression who have refused to surrender themselves to shame and ostracism.[16]

Bogdan dispenses with much of the moralizing that, implicitly or explicitly, is found in some of these views. He also is not concerned directly with the psychology of the audience, though such inquiry might help us understand the long-abiding fears and obsessions that explain the desire to gawk at the physically atypical, from the distant past to the present. The feeling of being on display is something with which almost all disabled people have had to deal; it is, in fact, a singular form of oppression—the oppression of unwanted attention—that disabled people share with few others. We need to return to this point later, because it is central to the issue of the freak show's exploitation of those with physical anomalies.

Instead, because he is interested in the larger question of the social construction of freakishness, Bogdan is concerned with the strategies developed for attracting an audience. For him, the story of the freak show is a chapter in the development of modern show business. Although he briefly acknowledges earlier precedents for the display of what he calls "human oddities," for Bogdan the history of the freak show begins with Barnum's successful efforts to tap the growing urban market for amusements by exhibiting "Tom Thumb" (Charles Sherwood Stratton) and other dwarfs for money. For Bogdan, therefore, the question is not why do people go to freak shows, or, relatedly, whether we should be troubled by the existence of freak shows. He sees the freak show as a business specializing in stylized performances, the "freak" as a player trained for his or her role, and the audience more or less as what Barnum and a host of lesser showmen thought it to be: a motley collection of suckers credulous enough to pay the price of admission. Bogdan's analysis centers around the freak show as a medium for developing ways of exhibiting such people as conjoined twins, dwarfs, the very tall, the ultra-obese, and microcephalics in order to enhance their otherness and exotic qualities. The test of these modes of exhibition is that they proved attractive enough to mold the public into an audience. Bogdan does not analyze the psychologies that might account for why people joined this audience, but rather the modes of display that showmen created. These showmen and the illusions they created to befuddle, amuse, and horrify the gullible public engage Bogdan because it is this creative process that serves to construct the freak. Thus the age-old display of people with deformities and other anomalies rests at the level of surfaces and impressions upon which the showmen themselves placed it.

Bogdan convincingly ties the evolution of styles of display and the formation of the freak show audience to two related historical developments that showmen exploited. First, the expansion of Western exploration and imperialism created a fund of popular impressions of previously remote areas of the world and a hunger for exotica. Human exhibits were often presented as originating in distant lands, as some actually did, and their oddity was enhanced through foreign dress and ambience. Second, in its popularized form the new science of evolution created various pseudoscientific knowledge categories, such as "throwback" and "missing link," that could be exploited in exhibiting individuals. Here, too, dress (for example, an ape suit) and ambience (a jungle setting) could be employed, separately or in combination, to enhance the presentation and make it knowable to the audience. Through a process of innovation and experiment, showmen learned how to make people who simply looked different into "freaks." They might train the very tall to act as if they were the remnants of a race of giants, and they might present microcephalics as the missing link. All the while they continued the age-old practice of displaying those with congenital limb deficiencies and deformities, dwarfs, conjoined twins, and others who might not necessarily be tied to remote areas of either the globe or evolutionary history, but who were nonetheless of continuing fascination.

Bogdan offers a compelling, though limited, explanation of the gradual decline of the freak show. He fixes mostly on the medicalization of disability and the rise of gene theory, to the near exclusion of political explanations focusing on the growth of ideologies and social movements concerned with minority rights, and the evolution of new media and of new genres of entertainment, such as the horror film, which may have served as outlets for the same emotional impulses as the freak show.[17] He shows how medicalization transformed public consciousness of people with physical anomalies, who now went from being human oddities or monsters to sick people, with some clinically identifiable syndrome requiring surgery, prosthetics, or sterilization. The vulgar categories of showmen were replaced by a medical diagnosis. The "giant" was now said to be suffering from acromegaly, the "ossified man" from polyarthritis deformens, and the "dog-faced boy" from hypertrichosis. As a sick person, the former freak was no longer to be exhibited for profit or in public — as opposed to before interns and specialists in hospital wards and medical textbooks.

One feels the weight of familiar and very legitimate grievances against the professional impositions and pretensions of medical doctors in this explanation. But the discussion seems problematic, and not merely because Bogdan underplays other sources of the freak show's decline. He is unwilling to credit the efficacy and legitimacy of, let alone personally embrace, the explicitly moral rejection of the freak show. Although he finds this moralism plausible, he seems more sympathetic to the arguments for the freak show — that it created opportunity, status, and enhanced power over their lives for the people employed in it.

In analyzing Bogdan's conception of the freak show and his views of its demise, we must deal with the related problems of volition and valorization. In regard to volition, Bogdan generally assumes the willingness of people to be human exhibits. In regard to valorization, he tries to give value, legitimacy, and respectability to the roles of those exhibited and to treat them as performers rather than as exploited victims, because that is the way, he believes, the majority of them saw themselves. He argues that people chose to become and to remain freaks because they valued what the role brought them and because they understood that role to be valuable in and of itself. If, therefore, the case for *valorizing* the role of the freak proves weak, the case for *volition* also would seem to weaken.

To examine the question of valorization is ultimately to ask again why people spent money to gain admittance to freak shows — why, in fact, able-bodied people seem compelled to stare at those with physical disabilities and deformities. How did audiences see these exhibitions and what did they take them for? Did the audience understand the show as a *performance* and attach value to those who were at the center of it? Or did people come to be fascinated by the unusual, to stare, to be horrified, and to engage in loathing at a *display*? Freak shows actually consisted of two types of individual representations, one involving a performance, the other certainly not. An armless man such as the famed German sideshow performer and vaudevillian Carl Unthan, a classically trained musician who played the violin with his feet,[18] is indeed engaged in a performance that may be appreciated for its skill, discipline, and difficulty as well as its aesthetic value. But Unthan and those like him were decidedly in a minority. More common was, say, the giant or the bearded lady who did little beside attempt, through environmental props and clothing, to look even taller or hairier, while perhaps carrying on some monologue or sometimes perfunctorily, and usually poorly, singing a song. Or what of the legless man who attained high speeds walking on his hands, demonstrating what for him was a necessary survival skill? In all of these cases we are speaking less of a performance than a display—in other words, merely an appearance in which talent, when it existed at all, was beside the point. We are left with the likelihood that a large dose of contempt, mockery, or hunger for bizarre spectacle lay behind the popularity of the freak show, because it offered the audience nothing else. If this is so, then it is difficult to valorize the role of freak.

It is no wonder that the fear of being placed on exhibit has haunted, and continues to haunt, people with physical anomalies. For example, Harold Russell, who became a bilateral hand amputee as a result of a military training accident in 1944 and went on to become a leading American advocate of expanding employment opportunities for the disabled, records at a number of points in his memoirs the fear that plagued him during the first months after his accident: that the only way he would be able to make a living would be displaying himself in a sideshow—this, at a time when there were many freak shows in existence. Russell, who was proud of his recent paratrooper training, recalls reflecting bitterly from his bed in Walter Reed Army Hospital, "Maybe I'd be able to get a job in the circus: The Handless Freak that Jumps Through the Air with the Greatest of Ease."[19] The oppression of unwanted attention permeates the narrative of Russell's convalescence.[20] More recently, Gelya Frank has written about the lives of congenitally limbless or limb-deficient young adults, and finds a number of them engaged in strategies of aggressive normalization and public self-presentation in order to counter being regarded as freaks and thereby devalued.[21] One of Frank's informants, Diane DeVries, continues to be offended by a well-meaning letter she received years afterward from someone who had admired her when she was a poster child engaged in fund raising, and who suggested she meet a certain sideshow celebrity, possessing some physical anomaly, for inspiration. Frank records that rereading this letter today, DeVries, who was born without legs and whose arms are greatly foreshortened, remains "repelled by [the] patronizing tone and content, which could be taken to suggest that she belongs in a circus."[22] The same revulsion at the dehumanization that is part of such displays, mixed with horror at the sadism that "dwarf bowling" and "dwarf tossing" reveal, has led the Little People of America, an advocacy organization for dwarfs, to lobby against these new "sports." Here dwarfs, no strangers to exploitative display, are employed to allow themselves, for example, to be thrown at bowling pins to the amusement of spectators.[23] The word "freak" continues to serve as a powerful, aversive metaphor for people with disabilities or physical anomalies, even such innocuous ones as relatively thick facial hair on women. It encodes negative meanings and the memory of painful experiences—ostracism, the oppression of unwanted attention, and the label "abnormal."[24]

But what of the individual, such as the tossed, bowled, or merely displayed dwarf, who believes that he or she is the star of a performance? Any argument advancing the view that the freak show was not in and of itself necessarily exploitative and dehumanizing clearly depends on this individual. It is also the case that highlights most powerfully the problem of choice and consent. To evaluate this we need to shift the basis for conceptualizing the role of freak away from the assumptions, framed by labeling theory and symbolic interactionism, that have guided Bogdan. For Bogdan, the freak show was a social construction built on a structure of manipulated perceptions and beliefs. Freaks knowingly colluded in creating these illusions, the argument runs, so one could hardly say they were the victims of the situation. In this Goffmanesque formulation, the freak show is another context for individuals to assume their role in the endless masquerade that constitutes so much of social life.[25]

There is a powerful insight here: the role of freak is certainly not inherent in having a disfiguring condition. But neither is participation in a freak show. If we proceed on the assumption that, like Harold Russell and Diane DeVries (admittedly of a later era than the classic epoch of the freak show), others, too, might have been disgusted by the thought of becoming sideshow attractions, we then have to try to understand why it was that they ended up doing so. One particularly significant problem with Bogdan's conception of the freak show is his reluctance to see the situation in light of the fact that those (showmen, human exhibits, and the audience) involved had vastly unequal powers to effect the course of their lives. For this reason, a conceptualization of the freak show framed by a minority group model is in order. Only by understanding the social oppression, exploitation, and degradation experienced by the sort of people who became freaks can we understand the choices, where indeed we find anything resembling choice, that led some, including those who claim to have valued and profited from their role, to appear to consent to be exhibited. In effect, in the case of the freak show, the minority group model serves to join a respect for social process to the power of social constructionism. It provides us with a plausible way of asking questions about who became a freak that may complement our understanding of how the role of freak was framed in cultural terms. Moreover, only by understanding that social context can we come to understand that the freak show was something qualitatively distinct from, even if related to, ordinary show business. Conventional performers and artists may be exploited by greedy managers and promoters, and they may be party, wittingly or unwittingly, to the creation of all sorts of stupefying illusions, including ones that are also self-deprecating. But, as a class, they have not been driven into their work by a lack of options and a desire to escape from a hostile world. Indeed, most of them have aspired to it, attracted by the opportunity for fame, wealth, glamour, and the chance to develop their art. But, unless the examples of Russell and DeVries are unusual, it is difficult to imagine people who would aspire to be in a freak show. Indeed, as we shall see, looked at systematically according to Herzog's exacting criteria, the volition of the types of people who regularly appeared as freaks seems dubious, even in the instances when it was formally free.

Becoming a "Freak"

Let us now review the quality of volition in various typical classes of "freaks." My method here is to recontextualize the facts as Bogdan presents them, using historical evidence and the perspectives and moral insights of both the minority group model for conceptualizing disability and Herzog's critique of consent theory. What this reveals is that the volition of those displayed was sharply proscribed not only by their disabilities and physical anomalies, but also by such social characteristics as age, class, race, and gender. The physically atypical particularly have historically existed in society under conditions of ostracism and stigmatization, and have had to endure the oppression of unwanted attention—that desire of others to stare at them that forms a basis of the marketing power of the freak show. An alternative to suffering these conditions has been to become a human exhibit, or to have a parent or guardian push one in that direction. At least then one might be paid for being stigmatized. It is possible, therefore, to speak of people with sharply limited options being tracked into becoming freaks.

Sometimes the thinness of the historical record is a consequence of the social structures and circumstances within which it is created. Documents are artifactual, and some actors in history have not had the power to create artifacts that they might leave behind to explain themselves. One group of freak show participants who probably could not have left any self-explanatory documents were microcephalics ("pinheads")—a standard exhibit in larger sideshows during the classic era of the freak show. Microcephalics are invariably developmentally impaired, though they may be high functioning individuals. Add to this the fact that a significant number of the microcephalics exhibited also were African-Americans or were from impoverished non-Western lands, and one sees that racism and colonialism add to the social disabilities that involved them in vastly unequal power relations. (Racial minorities are also found in other classes of displayed individuals.) To further compound their powerlessness, some of these microcephalics from outside the European world were sold or given away as children to showmen, who toured the world looking for human anomalies to display. Their parents were desperately seeking cures for them, or they were unwilling to live with the tremendous stigma their cultures attached to physical difference and believed their children might have a better life in another land. (Others also entered the freak show world as children.)[26] Obviously, choice and consent are irrelevant in evaluating this class of exhibits. If less severely disabled people found it impossible to support themselves in the past, how could such impaired and deformed people do so, especially when they were foreign and nonwhite, and had been immersed in the insular world of the freak show from childhood? Without some sort of guardian like the freak show entrepreneur, these docile children, who could never really grow up, were doomed. That, as Bogdan notes, freak show entrepreneurs often took this guardianship seriously and acted responsibly toward their charges within the limits of the situation, even while exhibiting them as exotics and monsters, surely does not seriously qualify the point that these people had few real choices in making lives for themselves.

Otis "the Frogman" Jordan, a physically anomalous but not developmentally impaired individual, provides another, seemingly more illusive, example of the dubiousness of choice and consent. Jordan becomes prominent in Bogdan's argument as an example of the weakness of the moral case against the freak show before the force of individual volition and empowerment. Jordan, an African-American with deficient, poorly functioning limbs, was blocked from appearing at the 1984 New York State Fair after protests on moral grounds by Barbara Baskin, a disability rights activist. Baskin had no ethical qualms about sitting in judgment of Jordan's appearance before audiences. Jordan, however, argued on behalf of his right to appear and do his act, which consisted, among other things, of an old freak show feature of those without arms—the survival skill of rolling, lighting, and smoking a cigarette, all with his lips. Prior to becoming a freak, Jordan had spent nearly three decades attempting, with poor results, to support himself. He sold small items from a goat-drawn cart along the back highways of the American South. One day a carnival came to town. He did his cigarette stunt before one of the showmen and was hired on the spot. Bogdan notes that according to Jordan himself, "It was the best thing that ever happened to him. He likes to travel and meet people and his new profession enabled him to buy a small house back home he lives in when the show winters. He has no complaints except one. He thought the woman who was complaining about his being exploited ought to talk to him about it. He would tell her there wasn't anybody forcing him to do it." If this were the end of Jordan's testimony, we would be placed in the difficult, but as I have suggested, not necessarily ethically compromising position, of having to argue with him about his situation. We would need to question him about the range and the quality of the choices he has actually had in his life, and to probe to see whether he believes being a freak is something to aspire to, rather than merely to fall back on. But, according to Bogdan, this is not all "the Frogman" had to say. He closed his testimony by actually revealing the grounds on which it would be possible to argue with his appraisal of his own situation. Speaking of Baskin, Jordan said, "I can't understand it. How can she say I'm being taken advantage of? Hell, what does she want for me—to be on welfare?" Bogdan concludes from Jordan's testimony that Jordan sees himself as "a showman: proud and independent." While acknowledging that Jordan's work as a freak probably does not advance the cause of the rights of people with disabilities, Bogdan is unwilling to criticize Jordan's understanding of his career. Indeed, he actually goes beyond Jordan's understanding, using language ("proud and independent") considerably more inflated in its valorization of Jordan's role and what he derives from it.[27] But if Jordan's choices in life have been reduced to participating in a freak show or "being on welfare," it really does not appear that he has had much choice at all. Whatever we may make of his pride, about which he himself actually says nothing, his independence certainly seems tenuous. Perhaps all we can say of his participation in the freak show world is that he has made the best of a bad situation, while noting, too, that the cause of Jordan's dignity would be better served if our social arrangements allowed him to earn a decent livelihood from mainstream employment.

Finally, let us look at the situation of dwarfs, people who have been used as human exhibits for many centuries. Dwarfs were Barnum's first successful human exhibits, and they were to remain thereafter a staple item of all large freak shows. It remains an important case, too, because though the freak show seems moribund, at least at the present time, people are still finding ways to exhibit dwarfs because of their physical condition, as the contemporary appearance of dwarf bowling and dwarf tossing has revealed. And it is of special concern to us here, because, as Little People of America has noted, dwarfs are allowing themselves to be tossed and bowled.[28] We may even find one who voices pride in his performance. How are we to evaluate the participation of dwarfs in such rituals of debasement?

A hereditary disorder, dwarfism is frequently a deforming condition, though not necessarily a disabling one, in spite of the health problems dwarfs often do experience. Without mental or serious physical impairments, the lives of dwarfs could be completely normalized, with necessary adjustments made for logistical and sizing difficulties.[29] But this has hardly been their history. In the Western world, and outside it, too, short stature is one of the oldest sources of the perception of human difference, and generally it has been a source of stigmatization. Even within the normal range, shortness has signaled immaturity and powerlessness. When coupled with the bodily disproportions common to many dwarfs, furthermore, shortness has been regarded as grotesque and has been an even more likely cause for ridicule and mocking, if at times also affectionate, humor.[30] In Egyptian tomb paintings and the works of the early modern European masters, in folklore, and in much written documentation, all manner of Western and non-Western cultural representations establish the segregation of dwarfs in special roles in which they have been employed for amusement and diversion: court jesters, circus exhibits and performers, and pets and mascots of powerful and prestigious individuals.[31] Though in this century medicalization and gene theory replaced folkish super-stition in understanding their condition, this has not guaranteed them equality. Many conventional public, adult roles remain closed to dwarfs, and they have experienced comprehensive employment discrimination.[32] For want of alternatives, the entertainment industry has continued to loom large in the imagination of American dwarfs as a quick route to success, mostly because they were once featured in some vaudeville routines and sideshows and in bizarre roles in a few films, most notably as "munchkins" in *The Wizard of Oz* (1939). In reality, there have been few film or television roles of any sort available to them. Those roles that have been available have mostly dwelled on their condition and failed to present them as ordinary human beings. As media reviewer John Corry said, reflecting on the dwarfs who appeared in *The Wizard of Oz*, "They were curiosities; adults who looked like children. Moviegoers presumably found them cute."[33] Few if any of them had acting training or ability, nor was it asked of them, for the only requirement of their role was their appearance.

Infantilized, patronized, stared at, mocked, and lacking significant power over much of their lives, many dwarfs have had problems with self-esteem and have experienced arrested psychosocial and sexual development. This psychological syndrome has been especially the case for males, because of the salience size, as a means for projecting power, has had in the social appraisal of men. Moreover, since their condition cannot be corrected and they are not chronically ill, dwarfs have frequently been found to show strong tendencies toward denial, which manifests itself in refusing to look in the mirror or to make eye contact with one another. They also commonly develop a veneer of cooperation and cheerfulness intended both to make others comfortable around them and to play to some of the positive aspects of the popular stereotype of them. Little People of America was founded to be a self-help as well as an advocacy organization, precisely because of the need to deal with these psychological consequences of stigmatization, which have caused some dwarfs to participate in their own debasement and most to experience doubts about their worth.[34]

Dwarfs attempt to be active and creative agents in their lives and have naturally placed emphasis on those aspects of life that allow them to effect their own normalization. But still they have faced significant impediments. Marriage has been difficult to arrange because of the problem of finding partners of similar size, and dwarf couples have had low birth rates historically, in part because of biological difficulties, but also in part because of personal ambivalence about reproducing. They, too, perceive wearing stylish clothes as a sign of taste and maturity, but it has been difficult for dwarfs to find clothing in their sizes. Employment is so prized among dwarfs as a sign of adult status that it has been common for them to take considerable abuse on the job, often in the form of constant remarks about height, in order simply to stay employed.[35]

This is vital background that may help us to understand the participation of dwarfs in freak shows. Clearly in their case consent to be displayed has to some indeterminate, but probably significant, extent been premised on a lack of opportunity to earn a living and to acquire status in the conventional ways, a point made by Little People of America in explaining why some dwarfs would allow themselves to be bowled or tossed.[36] Once having taken the step to become a freak, however, couldn't it be argued that Charles Sherwood Stratton ("Tom Thumb") and others enjoyed full, affluent, and interesting lives that hardly made being a freak an ordeal, and made their continuing in that role a matter of conscious consent?

It is plausible, but the type of life led by even so acclaimed a human exhibit as Tom Thumb does not give us complete confidence in that comforting argument, in which, unlike the world as we know it, there are no losers. It was Barnum's sound intuition that he could make money displaying those finely proportioned dwarfs popularly known as "midgets," who lacked atypical proportions and were simply very short. People seemed to feel affectionate toward these miniature adults in the way one feels toward a pet. He heard about Stratton, who had stopped growing in infancy, while recruiting exhibits for the American Museum. He used his considerable powers of persuasion to talk Stratton's working-class parents, people of narrow means, to allow him to display the boy, who was then almost five, in New York City. Thereafter, Barnum was the principal influence in Stratton's life. Barnum certainly did treat Stratton well, paying him a large salary, having the finest clothes made for him, and affording him access to other fine things that his family could never have possessed. But Stratton was too young at the inception of his career as an exhibit to know what would be done with him. He was raised to be a freak—it was the only life he knew.

An atmosphere of pathos and farce hung over much of his life. It was Barnum who gave him the mock-heroic name, General Tom Thumb, just as he gave the other male dwarfs he displayed aggrandizing titles such as "Commodore." Largely for promotional purposes, Barnum put him in contact with many important people of the time, who treated him with genial good will. Barnum also opened intimate aspects of his life to public observation in order to create publicity. Stratton's marriage to Lavinia Warren, also a dwarf, seems to have been a product of mutual devotion, though there were always suspicions that Barnum had initially arranged the union for his own purposes. The marriage ceremony, to which tickets were sold, was a public spectacle elaborately stage-managed by Barnum. The couple then embarked on a European tour, during which they were everywhere displayed in their wedding finery. Though Lavinia very much wanted a child, she was not able to conceive. Barnum understood that the only act that could follow the wedding extravaganza was the birth of, as Bogdan puts it, "a little Thumb," so infants were rented for the couple to display as if they were their own.

What of Stratton the performer? Could he derive a positive sense of himself from his stage career? He had little talent, even for such farcical vaudeville routines (a song, some dance steps, effecting a pose as Samson or some other mythological or historical hero, etc.) as he performed. The saving element in these routines was his refusal to play them seriously, tellingly keying the audience into the awareness that he knew that they knew that the whole affair was a joke anyway. But as he grew older, Stratton's capacity for this masquerade declined, and a note of gravity entered his personality, as if he wished to be taken more seriously or at least to take himself more seriously. In later years, he ceased doing his self-mocking routines altogether, and simply made personal appearances. His career did bring him wealth, but he spent money with an abandon that suggests compensatory striving. He was able to leave his wife only a small amount of the fortune he had made when he died of a stroke at age forty-five in 1883.

This sketch of Stratton's life is based on the facts presented in Bogdan's book. Given the same facts, however, Bogdan and I see their meanings differently. I have seen Stratton as tragic, a prisoner of conditions over which he, as a dwarf, had little control and that both profited and humiliated him. While Bogdan does acknowledge that all did not go well with Stratton, he does not seek to understand why. Instead, impressed by Stratton's affluence and his participation in Barnum's outrageous promotional schemes, he attempts, in effect, to explain Stratton's life as if it were a real-life correlative to the aggrandized, mock-heroic character of Tom Thumb, the suave, petit, urbane gentleman, that Barnum developed for purposes of display. Stratton himself thus appears not as a sad, unfulfilled figure, but as the huckster-charlatan that was the essence of General Tom Thumb.

It seems a logical result of Bogdan's understanding of the freak show that the dancer must ultimately be confused with the dance—or the human being with the freak. In this confusion, we lose the capacity to recognize the deeper humanity of Stratton and others like him and the pathos of their lives. Bogdan refers to such talk as "the pity approach," and sees it as evidence of condescension on the part of the analyst.[37] If by "pity" here we mean "sorrow" and "regret" about the course of a life such as Stratton's, it is not necessarily something for which to apologize. If as an approach "pity" offers us "empathy," with all of its well-known analytical pitfalls, that, too, is not necessarily something to avoid. From an analytical viewpoint, if our goal is to understand the freak show, are we really better off not attempting to ask ourselves what it must have been like, in an era long before disability rights advocacy and the independent living movement, to be General Tom Thumb or some other famous human exhibit? Stratton can also be viewed as a mature man with the intellectual resources to see that much of his life was a masquerade. If, as his emotional development during his adult years suggests, he did come to this understanding, it was evidently too late for him to choose to change his situation. Besides, what else was there for him to do?

One imagines Stratton and many other human exhibits adopting some of the defensive solidarity and cynical insularity of the carnival world, and ultimately consoling themselves with the thought that they were exacting some revenge on a hostile, insensitive world of ignorant suckers by exploiting their vulgarity and credulity, and rather effortlessly taking their money. At the same time, we should not be surprised by another state of mind, perhaps coexisting and competing with this cynicism. In the narratives of freaks who retrospectively interpreted their lives in terms of the progress of their careers, we see evidence of the effort to give coherence and meaning to life by seeing it in terms of volition and unfolding purpose rather than oppression and victimization. Thus, the element of self-aggrandizement, through which Stratton and others ultimately might become the victims of their own publicity, may well be a gesture of defiance. At this point, however, we are talking about a state of mind that is considerably more complicated than even such fertile concepts as "choice" and "consent" can help us to comprehend.

NOTES

1. Brief portions of this chapter were initially published as "Pornography or Entertainment? The Rise and Fall of the Freak Show," *Reviews in American History* 18 (March 1990): 15–21. This chapter is a revision of an article published under a similar title in *Disability, Handicap and Society* (now called *Disability and Society*) 7, no. 1 (1992): 53–69. The present chapter also incorporates ideas contained in my response to Robert Bogdan's critique of my original essay. That response was published as "Interpreting Freak Show and the Freak Show," *Disability, Handicap and Society* 8, no. 4 (1993): 435–36.

2. Robert Bogdan, *Freak Show: Presenting Human Oddities for Amusement and Profit* (Chicago: University of Chicago Press, 1988); and "In Defense of Freak Show," *Disability, Handicap and Society* 8, no. 1 (1993); 91–94 (quotes on pp. 92, 93; see also *Freak Show*, 70).

3. Don Herzog, *Happy Slaves: A Critique of Consent Theory* (Chicago: University of Chicago Press, 1989), 237, suggests these responses, with their different ethical and interpretive weights, in evaluating choice.

4. Ibid., 1.

5. Ibid., 5–71.

6. Ibid., 182–247.

7. See ibid., 215–47, for the basis for these questions and responses.

8. Ibid., 231.

9. Yi-Fu Tuan, *Dominance and Affection: The Making of Pets* (New Haven: Yale University Press, 1984), 154–61.

10. Ottavia Niccoli, " 'Menstruum quasi Monstruum': Monstrous Births and Menstrual Taboo in the Sixteenth Century," in *Sex and Gender in Historical Perspective,* ed. Edward Muir and Guido Ruggiero (Baltimore: Johns Hopkins University Press, 1990), 5.

11. Leslie Fiedler, *Freaks: Myths and Images of the Secret Self* (New York: Simon and Schuster, 1978); Bogdan, *Freak Show,* 62–68, 267; Neil Harris, *Humbug: The Art of P. T. Barnum* (Chicago: University of Chicago Press, 1973).

12. Bogdan, *Freak Show,* 3, 285.

13. Tuan, *Dominance and Affection,* ix, 4–5, 15–17.

14. Hanoch Livneh, "Disability and Monstrosity: Further Comments," *Rehabilitation Literature,* November-December, 1980, 280–83.

15. Fiedler, *Freaks,* 31–36.

16. Frederick Drimmer, *Very Special People: The Struggles, Loves, and Triumphs of Human Oddities* (New York: Bantam, 1976).

17. Peter N. Stearns and Timothy Haggerty, "The Role of Fear: Transitions in American Emotional Standards for Children, 1850–1950," *American Historical Review* 96 (February 1991): 93–94.

18. Carl Unthan, *The Armless Fiddler: A Pediscript, Being of a Vaudeville Man* (London: Allen and Unwin, 1935).

19. Harold Russell, *Victory in My Hands* (New York: Creative Age, 1949), 70; see also pp. 16, 42, 150.

20. David A. Gerber, "Anger and Affability: The Rise of a Repertory of Roles and Motives in the Life of a Disabled Veteran of World War II," *Journal of Social History* 27 (Fall 1993): 1–27.

21. Gelya Frank, "The Life History Model of Adaptation to a Disability: The Case of a Congenital Amputee," *Social Science and Medicine* 19, no. 3 (1984): 639–45; and "Beyond Stigma: Visibility and Self-Empowerment of Persons with Congenital Limb Deficiencies," *Journal of Social Issues* 44, no. 1 (1988): 95–115.

22. Frank, "Beyond Stigma," 104.

23. "Snow White's an Activist?" *Disability Rag* January-February, 1990, 21; "Little People Oppose Events in Which Dwarfs Are Objects," *New York Times,* 3 July 1989, 1; untitled, *New York Times,* 25 July 1990, B2 (on the passage of anti-dwarf bowling legislation in New York State).

24. For examples of "freak" as aversive metaphor, see Rebecca Bates, "The Oppressed —The Oppressor," *Disability Rag,* July-August, 1990, 20 (for the memory of growing up with a disabling muscle condition); and Holly Devor, *Gender Blending: Confronting the Limits of Disability* (Bloomington: Indiana University Press, 1989), 124 (for the testimony of a woman with thick facial hair).

25. Erving Goffman, *The Presentation of Self in Everyday Life* (Garden City, N.Y.: Doubleday Anchor, 1959); and *Stigma* (Englewood Cliffs, N.J.: Prentice-Hall, 1963).

26. Bogdan, *Freak Show,* 127–46.

27. Ibid., 280–81.

28. "Little People Oppose Events in Which Dwarfs Are Objects."

29. Joan Ablon, *Little People in America: The Social Dimensions of Dwarfism* (New York: Praeger, 1982), 1–3, 29–30; Anthony Smith, *The Body,* rev. ed. (New York: Viking, 1986), 214, 235, 295–96.

30. Joan Ablon, *Living with Difference: Families with Dwarf Children* (New York: Praeger, 1988), 50–52, 120; and *Little People in America,* 6–9, 25–28, 47–54, 81; Barry Worth, "How Short Is Too Short? Marketing Human Growth," *New York Times Magazine,* 16 June 1991, 14–17, 28–29, 42.

31. Ablon, *Little People in America,* 4–5; Tuan, *Dominance and Affection,* 154–61. If Paul Theroux's experience is representative, apparently the stigmatization of dwarfs is not limited to the West. Theroux observed a crowd, including a number of deaf people, taunting a dwarf in a Peijing railroad station;

see Paul Theroux, *Riding the Iron Rooster: By Train through China* (New York: Ballantine, 1988), 195–96.

32. Ablon, *Little People in America*, 67, 72.

33. John Corry, "Little People Looks at the Lives of Dwarfs," *New York Times*, 17 July 1984, C18.

34. Ablon, *Little People in America*, 91–163.

35. Ibid., 57, 67–72, 75; Smith, *The Body*, 214.

36. "Little People Oppose Events in Which Dwarfs Are Objects."

37. Bogdan, "In Defense of Freak Show," 93.

FOUR

Intolerable Ambiguity: Freaks as/at the Limit

ELIZABETH GROSZ

> But, I that am not shap'd for sportive tricks,
> Nor made to court an amorous looking-glass;
> I, that am rudely stamp'd, and want love's majesty
> To strut before a wanton ambling nymph;
> I, that am curtail'd of this fair proportion,
> Cheated of feature by dissembling nature,
> Deform'd, unfinish'd, sent before my time
> Into this breathing world scarce half made up,
> and that so lamely and unfashionable
> That dogs bark at me as I halt by them—
> —SHAKESPEARE, KING RICHARD III, I.I.14–23

Any discussion of freaks brings back into focus a topic that has had a largely underground existence in contemporary cultural and intellectual life, partly because it is considered below the refined sensibilities of "good taste" and "personal politeness" in a civilized and politically correct milieu, and partly because it has required a new set of intellectual tools, which are still in the process of development, to raise it above being an object of prurient speculation. I am interested in the question of human freaks not simply for voyeuristic reasons—although these must no doubt play a part—but also because I am interested in the psychical, physical, and conceptual *limits* of human subjectivity, that is, what the nature and forms of subjectivity consist in and the degree to which social, political, and historical factors shape the forms of subjectivity with which we are familiar; and the degree to which these factors are able to tolerate anomalies, ambiguities, and borderline cases, marking the threshold, not of humanity in itself, but of acceptable, tolerable, knowable humanity. Closely related to the question of the psychical conditions of subjectivity (a field that psychoanalytic theory has tended to dominate) is a concern about the corporeal limits of subjectivity. The ways in which the body is lived and represented, the inputs and effects of the subject's corporeality on its identity, seem crucial if usually underestimated factors in any account of the subject.

I will explore some of the most severe and gross physical disorders afflicting those human beings who have been coarsely categorized as "freaks," "curiosities," "prodigies," and "monstrosities," poor suffering individuals with observably disturbing bodily disorders, stunted limbs, distorted figures: Siamese twins, dwarfs, giants, hunchbacks, humans with parasitic or autositic attachments, so-called legless or armless wonders, half-creatures, hermaphrodites, rubber men, and so on. The simultaneous horror and fascination with these people, and the fact that many exist in the world of entertainment and gain their livelihood from being commercially exhibited, need to be explained. In the so-called normal subjects who constitute the paying audience for freak shows, this fascination amounts to both willingness and shame. The sometimes overpowering need to look and a horror of and pity toward what is seen are important elements in understanding the psychologies and the body-images of "normal" subjects, attesting to what is and is not tolerable or incorporable into normality. Moreover, in attempting to understand the freak's own body-image and psychological structure—the kinds of social, interpersonal, and narcissistic images freaks internalize and the ways in which their bodies are inscribed and made socially meaningful, medicalized, and rendered into a typology—may also prove invaluable to understanding subjectivity and corporeality in their most general outlines, and in their most extreme forms.

First, however, it is necessary to specify what I mean by "freaks." This is not an easy concept to define. I use this term in part, not as a description or a mode of moral evaluation, but as something of a political gesture. Like a series of other negative labels ("queer" comes most clearly to mind), it is a term whose use may function as an act of defiance, a political gesture of self-determination. For this reason I prefer it to euphemistic substitutes: it makes clear that there are very real and concrete political effects for those thus labeled, and a clear political reaction is implied by those who use it as a mode of self-definition. First, let me clarify what I do *not* mean by the term: I wish to exclude from my discussion the more commonplace bodily infirmities and deficiencies—those born with nonfunctional or improperly functional limbs and organs, the blind, those who are unable to walk, and those with cerebral palsy and other medical disorders. While these persons may be as or more disabled than those categorized as freaks, they do not exert the same ambivalent appeal. Nor do I wish to include those with congenital abnormalities in internal organs (heart, lung, kidney, etc.). Nor do I include the accidental tragedies in which individuals are maimed or wounded (e.g., amputees, brain damage cases, orthopedic problems, etc.). The term *freaks* does not simply refer to disabilities of either a genetic, developmental, or contingent kind. Indeed, some classified as freaks (such as the bearded lady or the human skeleton) are not necessarily physically incapacitated at all, although, of course, many are. All suffer a certain social marginalization. I also do not refer to those particularly gifted with unusual aptitudes, such as the athlete or technically skilled performer, although many freaks do fall into this category. Freaks are not just unusual or atypical; more than this is necessary to characterize their unique social position. The freak is thus neither unusually gifted nor unusually disadvantaged. He or she is not an object of *simple* admiration or pity, but is a being who is considered simultaneously and compulsively fascinating and repulsive, enticing and sickening.

Many freaks are the result of genetic or hereditary factors: abnormal elasticity of the skin, albinism, the growth of human horns, microcephaly (pinheads), dwarfism or gigantism, multiple births, and so on are commonly observed in disproportionate numbers in certain families. Others, it seems, are the result of embryological or histological conditions, in which fetal development is hindered or altered in utero (e.g., conjoined twins and hermaphrodites). Others are the result of medical factors that emerge after birth: dwarfism is commonly the result of tumors on the pituitary gland; obesity and extraordinary thinness are usually the result of overeating or disgust of food. Some freaks are the result of conscious efforts on the part of individuals to maim, cripple, or distort the human body (there are many cases where limbs have been amputated by unscrupulous individuals, commonly parents, for profit or pity). Perhaps more alarmingly, some within the medical and veterinary sciences seem to have had a passion for experimentation in controlled mutation, cross-breeding, and genetic engineering in which, like Dr. Moreau, they create two-headed creatures, hermaphroditic cattle, freemartins,[1] and interspecies hybrids for (pseudo)scientific or perverse reasons.[2]

The freak is an object of simultaneous horror and fascination because, in addition to whatever infirmities or abilities he or she exhibits, the freak is an *ambiguous* being whose existence imperils categories and oppositions dominant in social life. Freaks are those human beings who exist outside and in defiance of the structure of binary oppositions that govern our basic concepts and modes of self-definition. They occupy the impossible middle ground between the oppositions dividing the human from the animal (Jo-Jo, the dog-faced boy; Percilla, the monkey girl; Emmitt, the alligator-skinned boy; the "wild man" or "geek"), one being from another (cojoined twins, "double-bodied wonders," two-headed or multiple-limbed beings), nature from culture (feral children, the "wild men of Borneo"), one sex from the other (the bearded lady, hermaphrodites, Joseph-Josephines or Victor-Victorias), adults and children (dwarfs and midgets), humans and gods (giants), and the living and the dead (human skeletons). Freaks cross the borders that divide the subject from all ambiguities, interconnections, and reciprocal classifications, outside of or beyond the human. They imperil the very definitions we rely on to classify humans, identities, and sexes—our most fundamental categories of self-definition and boundaries dividing self from otherness.

The study of monstrosities, whether human or animal, has long preoccupied physicians, magicians, sages, and soothsayers. "Teratology," the science of monsters, is almost as old as our culture itself, and the study of monstrosities has produced all sorts of peculiar associated knowledges, including fetomancy and teratoscopy, which regard monstrous births as omens or predictions of the future. The Greeks regarded minor and major terata with the greatest curiosity, holding them to be divine warnings of the future and/or symptoms of past indiscretions. Greek mythology abounds in representations of monsters, combinations of human and animal, centaurs and minotaurs, the cyclops, giants, and hermaphrodites. Empedocles, Democritus, Hippocrates, Aristotle, Galen, and Pliny all describe in considerable detail various human and animal deformities. Indeed, stories of double-monsters, individuals with two heads, and mixtures of animals and humans seem to litter the (pre)history of every race. Speculation that monstrosities were the result of carnal indulgences, and particularly of bestiality, was rife in the Middle Ages, when freaks and human monsters were regarded as divinations, forebodings, and examples of the wrath of God, as well as forms of glorification of God's might and power. These were usually seen as forms of divine punishment meted out to individuals, communities, or even nations.

Teratology was largely a mystic and superstitious doctrine until it was linked more closely to the medicalization of bodily regulation in the sixteenth century and became a category of illness for the first time. The management of teratology by medicine seems to have had a mysterious power to render what is horrifying and fascinating about such individuals into "neutral" facts, described in scientific terminology, as part of a meticulous classificatory system that explains anomalies and renders them more "normal," or at least places them within a broad continuum containing the "normal" as its ideal. Ambroise Paré classified and organized the monstrous in (pseudo)scientific form according to the (presumed) causes of terata. He postulated three major categories of monstrosities: anomalies of excess, of default, and of duplicity. This classificatory schema, with its impulse for tables, categories, forms, and order, was refined and augmented with medical descriptions only in the eighteenth century, and reached its pinnacle toward the end of the nineteenth century. In *Anomalies and Curiosities of Medicine* (1897), George M. Gould and Walter L. Pyle date the emergence of "modern" teratology in the nineteenth century from the work of Isidore Geoffroy Saint-Hilaire, who was not only committed to advancing a methodological study of human deformities, but also to combating what he believed were the naive and superstitious myths surrounding them.[3]

Space permits me to concentrate on only two forms of monstrosity here, though I would have liked to discuss others. Nor can I direct adequate attention to the implications of medical discourse and practice in the simultaneous normalization and pathologization of the corpore-ally unclassifiable. I focus on those two examples of monstrosity that most tangibly present the human subject as ambiguously one identity and two, or one sex and the other: conjoined twins and hermaphrodites. Both are relatively regular occurrences today,[4] and therefore are the continuing objects of medical investigation and surgical intervention. They are not usually subject to infantile euthanasia, as commonly occurs in other cases of gross deformity (which may explain the increasing rarity of so-called limbless wonders and other severely damaged individuals). And they continue to hold a place of public fascination, even if they are no longer exhibited in sideshows and as forms of public entertainment. This can be seen by the extensive coverage granted in the popular press to the birth of Siamese twins and hermaphro-dites. In the last few years, for example, there have been detailed, globally circulated reports in newspapers on the birth or separation of conjoined twins, as well as on the medical interventions into the sexual typology of hermaphrodites.

Hermaphrodites have long been recorded in Western history and are referred to frequently in classical literature. Herodotus, for example, refers to the "Scythians," a race of soothsayers and prophets, comprised of women-like men who predicted the future by reading the inner bark of the linden tree. Plato, by contrast, attributes no mythical or religious powers to an ambisexual tribe, but regards them instead as the (mythical) origins of our own race. In *The Symposium*, he states: "the original human nature was not like the present, but different. In the first place the sexes were originally three in number, not as they are now; there was man, woman and the union of the two having a double nature; they once had a real existence, but it is now lost, and the name only is preserved as a term of reproach" (quoted in Jones and Scott 1971, 3).

The hermaphrodite was the child of Hermes (the god of invention, athletics, secret or occult philosophy) and Aphrodite (the goddess of love). In about 60 B.C., Diodorus speaks of Hermaphroditus "who was born of Hermes and Aphrodite, and received the name which was a combination of his parents. Some say that Hermaphroditus is a god . . . [who] has a body which is beautiful and delicate like that of a woman, but has the masculine quality and vigor of a man, but some declare that such creatures of two sexes are monstrosities" (quoted in Jones and Scott 1971, 4). It seems clear from these and other accounts that ambisexual or intersexual individuals were a recognized, if not accepted, part of Greek and Roman life.

But it seems likely, given that there are many forms of hermaphroditism, that the Greeks and Romans were familiar with only one or two types, those in which the genitalia of one sex are coupled with the secondary sexual characteristics of the other in a visible, observable mismatch (Klinefelter's syndrome and testicular feminization). In the light of development in

Mendelian genetics, and in view of more detailed studies of the nature of the sex chromosomes, it has become apparent that there are far more abnormalities of the sex chromosomes than are manifested in external sexual characteristics. It is now commonly accepted that the category of sex can be determined by at least six different criteria, which so-called normal subjects exist in agreement but intersexes or hermaphrodites exist in conflict with each other. There is genetic sex, which is the sex exhibited by the sexual chromosomes (XX in the case of females, XY in the case of males); gonadal structure (i.e., whether the organs of generation are testes, ovaries, or some other alternative such as an ovotestis or a "streaklike" gonad); the morphology of external genitalia (which, incidentally, is the most common criterion for assigning sex to the newborn infant); the morphology of the internal genitalia (i.e., whether the wolffian ducts predominate as in males, or the müllerian ducts, as in females); hormonal constitution (in which the predominance of androgens, testosterone, or estrogen dictates secondary sexual characteristics); and the sex of rearing (which may confirm or conflict with the anatomical, hormonal, and functional aspects of the individual). John Money's various researches into intersexuality and sex change indicates that, paradoxically, the most difficult aspect of the individual's sexuality to change is the sex of rearing, and his advice to doctors and intersexed individuals is, where possible, to use surgical and hormonal procedures to approximate the sex of rearing rather than, as one would expect, change the sex of rearing to conform to the child's anatomical form or chromosomal structure—a point to which I will return later. Wherever there is some discordance between any of these criteria, we are justified in talking about an intersexed subject, one who is anomalous in terms of our everyday conceptions of the clear-cut, binarily opposed notions of male and female.

Within the medical literature, sexual disorders are usually attributed to one or more of three possible causes: (1) errors present in the parents prior to conception (chromosomal anomalies); (2) errors that occur subsequent to conception, from the first division of cells to postnatal life (hormonal or gonadal anomalies); (3) errors in which sex determination is normal and sexual differentiation is abnormal (as in testicular feminization or gonadal dysgenesis). This leads to a variety of different types of intersexuality:

1. *Turner's syndrome,* in which the subject is chromosomally female but has primitive "streaklike" gonads in place of the ovaries. Here the subject is generally of short stature, has neck webbing and immature development of breasts and genitals, and is infertile;
2. *Klinefelter's syndrome,* in which the subject is chromosomally male but may have undersized or nonfunctional testes. In this case as well, the subject is infertile. Occasionally there is also gynecomastia, meaning that breasts develop after puberty. This type is most commonly represented in popular images of the hermaphrodite—the subject who has both a penis and breasts;
3. *Chromosomal mosaics,* in which there is a shortfall in the number or quality of chromosomes (the normal complement is forty-six). Where the subject has forty-five chromosomes in some cells and forty-seven in others, we can speak of a mosaicism (XO/XXX). Here the subject's sexual phenotype is female, yet the external genitalia are undeveloped, the vagina is absent, and there is no breast development. (This type comes closest to an anatomical equivalent of the celibate—a "sexless" subject);
4. *Testicular feminization,* in which genotypic males develop into female phenotypes. Here the chromosomal sex is female, but the subject has male gonads and, consequently, with the

onset of puberty becomes masculinized through increases in circulating male hormones, developing hirsutism and a deeper voice, with little or no breast development;

5. *Gonadal dysgenesis,* in which the subject is chromosomally female but the gonads are neither male nor female, instead exhibiting the streaklike characteristic already mentioned. The subject in this category is described as a tall, eunuchoid female, with primary amenorrhea and underdeveloped breasts and genitalia; and

6. *"True" hermaphroditism,* in which the chromosomal sex is usually female but the subject has both testicular and ovarian tissue. Here there are a number of possibilities: the subject may have an ovary on one side of the body and a testis on the other. The testis may be undescended and undetected, or may take up its place in the scrotal sac. Or the subject may have a combined ovotestis on one or both sides, or an ovotestis on one side and a primitive gonadal streak on the other.

In addition to these quite distinct types of hermaphroditism, there are also various grada-tions of intersexuality—depending on the strength, degree, and effectivity of hormonal, gonadal, and chromosomal anomalies—leading to a number of variations from "normal" sexual identity.

This has been an extremely brief overview of a complex set of categories common in the current medical literature, categories that are not without problems of their own. The effects of taxonomic schema on the groupings and regroupings of individual bodies is capable of catastrophic effects such as those outlined in Foucault's account of the reclassification of the hermaphrodite, Herculine Barbin: such reclassification has massive personal effects on the ways individuals live their bodies and their lives. Nevertheless, there are a number of points of interest I would like to draw out of the various scientific and historical data available on the question of intersexuality.

First, what is normally seen as a sexual polarity, with the female at one extreme and the male at the other, could, based upon medical evidence and the existence of ambisexual subjects, be represented differently. Rather than presuming two binarily opposed sexes, sexed subjects could be seen to occupy a position within a sexual continuum. This spectrum would contain a broad range of different forms of sexuality, some located at the male and some at the female poles, with others occupying intermediary positions with varying mixtures of male and female attributes. Perhaps more accurately, rather than a continuum (which implies the smooth transition between intermediate categories), the sexes can be regarded as a (relatively discontinuous) *series.* There are *n*-sexes rather than two, but these *n*-sexes have only ever been defined relative to the two. Indeed, the series is established as such only *between* male and female, which continue to function as the limits within which anomaly is to be mapped.

Second, medically oriented studies of hermaphroditism have indicated that the primacy given to the visible or manifest differences between the sexes is biologically unwarranted. The morphology of external genitalia does not provide a clear-cut delineation of the differences between the sexes, even if it does provide the usual criterion for determining sex in the neonate. Sex is a multilayered phenomenon, in which a variety of different levels coalesce: these include organic, genetic, somatic, but also behavioral and psychological factors. Sex is thus a much more complicated matter than the information afforded by vision; yet our lived (as opposed to scientific) understanding of sexual difference is focused on the presence (or absence) of visible genitalia.

Third, there has been a remarkable medicalization of the hermaphrodite, so that today virtually the only discourses available on intersexuality are those provided by clinical and scientific disciplines. The mythical, religious, dramatic, and exhibitionistic context in which hermaphroditism has been positioned is a thing of the past. The awe and horror, the special privilege (in some cultures), and the very real dangers (in other cultures) facing the hermaphrodite are today neutralized and normalized through the processes of medicalization. In so positioning hermaphroditism, the question of medical intervention, "correction," is rendered predictable and necessary, and specific treatments can be prescribed.

It is therefore ironic, given the primacy accorded to medical discourses, and given medicine's recognition of the complex factors constituting a subject's sexuality, that nevertheless the primary concern of surgeons, pediatricians, endocrinologists, cytologists, and psychiatrists has been the surgical correction of the subject's nonconforming sexuality so that it comes to approximate one or the other category of sexual identity. Underneath its manifest or latent complexity, it is presumed that there is a true sexuality, which is simply inadequately formed, rather than an anomalous, nonconformist, or multiformed sexuality. One quote from recognized authorities on intersexuality will illustrate this:

> To visualise individuals who properly belong neither to one sex nor to the other is to imagine freaks, misfits, curiosities, rejected by society and condemned to a solitary existence of neglect and frustration. Few of these unfortunate people meet with tolerance and understanding from their fellows, and fewer still find even a limited acceptance in a small section of society: all are constantly confronted with reminders of their unhappy situation. The tragedy of their lives is the greater since it may be remediable; with suitable management and treatment, especially if this is begun soon after birth, many of these people can be helped to live happy well-adjusted lives, and some may even be fertile and be enabled to enjoy a normal family life. (Dewhurst and Gordon 1969, vii)

Finally, it is significant that there remains a wide schism between medical understandings and popularized representations of hermaphroditism: the most common sideshow and carnival images present a graphic, nongenital, lateral hermaphroditism by splitting the subject down the middle and dressing one half as male and the other as female. The Victor-Victoria, John-Jane image has no known medical correlate: these individuals have probably had plastic surgery or wear implants on the one side (to create the impression of breasts) or have had one breast removed.[5] In other words, in popular, nonmedical discourses, there seems to be something intolerable, not about sexual profusion (a biological bisexuality that is fascinating and considered worth paying for by audiences) but about sexual *indeterminacy:* the subject who has clear-cut male and female parts seems more acceptable than the subject whose genitalia is neither male nor female. These subjects imperil the very constitution of subjectivity according to sexual categories. I will return to this.

I would like now to turn briefly to that category of monstrosity that is today named after its most famous examples, "Siamese" (or conjoined) twins, after Chang and Eng (who, incidentally, were Chinese, not Siamese). Born in Siam in 1811 of Chinese parents, the pair was discovered by the merchant Robert Hunter in 1824, who obtained the permission of their parents and the king to take them to the United States and Europe for exhibitions. Significantly, they were first exhibited before doctors (at Harvard University in 1829), legitimized and authenticated, and then exhibited before the general public. When they were forty-two, they took the name "Bunker," married two sisters, English women aged twenty-six and twenty-eight, and for a number of years lived together in one house. When their families became too large, they moved into separate residences, the twins spending three days with one woman then three with the other in alternation until their deaths. Between them, they had twenty-two children and more than two hundred grandchildren. Apparently their descendants now number several thousand, many of whom live in the same region today as the twins did.

Although they were examined by dozens of doctors, and in spite of the fact that as they grew older, they fought more and more bitterly, it was decided not to attempt to separate them. Conjoined twins had been successfully separated as early as 1690, when two Swiss sisters joined belly to belly were separated by ligature and a simple operation (Gould and Pyle 1897, 172). In Chang and Eng's case, however, it was decided that surgery would endanger the survival of both. Moreover, Chang and Eng were so dispirited by the idea of separation that, at least in the first forty years of their lives, they would weep if it was even mentioned. It is significant that today the lives of conjoined twins are considered tragic if the operation to separate them is not feasible. This does not always accord with the feelings of the conjoined twins themselves.

Conjoined twins are relatively rare, and first-person (singular or plural) accounts are even rarer, so it is difficult to know what the experience of a permanent coupling is like. There are now, in the late twentieth century, usually only two possible fates for conjoined twins: separation, with the attendant dangers it poses for the children's physical and emotional well-being; or isolation from society, either through institutionalization or through a kind of self-imposed segregation. Probably the most famous adult conjoined twins in recent times are the McCarther twins, Yvonne and Yvette, who were born in 1949 joined at the top of the head, and who died in 1992. Their story made newspaper headlines worldwide when they emerged from thirty-eight years of being housebound—as they put it "just (lying) around the house all day, watching TV and being worthless"—to enroll in college in Los Angeles.

The Siamese twins and the McCarther twins are the only conjoined twins I know of who have given some public indications of their psychical states of being. There are a number of striking similarities between them. It is clear for both sets of conjoined twins that they are two separate subjects, in the sense that they have different personalities, preferences, and styles. Yet it also seems evident that the usual hard and fast distinction between the boundaries of one subject and another are continually blurred: speech patterns and even sentences are shared; all their experiences are shared; they do not need to consult over decisions but make them in unison automatically. Chang and Eng, for example, even wrote their letters in the first person singular, using "I" where others would have presumed a "we" was appropriate, and signing themselves in the joint name "ChangEng."

It seems to be an affront to the common sense of identity that two individuals, even identical twins, should submerge themselves so completely in an identification with another person as to lose all trace of their singularity. However, in the case of both of these sets of twins, every attempt to individuate them in terms of dress, appearance, and behavior was frustrated. It seems that both sets were more than happy to wear the same clothes, eat the same food, and do whatever they could to act and appear the same. Chang and Eng always bought their clothes at the same time, having two suits made in identical styles from the same materials. Admittedly, it would have been difficult for them not to at least shop at the same time, but their refusal, for example, to use up material that would have made a suit for one but not for two, indicated that even where it may have been more convenient and cheaper to dress differently, they refused to do so. A *Los Angeles Times* article indicates that the same voluntary identification occurred with Yvonne and Yvette: "As usual, they dressed identically, from head to toe. Even their purses contain matching sets of everything from vitamin jars to wallets with exactly the same family photos." Ironically, the linkages between conjoined twins, which seem so pitiable and horrifying to us, are not considered problematic by the twins themselves. A contemporary report on Chang and Eng, from London's *Examiner*, succinctly puts the tragedy of their existence into words:

> It is a mournful sight, to behold two fellow-creatures thus fated to endure all the common evils of life, while they must necessarily be debarred from the enjoyment of many of its chief delights. The link which unites them is more durable than that of the marriage tie—no separation can take place, legal or illegal—no Act of Parliament can divorce them, nor can all the power of Doctors' Commons give them a release even from bed and board. (Quoted in Wallace and Wallace 1976, 80)

However, the twins themselves seemed far more content than this, being limited more by the social necessity of their economic survival in a culture puzzled and horrified by them, and aware of their peculiarity only from others.

The conjunction of twins is made more stark, and the divisions between one existence and another more blurred, in the case of parasitic twins, where only one of the twins is fully formed and organically functional and the other is embedded in the body of the first. In such cases, it is exceedingly rare that the head of the parasitic twin is developed or formed; more commonly, the limbs exist in atrophied form, so that either a torso protrudes from the torso of the fully formed twin, or she or he has extra limbs in unexpected places. In such cases, it is no longer clear that there are two identities, even if the bodily functions of the parasitic twin occur independently of the will or awareness of the other. In such cases, is there one subject or two? If the subject is considered a single being, what kind of body-space does he or she occupy? Given that the sensations of the parasitic twin are not always perceived by the autositic twin, does the body-image include the parasitic body? What kind of body image must it be if the body is to include sensations and experiences the subject cannot experience in the first person?

The presence of conjoined twins raises a number of points of interest, some of which are similar to those raised by hermaphrodites. First, just as sexuality is best regarded in terms of a series of sexual morphologies and positions, so, too, in the case of conjoined twins there seems to be a continuum of identities, ranging from the so-called normal, individuated singular subject, to a nonindividuated, collectivized multiple subject.

Second, the subject is not given an identity independent of his or her bodily morphology—either sexual or more broadly corporeal—but acquires an identity in the relation to the body. The range of peculiarities and biological anomalies to which the body is liable clearly make a difference to the kind of body-image and consequently to the kind of identity the subject (or subjects) attributes and finds others attributing to itself. If it is uncertain where one body ends and another begins, the subject's identity too must remain undecidably singular and plural, individual and collective.

Third, as in the case of hermaphroditism, it is significant that, in spite of the state of health of conjoined twins, there appears to be a medical imperative for surgical intervention and normalization, even if surgery may actually endanger lives that may otherwise remain healthy. It seems that the permanent conjunction of individuals is socially intolerable, and that it is unimaginable to others that these subjects themselves would not wish to be able to lead "normal" lives. Surgery, it is argued, provides the only hope of such a normality, and surgical intervention clearly functions more successfully the earlier it occurs: the younger the children are, the less formed their body-image is.

Finally, the existence of conjoined twins, whether autositic or parasitic, raises the question of the nature of bodily boundaries and the distinctions that separate one being from another. While psychologically distinct individuals, conjoined twins are nevertheless far closer than any other two beings ever could be, and while there are two identities, they are not sharply distinguished from each other. In separating conjoined twins, one does not thereby create two autonomous beings, only as close as identical twins; conjoined twins are bonded through the psychical inscription of their historical, even if not current, corporeal links. Those who have shared organs, a common blood circulation, and every minute detail of everyday life can never have this corporeal link effaced.

In conclusion, I would like to return to one of the concerns I mentioned at the beginning of this chapter: not to so-called freaks themselves, but to what is freakish among those who are not freaks—that is, the dual horror and fascination others have toward those they label freaks. This mixture of reactions is a peculiar one that requires some kind of explanation. Why are people horrified at seeing deformities and human anomalies? Why do they classify such anomalies as freaks? What is so unsettling about freaks? I suggest that it is not gross deformity alone that is so unsettling and fascinating. Rather, there are other reasons for this curiosity and horror. First, it seems to me that the initial reaction to the freakish and the monstrous is a perverse kind of sexual curiosity. People think to themselves: "How do they do *it?*" What kind of sex lives are available to Siamese twins, hermaphrodites, bearded ladies, and midgets? There is a certain morbid speculation about what it would be like to be with such persons, or worse, to be them. It is not altogether surprising that a very large percentage of freaks I have researched were married or involved in sexual liaisons. As Victor Hugo writes in *The Man Who Laughs,* "You are not only ugly, but hideous. Ugliness is insignificant, deformity is grand. Ugliness is a devil's grin behind beauty; deformity is akin to sublimity."

The perverse pleasure of voyeurism and identification is counterbalanced by horror at the blurring of identities (sexual, corporeal, personal) that witness our chaotic and insecure identities. Freaks traverse the very boundaries that secure the "normal" subject in its given identity and sexuality. Monsters involve all kinds of doubling of the human form, a duplication of the body or some of its parts. The major terata recognized throughout history are largely monsters of excess, with two or more heads, bodies, or limbs, or with duplicated sexual organs. One might ponder why the excess of bodily parts is more discomforting than a shortage or diminution of limbs or organs. Perhaps our fear of the immersion or loss of identity with another is greater or more pervasive than our fear of bodily incompletion. This fear, like the fear and horror of ghostly doubles or Doppelgänger, is a horror at the possibility of our own imperfect duplication, a horror of submersion in an alien otherness, an incorporation in and by another.

The freak illustrates our so-called normal pleasure and fascination with our mirror-images, a fascination with the limits of our own identities as they are witnessed from the outside. This is a narcissistic delight at the shape of our own externality, which is always inaccessible to us by direct means and is achievable only if we can occupy the perspective others have on us. The relation we bear to images of ourselves is drawn from this simultaneous and ambivalent reaction: the mirror-image threatens to draw us into its spell of spectral doubling, annihilating the self that wants to see itself reflected. At the same time, it gains pleasure from the access it gives to the subject's exteriority, from an illusory mastery over its image. Fascination with the monstrous is testimony to our tenuous hold on the image of perfection. The freak confirms the viewer as bounded, belonging to a "proper" social category. The viewer's horror lies in the recognition that this monstrous being is at the heart of his or her own identity, for it is all that must be ejected or abjected from self-image to make the bounded, category-obeying self possible. In other words, what is at stake in the subject's dual reaction to the freakish or bizarre individual is its own narcissism, the pleasures and boundaries of its own identity, and the integrity of its received images of self.

Notes

This chapter was written in 1986, under the auspices of and with funding from the Humanities Research Centre, The Australian National University. It was published as "Freaks: An Exploration of Human Anomalies" in *Social Semiotics* 1, no. 2 (1991): 22–38. It has been rewritten for this collection.

1. A freemartin is a sterile twin in cattle, sheep, goats and pigs, in which the female twin is masculinized when the male hormones secreted by the male twin enter the female twin through common blood circulation. See Mittwoch (1973), 60ff.

2. I was recently alarmed to read in my local newspaper a report on the experiments of scientists who, as part of the human genome project, are trying to map the genes relevant to sight. They have, through gene-splicing, been able to induce the development of up to fourteen eyes on a single fly, in unlikely and dysfunctional sites (e.g. on the end of antennae, on legs, on the thorax or back). Sadly, it seems, the more information about genetics and genetic manipulation is developed, the more bizarre and extreme are its experimental implications.

3. Geoffroy Saint-Hilaire's teratological classifications were as follows:

CLASS 1—Union of several fetuses. CLASS 2—Union of two distinct fetuses by a connecting band. CLASS 3—Union of two distinct fetuses by an osseous junction of cranial bones. CLASS 4—Union of two distinct fetuses in which one or more parts are eliminated by the junction. CLASS 5—Union of two fetuses by a bony union of the ischii. CLASS 6—Fusion of two fetuses below the umbilicus into a common lower extremity. CLASS 7—Bicephalic monsters. CLASS 8—Parasitic monsters. CLASS 9—Monsters with a single body and double lower extremities. CLASS 10—Diphallic terata. CLASS 11—Fetus in fetu, and dermoid cysts. CLASS 12—Hermaphrodites. (Quoted in Gould and Pyle 1897, 167)

4. An estimated three hundred conjoined twins have survived beyond a few months of age in recorded history, although the success rate in separating conjoined twins is increasing with advances in the techniques of microsurgery. In the case of intersexuality, however, the rate is much more frequent, perhaps being one in two thousand.

5. Significantly, probably the most striking mass culture representation of the hermaphrodite, in

Federico Fellini's *Satyricon,* in which there is a closer correspondence with medicalized images, was played by a sexually immature boy who, through the help of make-up, was given the appearance of breasts.

BIBLIOGRAPHY

Dewhurst, Christopher J., and Ronald R. Gordon. 1969. *The Intersexual Disorders.* London: Baillière Tindall/Cassell.

Drimmer, Frederick. 1973. *Very Special People.* New York: Amjon.

Fiedler, Leslie. 1978. *Freaks: Myths and Image of the Secret Self.* New York: Simon & Schuster.

Gould, George M., and Walter L. Pyle. 1897. *Anomalies and Curiosities of Medicine.* Philadelphia: W. B. Saunders.

Hirst, B. C., and G. A. Peirson. 1893. *Human Monstrosities.* Philadelphia: Lea Brothers.

Jones, Howard W., and William W. Scott. 1971. *Hermaphrodites, Genital Anomalies and Related Endocrine Disorders.* Baltimore: Williams and Wilkins.

Josso, Nathalie, ed. 1981. *The Intersex Child.* Basel: S. Karger.

Lifson, Robert. 1983. *Enter the Sideshow.* Bala Cynwyd, Pa.: Mason Publishing.

Mittwoch, Ursula. 1973. *Genetics of Sexual Differentiation.* London and New York: Academic Press.

Money, John. 1968. *Sex Errors of the Body: Dilemmas, Education, Counselling.* Baltimore: Johns Hopkins University Press.

Nishimura, Hideo, and James R. Miller. 1969. *Methods for Teratological Studies in Experimental Animals and Man.* London: Pitman Medical Publishing.

Rubin, Alan. 1967. *Handbook of Congenital Malformations.* Philadelphia: W. B. Saunders.

Smith, David W. 1976. *Recognizable Patterns of Human Malformation.* Philadelphia: W. B. Saunders.

Wallace, Irving, and Amy Wallace. 1976. *The Two.* London: Cassell.

Wilson, James G. 1973. *Environment and Birth Defects.* New York: Academic Press.

PART II

Practices of Enfreakment

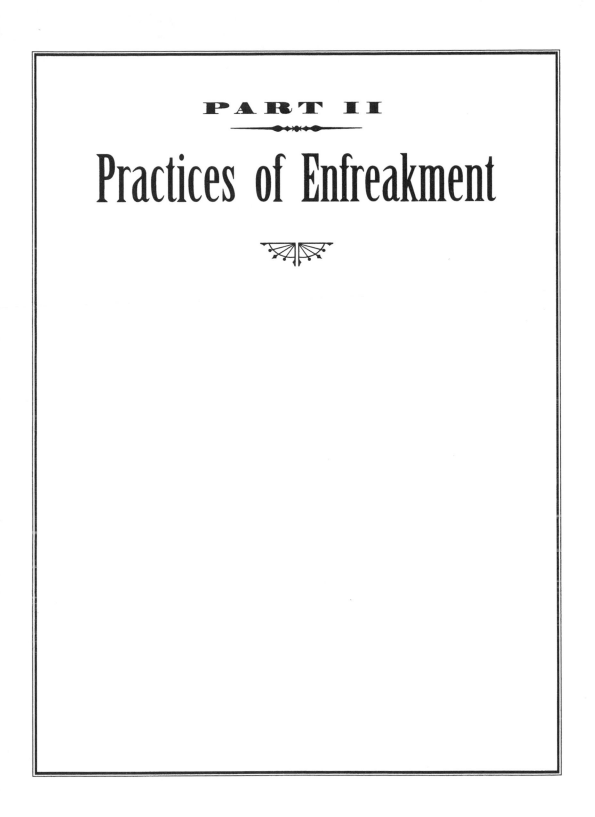

Monsters in the Marketplace: The Exhibition of Human Oddities in Early Modern England

PAUL SEMONIN

The publication of Jonathan Swift's satire *Gulliver's Travels* in 1726 signaled the decline of an era in which the taste for monsters had become an almost universal craze among English citizens of all ranks. Swift's tales parodied many different aspects of English society, but the central motif for his beleaguered hero in the novel *Voyage to Brobdingnag*, "the Ignominy of being carried about for a Monster," was borrowed from a centuries-old fixture in English popular culture, the display of monsters in the marketplace.[1] Though he scornfully mocked the "monster-mongers and other retailers of strange sights" in an earlier work, *A Tale of the Tub*, Swift himself was a connoisseur of these strange sights, being among the first to see the seven-year-old Hungarian sisters, Helena and Judith, twins joined at the backs, who were typical of the so-called monsters that had thrilled learned Englishmen since the Restoration. Only a month after a scholarly description of these twins was read before the Royal Society on May 12, 1708, Swift commented on their impact on him, remarking that seeing them "causes many speculations; and raises an abundance of questions in divinity, law and physic."[2]

For many observers, the decadence at the court of Charles II heralded the resurgence of interest in monsters that swept through England in the late seventeenth century, a phenomenon that drove historian Henry Morley to declare that after the Restoration "the taste for monsters became a disease."[3] Though dwarfs had always played a role in court society, the increased demand for them, along with armless and legless performers, hermaphrodites, scaly boys, and many other performers with natural deformities, brought fame, though not very often fortune, to the most versatile of these entertainers. Matthew Buchinger, the armless and legless German dwarf, whose virtuosity with a pen, musical instruments, playing cards, cups and balls, and witty repartee made him a court favorite, appeared at the Blackmoor's Heads in Holburn, near Southampton, in 1723, a few years before Swift's *Gulliver's Travels* was published.

At the peak of their popularity after the Restoration, the term "monsters" applied to many types of exotic exhibits besides those natural anomalies that fell into the category of monstrous births. Even these prodigies, which had come to be viewed as wonders of God's nature, included an assortment of fabulous creatures, whose pedigrees clearly went well beyond the limits of natural conception into the realm of the mythical. From Elizabethan times, when the first inhabitants and specimens of animal life from the New World began to arrive in England, there appeared among the exhibits a startlingly diverse array of monstrous creatures, many of whom were already familiar to their audiences through popular fables, the bestiaries, pictorial prints, and biblical lore. Late seventeenth-century handbills, many from Sir Hans Sloane's collection, announced such hybrid creatures as the hand of a Sea Monster, half man and half fish; a Man-Teger [sic] from the East Indies, "from the Head downwards resembling a Man, its fore parts clear, and his hinder parts all Hairy"; a "strange and monstrous Female Creature that was taken in the woods in the Deserts of Aethiopia in Prester John's Country, in the remotest parts of Africa"; and a monster from the "Coast of Brazil, having a Head like a Child, Legs and Arms very wonderful, with a Long Tail like a Serpent, where with he feeds himself, as an Elephant doth with his Trunk." In addition to the hermaphrodites, dwarfs, giants, and giantesses who were standard fare at these shows, there were also a wide variety of persons with natural anomalies, including a woman with three breasts, a boneless child, and a monster with one body, two heads, four arms and four legs, with teeth in each mouth.[4]

Throughout the seventeenth century, the London monster shows were the occasion of a mingling of the classes that may have been unprecedented. Foreign visitors to England declared the wide appeal of these exhibits to be one of the characteristic traits of the English people. While the top acts entertained the royalty at court, wealthy connoisseurs could obtain private audiences by paying the showmen to bring these curiosities into their homes. Inns were regarded as the most eligible show places for upscale public viewing, since the common practice of renting lodging to a monster during fairs often attracted customers to these establishments. The cheapest shows were those of itinerant showmen who set up their displays in the streets near taverns or coffeehouses. Don Saltero's Coffeehouse, London's first public museum, advertised such exhibits in *Mist's Weekly Journal* in 1723: "Monsters of all sorts here are seen, Strange things in nature as they grew so."[5]

For ordinary Londoners, the tumultuous throng that often provided the burgeoning mass audience for the monsters, there were the penny shows in the streets and at the fairs, which were also frequented by a surprising number of the penny-pinching better sort. A midget named the "Corsican Fairy," normally shown in Cockspur Street for two-shillings and six-pence, could be seen at Bartholomew Fair at three-pence for "Working People, Servants and Children," but six-pence for "Gentry."[6] Henry Morley's history of Bartholomew Fair points out that the cheap shows there were not rarities to be seen only at the fair, but rather entertainments of the regular London showmen, normally scattered about the city during the rest of the year.

Among the most ardent admirers of these monsters were many of the luminaries of the London literary scene, especially budding naturalists. Diary entries by John Evelyn, Samuel Pepys, and Robert Hooke, all members of the Royal Society, record their visits to the cheap exhibits, as well as the more expensive. Scholarly descriptions of the monsters appeared frequently in the early issues of the Royal Society's journal. Pepys's servant, James Paris du Plessis, produced an early chronicle of these exhibits, a three-hundred-page book entitled *A Short History of Human Prodigies and Monstrous Births, of Dwarfs, Sleepers, Giants, Strong Men, Hermaphrodites, Numberous Births and Extreme Old Age, Etc.*, which included fifty-four hand-colored drawings of these figures. The physician Sir Hans Sloane, an eminent collector of curiosities and founder of the British Museum, sent a draughtsman to make drawings of the monsters and compiled the most extensive collection of handbills advertising them. Exhibitors were obviously aware of the interest among learned naturalists in their audience and worded their handbills to highlight such appeal: "For the satisfaction of all curious enquirers into the Secrets of Nature, is to be seen a Woman Dwarf, but Three Foot and one Inch high, born in *Sommersetshire*, who discourses excellently well, and gives great Satisfaction to all that ever saw her."[7]

The intellectual fascination for monsters among the naturalists was testimony to the enduring scientific interest in them engendered by Francis Bacon during the early seventeenth century. In 1620, Bacon had given monstrous births a strategic place in his tripartite schema for the study of natural history, arguing that they should constitute a special category, the preter-natural, which he saw linking the other two categories, the natural and the artificial. His principal concern was to separate monstrous births from the long tradition of supernatural explanations of such phenomena. As Katherine Park and Lorraine J. Daston note, "Bacon was at pains to distinguish his history of marvels from 'books of fabulous experiments and secrets' which served up a jumble of fact and fable to 'curious and vain wits.' "[8]

Even within the narrow world of natural history, such efforts to confine monsters to a strictly scientific niche only succeeded eventually in hastening their departure from the polite company of learned society. The principal legacy of this demythification was the establishment of a secular yardstick for measuring the credulity of those who still attended the shows in the marketplace. From the early days of the English Renaissance, there had been a growing criticism of the gullibility of the penny audience, the "Mob," which patronized the monster shows. "By the mid-eighteenth century an appetite for the marvelous had become, as Hume declared, the hallmark of the 'ignorant and barbarous,' antithetical to the study of nature as conducted by the man of 'good-sense, education and learning.' "[9] Monsters came to symbolize the imbecility of popular beliefs, the perfect metaphor for decrying the sheep-like mentality of the masses, who were the butt of ridicule by everyone from satirists to scientists.

Efforts by modern scholars to understand the popular appeal of monsters have been hampered by their tacit acceptance of this gullibility thesis. In their comprehensive study of early modern monster literature, Park and Daston frame their argument in terms of a struggle between the Protestant reformers, who viewed monstrous births primarily as ominous signs of God's displeasure with sinful behavior, and the nascent scientific mentality that sought to strip away any religious significance in order to interpret them mainly within the realm of medical pathology. For Park and Daston, the transition from popularly based broadside ballads by Protestants to the learned clinical treatises by scientists paralleled the withdrawal of the educated classes from popular culture, ending finally with the predominantly secular opinion that popular beliefs about monsters were symptoms of ignorance and superstition. "In the early years of the Reformation, the tendency to treat monsters as prodigies—frightening signs of God's wrath dependent ultimately or solely upon his will—was almost universal. By the end of the seventeenth century, only the most popular forms of literature—ballads, broadsides and the occasional religious pamphlet—treated monsters in this way."[10]

Although Park and Daston seem well aware of the ancient tradition of monster culture pre-dating the Reformation, they make only passing reference to its manifestation in popular culture, preferring instead to highlight its influence upon medieval writings and the new Renaissance genre of wonder literature, where the strictly religious treatment of monsters as prodigies was replaced by an encyclopedic interest in them as marvels of nature. The cosmographies of Konrad von Gesner and Pierre Belon were typical of this new genre, which had its roots in the efforts by late medieval Latin humanists to compile encyclopedic treatises, including Albertus Magnus's *De secretis naturae*. German and Swiss scholars borrowed heavily from ephemeral literature on monstrous births to create learned Latin treatises on the subject in the sixteenth century, and these works were quickly vulgarized by authors who either translated them into the vernacular or simply plagiarized them to produce the popular prodigy books. Though the distinction between the prodigy books and the wonder literature often seems overwrought, there can be little doubt that both had a tendency to secularize the subject, since they inevitably included clinical descriptions of the monstrous births with occasional accounts of mythical creatures. In many respects, it seems more appropriate to identify learned prodigy books such as Pierre Boaistuau's *Histoires prodigieuses* and Ambroise Paré's *Des Monstres et prodiges* (see fig. 5.1) with the protoscientific Baconian tradition. Jean Céard, a French authority on Paré, considers *Des Monstres et prodiges* "the most sustained attempt (during the sixteenth century) to 'naturalize' monsters."[11] Nonetheless, Jurgis Baltrusaitis's remark about Paré's contribution to this new genre of medicalized monster lore suggests that scientific imagery was capable of creating its own fantasy world: "The fantastic realism of the image-makers is joined here to the awakening of a realistic [scientific] mind."[12]

Even though vulgarizers of this new wonder literature, like Thomas Lupton, the late sixteenth-century English author of the catalogue of natural marvels *A Thousand Notable Things*, wrote in a plain style aimed at "the slenderly learned and common sorte," it should be evident by now that we must use the word "popular" advisedly when dealing with the new audience of lay readers—especially if we are to maintain any integrity to a notion that previously, if not primarily, was applied to the folk beliefs of semiliterate and illiterate peasants, laborers, and migrant workers. For Park and Daston, "vulgarization" is relevant mainly to the emerging middle-class lay readers rather than the "mob." This is evident in their efforts to link the wonder literature to the conversation manuals, both of which "presented a new, civil ideal of culture, opposed to both popular ignorance and the solitary efforts of the professional scholar, and identified with the culture of the educated layman—the lawyer, the businessman, the government official, and their wives and daughters."[13] "While popular literature retained its traditional prodigious and prophetic thrust," they argue, "educated culture, in this and other areas, was tending to detach itself from what it perceived as the ignorance and superstition of the folk—'the most deceptable part of Mankind,' as Thomas Browne called them in *Pseudodoxia epidemica*."[14]

The broadside ballads, on which the edifice of Protestant prodigy literature rested, actually served in many ways to obscure the popular meaning of monsters in the marketplace. The ballads sought to instill fear instead of wonder in the hearts of the common people, to whom the dreadful litany of God's wrath must have become a numbing routine. In the late sixteenth century, "A mervaylous strange deformed Swyne" brought from Denmark to England for display occasioned a ballad whose verse was typical of the Protestant sentiments:

> *Come neere, good Christians all,*
> *Beholde a monster rare,*
> *Whose monstrous shape, no doubt, fortels,*
> *Gods wrath we should beware.*[15]

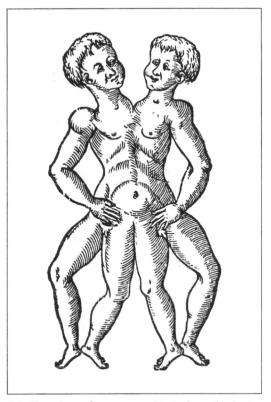

5.1. Drawing of monstrous birth from Ambroise Paré's *Des monstres et prodiges* (Geneva: Librairic Droz, 1971; orig. 1573), 14.

By 1637, a Protestant minister's sermon against the showing of monsters in the marketplace acknowledged the declining popular interest in prodigies: "The common sort makes no further use of prodigies and strange-births, than as matter of wonder and table-talk."[16] Even though these ballads were "sung" by the peddlers who sold them, it was often not a song in the traditional sense, but rather a crying of the news, that they most resembled. Lyric ballads like *Chevy Chase* and *Barbara Allen*, Peter Burke notes, were "swamped by new ones which often dealt with current events; battles, murders, witchcraft, monstrous births and other prodigies."[17] Often the ominous ballad lyrics, as the broadsides themselves indicated, were to be sung to music from other songs, whose incongruous titles sometimes suggest an almost satiric tone was sought in their actual singing.

Such patently journalistic headlines were typical of the broadsides. By the late seventeenth century, a ballad about a woman who gave birth to a toad, a serpent, and a child announced the event under the rubric of "True wonders and strange news," while retaining elements of the familiar prodigy formula in its verse: "Strange miracles the Lord has sent, that we our sins may lay aside."[18] From the earliest broadsides, the element of wonder seems to have been an important ingredient in this genre, since the monstrous births, the signs of God's wrath, were also considered miracles, indications of God's power over nature. However, the sense of wonder was undercut, if not entirely negated, by a stark realism evident in the detailed description of the monstrous birth, which had none of the fanciful spirit of the showman's handbills. An early seventeenth-century broadside, headlined "The true picture of a Female Monster born near Salisbury" (fig. 5.2), was accompanied by an anatomical sketch and announced "a wonderful Creature, which cannot be otherwise accounted than a Monster: It having two Heads, four Arms, and two Legs."[19]

Even these prodigies were often brought to the marketplace, not for religious purposes, but for commercial display to curiosity seekers. In 1664, a broadside described how the embalmed bodies of two monstrous twins, Martha and Mary, joined together at the navel, were brought to London where the father, a poor man, had "twenty pounds given him the first day, by persons of Quality."[20] By viewing these events mainly through the broadside ballads, as manifestations of religious sentiments engendered by the Reformation, we run the risk of ignoring their wider nonreligious significance in the marketplace. After all, a person there could see a monster for the one-penny price of a broadside ballad. The ballads themselves were sold and sung by peddlers in the marketplace, where they competed with the handbills of showmen for the attention of the assembled throng. In many respects, the realistic tone of these broadsides may have had more in common with the secular scientific tradition of the learned naturalists than with the popular mentality of the marketplace, which both Protestant reformers and the secular naturalists eventually condemned with equal ferocity. What these groups had in common only becomes readily visible when both are set off against the profoundly different folk mentality of the popular mind, which tends to remain submerged in the background of early modern monster lore so long as we rely so heavily upon the literary evidence, whether it be broadsides or Latin treatises. Even within the literary tradition itself, the popular taste for monsters, with its decidedly folkloric conception of them, constitutes a well-documented outlook that is later dismissed simply as credulity.

Beneath the surface of the documentary evidence, with its thinly veiled contempt for popular beliefs, lies a shadow world of monster lore that is surprisingly visible, if we look at the cultural environment in which these people lived. In the medieval bestiaries, the crab crawling sideways symbolized the fraudulent; ironically, it is to the fabulous, imaginary creatures that we must turn for further insight into the popularity of monsters in the marketplace. While Protestant divines and naturalists were busy trying to separate humankind from nature, the popular mind still felt at home in a mental world inhabited by fabulous creatures, a realm of natural wonders based upon the ancient assumption that human beings and nature were locked into one interacting world.

Early Christianity had adopted a hostile attitude toward the animistic beliefs common in pagan cultures, and it promoted a distinctly antimythical doctrine in which humankind's separation from nature was symbolized by the expulsion of Adam and Eve from the Garden of Eden. In his timely study *Man and the Natural World,* Keith Thomas has explored some of the consequences of this dichotomy, pointing out that among them was the repudiation of the tradition in classical Greek culture that man was descended from animals.[21] By the early modern era, the boundary between the human and animal worlds had become the battleline in the war against popular beliefs. "Wherever we look in early modern England," says Thomas, "we find anxiety, latent or explicit, about any form of behaviour which threatened to transgress the fragile boundaries between man and the animal creation."[22] In the popular monster lore, this boundary between beasts and humans was virtually nonexistent and was crossed over frequently in a bestiary tradition dating back to antiquity that included centaurs,

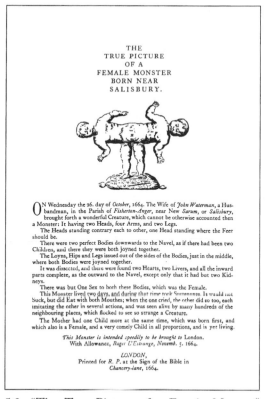

THE
TRUE PICTURE
OF A
FEMALE MONSTER
BORN NEAR
SALISBURY.

ON Wednesday the 26. day of *October*, 1664. The Wife of *John Waterman*, a Husbandman, in the Parish of *Fisherton-Anger*, near New *Sarum*, or *Salisbury*, brought forth a wonderful Creature, which cannot be otherwise accounted then a Monster: It having two Heads, four Arms, and two Legs.

The Heads standing contrary each to other, one Head standing where the Feet should be.

There were two perfect Bodies downwards to the Navel, as if there had been two Children, and there they were both joyned together.

The Loyns, Hips and Legs issued out of the sides of the Bodies, just in the middle, where both Bodies were joyned together.

It was dissected, and there were found two Hearts, two Livers, and all the inward parts complete, as the outward to the Navel, except only that it had but two Kidneys.

There was but One Sex to both these Bodies, which was the Female.

This Monster lived two days, and during that time took Sustenance. It would not Suck, but did Eat with both Mouthes; when the one cried, the other did so too, each imitating the other in several actions, and was seen alive by many hundreds of the neighbouring places, which flocked to see so strange a Creature.

The Mother had one Child more at the same time, which was born first, and which also is a Female, and a very comely Child in all proportions, and is yet living.

This Monster is intended speedily to be brought to London.
With Allowance, *Roger L'Estrange, Novemb.* 5. 1664.

LONDON,
Printed for *R. P.* at the Sign of the Bible in
Chancery-lane, 1664.

5.2. "The True Picture of a Female Monster" (London, 1664), broadside, reprinted in *The Pack of Autolycus*, ed. Hyder E. Rollins (Cambridge, Mass.: Harvard University Press, 1927), 140.

satyrs, and minotaurs, not to mention the dog-headed men, pygmies, and troglodytes who constituted the monstrous races believed to inhabit remote parts of the earth.[23]

Naturalists seeking knowledge of plant life from rural folklore found that "for most people in the early modern period the plant world was alive with symbolic meaning."[24] Even plants could give birth to monsters. Learned sixteenth-century herbalists saw further evidence of popular credulity in the fantastic stories surrounding the mandrake root, a plant that popular lore held grew beneath the gallows from the seed of hanged men. The mandrake plant, which has narcotic properties, produces a forked, fleshy root shaped like a human figure, which popular lore maintained was so full of animal life it gave a shriek and dropped human blood when torn out of the ground. In medieval times these roots were made into charms, and by the Tudor era they were being sold as puppets by itinerant peddlers at Bartholomew Fair, where they aroused an indignant warning from William Turner, author of *A New Herball*, that they were the fabrications of confidence men.[25] The mandrake charms are concrete evidence of the monster lore that crossed over from medieval popular beliefs into the early modern marketplace despite efforts to suppress it. In 1611, they posed a haunting question to the schoolmaster and author Henry Peacham:

Why doe the rude vulgar so hastily post in madnesse
To gaze at trifles, and toyes not worthy the viewing?
And thinke them happy, when they may be shew'd for a penny
The Fleet-streete Mandrakes, that heavenly Motion of Eltham.[26]

For anyone seeking the answer to Peacham's question, Bartholomew Fair represents a rare vista in the landscape of early modern popular culture, a monumental assemblage of the strange and exotic that the English poet William Wordsworth described at the beginning of the nineteenth century as the "Parliament of Monsters." From its inception in the early twelfth century until its final suppression in 1855, the fair was a living museum of the monstrous, which survived everything from the Reformation to the Civil War, before finally falling victim to the middle-class decorum of the Victorian era.

By the Elizabethan age, Bartholomew Fair was already an "ancient custome," having been first chartered over four hundred years earlier in 1133 by a monk named Rayer, who had been court jester to Henry I. Beginning on the eve of St. Bartholomew's Day in the month of August, the fair was celebrated for three days each year at the Priory of St. Bartholomew, located in West Smithfield, just beyond Alder Gate outside the London city wall. Until 1614, when Smithfield was first paved, the site remained, in Henry Morley's vivid words, "a broken plain of mud" full of the filth of men and beasts, at the edge of London, where paths from the countryside met uninhabited lanes from the city. Originally the site of the king's market held every Friday, the large open field before the priory eventually became a daily gathering place for Londoners seeking recreation, and it was the scene of great jousting tournaments, wrestling, and ninepins. The city gallows there were the site of public executions, while the open field also became a place of martyrdom for heretics burnt alive and was a public burial ground for plague victims.

Everywhere in England the first fairs had originated as gatherings of worshipers and pilgrims at sacred places, on the feast days of saints enshrined in the nearby abbeys and cathedrals. They were held within the church itself until this practice was prohibited, shifting their locale to the churchyard and the surrounding neighborhood. The Priory of St. Bartholomew operated a hospital for the poor, and under Rayer's tutelage the site quickly became a "wonder-working shrine," a place of pilgrimage famous for miraculous cures. Rayer himself staged numerous "miracles" to attract people to the Fair, and although they were denounced later by the church they continued to occur even after his death.

From its inception, on the feast days during the fair St. Bartholomew's was the scene of wondrous entertainments, intermixed with sinful excesses. Morley provides an atmospheric description of the fair based upon drawings from the Decretals, thirteenth-century illuminated manuscripts prepared by monks depicting life around the priory:

We have but to give voice and life to all those pictures, and we have the spirit of the concourse at the Fair. Cripples about the altar, miracles of saints, mummings of sinners, monks with their fingers in the flesh-pot, ladies astride on the high saddles of their palfreys, knights, nobles, citizens and peasants, the toilers of idleness and industry, the stories that were most in request, lax morality, the grotesque images which gave delight to an uncultivated people.[27]

From the same manuscript drawings, we can see that Bartholomew Fair was the site of miracle plays, the mysteries and the moralities, for they depict a stage scene with the devil emerging from a Hell-mouth, the grotesque animal's head that was the traditional medieval stage device through which these monstrous creatures came and went. But in these productions, as Morley points out, the devil was always portrayed as a comic character, wearing a leather dress trimmed with feathers or hair.

Bartholomew Fair eventually became a sort of mecca for monsters, a place of pilgrimage whose aura of the miraculous survived even after the dissolution of the monasteries. The monsters appeared there in a carnival setting, along with a corps of professional entertainers including rope dancers, puppeteers, posture-masters, fire-eaters, and animal trainers, all immersed in a cacophony of rumbling kettle drums, penny trumpets, bagpipes, and fiddlers. "It is there you will see the Italian Scaramouch dancing on the Rope," cries a handbill, "with a Wheel Barrow before him with two Children and a Dog in it, and a Duck on his Head, who sings to the Company, and causes much laughter."[28] While the puppet shows echoed the miracle plays and moralities of medieval times, the "drolls," short comic performances, often featuring dwarfs, trained animals, and persons with natural anomalies, provided an array of theatrical shows that were not shut down even when London's playhouses were silenced during the Commonwealth. In many respects, Bartholomew Fair was a theatrical extravaganza in which the monsters were normal and their extraordinary form became part of a spectacle of the unnatural, the grotesque, and the lewd. A pamphlet from 1641, the earliest tract describing the Fair, captures this intermingling of the monstrous with the theatrical among the crowds of people:

> Here a Knave in a fooles coate, with a trumpet sounding, or on a drumme beating, invites you and would faine perswade you to see his puppets; There a Rogue like a wild woodman, or an Antick shap like an Incubus, desires your company to view his motion; on the other side, Hocus Pocus with three yards of tape or ribbin in's hand, shewing his art of Legerdemaine, to the admiration and astonishment of a company of cocko-loaches.[29]

In the early Tudor period, the word "anticke," derived from the Italian *antico*, was synonymous with the term grotesque, which was used to describe various monstrous forms, including the diabolical genre of paintings and prints from continental artists. Breughel's painting of the torments of St. Anthony, with its dream-like Germanic style full of demons and hybrid creatures, was typical of this genre. The German painter Hans Holbein's prints depicting the ridiculous antics of folly and death introduced England to *diablerie* and were extremely popular there.[30] The weird figures in these "lewd" prints, often satyrs, fauns, griffins, and harpies derived from Roman myths, were called "antics" by their critics. French artist Jacques Callot's inexpensive prints, which became popular in England during the early seventeenth century, included figures with natural anomalies as well as fantastic hybrid creatures.

While the clergy saw these "anticke" images as diabolical, to the popular audiences such fabulous creatures, including the Devil, were often comic characters, whose mirthful qualities were derived from older pagan mythologies. "The demons of the monkish legends," Thomas Wright reminds us, "were simply the elves and hobgoblins of our forefathers, who haunted the woods, and fields, and waters, and delighted in misleading or plaguing mankind, although their mischief was usually of a rather mirthful character."[31] Even in the old mysteries or religious plays in which these demons appeared, their roles were the comic scenes, or farce, of the piece. "The devils are droll but not frightful; they provoke laughter, or at least a smile, but they create no horror," observes Wright.[32] The spirit of these medieval monsters—hairy, shaggy creatures with horns, hoofs, and tails—was that of the ludicrous, where the monstrous expressed the love of burlesque and caricature in the popular tradition.

The seventeenth-century English poet John Dryden, himself an ardent critic of the "anticke," divided comedy into two categories—the naturalistic and the fantastic. For him, naturalistic comedy, which was the acceptable form, was a comedy of natural deformity, based upon Aristotelian rules. By contrast, the fantastic was a meaningless exercise, a distortion of the real world, which, ironically, he associates with the monsters at Bartholomew Fair:

> The persons and actions of farce are all unnatural, and the manners false, that is inconsisting [sic] with the characters of mankind. Grotesque painting is the resemblance of this; and Horace begins his *Art of Poetry* by describing such a figure, with a man's head, a horse's neck, the wings of a bird, and a fish's tail; parts of different species jumbled together according to the mad imagination of the dawber; and the end of all this, as he tells you afterwards, to cause laughter; a very monster in Bartholomew Fair, for the mob to gape at for their two-pence.[33]

By transposing Dryden's metaphor, we can see that in the popular tradition monsters were actors in a drama, rather than merely symbols of God's wrath or specimens of scientific interest. They were characters of comic horror intimately connected to an ancient tradition of folk humor, which provides the best insight into the enigma of their enduring appeal in the marketplace. After the Restoration, when the taste for monsters had become so widespread, the term "grotesque" became "the generic designation for all low comic characters, whether fantastic or merely naturally deformed."[34] The use of grimacing figures, obscene language, and bawdy jests were then considered only suitable for vulgar street plays.

Among the monsters exhibited in London in this period, we find a creature who illustrates the comic character of the monstrous. In a handbill advertising his show, he was called the "Bold Grimace Spaniard," a "wild man" captured in the mountains where he had lived for fifteen years after being snatched from his cradle by a savage beast. His performance consisted of the following grimaces:

> He lolls out his Tongue a foot long, turns his Eyes in and out at the same time; contracts his face as small as an Apple; extends his Mouth six inches and turns it into the shape of a Bird's beak, and his eyes like to an Owl's; turns his mouth into the Form of a Hat cock'd up three ways; and also frames it in the manner of a four-square Buckle; licks his Nose with his Tongue, like a Cow; rolls one Eyebrow two Inches up, the other two down; changes his face to such an astonishing Degree, as to appear like a Corpse long bury'd.[35]

While wild men were stock figures in medieval monster lore, the Bold Grimace Spaniard also embodied the traditional peasant entertainment of grinning through horse collars, which was popular at country fairs. This innocuous sideshow amusement, with its blending of the monstrous with the comic, might be regarded simply as a cony-catching ruse for the rustic countrymen were it not for the fact these same facial contortions descended from an ancient comic tradition dating back to the clowns and buffoons of antiquity, who employed the same expressions in their mimicry.

The grimacing faces in the marketplace echoed the grotesque and monstrous heads found in the stone sculpture and wood carving decorating medieval churches. Three "grimacers" found on the carved wooden stalls at the church of Stratford-upon-Avon were typical of this popular art form found in many English ecclesiastical buildings. "This grinning face with tongue out was not a fanciful mode of making the demon appear more repulsive, but was adopted from a classical source."[36] The frightful face with the tongue lolling out took the form of Gorgon in ancient Greek mythology, and dated back to the Egyptian monster Typhon, "the apparent origin of a long series of faces, or masks, of this form and character, which are continually recurring in the grotesque ornamentation, not only of the Greeks and Romans, but of the middle ages."[37] Wright maintains that many of these grotesque forms were handed down to medieval times directly from antiquity by the stone carvers themselves. Along with the many other monstrous creatures found in medieval church decorations, from the legendary monstrous races of the "Indian wonders" to the Germanic wild men, these figures bear silent witness to a long tradition of popular folk humor, in which the monster was a mythological figure, imbued with an essentially comic meaning for its audience in the marketplace. Even though figures with natural anomalies were relatively rare in the carvings, their infrequent appearance there should be sufficient to link them, along with their living counterparts in early modern England, to an enduring folk attitude toward the monstrous that is quite distinct from either the Protestant prodigies or the protoscientific natural wonders.

In contrast to the frivolity of popular attitudes toward the monstrous, the Puritan attacks upon these "anticke" figures often shrouded them in shame and fear. Yet, for all the foreboding portents in their prodigies, the Puritan critics clearly understood an important element of the psychology of the monstrous, even while they attempted to strip away the symbolic significance of the ludicrous. Sir John Davis, the Calvinist author of *Nosce Teipsum*, a collection of verse published in 1599, believed that men were afraid and ashamed of the "antickes" and "chimeras" because they were part of the inner self, what the soul saw when it looked at its own image.

> E'en at first reflection she espies
> Such strange chimeras and monsters there,
> Such toys, such anticks, and such vanities
> As she retires and sinks for shame and fear.[38]

Many modern scholars believe that the ludicrous spirit of the grotesque style of modern literature is an effort to disarm these primordial fears, to subdue the demonic aspects of the world. But, as Frances Barasch points out in her illuminating introduction to a reprint of Wright's study, these modern critics generally ignore the popular tradition, the idea that "medieval frivolity was man's attempt to effect a 'secret liberation' from his sense of help-lessness and horror."[39]

In his classic study of the popular roots of the grotesque in Rabelais, the Russian literary theorist Mikhail Bakhtin argues that the monstrous images in popular folk humor are intimately related to the primordial fears that the Calvinists saw in the soul, only the response in popular culture is laughter instead of shame and guilt. By the early modern period, the Hell-mouth, the monstrous animal's head from the miracle plays, had moved into the marketplace, where it became part of the carnival processions there. "This grotesque image," says Bakhtin, "cannot be understood without appreciating the defeat of fear. The people play with terror and laugh at it; the awesome becomes a 'comic monster.'"[40] For Bakhtin, the monstrous represents the essence of popular culture, the master metaphor for the debasing power of the people's laughter, which lies beneath the placid surface of official culture, only to rear its ugly head from time to time, to remind the world of its humanity. "The essential principle of grotesque realism is degradation, that is the lowering of all that is high, spiritual, ideal, abstract; it is a transfer to the material level, to the sphere of earth and body in their indissoluble unity."[41] Bakhtin links the grotesque imagery of popular culture directly to the literary and pictorial tradition that was such an important legacy from antiquity for popular monster lore, including the legends of the Indian Wonders and medieval demonology.

In her essay "Proverbial Wisdom and Popular Errors," which deals with the changing attitude of learned scholars toward popular proverbs, Natalie Zemon Davis frames her argument with references to a fifteenth-century woodcut depicting the famous dialogue between the scholarly king Solomon and the peasant Marcolf.[42] While the actual identity of Marcolf remains as obscure as the source of this cycle of stories, Davis identifies him as a "barefoot rustic," whose ribald responses to the learned Solomon's proverbs in the monkish legend raise many poignant issues of interpretation for modern scholars of popular culture. Interestingly enough, Marcolf, or Morolf, also appears in Bakhtin's study of Rabelais, where he is referred to only as a "clown," an example of the debasing humor of an ancient folk tradition. However, Barasch adds an intriguing new dimension to this speculation about Marcolf's identity when she points out that during the English Renaissance the comic horror of medieval monsters was transferred to comic types such as Puck, Robin Goodfellow, Till Eulenspiegel, and Marcolf, whom she identifies as a hunchback or dwarf: "The career of the comic hunchback Marcolf—perhaps a survival of the ancient comic dwarf Maccus—has also been traced from the gleeful medieval demon to the clown and fool of Renaissance comedia and jest books."[43] The dwarfish figure from the fifteenth-century woodcut that Davis used to illustrate her essay lends support to Barasch's characterization of Marcolf as a monster.

The monsters in the marketplace of early modern England embodied elements of an ancient comic tradition. The comic horror of monsters and fabulous creatures has been effaced by the prodigy literature of Protestant reformers and the naturalistic mindset of modern scholars. Recovering this link, however, should alter fundamentally our perception of the role of monsters in popular culture.

NOTES

1. For a full discussion of Swift's legacy to the London monster shows, see Aline Mackenzie Taylor, "Sights and Monsters and Gulliver's Voyage to Brobdingnag," *Tulane Studies in English* 7 (1957): 29–82.

2. Richard Altick, *The Shows of London* (Cambridge: Harvard University Press, 1978), 37.

3. Henry Morley, *Memoirs of Bartholomew Fair* (London, 1892), 246.

4. Ibid., 252–56; see also John Ashton, *Social Life in the Reign of Queen Anne* (London: Chatto and Windus, 1925), 204.

5. Altick, *Shows*, 17.

6. Morley, *Memoirs*, 336–37.

7. Ibid., 257.

8. Katherine Park and Lorraine J. Daston, "Unnatural Conceptions: The Study of Monsters in Sixteenth- and Seventeenth-Century France and England," *Past and Present* 92 (1981): 45.

9. Ibid., 54.

10. Ibid., 24.

11. Jean Céard, introduction to *Des Monstres et prodiges* by Ambroise Paré (Geneva: Librairie Droz, 1971), xiv.

12. Baltrusaitis's remark appears in Janis L. Pallister, introduction to *On Monsters and Marvels* by Ambroise Paré (Chicago: University of Chicago Press, 1982), xiii.

13. Park and Daston, "Unnatural Conceptions," 39.

14. Ibid., 41.

15. Joseph Lilly, *A Collection of Seventy-Nine Black-Letter Ballads and Broadsides* (London: J. Lilly, 1870), 187.

16. Park and Daston, "Unnatural Conceptions," 35.

17. Peter Burke, "Popular Culture in Seventeenth-Century London," in *Popular Culture in Seventeenth-Century England*, ed. Barry Reay (London: Croom Helm, 1985), 49.

18. Hyder Edward Rollins, *The Pack of Autolycus* (Cambridge: Harvard University Press, 1927), 192.

19. Ibid., 140.

20. Ibid., 145.

21. Keith Thomas, *Man and the Natural World* (New York: Pantheon, 1983), xx.

22. Ibid., 38.

23. Rudolf Wittkower, "Marvels of the East: A Study in the History of Monsters," *Journal of the Warburg and Courtauld Institutes* 5 (1942): 159–97, surveys the genealogy of the monstrous races.

24. Thomas, *Natural World*, 79.

25. Ibid., 75.

26. Altick, *Shows*, 7.

27. Ibid., 49.

28. Ashton, *Social Life*, 190.

29. *Bartholomew Faire* (London, 1641); facsimile reprint, ed. E. W. Ashbee (London: John Tuckett, 1868), 4.

30. See Frances Barasch's excellent discussion of the history of the grotesque style in her introduction to *A History of Caricature and Grotesque* by Thomas Wright (New York: Frederick Ungar, 1968; orig. 1865).

31. Wright, *Caricature*, 61.

32. Ibid., 73.

33. From John Dryden's preface to his translation of Charles Du Fresnoy's *De Arte Graphice*.

34. Barasch, introduction to Wright, *Caricature*, xxxv.

35. Morley, *Memoirs*, 250.

36. G. C. Druce, "Some Abnormal and Composite Human Forms in English Church Architecture," *Archaeological Journal* 72 (1915): 153.

37. Wright, *Caricature*, 9.

38. Sir John Davis, *Nosce Teipsum* (London, 1599), cited by Barasch, introduction to Wright, *Caricature*, xxx.

39. Barasch, introduction to Wright, *Caricature*, xiv. Leslie A. Fiedler's *Freaks: Myths and Images of the Secret Self* (New York: Simon and Schuster, 1978) is an exception to the dearth of serious treatment of this topic.

40. Mikhail Bakhtin, *Rabelais and His World* (Bloomington: Indiana University Press, 1984), 91.

41. Ibid., 19.

42. Natalie Zemon Davis, *Society and Culture in Early Modern France* (Stanford: Stanford University Press, 1975), 226–27.

43. Barasch, introduction to Wright, *Caricature*, xxxii.

SIX

Death-Defying/Defining Spectacles: Charles Willson Peale as Early American Freak Showman

EDWARD L. SCHWARZSCHILD

Preserving and Displaying the Dead for the Life of the Nation

It is my ardent wish to bring this Museum into such consideration, as to make it worthy the public protection; and at the same time, that my family may not lose the benefits of my assiduous labors of years past, and to enable my children to contribute their future aid to this my favorite undertaking, I am teaching them the methods I use to preserve subjects.[1]

Charles Willson Peale (1741–1827)—American painter, inventor, ethnographer, writer, collector, curator—was also one of his era's most avid taxidermists and portraitists, and he prided himself on his ability to preserve the dead. Throughout his life and many of his myriad endeavors, Peale sought to use his skills at preservation—chemical as well as pictorial—to both evoke and erase the effects of death. Peale struggled, in essence, to make of death a controlled spectacle, to distance himself from the clutches of death even as he strove to gain individual and national distinction by displaying a dramatic control over human mortality. Assessments of the diversity of Peale's substantial achievements have not traditionally discussed him as a pioneer of freak show culture in the United States. I argue, however, that the particular manner in which his most prominent lifelong projects—his portrait painting and museum-making—revolved around an interest in taxidermy, preservation, and death establishes his importance to understanding the shape and significance of freak shows in American culture.

Recent analyses of cultural institutions—from all bands of the political spectrum—forcefully evidence that museums can function as "powerful identity-defining machines," capable of determining and displaying how a community sees itself and, simultaneously, how it views and interprets "others."[2] Understood broadly, museums offer carefully designed, framed spectacles, enabling and encouraging visitors to form various distinctions, be they aesthetic, social, racial, national, or historical. Freak shows, of course, function similarly. Unlike the participatory structure of carnivals, which can hinge on an almost democratic reciprocity and blurring of extant boundaries, the framed spectacles of museums and freak shows tend to be structured by distance, by marked divisions between "us" and "them."

The fact that Peale, in his museum and in many of his portraits, often presented death as a "freak of nature" helps to clarify his connection to freak shows. Susan Stewart, echoing the work of Leslie Fiedler,[3] has emphasized that the so-called "freak of nature" needs to be understood as "a freak of culture": "His or her anomalous status is articulated by the process of the spectacle as it distances the viewer, and thereby it 'normalizes' the viewer as much as it marks the freak as an aberration." This dynamic is akin to colonization: "The body of the cultural other is by means of this metaphor both naturalized and domesticated in a process we might consider to be characteristic of colonization in general. For all colonization involves the taming of the beast by bestial methods and hence both the conversion and projection of the animal and human, difference and identity. On display, the freak represents the naming of the frontier and the assurance that the wilderness, the outside, is now territory."[4] For Peale, death was grotesque and aberrant, an inscrutable if unavoidable freak of nature that he sought to make simultaneously separate, controlled, and artistic. Peale would colonize death, making it his territory. Just as freak shows work to establish the normalcy and authority of the spectators, Peale's pictorial, chemical, and curatorial efforts were part of a larger attempt to normalize and empower his self and his nation. To preserve and command the realm of the dead would testify to the authority and permanence of Peale's still fledgling country. Freaks, however, are never as "other" as the shows suggest; similarly, Peale's freak of nature refused to stay separate, forcing him to realize that death remained beyond his control, undermining his drive for order, his quest for individual and national distinction.

As with the divisions posed by freak shows, Peale's order and power were called into question most insistently by the shared human condition of corporeality. Still, at times Peale was confident in the extent of his command over death, widely publicizing and celebrating the significance of his ability to arrest this inevitable process. For instance, after 1787, when writing of his accomplishments, lobbying for the nationalization of his groundbreaking Philadelphia museum, and petitioning federal and state governments for financial support, Peale regularly emphasized that the method he had devised for dressing "Animal subjects" was "much superior to those in general use in Europe"—he saw his taxidermic method not only as an individual accomplishment, but also as a national triumph (2.1:388). Yet the component parts of the process he detailed for his friends and for posterity were rather straightforward. His 1787 "Directions for Preserving Birds, &c.," for example, called for simple skinning and stuffing—rote evisceration:

Those birds which are large . . . may be skinned in the following manner, Vizt. open with a sharp pen knife from the vent to the breast and separating the skin on each side until the thighs may be drawn through the skin and cut off at the joint of the legs, do the same with wings to the pinion, and in the pinion part of the wing draw out all the flesh you can get out with the hooked wire . . . , then draw the neck through the skin until you can cut off the neck close to the skull, and cutting off the body and the tail, having thus the skin separated from the body hook out all the brains through the back part of the skull where the neck was cut off. Cut out the roof of the mouth, take out the eyes by means of the hook from the inside of the mouth. . . .

All sorts of beasts may be skinned by opening the belly and drawing the legs and cutting off at the joint of the feet, if very small the whole skin may be left & treated and with the larger birds, but the larger beasts it will be sufficient to cut off from the head such part as will show the upper & under teeth, which may be left attached to the skin—salt may be put on the skins of beasts but never in the birds. (1:488–89)

Such thorough directions reflect not only a familiarity with the material of bodies, but also a physical mastery of the corporeality of other life. Peale, as naturalist and instructor, presents himself in complete control, reigning supreme over the bodies of "all sorts of beasts," educating his contemporaries in his method.

Peale's cherished taxidermic originality ultimately resulted from his experiments with a new form of preservative, but his discovery is shadowed by the very vulnerability he worked to defeat and master. As early as 1788, instead of using the powders of dried herbs, spices, and lime or alum popular with his contemporaries, Peale was dipping his specimens into mixtures of hot water and arsenic (1:487). The advantage of this mixture was, as he explained to his friend and correspondent Thomas Jefferson, that it kept the skins "free from the depredation of insects a great length of time" (2.2:929). Yet the arsenic solution was not without its own depredatory side effects, as one of Peale's complaints to his diary indicates: "continued my labour this whole day in washing my birds & beasts in the arsenic water, having my hands continually wet, I find a considerable soreness at the ends of my fingers, so much that I had a small fever at night & some restlessness" (1:512). These lines, while they suggest the ill effects of arsenic, also starkly describe the inherently self-reflexive dynamic that pervades Peale's efforts to preserve his museum displays. Peale's observation points out that his process of preservation, in the midst of attempting to prevent the physical decay of the dead, reveals the corporeal vulnerability of the living; in other words, the process he embraces calls attention to the fragility of both one's own body and the bodies of others.[5]

This vulnerability is a stubborn fact, one that testifies to the deeply paradoxical nature of Peale's attempt to interpret his taxidermic success as an enduring individual and national triumph. What Donna Haraway has written of early twentieth-century American taxidermy illuminates Peale's lifelong struggle to preserve and publicly exhibit the dead: his museum full of specimens is predicated on the belief that "the body can be transcended," as if it were possible to birth a "better than life" world "from dead matter." Haraway argues that "taxidermy was about the single story, about nature's unity, the unblemished type specimen. . . . The power of this stance is in its magical effects: what is so painfully constructed appears effortlessly, spontaneously found, discovered, simply there if one will only look. . . . This art repays labor with transcendence."[6] To maintain the control he desired, Peale worked to suppress his own physical vulnerability: he would magically find only transcendence—both national and individual—in his painfully constructed museum world; he would create permanent order and distinction out of an innovative chemical practice that at once revealed and obscured the evanescence of the corporeal.

The spectacle of death Peale sought to create would ideally transform the fact of physical vulnerability into a didactic, carefully organized, self-serving and self-saving freak show; the pictures and objects he exhibited were poised precariously between life and death, placed in something of a hybrid, unnatural, "other" world against which Peale could define himself and his desired world. In seeking to control the re-presentation of death in the early United States, Peale operated like a national colonizer, hoping to claim a future and a past for America that could transcend death and decay. Like a showman, he hoped to tame and display death for posterity, presiding over his chosen territory, keeping his body and his self invulnerable.

After providing some additional biographical information, I will focus on several of Peale's portraits—most particularly his famous 1822 self-portrait, *The Artist in His Museum*—and on his relations with Benjamin Franklin in order to show in greater detail how Peale, while painting and museum-making, strove impossibly but insistently to separate self from other, freak from normal, death from life—all in the name of strengthening himself, his family, and his nation.

PORTRAIT PAINTING, SHOWMANSHIP, AND THE SPECTACLE(S) OF BENJAMIN FRANKLIN

Sorry I am, that I did not propose the means of . . . preservation to
that distinguished patriot and worthy philosopher, Doctor Franklin.
(2.1:15)

From his childhood forward, Peale's identity was bound to a concern with corporeality and transitoriness—more literally, with skin and timepieces. Apprenticed at age nine to a saddlemaker, he learned to handle leather and, at the same time, taught himself to make and repair watches. Preservation was indeed Peale's central and lifelong occupation. In fact, in order to receive his first instruction in painting, he exchanged "one of his best saddles" for three lessons from the portraitist John Hesselius: it is, we might say, Peale's skin trade that links his work in preservation to his work in art (1:33). He went on to gain a reputation as a portrait painter, able to list among his sitters numerous heroes of the young United States: Benjamin Franklin, George Washington, Baron von Steuben, the Marquis de Lafayette. In the sixty-six-foot-long gallery that he built onto his house (the first sky-lit gallery in America), Peale gathered and displayed his images of the famous, hoping eventually to "make such a collection of portraits to fill his gallery as might be valuable in a future day" (1:375). In addition to presiding over his portraits, in 1785 Peale converted one end of his gallery into a theater for the viewing of what he came to call "Moving pictures with changeable effects." When this imitation of Philip James de Loutherbourg's London "Eidosphusikon" ("image of nature") proved unprofitable, he "quitted" it, as he wrote Benjamin West in 1788, "for a new, but no less arduous undertaking. That is the preserving of birds, beast, &c to form a Museum" (1:544).[7] As his career shifted from one undertaking to another, Peale used the images and bodies of others to create a public self; he emerged as a figure who ordered, preserved, exhibited, and presided over visions of his nation.

Consistently, Peale's various exhibitions owed much of their power and popularity to a conscious appeal to nationalistic sentiment. One of his earliest works on canvas (1768) offers an emblematic image of William Pitt dressed classically in the robes of a Roman republican.[8] In an effort to both guide interpretation and build a reputation, Peale issued, together with the mezzotint of the portrait, a prose broadside that emphasized Pitt's work on behalf of the American colonies (he had recently opposed the Stamp Act). The broadside also praised the "natural *Faithfulness* and *Firmness* of AMERICA," and explicated the portrait as a representation of "the Gratitude of AMERICA to his Lordship" (1:76). Similarly, to fill out his "Collection of Illustrous Personages," he took advantage of his Philadelphia location by capitalizing on opportunities for sittings provided by the presence of the Continental Congress, effectively tying his professional career to the formation of the new nation (1:412). And when his moving picture show was failing to make money, he added to the conventional views of dawn, dusk, rainbows, and "Pandemonium" (all previously executed by de Loutherbourg) a patriotic scene that showed John Paul Jones's *Bonhomme Richard* capturing the British ship *Serapis* (1:141). Further, Peale long envisioned his museum as a nationally sanctioned establishment, an institution that would ultimately stand above "all the splendid Museums of the great European nations" (2.1:10). Each of these "splendid" European institutions had, Peale reminded the public, "risen from . . . foundations laid by individuals" and gone on, once adopted by the government, to represent national power and enlightenment (2.1:10). The construction of an American museum, Peale believed, would, like his portraits and his moving pictures, come to represent the accomplishment of the United States; it would become a central monument testifying to the force, distinction, and permanence of an American national identity.

But just as the work with arsenic solution suggested that Peale could not ignore the role his own hands played in the process of preservation, the creation of his museum, the projection of his moving pictures, and the organization of his gallery all stand as structuring acts shaped by a certain self-interest, acts marked by strategic personal involvement. The quests for national and individual identity were inextricably linked. Each display represented not only the accomplishment of the United States, but also, and perhaps more immediately, the accomplishment of Charles Willson Peale. Influenced by and, he hoped, influencing the new nation forming around him, Peale repeatedly attempted to achieve his individual goals; he strove both to affect a changing society and to secure a privileged place in that society. Throughout his showman-like career, Peale's curatorial actions stemmed from a complex network of personal and national motivations.

His motivations and showmanship coalesced around a desire for individual control and distinction, a desire made very clear in his attempt to gain Jefferson's support for the "national establishment of [his] Museum" (2.1:386). When he described his hope in a letter to the president, Peale also mentioned that he would soon be offering the museum to the state of Pennsylvania. A rhetoric of salesmanship pervades Peale's letter: he explains that the "income by visitations to a museum [in Washington, D.C.] would be far short of what may be had in any of our larger cities for many years to come," but he would make the sacrifice, provided the federal government act without delay (2.1:388). For emphasis, Peale appended to his letter the text of the address he planned to deliver to the state legislature. The museum had become a time-consuming burden; Peale explained how he valued its "public utility" but also valued his private life and, consequently, wanted a government, *any* government, to help provide for, in his phrase, the "main tenance" of the museum (2.1:388). Seeking to gain private profit, freedom, and fame from skillful, strategic public presentation, Peale used his address to the legislature to sow seeds of competition:

> The time is now fully arrived when it has become expedient to decide the fate of the Museum. . . . [F]rom the uncertain tenure of human life it may not long continue in the same circumstances in which it has progressed, and means must be devised for its durability, perfection and public utility. . . . It must either continue private property or become a public one; if private, the place where suitable encouragement is given must

possess it; if public, some of the states or the United States, may secure all the advantages of such an institution, by an inconsiderable appropriation.

To Pennsylvania the *first offerings* are now tendered. (2.1: 388–89, emphasis in original)

Despite the urgent tone of these lines, which he sent to Jefferson in January 1802, Peale continued to preside over the museum until 1810, when he retired to a farm in Germantown, only to take up control of the museum again in 1822, remaining in charge until his death in 1827. Thus, in some respects, this address, with its reference to "the uncertain tenure of human life," reveals that the preservation of Peale's individual and national accomplishments was interwoven with an anxious recognition of his mortality. At the same time, however, the crisis alluded to here was hardly imminent. Indeed, Peale seems to have *used* the specter of death as a marketing ploy, a bargaining tool, as if mortality were something he could wield and manipulate.

This simultaneously anxious and confident sense of mortality appears more dramatically in Peale's relationship with Franklin. Early in his autobiography, Franklin expressed a strong, unconditional desire to relive his life. But, he explained, "since such a Repetition is not to be expected, the next Thing most like living one's Life over again seems to be a *Recollection* of the Life," a recollection, Franklin added, that should be made "as durable as possible." Franklin here posited the construction of collections as a substitute for rebirth. He also confessed that, in his own recollection, he would "a good deal gratify" his "own *Vanity*." He would attempt to make "as durable as possible" an ideal version of his life.[9]

As the quintessential self-made man, a man with wide-ranging interests, capable of strategically refashioning his public identity with the images that surrounded him, Franklin was a powerful model for Peale. In fact, Franklin was such a powerful model that Peale desired not only to emulate, but also to embalm him: "Sorry I am," Peale confessed in the midst of his 1792 speech to his Museum's trustees, "that I did not propose the means of . . . preservation to that distinguished patriot and worthy philosopher, Doctor Franklin . . . it is not improbable that . . . he could have been prevailed on, to suffer the remains of his body to be . . . in our view." This curious desire to execute and publicly exhibit *human* taxidermy is merely the natural extension of Peale's devotion to preservation and the framed spectacle. In addition to hundreds of taxidermic specimens, his museum also displayed mummies, and, on at least one occasion, he tried assiduously to procure for exhibition the body of an embalmed child (2.1:21n. 4). Human taxidermy could, Peale imagined, "hand down to succeeding generations, the relicks of such great men"—the "actual remains" would provide posterity with information and knowledge which could not possibly be gleaned from mere painted portraits; a gallery of stuffed, famous men would enable his nation's citizenry to better appreciate the distinctions and successes of its antecedents (2.1:14–15). Such a display, of course, would also foreground human mortality and a sense of the impermanence of such human constructions as identity and culture, but Peale presents himself as firmly in control, capable of making the dead bodies "speak" only of progress, potential, and unity.[10] Thus, Peale's desired treatment of Franklin forcefully reiterates that in museums the triumphant idealization of oneself or one's culture is invariably dependent upon the subordination of others, or, as John R. Gillis explains, national memory is formed "as much by forgetting as by remembering."[11] This subordination and suppression can be lodged in corporeality, in one's apparent bodily power over life and death.

To sharpen further our sense of Peale's subordinating practices, we need only juxtapose for a moment an 1804 self-portrait by Peale with his well-known 1785 portrait of Franklin. When Peale listed *The Artist in His Museum* in the 1822 catalogue of the Eleventh Annual Exhibition of the Pennsylvania Academy of the Fine Arts, he described his painting briefly as a "Portrait of C.W. Peale, Esq. proprietor of the Museum painted in the 81st year of his age without spectacles."[12] As in the painting itself, Peale sought in this catalogue entry to emphasize and preserve an enduring power: though he was eighty-one at the time, he insisted that he required no glasses, that is, no mediation between himself and his work. He owned spectacles, as the 1804 image makes clear, but he did not need to use them. When we examine Peale's 1785 portrait of Franklin, we can better appreciate what it means, in Peale's taxidermic terms, "to suffer the remains of [a] body to be . . . in our view." In this portrait, painted a few months before Franklin's own eightieth birthday, the bifocals are perhaps the most prominent feature. Not only do these spectacles seem to distort Franklin's face, but, in light of Peale's later comment about his own remarkable physical constitution, the distortion of Franklin's features suggests a corresponding corporeal weakness, one decidedly not suffered by Peale. To suffer one's body to be a part of another's display is to yield power, to submit oneself to the control of another. The glasses are a visible representation of the vulnerability associated with a reliance on such mediation. Peale, as showman, painter, taxidermist, and curator, would prefer to stand apart, separate from his audience, separate from those condemned to decay and death. From his safe position of remove, he would determine how these visitors and subjects would appear to themselves and to future generations: they would appear as if they were objects on display, balanced precariously between the revered and the freakish, caught in a world structured by spectacles. And the pun on spectacles here marks a critical convergence, for it registers, visually and verbally, the interwoven relations between vision and power that pervade Peale's life's work.[13]

THE DEATH OF *THE ARTIST IN HIS MUSEUM*

> I think it is important that I should not only make it a lasting ornament to my art as a painter, but also that the design should be expressive that I bring forth into public view the beauties of nature and art, the rise and progress of the Museum.[14]

In *The Artist in His Museum* we can see more clearly how Peale worked to strengthen his own image through the erasure and depiction of "glasses" (fig. 6.1). This image stands as Peale's most nuanced attempt to reconcile his desire to preserve with the fact of his mortality. Peale's collection of portraits holds the highest position on the walls of the museum, but these images of famous men are not the only portraits apparent here. Denied any sense of spatial depth or three-dimensionality, the cabinets, as they frame the preserved specimens, have the look of paintings; though more carefully rendered than Peale's illustrious personages, these glass-covered cabinets also appear as portraits. It is, perhaps, as a result of this erasure of depth that critics of Peale's work do not attend to the sheets of glass that cover the cabinets behind the plush curtain. But it is this glass that provides a perfect figure for understanding Peale's position in the world he paints. The rendering of light was central to the composition of the painting—seeking to avoid creating "a picture such as are usually done in common Portraits," Peale made what he described as a "bold attempt" to use light in an original fashion.[15] In

6.1. Charles Willson Peale, *The Artist in His Museum* (1822). Oil on canvas, 103³/₄″ x 79⁷/₈″. Courtesy of the Pennsylvania Academy of the Fine Arts, Philadelphia. Gift of Mrs. Sarah Harrison (The Joseph Harrison, Jr. Collection).

preparatory studies for the portrait, Peale had worked to make the surface of the glass visible, as he had worked to convey the depth of the cabinets.[16] In the final, publicly displayed version, however, the glass that encloses Peale's objects and separates his visitors from the portrait-like exhibits is, it seems, completely transparent. The artist of the painting offers his museum as a work of art that he has the power to give directly, independent of intermediaries other than himself.

In addition, the apparent transparency is offered in direct opposition to the nature of the physical material available to Peale. During the early nineteenth century, as Peale wrote in an 1809 letter to the botanist Stephen Elliot, "Good Glass [was] not to be had" in Philadelphia. It was difficult to find glass that was not "thin, uneven & coloured" (2.2:1179). Richard Sennett has suggested that plate glass has always been a "material which lets [one] see everything inaccessible to desire"—it allows vision, but prohibits touch.[17] Revealing and reflecting, sheets of glass function as both windows and mirrors. On one level, then, Peale's elimination of the glass represents an attempt to move from a desired order to an achieved order. On another level, however, the production of this utter transparency speaks to the physical impossibility of Peale's desire. The construction of a durable recollection, the preservation of an idealized identity, and the defeat of an imminent death cannot be achieved except through distortion. Peale sought a transparency that would enable him to display evidence of impermanence as contributing to a careful narrative of individual and national progress; as in the gallery of human taxidermy he envisioned, this drive for transparency testifies to human evanescence, even as it strives to instantiate an enduring, idealized American order.

The removal of the glass, and the contingent depiction of transparency, is only one example of the distortions that disrupt the self-portrait Peale himself described as his own "lasting monument." In fact, much of the painting's considerable force comes from the tension that pits the desire for life and idealized recollection against the inevitability of death and unregulated memory: cognitive discord repeatedly manifests itself as painterly disruption. In this attempt to control the appearance of life and to conceal the fact of death, bodies necessarily occupy a central position, revealing, as in the Franklin portrait, the corporeal consequences of Peale's curatorial power. The four museum visitors who stand on the other side of the raised curtain are dwarfed by Peale's gigantic, black-clothed, curiously amorphous body. Like the specimens of taxidermy, these visitors can be seen as part of Peale's displayed collection; and like the trustees from whom he received financial backing, and his audience generally, these small figures appear as objects he wanted to arrange in order. In their traditional postures, they stand as cultural types: the astonished woman, the instructive father with his obedient child, and the enlightened young man seem linked together in a didactic vision of domestic union. That Peale has raised the curtain that could cover them and make them invisible testifies to his power—a power that seems capable of both reducing the size and determining the shape of the public's image. He further emphasizes his control by skewing the perspectival construction of the room, making himself appear all the more towering.

In the painting Peale proudly displays himself, his mastodon skeleton, and his carefully organized exhibits in an indisputable position of national importance—the second floor of the Pennsylvania State House, now known as Independence Hall, where the Declaration of Independence, the Articles of Confederation, and the Constitution had been debated and signed. This room was part of the space that the museum had occupied since 1802. The mastodon skeleton, however, never stood in the Long Room or in the State House but was located in a nearby building. In order to place himself alongside his most renowned object, Peale has here altered the arrangement of his museum and distorted its actual structure: he wanted posterity to associate his image with the extraordinary achievement of exhuming the mastodon, an event which he recorded in another well-known painting.[18] This distortion, like the desire to embalm Franklin, is merely the natural extension of Peale's particular commitment to preservation and framed spectacles: he would reconstruct and display the dead for his own benefit, thereby subordinating others to his own idealized version of reality.

Peale's imaginary space works to eliminate evidence of mediation, to create an impossible perspective, and to image an ideal individual and national union. Denying physical limitations, Peale's ideal museum and his presence in it suggests that the artist/showman's desires will always outstrip what he is actually, physically capable of achieving. Ultimately, these distortions disrupt Peale's monument for posterity and point to the tensions undergirding the museum. Within the Long Room of Independence Hall, death and regeneration collide, leaving a vision of an exceedingly fragile order. The museum is full of animals grouped in cabinets, offering by their proximity and pairing a visual promise of reproduction. The family stands in the plane of the cabinets, and these cultural types also seem to exhibit a certain promise for coming generations—the American family stands harmoniously alongside the family of Nature. But, of course, the animals are all dead, eviscerated, and stuffed—bathed in arsenic and utterly sterile. It is from these sterile objects that the painting shows the child obediently receiving his education. The painting's discourse, in the end, is strangely terminal. Peale's self-portrait resonates with Theodor Adorno's observation that "museum and mausoleum are connected by more than phonetic association."[19] Peale raises the billowy curtain, he lifts the crimson veil, but this spectacular act reveals a world and a country, quite literally, drawn to death. Although he attempted to depict death as a "freak of nature" he could escape and control, Peale's most "lasting ornament . . . as a painter" offers a visual record of death's persistent presence—the culminant self-portrait in the museum shows how the fact of mortality continually threatens to dissolve even the most carefully constructed, strongly guarded distances and divisions.

CODA: *RACHEL WEEPING* OVER PEALE'S DESCENDANTS

> Draw not the curtain, if a tear
> Just trembling in a parent's eye
> Can fill your gentle soul with fear
> Or arouse your tender heart to sigh.
>
> A child lies dead before your eyes
> And seems no more than molded clay,
> While the affected mothers cries,
> And constant mourns from day to day. (1:380)

The above poem, written by Peale in the early 1780s, was part of a display that anticipated the design both of *The Artist in His Museum* and of freak shows. The poem came to accompany Peale's *Rachel Weeping*, a painting he worked on between 1772 and 1776, that

6.2. Charles Willson Peale, *Rachel Weeping* (1772–76). Oil on canvas, 37¹/₈″ x 32¹/₄″. Courtesy of the Philadelphia Museum of Art: given by the Barra Foundation, Inc.

took as its subject the death of his fourth child, Margaret Bordley Peale (fig. 6.2). Apparently because his wife Rachel could not bear to look at the image, Peale placed it behind a curtain, using his lines of poetry to warn potential viewers of his painting's subject and power. *The Freeman's Journal* of December 4, 1782, described the poem as "found in Mr. Peale's New Room, pinn'd to the curtain which hangs before the portrait of Mrs. Peale lamenting the death of her child." [20]

As Susan Stewart has pointed out, "*Rachel Weeping* is only the first example of Peale working through, via his painting and collecting activities, an anxiety regarding death." And she goes on rightly to note that the painting materializes his questioning "the meaning of nature's lessons when such lessons were clearly unnatural, even monstrous." [21] How, Peale seems to ask, is one to understand this "freak of nature"? How is one to find order in the death of an infant? At the same time, it is important to note that these questions are inextricably linked to more market-oriented, showman-like interrogations: How is one to display and thereby control death? How is one best to represent death to the paying public? The curtain and the poem suggest that, several years before his pioneering work in arsenic and hot water, forty years before the painting of *The Artist and His Museum* and its own billowing red curtain, Peale was concerned with preserving death in such a way that he could make of it a controlled spectacle, something he could aestheticize and from which he could distance himself.

"I am teaching [my children] the methods I use to preserve subjects," Peale wrote, explaining that he wanted his many descendants to be able to contribute to his "favorite undertaking." They, too, would have to learn how to confront the child that "lies dead before your eyes"; they would have to find their own success between the tasks of mourning and preserving required for survival. Had he been able, Peale would surely have bequeathed to all his descendants and heirs a world carefully constructed, completely curated, free from chaos. But, failing that, he left them with the tensions that had shadowed him, with the delicate balances he had sought to maintain. Some of his children pursued careers as painters, museum-makers, and naturalists. A son (Titian Ramsay Peale II) and a grandson (Coleman Sellers) became avid photographers, colonizing for themselves another territory where death and life, self and other, freak and normal are complexly, inextricably linked. And Phineas T. Barnum, though not a family relation, became heir to Peale's collections. In 1850 he purchased what remained of the Philadelphia museum, and he went on to reach new heights in the marketing of framed spectacles, combining the cultural spaces of museums and freak shows more thoroughly than Peale ever dared.

It is fitting that, late in life, when Peale was planning to re-exhibit a retouched *Rachel Weeping* in the Pennsylvania Academy's annual exhibition in 1818, he reconsidered and finally withdrew the painting—he could not bring himself to expose this image of mourning once more to the public. [22] Just such moments of decision and indecision give force to *The Artist in His Museum*. Indeed, this movement back and forth between exhibiting human impermanence and attempting to conceal it, between displaying the fact of mortality and hoping to control it, between defining death as "other" and as inseparable from oneself, pervades Peale's lifetime of work. The painters, curators, photographers, freak show makers, and spectators who have come after Charles Willson Peale have recapitulated but have yet to resolve the life-and-death struggle he left to posterity. [23]

NOTES

1. All quotations from the papers of Charles Willson Peale, unless otherwise noted, refer to *The Selected Papers of Charles Willson Peale and His Family*, ed. Lillian B. Miller (New Haven: Yale University Press; Washington, D.C.: National Portrait Gallery and the Smithsonian Institution, 1983–88). These widely available volumes provide exact transcriptions of the Peale documents; I have normalized spelling and capitalization in order to clarify meaning. Here I cite 2.1:19; all further references to this work are cited in the text by volume and page number.

2. Carol Duncan, "Art Museums and the Ritual of Citizenship," in *Exhibiting Cultures: The Poetics and Politics of Museum Display*, ed. Ivan Karp and Steven D. Lavine (Washington, D.C.: Smithsonian Institution Press, 1991), 101–2. The entire collection offers useful perspectives on current debates in museum studies. See also Daniel J. Sherman and Irit Rogoff, eds., *Museum Culture: Histories, Discourses, Spectacles* (Minneapolis: University of Minnesota Press, 1994).

3. See Leslie Fiedler, *Freaks: Myths and Images of the Secret Self* (New York: Simon and Schuster, 1978), 13. See also Robert Bogdan, *Freak Show: Presenting Human Oddities for Amusement and Profit* (Chicago: University of Chicago Press, 1988). Bogdan rightly stresses the inherently constructed nature of the distance desired and/or observed between the "freak" and the "normal": "Our reaction to freaks is not a function of some deep-seated fear or some 'energy' that they give off; it is, rather, the result of our socialization, and of the way our social institutions managed these people's identities. Freak shows are not about isolated individuals, either on platforms or in an audience. They are about organizations and patterned relationships between them and us. 'Freak' is not a quality that belongs to the person on display. It is something that we created: a perspective, a set of practices—a social construction" (xi).

4. Susan Stewart, *On Longing: Narratives of the Miniature, the Gigantic, the Souvenir, the Collection* (Durham, N.C.: Duke University Press, 1993), 109–10.

5. The ill effects of this mixture are at the center of Phoebe Lloyd's recent argument that Peale's son Raphaelle died in 1825 from arsenic poisoning brought on by his taxidermic work for the museum. See Lloyd, "Philadelphia Story," *Art in America* 76 (November 1988): 154–71, 195–203.

6. Donna Haraway, *Primate Visions: Gender, Race, and Nature in the World of Modern Science* (New York: Routledge, 1989), 28, 38.

7. The editors of the Peale papers provide this description of the "moving pictures":

Peale's "moving pictures" were patterned closely after the novel and widely acclaimed "Eidophusikon" (or "image of nature") created by Philip James de Loutherbourg (1740–1812). . . . De Loutherbourg's scenes were shown on a "stage" about ten feet wide, six feet high, and eight feet deep, lit from above by the recently invented Argand lamps, which by means of an oil-burning wick placed between two concentric tubes produced a concentrated and steady light capable of being focused and projected by a lens. A variety of materials—pasteboard, cork covered with mosses and lichens, wooden figures, strips of linen and transparencies—made up several layers of scenery. Color effects were produced by placing slips of stained glass over the lamps and sound effects by such devices as tambourines, a sheet of copper to produce thunder, and boxes of shells, peas, and light balls.

Peale's moving pictures were based upon transparencies and lit also by Argand lamps. We have no other information concerning their construction. (1:428)

8. For a discussion of Peale and the tradition of the emblematic portrait, see Roger B. Stein, "Charles Willson Peale's Expressive Design: The Artist in His Museum," *Prospects* 6 (1981): 139–85.

9. Benjamin Franklin, *The Autobiography of Benjamin Franklin*, ed. Leonard W. Labaree (New Haven: Yale University Press, 1964), 43–44.

10. David Steinberg is concerned with Peale's rendering himself as divinely empowered. While it is vital to appreciate Peale's desire to wield an overarching power, it is equally vital to see both the national context and individual context of this desire. See "Charles Willson Peale: The Portraitist as Divine," in *New Perspectives on Charles Willson Peale*, ed. Lillian B. Miller and David C. Ward (Pittsburgh: University of Pittsburgh Press, 1991), 131–43.

This national and individual convergence is reflected in the singular bald eagle imaged in *The Artist in His Museum*. The only animal cabineted without a mate is particularly significant, for this was an eagle that Peale himself had raised from an eaglet. In fact, as Stein has noted, the eagle, with its white head and black-feathered body, resembles the bald-pated, black-clothed Peale—the common features, to a certain degree, pair the eagle with Peale (see Stein, "Peale's Expressive Design," 182). Just as he sought power from his connection to the mastodon skeleton that stands as a symbol for a mighty American past, he also linked himself visually to the symbol of the new nation. In his third-person autobiography, Peale wrote of his attachment to this symbol of the United States: "This Eagle had been so long domesticated, that Peale could without fear stroke him with his hand, nay it knew well that when [Peale] was walking in the State House Garden, it would utter cries expressive of its pleasure on seeing him. He had in Gold Letters on his cage *Feed me daily 100 years;* however it did not live in captivity only 15 years." Peale domesticated the national symbol, freely exercising physical control over the eagle. The country's icon, content in its containment, revered its keeper. But despite the "Gold Letters" printed across the cage Peale provided, the bird did not endure. Death ignored Peale's privileged sign, undermining both his individual and national control. See Edgar P. Richardson, Brooke Hindle, and Lillian B. Miller, *Charles Willson Peale and His World* (New York: Harry N. Abrams, 1983), 114.

11. See John R. Gillis, ed., *Commemorations: The Politics of National Identity* (Princeton: Princeton University Press, 1994), 7.

In a recent study of Peale's museum and its audience, David R. Brigham importantly shows how Peale's displays of "human difference" worked to promote a vision of social harmony predicated on hierarchy and subordination: "Embodied within Peale's representation of humanity was the assumption that a consensus was possible that benefitted all races, classes, genders, and people of various physical capacities. Yet this harmonious vision depended upon resignation to unequal social and material circumstances. Resistance to one's station was perceived to be a disruptive response to natural order. Slaves who resisted their master's authority, Native Americans who fought displacement from their land, and the lower sort who disrupted public gatherings were particularly guilty" (144). See Brigham, *Public Culture in the Early Republic: Peale's Museum and Its Audience* (Washington, D.C.: Smithsonian Institution Press, 1995), 122–44.

12. Anna Wells Rutledge, ed., *Cumulative Record of the Exhibition Catalogues: The Pennsylvania Academy of the Fine Arts, 1807–1870* (Philadelphia: American Philosophical Society, 1955), 163.

13. Peale's desire to preserve bodies also animated his commitment to the mechanical arts. As Sidney Hart has observed, he "manufactured artificial teeth, ground lenses for spectacles, and built an artificial hand for a member of the Pennsylvania state legislature." See Hart, " 'To encrease the comforts of Life': Charles Willson Peale and the Mechanical Arts," in Miller and Ward, eds., *New Perspectives on Charles Willson Peale,* 240.

14. Peale to Rembrandt Peale (23 July 1822), in Lillian B. Miller, ed., *Peale Family Papers,* microfiche, American Philosophical Society Library.

15. Charles Coleman Sellers, "Portraits and Miniatures by Charles Willson Peale," *Transactions of the American Philosophical Society* 42, Part 1 (1952): 161.

16. That Peale attached great importance to this late painting is evidenced by the fact of these preparatory studies; he did not make such studies for most of his other paintings, preferring to work directly.

17. Richard Sennett, "Plate Glass," *Raritan* 6, no. 4 (Spring 1987): 1–15.

18. See Lillian B. Miller, "Charles Willson Peale as History Painter: *The Exhumation of the Mastodon,*" in Miller and Ward, eds., *New Perspectives on Charles Willson Peale,* 145–65.

19. Theodor W. Adorno, "Valery Proust Museum," in *Prisms,* trans. Samuel Weber and Shierry Weber (London: Neville Spearman, 1967), 173–86.

20. See Phoebe Lloyd's discussion of *Rachel Weeping,* "A Death in the Family," *Philadelphia Museum of Art Bulletin* 78 (1982): 3–13, esp. 3–7. See also Susan Stewart, "Death and Life, in that Order, in the Works of Charles Willson Peale," in *The Cultures of Collecting,* ed. John Elsner and Roger Cardinal (Cambridge: Harvard University Press, 1994), 204–23, esp. 209–13. While Stewart sees the validity of an interpretation that attends to the nation-making role of Peale's work, she forcefully argues that the construction of Peale's museum was also importantly tied to his interrogation of deism's doctrinal relation to death. Along with many of his contemporaries, Peale struggled to reconcile his religion's denial of divine interposition with his own desire to see a nature composed of something other than indifference and disorder (207–11).

21. Stewart, "Death and Life, in that Order," 211.

22. Lloyd, "A Death in the Family," 9.

23. I would like to thank the American Philosophical Society Library for the Mellon Resident Research Fellowship that made this work possible—I am particularly indebted to Martin L. Levitt, Elizabeth Carroll-Horrocks, and Roy E. Goodman of the Library. I am grateful as well to Susan Stewart, who kindly provided me with an early draft of her essay on Peale. I would also like to thank Robert Jensen for his comments on an earlier draft of this essay, and Rosemarie Garland Thomson for her crucial suggestions and insights. A Grant-in-Aid Award for Research and Scholarship from Sweet Briar College helped to secure the images for this essay.

SEVEN

P. T. Barnum's Theatrical Selfhood and the Nineteenth-Century Culture of Exhibition

ERIC FRETZ

P. T. Barnum performed a remarkable kind of cultural work in nineteenth-century America. He orchestrated performances and exhibitions, produced narratives and advertisements for public consumption and debate, and achieved a public role as the nineteenth century's greatest showman. From his initial foray into the popular entertainment world of New York City in the early 1830s until his death in 1891, Barnum firmly held his position as the public manager of nineteenth-century American popular culture.

In 1834 Barnum moved his wife and child to New York City in order to fulfill his dream of owning a public exhibition: "I had long fancied that I could succeed if I could only get hold of a public exhibition."[1] The nineteenth-century culture of exhibition was wide and varied, involving the public display of natural curiosities, technological advances and demonstrations, and medical/psychological treatments. Cultural phenomena such as mesmerism, phrenology, animal magnetism, and the art of daguerreotyping were all displayed on the exhibition stage of nineteenth-century America. The public lectures and lyceums that became popular during the 1830s and the grand revival traditions of the same decade also contributed to the larger exhibition culture of the period. Barnum participated in and used all these aspects of the culture of exhibition—he gave lectures (his most famous was entitled "The Philosophy of Humbug"), exhibited mesmerized subjects in his "Lecture Room" and even addressed congregations of America's churches.[2]

Barnum's participation in the mid-nineteenth-century exhibition culture represents a fundamental shift in the way Americans perceived the individual within the public sphere. According to Jay Fliegelman, Revolutionary Americans considered the public adornment of the private man or woman a nefarious threat to the new republic. Reacting against the Enlightenment's formalized and hierarchical use of language, the Revolutionary leaders set out to discover and employ a natural language that would reveal the true motivation of the speaker and mitigate, even preclude, the duplicitous representation of self. In the Revolutionary period, the "unadorned public man" who was free from the ostentations and chimeras of affected public life became the ideal.[3]

By the mid-nineteenth century the ideal of the unadorned private man had given way to the reality of the public confidence man, or painted woman, who concealed or transformed his or her private nature in the construction of a public identity.[4] Barnum, and the antebellum exhibition culture in which he participated, celebrated the individual's ability to stylize a public persona and assert these artificially constructed identities into the public sphere. Barnum exhibited both himself and his freaks as commodities in an era of exhibitionism that privileged appearance over essence. When Barnum exhibited himself in his autobiography and his freaks and dwarfs on the public stage, he was challenging the American public to accept the pliant and adorned nature of self; Barnum displayed theatrical Selfhood to the public—and they bought it.

In his autobiography, as well as his life, Barnum worked out the problem of selfhood on the debit and credit sheets of his financial records. For Barnum, it does not matter that "things are not what they seem."[5] "Not knowing" or the inability to distinguish illusion from reality is no longer an epistemological conundrum posing a threat to the republic and the good order of society. The gulf between public and private perception, or between reality and illusion, seems less threatening when someone like Barnum—a public figure who strove for middle-class respectability—is orchestrating the public perception of the self. By mid-century, this theatricality of self had become a normal part of American life that entertained, diverted, and challenged the masses. The performing selves that Barnum displayed for the public gaze—whether they were the different Barnums of his autobiography or the many human exhibitions he displayed throughout his career as a showman—were gleefully applauded and consumed. Barnum recasts the problem of self-representation of the post-Revolutionary period by turning the problem into an entertainment for the masses.

RE-MAKING THE AUTOBIOGRAPHICAL SELF

P. T. Barnum fashioned an autobiographical self that surreptitiously celebrated theatrical selfhood. Barnum was only forty-five when he wrote the first of three versions of his autobiography. Published in 1855, *The Life of P. T. Barnum, Written by Himself* promptly sold 160,000 copies in the States.[6] Pirated editions soon appeared in Germany, France, Holland, and Sweden. Never happy with the 1855 version, Barnum considered the first autobiography to be a form of advertisement, explaining that it was designed "for the purpose, principally, of advancing my interests as proprietor of the American Museum."[7] When the sales of *Life* started to decline, Barnum destroyed the plates, intent on publishing another version of his life. The second autobiography, updated, altered, and renamed *Struggles and Triumphs: Or, Forty Years' Recollections of P. T. Barnum,* was published in 1869. Half a million copies were in print by 1882, and by 1888 the figure had reached one million. The final version of Barnum's life appeared in 1889, two years before his death, under the same name as the 1869 version.[8]

If any book of the nineteenth century is worth considering for its circulation within the culture, it is surely the three versions of Barnum's autobiography. Each version has a tenor and tone of its own, and each constructs a different Barnum as well as reflecting the changing cultural climates of mid-century America. The 1855 edition is anecdotal, primarily concentrating on Barnum's early life. Spontaneous, artless, and full of the "confessions" of the narrator, Barnum's *Life* has all the stylistic attributes of autobiography. The first hundred pages read like the tale of a Yankee trickster and work to establish Barnum as a born jokester who, as "The Prince of Humbugs" and "The Prince of Showman," is merely acting out his innate talents. Barnum's first autobiography incorporates aspects of the picaresque novel, instructional literature, and Yankee trickster/Southwestern humor tales, all told in an authorial voice that explicates, narrates, and even confesses the actions and events of the life of P. T. Barnum. *Life* is a cornucopia of American literary traditions; the shadows of Ben Franklin, Stephen Burroughs, and Jonathan Edwards and the legends of Mike Fink and Davy Crockett are lurking within its anecdotal, bombastic, and didactic rhetoric. The apparent lack of narrative direction and the homely metaphors and anecdotes give *Life* its native charm. Yet the linear progression of a self that moves from a small-town wag to a big-shot showman who occupies and manipulates the public mind of the nineteenth-century becomes the strongest selling point of this most American of books.

Barnum trimmed down the anecdotes for the 1869 version, spending more time on Tom Thumb and the Jenny Lind enterprise, but the book was still a formidable affair, running over seven hundred pages (the 1855 version is just over four hundred). The 1869 version appeared in a dazzling number of different editions—small print, large print, abridged editions, and both cheap and expensive styles of the autobiography inundated the American and English reading public. Moreover, Barnum persisted in making unprecedented autobiographical moves by continuing to write chapters and tacking them on to new editions of the 1869 version. In 1884 Barnum waived the copyright contingencies and announced that the autobiography was open for publication by any interested party. Throughout the 1880s, Barnum nearly gave the book away during his circus performances—paying spectators received complimentary copies of the book, and the showman remarked that the crowds leaving his bigtop looked "as if they were coming out of a circulation library."[9]

Barnum exhibits a dynamic sense of selfhood in his autobiographies; with each new version, he creates a new P. T. Barnum, replacing and adding on to the former. The 1855 version uncovers the inherent subjectivity of writing a life by flamboyantly flaunting that life's malleability in the face of the reader. The revisions of Barnum's autobiography demonstrate a malleable self that transforms itself with the passage of time and the continual (re)act of writing. Barnum's notion of a dynamic self, illustrated in each rewriting of the autobiography, exposes the elusiveness of essential self-identity. With the subsequent publications of the autobiography, Barnum validated a sense of stylized selfhood in American culture. The autobiographical act corrals experience, forming a public self; in this way, autobiography becomes an achievement of self-construction and the rhetorical shaping of a public persona.

Despite the confessional tone and the occasional attempts to reveal a private self, Barnum's autobiographies remain highly stylized narrative constructions and, consequently, incline toward fiction. Less than "self biography" and tending more toward the fictive invention of self, Barnum's *Life* becomes a "hopelessly subjective" autobiographical fiction.[10] Thomas Couser finds this problematical, complaining that the *Life* "very nearly makes an autobiography out of practical jokes, and a joke out of autobiography." Ultimately, argues Couser, the "effect of his prolific production and circulation of different accounts of his life during the second half of the nineteenth century was to undermine the authority of his own autobiography and, by implication, that of the genre as a whole."[11] Possibly. But Barnum was never one to be overly concerned with authority, and, like his contemporary, Walt Whitman—who published the first of nine editions of *his* autobiography in 1855—Barnum multiplied the autobiographical moment as an act of self-advertisement.

In the emerging market economy of mid-century America, the creation and manipulation of self determined success. Closing his autobiography with a section titled "Rules for Success in Business," the showman encourages fortune hunters and speculators to "put on the *appearance* of business and the reality will follow" (*Life*, 396). For some critics Barnum's book is a dark derivation of Franklin's autobiography and suggests the potentially subversive elements of American democracy.[12] Yet a quick survey of the public reception of *Life* (and the subsequent versions) reveals that many nineteenth-century Americans distinguished Barnum's book as a model of American virtue, piety, and ingenuity.[13] As the reviews suggest, Barnum's book did the kind of cultural work that confirmed the values of a mid-nineteenth-century market economy as it spread across space and time. Read as a handbook for survival in a burgeoning market economy, the text, which glorified dynamic selfhood as it exhibited its central figure, established the general acceptance of theatrical selfhood in a socially and economically turbulent time. "To Barnum's admirers," explains Neil Harris, "his autobiography was simply a road map of the route to success,"[14] and George Bryan reminds us that the autobiography was used as a manual for common business sense.[15] John Fitch, a contemporary of Barnum, told the showman: "I know every line in your book . . . and I have conducted my business on the principles laid down in your published 'Rules for Money-Making.' I find them correct principles; and [I] thank you for publishing your autobiography, and tell you that to act of yours [*sic*] I attribute my present position in life."[16] Harris reports an American lecturer who reasoned that he knew "of no book which is better adapted to become a thoroughly instructive and agreeable guide through life,"[17] and Bryan reprints advertisements for *Struggles and Triumphs* declaring "Every young man should read it." Furthermore, that other instructor of young men, Horace Greeley, explained (this is according to Barnum) that the book and the lecture on the Art of Money-Getting "was worth a hundred-dollar greenback to a beginner life."[18] A. S. Saxon notes that Barnum boasted (in an unpublished letter dated 13 March 1855) that his publisher had received over one thousand auspicious reviews of *Life* since its publication in December of the preceding year. Saxon reprints a "fair example" of one of those reviews:

THE MORAL OF BARNUM'S BOOK. If this book be not *superficially* read, it is easy to see that, under a cloak of fun, jokes and good humor, the author intends to teach and press home the lesson that mere humbugs and deceptions generally fail, and that money acquired in immoral occupations takes to itself wings and flies away. . . . Thus he shows . . . his "humbugs" were no source of direct profit to him, but were used merely as advertisements, to attract public attention to himself, and to gain public support for his real and substantial exhibitions, such as his Museum, Tom Thumb in England, and Jenny Lind.[19]

In his encouragement of the reader to take Barnum's book seriously and engage it on a deeper level of meaning (a level similar, perhaps, to the way nineteenth-century readers would have been encouraged to read the Bible), the writer of this article suggests the comfort that American culture, by 1855, had with individuals engaging in plots of mistaken identity and games of duplicity, arguing that the public hoaxes were all for the "greater good" of Barnum's "real" and "substantial" (could this be thick irony?) public displays.

STYLIZATION OF PUBLIC SELVES AND AN ANTEBELLUM CULTURE OF EXHIBITION

In his autobiography, Barnum invented his life and made it palpable for middle-class consumption. But *Life* is primarily made up of accounts of Barnum's attempts to theatricalize the lives of others. Indeed, Barnum made a name for himself by stylizing the lives of others and packaging them for public consumption.

Barnum was working in a tradition of public exhibition whose development from the post-Revolutionary period to the mid-nineteenth century we might pause to adumbrate. Before the Revolution, traveling showmen roamed the colonies exhibiting natural curiosities for profit.[20] But by 1850, when Barnum introduced Jenny Lind to America, "exhibiting" had become a formalized extravaganza yielding high profits and intense public fervor.

Barnum's most famous predecessor in the area of public exhibitions was Charles Willson Peale, the eccentric developer of America's first museum of indigenous artifacts and natural history. Peale's museum, which he opened in Philadelphia in 1784 and passionately developed until he retired in 1810, was a product of an Enlightenment mind that believed in the essential perfection of the natural order. For Peale, humans who copied and learned from Nature led happy, righteous lives, and he exhibited Nature in order to teach and instruct: "I love the study of Nature," he once said, "for it teacheth benevolence."[21]

After Peale retired, he gave the museum management to his sons, Rembrandt and Reubens, post-Enlightenment subjects who found it impossible to maintain the didactic mission of the museum. The exhibition of Nature gradually gave way to public demand for fantastic and exotic displays and performances. Gradually, the function of the museum moved from an institution benefiting the public good to a money-making device as Reubens, late in the first decade of the nineteenth century, began to use lecturers, performers, and experimenters to attract more customers.[22] By 1817, Reubens conceded that the museum could only survive by pursuing profits, so he added catchpenny shows and a pandean band (a one-man musical show). By 1838, three years prior to the opening of Barnum's American Museum, Peale's museum was displaying Negro bands, Yankee impersonators, Hungarian minstrels, and musical ladies. Tom Thumb appeared on the Museum stage in 1845. The museum stayed on this course until Barnum purchased it in 1850.

The spectacular and bizarre captured the imaginations of early nineteenth-century Americans,[23] and Barnum capitalized on this captivation by stylizing the public display of others. By the mid-1840s, Barnum's American Museum was in full swing, attracting audiences who were able to view freaks of all sorts. From the Bearded Lady to the "Nova Scotia Giantess," from the Leopard-Skinned Boy to Zalumma Agra, the famous "Circassian Girl," and from the Chinese family to the Albino family—if they were deformed, exotic, disproportioned in any way, or simply inclined to be transformed into one of Barnum's freaks (he exhibited a "Yankee Man" at one point), the great showman would put them on the stage of his "Lecture Room" for the inspection of the masses.

"Freak shows," or the exploitation of human strangeness, was a theatrical performance grounded in the disguise of the (mostly) nonwhite subject. Blacks acted out aboriginal roles, often being represented as "missing links"; Native Americans performed rituals and dances that confirmed their primordial type; and Gypsies and Bohemians (usually women) were represented as lusty, exotic beauties. The "freaks" would perform according to their public roles: sartorial significations suggested their foreignness, and their stage presence would correspond to stereotypical roles—Native Americans would whoop and chant, "savage" blacks would grunt, and Asians would affect a demure and sedate demeanor.[24]

Ironically, as the freak shows were entertaining the urban masses, criminal penitentiaries and insane asylums—institutional homes for humans with "aberrational" tendencies—were becoming an integral part of the American reform culture. America was the site of the world's first penitentiary system; the French government sent Alexis de Tocqueville to America in 1832 to observe the new penitentiary system. Prior to the rise of the asylum the poor and the insane were assimilated into the community. By the 1830s, a Lockean way of viewing human behavior demonstrated that society itself was corrupt, and a burgeoning reform tradition gradually developed the idea that criminals and the insane could be reformed of their problems by removing them from the social (dis)order. The implication was that separation from the social milieu and a good dose of moral reform would rejuvenate rational behavior.[25] Reformers carted aberrants away, sequestering them behind institutional walls while showmen like Barnum paraded "defective" individuals before the wondering and paying public gaze. As far as we know, Barnum did not search out his "freaks" from neighboring asylums or penitentiaries. Yet the irony of a society that has made room for human aberrations in the forum of a culture of exhibition and, at the same time, demanded the removal of social pariahs, illustrates one of the paradoxes of the tension-filled nineteenth century.

When Barnum exhibited Otherness on the nineteenth-century stage, he ceded authorial control to the human aberrations he chose to display. Consider Barnum's initial foray into the exhibition culture of antebellum America. In 1835, the "Prince of Humbugs" began his career as a showman by becoming a slaveholder. Keen on the public demand for the exhibition of race and difference on the public stage, Barnum made every possible effort to supply the public need.[26] He purchased Joice Heth, the alleged 161-year-old woman who was displayed before the public as George Washington's nursemaid, in June of 1835 and began to exhibit her at Niblo's in New York City in August. Shortly before he purchased Heth, Barnum visited Scudder's Museum (which he would purchase six years later) to bargain on the purchase of a Hydro-Oxygen Microscope that the owner guaranteed would "secure its owner an independence" if the invention were exhibited throughout the country (*Life*, 144). The two-thousand-dollar price tag was more than Barnum was able to pay, though. Shortly thereafter Barnum discovered Heth and does not seem to have had much trouble talking her owner down from the three-thousand-dollar asking price to one thousand: it was more profitable in antebellum America to exhibit fantastic African Americans than it was to offer close-up glimpses of nature through a microscope. On a pragmatic level, Barnum certainly made the right choice in choosing Heth over the microscope. The fantastic claim of her age and the mythical connection to Washington was ripe for the spectacular imagination of the 1830s. Barnum only enjoyed Heth's services for seven months; she died on 19 February 1836. A public autopsy revealed her age to be no more than eighty years, and Barnum came under public suspicion for his blatant humbuggery. He managed to make Heth the subject of public controversy and to profit considerably from her exhibitions. Indeed, Joice Heth became the first of a multitude of subjects that Barnum exhibited and stylized for public consumption. Yet, Heth authored herself as much as Barnum created her character. The dynamics between Barnum's manipulation of Heth and her presentation of her public self makes this incident important here.

According to Barnum's description, Heth was a wonder to look at: He says he was "favorably struck with the appearance of the old woman" who "might almost . . . have been called a thousand years old" (*Life,* 148). Toothless, blind, and nearly completely paralyzed, her eyes "were so deeply sunken in their sockets that the eyeballs seemed to have disappeared altogether." Her decrepit hand bent inward and the fingernails projected beyond her wrist. Rounding out the picture, Barnum tells us, "The nails upon her large toes also had grown to the thickness of nearly a quarter of an inch" (*Life,* 148–49).

Heth mixed her grotesque features with a fine sense of histrionics when she passed herself off as George Washington's nursemaid: She was "sociable" and talked "incessantly" to her public viewers. Heth performed on her own volition; unlike Tom Thumb, her successor in the world of Barnum's exhibitions, she did not rely on Barnum for any prompting or training (*Life,* 148). She sang hymns, spoke of the first president as "dear little George," and proudly claimed to be present at his birth. " 'In fact,' said Joice, and it was a favorite expression of hers, 'I raised him.' " Appealing to the piety of her viewers, Heth moved from anecdotes of Washington's childhood to religious subjects, "for she claimed to be a member of the Baptist Church," which "rendered her exhibition an extremely interesting one" (*Life,* 149).

Joice Heth, ultimately, had the last laugh on P. T. Barnum. Throughout his career, Barnum submitted that he was astonished when the physicians who examined her corpse discovered that Joice was no more than eighty years old. It is important that Barnum maintains his innocence in this alleged humbug. In his *Life,* he willingly reveals previous public deceptions. He happily confessed to his organization of the Great Buffalo Hunt hoax of 1843—an event in Hoboken, New Jersey, that attracted spectators by advertising a frontier simulation of a wild buffalo hunt, complete with real cowboys and Indians. The event never reached the level of simulation that Barnum advertised because the seven hundred buffalo, terrified by the crowd, headed straight for the nearest swamp upon being released from their cages. Moreover, Barnum freely admitted his participation in the Woolly Horse hoax of 1848 when he purchased an odd-looking horse from an Indiana native and passed it off to the public as one of the animals that General Fremont had brought back from his expedition to the Rocky Mountains. As any reader of the autobiography can see, Barnum was not averse to uncovering former deceptions, but by maintaining his ignorance of Joice Heth's age, he admits that he has been duped by the histrionics of the clever old woman. In his *Life,* Barnum was still asserting his innocence in the Heth hoax, arguing that he bought her in *"perfect good faith,"* and that he was duped by a *"forged bill of sale* purporting to have been made by the *father* of George Washington." Barnum argues that he "honestly *believed"* the false document and laments the fact that he "has ever since borne the stigma of *originating* that imposture" (155, italics in original). The uncomfortable situation of owning an African American and profiting from her performances does not seem to have affected Barnum's conscience. It probably hurt Barnum more to admit his unwitting role in the falsification of Joice Heth's character because, by doing so, he was admitting that she duped him. Heth, not Barnum, displayed the most crafty sense of showmanship in the Joice Heth affair. Throughout the autobiography, Barnum goes to painstaking lengths to prove to the reader that no one can outsmart him, yet Joice Heth out-theatricalizes "The Prince of Humbugs" at the start of his illustrious career. She performed her role so well that it was only death that could uncover her mask of deception.

With Joice Heth, Barnum used blackness as an integral part of the national past; he stylized a public performance that marked the ironies of a nation that subscribed to the notions of the Declaration of Independence yet institutionalized African American slavery. Barnum was colorblind only when it came to exhibiting human aberrations on the public stage. White, brown, black, or red; man, woman, or child—Barnum was satisfied if he could profitably present any "body" into the public sphere. However, as we saw in the Joice Heth episode, the bodies that Barnum exhibited were not selfless and will-less mannequins. And it is their assertion of self as it conflicts with Barnum's presentation of them that makes Barnum's participation in the exhibition culture interesting.

Following the Joice Heth affair, Barnum continued to receive dividends from his investments in black culture. In a curious incident in *Life*, Barnum performed race on the public stage when he assumed the role of an African American by blacking his face and participating in the American minstrel tradition—a cultural practice that struck to the heart of race relations in antebellum America. In the spring of 1836 Barnum was managing a traveling circus. On a jaunt through South Carolina a minstrel singer named Sanford flew the company, leaving Barnum with a problem.

> I had advertised Negro songs; no one of my company was competent to fill [Sanford's] place; but being determined not to disappoint the audience, *I blacked myself thoroughly*, and sung the songs advertised, namely, "Zip Coon," "Gittin up Stairs," and "The Raccoon Hunt, or Sitting on a Rail." It was decidedly "a hard push," but the audience supposed the singer was Sanford, and, to my surprise, my singing was applauded, and in two of the songs I was encored! (*Life*, 189, emphasis in original)

Blacking himself and performing black culture represent Barnum's ultimate attempt to stylize and control the black body. Perhaps he learned a lesson from the Joice Heth affair and realized the black subject's ability to stylize a self that undermined Barnum's own cultural authority. The nineteenth century's consummate showman rarely appeared onstage in a costume other than his own self. Barnum orchestrated his own life and the lives of others, but his stage was the *theatrum mundi*. It is curious, then, that when Barnum does assume another character it is done by blacking his face and improvising a minstrel act. His rationalization for blacking up—that no one in the company was "competent" enough to perform—seems disingenuous. Barnum simply delighted in the prospect of the performance. His comment about the "competence" required in minstrelsy suggests both the professionalization and the specialization of the practice. What, then, made Barnum qualified to perform the minstrel routine? The minstrel show was a performance of blackness based on a white invention, and as Barnum demonstrates here it was used as a cultural commodity. Here, Barnum reaps the rewards of reification through his investment in black culture. Mimicry required study and observation, and the minstrel singers who confused the empirical boundaries between black and white entered into black culture in order to present it (in a highly artificial, distorted manner) to their white audiences were engaging in some form of cultural exchange.[27]

Barnum concludes this foray into nineteenth-century issues of race with a final anecdote: "After singing my negro [sic] songs one evening, and just as I had pulled my coat off in the 'dressing room' of the tent, I heard a slight disturbance outside the canvas. Rushing to the spot, and finding a person disputing with my men, I took their part, and spoke my mind to him very freely" (*Life*, 189). Barnum did not simply fill in for Sanford for one night, and he makes no mention of searching for another minstrel singer. Indeed, he had found the minstrel he was looking for in himself, and the subtle reference to continuing performances ("After singing my negro songs one evening") is intriguing; Barnum has performed the songs on a number of occasions, and, moreover, he has made them *his;* that is, he has taken stock in his "negro songs" and made a repertoire from them. In the preceding passage, Barnum never tells us what the disturbance was about; indeed, when he emerged from the tent disguised as a black man and began haranguing the stranger, a new problem quickly arose: "He instantly drew his pistol, exclaiming, 'You Black scoundrel! dare you use such language to a white man?' and proceeded deliberately to cock it. I saw that he supposed me to be a negro *[sic],* and might perhaps blow my brains out. Quick as thought I rolled up my shirt sleeves, and replied, 'I am as white as *you* are, sir.' He absolutely dropped the pistol with fright! (*Life,* 189). The psychosexual overtones of this passage (the gun as phallus, and the imagery associated with the man "deliberately" cocking his pistol) are examples of the white male's latent fear of miscegenation and the homoerotic fascination of the black body that Leslie Fiedler first noticed in 1948.[28] Moreover, this incident is of interest to us for the way it demonstrates the lack of control Barnum (or anyone who "blacked up") had over the role they were performing. Whites mistook the minstrel singers for "real" African Americans. Eric Lott remarks, "When, in the decades before the Civil War, northern white men 'blacked up' and imitated what they supposed was black dialect, music, and dance, some people, without derision, heard Negroes singing." Barnum's anecdote demonstrates that this racial conflation occurred offstage as easily as it did under the footlights.[29]

It is probably too easy to chastise Barnum for "not moralizing on race at this opportune narrative moment," and treating "it as a contingent phenomenon, allowing the incident to stand as a practical joke that nearly backfired."[30] Barnum's views on slavery were characteristic of many Northern Democrats. On the one hand, he could write the following to Thomas Wentworth Higginson in April of 1855: "I have spent months on the cotton plantations of Mississippi, where I have seen more than one 'Legree' "; on the other hand, he could argue for the continuing enslavement of blacks on the grounds that emancipation would put them in an inferior position to the whites.[31] It was no accident that Barnum omitted this incident from the 1869 version of the autobiography. The racial "problems" relating to black slavery in antebellum America that were lost on Barnum in the 1855 version are considerably absent from the 1869 version, as were the blackfacing episodes. The Joice Heth affair remained a sore spot for Barnum, and he continued to talk about it in the subsequent versions of his autobiography, but without the aplomb he exhibited in *Life.*

Conclusion: Negotiating Theatrical Selves in the Public Sphere

The exhibition culture of the nineteenth century was a site of cultural exchange and conflict, and the public display of theatrical selfhood both confirmed and implicitly challenged middle-class values. The public selves on display became ideological mirrors that reflected the values of a developing American middle class by confirming notions of success, otherness, and, in some instances, blackness. Hegemonic and peripheral voices mingled in the sites of public pleasure created by public exhibitions. The exhibition textualized the public self and highlighted the subjectivity of the exhibit. Like the act of writing autobiography, the exhibition defied official closure. To exhibit is to hold something up for question, to deny its totalizing teleology. Audiences and performers struggled to make meaning of the self on display, but neither the seer nor the seen were able to control the interpretation of bodies. Cultural meaning is the result of negotiation between the audience's and the performer's interpretation of the public self. "Culture is neither autonomous nor an externally determined field," remarks Richard Johnson, "but a site of social differences and struggles."[32] Yet the reflecting mirrors were distorted—like the funhouse mirrors at a carnival. The freaks on display disturbed the audience's interpretation and established authorial autonomy through their public performances.

P. T. Barnum validated theatrical selfhood in nineteenth-century America. Even after Joice Heth's death, Barnum (with Levi Lyman's help) shamelessly continued the charade by starting a rumor that Heth was not really dead but alive and well in Hebron, Connecticut, and that the woman's body on whom the doctors performed their autopsy was one "Aunt Nelly," whose dead body was brought as a stand-in for Heth. Similarly, each of Barnum's many editions (additions) to his *Life*, is a narrative display of a temporal slice of an ever-changing P. T. Barnum. Barnum as much as admitted this in the preface to *Struggles and Triumphs*: "If my pages are as plentifully sprinkled with 'I's' as was the chief ornament of Hood's peacock, 'who thought he had the eyes of Europe on his tail,' I can only say, that the 'I's' are essential to the story I have told. It has been my purpose to narrate, not the life of another, but that career in which I was the principal actor."[33]

Barnum's use of the image of a peacock with ornamentation illustrates how far selfhood had come in American discourse since the Revolution. Fliegelman terminates his study of an American culture of performance with the culmination of the Revolution, when the unadorned public man proudly exhibits his private self in the public square. Barnum, however, becomes an example of the *adorned* public man of the mid-nineteenth century—a man of varying social selves who stylizes his life, as well as the public lives of others, to become the quintessential public man of the age.

Notes

1. P. T. Barnum, *The Life of P. T. Barnum, Written by Himself* (New York: Redfield, 1855), 143. Hereafter cited in the text as *Life*.

2. See David Reynolds, *Walt Whitman's America* (New York: Knopf, 1995), for a discussion of nineteenth-century pseudosciences. On public oratory, see Carl Bode, *The American Lyceum: Town Meeting of the Mind* (New York: Oxford University Press, 1956); Donald Scott, "The Popular Lecture and the Creation of a Public in Mid-Nineteenth-Century America," *Journal of American History* 66 (1980): 791–809. For a discussion of enthusiastic religion, see Whitney Cross, *The Burned-Over District: The Social and Intellectual History of Enthusiastic Religion in Western New York, 1800–1850* (Ithaca: Cornell University Press, 1950). For a discussion of Barnum's political activities in the early 1830s and his reactions against "hysterical Christianity," see A. H. Saxon, *P. T. Barnum: The Legend and the Man* (New York: Columbia University Press, 1980), 40.

3. Jay Fliegelman, *Declaring Independence: Jefferson, Natural Language, and the Culture of Performance* (Stanford: Stanford University Press, 1993).

4. See Karen Halttunen, *Confidence Men and Painted Women: A Study of Middle-Class Culture in America, 1830–1870* (New Haven: Yale University Press, 1982); and Gary Lindberg, *The Confidence Man in American Literature* (New York: Oxford University Press, 1982).

5. The allusion is to Henry Wadsworth Longfellow's "A Psalm of Life," a popular nineteenth-century poem published in *Knickerbocker* in 1838.

6. Carl Bode, introduction to *Struggles and Triumphs; or Forty Years' Recollections of P. T. Barnum* by P. T. Barnum (New York: Penguin, 1981), 19.

7. George Bryan, introduction to *Struggles and Triumphs: or, The Life of P. T. Barnum, Written by Himself* (New York: Knopf, 1927), xviii.

8. For a detailed printing history of Barnum's autobiographies, see Raymond Toole-Stott, *Circus and the Allied Arts* (Derby: Harpur, 1971), 4:9719–41.

9. Bryan, introduction to *Struggles and Triumphs*, xx.

10. William Spengemann, *The Forms of Autobiography: Episodes in the History of a Literary Genre* (New Haven: Yale University Press, 1980), xiii; Thomas Couser, *Altered Egos: Authority in American Autobiography* (New York: Oxford University Press, 1989), 66.

11. Couser, *Altered Egos*, 53–54.

12. Ibid., 53.

13. The book had detractors. See Neil Harris, *Humbug* (Boston: Little, Brown, 1973), 224–31.

14. Ibid., 224.

15. Bryan, introduction to *Struggles and Triumphs*, xxx.

16. Quoted in ibid., xxx.

17. Harris, *Humbug*, 224.

18. Quoted in Bryan, introduction to *Struggles and Triumphs*, xxxi.

19. Saxon, *P. T. Barnum*, 12.

20. Brooks McNamara, "'A Congress of Wonders': The Rise and Fall of the Dime Museum," *Emerson Society Quarterly* 20 (1974): 218.

21. Quoted in Charles Sellers, *Mr. Peale's Museum: Charles Willson Peale and the First Popular Museum in Natural Science and Art* (New York: Norton, 1980), 15.

22. See ibid., Chap. 6.

23. Constance Rourke, *Trumpets of Jubilee: Henry Ward Beecher, Harriet Beecher Stowe, Lyman Beecher, Horace Greeley, P. T. Barnum* (New York: Harcourt, Brace, 1927), 291.

24. Robert Bogdan, "The Exhibition of Humans with Differences for Amusement and Profit," *Policy Studies Journal* 15 (1987): 537, 540.

25. See David Rothman, *Discovery of the Asylum: Social Order and Disorder in the New Republic* (Boston: Little, Brown, 1971).

26. On the representation of African Americans and Native Americans on the American stage, see Richard Moody, *America Takes the Stage: Romanticism in American Drama and Theatre, 1750–1900* (Bloomington: Indiana University Press, 1955), especially Chap. 2.

27. Eric Lott, *Love and Theft: Blackface Minstrelsy and the American Working Class* (New York: Oxford University Press, 1993), 39. The critical response to the minstrel tradition, a highly popular nineteenth-century entertainment, has exposed the phenomena as a racist attempt by white culture to lampoon black culture, and so it was. Yet, despite its mockery, as Lott argues, the minstrel tradition was the first white recognition of black culture, and the first American cultural practice to establish avenues of exchange between black and white culture. Whites commodified blackness by investing their interests in black culture (learning dialects and songs, aping gestures and mannerisms) and then selling transmogrified versions of blackness to white audiences.

28. See Leslie Fiedler, "Come Back to the Raft Ag'in, Huck Honey," in *The Fiedler Reader* (New York: Stein and Day, 1977), 3–12.

29. Lott, *Love and Theft*, 57, 17.

30. Couser, *Altered Egos*, 57.

31. P. T. Barnum, *Selected Letters of P. T. Barnum*, ed. A. H. Saxon (New York: Columbia University Press, 1983), 86.

32. Richard Johnson, "What Is Cultural Studies Anyway?" *Social Text* 16 (1986): 39.

33. Barnum, *Struggles and Triumphs*, 46.

EIGHT

Social Order and Psychological Disorder: Laughing Gas Demonstrations, 1800–1850

ELLEN HICKEY GRAYSON

Between 1845 and 1848, Dr. Gardiner Quincy Colton traveled throughout the eastern United States exhibiting the colossal thirteen-by-twenty-four-foot temperance painting, *Court of Death*. At twenty-five cents, the price of admission to see the painting was comparable to a ticket to the circus or a cheap seat at the theater. Together with Colton's popular science and telegraph demonstrations, the exhibition packed thousands of viewers into hotel ballrooms, Masonic halls, lyceums, and young men's associations, especially in towns along the Erie Canal where the message of spiritual redemption and economic progress appealed to ministers, civic leaders, and moral reformers. Eager to assert cultural authority and advance their own agendas, these individuals comprised an elaborate promotional network capable of mobilizing large audiences. As the exhibition traveled further west, however, in commercial centers where the promotional infrastructure was less highly developed, attendance figures tapered off. Faced with diminishing revenues, Colton resorted to laughing gas demonstrations. Drawing record crowds in Pittsburgh, Cincinnati, Louisville, St. Louis, New Orleans, and Mobile, the demonstrations were far and away the most lucrative element in Colton's exhibition package. Indeed, they proved more successful in mobilizing audiences than even the most highly developed network of ministers and moral reformers. And although the media differed, both the demonstrations and the painting achieved the same ends.

In order to understand why these laughing gas demonstrations were so popular and how they became a legitimate form of commercial entertainment, it is useful to trace the history of the interpretive frameworks associated with nitrous oxide.[1] During the first decades of the nineteenth century, responsibility for constructing these frameworks shifted from the scientists who recorded the effects of the gas in experiments to newspapers and lecturers who promoted the demonstrations as a form of commercial entertainment. Once subject to the dictates of the marketplace, new interpretive frameworks gradually neutralized the demonstrations' potentially subversive effects. And while the specific content of the interpretive frameworks changed, the role of the demonstrations, as an antidote to broader cultural concerns, remained the same.

Unlike the freak shows featured in Barnumesque museum exhibitions, volunteers from the audience were the subject of the spectator's gaze in laughing gas demonstrations. Instead of defining the parameters of normalcy in physical terms, laughing gas performances exhibited cultural aberrations or "otherness" in psychological terms. And rather than focusing on surface contours, the performances were believed to expose character traits normally hidden within. By placing defects of character on display, audiences exorcised aberrant behavior within the collective whole.

The success of the laughing gas performances during the 1840s tour of *Court of Death* demonstrates the extent to which market capitalism incorporated seemingly subversive elements into commercialized forms of entertainment, which in turn reinforced the existing social order. Shifts in the interpretive frameworks associated with the demonstrations indicate how audiences and the marketplace adapted and adopted cultural products to suit their own purposes. Even as the laughing gas performances suggest a collective ambivalence toward the role of irrational passions amid expanding democracy and advancing capitalism, they also demonstrate how new forms of commercial entertainment reinforced the parameters of middle-class respectability.

In 1773, Joseph Priestley first identified nitrous oxide as "Dephlogistic Nitrous Air." Priestley believed the gas to be poisonous.[2] Twenty-six years later, in 1799, the young British chemist Humphry Davy set out to challenge Priestley's conclusion by developing a means of purifying nitrous oxide so that it was safe to inhale. He succeeded on April 11 of that year.

The circumstances under which Davy conducted his experiments established the initial interpretive framework associated with the gas. Davy conducted the experiments in Clifton, a suburb of Bristol, where he was employed at the Pneumatic Institute, a facility established in 1798 to treat illnesses with doses of inhalable gases. Many of the participants in the experiments were friends or associates of the founder of the Institute, Thomas Beddoes, a physician, former lecturer in chemistry at Oxford, and outspoken liberal democrat, who expressed his political opinions in *The Watchman*, a short-lived, bimonthly journal edited by Samuel Taylor Coleridge.[3] Together with Robert Southey, Robert Lovell, Joseph Cottle, and Thomas Wedgwood, Coleridge and Beddoes formed a circle of poet-scientist-philosophers who shared an interest in liberal politics and romanticism.[4] Interrelated through marriages and sources of patronage, the members of the group espoused German aesthetic philosophy, especially the work of Immanuel Kant.[5] Davy's account of the experiments, with his emphasis on subjective experience, reflects this shared philosophical orientation.

In his five-hundred-page treatise *Researches, Chemical and Philosophical, Chiefly Concerning Nitrous Oxide*, Davy recounted in minute detail experiments performed primarily on himself.[6] Over a period of fourteen months, Davy inhaled from six to twelve quarts of the gas four or five times a week and sometimes as many as three or four times a day. He described the sensations produced by the gas as "intense intoxication" and "sublime emotions connected with highly vivid ideas" eliciting "thrilling and other pleasurable feelings" and, afterwards, "vivid and agreeable dreams."[7] Aiming to observe the effects of the gas under different physical circumstances, Davy inhaled doses at various times of the day (after he had eaten, fasted, slept, not slept, in the company of others, in solitude, etc.). The experiments culminated with a procedure on December 26, 1799, when Davy "resolved to breathe the gas for such a time and in such quantities, as to produce excitement equal in duration and superior in intensity to that occasioned by high intoxication from opium or alcohol."[8] Emerging from an airtight breathing box and immediately inhaling twenty quarts of pure nitrous oxide, Davy recalled having "lost all connection with external things; trains of vivid visible images rapidly passed through my mind, and were connected with worlds in such a manner, as to produce perceptions perfectly novel. I existed in a world of newly connected and newly modified ideas. I theorized—I imagined that I made discoveries."[9] When he awoke from "this semi-delirious trance," although his recollection of his "imagined discoveries" was "feeble and indistinct," Davy proclaimed, "in prophetic manner, Nothing exists but thoughts!—the universe is composed of impressions, ideas, pleasures and pains!"[10] The fact that Davy assigned to the experience such profound insight into the subjectivity of human perception indicates the extent to which he was willing to use his accounts of the experiments to promote Kantian aesthetic philosophy and furnish a scientific basis for the link between chemistry, human physiology, and subjective experience.

Descriptions of other responses to inhaling the gas replicated Davy's findings. In his *Researches,* Davy included the responses of eighteen participants, most of whom inhaled six to seven quarts of the gas four or five times over a period of days. They described unsuppressible laughter, heightened sensory perception, enhanced physical strength, and general euphoria, and attributed the source of their pleasure to "effects on the nervous system," or "delicious tremours," which "thrilled all through" one inhaler and caused another to "faint in extacy [sic]."[11] Although some experienced weightlessness, drowsiness, or a sense of serenity and tranquility, most reported feelings of "irrepressible muscular strength."[12] Often at a loss for words to describe the sensations, participants searched for analogous situations, such as the feelings elicited by climbing high mountains, hearing "great choruses of the Messiah" from seven hundred instruments in Westminster Abbey, witnessing heroic acts on the stage, or reading a sublime poetic passage.[13] Davy himself observed that he had sometimes experienced "sensations similar to no others, and they have consequently been indescribable."[14] This emphasis on unprecedented, ineffable feelings challenged Lockean theories of sensory perception, which stipulated that all interior thoughts or perceptions originate in external stimuli.

The publication of Davy's *Researches* established his credentials as a scientist. In the spring of 1801, Davy left Bristol for London, where he delivered three addresses at the Royal Institute, a scientific organization recently established under the direction of Count Rumford for the "diffusion of knowledge." Davy's experiments helped him to secure a position as lecturer in chemistry at the Royal Institution, where on June 20, 1801, he presented his findings to an audience of five hundred who, according to Davy, responded with "unbounded applause." The following day, a "party of philosophers" met at the Institution to inhale the "joy inspiring gas," which produced "a great sensation."[15] Reviews of Davy's demonstrations were published in the *Philosophical Magazine,* the *Monthly Magazine and British Register,* and the *Monthly Review or Literary Journal.*[16]

Despite a generally favorable reception, not everyone took the laughing gas demonstrations seriously. In 1802, artist James Gillray published an engraving of the demonstrations that satirizes the learned pretensions of both the scientists and their audiences (fig. 8.1). Maria Edgeworth, whose brother Robert Lovell participated in Davy's experiments at the Pneumatic Institute, observed that a predisposition to perform was necessary to fully experience the effects of the gas: "faith, great faith, is I believe necessary to produce any effect upon the drinkers, and I have seen some of the adventurous philosophers who sought in vain for satisfaction in the bag of *Gaseous Oxyd,* and found nothing but a sick stomach and giddy

8.1. In his parody of pneumatic research, artist James Gillray depicts Humphry Davy working the bellows as Professor Thomas Young administers gas to Sir John C. Hippisley. Count Rumford stands at the extreme right. James Gillray, *Scientific Researches! New Discoveries in Pneumaticks! or an Experimental Lecture on the Powers of Air*, colored etching, 1802. Print Collection, Miriam and Ira D. Wallach Division of Art, Prints and Photographs, The New York Public Library, Astor, Lenox and Tilden Foundations.

head."[17] Cottle recalled that the laughing gas experiments "quite exorcised philosophical gravity, and converted the laboratory into a region of hilarity and relaxation."[18] Physician William Paul Crillon Barton, who later experimented with nitrous oxide in Philadelphia, noted that Davy's observations on the effects of nitrous oxide were "derided as extravagant and imaginary" and efforts were made to expose "the delusion . . . and to laugh it into contempt."[19]

For others, the laughing gas experiments were neither amusing nor benign. Davy himself recognized the addictive qualities of the gas, confessing in his *Researches* that "the desire to breathe the gas is awakened in me by the sight of a person breathing, or even by that of an air-bag or air-holder."[20] George Burnet admitted to an "irresistible *appetite* to repeat it."[21] Maria Edgeworth concluded that "Pleasure even to madness is the consequence of this draft."[22] Years later, in his reminiscences of Coleridge and Southey, Cottle recalled "the appalling hazards encountered by M. Davy, in his intrepid investigation of the gases." These "destructive experiments," according to Cottle, "probably, produced those afflictions of the chest to which he was subject through life, and . . . beyond all question, shortened his days."[23] Davy admitted that during the course of his experiments his health had been "somewhat injured": he slept less than usual, experienced an "uneasy feeling . . . analogous to the sickness of hope," became more irritable, and lost physical strength.[24] Questionable procedures at the short-lived Pneumatic Institute further undermined the perception of experiments with nitrous oxide as a valid course of scientific inquiry. Less than one year after the Institute opened its doors, attendance figures had dropped so low that Beddoes was forced to pay patients to receive his gaseous treatments.[25]

After his demonstrations at the Royal Institution, Davy abandoned nitrous oxide experiments. Although in his *Researches,* Davy briefly noted its potential use as an anesthetic, neither he nor any of his contemporaries pursued the possibility further. Nitrous oxide was never fully divested of its association with the "philosophic revelers" at the Pneumatic Institute nor the Kantian aesthetic philosophy and liberal politics they espoused. Indeed, the most significant impact of Davy's *Researches* was to promote Kantian subjectivity and provide a scientific basis for the link between human physiology and the aesthetic sublime.[26] With no immediate medical or scientific application and little relevance outside the rarefied circles of London's scientific and literary elite, the discovery of nitrous oxide would appear to have reached its logical conclusion. The commercial applications of the gas, however, had yet to be fully explored.

William Paul Crillon Barton's *Dissertation on the Chymical Properties and Exhilarating Effects of Nitrous Oxide Gas,* published in Philadelphia in 1808, drew directly upon the interpretive framework established by Davy's *Researches.*[27] Like Davy, Barton performed the experiments primarily on himself. Although his descriptions were far more detailed than Davy's, Barton nevertheless had difficulty putting his feelings into words.[28] He equated the sensation to that which he had "often experienced in a state of voluptuous delight, vibrating between a waking consciousness and the torpor of sleep."[29] Feeling "furnished of two separate minds" in this "semi-conscious, semi-delusive state," Barton described becoming equally convinced of two conflicting ideas at once: "the one confirmed what I fancied, the other convinced me that it was all imaginary."[30] Like Davy's conclusions, Barton's observations challenged the basic tenets of the Enlightenment understanding of reason, especially the belief that the mind cannot contain two contradictory ideas at once.

Barton also briefly notes possible anesthetic applications for nitrous oxide, especially after experimenting with the gas while still suffering from a head injury. Yet never in his subsequent career as a Navy surgeon did Barton use the gas for that purpose.[31] Rather than pursuing its application as a painkiller that would render the individual passive, neutral, and without the use of will or reason, Barton envisioned a role for the gas in terms of human perfectionism — the answer to Benjamin Rush's search for "some production of nature or art, yet undiscovered, that shall act in such a manner upon the brain, as to enlarge and strengthen the intellectual faculties."[32] Such an application would seem entirely fitting, given the importance of social mobility and competitive individualism in the context of expanding democracy and advancing capitalism.[33] The neutralizing effects of laughing gas, however, proved even more appealing to those concerned about the volatility of the democratic masses. To this latter concern, the interpretive framework gradually responded.

Within the first decade of the nineteenth century, nitrous oxide demonstrations, which had been confined to relatively small scientific circles in Philadelphia and New York, were adapted as a form of commercial entertainment, now reaching much broader audiences. With commercialization, the medium establishing the interpretive framework shifted from written texts, focusing on interior sensations to outward, visual displays of its effects. Central to this interpretive shift was a new emphasis on the dangers of the gas, especially its ability to unleash irrational passions. Whereas only two of the participants in Davy's experiments characterized the sensations produced by laughing gas as a loss of control, early accounts of laughing gas performances in America emphasized uncontrollable passions and physical aggression.[34]

A political tract published in Philadelphia in 1814 on the anniversary of the birth of George Washington helped to establish this new framework.[35] The treatise opens with an account of a demonstration at which four young men between the ages of fifteen and twenty-five inhaled the gas and stormed around the lecture hall, assuming military postures, leaping over furniture, and attacking members of the audience. The unidentified author of the treatise equates these performances to the mood of the nation, warning that America should not retaliate against Britain on the eve of peace negotiations for the end of the War of 1812. The young men whose rational understanding was rendered powerless by the nitrous oxide, to this author, personified the volatility of the democratic masses. Asserting that the entire country was "in a state of political intoxication," and that nothing could be more natural than "young men . . . in a state of inconceivable excitation" resorting to irrational retaliation, the author condemns the policies of "self-styled republicans" and "demagogues of democracy." By referring to the gas as "potent doses of the delicious poison" and noting that the ladies were instructed to "place themselves upon the hindmost seats . . . out of harm's way," the author emphasizes the element of danger posed by the gas.[36]

Partially in response to concerns about the loss of reason and unleashed passions, the interpretive framework for nitrous oxide demonstrations began to emphasize the ability of the lecturer (usually a scientist, chemist, druggist, or doctor) to control the volunteers from the audience who inhaled the gas. Newspaper announcements elevated the status of the lecturer by emphasizing his expertise and mystifying the performance. The *New York Evening Post* warned, "If the gas be not pure it might produce serious consequences to those who aspire it, not only in lasting injury to the lungs, but immediate death."[37] The proliferation of quacks and competition among lecturers intensified such rhetoric. Dr. Preston, who performed demonstrations in 1821 at the City Hotel in New York, complained that "some persons, who have no pretensions to chemistry, have advertized such exhibitions." Fearing that he may "in some measure [be] implicated if any melancholy event should transpire from impure gas, even exhibited by other persons," Dr. Preston insisted that the preparation of the gas be supervised by not simply a "scientific," but also a "practical chemist."[38] Incidents such as when a young man was found comatose beside the open spigot of the gasometer after a demonstration performed in Utica, New York, in 1821, further heightened the sense of danger.[39]

Robert Seymour's satirical print *Living Made Easy: Prescription for Scolding Wives* dramatizes the balance of power between the lecturer and the inhaler by introducing the issue of gender (fig. 8.2). A thinly disguised metaphor for male sexual prowess, laughing gas is portrayed as a sedative. In the central grouping, later used in broadsides, the husband stands astride his seated wife (fig. 8.3). Holding the back of her neck in a vice-like grip, his leg separating her legs, he forces the inflated bag of gas into her mouth as she tips backwards, eyes bulging and hands cringing in horror. In the background a satisfied husband, his bag deflated, gestures toward his wife, who sits in a chair facing a wall, giddy with laughter and, apparently, sedated.[40]

8.2. The issue of gender dramatized the power relationship between the lecturer and the inhaler and emphasized the ability of the gas to neutralize the uncontrollable masses. Robert Seymour, *Living Made Easy: Prescription for Scolding Wives*, colored etching, London, 1830. National Library of Medicine.

8.3. The central grouping from Seymour's engraving was used on broadsides advertising the demonstrations in the 1840s, even after the interpretive framework shifted to emphasize the audiences' ability to discern "true character." *A Grand Exhibition of . . . Laughing Gas!*, ca. 1845. Broadside. Buck Hill Associates, Johnsburgh, New York.

During the 1840s, the interpretive framework for laughing gas again began to shift. The power of the lecturer to mystify and sedate members of the audience with his scientific expertise no longer suited the concerns of a society that considered the charismatic powers and mystical practices of Mormons, Catholics, and Freemasons to be a threat to the state.[41] Instead, the interpretive framework began to emphasize the ability of the gas to reveal "true character." In so doing, it shifted authority from the lecturer to the audience, who, with their spectating gaze and vocal laughter, discerned "true character" and censured aberrant behavior.[42] The interpretive framework for the laughing gas demonstrations included on the 1840s tour of *Court of Death* illustrates the reasons why this shift took place.

At first it would seem that Colton's laughing gas demonstrations subverted the message of temperance and control of the passions represented in *Court of Death*. By providing socially sanctioned space for the display of irrational passions, these performances would seem to validate the very thing that supposedly threatened to undermine the moral fabric of society. Indeed, the performances included several characteristic features of the carnivalesque—especially laughter, masks, and the grotesque with its emphasis on orifices and bulging body parts—that Mikhail Bakhtin described in his study of seventeenth-century society, *Rabelais and His World*.[43] Far from the scenes of masked revelry erupting in seventeenth-century town squares, however, both the audiences and the performers in nineteenth-century laughing gas demonstrations were carefully regulated.

Newspaper announcements regarding safety precautions offered readers both reassurance and titillation. Notices consistently insisted that the gas was medically safe, that the sensations were "perfectly delightful," and that "no impropriety need be anticipated."[44] Nevertheless, twelve "strong men" were engaged to stand on the stage built with a railing around it in order to protect "those under the influence of the gas from injuring themselves or others."[45] An officer was stationed in the balcony, where "no boys were admitted," and dress seats on the parquet were reserved for "the ladies."[46] Assurances were made that the gas would be administered only to "the first class of gentlemen." Such arrangements aimed "to prevent the excited participants from cutting up and extravagant extras," and to assure that the same "intelligent, respectable audiences" who attended the exhibition of *Court of Death* would also comprise the audiences for the laughing gas demonstrations.[47] "The whole entertainment," announced the *Pittsburgh Gazette*, "will be calculated with the propriety and decorum which shall deserve the patronage of an intelligent class of ladies and gentlemen."[48]

The new interpretive framework of revealed character further mitigated the potentially subversive aspects of the demonstrations. Instead of exposing seemingly disruptive passions under the anonymous cover of the street crowd and carnival mask, laughing gas demonstrations placed individuals from the audience onstage and, one by one, subjected them to the scrutiny of the audience.[49] As a means of revealing "true character," laughing gas was claimed to be more accurate than phrenology.[50]

Both participants and audiences were nevertheless profoundly aware of prescribed parameters of disclosure, especially for women, who restricted their performances to demonstrations of moral virtue. Most recited scripture, broke into song, or lapsed into poetic verse. Those women who revealed inappropriate character traits, like the woman in St. Louis who, according to the *Daily Union*, "let the cat out of the bag," rendered themselves subject to public censure and humiliation.[51] So strong was the tendency towards self-censure among women that during afternoon auditions for evening performances, Colton actively encouraged more "interesting"—if not deviant—behavior. Among twenty women wishing to inhale the gas in Mobile, Alabama, Colton announced that only four or five of the "most interesting subjects" would be selected to perform in public.[52]

Descriptions of performances by male volunteers encompassed a wider range of behavior, including political harangues, performances of high tragedy, military maneuvers, and song. The interpretive framework of revealed character, nevertheless, structured these performances according to ethnic and class stereotypes. Reports on performances by Irishmen and working-class firemen confirmed stereotypes that these individuals were especially prone to violence.[53] Middle-class or elite professionals, such as the young lawyer who "threw himself into an attitude and recited three stanzas from Bryant," demonstrated how cultivated passions could be appropriately channeled into poetic sentiment.[54] Occasionally performances subverted outward appearances, as when a "gentleman" danced a "magnificent breakdown," a dance specifically associated with the Bowery b'hoys and urban, potentially deviant youth. Performed unaccompanied, the dance epitomized the refusal of the unassimilated male youth to conform to domesticated codes of decorum. Equally ominous was the performance of "a merchant, well known as a very amiable young man" who "proceeded to kick and knock every body about on the stage," appearing to be "in a great rage." The reviewer concluded that, despite outward appearances, "our quiet young friend must be a regular destructive in disposition."[55]

Disjunctures between revelations of inner character and outward appearances, however, were rare. More often the laughing gas demonstrations merely confirmed public perception of character, as when an editor moved across the stage "very gravely and with great dignity . . . being doubtless, in secret, a diplomatist," or when a man identified as a "philanthropist" in St. Louis "opened his pocket book, handed the lecturer a five dollar bank note—then, as if he had not done enough, thrust the pocket book on him—then gave his purse, and finally felt his vest, pantaloons and coat pockets apparently for more. The countenance expressed extreme benevolence—tears even starting in his eyes."[56] Newspaper accounts reported that lawyers and "gentlemen" revealed virtuous characteristics far more frequently than performers identified by working-class occupations or ethnic origin.

In the end, laughing gas demonstrations were hardly subversive, in the Bakhtinian sense or otherwise. By ritualizing the unveiling of character under the auspices of science, laughing gas performances, rather than refuting the moral philosophy represented in *Court of Death*, in fact affirmed the dominant values of bourgeois respectability. According to newspaper accounts of the demonstrations, it was not the effects of the laughing gas in revealing true character that were most amusing, but rather watching the participant's reaction as the nitrous oxide wore off. Like twentieth-century television audiences for Allen Funt's "Candid Camera," nineteenth-century audiences were as amused by the embarrassment of revealed character as by the performance itself. The effect of both exercises was to collectively impose a self-consciousness upon participants and viewers, reinforcing a profound awareness of behavioral norms and the parameters of respectability.

There seems to be something uniquely American, disturbingly familiar, and rather pathetic about the image of the isolated individual, venting deep-seated social frustrations onstage before a large and vocal audience, whose moral code of conduct was advertised on a billboard-sized painting serving as a backdrop to the performance. Compare, for example, the isolated figure of Joe, thumbing his nose at the audience in Pittsburgh, to individuals losing themselves among crowds of masked revelers.[57] *Court of Death* embodied the dominant code of moral values that made audiences laugh when individuals like Joe—only under the guise of science—were licensed to reveal their true characters. The scientific nature of the exhibitions made them seem controllable and safe.

Taken as a whole, the traveling exhibition package of *Court of Death* offers two models of cultural hegemony. In towns along the Erie Canal, known for the religious revivals that took place there during the Second Great Awakening, powerful cultural mediators and an elaborate network of ministers, newspapers, and moral reform institutions mobilized large audiences to see the painting and advance the message of moral reform. In towns throughout the Midwest and South, where this infrastructure was not as highly developed, laughing gas demonstrations accomplished the same ends. Having internalized the moral philosophy represented in the painting, audiences, through their laughter, reinforced the parameters of middle-class codes of decorum.

The history of laughing gas during the first half of the nineteenth century ultimately links the Kantian aesthetic philosophy espoused by a circle of liberal, scientific, and literary elites in England to the self-promoting, upwardly mobile, rugged individualist of antebellum America. Advancement and, often, survival in a democratic society and market economy demanded enormous energies of self-fashioning. But the liberating aspects of expanding democracy gave pause to those concerned about the volatility of the democratic masses. And even as advancing capitalism fostered rugged individualism and competitive entrepreneurship, it also imposed the regimentation of wage labor and mass production. The shifting interpretive framework for laughing gas demonstrations mirrored this tension between expansion and restraint. In responding to one set of concerns, the laughing gas demonstrations raised a new set of issues, which in turn were revised by yet another set of cultural imperatives. In response to concern about the volatility of the masses, the laughing gas lecturer became the embodiment of scientific (rather than religious) social authority, capable of exerting control over audiences and performers, a metaphor for the body politic. Mystifying audiences with feats of scientific mastery, the lecturer neutralized the masses, as the husband in Seymour's engraving sedates the wife. In time, the very mystifying quality of the lecturer's power also proved unsettling, and the interpretive framework again adjusted itself by investing the audience with the means to discern "true character."

Colton himself embodied this tension between expansion and constraint: the expansiveness of romantic wanderings and opportunities for self actualization versus the imperatives of market capitalism, the constraints of bourgeois respectability, and the isolation of rugged individualism. Audiences remarked on his "gentlemanly bearing" and his "perfect understanding of the subject." [58] Yet under the veneer of gentility, Colton was as much a man on the make as the next showman.

Fittingly, just as Colton maximized nitrous oxide's potential as a form of commercial entertainment, so too did he exploit it as an anesthetic. Almost by accident, a medical application for nitrous oxide was finally established, not within the sterile halls of scientific institutions, but rather within the chaotic atmosphere of the sensationalized public exhibition. During one of Colton's demonstrations in Hartford in 1844, a drugstore clerk, while under the influence of the gas, ran into a bench and lacerated his leg. Observing that the clerk had felt no pain, Horace Wells approached Colton afterwards and asked him to administer the gas while Wells had a wisdom tooth extracted. The procedure was successful and is cited as a seminal moment in the establishment of nitrous oxide as an anesthetic. Although credited with the discovery, Wells did not live long enough to reap any financial rewards. Addicted not only to nitrous oxide but also to ether and chloroform, Wells committed suicide in 1848 while imprisoned in New York's city jail. The ever-resilient Colton, however, returned to New York after a stint managing a silver mine in California and in 1864 established the Colton Dental Association. By 1886, Colton had several branch offices along the East Coast. At the end of his career, Colton is said to have administered nitrous oxide as an anesthetic more than 125,000 times, painlessly extracting hundreds of thousands of teeth.[59]

On the eve of the American Revolution, fearing that moral degeneracy would jeopardize public virtue, the First Continental Congress instituted codes of conduct that outlawed theatergoing, cockfighting and horseracing.[60] At the close of the war, the codes of conduct were repealed, once again placing the moral fiber of society at risk. The evolution of the interpretive framework for laughing gas performances indicates that such fears were unfounded. By the 1840s new forms of commercial spectacle furnished the means to preserve codes of conduct and delineate the parameters of middle-class respectability with greater effectiveness than abstinence from the theater or horseracing could ever have hoped to accomplish. Advancing capitalism and expanding democracy proved remarkably adept at producing commercial spectacles that would promote the survival of their own social and economic structures.

NOTES

1. Usually applied to reader response in literary analyses, the term "interpretive framework" works equally well for studies of audience response to visual spectacle. In the case of the laughing gas demonstrations, the term refers specifically to the written texts (scientific accounts, political treatises, and newspaper reviews) that shaped viewers' understanding of the performances. For further discussion of the term, see the introduction in Stanley Fish, *Is There a Text in This Class? The Authority of Interpretive Communities* (Cambridge: Harvard University Press, 1980).

2. Samuel Latham Mitchill reiterated Priestley's understanding that the gas was poisonous in his *Remarks on the Gaseous Oxyd of Azote and of Its Effects* (New York, 1795). See David Knight, *Humphry Davy: Science and Power* (Oxford: Blackwell, 1992), 28.

3. Anticlergy, protemperance, and abolitionist, *The Watchman* attacked William Pitt's policies, condemned the intensification of the war with France, and exposed corrupt magistrates in Birmingham. Dorothy A. Stansfield, *Thomas Beddoes, 1760–1808, Chemist, Physician, Democrat* (Dordrecht: D. Reidel, 1984), 132; Trevor H. Levere, "Dr. Thomas Beddoes and the Establishment of His Pneumatic Institution: A Tale of Three Presidents," *Notes and Records of the Royal Society of London* 32 (July 1977): 41–51.

4. For discussion of conflicting political attitudes in British scientific circles, see Maurice Crosland, "The Image of Science as a Threat: Burke versus Priestley and the 'Philosophic Revolution,'" *British Society for the History of Science* 20 (July 1987): 277–307.

5. In 1794 in Bristol, Coleridge, Southey, and Lovell developed plans for a utopian community to be located on the banks of the Susquehanna in Pennsylvania and resolved to marry the Friker sisters, Sarah, Edith, and Mary. Cottle, a bookseller who published Southey's *Joan of Arc* (1796) and Coleridge's *Lyrical Ballads* containing the "Ancient Mariner" (1798), was also a member of this circle. Wedgwood, the son of ceramic manufacturer Josiah Wedgwood, became the chief benefactor of Coleridge and principal investor in Beddoes's Pneumatic Institute. Wedgwood also financed Coleridge's trip to Germany. As early as 1793, Beddoes included excerpts from Kant's *Critique of Pure Reason* in his *Observations on the Nature of Demonstrative Evidence.*

6. Humphry Davy, *Researches, Chemical and Philosophical, Chiefly Concerning Nitrous Oxide* (London: J. Johnson, 1800).

7. Ibid., 463, 492–93.

8. Ibid., 187.

9. Ibid., 289–90.

10. Ibid.

11. Participants used terms such as "glowing warmth," "senses more alive to every surrounding impression," and an "almost delirious but highly pleasurable sensation in the brain" to describe their experiences. While Southey described the sensations produced by the "bag of nitrous oxide with which he [Davy] generally regaled me" as "perfectly new and delightful," Coleridge reported "great extacy [sic]" and "unmingled pleasure." Davy, *Researches*, 499, 501, 505, 508, 520; Robert Southey to Humphry Davy, 4 May 1799, cited in Stansfield, *Thomas Beddoes*, 172; Suzanne R. Hoover, "Coleridge, Humphry Davy, and Some Early Experiments with a Consciousness-altering Drug," *Bulletin of Research in the Humanities* 81 (Spring 1978): 9–28.

12. Davy, *Researches*, 499, 503, 514, 519.

13. Ibid., 501, 521, 525.

14. Ibid., 405.

15. *Fragmentary Remains, Literary and Scientific, of Sir Humphry Davy, Bart.*, ed. John Davy (London: J. Churchill, 1858), 64.

16. June Z. Fullmer, *Sir Humphry Davy's Published Works* (Cambridge: Harvard University Press, 1969), 30.

17. Maria Edgeworth to Mrs. Ruxton, 26 May 1799, in *Life and Letters of Maria Edgeworth*, ed. Augustus J. C. Hare (London: E. Arnold, 1894), 165–66.

18. Joseph Cottle, *Early Recollections, Chiefly Relating to the Late Samuel Taylor Coleridge*, 2 vols. (London: Longman Rees, 1837), 2:37.

19. William Paul Crillon Barton, *A Dissertation on the Chymical Properties and Exhilarating Effects of Nitrous Oxide Gas, and Its Application to Pneumatic Medicine, Submitted as an Inaugural Thesis for the Degree of Doctor of Medicine* (Philadelphia: Lorenzo, 1808), xiv.

20. Davy, *Researches*, 493.

21. Ibid., 308.

22. Ibid., 312.

23. Joseph Cottle, *Reminiscences of Samuel Taylor Coleridge and Robert Southey* (London: Houlston and Stoneman, 1847), 269–70.

24. Davy, *Researches*, 464, 478.

25. Within months of the opening of the Pneumatic Institute in 1798, the opinion prevailed among the patients that "they were merely made the subjects of experiment." Cottle, *Reminiscences*, 267, 270; See also "Review of Thomas Beddoes' *Notice of some Observations made at the Medical Pneumatic Institution*," *Anti-Jacobin Review and Magazine* 6 (1800): 424–28.

26. For discussion of a similar relationship between mesmerism and radical politics in France, see Robert Darnton, *Mesmerism and the End of the Enlightenment in France* (Cambridge: Harvard University Press, 1968), 83–125.

27. James Woodhouse, Barton's lecturer in chemistry at the University of Pennsylvania, performed nitrous oxide experiments upon his return from London in 1802, as did fellow lecturer in chemistry John Griscom in New York. Barton, *Dissertation*, 4, 51.

28. Barton's experiences typically began with a "warm glow" and sense of expansion in the chest followed by a "thrilling or titillating sensation that extended to every part of my frame." Subsequent feelings of "rapturous delight which then entranced my faculties" and an "indescribable extacy [sic]," he concluded, "*must* be what *angels* feel." Ibid., 55, 57.

29. Ibid., 59.

30. Ibid., 61.

31. Ibid., 74.

32. Ibid., 80.

33. Hoping that the gas could "invigorate memory and increase the quantum of genius in our country," Barton envisioned applications for nitrous oxide comparable to the longings of a young Dr. Frankenstein. Citing *The Life of Darwin* by Anna Seward, Barton refers to the transfusion of blood from young people and animals into old people as a precedent for such an application. Ibid., 82.

34. Davy, *Researches*, 528, 531.

35. *A Cursory Glimpse of the State of the Nation on the Twenty-Second of February, 1814, Being the Eighty-First Anniversary of the Birth of Washington, or A Physico-Politico-Theologico Lubrication upon the Wonderful Properties of Nitrous Oxide Newly Discovered Exhilirating Gas in Its Effects Upon the Human Mind and Body* (Philadelphia: Moses Thomas, 1814), 5.

36. Ibid., 8–9.

37. *New York Evening Post*, 7 March 1820, sec. 3, p. 1.

38. Ibid.

39. G. Foy, *Anaesthetics, Ancient and Modern* (London: Balliere, Tindall and Cox, 1889), 25–27, cited in Elizabeth A. M. Frost, "A History of Nitrous Oxide," in *Nitrous Oxide,* ed. Edmond I. Eger (New York: Elsevier, 1985), 9–10.

40. Women generally did not participate in public performances of laughing gas demonstrations until the 1830s and 1840s. Still, their attendance in the audience was crucial to legitimizing the exhibitions. For Preston's performances in New York, a single ticket admitted two women if accompanied by a man. Tickets were sold at the Ladies Literary Cabinet, and the Female Assistance Society sponsored one of the evening's demonstrations. *New York Evening Post*, 2 March 1821, sec. 3, p. 2; 4 March 1821, sec. 3, p. 1.

Although the single account of a woman inhaling the gas in Davy's *Researches* suggests that women responded to the gas by experiencing languor, Cottle's later account of the woman running out of the Pneumatic Institute indicates that women also responded to the gas with increased physical vigor, similar to that experienced by men. Cottle claims that this incident so appalled the other female patients at the Institute that they subsequently refused to inhale the gas. Davy, *Researches,* 530; Cottle, *Reminiscences,* 267, 268.

41. For further discussion of countersubversive movements, see David Brion Davis, "Some Themes of Counter-Subversion: An Analysis of Anti-Masonic, Anti-Catholic, and Anti-Mormon Literature," *Journal of American History* 47 (September 1960): 205–24.

42. For further discussion of the desire to discern true character in the era of the confidence man, see Karen Halttunen, *Confidence Men and Painted Women: A Study of Middle-Class Culture in America, 1830–1870* (New Haven: Yale University Press, 1982), 1–32.

43. Mikhail Bakhtin, *Rabelais and His World* (Cambridge: MIT Press, 1968), 9–12, 26, 423, 432–47; idem, *The Dialogic Imagination* (Austin: University of Texis Press, 1981), 36–37, 54–58; Dominick La Capra, *Rethinking Intellectual History: Texts, Contexts, Language* (Ithaca: Cornell University Press, 1983), 291–324.

44. *Cincinnati Gazette*, 3 October 1847, p. 2; 9 October 1847, p. 2.

45. *Pittsburgh Daily Gazette*, 1 September 1847, p. 2.

46. *Pittsburgh Daily Gazette*, 3 September 1847, p. 2.

47. *St. Louis Reveille*, 7 December 1847, p. 2.

48. *Pittsburgh Daily Gazette*, 1 September 1847, p. 2.

49. After inhaling the gas, explained one notice, the "restraints which usually hide the real character of the man, disappear." *Cist's Weekly Advertiser* (Cincinnati), 12 October 1847, p. 2.

50. Ibid.

51. *The Daily Union* (St. Louis), 20 December 1847, p. 2.

52. *Mobile Register and Journal*, 5 April 1848, p. 2.

53. *Daily Commercial Journal* (Pittsburgh), 2 September 1847, p. 2; *Cist's Weekly Advertiser* (Cincinnati), 12 October 1847, p. 2.

54. *Daily Commercial Journal* (Pittsburgh), 2 September 1847, p. 2.

55. Ibid.

56. *Cist's Weekly Advertiser* (Cincinnati), 12 October 1847, p. 2.

57. *Daily Commercial Journal* (Pittsburgh), 2 September 1847, p. 2.

58. *New-York Tribune*, 19 December 1845, p. 2.

59. Frost, "History of Nitrous Oxide," 11–14.

60. For analysis of the cultural implication of these codes of conduct, see Ann Fairfax Withington, *Towards a More Perfect Union* (New York: Oxford University Press, 1994).

NINE

Photography and Persuasion: Farm Security Administration Photographs of Circus and Carnival Sideshows, 1935–1942

RONALD E. OSTMAN

Persons who differ from the physical norm have been exhibited throughout history (Thompson 1931), and the reaction of viewers has run the gamut from revulsion to terror to sympathy to awe to mirth. Aristotle taught that persons who are considered "human oddities" were *lusus naturae,* or "jokes of nature" (Fiedler 1978). Those who accepted this explanation reacted to viewings with amusement and were inclined to tease and mock. Those subscribing to supernatural or religious views sometimes saw a satanic or sinful ontogeny and felt justified in killing, torture, and cruelty. Others saw the uniqueness of human oddities as a possible sign of supernatural or divine intervention and/or favor.

When human oddities have been exhibited, persons from all stations of life have been willing to pay for the privilege of viewing. For the most part, potential viewers were fascinated with the idea of what they were promised but remained skeptical. Therefore, persuasion usually was necessary in order to extract payments from them. Sometimes persuasion was necessary only at first—once a few people had viewed the promised sights they could be counted upon to spread the word, thus reducing others' reluctance and reticence. Exhibitors of human oddities in circus or carnival sideshows during the early twentieth century faced genuine resistance from potential viewers, who were very skeptical of the sideshow's honesty. It usually was necessary to show them a taste of the real thing to persuade them to buy a ticket to see the whole show. Because of the ever-changing nature of the transitory, milling crowds, it was necessary to continually convince potential customers to pay to see the promised human oddities of the sideshow.

RECENT HISTORICAL BACKDROP

In the New World, itinerant promoters of human oddities toured from tavern to tavern, inn to inn. The first human oddity to be exhibited in the United States was a "maiden dwarf," Miss Emma Leach, who was shown in Boston in 1771 for one shilling a visit (Durant and Durant 1957). The practice stabilized and became an institution when Phineas Taylor

Barnum established his American Museum in 1842, collecting at one permanent site a group of human oddities for paid exhibition. Thus, the crowds came to the human oddities rather than vice versa. Barnum expanded upon this theme, creating both location-bound exhibits and traveling shows for the next fifty years. Michael Mitchell (1979) notes that private dime museums featuring human oddities could be found throughout the growing urban areas of the United States after the Civil War, and that the rapid expansion of the railroad system permitted fast and widespread travel of human oddities to ever more remote areas, often to their vast financial benefit. During this same period, the classic American circus was formulated, and elaborate touring shows invariably carried a sideshow exhibition of human oddities. By the end of the nineteenth century, however, small-town preachers and editors were complaining quite loudly about the proliferating tent shows that infiltrated county fairs (Sears, Belsky, and Tunstell, 1975).

The invention of photography by French physicist Joseph Nicéphore Niepce in 1824 and the subsequent improvements leading to commercial practicality by Louis Daguerre in 1837 led to its rapid expansion shortly thereafter (Becker and Roberts 1992). Most people were willing to accept as objective and true any evidence that was captured by photography. Photographs removed some of the doubt from the population's beliefs concerning human oddities, but because they revealed so much they were not often used as a means of promoting human oddity exhibits. Artistic renditions of human oddities, often exaggerated and romanticized, continued to be the norm. Therefore, the exhibitor still faced the challenge of convincing potential paying customers that what could be seen for a fee was bona fide.

Another use of photography was of direct benefit to exhibitors and human oddities. Many human oddities were photographed and had *carte de visite* or *cabinet* portraits produced by the bulk lot, individual copies of which were sold to exhibit viewers as souvenirs (Coleman 1977). Not only did this increase the income beyond the initial entrance fee, it also provided the possibility of yet a third fee if the viewer wanted the photographic copy autographed (assuming the human oddity was able to do so, of course). Moreover, the photographs helped sell future exhibition tickets once the purchasers took them back out on the streets and into their neighborhoods and homes. Here was evidence that the phenomenon was real and that when one bought a ticket to see it, one wouldn't be tricked or taken for a sucker.

FARM SECURITY ADMINISTRATION PHOTOGRAPHY

The Farm Security Administration (FSA) was a New Deal government agency. It grew out of the Resettlement Administration, begun in 1935 to resettle poor farm families away from their worn-out land, and to make grants and loans for new starts. Ultimately, the Resettlement Agency evolved into the FSA, which had the general mission of assisting farmers and others associated with agriculture — including migrant workers, sharecroppers, tenant farmers, and experimental communalists — who were in economic trouble because of the depression. The Historical Division of the FSA was charged with the responsibility of photographing government activities toward that end. Only a handful of photographers were hired during the agency's existence from 1935 to 1942, but they were among the best documentary photographers working in the United States. Some quarter of a million images were made over that period, some of which have achieved icon status (Stott 1986; Zakia 1993).

Roy Stryker, head of the FSA Historical Division, said in 1935 that "it might be appropriate to gather together a collection of photographs of all aspects of American rural life, with [an] emphasis on what had gone wrong: deforestation, soil erosion, migrant fruit pickers, and hungry children" (Guimond 1991, 110). By the early 1940s, Stryker was telling his photographers to take positive photos that showed the successes of New Deal programs and the strength of the American people and land. His photographers were only too happy to oblige. They were seeing many interesting and stimulating things during their journeys, and they were creative and independent artists who sometimes resented being told exactly what type of dull, unimaginative photograph to take by some regional FSA worker who wanted publicity in a local newspaper.

State and county fairs were a natural venue for FSA photographers on the prowl for photos that would satisfy Stryker's desire to show American farming and life *au naturel*. There, images could be made of prize livestock, new farming equipment, crafts, food preservation, and a myriad of topics that fit the practical needs of the FSA Historical Division. More importantly, for present purposes, state and county fairs also featured circuses and carnivals, which offered human oddity sideshows as a regular part of their entertainment. The FSA files contain many images of these sideshows. The ten images shown here were taken by a variety of photographers in various U.S. locations during the years 1938–42. Based on these images we can reconstruct the process of persuasion right up until the customer stepped inside to see the real show. Anecdotal evidence permits a further understanding of what happened once the ticket was collected.

Suckers/Towners

P. T. Barnum reportedly said, "There's a sucker born every minute." He spoke the right lingo, according to Joe McKennon (1980), who lived the life of a circus trouper and made an effort to preserve circus and carnival language. McKennon's dictionary permits us to reconstruct what is going on in the FSA photographs. In figure 9.1, for example, Arthur Rothstein photographed seven men waiting for . . . well, waiting. They're in Marshalltown, Iowa, in September 1939, at the Central Iowa 4-H Club Fair. Seeing the Reynolds & Wells United Show's "Oddities of the World" sideshow banner (which the troupers sometimes called "valentines") before they sat down was exciting and almost exotic considering they spent the summer farming, small-town clerking, or maybe banking. Not that any of them intend to see the human oddities: the half-crab-half-human, the two-headed-one-bodied baby, the four-legged woman, the Siamese twins, the jungle woman with the huge disk lips, the mermaid, the human-with-a-mule-face, or the dwarf (called "runts" by circus and carnival folk). They figure the show probably has a lot of fakes. Besides, with 9.4 million Americans (17.2 percent of the workforce) still unemployed a decade after the Great Depression began, a dime is something you don't throw away (McElvaine 1993). These, then, are the "suckers" or "towners" that circus and carnival folk will soon convince that "one thin dime, the tenth part of a dollar" is a trifle and that the world oddities inside the midway tent are well worth the cost of a ticket. How is that accomplished?

9.1. Marshalltown, Iowa, September 1939. The Central Iowa 4-H fair. A show on the midway. Photo by Arthur Rothstein. U.S. Farm Security Administration Collection, Prints and Photographs Division, Library of Congress.

THE TALKER TROUPERS

The search for money drives the circus and carnival workers. Their language is spiced with references to "jitneys" (nickels), "dimers," "quaters," and so on. Many spend most of their idle hours fishing in their "grouch bags" or "pokes" (the place where they keep their cash) for the "blanket game" (gambling with other show folks). If they are lucky enough to leave their gambling with any money, they are said to be "holding." If they are broke and are forced to live on credit from the show's management, they are "on the burr" or "on the nut." When they are asked to "up it," they are being requested to pay back what they owe (with an implied "or else"). Everyone is constantly on the lookout for "queer" (counterfeit money). Day in and day out, they have to "crack the nut," meaning there are the daily expenses to be made before a profit can be counted from the "take." Since they're only in the area for a few days before moving on to the next location, they aren't particularly scrupulous in how they "work on the suckers" (and empty the "natives'" pockets, if possible). If it takes a bit of dishonesty, well, then it takes a bit of dishonesty. In their lingo, they will "work strong" (do what it takes) to accomplish their goal.

In fact, many of the human oddities are legitimate. For example, there really *is* a four-legged woman who will help "clean" the patrons. But the suckers only think they're seeing a mermaid. That little piece of thievery will help "skin" the "sucks" slick and clean. Figure 9.2, a photograph made by Jack Délano at the Vermont State Fair in Rutland, September 1941, features a "single-o," or single attraction that probably is legitimate. Pictured is a "talker" (also

9.2. Rutland, Vermont, September 1941. A sideshow at the Vermont State Fair. Photo by Jack Delano. U.S. Farm Security Administration Collection, Prints and Photographs Division, Library of Congress

known as a "spieler" or "grinder") dressed in a nurse's uniform. She is trying to "turn the tip" (convince the patrons that what she says is truthful, that there really is a "first in medical history" inside the tent, and that they should pay their dime to see the Strong twins). The "nurse" talks smoothly about the "blessed event" that led to the "world's most famous twins" and invites the tip to meet their mother inside. She assures the patrons that the twins are alive and cites confidence-building information as printed by the *Sunday News*. "One has brown eyes, one has blue," she claims. "One is a caucasian baby and the other one is negroid. They were born one right after the other, from the same mother, less than ten minutes apart." The single-o talker relies heavily on her charismatic ability to gain the tip's trust, because there will be no "ballyhoo" (a short free show on the platform prior to ticket sale). The tip has to be turned with words alone.

Many sideshows combined this mixture of entertainment and seemingly scientific information. Often, such a show would have a second person inside, called a "lecturer," who would deliver a talk that simulated an educational classroom, with the patrons as students. These "educational" shows were photographed by FSA photographers along with the other sideshows. Their banners described "The Unborn" or "Life Unborn," for example. The unborn usually consisted of fetuses preserved in jars. Often these were abnormal and malformed fetuses, such as two-headed babies and conjoined twins, born prematurely or aborted, and unceremoniously called "pickled punks" in private by the troupers. Other shows of this genre included "The Hall of Science" (which presented a talk on whether or not "Dr. Carrell & Col. Lindbergh will be able to grow human beings in bottles. 40 people from all nations. Can it penetrate the eternal mystery of life? Here is science's supreme adventure.") The same Hall of Science promised an examination of the "Sins of Marriage" and presented "Beautiful Princess Mary, the Shrunken Headed Girl." It also was dedicated to "Exposing Birth Control" and featured "Dr. R. Garfield, Robt. L. Ripley's 'Believe It Or Not' The Man Without a Skull. Alive." If that wasn't enough, the patron would also learn "The Laws of Nature" while attending to "Knowledge Concerning Life." If the patron was still not convinced, a sign promised the *pièce de résistance:* "Extra! Delivered by Dr. Sterling. Added attraction. Clinton Mystery. Twins born to live. 3 heads 2 bodies. Born Clinton, N.C. June 12, 1935. Baffled medical science." All this could be had for only ten cents, the tenth part of a dollar.

THE BALLYHOO

The ballyhoo or "bally" gives the crowd enough of a taste of the real thing to stimulate their appetite for more, which could be satisfied inside the tent for ten, fifteen, or twenty cents. The bally consists of a free show outside the sideshow tent to attract a crowd and to convince them that what is inside will be even more elaborate, spectacular, and irresistible. "Tomorrow, we'll be gone," the talker says, "and your friends and neighbors will be bragging about what they've seen in here today and you'll be sorry if you don't go inside. Tomorrow all that'll be left is wagon tracks and empty popcorn sacks. Only a dime! Surely, you can spare a dime to see these spectacular wonders of the world!" In Figure 9.3, also taken by Délano at the Vermont State Fair, the talker points to the banner, referring to the amazing sights inside. To his right stand two human oddities and to his left a "pinhead" (microcephalic). This is part of the World of Mirth sideshow, which features "strange human freaks alive"—the third sex family, the backward boy, Boko the alligator skin boy, Zip and Pip the pinheads, and Betty Williams, the genuine double-bodied girl with four legs ("Alive! Not in a bottle, not a trick!"), among other attractions. The pinhead's hair has been shaved to show the upward sloping volcanic-shaped skull. A small tuft of hair at the very pinnacle is tied up with a bow so that the hair spills over like lava. The backward boy to the talker's right is Demetrio Ortiz, listed in Ripley's "Believe It Or Not" as "the only man living who can twist his body completely around while his feet remain stationary. When the lower half of his body is facing in one direction, the other half is in the opposite direction, and he can walk in that position. Señor Ortiz is from Mexico."

While showing the bally, the talker delivers a steady stream of words, modulating his tone up and down the scale. He refers to the human oddities on the platform and describes their actions, and marvels on the wonders that they are yet to do inside the tent. He also refers frequently to the banners behind them: "That's the way she looks, ladies and gents, boys and girls! You'll find them on the inside just as they are represented on the canvas! Step right up and the gentlemanly usher will escort you to points of vantage! One thin dime, the tenth part of a dollar!" Sometimes, the bally would feature others from among the human oddities. When dwarfs were on the platform, the talker would say: "Now, ladies and gentlemen, boys and girls, if you please, step over here and see the world's tiniest people. Note the yardstick—an accurate, an exact, a perfectly calibrated instrument against which to measure the height of these minuscule humans, some of them members of the foreign titled aristocracy! (Step forward, Count, and you too, Baron, and stand by the yardstick.) Each and every one of these

9.3. Rutland, Vermont, September 1941. Outside a freak show at the Vermont State Fair. Photo by Jack Délano. U.S. Farm Security Administration Collection, Prints and Photographs Division, Library of Congress.

9.4. Donaldsonville, Louisiana, November 1938. A talker at a sideshow with human oddities at the South Louisiana State Fair. Photo by Russell Lee. U.S. Farm Security Administration Collection, Prints and Photographs Division, Library of Congress.

little people, ladies and gentlemen, girls and boys, is a full-grown human being! (Thank you, Count. Thank you, Baron.)"[1]

Figure 9.4 provides a closer view of the talker and his bally review. This image was made by Russell Lee in Donaldsonville, Louisiana, in November 1938. The only pictured bally performer for whom information exists is the man in a Native American feathered headdress at the talker's far right, who was identified in a different photo as "an Indian glass eater." The banner shows the English bulldog girl on all fours coming out of a doghouse. Also pictured are a three-legged woman, pinheads, a doubled-bodied man, midgets, a thin man, and a fat woman. Part of a drum can be seen at the far right edge of the photo.

A drum also can be seen in figure 9.5, immediately behind the talker. Drums often were used as attention-getters during the initial portion of the spiel, hence the expression "drumming up business." The banner in the background shows an armless, legless woman, a double-bodied man, a three-legged man, Siamese twins, and midgets, among other unidentifiable human oddities. The double-bodied man image appears to be based on a photograph of Jean and Jacques Libbera, born in Rome in 1884 and shown by Barnum and Bailey in the United States as early as 1907. Whether Jean and Jacques were part of this particular sideshow of "freaks, strange people, oddities" is unknown. Equally mysterious in this photo are the evidently humorous comments being made by the talker and the strange demeanor of the woman with a cloth covering her head. Other photographs in the series, made by Russell Lee at Klamath Falls, Oregon, in July 1942, show that she remained rigid throughout the spiel. Detail in the additional photos also reveals that this particular sideshow was labeled an "Odd 'i' torium" and featured attractions from "past and present," including a bearded lady, midget oriental dancers, and an elephant-skinned man.

Obese people in the "fat show" have always been crowd pleasers. Perhaps more than other human oddities, these individuals have been held accountable by the public for their physical condition. The popular criticism has been that they are obese because they eat too much. However, Tom Ogden (1993) offers a more charitable explanation that they suffer from hormonal imbalances. There is evidence that the condition is familial. Jack Délano's photo of one member of the "world's fattest family," taken in Rutland, Vermont, in September 1941 (fig. 9.6) shows an individual who does not look terribly obese to the modern eye. The banner for this particular sideshow depicts "Sister Violet" at 531 pounds, "Mother" at 648 pounds, "Father" at 702 pounds, "Baby Ruth" at 409 pounds, "Brother Bill" at 518 pounds, and "Brother Burvia," whose weight is not visible in the image. They are, the banner says, "Just one big fat family." The banner further depicts them as a musical family—Burvia holds a saxophone, Violet plays the drums, father holds a trumpet, Baby Ruth strums a guitar, Bill plays a horn, and mother is seated at the piano, presumably on a reinforced piano seat. They will, the talker promises as he points to a sign, perform "ten big vaudeville acts. Ten! The family sings 'Hello Everybody.' Willie does a whistling solo. Ruth favors you with a tap dance. Burvia gives a stirring sax solo. Ruth follows with an acrobatic number. Not to be left out, Ma and Pa will dance. Sibling rivalry? The fat family's got it and Will and Burr will have a boxing match. Violet calms things down with a Hawaiian hula so realistic you'll think you're on Waikiki Beach with soft ocean breezes and the fragrant scent of flowers. Ruth provides a soulful song of blues. And last, certainly not least! Will and Violet show you how the jellyrolls shake with a fast, modern jitterbug! Oh, you won't want to miss it. We've had to bring in structural engineers to figure out how to hold up the stage floor with all that blubber shaking

9.5. Klamath Falls, Oregon, July 1942. Sideshow at the circus. Photo by Russell Lee. U.S. Farm Security Administration Collection, Prints and Photographs Division, Library of Congress.

9.6. Rutland, Vermont, September 1941. A fat man at the Vermont State Fair. Photo by Jack Délano. U.S. Farm Security Administration Collection, Prints and Photographs Division, Library of Congress.

and shifting, putting such a strain on that poor floor. Fat? I'll say! Talented? You bet! Six people and more than 3,500 pounds. Use your fourth grade math. That's *an average* of nearly 600 pounds each. How much does *your* family weigh? You'll be lucky if your family weighs an average of 150 pounds per individual. See them quiver and shake! I don't even want to tell you how much food this family consumes on a regular day. And Thanksgiving? Oh, my! Thanksgiving they eat enough to keep a small town fed for several days! Oh, you won't want to miss it. You can't miss it. You shan't miss it, either, for the price of fifteen cents adults, ten cents for children under twelve. Let your children see this show, ladies and gentlemen. Let it be an object lesson to them. Imagine, ten big vaudeville acts, at a cost of only one cent per act for the kiddies, a penny and a half per act for the adults. The fat family. See them now. You'll never see a fatter family in all your born days. You'll remember this act, folks, long after you've forgotten everything else that transpired here today! Oh! They are fat. So terribly, terribly, terrifically fat."

Marion Post Wolcott's March 1939 photo of "Dolly Dimples, Personality Fat Girl" (fig. 9.7) was taken at the Strawberry Festival and Carnival, Plant City, Florida. Dolly is posed as an odalisque, reclining on billowy soft pillows and couch. Gauze and veils do a flimsy job in attempting to cover her ample, suggestive body. Personality girl or not, however, Dolly is daily insulted, as the adjacent banner depicts. A taxi driver responds to her wave for a ride with the curt, "You can never get in the door. You will have to ride in a truck." In another banner, shown in a different photo, Dolly is being measured by a tailor for a dress. He wraps a fabric around her, exclaiming, "Just one more bolt of cloth will make it." Dolly traveled a far-flung circuit. FSA photographer Ben Shahn photographed these banners earlier at a county fair in Central Ohio in August 1938. She did not command the price that Délano's fat family did, however. The posted price at the ticket seller's booth was ten cents for adults and five cents for children.

Another group of human oddities was what Ogden (1993) calls "self-made freaks," such as tattooed people, glass eaters, human pincushions, sword swallowers, and so on. Preying on people's almost universal revulsion for rats, bats, snakes, and the like, the "geek" shown in figure 9.8 presumably earned his living by tearing the flesh from snakes and eating it. This (purportedly) African man, who in all other respects appeared "normal," was part of a sideshow cleverly labeled with large lettering proclaiming "Believe It Or Not" on the top line and, in equally large lettering, "A Ripley Show" on the bottom line. The casual viewer probably didn't see the middle line, in much smaller lettering, which said, "this is not." The come-on for this Congo show, as it was known, sounded like this: "This man, ladies and gentlemen, girls and boys, looks like an ordinary person." (The man shuffles onto the stage for the bally, smiling a simpleton's blank smile.) "He was brought to this country from the Congo in deepest, darkest Africa some years ago. And while we've been able to dress the savage up like a person you might meet on the street, I want you to know he's no ordinary man. No. Beneath those clothes of civilization lies a jungle beast who has refused to eat what you or I might prefer." (Here, the "savage" reaches into a box and withdraws a long snake, which is nearly as long as he is and as round as his wrist. The talker shudders with distaste and grimaces.) "No, he never learned to appreciate the taste of civilized food." (The talker, who had been looking away from the man, now looks at him and immediately increases the volume and pace of his delivery.) "HE IS GOING TO EAT ... CAN IT BE? LADIES AND GENTLEMEN, GIRLS AND BOYS, I THINK HE'S GOING TO *eat that snake!* oh oh oh my my my ...

9.7. Plant City, Florida, March 1939. A Strawberry Festival and Carnival fat lady show banner. Photo by Marion Post Wolcott. U.S. Farm Security Administration Collection, Prints and Photographs Division, Library of Congress.

9.8. Donaldsonville, Louisiana, November 1938. A man chewing a piece of snake which he has just bitten off at the South Louisiana State Fair. Photo by Russell Lee. U.S. Farm Security Administration Collection, Prints and Photographs Division, Library of Congress.

he's going to . . . is he? I think he is. Oh how terrible!" The man caresses the snake. He licks the snake's skin. He gingerly places the snake in his mouth, taking care to grasp it just behind the head. His free arm comes up. You can see him grinning even as he tightens his jaw muscles. Then, he releases the snake from his mouth and playfully shoves it toward those in the front row of the crowd. They push back. "Aren't you going to eat that snake?" The talker seems both relieved and annoyed at the same time. The man turns toward the talker, allowing the crowd to press forward again. "Ain't you hungry? I thought you said you was hungry?" The talker chides the man, who continues to hold the snake. The audience can't tell if the snake is alive or not, because the man keeps moving it. "If you're going to eat that snake, EAT IT! YOU DON'T NEED TO TEASE THESE GOOD FOLKS!" The talker's voice becomes more strident. The man grasps the snake with his other hand and brings it toward his mouth. His white teeth glisten, showing a gap where a front tooth is missing. The diamond texture of the snake is clearly visible. The man again thrusts the snake toward his mouth in a sudden motion, shutting his eyes as he bites and tears flesh with an audible grunt, then rips the snake away from his mouth in a spasmodic, writhing snarl. He moves quickly about the stage, holding the coiling snake, which he finally throws back into the box. In his mouth is a bloody piece of snake. He chews, grinning, bloody red liquid flowing down from the corners of his mouth, oozing down his chin, inching closer and closer to that nice white shirt he's wearing. Some in the audience look as if they might be sick as they search for handkerchiefs, their cheeks puffing out, lips tightly together, and their heads bobbing forward. With a final snarl, the "Congo savage" disappears behind a canvas flap. "There he goes, there he goes. But he only got one good bite. He'll be wanting more to eat when you see him inside the tent, ladies and gentlemen, girls and boys. He'll eat more snakes. Oh?! Did I tell you that he also eats rats and bats and mice and lice and bites the heads off live chickens?" (Thus the man was not only a geek, but a "gloamer," a "gloaming geek.") "Oh, yes. If you had trouble believing what you just saw, what your eyes just told you, well, you're going to be absolutely flabbergasted what you see on the inside!" Thus, the talker begins his windup, pushing toward the final sell, the clincher, the closer that will separate the suckers from their dimes.

SHILLS AND TICKET SELLERS

When it comes time to move the tip from rapt bally audience to ticket purchasers, the talker tries to rely on whatever energy he can whip up when ending the bally. This done, the stage empty, the human oddities all back inside the tent, only the ticket seller stands between the crowd and the show inside (see fig. 9.9). The natural human impulse under these conditions, unfortunately for the ticket seller, is inertia. For that reason, circuses and carnivals used "shills," individuals who dig for their dimes and move to "purchase" a ticket. The crowd, seeing brave souls move forward to buy the first tickets, moves lemming-like into line as the talker continues: "Now, don't push, ladies and gentlemen, boys and girls. There's room inside for everyone, including the family dog if you happen to have brought Fido along, and the show won't start until you're all safely inside. Just watch the speed of that ticket seller! Say, here's a show in itself. Just see how fast he can sell those tickets!" The talker has two purposes for talking up the ticket seller's speed. One is to get people in line so they can see for themselves how fast he is. The other, hardly surprising perhaps, is to assist the ticket seller in bilking the crowd by practicing "short cake." Patrons will be short changed by the ticket seller,

9.9. Central Ohio. Selling tickets to the county fair sideshow. Photo by Ben Shahn. U.S. Farm Security Administration Collection, Prints and Photographs Division, Library of Congress.

who also often is a "grinder," taking up the banter as the talker trails off. This is done several ways. In a "grift show," where the entire circus or carnival operation is set up to clean the suckers, ticket boxes are purposely built high to prevent the patron from seeing the change as it is laid down (never counted). Sometimes, change inadvertently will be left on top of the ticket box by customers (who are then called "walkaways"). Change is made with one hand for the first customer, tickets are torn with the other hand for a second customer, while at the same time the ticket seller is asking a third patron "How many, please?" If the ticket seller hands the money to a patron (again, never counting it), it is almost certain that he is "duking" them. Because of the distraction and confusion of the "speed show," the ticket seller can get away with "clipping" or "cloating" the entire line of patrons. In the event that an earlier patron counts his or her change and finds it short, it will be difficult to interfere with the speed selling show and the mob of moving customers. If the short-changed sucker makes a fuss nonetheless, he or she probably will be reimbursed for the amount declared missing, but in such a way as to discount their claim and to chide them for spoiling the ticket selling show.

ON THE INSIDE

There are two basic physical layouts for the human oddities sideshow. One is the "pit." Typically, this is a small (eight- or ten-foot square) canvas enclosure where human oddities are exhibited and do a "pit show." Spectators stand around the four sides and look down. The other layout is the "platform show." Customers walk up to see the human oddities, sometimes traversing a "walk over bally." Circuses and carnivals generally find that this more elaborate setup does more business, because the customers themselves are on view from the outside. Sometimes, it takes customers to "take" customers (bring in cash from a performance). As a final ploy to bilk patrons, the most spectacular of the promised events sometimes are available for viewing only if an additional fee is paid once inside and once the regular show is concluded. This is the "blowoff" and might feature, for example, a naked fat lady or a viewing of the private parts of a "half-and-half" (hermaphrodite). The blowoff event is never promised in advance and is suggested only after the patron has had his or her appetite whetted for a "special" that is not part of the regular show.

On the outside, the talker judges when the crowd inside has thinned sufficiently to begin to attract a new crowd. "It's never over. It's never out. Round and round the sideshow goes, when we'll stop, nobody knows. What's that young man? You say, 'What's that hole in the platform?' There's no trapdoor in the platform, young man. You want the people to see the hole in the platform? Well, if you want to see it, folks, you'll have to come in nice and close." (Pause.) "Thanks for coming in real close, folks. But I told you, son: It's not a trapdoor. No, it's just a knot hole. But thanks for coming in close, because we have an amazing show here today."

The Demise of the Sideshow

With the death of the large traveling circuses and the death throes of the smaller carnivals in the late 1950s, coupled with growing sentiment against public exhibition of those deemed "less fortunate," the old sideshow seen in figures 9.1 through 9.9 is largely extinct. For awhile, the economics were such that relatively stationary "museums" of the same basic content (see fig. 9.10) were able to survive in larger population centers. With the museum, the old talker had disappeared, replaced by window displays, neon signs, and "point of purchase" exhibits promising "living oddities," "big acts," and "all alive freaks" to capture patrons' interest.

Essentially, however, the days of human oddities attractions were over.

> Most freaks never felt themselves to be outcasts, surely not monsters. Some considered themselves quite "special" or "touched by God." In the latter 20th century, however, public sympathies largely turned against the exhibition of the human eccentricities, and laws were passed in many states barring the display of humans. As the same time, many circuses were moving into arenas or, at the very least, abandoning their sideshows due to escalating costs. Although some indoor shows continued to carry a sideshow for a few years, by the time John Ringling North made his historic 1956 announcement that the days of the tented circus were over, the heyday of the "freak show" was already a part of the circus's past." (Ogden 1993, 167)

To the end of the exhibition of a long cast of human oddities stretching over centuries, some would say, "Good riddance." Others, however, look back at that era and see positives. The FSA and other documentary photographs remain to inform us of a common cultural event experienced with some degree of humor and affection by many past generations of Americans. Stryker perhaps said it best in a letter to Russell Lee in October 1937: "But I know that you and I share an urge alike, that is, a desire to photograph the whole United

9.10. Norfolk, Virginia, March 1941. West Main Street World Fairs Freak Museum entrance. Photo by John Vachon. U.S. Farm Security Administration Collection, Prints and Photographs Division, Library of Congress.

States at once. I have a feeling that if we don't do it this year, it may blow away by next" (Fern and Worth 1985, 130).

NOTE

1. The talkers' quotes are taken, with slight modifications, from McCullough's (1957) book on Coney Island. Many circus and carnival troupers found themselves at Coney Island from time to time. Other talkers' quotes stem from Durant and Durant (1957) and Ogden (1993). Still others are from the author's imagination.

REFERENCES

Becker, Samuel L., and Churchill L. Roberts. 1992. *Discovering Mass Communication*. New York: HarperCollins.

Coleman, Allan D. 1977. *The Grotesque in Photography*. New York: Ridge Press and Summit Books.

Durant, John, and Alice Durant. 1957. *Pictorial History of the American Circus*. New York: A. S. Barnes.

Fern, Alan, and William Worth. 1985. "Taking Photographs of the History of Today." In William Worth, ed., *Russell Lee's FSA Photographs of Chamisal and Peñasco New Mexico*. Santa Fe: Ancient City Press.

Fiedler, Leslie. 1978. *Freaks: Myths and Images of the Secret Self*. New York: Simon and Schuster.

Guimond, James. 1991. *American Photography and the American Dream*. Chapel Hill: University of North Carolina Press.

McCullough, Edo. 1957. *Good Old Coney Island: A Sentimental Journey into the Past.* New York: Charles Scribner's Sons.

McElvaine, Robert S. 1993. *The Great Depression: America, 1929–1941.* New York: Times Books.

McKennon, Joe. 1980. *Circus Lingo.* Sarasota, Fla.: Carnival Publishers.

Mitchell, Michael. 1979. *Monsters of the Gilded Age: The Photographs of Charles Eisenmann.* Toronto: Gage.

Ogden, Tom. 1993. *Two Hundred Years of the American Circus: From Aba-Daba to the Zoppe-Zavatta Troupe.* New York: Facts on File.

Sears, Stephen W., Murray Belsky, and Douglas Tunstell. 1975. *Hometown U.S.A.: America at the Turn of the Century.* New York: Barnes and Noble.

Stott, William. 1986. *Documentary Expression and Thirties America.* Chicago: University of Chicago Press.

Thompson, C. J. S. 1931. *The Mystery and Lore of Monsters: With Account of Some Giants, Dwarfs and Prodigies.* New York: Macmillan.

Zakia, Richard. 1993. "Farm Security Administration (FSA)." In Leslie Stroebel and Richard Zakia, eds., *The Focal Encyclopedia of Photography.* Boston: Focal Press.

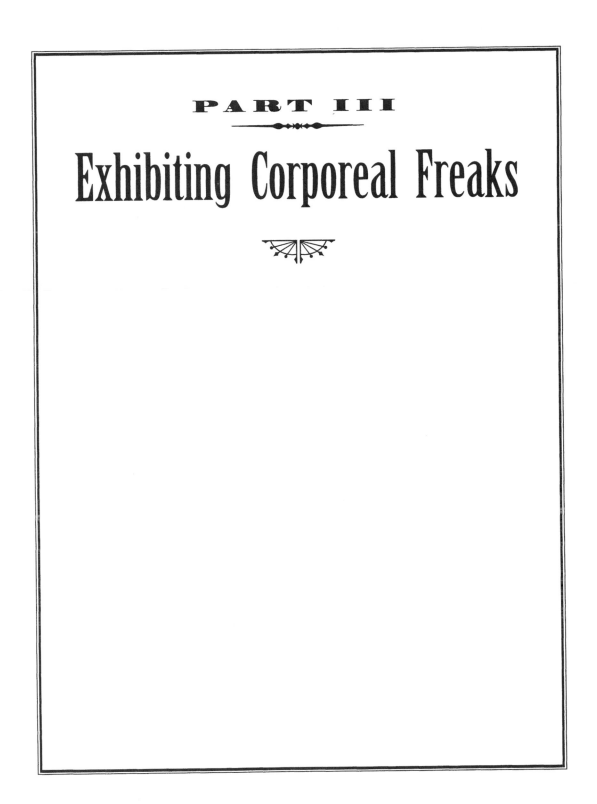

PART III

Exhibiting Corporeal Freaks

Of Men, Missing Links, and Nondescripts: The Strange Career of P. T. Barnum's "What is It?" Exhibition

JAMES W. COOK, JR.

For some days past, all the brick piles in the City—which, by the way are neither few nor far between—have been postered with a pertinacious query, printed in extremely interrogative type and to the effect: "What is It?" The public knowing by long experience that an answer would be vouchsafed in due time, waited, and on Monday received light from Barnum's Museum. The proprietors of that establishment, it seems, have secured what they are pleased to term a nondescript.

—*New York Times*, 5 MARCH 1860

Over the course of his long nineteenth-century career as showman, P. T. Barnum employed a wide range of exhibition strategies, each conceived with one grand design: to seize the public's "curiosity," to make people look, think, wonder, and talk about his productions—and, above all, to pay him for these privileges.[1] During the early 1850s, this considerable promotional energy focused on the Swedish opera singer Jenny Lind, whom Barnum hoped to convince New Yorkers was both the world's greatest soprano and the very model of virtuous Victorian womanhood. The goal here, as he later explained, was to consolidate public opinion around a particular set of cultural values, to locate the European star's extraordinary, but as yet unheard, vocal talents within a nexus of aggressively advertised, generally agreed upon claims of character.[2] As was often the case, Barnum's offering proved enormously persuasive: before a single note had been sung, thousands of New Yorkers cheered Lind's arrival at the docks and followed her every move around the city.[3]

On numerous other occasions, however, Barnum went to great pains *not* to tell his audience what to think, opting instead to maintain a highly visible, self-effacing silence in the middle of heated popular controversy. Was Joice Heth (1835) the 161-year-old nurse of George Washington or simply an elderly African-American woman who told amusing stories? Did the Feejee Mermaid (1842) prove the existence of a long-rumored mythological creature or merely demonstrate some artisan's skillful fusion of monkey and fish? Was the Colorado Giant (1878) a petrified example of prehistoric man or a recently manufactured piece of plaster, planted in the ground suspiciously near the showman's Western property? Again and again, Barnum circulated stories supporting *both* positions, feigned ignorance on his own behalf, and deferred to viewers for answers. These perplexing questions were, as his ubiquitous advertisements insisted, "for the public to decide."

It was this second, nondidactic mode of "exciting" popular curiosity—the carefully produced, deliberately unsolved visual *riddle*—that Barnum turned to once again in February 1860, as he put into place what was perhaps the most complex, daring, and (to our eyes at least) disturbingly cruel enterprise of his long tenure as manager of the American Museum: the exhibition, or rather series of exhibitions, that appeared under the banner, "What is It?" (fig. 10.1). Even for the self-proclaimed "Prince of Humbug," the timing of this debut was remarkably bold. Coming only three months after the publication of Darwin's *Origin of Species*, Barnum promoted his new, dark-skinned performer as a possible "missing link" between man and animal—an intriguing, though potentially heretical, idea in late antebellum America. Yet, as both the showman and his audience clearly understood, such complicated "scientific" questions also quickly spilled over into even more controversial questions of racial definition, politics, and property. If man was perhaps descended from animals, what were the implications of suggesting that the "proof" of this descent had the face of "a full blooded African?"[4] Did such proof ultimately affirm the "brutishness" of those with dark skin, and thus the legitimacy of their political and economic subjugation? Or did it establish instead a fundamental commonality—at least on some abstract, prehistoric level—between "What is It?" and the thousands of white New Yorkers who flocked to see him? What, if any, political function might these playful public deliberations about race and human definition have served during the first months of 1860, as a whole host of equally complex and racially charged "sectionalist" controversies pushed the country closer and closer to full-blown warfare?

Precisely because of its proximity to these interconnected theological, scientific, legal, and political debates, "What is It?" carried the potential for generating both lucrative public excitement or, if handled recklessly, intense public condemnation. Barnum thus chose his terms carefully. The figure that appeared at the American Museum, he explained to New Yorkers, was simply "indescribable"—neither "man" nor "monkey," a creature demonstrating characteristics "animal" as well as "human," "civilized" as well as "brutish." It was, as his relentless stream of promotional materials insisted, a *nondescript*: a "living curiosity" in need of more precise classification, yet remarkably resistant to the management's "best efforts" to do so. While numerous previous American Museum promotions had banked on such winking seductions, this new attraction elevated the showman's calculated imprecision to new heights. In both its name ("What is It?") and its ingeniously evasive classification-type ("nondescript"), Barnum's early 1860 hybrid both literally and figuratively begged the public to fill in the blanks.

"What is It?": The Actors, Barnum's Character, Its Category

Perhaps the most disturbing feature of the eighty-year history of "What is It" is that we simply do not always know with certainty who was standing on the exhibition platform, or what this person might have thought or said about his career as "nondescript." Any history of the exhibition thus to some extent perpetuates Barnum's caricature: what we see in retrospect is a manufactured image—a *character* called "What is It?"—rather than the actual human beings who embodied these fictions. We do know at least two different men performed the role: Hervey Leech, a New York actor who played the character briefly in London in 1846;

10.1. An artist's representation of "What is It?" and his white, middle-class audience. Unlike later "freak" productions, "What is It?" was considered perfectly appropriate for family viewing, even for well-dressed Victorian New Yorkers such as these. Currier and Ives lithograph, circa 1865. Courtesy of Hertzberg Circus Collection and Museum, San Antonio, Texas.

and William Henry Johnson, a mentally retarded man from New Jersey, who seems to have been sold or rented into Barnum's service around 1860.

Leech, according to most accounts, was born in Westchester County, New York, in 1804 and worked a number of show business jobs under the theatrical nom de guerre "Signor Hervio Nano." Both this Italianate title and contemporary portraits suggest that Leech was probably Caucasian. According to a newspaper article from 1847, his only "remarkable" physical feature was the size of his legs, which were unusually small in proportion to the rest of his powerful body: "This extraordinary cripple . . . exhibits the very rare combinations of perfect symmetry, strength, and beauty, with a great amount of deformity. The head is remarkably fine in form, and the expression intelligent and benign; the chest, shoulders, and arms form a perfect model of strength and beauty. . . . In the place of legs there are two limbs, the left about 18 inches from the hip to the point of the toes, the right about 24 inches from the same points. The feet are natural."[5] Such an "arrangement," this author suggested, gave Leech "double power" between his feet and hands, and allowed him to demonstrate "extraordinary feats of leaping."

It also allowed him to play numerous "monkey" characters in the imaginary space of the mid-nineteenth-century stage: "Jocko, the Brazilian Ape" at the Chatham Theater in New York; "Bibbo, the Patagonian Ape" at Palmo's; an "Ape" of unspecified origin at the Bowery Theater. His most successful and enduring role, however, was the "Gnome Fly," a kind of dramatic triptych that debuted at the Bowery Theater in January 1840 and required Leech to transform himself first from the gnome "Sapajou" into a "baboon," and later—through a "wonderful flight, in magnificent costume . . . from the ceiling, back of the gallery, to the back of the stage, a distance of 250 feet"—into a "blue-bottle fly."[6] Barnum, who was then working as a New York theatrical manager, must have heard a great deal about the new production; indeed, one imagines the young showman mesmerized by the strangeness of Leech's performance, his mind racing with ideas about future schemes for the diminutive star. Whatever the precise circumstances, by August 1846 a deal had been struck between Barnum and Leech for the showman's second European tour. Leech acquired a "hair dress" from a New York wigmaker and "stained" his hands and face. Barnum rented a room in London's "Egyptian Hall," and citizens of the British capital began to read advertisements about a strange, new American curiosity set to open.[7]

The exhibition, which consisted of Leech standing in a cage, grunting, jumping, and eating raw meat, lasted less than a half hour before being exposed by a rival showman, who, in spite of Leech's elaborate "disguise," immediately recognized the well-known American actor and entered the cage to greet him. In the broad span of Barnum's volatile but mostly successful career, it was a minor incident, one of many quick failures with relatively little financial damage. During the next fourteen years, he kept the unrealized scheme filed away, perhaps to be used again when the right moment presented itself. Meanwhile, he laughed about the escapade in the 1855 edition of his autobiography and professed total ignorance about who might have been behind it.[8]

For Leech, however, this botched impersonation seems to have had a more lasting impact. According to a "sidewalk strongman" interviewed by Henry Mayhew for his 1861 history of the "London Poor," Leech never quite recovered from the embarrassment of public exposure: "That 'What is It,' at the Egyptian Hall killed him. They'd have made a heap of money at it, if it hadn't been discovered. He was in a cage, and wonderfully got up. He looked awful. A friend of his comes in, and goes up to the cage, and says, 'How are you, old fellow?' The thing was blown up in a minute. The place was in an uproar. It killed Harvey [sic] Leach, for he took it to heart and died."[9] Given Mayhew's working-class sympathies and propensity for sensationalism, this may be nothing more than the first installment in a long trail of "What is It?" apocrypha.[10] Yet there is no denying the final result of Leech's London tour: within six months of the incident, he was dead at the age of forty-three. As was so often the case with "curious" nineteenth-century bodies, Leech's remains were eventually transferred to a museum display case.[11]

The details of William Henry Johnson's tenure are even harder to nail down with any precision. Numerous publicity photographs suggest that he was a short, African-American man with a sharply sloping brow line, though as one writer observed at his funeral, out of costume there was really nothing particularly exceptional or unique about his head.[12] We also know that Johnson played the character for decades before his death in 1926, and that most early twentieth-century observers, including many long-term Barnum employees, described him as the "original What is It?" from the 1860s, a theory bolstered by two early Mathew Brady portraits that seem to be the same man who appears in much later images of the character (fig. 10.2).[13] If Barnum hired other "What is It?" actors during the early 1860s

10.2a, b. Mathew Brady's early portraits of William Henry Johnson as "What is It?" Note the various ways—the fur suit, Johnson's shaved head, the walking stick, the exotic backdrop—in which these images visually reinforce and produce Barnum's caricature. Circa 1865, by Mathew Brady. Courtesy of Meserve Collection, National Portrait Gallery, Smithsonian Institution, Washington, D.C.

before coming upon Johnson, no contemporary photographer or writer noted the change in personnel.

Less clear is how Johnson even ended up in Barnum's employ, or how much control he might have had over his sixty-year service with Barnum's museums and circuses. The only clue from the showman himself appears in an early 1860 letter, where he simply noted: "A certain museum proprietor in St. Louis—I don't know his name—saw a queer little crittur exhibiting in Phila. a few months since. I have since secured it, and we call it 'What is It?' "[14] Whether this was in fact Johnson, or what exactly Barnum's methods for "securing" his performer included, remain hard to pinpoint. Years later, a woman claiming to be the Johnson's sister told reporters that he grew up in Bound Brook, New Jersey (a small town about halfway between Philadelphia and New York), and at the age of four "was sold into the circus side-show by his parents in need of funds."[15] Such a transaction would have been consistent with Barnum's other dealings for "human curiosities"; during the 1830s and 1840s, for example, both Joice Heth and Tom Thumb were similarly "sold" into their roles as professional entertainers. Johnson, moreover, was a young, African American at a time when Northern blacks enjoyed few political or legal protections, and he appears to have suffered from a mental disorder called "microcephally"—all of which would indicate he probably had little control over his entrance into show business.[16] According to one obituary, for nearly ten years Johnson "had almost to be forced to mount the platform."[17]

Sadly, however, neither Barnum's inhumane treatment of his performers nor the various attitudes and prejudices behind this treatment were particularly unusual for their day. Indeed, both as a popular museum manager and as a white, antebellum New Yorker, Barnum's handling of the entire "What is It?" episode placed him squarely within the ideological mainstream of his social milieu.[18] The more relevant question here seems to be not simply *whether* "What is It?" was a product of racism or to what degree, but *how*—and to what end? How did Barnum's new exhibition fit within the aesthetic conventions of earlier, similar kinds of racially inflected carnival and museum characters? What did Barnum offer to mid-century New Yorkers that they could not receive elsewhere in the city's wealth of theaters and exhibition rooms?

One good place to begin answering these questions is with the "savage man" or "Homo Ferus" character, an old and complicated figure in Western culture that "What is It?" seems to simultaneously grow out of and supersede. Much like Shakespeare's late sixteenth-century island-dweller, Caliban, for example, Barnum located all of his character variations in some exotic, vaguely sketched, aboriginal context.[19] While Shakespeare's "monstrous" creature dwelled alone in an unspecified spot in the "stormy Bermoothes," the 1860 "What is It?" was said to have been captured in "the interior of Africa," where it had simply been "living in a tree."[20] Similarly, the most frequent costume for "What is It?"—a suit of black hair covering most of the performer's body—followed in the tradition of eighteenth-century European carnival "savages" such as "The Black Hairy Pigmy from Araby," which employed fur as a multidimensional signifier for non-Western geography ("Araby"), race/ethnicity ("Pigmy"), and physiological proximity to non-Western animals ("Black," "Hairy").[21] Even the character's various titles were partially recycled. Whereas Charles Willson Peale presented an orangou-tang as "The Wild Man of the Woods" at his Philadelphia Museum in 1799, Barnum offered Leech to Londoners as "The Wild Man of the Prairies."[22]

Yet, as this subtle transmutation of Peale's anthropoid ape also clearly demonstrates,

Barnum never simply rehashed the tired wares of his competitors, never limited himself to permanently fixed or one-dimensional characters. For this particular exhibition, in fact, he developed three separate inflections. The short-lived London character was said to have been discovered in "the wilds of California," where "for the last 10 months it has been with a tribe of Indians." In New York, by contrast, Barnum shifted the character's "habitat" to "the African jungle" and gave him a new nickname, "the Man Monkey." Around the turn of the century, this persona, too, was modified. Though the actor, costume, and older "missing link" rhetoric remained consistent, promotional materials added a less geographically specific moniker ("Zip"), as well as a more fantastic place of origin ("the land beyond the moon").

Visual representations of the character nicely illustrate these shifts. The somewhat contorted feet depicted in an 1860s Currier and Ives lithograph (fig. 10.3), for example, suggest those of an animal, with but two large toes. The upper portion of the body, however, appears human, or at least something close to what a white, antebellum New York artist might have imagined a "wild African" to look like. As in the Brady photographs from the same period, the character stands alone before a wooded background, hunched over a bit and carrying a supportive stick, as if just now learning how to walk upright. These antebellum images suggest a biological work in progress: "man" on top, "monkey" on the bottom. By 1908, however, the jungle motifs and Darwinian themes were beginning to disappear from the character's promotional materials (see fig. 10.4). Though Johnson's fur suit and bald head remain prominently featured, he now stands before a plain, white background, smiling and shrugging his shoulders, as if to evoke—through comic body language rather than context—his categorical imprecision.

Much of this flexibility in the character's construction, one suspects, followed the prevailing tides of public opinion. In London, for example, Barnum probably designed his "Wild Man of the Prairies" production with the hope of capitalizing on the same enthusiasm for things Western that had carried George Catlin's American Indian exhibit to enormous success at the Egyptian Hall only a year or two before. Yet it is also easy to exaggerate, or at least overemphasize, this kind of simplistic, one-to-one influence on Barnum's production schemes. Writing to Moses Kimball two weeks before the London opening, Barnum seems to have been largely uninterested in his new character's geographic or racial details. These he threw off quickly and carelessly, focusing instead on two other issues—the character's more basic hybrid status, somewhere between man and animal, and his desire to pitch the exhibition in such a way as to encourage public debate about this hybridity: "The *animal* that I spoke to you & Hale about comes out at Egyptian Hall, London, next Monday, and I half fear that I will not only be exposed, but that *I* shall be *found out* in the matter. However, I go it, live or die. The thing is not to be called *anything* by the exhibitor. We know not & therefore do not assert whether it is human or animal. We leave that all to the sagacious public to decide. The bills & advertisements will be headed as follows: 'What is It?' Now exhibiting at Egyptian Hall &c. &c. found in the forests of California &c. &c."[23] Whether his "animal" came from the "forest" or the "prairie," "California" or "Araby," seems, in the larger scheme of things, to have been a secondary concern. At the very core of Barnum's new character idea was simply the desire to create a fundamentally *liminal* creature ("the thing is not to be called anything by the exhibitor"), onto which numerous geographic, racial, and cultural templates could be applied, each according to the contingencies of the showman's transatlantic exhibition schedule and the vagaries of shifting, contemporary public curiosity.

10.3. "What is It?" in its most elaborate and fantastic version of the missing link theme. Almost every feature of Johnson's body has been transformed to suggest a kind of hybridity between man and monkey. Currier and Ives lithograph, 1860s. Courtesy of the Shelburne Museum, Shelburne, Vermont, photograph by Ken Burris.

10.4. During the early twentieth century, promotional images of "What is It?" abandoned the African jungle settings and walking stick in favor of a more clownish persona, with no specific geographic context. Johnson's promoters also added a new name—"Zip"—reminiscent of a famous minstrel show character. 1908 photograph. Courtesy of Hertzberg Circus Collection and Museum, San Antonio, Texas.

In many ways, then, the character "What is It?" developed much like Leech's "gnome fly," transmutating across time and space from the "Wild Man of the Prairies" into the African "Man-Monkey," and then, as a kind of final act, into the early twentieth-century circus star, "Zip." Barnum's aesthetic innovation, however, was not limited to these variations on the Homo Ferus theme. Almost simultaneously, he began to refine the broader conception of physical and cultural hybridity upon which the "savage man" and so many other standard nineteenth-century "freak" characters were based. Just as he decided not to *call* his "What is It?" "anything," he also chose to *position* this liminal creature outside, or in opposition to, the very idea of social categorization. In his best, most equivocal dime museum bluster, Barnum pronounced his new character a "nondescript."

Significantly, it is at this very moment—as Barnum is searching for the right language to describe his new character—that the term "nondescript" first appears in the English language as a noun defining "a person or thing that is not easily described, or is of no particular class or kind." [24] For two centuries previously, the word had referred rather to a *lack* of description, a thing or person not *yet* described. Thus, a hitherto unknown but recently discovered species might have been labeled in eighteenth-century scientific discourse as a "nondescript"—*until* it received official classification. This, of course, had resonance for Barnum's character-in-the-making: it is precisely the kind of new and previously unseen animal or species he is trying to describe. By the first decades of the nineteenth century, however, the word was also taking on a distinct, secondary meaning: the more liminal sense of *resisting* classification, or *straddling* descriptive boundaries. So while the older definition of "nondescript" provided Barnum with a means of capturing the novelty of "What is It"—his pristine status as the aboriginal inhabitant of some far-off land—the term's newer, secondary meaning offered a subtle linguistic tool for talking about this aborigine's visual and behavioral ambiguities. [25]

Barnum began to use the term publicly in 1849, sometimes to describe new animal attractions such as the "Woolly Horse" ("Col. Freemont's Nondescript," the "ambiguous quadruped"), which debuted under an assistant's charge in Philadelphia; on other occasions it specified a particular category of museum display, as in the lengthy title of a guidebook from the same year: *Sights and Wonders in New York; including a description of the mysteries, marvels, phenomena, curiosities, and nondescripts, contained in that great congress of wonders, Barnum's Museum.* [26] This title may have been referring to any number of American Museum exhibits—his orangoutang, for example, or perhaps the flying fish, or "Ornithoryncus" (duck-billed platypus)—all of which had been hailed previously by scientists as possible intermixtures of species and had appeared in natural history collections for quite some time (e.g., in Peale's 1799 "Wild Man of the Woods" exhibit). [27] What Barnum was actually innovating here was not so much the basic idea of the exotic hybrid, but rather the more precise language necessary to emphasize and differentiate this theme of "intermixture" from the thousands of other, less categorically uncertain "curiosities" (stuffed eagles, fossils, ethnic artifacts, automata, rare coins) that filled the rest of his hundreds of museum display cases.

To move from nondescript horses and flying fish to nondescript *people*, however, represented a significant conceptual leap, one Barnum appears not to have fully undertaken until the American debut of "What is It?" in 1860. Above all, it required far more attention to "manners" and "actions" than Barnum had attempted in any of his previous liminal productions. In the 1849–50 "Woolly Horse," for example, liminality remained mostly a function of ambiguous surfaces and complicated physical markings: "This most astounding of all flesh is, in size, like the ordinary Horse; but exhibits portions of the Buffalo, Camel, Deer, Elephant, and [is] covered with FINE CURLY MATTED SILK of the colour of camel's hair. He has not the mane or the tail of the horse, but *the tail of the Elephant!* Old trappers were ignorant of such an animal." [28] Of the behavior of this astounding creature, Barnum noted only that it "bounds twelve or fifteen feet high"; how exactly "old Woolly" ate, ran, or slept—or which "animal" in his "ambiguous composition" had produced such remarkable "bounding" skills—Philadelphians were left to ponder for themselves.

By contrast, the "What is It?" campaign of 1860 wove such ambiguous physical descriptions into a far more complex package, one equally dependent on "habits" and "features." "The curious creature is two thirds [the] size of Man. Laughs, but can't speak," noted one of

Barnum's ads in the New York papers.[29] Exclaimed another: "Looks like a Man! Acts Like a Monkey!"[30] Though his "natural position" was "on all fours," the creature could, with effort and the careful guidance of his "trainer," slowly assume the natural, bipedal position "of man"—an important distinction from the rest of "brute creation," which, by definition, is wholly incapable of "cultivation" or "reform." Yet, other aspects of his behavior simultaneously distanced him, as if due to some deeper, atavistic urge, away from "mankind." "When he first came," noted Barnum's exhibition program in a series of rapidly shifting qualifications, "his only food was raw meat, sweet apples, oranges, nuts, &c., of all of which he was very fond; but he will now eat bread, cake, and similar things, though he is fonder of raw meat, or that which, when cooked, is rare."[31] Faced with Claude Levi-Strauss's famous anthropological choice between "the raw" and "the cooked" (and, by implication, "nature" versus "civilization"), old "habits" often appear to have gotten the best of "What is It."[32]

Similarly, the "animal" portions of his body—at least in Barnum's grossly exaggerated caricature—seemed to push "What is It?" back into the trees:

> The formation of the head and face combines both that of the native African and of the Ourang Outang. The upper part of the head, and the forehead in particular, instead of being four or five inches broad, *as it should be, to resemble that of a human being,* is Less Than Two Inches! . . . The ears are set back about an inch *too far for humanity,* and about three fourths of an inch too high up. They should form a line with the ridge of the nose *to be like that of a human being.* As they are now placed they constitute the perfect head and skull of the Ourang Outang, while the lower part of the face is that of the native African.[33]

For every "human" feature that could be discerned in the character's "formation," Barnum counterposed an equally "brutish" trait, each designed alternatively to link and mark distance between "What is It?" and his audience of armchair physiologists.

As disturbing as these descriptions seem today (especially given the fact that Barnum was probably describing a mentally retarded boy from New Jersey), they did represent a new level of aesthetic subtlety vis-à-vis the typical, mid-nineteenth-century "wild man" production. For example, an 1850 ad in Philadelphia had promised "The Wonder of the World at Last"— "To be seen alive, the Bush Negro, or *Wild Man of the Woods.* . . . This creature seems to be the connecting link between the brute and human species, and it is difficult [to determine] to which race it belongs." Barnum thoroughly reworked this caricature, however, on one hand adding layers of descriptive detail, on the other making any "determination" of the detail's ultimate meaning harder to establish.[34] Though "What is It?" walked naturally on all fours, it could be trained to stand on two. The top half of its head was clearly "too small for humanity," yet the lower part of its face was just as clearly "that of the native African."

Above all, Barnum never used the word "negro"—not even a modified, more ambiguous version of the term, like "Bush Negro"—to describe his character. Rather, he offered a kind of categorical stand-in: a racially undefined persona that included clear physical signifiers of "blackness," but allowed public discussion of this "blackness" to take place in a kind of abstracted, liminal space.[35] Or to put it a bit more directly: by positioning his dark-skinned Museum character as "nondescript" rather than "Negro," Barnum provided white mid-century New Yorkers with an arena in which to talk openly about black people, often in brutally dehumanizing ways—to glide seamlessly between straightforward physical description and gross cultural caricature, and thus to alternate between the guises of armchair biologist and political juror—without even acknowledging *who,* exactly, they were talking about.

Of course, to say as much is to beg a far trickier and more audience-oriented kind of question: Why was such pseudoscientific obfuscation and cultural double-speak even *neces-sary?* Why not simply come out and attach these racialist stereotypes and categorical distinctions to their usual African-American targets, as was so commonly practiced in virtually every other corner of white, Northern, mid-nineteenth-century urban popular culture? Certainly, no contemporary minstrel show audience had any problem at all identifying the conventional caricatures of blackface as "Negro," nor did they require a deracialized rhetorical space to talk about the "brutishness" of the Sambos and Jim Crows that routinely appeared on the antebellum Northern stage. Indeed, such deliberate character abstraction would have been largely antithetical to the whole project of the antebellum minstrel show, which was constructed in large part to define, reify, and essentialize a certain set of physical and cultural attributes as *authentically* "Negro," at least in the eyes of those Northern non-negroes who regularly performed and went to see them.[36]

Barnum, by contrast, appears to have been offering up something a bit different (and a bit riskier perhaps) during the winter of 1860: a staged hybridity in many ways more cruel and dehumanizing even than the minstrel show's brand of racial caricature (instead of "blackface" on "white," what might be termed "bruteface" on "black"), as well as a new form of cultural double-entendre (not simply white men playing with "blackness," as in the minstrel show, but an actual African-American man playing a "nondescript"). All of this seems to have been designed to absolve the showman of any definitional agency in the whole matter, or at least to place the *final act of definition* in the hands of his audience; rather than actually *say* what "What is It?" was, Barnum only offered *possibilities.* But in so doing, he also seems to have offered something else: an arena in which the process of human definition itself was becoming more ambiguous and fluid, more prone to manipulation and experimentation; a place where New Yorkers could freely associate and signify identity in all sorts of ways, some of them even quite controversial and transgressive.

THE POLITICS OF NONDESCRIPTION

Consider the function of "What is It" as late antebellum political discourse—a function that, at least initially, seems almost antithetical to Barnum's well-known public credo of constructing "harmless amusements" for all kinds of "honest Republicans."[37] Yet, as Eric Lott has demonstrated recently, Barnum was a serious player in the "sectional controversies" of the 1850s, especially in his politically charged decision to run H. J. Conway's version of *Uncle Tom's Cabin* in direct competition to the more famous (and now canonical) George Aiken production.[38] Only a few decades earlier—following the Missouri Compromise of 1820—such direct public discussion about slavery's moral legitimacy remained largely unheard of on the New York stage. While the melodramas and minstrel shows of the 1830s and 1840s had lots to say about "race" and African-American "degradation," they usually did so in the same manner as most antebellum politicians: without specifically addressing the potentially volatile political repercussions of African-Americans' legal status in the South or West.[39]

As this tenuous national silence began to unravel during the late 1840s and early 1850s, however, New York theatrical managers quickly followed suit, using different adaptations of Harriet Beecher Stowe's novel as a battleground for either endorsing or opposing abolitionist ideas—though often, like the novel itself, with subtle intermixtures of both positions. Whereas Aiken's National Theater production offered *Uncle Tom* as a "sentimental," tear-soaked tragedy, designed to provoke sympathy for its Christ-like protagonist and the "pathos" of his unjust plight, Barnum's version highlighted "slaves singing blackface choruses," a difference in racial representation that infused the play with a more "comic," ridiculing tone.[40] Of the latter production, which actually began with a full-blown minstrel routine, William Lloyd Garrison's *Liberator* vehemently complained: "Barnum has offered the slave-drivers the incense of an expurgated Uncle Tom. He has been playing a version of that great story at his Museum, which omits all that strikes at the slave system, and has so shaped his drama as to make it quite an agreeable thing to be a slave."[41]

Such complaints, of course, expressed a strongly partisan and probably minority position; other Northern press commentators were far less critical of Barnum's racial politics and even defended them as appropriately evenhanded. But that is precisely what made this particular theatrical rivalry so engaging: unlike his earlier Lecture Room theatrical successes (e.g., *The Drunkard*, a popular temperance melodrama), Barnum was now constructing public entertainments that aggressively courted sectional controversy—indeed, that made this kind of controversy their principal drawing card. As Lott explains, "the *Uncle Tom's Cabin* plays institutionalized the social divisions they narrated. Sectional debate henceforth became theatrical ritual, part of the experience of *Uncle Tom*."[42]

Barnum's foray into sectional politics did not end with Conway's controversial adaptation of *Uncle Tom*. By the time "What is It?" made its 1860 American Museum debut, in fact, Barnum was offering two other, equally provocative entertainments upon which New Yorkers could express sectional opinions: a collection of artifacts from John Brown's raid on Harper's Ferry (including a wax statue of the radical abolitionist himself); and a production of Dion Boucicault's *The Octoroon*, which told the tragic story of a mixed-blood Louisiana free woman, courted by the son of a wealthy white judge, but ultimately sold into slavery to save her family from financial ruin.[43] According to a *New York Tribune* review, a number of "touchy students from the South" had initially tried to block the play's opening in Philadelphia; the "excitement," explained the author, "fully parallels the enthusiasm that was excited here by the same play, and the best seats are all taken a week in advance."[44] Joseph Jefferson, star of *The Octoroon*, recalled a similar pattern, noting that this combination of heated debate and packed houses seemed to grow out of the play's ability to provoke public support for both sides of the controversy: "When Zoe, the loving octoroon, is offered to the highest bidder, and a warm-hearted Southern girl offers all her fortune to buy Zoe, and release her from threatened bondage . . . the audience cheered for the South; but when again the action revealed that she could be bartered for, and was bought and sold, they cheered for the North, as plainly as though they said, 'Down with slavery.'"[45]

Was Barnum's "What is It?" exhibition an extension of this deliberately provocative though ambiguous "sectionalist" cultural program—one built, like *The Octoroon*, around a politically slippery cultural representation of hybrid black identity? In many ways, certainly, "What is It?" provided a kind of exhibition-room analog to one of sectionalism's defining events: the landmark Supreme Court case *Dred Scott v. Sandford* (1857), in which Scott, a former

Missouri slave, became the focus of a national dialogue on the intricacies of African-American political identity. The chronology of Barnum's exhibition parallels Scott's long-running legal battle almost exactly. Both began rather quietly in 1846 (the same year, intriguingly, as the Wilmot Proviso, a controversial piece of early sectionalist legislation that ushered in the political crises of the 1850s) and drifted out of public consciousness for over a decade, returning with a bang just before the Civil War. Both returns, moreover, were played out within the context of bitterly fought presidential campaigns, in which the nagging question of how to define the legal status of African Americans in the Western territories emerged as the central point of partisan contention.[46]

Whereas Scott's lawyers described their client as a "quasi-citizen," born a slave but seemingly emancipated by his temporary residence in two free states, Barnum offered "What is It?" as the world's first *quasi-man*, born a "brute" in the African jungle, but now beginning to take on various "human," more "civilized" features during his stay in New York. In both ideological arenas, the theoretical problem confronting white jurors boiled down to one of innate qualities versus environmental impact. Was the African brutishness of "What is It" simply intrinsic, or did it somehow fade away when removed from its original context? Was Scott's identity as slave defined forever by his African ancestry, or did it instead fluctuate as he moved across the jurisdictions of different states in the Western portion of the country? Not surprisingly, the actual African-American men at the center of these public debates quickly became secondary to the larger categorical groups they represented. In much the same way that Chief Justice Robert B. Taney decided to use Scott's appeal for freedom as an opportunity to offer partisan opinion on the legal history of all American Blacks, Barnum's audiences responded to "What is It?" as a test case through which to speculate on the basic humanity of "wild Africans" in general.

In both cases, however, the rhetorical route toward judgment was lined with sharp turns and equivocations. Just as historians now still argue over the implications of the Taney Court's split vote and stinging opinion that African Americans had been "excluded" from the Declaration of Independence—perhaps a ruling on "Negro citizenship," perhaps a recision of the Missouri Compromise, perhaps nothing more than the reversal of an earlier state court decision freeing Scott—it is often hard to tell exactly what the New York press ruled on "What is It?" except perhaps that he represented a "lower order of being."[47] In its first review, for example, the *New York Herald* described "What is It?" as "a most extraordinary freak of nature, consisting of a creature supposed to belong to our ourang outang species"—a remarkably ambiguous evaluation, on one hand suggesting the character's proximity to a familiar simian reference point, yet simultaneously designed to pull this analogy back towards humanity with the more inclusive pronoun "our." Later on, the *Herald* reviewer waffled again, arguing that "What is It?" has "all the appearance of a human being," only to assert a few lines below that "the formation of its hands, arms, and head are those of an ourang outang" (this time without the inclusive semantics). "A cloud of doubt and uncertainty," the article concluded, "hangs about the exhibition room."[48] A reporter from the *Sun* moved in the opposite interpretive direction, going to great initial pains to explain what was physically different about "What is It?" from a "typical" African-American man: "the ears are far too high and too much back for a negro; the arms are several inches too long in proportion, and the jaws and teeth are entirely animal." Yet, the review's final analogy made it clear what kind of human being he thought "What is It?" most closely resembled. "Dan Rice in his palmiest days," noted the author, "never could produce a heartier Jim Crow laugh than this creature gets out on the slightest occasion."[49]

Other 1860 New York commentators repeated and expanded this "cloud of uncertainty" ad nauseam, providing one lengthy description after another of the hybridized grin (deemed both "idiotic" and "friendly"), posture ("exceedingly awkward" yet nonetheless "erect"), precarious bi-pedal walk (sometimes "elderly" or "animal," on other occasions "child-like" or "sportive"), and temperament ("not at all vicious," but also "enjoying a distinguished reputation for ferocity").[50] All of which simply suggests that the New York press treated "What is It?" much like any other contemporary black person: as a kind of hybrid being whose "true" identity depended upon the circumstances and contexts of conversation.[51] "What is It?" was docile enough to demonstrate the complete control of his trainer, as well as ferocious enough to demonstrate the need for such control; savage enough to imply genetic inferiority, but civilized enough to inspire evolutionary hope for the future; strange enough to become a museum curiosity, yet also familiar enough to be routinely compared to ordinary African Americans.

Here, in other words, was much the same nineteenth-century pattern of racial objectification and contradictory labeling described by W. E. B. Du Bois as "double consciousness," in this case staged as a form of popular visual entertainment: a "dark body" whose "twoness" was both created and imposed "through the eyes of others"; a "soul" measured "by the tape of a world that looks on in amused contempt and pity."[52] The precise equation of "contempt" and "pity" rendered by 1860s New Yorkers, however, was far from predetermined. Indeed, as nineteenth-century racial caricatures went, the figure of the nondescript was a remarkably flexible ideological tool. Did Barnum's hybrid simply reinvent a much older brand of European racism common during the earliest days of the African slave trade, one that, as Winthrop Jordan has demonstrated, equated "blackness" with the "savage," the "low," the "ape-like," and then used this differentiation as the basis for social subjugation?[53] Certainly, this seems to be the case in one typical review from the *Courier and Inquirer,* which makes a seamless leap of logic from conventional nineteenth-century racial stereotypes to a coldly dispassionate verdict of inhumanity: "The head is shaped like that of a monkey, but the face is more like that of an African negro of the lower order. The creature moves along with a shuffling gait very much like an elderly negro. . . . It has been pronounced by naturalists as a specimen of the connecting link between man and monkey."[54] Likewise the "joke" that appeared in *Frank Leslie's Illustrated Newspaper:* "The 'irrepressible conflict' still rages in the Zoological world as to what the 'What is It?' is. Some people think it has too much intelligence for a nigger, and not enough for a monkey."[55]

On other occasions, however, Barnum's caricature served as the basis for establishing a subtly different kind of racial categorization, one that presumed that even the "lowest order" of African contained and was capable of basic, universally shared "human" qualities. A writer from the *New York Tribune,* for example, lauded "the brightness of its eye, and intelligent response to the words and motions of the person in charge," which "at once relieve it of the imputation of imbecility."[56] Other commentators similarly focused on the propensity of "What is It" for rapid physical and cultural development—"like a child just learning," according to the *New York Express*—which, for a moment at least, seemed to undermine or at least temper those very same racialist hierarchies constructed by American Museum viewers to establish the subhuman status of "What is It" in the first place.[57]

Of course, both "What is It?" inflections involved some attempt to create a vertical, racially defined social order: either an evaluation of out-and-out degradation within an immutable racial hierarchy, or a somewhat less rigid verdict of partial degradation that allowed for small degrees of paternalistic reform. At this point, though, we would do well to think more specifically about what *kind* of social blueprint was being drawn from such calculated cultural equivocations. After all, given the timing of this exhibition—right in the middle of Lincoln's 1860 run for president—as well as the presence of a controversial slavery melodrama right next door, it seems at least a little surprising to find absolutely no overt references to the "peculiar institution" in Barnum's exhibition room, or even any implied discussion of the possible function of "What is It?" as a "worker" in the service of white society. Though quite consistent in their efforts to use this caricature as an instrument for establishing racial superiority, Barnum and his viewers also consistently avoided at least *one* of the most common ideological weapons of antebellum white supremacism: the notion, usually propagated by proslavery theoreticians, of a basic "negro predisposition" for agrarian labor. Whereas George Fitzhugh, for example, routinely crafted images of African Americans as "natural," "productive," and "happy" field workers requiring the paternalistic control of a slave economy, Barnum's Northern brand of racial paternalism made little if any reference to physical ability or productive capability.[58] On the contrary, his advertisements were quite insistent about the fact that "What is It?" could barely walk or stand up, let alone perform exhausting manual work.

How, then, are we to explain the ideological *utility* of this cultural phenomenon: a mode of public discourse clearly shaped by the sectional controversies of the 1850s, yet also lacking any clear references to slavery; a hybrid caricature of blackness which easily absorbed both hard-line and reformist visions of a white dominated, racially determined social hierarchy, yet which also remained staunchly uncommitted to either ideological position? Did such forms of evasiveness somehow make "What is It?" *less* political than *The Octoroon*, which offered a readily identifiable social problem (the impact of chattel slavery on a racially mixed woman) and context (a Louisiana plantation, on the verge of dissolution)? The answer, it seems to me—and I intend absolutely no evasiveness on my part here—is both yes and no: *yes* in the sense that Barnum and his New York audiences seem to have used "What is It?" as a tool for consensus-building, one that allowed for spirited public discussions about the racial boundaries of "humanity" without specific reference to *any* of the dangerous subtexts normally fundamental to such discussions (e.g., the Christian ethics of slavery as an institution); and *no* in the sense that this activity of building consensus around caricatured abstractions of "black brutishness" was itself *deeply* political, since it served to maintain and justify the North's racial caste system, even as the institution of slavery was finally being abolished from American society.

What Barnum seems to have been particularly adept at representing and promoting through the figure of the nondescript were the various points of ideological overlap on racial matters which *connected* the antebellum North's diverse political factions.[59] From Northern Whigs and Republicans, he took the moderate or "soft racist" notion of paternalistic reform, which posited that Africans would benefit from the ameliorative influence of Anglo-Saxon culture (evidenced in this case by the shift from a quadrupedal to bipedal stance, and raw to cooked food), as well as a fixed social order that allowed for charitable guidance from on high (symbolized by Barnum's white trainer—always above his black student, yet aiding his gradual uplift). From Northern Democrats, Barnum took the "hard racist" notion of biological competition, which posited the existence of intrinsic physiological differences between blacks and whites (demonstrated by measurements of the facial angle of "What is It," and lack of speech), as well as a more egalitarian vision of white society within which Africans needed to be aggressively confined to the lowest rungs (articulated through the ventriloquist voice of unnamed "naturalists," who were said to have simply "ruled" upon the subhuman status of Barnum's "creature").[60]

"What is It?," in other words, expressed—or more specifically, *embodied*—virtually *all* of the disparate strands of white Northern racialist thought common before and during the Civil War. But he also embodied something else: the deep contradictions and ideological slippages within Northern ideas about race. Horace Greeley's *New York Tribune*, a Whig-supported paper with consistent antislavery leanings, railed against other newspaper reviewers' attempts to condemn "What is It?" to "imbecility," but also routinely described the man playing this character, William Henry Johnson, as an "animal."[61] Benjamin Day's *Sun*, a Democratic organ, predictably emphasized the "small brain," "exceedingly awkward walk," and "Jim Crow laugh" of "What is It" but could also remark—like Greeley's *New York Herald* reporter—upon its "bright and intelligent eyes."[62] None of these odd ideological intermixtures could compare, however, to the incongruity that took place during a "Freedman's Society" benefit held at the Cooper Institute in 1864. Though designed to raise money for recently emancipated slaves and presumably attended by at least a few orthodox abolitionists, Barnum "contributed" to the cause by offering "What is It?" as an entre-act entertainment—a decision that, according to the *New York Tribune*, left the Cooper Institute audience in "an almost continual roar of laughter" and "much gratified."[63]

That such "laughter" and "gratification" could have taken place at all at a Freedman's Society benefit (and that Barnum, one of the great judges of nineteenth-century public opinion, seems to have had few misgivings about pairing this act and audience) only reinforces a troubling paradox long ago uncovered by historians of abolitionism: even those white Northerners most deeply involved in the crusade to dismantle slavery often questioned the full humanity, not to mention the full equality, of their beneficiaries.[64] The contrast here with Barnum's earlier *Uncle Tom's Cabin* production and its strongly partisan press reception is striking. Now, instead of noting abolitionist outrage and condemnation from the *Liberator*, New York writers commented only on the Cooper Institute audience's unqualified "amusement."

This shift in reception, I would argue, had less to do with abolitionism itself—which as an ideological posture remained mostly unchanged over the course of the decade—than Barnum's increasing skill at weaving together the common threads of white Northern racism, as well as eliding any potentially volatile partisan differences contained therein. Like the competing *Uncle Tom's Cabin* productions that had dominated New York popular entertainment during the mid-1850s, "What is It?" reflected the era's deeply conflicted racial politics. By 1860, however, Barnum seems to have devised a strategy with which not only to include, but also placate all Northern sides of the sectionalist debates in a *single* entertainment offering: first, position this offering's "blackness" somewhere between the conflicting racial stereotypes and social blueprints espoused by the leading political parties; second, remove slavery from the discussion altogether, and define the African-American object of discussion as something else—a nondescript—so as not to offend the more delicate sensibilities of antislavery advocates; and, finally, use this new brand of caricature to provoke a public "controversy" about the terms—rather than the existence—of Northern society's deeply entrenched racial hierarchy, one that allowed for vigorous debate over the degree, causes, and mutability of "African brutishness," yet also (precisely because of the highly circumscribed quality of the questions being posed) appealed to white artisans and abolitionists alike.

Notes

1. For help with this chapter, I would like to thank Lawrence W. Levine, Margaretta Lovell, Patrick Rael, and Rita Chin.

2. P. T. Barnum, *Struggles and Triumphs* (New York: Viking Penguin, 1981), 184.

3. For a discussion of Lind's manufactured "celebrity," see Peter Buckley, "To the Opera House: Culture and Society in New York City, 1820–1860," (Ph.D. diss., State University of New York at Stony Brook, 1984).

4. *New York Herald*, 2 March 1960, 7.

5. *London Times*, 27 April 1847.

6. George C. D. Odell, *Annals of the New York Stage* (New York: Columbia University Press, 1928), 4:368.

7. *Wemyss' Chronology of the American Stage from 1752 to 1852* (New York: William Taylor, 1852), 92; P. T. Barnum, *The Life of P. T. Barnum, Written by Himself* (New York: J. S. Redfield, 1855), 346; *London Times*, 29 August 1846.

8. Barnum, *Life*, 346; Richard Altick, *Shows of London* (Cambridge: Belknap, 1978), 266–67.

9. Henry Mayhew, *London Labour and the London Poor* (London: Charles Griffin, 1861–62), 3:111.

10. In 1852, Wemyss wrote that "poor Leach" [sic] was "maltreated" and died soon afterward—which led subsequent late nineteenth- and early twentieth-century theater historians to conclude that Leech was actually attacked by the crowd at Barnum's exhibition. As Richard Altick has argued, however, this was probably not the case. *Wemyss's Chronology of the American Stage*, 92; Altick, *Shows of London*, 266–67.

11. *London Times*, 27 April 1847; George M. Gould and Walter L. Pyle, *Anomalies and Curiosities of Medicine* (New York: Bell, 1896), 266.

12. "Zip Grins in Death, Mask Off at Last," *New York World*, 29 April 1926, 17.

13. "Zip, Barnum's Famous 'What is It?' Freak Dies of Bronchitis in Bellevue; his Age Put at 84," *New York Times*, 25 April 1926, 1. The Brady photographs are undated, but the fact that they are in the carte-de-visite format virtually guarantees that they were taken in the 1860s. A magazine article by Dorothy Meserve Kunhardt states that the collection is from the "middle 1860s." "Barnum and Brady, Pictures from the Collection of Frederick Hill Meserve," *Colliers*, 29 April 1944, 21.

14. P. T. Barnum to Sol Smith, American Museum, 4 April 1860. Reprinted in A. H. Saxon, ed., *Selected Letters of P. T. Barnum* (New York: Columbia University Press, 1983), 104.

15. This information appears in a somewhat unreliable article from the *New York World*, 29 April 1926, 8. At least parts of the story, however (that Johnson had a sister named Sarah Vanduinne and was born in Bound Brook), are confirmed by a number of other sources. See, e.g., "Many Circus Folk at Zip's Funeral," *New York Times*, 29 April 1926, 48, which states that both Vanduinne and a brother, Theodore Johnson, attended their sibling's funeral in Bound Brook. Robert Bogdan (*Freak Show, Presenting Human Oddities for Amusement and Profit* [Chicago: University of Chicago Press, 1988], 293) notes a grave for Johnson in Bound Brook as well as a plaque claiming the town as his birthplace.

16. Bogdan, *Freak Show*, 134, 293.

17. This again is from the woman who claimed to be Johnson's sister, Sarah Vanduinne. *New York World*, 29 April 1826, 17.

18. Leon Litwack, *North of Slavery: The Negro in the Free States, 1790–1860* (Chicago: University of Chicago Press, 1961), 15–17. A. H. Saxon, *P. T. Barnum: The Legend and the Man* (New York: Columbia University Press, 1989), chaps. 1 and 6.

19. Leslie Fiedler, *Freaks: Myths and Images of the Secret Self* (New York: Anchor, 1979), 259. The term "Homo ferus" comes from the eighteenth-century European naturalist Linneaus.

20. *New York Herald*, 19 March 1860, 1.

21. Altick, *Shows of London*, 265.

22. David Rodney Brigham, "A World in Miniature: Charles Willson Peale's Philadelphia Museum and Its Audience," (Ph. D. diss., University of Pennsylvania, 1992), 589.

23. P. T. Barnum to Moses Kimball, Brighton, England, 18 August 1846. Reprinted in Saxon, *Selected Letters of P. T. Barnum*, 35–36.

24. *Oxford English Dictionary*, 2d ed., s.v. "non-descript."

25. The *OED*'s earliest reference for this second sense of "non-descript" is from 1811: "The House contains about 250 country gentlemen, 120 courtiers [etc.]. The rest are non-descripts."

26. *Philadelphia Public Ledger*, 22 December 1849, 3. The guidebook was published in New York by J. S. Redfield.

27. Ramona Morris and Desmond Morris, *Men and Apes* (New York: McGraw-Hill, 1966).

28. *Philadelphia Public Ledger*, 21 December 1849, 2.

29. *New York Herald*, 8 March 1860, 1.

30. *New York Herald*, 15 March 1860, 1.

31. This program is reprinted in Bernth Lindfors, "P. T. Barnum and Africa," *Studies in Popular Culture* 7 (1984): 21–22. Barnum also frequently used this text in ads, e.g., *New York Herald*, 19 March 1860, 1.

32. Claude Levi-Strauss, *The Raw and the Cooked: Introduction to a Science of Mythology*, vol. 1, trans. John Weightmann and Doreen Weightmann (New York: Harper and Row, 1969).

33. *New York Herald*, 19 March 1860, 1 (my emphasis).

34. *Philadelphia Public Ledger*, 30 April 1850.

35. My use of this term has been heavily influenced by Eric Lott's important study, *Love and Theft: Blackface Minstrelsy and the Working Class* (New York: Oxford University Press, 1993). "Blackness" in Lott's conception refers not to some aspect of African-American culture or physiology, but to white projections, prejudices, and fantasies about these things; it is, as Lott explains, "not innate but produced, a cultural construction" (36).

36. Lott, *Love and Theft*; Robert Toll, *Blacking Up: The Minstrel Show in Nineteenth-Century America* (New York: Oxford University Press, 1974); and Alexander Saxton, *The Rise and Fall of the White Republic: Class Politics and Mass Culture in Nineteenth-Century America* (London: Verso, 1990).

37. For a more detailed discussion of the mid-century social meanings of "What is It"—including the character's relationship to Darwinism, polygenesis, and Victorian respectability—see my "Masters of Illusionism: A History of Victorian America and its Puzzling Visual Culture" (Ph.D. diss., University of California, forthcoming).

38. The discussion that follows is a somewhat abbreviated version of the argument in Lott's final chapter of *Love and Theft*, "Uncle Tomitudes: Racial Melodrama and Modes of Production."

39. There are numerous books on the emergence of "sectionalism" before the Civil War. See, e.g., David Potter, *The Impending Crisis* (New York: Harper and Row, 1976); and Kenneth Stampp, *America in 1857: A Nation on the Brink* (New York: Oxford University Press, 1990).

40. Lott, *Love and Theft*, 213–33.

41. *Liberator*, 16 December 1853. Quoted in Lott, *Love and Theft*, 218–19.

42. Lott, *Love and Theft*, 223.

43. On the John Brown materials, see *New York Times*, 2 January 1860, which promised a "Wax Figure of Ossawatomie Brown. Two Spears From Harper's Ferry. Link of the Shackles That Were Cut by Coppic and Cook. Autograph Letter from John Brown." Boucicault's text is reprinted in Peter Thompson, ed., *Plays by Dion Boucicault* (New York: Cambridge University Press, 1984).

44. *New York Tribune*, 2 March 1860, 7.

45. Odell, *Annals of the New York Stage*, 7:213.

46. For a focused treatment of this enormously complex event, see Don E. Fehrenbacher, *Slavery, Law, and Politics: The Dred Scott Case in Historical Perspective* (New York: Oxford University Press, 1981); and Stampp, *America in 1857*, especially chap. 4.

47. Fehrenbacher, *Slavery, Law, and Politics*, 173; Stampp, *America in 1857*, 93–98.

48. *New York Herald*, 28 February 1860, 2.

49. Quoted in *New York Herald,* 1 March 1860, 7.

50. *New York Times,* 5 March and 7 April 1860; *Sunday Times,* 25 February 1860; *New York Herald,* 28 February 1860; *New York Evening Post, Sun,* and *Express* (no dates), reprinted in *New York Herald,* 1 and 2 March 1860; *Commercial Advertiser, Courier and Inquirer* (no dates), reprinted in *New York Herald,* 16 March 1860; *Tribune,* 27 and 29 February and 12 March 1860; *Frank Leslie's Illustrated Newspaper,* 3, 10, and 24 March 1860.

51. Ronald T. Takaki, *Iron Cages: Race and Culture in Nineteenth-Century America* (New York: Oxford University Press, 1990), esp. chap. 6.

52. W. E. B. Du Bois, *The Souls of Black Folk: Essays and Sketches* (1903; reprint, New York: Fawcett, 1961), 17.

53. Winthrop Jordan, *White over Black* (New York: W. W. Norton, 1977), 29–32.

54. Quoted in *New York Herald,* 16 March 1860, 7.

55. *Frank Leslie's Illustrated Newspaper,* 24 March 1860, 257.

56. *New York Tribune,* 29 February 1860, 7.

57. *New York Express,* quoted in *New York Herald,* 1 March 1860, 7.

58. Takaki, *Iron Cages,* 124; George Fitzhugh, *Sociology of the South; or, the Failure of Free Society* (New York: Burt Franklin, n.d.).

59. My argument here draws from Saxton, *The Rise and Fall of the White Republic,* parts 1 and 2. The terms "hard" and "soft" racism are his.

60. For an analysis of cultural "ventriloquism," see Michael Denning, *Mechanic Accents* (London: Verso, 1987).

61. *New York Tribune,* 29 February 1860, 7; 12 March 1860, 7. For a discussion of the politics of the antebellum "penny press," see Alexander Saxton, "Problems of Class and Race in the Origins of the Mass Circulation Press," *American Quarterly* 36, no. 2 (1984): 211–34.

62. Quoted in *New York Herald,* 1 March 1860, 7.

63. *New York Tribune,* 28 January 1864, 8.

64. Martin Duberman, ed., *The Antislavery Vanguard: New Essays on the Abolitionists* (Princeton: Princeton University Press, 1965).

ELEVEN

Aztecs, Aborigines, and Ape-People: Science and Freaks in Germany, 1850–1900

NIGEL ROTHFELS

Microcephalics must necessarily represent an earlier developmental state of the human being . . . ; they reveal to us one of the milestones which the human passed by during the course of his historical evolution.
—CARL VOGT (1867)

A 1905 postcard of the "Hamburger Dom"—the traditional Christmas fair for Hamburg and its surroundings—shows a muddy street full of men and women before a series of freak-show booths running along the left of the view.[1] The photographer's primary interest appears to be the life of the street itself; the figures milling about in dark overcoats on a grey and wet winter day are the first to attract our attention. The booths are removed from the public space; they form the backdrop, the sideshow. However fascinated the photographer may have been by the *flânerie* of the street, the story of this scene nevertheless seems to rest at least as much in the street's frame, the closed rooms of the freak shows.

As faces turn, crowds gather before the tents to see the wonders of humanity: "the largest," "the most amazing," "something never seen before!" The signs read: "Live! The Largest and the Smallest People in the World!" "The Atzteeken are Here!" "Frederke, the 15-Year-Old Pomeranian Colossus, Live!" Within the context of a carnival, these signs seem ordinary. Part of the task of this volume, however, is to seek out the lives behind the signs and to understand them as both extraordinary and ordinary. Most of those lives will nevertheless remain hidden in the historical record. Still, it remains possible to gain glimpses into the experiences of especially the more celebrated freaks, people who appear, paradoxically, both remote and somehow familiar. The paradox stems from a certain continuity in freakmaking over the last couple of centuries. Despite Franz Kafka's sense in 1929, for example, that along with many other unusual performers, the "hunger artists" had lost their place in European culture, neither the aestheticization of hunger nor the hunger artists themselves have disappeared. Nor have the sword swallowers, dwarfs, giants, tattooed men and women, Siamese twins, contortionists, and the armless and legless somehow vanished from our cultures. They still exist, they are still "freaked," and some still perform, albeit on such new venues as the daytime talk show. Despite the continuity of freakmaking in Western history, however, it is important to understand that freaking has a historical frame—the precise cultural interpretation of an unusual person has a great deal to do with the historical moment in which that person finds himself or herself freaked by his or her own or another culture.

In an effort to come to a deeper understanding of the relation between cultures and the process of freaking, this chapter examines the curious context in which one small freak show—the "Atzteeken" in the Hamburger Dom photograph[2]—which ran from the early 1850s to the first decade of the twentieth century came into contact with the German scientific community, and more particularly that community's leaders among the members of the Berlin Anthropological Society *(Gesellschaft für Anthropologie, Ethnologie, und Urgeschichte)*. Of course, neither the show nor the anthropologists existed in carefully sealed specimen bottles, and in order to clarify their relation we must look to other shows and larger cultural concerns in Germany and in the West more generally.

Some fifty years before the Hamburger Dom postcard appeared, a small octavo pamphlet was published entitled *An Illustrated Report of the Important Expedition to Central America from Which Resulted the Discovery of the Idol-Worshipping City of Iximaya in a Completely Unexplored Region.* The illustrated brochure related the story of a group of Mexican and "Yankee" bandits who managed to locate the hidden city of Iximaya and its temple cult in Central America. Despite unforeseen dangers, the desperados succeeded in abducting two "lilliputian" beings known as "Bartola" and "Maximo," believed to be the last descendants of an unusual race of people worshiped by the inhabitants of Iximaya. Perhaps not surprisingly, and despite great risk and expense, the young children were brought to Europe to be exhibited as anthropological phenomena of the highest interest, that is, as Aztecs.[3]

The true origins of the "Aztecs" "Bartola" and "Maximo" will probably never be known. Most of the scant history surrounding the two most famous microcephalics in the history of the freak shows begins with their exhibition in 1849 as children in New York. We know that especially in the early years of their tours many believed the pair could in fact have been representatives of a lost race of Aztecs. This argument was bolstered by resemblances between the physical appearance of "Bartola" and "Maximo" and certain ancient Central American drawings and sculptures. In 1856, for example, Carl Gustav Carus, one of the first German scientists to examine the children, formulated an argument still heard thirty and even forty years later that favorably compared the physiognomy of "Maximo" and "Bartola" to sculptures found in Chiapas.[4] While some observers found the purported history of the "Aztec" children plausible, most remained skeptical of the idea that the pair were the offspring of some lost civilization. The great Johannes Müller, for example, is said to have insisted in one of his last lectures on pathological anatomy in 1857 that the children were born to parents of mixed race still living in San Salvador. A travelogue of 1854, moreover, argued that the "Aztecs" were no more than the twin children of Innocento and Martina Murgos, who lived in the town of Tocoro in the Department of San Miguel. According to the travelogue, a Spaniard named Ramon Selva convinced the mother to let him take the children to America; instead, however, he exhibited them in cities throughout Central America and then sold them to an American entrepreneur who took them to Europe.[5]

The rest of the actual record of the pair's life experiences can sadly be summed in a handful of sentences. Their shows in Europe began in 1853. They were presented in the fairs and panoptica of the larger cities. They were shown to royalty and scientists at every opportunity.

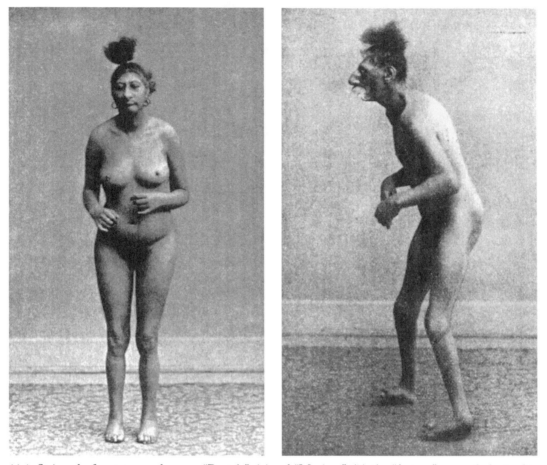

11.1. Stripped of costume and props, "Bartola" *(a)* and "Maximo" *(b),* the "Aztecs," are pathologized in these clinical photographs. Reproduced from *Verhandlungen der Berliner Gesellschaft für Anthropologie, Ethnologie, und Urgeschichte* 33 (1901): 349, 50.

They were "represented" by numerous figures over the next sixty years. Despite early claims that the two were siblings, they were married in 1867 under the names of "Maximo Valdez Nuñez" and "Bartola Velasquez." Through the many records of their bodies—from both scientific and souvenir photographs, such as those presented here (figs. 11.1a and b and 11.2), to the careful measurements of all their features—the curious and mundane physical aspects of the two have been preserved. "Maximo" died in 1913; the year of death for "Bartola" is unknown.

Despite the paucity of information about the actual lives of "Bartola" and "Maximo," however, they occupy a particularly important and almost unique place in the scientific and cultural history of nineteenth-century Germany. Precisely because they were microcephalic, because of the time of their discovery, and, in the end, because of their discovery in Central America, the bodies of "Bartola" and "Maximo" became for many—especially among the scientific community—the preeminent site on which to formulate and debate the technical

11.2. "Maximo" and "Bartola," the "Aztec Children," as presented in the entertainment discourse. Courtesy of the Ron Becker Collection, Syracuse University Library, Department of Special Collections.

and philosophical features of two of the most important scientific theories of the period: evolution and recapitulation.

Although the arrival of the "Aztec Children" in Europe in the early 1850s preceded the great surge of excitement in the idea of evolution, that idea was soon to become a major component in the enfreakment of a whole range of individuals, including the "Aztecs." With such sensational discoveries as the Neanderthal Man—one of the most important freaks of all time—in a cave outside Düsseldorf in 1856, and even more importantly, the publication in 1859 of Charles Darwin's *Origin of Species,* which was eagerly received by German scientists, the idea of evolution gained a scientific and popular currency in Germany that contrasts with reactions in other Western countries. Broad sectors of the public and scientific community became fascinated with what the theory of natural selection suggested about the development of man from nonhumanoid species, as well as with what it implied about the origins of races and cultures.[6] Recalling the acceleration of interest in evolutionary theory in Germany, anthropologist Carl Stratz noted in 1904 that "the various more primitive human races were examined for their resemblance to apes, . . . a list of pithecoid (ape-like) characteristics of man was compiled, and the missing link—the last connecting link between human and ape— was sought after with enthusiasm."[7] Looking back from our standpoint, it is important to recognize that the idea of a missing link made remarkably clear sense in the late nineteenth century. Because evolutionary theory suggested a continuity between different life forms, it was argued that creatures might be found who represented earlier stages in human development, who were, in some sense, "lost in time." Along with enthusiasm for the theory came, of course, a certain willingness to stretch the idea of what a missing link might be. Whereas unusual people with certain alleged "animalistic" characteristics had always found a place in collections of human oddities, in a cultural environment increasingly saturated with the discourse of evolution, these people became easily defined as "missing links" between human and other animal forms on an increasingly fluid chain of being.

To be sure, the scientific community and the "educated" tended to frown on claims by the exhibitors of "savages" and "ape-men" that the freaks were in fact the much-theorized missing links. The bourgeois magazine *Die Gartenlaube,* for instance, ran an article in 1888 entitled "The 'Savage' Human," which clarified for the public that while scholars had until recently widely believed that some sort of prehumans might be found, anyone familiar with current research must discount stories that "ape-people," "men with tails," or such creatures as the infamous "One-Leggers" who, it was claimed, could run and jump with remarkable proficiency through their native forests, would or even could be found. Despite educated skepticism, however, the popular *and* scientific interest in "missing links" rarely abated.

The reception of the famous "ape-girl," "Krao" (1876–1926), is in many ways typical of how individuals were freaked as "missing links" in the period. *Die Gartenlaube's* article briefly recalled the history of the child "undoubtedly familiar" to all its readers: "One day, a few years ago, stunned Europeans read in the daily papers that an 'ape-child'—a girl of 7 to 8 years old—had been captured in the forests of Laos and would begin a tour through Europe. In the reports, it was explained that from this extraordinary race an entire family had been captured, but because the father died of cholera in Laos and the ruler of the land forbade the exporting of the mother, the child was being brought alone."[8] The larger story circulated in

11.3. "Krao, the Ape Girl." Courtesy of Harvard Theatre Collection, The Houghton Library.

the brochures describing "Krao" (fig. 11.3) detailed the formidable efforts of the impresario Farini to bring one of the ape-people living in the forests of Laos to civilization. Having heard that a family of "hairy" people from Laos were being kept by the king of Burma, Farini sent an agent named Carl Bock to obtain one or more of the people for exhibition. Having little luck convincing the king, however, Bock organized an expedition to Laos to capture some of the ape-people for himself. Predictably, Bock claimed to have seen a whole tribe of the people living in tree-huts deep in the forest who fed on rice and raw meat. While he was, in the end, unable to capture any of these ape-people, Bock did eventually succeed in convincing the king to allow the export of "Krao," but only on the condition that she be adopted by Farini.

Despite the fact that the scientific judgment of "Krao" argued squarely that she was far from any "ape-girl" or "missing link," but rather "a typical Siamese" suffering from a pathological condition noted in representatives of diverse races,[9] "Krao" continued to be known as the "missing link" in the most respected and educated circles. Like "Julia Pastrana, the Girl with the Ape Face," who died in 1860 shortly after giving birth, but whose body continued to be exhibited well into the twentieth century,[10] the spectacle of "Krao"—her enfreakment—was a combination of fact and fantasy. When the facts fell short of the fantasy, they were largely ignored. Although the most respected anthropologists of the day, including Rudolf Virchow and Max Bartels, clearly diagnosed "Krao" as suffering from a rare but known pathology, the Zoological Gardens in Frankfurt—a virtual bastion of educated, bourgeois respectability—exhibited "Krao" in 1884 and 1894 as "The Missing Link." Posters for the shows reveal the pervasive narrative of evolution: the hairy child—indeed, much hairier than she was in real life—is drawn against a jungle background. For the 1884 exhibit, for example, a life-size poster of "Krao: The Missing Link" shows a hair-covered child, wearing only a loin cloth and metal bracelets, surrounded by verdant jungle growth as a lizard crawls through the grass at her feet.

As popular as the exhibits of such individuals as "Krao" were—the shows at the Frankfurt Gardens stand today among the most memorable of the zoo's nearly 150-year history[11]—and as much as "Krao" and others form a significant backdrop to the success of the "Aztecs," it is important to recognize that the "Aztec" exhibit stems from a parallel but slightly different tradition: the exhibition of foreign peoples and cultures. Based on the ancient practice of returning home from exploits in foreign lands with captives and representatives of conquered peoples, the display of foreign individuals and cultures only accelerated with the explorations of the early modern and modern period. By the nineteenth century, most cities of Europe had hosted regular exhibits of "strange" peoples, including the almost traditional appearances of Sub-Saharan Africans, Moors, Sami, and other Old World peoples, as well as such new arrivals as Native Americans, Inuit peoples, and South Sea Islanders. In the second half of the nineteenth century, both the frequency and diversity of the shows of "exotic" peoples grew steadily. Whereas in the early decades of the century, a show of "Eskimos" could still be counted among the unusual, by the *fin de siècle* the most important organizer of such shows in Europe, the firm of Carl Hagenbeck, was touring multiple "people shows" each year, with groups from tropical or temperate climates through the summer and others from Arctic and Antarctic lands through the winter.[12] The public and scientific interest in the shows of people varied, of course, according to time, the group exhibited, and even the individuals in that group.[13] Nevertheless, among the most consistently popular exhibitions in the latter half of the century in Germany were those that focused on "primitive" peoples, who could, like "Krao," somehow be freaked as evolutionary ancestors of modern Europeans.

The 1881 "Terra del Fuego" exhibit presents a classic case. Trying to explain the massive public interest in the four men, four women, and three children who comprised one of Carl Hagenbeck's most notable exhibits, Hagenbeck's early biographer, Heinrich Leutemann, quite typically concluded in 1887 that through the display, the public "could still see the human as he had been imagined, pushed back into the incalculable past, at the very beginning of his existence as human, after he had, that is, completely left the ape behind."[14] While most of Hagenbeck's shows relied on elaborate parades, the staging of wild and exciting performances (such as exotic dances by Singhalese women, Sami migrations, the milking of horses by Kalmucks, and Somali camel races), the "Fuegians" simply sat quietly, walked around the grounds, and prepared their food on an open fire without the use of pots. The public, despite the apparent mundaneness of these activities, was staggeringly enthusiastic. In Paris more than 50,000 people visited the show on one Sunday, and at the Berlin Zoological Gardens, "in order to avert the earlier wild scenes of the rush of the public, a large stage some four feet in height had to be erected upon which the Fuegians were situated."[15] Most of the public was clearly more than satisfied with simply gazing upon these apparently obviously "primitive people."

Fulfilling a traditional responsibility of testing the claims of the exhibitor, the chair of the Berlin Anthropological Society, Rudolf Virchow, insisted in his 1881 lecture titled "About the Fuegians" that every day new evidence proved the "authenticity" of the "Fuegians." Among that evidence, the most impressive, Virchow concluded, was the people's "astonishing capacity to withstand every disadvantage of weather (despite a completely inadequate costume), an ability which has not even been closely paralleled by any other people of the Earth, with the possible exception of the Kamchadals."[16] Regarding the cultural accomplishments of the "Fuegians," however, Virchow had little to say, believing that such observations were at best anecdotal and lacking in science. Nevertheless, despite both a number of his own conclusions and the general scientific discourse surrounding the "Fuegians" since Darwin's observations—which suggested that the people were the lowest of human forms yet discovered—Virchow argued that the "Fuegians" in no way represented some form of transitional stage between ape and man. Rather, he concluded, the people "could have progressed further if the adversity of their environment had not repressed them so much that they remained at the lowest level of social life."[17] Behind Virchow's insistence rested the active debate about the evolutionary status of "primitive peoples." Were they only different in appearances from European races, or were the differences deeper and more important? On the whole, the popular perception of the "Fuegians"—a perception rooted in the way the "savages" were displayed and enfreaked—tended to focus on deep differences between them and Europeans. Typical articles describing the "Fuegians" noted loose social structures, an absence of a "feeling of shame," "crude" methods of food preparation and cooking, and a lack of "civilized" standards of cleanliness. According to an 1881 article by Heinrich Steinitz in *Die Gartenlaube*, for example, the "poor wretched creatures were stunted in their growth; they had smeared their ugly faces with white paint, their skin was dirty and greasy, their hair tangled, their voices dissonant." Marking the cultural contrasts, Steinitz concluded for many scientists and the public at large (using Darwin's words from the *Journal of Researches* [1839]) that in "viewing such men, one can hardly make oneself believe that they are fellow creatures and inhabitants of the same world."[18]

While evolutionary theory propelled the search for individuals such as "Krao," and even whole peoples such as the "Fuegians," who could somehow be construed as representing links in human evolution, a corollary to evolutionary theory, focusing on the idea of recapitulation elaborated by German scientist Ernst Haeckel, began to shift the focus of evolutionary studies. Rather than looking to "primitive" peoples such as the "Fuegians" to find the precursors of modern man, Haeckel argued that every creature carried its entire evolutionary history within itself. More precisely, Haeckel's famous "biogenetic law" of 1866 argued that during the process of an individual organism's development from embryo to adult, it rapidly retraced the path of its genetic heritage ("that [its] ontogeny [was] a concise and compressed recapitulation of [its] phylogeny, conditioned by the laws of heredity and adaptation").[19]

Of course, by the time Haeckel's biogenetic law was unleashed, theories of recapitulation had already had a long and fairly complicated history on the continent. Their origins in Germany reached back to the biological studies of the *Naturphilosophen*, gracefully described by Stephen Jay Gould as "a group of late-eighteenth and early-nineteenth-century biologists [who] combined a progressivist view of nature with the romantic thought then current in philosophy and literature" producing a system of ideas with "an uncompromising developmentalism and a belief in the unity of nature and its laws."[20] Under the leadership of Lorenz Oken and, more importantly, J. F. Meckel—whose 1811 essay, "Sketch of a Portrayal of the

Parallels that Exist between the Embryonic Stages of Higher Animals and Adults of Lower Animals," remains one of the central pre-Haeckelian statements of the theory—recapitulation had a strong presence in German biological thought until nature-philosophic (or physio-philosophic) approaches fell into disfavor around the middle of the century. Among the French as well, recapitulation had been championed for decades. Some of the most significant work was produced in the 1820s and 1830s by Étienne Serres, who importantly expanded his studies into the field of teratology, arguing that malformations could be explained as either a deficiency or an overabundance of life force leading to either the arrested development or overdevelopment of body parts.[21] Nevertheless, it is with Haeckel that recapitulation and evolution were combined in their most popular form, which remained powerfully convincing for decades.

While evolutionary theory directed attention to peoples somehow "lost in the past," recapitulation theory led scientists to consider the possibility of finding two kinds of individuals, born of apparently "normal" parents, who could be seen as embodying the evolutionary past of man: (1) those whose entire embryological development remained fixed at a certain point and who, therefore, represented the mature form of an evolutionary predecessor of modern man; or (2) those whose embryological development remained fixed only in certain parts, and who, therefore, represented a blend of evolutionary creatures, or what anatomist Carl Vogt described in 1867 as "a mixed being . . . in which a notable combination of different types is fused into a whole."[22] According to this line of reasoning, because the complete phylogenetic history of the human was both present and recapitulated in the development of an individual, atavistic traits—that is, characteristics from the prehistory of modern man—could reasonably be expected to reappear in individuals who, for whatever reason, suffered a certain developmental arrest or fixation. Expanding on an idea explored by Serres by adding an evolutionary "look and feel," Vogt, for example, concluded: "We know so far that characters passed on latently can reappear after generations, after even very significant periods, even after geological epochs, and that in their reappearance they can modify only parts or even the entire organism."[23]

For Vogt and many of his colleagues, microcephalism provided the classic case for exploring the validity of recapitulation and the importance of arrested developments, and the most famous microcephalics of the period were the "Aztecs." "Bartola" and "Maximo," consequently, became a repeated fixture in the investigations of anthropologists across Germany. The two were measured in every possible way: their skulls (twenty-eight separate measurements by Rudolf Virchow in 1877 to be expanded upon in later examinations) were compared to those of apes; their hair, cropped peculiarly to further the theatrical presentation of difference, was compared to that of all the known races; eye and skin colors were compared on charts prepared by the various anthropological societies; the scientists discussed the vocalizations, expressions of will, and potential reproductive capability of the pair. In the end, however, neither the statistical information ascertaining ear height, forehead width, or distance from eye to eye, nor the comparative indices derived from these data, such as head length to head breadth, could validate or deny Vogt's more speculative assertion that the "Aztecs" might somehow represent "one of the milestones" of human evolution.[24]

As "milestones" the "Aztecs" could potentially qualify under two separate arguments. On one hand, if they were truly what their promoters claimed them to be—descendants of an apparently "primitive" people—then the two last survivors of the lost race of the Aztecs displayed an "apelike" cranial morphology that suggested a race somehow part human and part ape. As I have noted, however, despite some initial acceptance, the German scientific community seems to have generally greeted this idea with disbelief. Virchow, for example, after seeing an exhibition of the "Aztecs" in 1891 at Castan's Panopticum in Berlin, noted the "negative effect" of the presentation made by the pair's manager and added that "we have been convinced for decades that these 'Aztecs' are [simply] microcephalics, and the recent exhibition has only strengthened that determination."[25]

But if few were convinced that the "Aztecs" were truly Aztecs, or that the real pre-Columbian Aztecs were so severely limited in their cranial capacity, many others could nevertheless argue that the "primitive" crania of "Bartola" and "Maximo" were the specific result of a developmental arrest, and that, therefore, the skulls and brains of the "Aztecs" corresponded to the mature development of an ape, even if a very primitive ape. The most thorough presentation of this position was Carl Vogt's exhaustive 1867 study of microcephalism, *About the Microcephalics or Ape-People*, which on one hand built extensively on the teratological arguments of Meckel and Serres, while contributing on the other a firm belief in the evolution of man from ape-like creatures, if not some extant species of ape. In this remarkable work, which was discussed by members of anthropological societies throughout Germany for decades after its publication, Vogt attempted to survey all known materials about microcephalics, examining both living examples and the skulls, drawings, and models housed in museums and pathological institutes.

Vogt's central conclusions were that microcephalism was a "partial atavistic" reappearance of an earlier state of human evolution caused by an arrest in the development of the fetus's skull resulting in the formation of an ape-like cranium and brain, which, according to Vogt, explained the limited capacities of the microcephalics. Vogt writes, "the intellectual abilities [of the microcephalic] are those of the ape in every respect, from the expressions of will to the understanding of external objects, to comprehension, to articulated language (which is in no way used by these creatures to express their thoughts, but exists rather only as a product of imitation as with talking animals)." Referring to a monument supposedly erected by Frederick the Great to a much-admired woman that had read "Corpore femina, intellectu vir," Vogt substitutes the pithy description of microcephalism: "Corpore homo, intellectu simia." He concludes that the examination of microcephalics presents a body of evidence that leads backward through time to the "common ancestor of the primates, from which we as well as the apes have descended."[26]

In response to Vogt's startling conclusions, Virchow, who was always an opponent of far-reaching conclusions (including evolutionary theory), argued that the microcephalic could not represent an atavistic recurrence of the mature form of an extinct species or race simply because the microcephalic could in no way be considered fit for the struggle for survival. "If a developmental arrest," he concluded in 1867, "creates such a helpless, absolutely useless individual, such as a microcephalic, an individual which in its functioning in no way even approaches the ape, but rather which presents an absolutely pathological, a purely ill appearance, then I am not in the position to find therein proof that a primordial form has been brought to light."[27] Ten years later, and after his second extensive examination of "Bartola" and "Maximo," Virchow reached the same conclusion: "One cannot maintain that the human was ever at a state for which the microcephalic could be an analog, otherwise humanity would have become extinct before the beginning of history."[28] At the root of Virchow's critique was the recognition that although one could forcefully maintain that many human malformations were the result of developmental arrests suffered by the embryo, it did not necessarily follow that these arrested states either paralleled or actually embodied the forms of ancestors or lower creatures.[29]

If Virchow's 1877 conclusions have something seemingly final and incontrovertible about them—and, indeed, as chair of the Berlin Anthropological Society his judgments tended to be accorded great respect—one nevertheless needs to explain why both the "Aztecs" themselves and the arguments about them continued to attract scientific attention through the beginning of the twentieth century. The scientific photographs of "Maximo" and "Bartola" reproduced here, for example (figs 11.1a and b), come from the 1901 *Transactions of the Berlin Anthropological Society*—twenty-five years after Virchow's most extensive assessment of the pair and thirty-five years after he formulated the major contours of his critique. The two photographs, typical of the hundreds of "scientized" records of freaks and "exotic peoples" appearing in the publications of the Society and its members, present "Bartola" and "Maximo" stripped of all narratives of their lives; they are simply objects of scientific interest. But what, in the final analysis, was the interest? It is clear, for example, that enthusiasm for Vogt's explanation of microcephalism, as an arrested embryological development atavistically revealing a protohuman morphology, had more or less been discarded by the late 1880s. Still, as Virchow himself noted in 1891, the "appearance [of the Aztecs] has [nevertheless] *something unusual about it,* which arouses further *penetration into their history,* and no researcher has been able to resist this attraction."[30] The "Aztecs," then, continued to intrigue German scientists because they remained somehow "unusual."

The precise nature of that unusualness remains difficult to ascertain. We know that while the Berlin Anthropological Society had many opportunities to study, measure, and debate over microcephalics during the latter half of the century, these efforts were usually applied to continued debate about the "Aztecs." At one point, for example, Virchow became convinced that a microcephalic race called the Chua might exist in the Punjab region of India, but he turned his discussion of the Chua upon its relevance to the "Aztecs." In the end, it appears that researchers maintained an interest in the "Aztecs" over other microcephalics for two primary reasons. First, because "Bartola" and "Maximo" lived much longer than the other microcephalics studied, it was logically argued that they presented a unique opportunity to investigate how aging affected the physical and intellectual capacities of microcephalics. But curiosity about the processes of aging is only part of the story. Primarily, the "Aztecs" remained interesting to the scientific community for the same reason that they remained so for the public at large: the idea of two children found in a temple in the middle of the jungle who were the last survivors of their ancient race. That idea, told in a fantastic story of adventure and discovery, involving great risk and contact with "primitive" cultures, and related in a largely theatrical set with costumes, bizarre hair styles, and constant guidance by the impresario, was what made the "Aztecs" different from the other microcephalics brought to the Society, and that story served as the underlying theme in all studies of the pair. Even though scientist after scientist sought to disprove the tale of the "last surviving" Aztecs, "Bartola" and "Maximo" remained the "Aztecs," embodying the idea of primitives from deep in the Central American jungle. Thus, in his year-end report to the Berlin Anthropological Society in 1891, Virchow enthusiastically states:

No earlier year has brought to us such a wealth of exotic and unusual people as this last. Here in the Society we have seen Dualla from Cameroon and Negroes from the West Coast of Africa (they call themselves Dahome), Melanesians and Tagals, Lapps and "Aztecs." The most fantastic monstrosities have stepped before us: a heteradelphic Indian, xiphodymic Italians, a bearded woman from North America, a prematurely mature girl from Berlin—in short, each of our members, while also being at home, was able to complete his anthropological observations with personally experienced memories.[31]

Rather than grouping the "Aztecs" among the "fantastic monstrosities" seen at the Society—including such other sideshow freaks as the conjoined twins known as "Laloo" ("heteradelphic Indian"), the also conjoined twins Giovanni and Giacomo Tocci ("xiphodymic Italians"), and the bearded woman, Miss Annie Jones—Virchow places "Bartola" and "Maximo," despite all his conclusions over the years, at the end of a list of remarkable, if also freaked, cultures.

By placing the "Aztecs" with the freaked cultures instead of with the "fantastic monstrosities," Virchow and his colleagues[32] participated in the enfreakment of "Bartola" and "Maximo" as living Aztecs. Their doing so stems, it seems, from the essential role that storytelling, or the narrative of enfreakment, has always played in creating the wondrous, monstrous, or historical out of the simply unusual. Thinking back on the photograph of the Hamburger Dom, for example, we must remember the presence of the signs "The Atzteeken are Here!" and "Frederke, the 15 Year Old Pomeranian Colossus, Live!"; we must recognize that before audiences, including the scientists, saw "Bartola" and "Maximo," they had already been repeatedly told by newspapers, friends, colleagues, signs, and, of course, the impresarios the elaborate story of Aztec temples deep in Central America and the strange people who inhabited strange regions of the earth.

Indeed, the importance of the history of "jungles" and "strange peoples" in assessing the reception of the "Aztecs" should not be underestimated. As we have seen, the "Aztecs" shared with "Krao" and the "Fuegians" foundation narratives that emphasized the remoteness and primitiveness of the areas in which they were discovered. "Krao," though obtained from a court in Burma, was an alleged representative of a race of ape-people living in the trees of Laos; the "Fuegians" were inseparably connected to the extremely isolated and inhospitable islands off the southern tip of South America—a land where, it could easily be imagined, time itself could somehow have remained frozen. Similarly, the "Aztecs" were framed by the story of lost civilizations, temple cults, and architectural ruins thickly shrouded by prehistoric-looking vegetation in an area of the world closed off from European cultures. To be sure, freaks did not actually have to be found in a lost corner of the globe to be constituted as missing links. Those freaks like "Krao" who suffered from the excessive hirsuteness of hypertrichosis, for example, were almost uniformly presented as missing links despite their origins. Thus, although "Jo-Jo the Poodle Man" (1870–1903) was discovered in Russia, far from any primeval jungles, it was quickly alleged that he had been captured in the ancient Russian forests. Similarly, the Englishman who came to be known as "Rham-a-Sama" (born around 1860) had, despite the claims of impresarios, little if any background in jungle environs.[33]

The case of "Lionel the Lion Man" (fig. 11.4) presents the exception that proves the

11.4. "Lionel, the Lion-Faced Boy." Courtesy of Harvard Theatre Collection, The Houghton Library.

importance of the jungle narrative. Born Stefan Bibrowski in 1890 in the Russian-speaking Polish city of Wilezagora, "Lionel" began touring as a freak when only a child. He was a main attraction with Barnum and Bailey in the latter years of the century but spent most of his career in Europe, eventually dying in either 1930 or 1932 in Italy. "Lionel," however, was rarely cast as a missing link. Despite posters that enfreaked him with a pride of lions, most of the surviving pictures of "Lionel" show him attired in upper-class or even aristocratic clothing in stately and educated poses. One studio photograph, for example, which captures well much of the aura surrounding him, pictures "Lionel" bare-chested, wearing highly decorated leggings and holding a book, while reclining on one elbow upon an elaborate cushion.[34] Such a pose with its air of luxury was simply an impossibility for an "Ape-Girl," "Aztec," or "Fuegian" whose identity was so closely tied to the nonhuman.

In the final analysis, the only way to explain the prominent place that "Bartola" and "Maximo" came to assume in the scientific culture of Germany in the second half of the nineteenth century is to recognize that the particular form in which they were enfreaked by that culture was the result of a series of both scientific and nonscientific interests. The particular morphology that the "Aztecs" presented led scientists to debate the evolutionary and recapitulationary significance of the pair. However, to understand the continued scientific enthusiasm for the pair after their microcephalism had been accepted, we must recognize, as

Virchow himself did, that the "Aztecs" remained unusual for reasons beyond their microcephalism. Just as the broad range of associations generated in the period by such ideas as "primeval," "jungle," "ancient," "ruins," and "lost civilizations" constitute a crucial backdrop to the theories of evolution and recapitulation, these associations played a vital role for both the public at large *and* the scientific community in the enfreakment of the "Aztecs" as the "missing links."

NOTES

1. The photograph is reproduced in Carl Thinius, *Damals in St. Pauli: Lust und Freude in der Vorstadt* (Hamburg: Christian, 1975), 121.

2. It has remained impossible to determine whether the 1905 show of "Aztecs" pictured in the postcard presented the "Aztecs" "Bartola" and "Maximo" discussed in this article. Due to the success of the original exhibit, there were a series of imitators who claimed to present "Aztecs," including the "Last Female Aztecs" and "Assra, the Dwarf Aztec." See Hans Scheugl, *Show Freaks and Monster: Sammlung Felix Adanos* (Cologne: M. DuMont Schauberg, 1974), 105–8.

3. This summary of the brochure is taken from Robert Hartmann, "Azteken," *Verhandlungen der Berliner Gesellschaft für Anthropologie, Ethnologie und Urgeschichte* 23 (1891): 278–79. Hartmann's lecture of 21 February 1891 discussed the then almost forty-year-old brochure in order to lay the groundwork for the Society's visit to the Aztec show on 7 March. The visit was discussed in the next meeting of the Society on 21 March in a lecture by Rudolf Virchow, who noted that the pamphlet brought to attention by Hartmann was still being sold at the exhibit.

4. Carl Gustav Carus, "Ueber die sogenannten Aztekenkinder," *Berichte der Akademie in Berlin, Mathematisch Physikalische Classe* (Berlin, 1856); and "Die Azteken," *Berichte über die Verhandlungen der Kgl. Sächsischen Gesellschaft der Wissenschaften zu Leipzig, Mathem. phys. Classe I* (Leipzig, 1856).

5. Hartmann, "Azteken," 279.

6. For an idea of the popular-scientific form that evolutionary theory took in Germany, see the remarkable novel by David Friedrich Weinland, *Rulaman: Naturgeschichtliche Erzählung aus der Zeit des Höhlenmenschen und des Höhlenbären* (1878; Stuttgart: Deutsche Verlags Anstalt, 1986).

7. Carl H. Stratz, *Naturgeschichte des Menschen: Grundriss der Somatischen Anthropologie* (Stuttgart, 1904), 15.

8. "Der 'Wilde' Mensch," *Die Gartenlaube* 88 (1888). 874.

9. Ibid., 874.

10. Scheugl, *Show Freaks*, 35.

11. See Christoph Scherpner, *Von Bürgern für Bürger: 125 Jahre Zoologischer Garten Frankfurt am Main* (Frankfurt am Main: Zoologischer Garten, 1983).

12. In 1883 and 1884, for example, Hagenbeck's "people shows" included groups of Araucanians, Australian Aborigines, Singhalese, and Kalmucks. For an introduction to the Hagenbeck shows, see Hilke Thode-Arora, *Für fünfzig Pfennig um die Welt: Die Hagenbeckschen Völkerschauen* (Frankfurt am Main: Campus, 1989).

13. Clearly, the ideas behind such shows as the "Cameroon Show" of 1886 (set against the backdrop of the acquisition of Cameroon as a German protectorate in the winter of 1884–85) and the "Amazon Corps" of 1891 (a fantasy production of the legend of a female army in Africa featuring "a dozen brown-skinned beauties in fantastic costumes of shells and corals—otherwise, however, practically naked" [Thinius, *Damals in St. Pauli*, 35]), span a broad range of interests, even while both shows focused on African peoples.

14. Heinrich Leutemann, *Lebensbeschreibung des Thierhändlers Carl Hagenbeck* (Hamburg, 1887), 62.

15. *Die Neue Preussische (Kreuz-) Zeitung*, 18 November 1881.

16. Rudolf Virchow, "Über die Feuerländer," *Verhandlungen der Berliner Gesellschaft für Anthropologie, Ethnologie und Urgeschichte* 12 (1881): 375. For an introduction to Rudolf Virchow, see Manfred Vasold, *Rudolf Virchow: Der Grosse Arzt und Politiker* (Stuttgart: Deutsche Verlags Anstalt, 1988).

17. Virchow, "Über die Feuerländer," 385. Heinrich Steinitz, "Die Feuerländer," *Die Gartenlaube* 81

(1881): 732–35, however, noted French articles appearing about the group that agreed with earlier reports that the "Fuegians" were "repulsive creatures standing still at the very beginning of human culture, if one can even use such a term with them" (732).

18. Steinitz, "Die Feuerländer," 734.

19. Ernst Mayr, *The Growth of Biological Thought: Diversity, Evolution, and Inheritance* (Cambridge: Harvard University Press, 1982), 474.

20. Stephen Jay Gould, *Ontogeny and Phylogeny* (Cambridge: Harvard University Press, 1977), 35.

21. Meckel, it should be noted, also applied the idea of developmental arrests to explain certain teratological phenomena. For a clear presentation of the development of the "recapitulation debate," see Mayr, *Growth of Biological Thought*, 469–76; and Gould, *Ontogeny and Phylogeny*, especially 33–166. See also Frank Sulloway, *Freud, Biologist of the Mind: Beyond the Psychoanalytic Legend* (New York: Basic Books, 1979). Freud, of course, popularized recapitulation further with both his discussion of the mental life of children replaying various stages in human development and his use of fixation and regression to describe mental disturbances in adults.

22. Carl Vogt, "Ueber die Mikrocephalen oder Affen-Menschen," *Archiv für Anthropologie* 2 (1867): 268.

23. Ibid., 274. Vogt's argument for the appearance of "atavistic" characteristics was not in any way bizarre or extreme; indeed, it was widely regarded at the time as a demonstrable fact. In *The Origin of Species*, Darwin, for example, discussed what he termed "reversions" to explain the reappearance of characteristics in domestic breeds that clearly derived from the original wild stock. Discussing the manifestation of leg bars and shoulder stripes among domestic horses and asses, he concluded at one point, "I venture confidently to look back thousands on thousands of generations, and I see an animal striped like a zebra, but perhaps otherwise very differently constructed, the common parent of our domestic horse . . . , of the ass, the hemionus, quagga, and zebra" (*The Origin of Species by Charles Darwin: A Variorum Text*, ed. Morse Peckham [Philadelphia: University of Pennsylvania Press, 1959], 317). For only the most recent chapter in this line of reasoning, see Brian K. Hall, "Atavisms and Atavistic Mutations," *Nature Genetics* 10 (June 1995): 126–27.

24. Vogt, "Ueber die Mikrocephalen," 277.

25. Virchow, "Über die sogenannten Azteken und die Chua," *Verhandlungen der Berliner Gesellschaft für Anthropologie, Ethnologie und Urgeschichte* 23 (1891): 371.

26. Vogt, "Ueber die Mikrocephalen," 276–78.

27. "Referate," *Archiv für Anthropologie* 2 (1867): 503. Virchow is here arguing along a line developed to confront the early recapitulationists.

28. Virchow, "Ueber Microcephalie," *Verhandlungen der Berliner Gesellschaft für Anthropologie, Ethnologie und Urgeschichte* 9 (1877): 288. Virchow's first examination of "Bartola" and "Maximo" was in 1866.

29. Virchow shared this analysis with his great antirecapitulationist predecessor Karl von Baer. For a discussion of von Baer, see Gould, *Ontology and Phylogeny*, 52–63.

30. Virchow, "Über die sogenannten Azteken und die Chua," 370, emphasis mine.

31. Virchow, "Verwaltungsbericht für das Jahr 1891," *Verhandlungen der Berliner Gesellschaft für Anthropologie, Ethnologie und Urgeschichte* 23 (1891): 869.

32. Virchow lamented in 1901 that the "Aztecs" continued to be discussed by his colleagues in racial terms. See Virchow, "Die beiden Azteken," *Verhandlungen der Berliner Gesellschaft für Anthropologie, Ethnologie und Urgeschichte* 33 (1901): 348–50.

33. Scheugl, *Show Freaks*, 35.

34. See ibid., 40–41, for illustrations.

TWELVE

The "Exceptions That Prove the Rule": Daisy and Violet Hilton, the "New Woman," and the Bonds of Marriage

ALLISON PINGREE

To vaudeville crowds of the late 1920s, Daisy and Violet Hilton (fig. 12.1) presented a remarkable sight. The teenage girls with long, dark ringlets and fancy dresses danced, sang, and played the saxophone, seemingly unimpeded by the fact that made them famous: they were conjoined twins, fused together at the base of their spine.[1] Born in 1908 in England, Daisy and Violet were trained in performance arts early on and were exhibited in different parts of the world from the time they were three (Drimmer 1991, 54). After coming to America in 1916, they became vaudeville sensations, earning up to five thousand dollars a week and hobnobbing with such figures as Harry Houdini, Eddie Cantor, and Bob Hope. The twins eventually made their way to Hollywood, where they appeared in two films, Tod Browning's *Freaks* (1932), and *Chained for Life* (1951).

The allure that these joined twins held for their early twentieth-century American audience worked at many different levels; according to Robert Bogdan, spectators wondered such things as how the twins "performed such normal activities as walking and sitting. . . . Did they feel the same emotion? When one was touched, did the other sense it? How similar were they in personality and taste? . . . How intertwined were their bodies? Could they be separated?" (1988, 201).

Similar questions have intrigued the observers of conjoined twins in a variety of cultural contexts. For centuries, scientists, physicians, and philosophers in the Western world have been both plagued and fascinated by conjoined twins' confounding mathematics of personhood—the fact that they are both more than one yet not quite two. Teratological studies ranging from Ambroise Paré's *On Monsters and Marvels* (1573) to George M. Gould and Walter L. Pyle's *Anomalies and Curiosities of Medicine* (1897) include extensive taxonomies of various types of "in-betweenness"—of bodily absence and overabundance (of arms, legs, heads, genitals, etc.). As with other corporeal anomalies, the fleshy link between conjoined twins provokes a variety of emotional responses, from wonder to confusion, curiosity to pity, amusement to awe, and most of all, an intense desire to contain and interpret. More specifically, a survey of teratological treatises reveals that conjoined twins pose a most literal

12.1. Daisy and Violet Hilton. Courtesy of the Hertzberg Circus Collection and Museum, San Antonio, Texas.

challenge to the borders of personal identity by placing a multiplied self where there is usually only one, and by questioning where individual agency begins and ends.

Such concerns are particularly pressing in the American cultural context. Not surprisingly, America has long been transfixed by conjoined twins, beginning with the so-called "original" Siamese twins, Chang and Eng, whose popularity here in the early to mid-nineteenth century, widely promoted by P. T. Barnum among others, was so vast that the country of their origin, Siam, now is used to connote all joined twins.[2] Conjoined twins arrest the attention and imagination of the American public because they embody both a national fantasy and a national nightmare. That is, the prospect of merged selves corporealized in conjoined twins both reflects a democratic imperative—where all selves are in a sense the same, interchangeable self—and imperils the stability of unique selfhood so stressed by American individualism.

But the case of Daisy and Violet provoked even more particularized and historically grounded responses in the American populace observing them. When the Hilton sisters emerged as celebrities, certain questions dominated the cultural landscape—questions that applied very readily to the twins themselves. That is, dramatic changes in the political, economic, and domestic circumstances of women in the early twentieth century created a highly controversial environment for a figure that was doubly female.

The decades before and after 1920, the year when women achieved suffrage, were fraught with heated debates about women's roles in marriage, motherhood, politics, and employment. And such issues were certainly at play as American audiences viewed the Hiltons; Bogdan claims that marriage in particular was a "constant issue in full public view" for Daisy and Violet, and was one of the main sources of their "publicity," for it "titillated the general public. Being normal meant establishing nuptial ties, yet the intimacies of marriage were allowed only under the most private circumstances—to which, of course, joined twins had no access" (1988, 201).

A brief exploration of some of the changes fueling these debates over women's roles will show more clearly how and why representations of the Hiltons were so charged with cultural meaning. In *The Grounding of Modern Feminism*, Nancy Cott explains that in the early 1900s the increase of "women's new experiences in public, organizational, and occupational life marked one of the ways in which the outlines of twentieth-century America were already taking shape" (1987, 22). For example, while only 35 percent of all those in college in 1890 were women, by the 1920s, a full half of that group were (Cott 1987, 148). Moreover, between the 1870s and 1920s, while about 10 percent of all American women did not marry, of those who graduated from college 40 to 60 percent did not (Smith-Rosenberg 1985, 253). In short, the "noticeable growth of single women's employment outside the home, the diversification of living patterns and family relationships that implied, and the emergence to social concern of a new type of woman leader, educated in college and perhaps graduate school and trained to analyze social problems, set the stage for a new era in the woman movement" (Cott 1987, 22).

The "new type of woman leader" to whom Cott refers is frequently described as the "New Woman," a term, as historian Carroll Smith-Rosenberg explains, originally coined by Henry James. Smith-Rosenberg uses the phrase to refer to "a specific sociological and educational cohort of women born between the late 1850s and 1900" who, in "rejecting conventional female roles and asserting their right to a career, to a public voice, to visible power, laid claim to the rights and privileges customarily accorded bourgeois men" (1985, 176). Indeed, the New Woman "constituted a revolutionary demographic and political phenomenon. Eschewing marriage, she fought for professional visibility, espoused innovative, often radical economic and social reforms, and wielded real political power" (245). Not surprisingly, the New Woman—often educated at women's colleges—frequently spent more time in the company of women than men, and derived much of her own delight and empowerment there; in some cases, these female-to-female relationships had an erotic component, while others remained more platonic. Smith-Rosenberg claims that such a "loving world of female bonding and traditional female familial concepts" worked to the New Woman's great advantage, allowing her to "forge a network of women reformers and social innovators into a singularly effective political machine" (255).

Another development in the 1920s and 1930s that similarly challenged traditional roles of women in and outside the home was an increased emphasis on "companionate marriage." The label, originated by Judge Ben Lindsey of Colorado, contained several components: birth control; divorce by mutual consent for partners who had no children, with no automatic alimony payments to the divorced wife; and a program dedicated to educating "youth and married couples in the art of love, the laws of sex and life, to equip them better for the serious duties of marriage and parenthood" (Lindsey 1930, 195). As Cott explains, though conservatives very much opposed such notions, others supported them since they located the family as a "specialized site for emotional intimacy, personal and sexual expression, and nurture among husband, wife, and a small number of children" (1987, 156). Those advocating the companionate mode saw Victorian marriage as "hierarchical and emotionally barren, based on dominance and submission," and preferred an "ideal of intimate sexual partnership, in which female sexuality was presumed and marriage was valued for eliciting the partners' individuality as well as for uniting them" (157). The companionate marriage, then, was "symmetrical" instead of a "system of domination that imprisoned women's individuality" (158).

Because of both the rise of the New Woman and the popularization of companionate marriage, close relationships between men and women—and between women and other women—were seen very differently by the turn-of-the-century American public than by previous generations. Even as companionate marriage gave women some measure of greater equality within the home, marriage also came to be seen much more as "normal," "natural," and socially necessary; Lindsey's model, moreover, implied that a woman's economic place still was within the home (Cott 1987, 157–58). Predictably, female friendships were now more suspect; whereas in earlier decades—when male authority was less in question—close female bonds were seen with impunity, now "same-sex relationships came to be suspected as alternatives to women's relationships with men, and therefore threats to existing sexual and social order" (159). Moreover, the concrete emerging reality of "unmarried women's earning power" provoked a "specter" of "women who had no evident male partners or guides" (159). Similarly, as Smith-Rosenberg (citing Havelock Ellis) explains, the New Women, "unmarried, career-oriented, politically active, often lovingly involved with one another," were criticized as "selfish," " 'unnatural' " and androgynous and/or lesbian (278).

Representations of such radical changes in women, and of men's responses to them, took many forms. In 1928, Henry Carey published an essay in *Harper's* claiming that "woman's emancipation" was a "threat to family life"; while this argument was a predictable one, the title Carey chose was not: "This Two-Headed Monster—The Family."[3] It is striking indeed that Carey symbolizes domestic and marital transgression through the corporeal anomaly of conjoined twins.

In particular, Carey lays down two grievances: first, women's "financial independence," which creates an "unnatural" erosion of men's "authority" by turning things "upside-down"; and second, women's attitudes reflecting "the craze for independence" associated with the "feminist movement and its egocentric doctrines" (Carey 1928, 165–66). Arguing that " 'the very essence of feminine love lie[s] in the idea of surrender' " and that men seek women who will give themselves "with that completeness which alone can call forth [their] single-hearted and unselfish devotion" (169–70), he maintains that a "woman's chief function on this planet" is to "attract and hold a man, with the object of reproducing and educating children. Man's job has always been to feed the family. It is not natural that the role of woman should be so suddenly modified" (167). Indeed, he argues that if a woman "does her duty by the race" and raises her children "with tender care," then "she has all the career that she needs, and her outside interests will then take their proper place as hobbies or pastimes" (169).

In addition to this division of labor, another crucial element in Carey's model of an acceptable family is that the deciding vote, in the case of a difference of opinions, always lies with the man. Presenting a typical scenario of a disagreement between husband and wife, he exhorts the woman to yield, for "a wife who will not surrender . . . is, from a man's point of view, not a wife at all" (170). To intensify his argument he draws on the vivid imagery of conjoined twins: "Feminists, note this well! It is the double-headedness of the modern American family which is causing it so frequently to split down the middle, . . . The heads are at war with each other. The house divided against itself does not, we observe, stand" (170). Herein, Carey extends his rhetoric about the "unnaturalness" of women's independence by imaging a marriage of equals as a freakish, conjoined set of bodies. Indeed, instead of invoking such a bond as a harmonious symbol of married life, he uses it to critique contemporary developments in female emancipation, portraying them as monstrous.

Even though Carey does not mention Daisy and Violet directly, they certainly possess many of the characteristics he most fears in women. At a variety of levels, the Hiltons' celebrated union raises contested issues regarding women's power, voice, earning capabilities, and their right and ability to be "on their own," separate from and outside of marriage and the home. The twins were beautiful and flaunted that beauty for their own ends; they were (for most of their lives) single; they were never burdened with child rearing; and most importantly, they were very financially successful, becoming among the highest-paid performers in vaudeville and Hollywood during their career. They were women joined together, seemingly happy without men, just as the New Woman was with her feminist sisters. Indeed, the twins had the potential to be seen in the same way that Smith-Rosenberg describes the New Woman, as a "condensed symbol of disorder and rebellion" (1985, 247).

It is, of course, a great irony that the twins would be seen as reflections of the new, independent woman when neither Daisy nor Violet ever *was* "free"—in physical terms—for a day of her life. Yet it was precisely their attachment to each other, rather than to a man, that made them so threatening, and made their image more haunting to a conservative male audience than other female "freaks" who also might have been earning lots of money. That is, the conjunction of Daisy and Violet, one that literally and symbolically approximated the marriage bond, was precisely what made them so profitable and so dangerous. The power behind the image of Daisy and Violet was that they were both permanently single because they were permanently doubled. They were already each other's "other half"; their bond thus superseded, and rendered unnecessary, the companionate, heterosexual spouse. Indeed, instead of being fused in marriage to someone else, they were each fused to each other, and that very fusion—the "monstrosity" they displayed—was the key to their financial independence and thus to the economic power that Carey saw as a threat to marriage.

Representations of the twins, constructed mostly by men, responded to this power in various ways. Some attempted to control it, either by using the conjunction as a playful symbol of harmonious marriage or by representing the twins as espousing beliefs that counteracted the trends toward women's independence. Through normalizing narratives that used the twins' bond to reaffirm traditional women's roles, such representations strove to transmute them into safer feminine figures and to contain the chaos that their threatening bodies presented. Other representations depicted the dangers that the twins' bond presented in a more straightforward way, imaging them as domineering and emasculating. In short, the twins were used both as containers or embodiments of cultural danger, as well as symbolic representations of solutions to that danger.

Always, though, these representations betrayed a deep awareness of how, as a symbol, the twins' bond represented the power of women united together, and of how, as a concrete commercial fact, the bond ensured that the twins were independent, financially prodigious women. Indeed, for most of their performing years, the Hilton sisters embodied a threatening substitute for marriage, ironically, by enacting and literalizing the very things that conservative marital norms of the time advocated. The twins could not be governed by a husband because they were already physically fused to each other; they were unable to enter a companionate marriage because they already were each other's own symmetrical "companions"; and they undermined the distinction between public and private by constantly witnessing each others' lives, and by inverting their own intimate bond into economic advantage. The bodies of Daisy and Violet simply concentrated, onto one corporeal site, much broader cultural debates about gender, domesticity and power.

Two years before Carey published his article and six years after American women received the vote, Daisy and Violet performed on vaudeville a playful, lighthearted song that parallels their relationship with that of a heterosexual couple, and thus normalizes their potential danger. From the outset, "Me Too" (written by Harry Woods, Charles Tobias and Al. Sherman) presents itself as being about male-female romance; the cover drawing (fig. 12.2) boasts a young woman in the foreground and her well-dressed suitor in the sporty convertible behind her. She is drawn as shapely and high-heeled—flirtatious yet also demure; the lyrics reveal that "[i]n a bathing suit she looks great." This energetic romance leads up to marriage in verse two: "Got a ring and a horse and a horse and a ring / And we're ready to go / Giddyap! Giddyap! Giddyap! Giddyap! / Oh the parson will know / That I don't care I don't mind / Anywhere that she goes you'll find / Ho Ho! Ha Ha! ME TOO." Moreover, many lines imply that this marriage will be a companionate one: "She loves the things I do / Morning, noon and night / I'm right in her sight / She can't get away / . . . . I do what she does / And she does what I do / And I'll tell you right now / That I don't care I don't mind / Anywhere that she goes you'll find / Ho Ho! Ha Ha! ME TOO." Likewise, the affluent speaker treats his sweetheart to an elaborate vacation ("She wants to go to Europe / So I said 'Honey, that's O.K.' "). In short, when the assumed speaker of "Me Too" is male, the song is a model for a companionate marriage: man and woman enjoy the same things and go places together; satisfied as a consumer of sex and material goods, the woman plays her proper role as the wife.

However, the other image on that same cover—that of Daisy and Violet—reminds the audience of a different prospect altogether. That is, when sung by Daisy and Violet, the lyrics take on a different meaning—one of two women, rather than a man and woman, joined together. By putting into their mouths this heterosexual script, the Hiltons' promoters could attempt to reduce the threat the twins posed of two young women who go everywhere together—with no man in sight—and thoroughly enjoy themselves.

A similar vacillation between revealing the transgressive sides of the Hiltons and attempting to contain those threatening elements emerges in a variety of publicity material on the twins. One such example is an early pamphlet (circa 1926), *Souvenir and Life Story of San Antonio's Siamese Twins*, written most likely by Myer Myers, the twins' domineering manager.[4] At one point, the pamphlet relates that the sisters share an intense bond—one that could easily evoke what many feared about the New Woman and her female friendships: Daisy and Violet supposedly claim that they have decided never to marry, explaining that there is a "closer

12.2. "Me Too" with the Hilton Sisters, "San Antonio's Siamese Twins." Courtesy of the College of Physicians of Philadelphia.

spiritual cord between us than between other human beings" and that "[heterosexual married] love can only complicate the business of living for us" (13). Thus, they conclude, "there is no way for either of us to find happiness that others find in marriage" so instead, "we are merely spectators" (14). Such descriptions are exactly the kind of thing that, when spoken by independent women, would have threatened traditional marital patterns; they invoke feminist "sisters" bonded together by a "spiritual cord," in lives not "complicated" by men and marriage.

But such an admission is rare in the pamphlet; rather, the rest transmutes Daisy and Violet into representatives of more traditionalist norms, decrying the views that such feminist sisters would hold. It reads in part like a handbook on American girlhood, sketching out model feminine conduct and appearance. For example, it claims that the twins "radiate happiness" and have "all the joy that comes to those who really love to make other people happy"; similarly, the twins "have a home development that is both interesting and instinctive. . . . [They] love to sew, get meals, cook, sing, dance, swim, . . . romp, raise pets, play tennis, golf, handball, go to the theatre, the movies, read good books and converse with cultured people." Daisy and Violet, the text claims, are "stimulated by higher ideals and nobler aspirations" than common girls (3). Moreover, the pamphlet places an unquestioned emphasis on the necessity, timelessness, and "naturalness" of marriage as an institution: "That the thoughts of girls, budding into womanhood, turn naturally to marriage, has been a theory of mankind since the dawn of the ages, and it has been a theory borne out by facts. It is human nature, that's all" (12).

The text's most overt appropriation of Violet and Daisy as advocates for traditional roles for women comes when it presents them as purportedly "speaking for themselves"; therein, they offer direct injunctions on the proper role and behavior of women:

> We do not care much for women in business, in offices. We believe in the so-called bromide that "woman's place is in the home." . . . [W]e believe that the career of every woman is marriage, or should be. It seems to us that Nature meant the race to go on, or men and woman [sic] would not have been created in the first place. We seem to feel that a woman who puts marriage behind her for the sake of a business or artistic career is not doing her allotted task. (13)

Such advice—strongly reminiscent of Carey's rhetoric—is startling, coming as it does from two women whose lives were spent in continuous employment and who themselves eschewed marriage. The text attempts to explain this bizarre juxtaposition by having the twins claim, " 'We are the exceptions that prove the rule' " (13).

Such defenses of marriage and domestically inclined women, of course, beg the question of their necessity: if the value of traditional female roles were not in question, such moralizing most likely would be superfluous. It seems that Myers, intuiting the latent threat that the twins pose, forms them into mouthpieces of the conventional norms that must have seemed endangered by current cultural debates regarding marriage and women's power. By framing the Hiltons as the "exceptions to girls in everyday life," he could advocate certain traditional standards for what that "everyday life" should be.

Another publicity article, written in the early 1930s, reflects many of the ways in which the twins posed a threat to conventional marital roles and similarly moves between identifying the dangers the twins present and attempting to contain them. Unlike the souvenir booklet, which claims that the twins will not marry, "One of the Hilton 'Siamese Twins' to be Married" explores what might happen if they did. Announcing the engagement of Daisy to Jack Lewis, a young orchestra leader from Chicago, the article presents Jack as the protagonist in a melodrama, facing challenge after challenge in his love quest. Each impediment arises from the unchanging fact of the twins' bond, and the representation of each confrontation reveals the complications that the twins present. For example, the article implies that the marriage could become a "two against one" relation, with Daisy and Violet ganging up on Jack—and winning: "Anyone can see that if Violet disliked Jack he would have no chance at all." An image of double monstrosity follows, revealing the implicit power the twins wield over the male suitor: "Presumably, if Jack ever comes home at an unholy hour, he will face an angry double figure in a nightgown. Many a husband has faced just such a double menace, but he can always make the double figure turn into one by closing one eye. Jack cannot do this. He may expect the left half of the apparition, which is Daisy, to stretch out a hand and in a terrible voice, say: '. . . . I wish to speak with you.' " Even if, as a result of such domination, Jack wants a divorce, the article warns that such efforts will be in vain: "It would be hopeless to contest her divorce because Daisy has an eye-witness to corroborate every act of her life who was present at all of her conversations." While such descriptions undoubtedly could cause a chuckle in readers, they nonetheless bespeak the underlying threat that the twins represent.

Even more dangerous than the prospect of the overly powerful, doubled wife is the way in which the twins' physical conjunction collapses the border between public and private—between external, masculinized realms of politics, enterprise, and spectacle, and intimate, feminized realms of domesticity—upon which the ideology of traditional marriage depends. Once again, the article attempts to cast the problem in a humorous light by focusing (through description and a photograph) on a clever gimmick the twins have devised to ensure privacy in courtship: a phone booth with a wall that slides up and down, so that one twin can have a secret conversation by phone while the other waits outside.

But such attempts, of course, were really a fiction of privacy, since any romantic attempt would always be witnessed—and thus participated in—by both twins. Indeed, Jack is constantly confounded in his attempt simply to be alone with Daisy:

> Next to murder, love-making is about the most personal and exclusive job in the world. All the world may love a lover, but lovers don't want anyone in on the loving. The question at once arises as to how Mr. Lewis managed to woo and win Miss Daisy, with the inseparable Miss Violet always welded to her. . . .
>
> As many a man learns to his cost, courtship is impossible while a girl's young brother is hovering about the room. However, that can always be fixed. The suitor whispers a few words in the ear of the grinning boy, a piece of silver changes hands and the young nuisance abates himself. But millions could not bribe Violet to go away, because it would be death to both.

Violet's never ending presence appears again and again in the article, in terms that reveal an underlying anxiety: "Thus far he has managed to walk that tightrope without a slip, but what about the honeymoon and later more prosaic days of married life? In all the literature of the world there is not a word of advice on how to manage a bride when her sister is present on all occasions." In the end, despite its comic twists and gimmicks, this article betrays the intensity of the twins' threat in its extreme and often violent language.

Such a threat was made abundantly clear in the responses that Daisy and Violet received when they attempted to get married in actuality. The representations of those marriages (as well as of their foiled marital attempts) reflect the way in which, once again, the twins' conjunction eroded the boundary between the public and private and was thus met with moral outrage.

Violet and Daisy each had engagements with different men that were broken off for various reasons through the years, yet each eventually married—Violet in 1936 and Daisy in 1941. Of the frustrated attempts, those made in 1934 for a marriage between Violet and Maurice Lambert, a bandleader, were the most adamantly opposed. In fact, Violet and her beau went to twenty-one different states and were refused in all of them for essentially similar reasons: "on moral grounds"; "on ground that bride is a Siamese twin"; on "the question of morality and decency"; as "a matter of public policy."[5] Even when they did each marry, neither marriage lasted more than a few weeks or months—Violet's because it was staged for publicity reasons alone (taking place before 100,000 people at the Texas Centennial celebration in Dallas), and Daisy's because her new husband moved out after ten days, claiming: " 'I guess I just am not the type of fellow that should marry a Siamese twin. . . . As far as being a bridegroom under such conditions is concerned, I suppose I am what you might call a hermit' " (Drimmer 1991, 54). Thus, in both the article describing Daisy and Jack's engagement and in public responses to other marriage attempts of the Hiltons, there emerges a keen awareness of the ways in which as a doubled wife, Daisy and Violet may wield too much power, and of the ways in which their conjunction fundamentally destroys the adamantly defended boundary between public and private.

What is presented as a dangerous possibility in "One of the Hilton 'Siamese Twins' to be Married" becomes an actuality in Browning's film *Freaks*. Although the twins appear in only a few scenes of the film, the events depicted there resonate strongly, given the cultural context in which they appear. One scene in particular focuses on the transgressive and dangerous aspects of the twins in marriage. Daisy has recently married Roscoe, a fellow circus performer who stutters frequently and who dresses up as a woman for his act; Daisy and Violet are making the bed in their small bungalow, and upon hearing Violet mocking him ("Oh, well, if he's going to say anything, let him say it. Don't let him p-p-p-uh for an hour"), Roscoe enters. The ensuing dialogue depicts an uneasy back-and-forth movement of a husband fighting to maintain control of the married female body—where it will reside and what actions it will pursue:

ROSCOE: Say, you're going to d-d-d-do as I say. *I'm* the b-b-boss of my home.
VIOLET: Half of it, you mean. . . . Come on, Daisy, let's get out of here.
ROSCOE: Oh no she d-d-don't, she's going to stay right here.
VIOLET: Come on, *I* gotta go.
ROSCOE: (as the twins exit) Aw, pahooey, you're always using that for an exc-c-c, for an exc-c-c, for an alib-b-i.

In this scene, Violet embodies many frightening aspects of the New Woman: she speaks out, goes where she wants, and is not regulated by a husband. She implies that a man can, at best, be in control of only "half" of his house—himself. Tellingly, in a previous scene Violet has confronted Roscoe's male authority by taunting sarcastically, "her master's voice is calling" when Roscoe beckons to Daisy; by the end of the above scene, it is all too apparent how little "mastery" Roscoe truly has.

Likewise, in a scene soon following the domestic quarrel, after Violet accepts a marriage proposal she and her fiancé suddenly kiss with great passion; Daisy—who until then has been oblivious to them as she reads a book—looks up in surprise, closes her eyes, and relishes the erotic pleasure right along with her sister. Such a sequence serves, once again, to reveal the frightening prospects that the twins pose—prospects such as women sharing simultaneous sensual enjoyment, or husbands unable to control altogether when, where, and how their wives experience sexuality.

In short, the creators of *Freaks* spell out in no uncertain terms the threatening impotence men could feel when confronted with these joined women. Placed as a representative of all husbands, Roscoe is emasculated directly, through Violet's rebellions, and in more subtle ways—linguistically through his stuttering and visually through his female circus act. These emasculations, combined with the twins' undifferentiated sexual pleasure, ultimately comment not only on Daisy and Violet, but also on other types of single, yet united, women. Indeed, the scenes involving the Hiltons condense the gender politics drama playing itself out in America at the time the film appeared.

In the end, the popular reception of Daisy and Violet Hilton reflects mostly what surrounded them, for on the palimpsest of their bodies were written the contradictory messages of a culture at war with itself about women. By replicating, literalizing, and thus supplanting the marriage contract, their fleshy bond kept them single, facilitated their education and cultural training, and, most importantly, earned them large fortunes that guaranteed them a place as career women. The twins' particular form of aberration perfectly embodies what many by then had come to fear: that a woman's body might not be able to be controlled; that heterosexual, companionate marriage might not be the only form of intimate "bonding" between two people; and that the division between public and private might not be so clear after all. Despite a host of attempts—futile as they were—to master this enigmatic figure, the image of Daisy and Violet remained, like the New Woman, a symbol of "disorder and rebellion."

NOTES

1. I would like to thank for their invaluable assistance with this chapter the following people: Meredith McGill, Vincent Tompkins, and the other members of the Harvard History and Literature Writing Group; Gretchen Worden, Tracy Fessenden, and Richard Canedo; and the staff of the Hertzberg Circus Museum (San Antonio, Texas).

2. For my analysis of the cultural uses and representations of Chang and Eng, see "America's 'United Siamese Brothers': Chang and Eng and Nineteenth Century Ideologies of Democracy and Domesticity," in *Monster Theory: Reading Culture*, ed. Jeffrey J. Cohen (Minneapolis: University of Minnesota Press, 1996).

3. I am indebted to Cott (345n. 27) for introducing me to this article.

4. A full analysis of Daisy and Violet's relationship with Myers—which I lack the space to do here— would further enrich my argument about the twins' engagement of issues of women and power. According to many accounts, until the twins were twenty-three, Myers (who was their guardian as well as their agent) kept them in "virtual 'bondage,'" giving them none of the money they earned and never letting them out of his sight except to attend their voice lessons. Finally, in 1931, the twins caught the sympathetic attention of an attorney, who helped them escape Myers's domination in a highly publicized court trial in San Antonio (Vasquez 1969).

5. See "Bars License to Siamese Twin," *New York Times*, 26 January 1935, 13; "City Bars Wedding of Siamese Twin," *New York Times*, 6 July 1934, 19.

REFERENCES

Bogdan, Robert. 1988. *Freak Show: Presenting Human Oddities for Amusement and Profit.* Chicago: University of Chicago Press.

Carey, Henry. 1928. "This Two-Headed Monster—The Family." *Harper's Monthly Magazine.* January, 162–71.

Chained for Life. 1951. Dir. Harry Fraser. Classic Pictures.

Cott, Nancy F. 1987. *The Grounding of Modern Feminism.* New Haven: Yale University Press.

Drimmer, Frederick. 1991 [1973]. *Very Special People: The Struggles, Loves and Triumphs of Human Oddities.* New York: Citadel.

Freaks. 1932. Dir. Tod Browning. Metro-Goldwyn-Mayer Pictures.

Gould, George M., and Walter L. Pyle. 1897. *Anomalies and Curiosities of Medicine.* Philadelphia: W. B. Saunders.

Lindsey, Benjamin B. 1930 [1928]. "An Answer to the Critics of Companionate Marriage." In *Twenty-four Views of Marriage.* Ed. Clarence A. Spaulding. New York: Macmillan.

"One of the Hilton 'Siamese Twins' to be Married." Newspaper article, c. early 1930s. Hertzberg Circus Collection, San Antonio Public Library, San Antonio, Texas.

Paré, Ambroise. 1982 [1573]. *On Monsters and Marvels.* Trans. Janis L. Pallister. Chicago: University of Chicago Press.

Smith-Rosenberg, Carroll. 1985. *Disorderly Conduct: Visions of Gender in Victorian America.* New York: Oxford University Press.

Souvenir and Life Story of San Antonio's Siamese Twins, Daisy and Violet Hilton. Publicity pamphlet, c. 1920s. Hertzberg Circus Collection, San Antonio Public Library, San Antonio, Texas.

Vasquez, Juan M. 1969. "Siamese Twins 'Bondage' Trial Packed Courtroom." *San Antonio Express.* 8 January, 8-D.

Woods, Harry, Charles Tobias, and Al. Sherman. 1926. "Me Too." New York: Shapiro, Bernstein and Co.

THIRTEEN

Cuteness and Commodity Aesthetics: Tom Thumb and Shirley Temple

LORI MERISH

A 1994 issue of the *New Yorker* contains an article entitled "Ethnicity, Genetics, and Cuteness."[1] Parodying *The Bell Curve*'s racist pseudoscience, author Bruce McCall presents his "findings" in such statements as the following: "Fifty-two percent of white Americans in our meticulous study included the word 'dimples' in their definitions of cuteness, while a similar number of African Americans did not" (about which McCall queries, "are federally funded dimple-awareness programs the answer?"). McCall satirizes the scientific pretensions of such studies by emphasizing the empirical elusiveness of their objects of analysis; cuteness is, for McCall, plainly a cultural, rather than a biological, phenomenon. But the ludicrousness of efforts like *The Bell Curve* to naturalize social differences is driven home by McCall's selection of a criterion of evaluation that is apparently, for him, trivial and culturally meaningless.[2]

In her powerful first novel about the impact of mass culture on African Americans, *The Bluest Eye*, Toni Morrison suggests that while "cuteness" is certainly a culturally specific, rather than organically based, phenomenon, the values it expresses are by no means trivial in their political significance nor in their social or psychological effects. Set in a working-class urban black neighborhood in the 1930s and 1940s, *The Bluest Eye* tells the story of three young girls—two sisters, Frieda and Claudia, and their friend, Pecola—whose coming-of-age requires a complex negotiation with the dominant icons of white America. In Morrison's account, cuteness is a culturally marked aesthetic: specifically, the "cute" is an aesthetic marked by race, class, and gender, as well as by sexuality. In *The Bluest Eye*, cuteness is principally embodied by Shirley Temple and the "big, blue-eyed Baby Doll[s]" that Frieda and Pecola adore: as the narrator notes, "Frieda and [Pecola] had loving conversations about how cu-ute Shirley Temple was." But Claudia resists Shirley's "cuteness," principally because she sees that cuteness is a marker of racial distinction, and because she recognizes that cultivating the "proper" aesthetic response to Shirley would entail psychological alienation and self-hatred. As Claudia asks about the blue-eyed baby doll, "What was I supposed to do with it? Pretend I was its mother?" Instead of responding to the cuteness embodied in "big-blue-eyed Baby Dolls" as Frieda and Pecola do, with maternal desire—specifically, with preservative love and

protective cherishing (as we shall see, the culturally sanctioned response to the "cute")—
Claudia responds with what Morrison terms "unsullied hatred," expressing her rage by
"destroy[ing] white baby dolls"; these "same impulses," Morrison suggests, could have led her
to "axe" little white girls. The construction of cuteness as an aesthetic value that constitutes a
marker of racial distinction is driven home in the scene where the girls' neighbor Maureen
Peal, whom Morrison terms a "high-yellow dream child," gives explicit voice to what Claudia
merely suspects: Claudia describes how "Safe on the other side of the street, [Maureen]
screamed at us, I *am* cute! And you ugly! Black and ugly black e mos. I *am* cute!"[3]

In *The Bluest Eye*, Morrison is chiefly concerned with two aspects of cuteness: the symbolic
properties and qualities that define the cute in a white supremacist culture (white skin, blond
hair, blue eyes); and the culturally specific ways in which consumers or spectators learn to
"recognize" and "value" the cute. Morrison is especially concerned with the ways in which
appreciating cuteness becomes a normative aesthetic response. As a young girl, Claudia says
she "hates" Shirley Temple, Morrison writes in Claudia's voice, because Claudia "had not yet
arrived at the turning point in the development of my psyche which would allow me to love
her" (*BE*, 19). Claudia's resistance is specifically a refusal to "love" the cute—that is, to feeling
the culturally specified normative emotions. By hating Shirley Temple, Claudia is refusing to
perform her inclusion in the community of those who "recognize" cuteness: she refuses to
participate in the ritual of emotional display that transformed a little girl, Shirley Temple,
into the pop culture phenomenon of "America's Sweetheart." In an important sense, Claudia
resists the forms of emotional tutelage and emotional performance that have been principal
disciplinary features of middle-class sentimental culture since the mid-nineteenth century.[4]

Claudia's resistance to feeling the power of the cute is a resistance to a generalized (and
racialized) maternal response. That the cute *demands* a maternal response and interpellates its
viewers/consumers as "maternal" is indicated by the most common synonyms of "cute":
"adorable," and "lovable." Claudia's question about the blue-eyed baby doll, "What was I
supposed to do with it? Pretend I was its mother?" is thus entirely apt: the cute always in
some sense designates a commodity in search of its mother, and is constructed to generate
maternal desire; the consumer (or potential consumer) of the cute is expected, as Claudia
recognizes, to pretend she or he *is* the cute's mother. Valuing cuteness entails the ritualized
performance of maternal feeling, designating a model of feminine subjectivity constituted
against those (ethnic, class, or national) Others who lack the maternal/sentimental endow-
ments (and aesthetic faculties) to fully appreciate the "cute." The Hallmark store, as much as
the art museum and the opera, is a site for the interpellation of gendered/class/racial subjects,
a site in which those identifications are inscribed on citizens' very bodies.

Claudia's resistance to feeling the power of the cute is a refusal to accede to these culturally
specific identifications, to take on a new (maternal) body. But Morrison's insights into the
phenomenology of cuteness don't end here. Morrison also realizes that appreciating the cute—
loving the "adorable" as culturally defined—entails a structure of identification, wanting to be
like the cute—or, more exactly, wanting the cute to be just like the *self*. Appreciating cuteness
expresses the double logic of identification, its fundamental inseparability from desire: it
bespeaks a "presumption of identification" that is, in the words of Doris Sommer, "appropriation in the guise of an embrace."[5] Assimilating commodity desire into a structure of familial,
expressly maternal emotion, the cute generates an aesthetic response mediated through familial resemblance. Maternal desire becomes the vehicle through which being and having are

synthesized: the cute is identified as part of the "family," indeed part of the self; the pleasure of the cute involves "recognizing" it as such. The aesthetics of cuteness thus generates an emotional response in accord with what Mary Ann Doane has described as a commercial structure of "feminine" consumer empathy, a structure that blurs identification and commodity desire. Putting a feminist twist on Walter Benjamin's formulations, Doane sees a convergence between the intimate, emotional address of commodities and certain "feminine," empathetic structures of feeling. Grafting commodity desire onto a middle-class structure of familial, expressly maternal emotion, the cute *naturalizes* women's proprietary longings—a fact grasped by early market analysts such as Carl Naether, who recommended that advertisers picture children in their ads so that women's maternal sentiments could be "transferred" from child to commodity. The aesthetics of cuteness courts consumer empathy, generating a structure of emotional response that assimilates consumption into the logic of adoption. Thus, the special relevance of cuteness to one particular commodity: the doll.[6] (The Cabbage Patch dolls literalized this structure; their owners filled out "adoption papers.")

Below, I examine the significance of an aesthetics of cuteness for what Pierre Bourdieu calls a "sociology of taste."[7] What counts as cute is surely important; as Morrison suggests, cuteness is an aesthetic category saturated with racial, as well as class, meanings. It is also a historically, as well as a nationally, specific aesthetic: the cute appears to have emerged as a distinct cultural style in late nineteenth-century America. According to the *Oxford English Dictionary*—which defines the word "cute" as " 'pretty, charming' and 'attractive in mannered way' " the modern significance originated in "U.S. colloquial and School-boy slang" during the second half of the nineteenth century; many of the entries from the period contain the phrase "what the Americans would call 'cute.' " Like nineteenth-century sentimentalism, with which it is closely allied, cuteness is a highly conventionalized aesthetic, distinguishable both by its formal aesthetic features and the formalized emotional response it engenders. It is generically associated with the child, both in terms of the formal property of smallness or "miniatureness" (miniatures are often called cute) and in terms of the specific features of cute figures (e.g., the numerous anthropomorphized animals such as Garfield, Winnie the Pooh, and the Care Bears—in television commercials and children's books, cartoons, videos, and toys): cuteness is usually designated by roundness of form and thickness of limbs; roundness and flatness of face; largeness of eyes; and especially by largeness of head in proportion to the body—all attributes of the human infant. Because of its association with childhood, cuteness always to some extent aestheticizes powerlessness: often cute figures are placed in humiliating circumstances, such as Winnie the Pooh with his snout stuck in the beehive, or Love-a-Lot Bear in *The Care Bears Movie*, who stares disconsolately out at us with a bucket of paint overturned on his head. What the cute stages is, in part, a need for adult care.

But the chief social power of cuteness is exercised as a drama of socialization. Drawing affective force from the Victorian sentimentalization of childhood, cuteness enacts the fundamental ambivalence of the child in a liberal-capitalist order: as at once consenting "subject" and property "object."[8] Evoking an ideal of maternal or benevolent ownership, cuteness stages a problematic of identification that centers on the child's body. This problematic involved anxieties about the cultural "ownership" of the child, and the racial identifications of children, that were acutely felt in the late nineteenth and early twentieth centuries, a period of massive immigration into the United States along with renewed nativist concern with racial "purity" and the transmission of Euro-American culture.[9] Focusing on the child—the privileged locus for the transmission of culture and the ("uncivilized") Other in that culture's midst—cuteness represents lines of interpersonal, intergenerational identification, promoting affective bonds of social affiliation and cohesion. Specifically, cuteness engenders an affectional dynamic through which the Other is domesticated and (re)contextualized within the human "family." Cuteness aestheticizes the most primary social distinctions, regulating the (shifting) boundaries between Selves and Others, cultural "insiders" and cultural "outsiders," "humans" and "freaks."

As public, mass cultural event, cuteness activates an erotics of maternal longing: "exposure" in the public sphere generates an appropriative desire to "rescue" the cute object by resituating it within a properly loving and appreciative (i.e., affectionally normative) familial context.[10] Associated with the figure of the child and coded as a "feminine" cultural style, the cute seems to have emerged in conjunction with the rise of the woman consumer in the late nineteenth century. Indeed, the emergence of cuteness as a commercial style in the second half of the nineteenth century activated a structure of feminine spectatorship and identification and helped constitute a feminine consumer public.

Cuteness's preoccupation with Otherness is especially evident in the historical identification between the "cute" child and the "freak." After outlining some generic attributes of the cute, I trace a nineteenth-century genealogy of cuteness that begins with commercialized spectacles of midgets (or "little people") such as Charles Stratton ("Tom Thumb") and Lavinia Warren. In the performances of these diminutive prodigies, the cute emerged as a site for feminine identification as well as a strategy for domesticating (the) Otherness (of "freak," of child), annexing the Other to the Self. I then turn to a central cultural site where the aesthetics of cuteness has been constituted and displayed: that site, as Morrison so deftly understood, is Shirley Temple.

The Cult of the Child: Anatomizing Cuteness

Cuteness is an aesthetic that mobilizes proprietary desire, a peculiarly "feminine" proprietary desire that equates to a moral sentiment: the desire to care for, cherish, and protect. The cute contains within its address an invitation to ownership: hence, the particular relevance of cuteness in certain arenas where ownership is negotiated and established (such as adoption, pet ownership, and so on). Morrison acknowledges this dynamic when she describes the "magic" that "cute white girls" worked on women, noting in particular the "possessive gentleness of [women's] touch as they handled them" (BE, 22–23). Cuteness's maternal aesthetics is especially evident in the modern cult of the cute child. The modern cult of the cute has clear antecedents in the Victorian cult of the child; but as a post-Victorian category, the cute is secularized, divested of the moral seriousness and spiritual sanctity with which Victorian childhood was endowed. The emotional appeal of the cute is emptied of the sense of mystery and unknowability—the limits to (earthly) possession—with which the Victorian child was surrounded.

The cute child, unlike the Victorian sacred child, is pure spectacle, pure display. What is lost in this idealization of the cute is sexuality and the danger of its power: what is lost is the desire of the Other, absorbing that Otherness into the logic of the Same.[11] Cuteness performs the de-sexualization of the child's body, redefining that body from an object of lust (either sexual or economic) to an object of "disinterested" affection. Staging the disavowal of child eroticism and the sublimation of adults' erotic feelings toward children, cuteness is the sign of a particular *relation* between adult and child, simultaneously establishing the "innocence" of the child and the "civility" of the adult spectator. Cuteness is thus a realm of erotic regulation (the containment of child sexuality) and "protection" from violence and exploitation.

This sphere of protection is marked by class and race, as is evident in *The Bluest Eye*. Some bodies, Morrison makes clear, are positioned outside the realm of sentimental protection, within the sphere of economic/sexual exploitation and violence. While Claudia rejects cuteness's maternal erotics, Pecola identifies with Shirley Temple as a strategy to stave off sexual abuse and incest. Pecola correctly sees in Shirley Temple's cuteness an alternative to the historical sexualization of African American women's bodies. Pecola's fantasy—that she possesses the "bluest eyes"—constitutes an individual, psychological solution to a social problem, and thus represents in Morrison's novel a form of madness.

Signaling the boundaries of cultural desire, cuteness is thus a regime of emotional as well as physical discipline. For example, rage is not usually considered an emotion compatible with the cute, nor are certain physical processes (such as defecating or vomiting). For its spectators, cuteness stages the assimilation of the Other ("uncivilized" child and/or "freak") into middle-class familial and emotional structures. As a performance aesthetic, cuteness can serve to mediate the subject's relationship to ritualized forms of social control: it can constitute a highly theatrical way of enacting familial allegiance and *choosing* the compelled, displayed, and erotically objectified body.

FREAKS AND (CHILD) PRODIGIES: HISTORICIZING CUTENESS

Morrison's Claudia experiences her rejection of the iconic status of Shirley Temple as a sign of her own freakishness: it renders her, to family and friends, "incomprehensible." Refusing to identify with the aesthetic standard exemplified by Shirley, Claudia finds herself banished from the sphere of maternal protection generated by the cute. Comparing her own situation to "little white girls'" like Shirley Temple, Claudia wonders, "What made people look at them and say, 'Awww,' but not . . . me?" Situated beyond the reach of maternal recognition, Claudia resides in a realm of "disinterested violence," a realm that she finds intolerable. She ultimately takes "refuge" from sentimental banishment by succumbing to "love" for Shirley, though she herself assesses this emotional "conversion" as signaling "adjustment without improvement" (*BE*, 22–23). Strikingly, Morrison depicts cuteness as an aesthetic that polices the boundaries of culture, generating forms of cultural identification (sentimental love) and disaffection ("disinterested violence"). The social field in which these energies emerge is not static but rather is constantly being transformed: in Morrison's account, cuteness can operate to construct cultural differences (differentiating appealing child from unloveable "freak") and deconstruct those same distinctions (repositioning the "freak" within the human family).

As a strategy for managing the radical Otherness of the child, cuteness is thus intimately bound up with the history of the "freak." There are obvious parallels between child and freak: both are liminal figures, residing on the boundaries that separate the "fully human" from the "less-than-human."[12] That "cute" child and "freak" are reciprocally defined is supremely evident in the film *E.T.*, which constructs an identification between child and freak (only the children can communicate with E.T.) in order to position the freakish extraterrestrial as a (cute) monster to be adopted. The monstrosity of the "alien" E.T. does not diminish but rather intensifies his cuteness—in part because his desire for "home" (as well as his docility) renders him sentimentally recuperable, available to assimilation within normative domestic and affectional structures.

As the example of *E. T.* suggests, the categories of "cute" and "freak" have historically been mutually articulated. Indeed, the cute child can be situated in a historical lineage that extends from Hellenistic times through the Middle Ages and Renaissance when dwarfs and midgets were kept as accoutrements of court life, entertainers, and pets. In the eighteenth century such figures were put on display in public taverns and at carnivals and circuses; by the 1840s, these exhibitions were consolidated in the commercialized spectacles known as "freak shows."[13] Tellingly, a popular term for "freak show" was "kid show."[14] Midgets—a term reserved, in general usage, for perfectly shaped and proportioned "little people"—were especially popular in these shows, as well as in popular theater and, later, vaudeville.[15] In nineteenth-century popular culture, there was a productive exchange between the cute child's performance and the midget's commercial display: part of the pleasure of watching precocious child and "little person" perform derived from how they unsettled, in a contained but dramatic fashion, the conventional boundary between child and adult. This interplay between the categories of cute child and "little person" was registered by drama critic Laurence Hutton. Commenting in 1890 on the "Infant Phenomena" of the American stage, Hutton observed that entertaining and precocious children occupy "the neutral ground between the amateurs and the monstrosities, without belonging to either class."[16] The history of freakish spectacles of "little people" is embedded within the performance of the cute child.

Complaining of the conventional comparison between little person and child, Lavinia Warren (a Barnum exhibit and one of the nineteenth century's best-known midget performers) describes in her autobiography a visit from presidential candidate Stephen A. Douglas while she was touring the South: "He expressed great pleasure at again seeing me, and as I stood before him he took my hand and, drawing me toward him, stooped to kiss me. I instinctively drew back, feeling my face suffused with blushes. It seemed impossible to make people at first understand that I was not a child; that being a woman I had the womanly instinct of shrinking from a form of familiarity which in the case of a child of my size would have been as natural as it was permissable [sic]."[17] The desire to *touch* little people of all ages, evinced by Douglas and invoked by Warren as "natural," constitutes a form of "petting" that conflates person and domestic animal; it also bespeaks the erotic and proprietary dynamic essential to the structure of the cute child. Like the cute child, the little person (like all "freaks") is culturally positioned as an object, not a subject. But unlike other freaks, the little person—by virtue of her identification with the child—could be drawn into the cute's structure of maternal proprietorship and "protection"; invested with sympathy denied most other freaks, she could be drawn more completely into the realm of the "human."

In his fine book on the history of the freak show in the United States, Robert Bogdan describes the "high aggrandized style" (e.g., assigning exhibits titles such as "General," "Princess," and "Count," and exaggerating their skills) that has characteristically been used to present midgets. Devised by showmen like P. T. Barnum, the style made exhibited little people seem, in Barnum's term, "diminutive prodig[ies]."[18] Much like the "overblown titles" (such as "senator," "colonel," "Prince," and "Apollo") assigned black comic figures in minstrelsy and vaudeville, as well as print culture, the high aggrandized style used in conjunction with little people made comic capital out of the blurring of "high" and "low"; in particular, it ridiculed the pretensions of the "low" to the status and privileges of the "high." Charles Stratton (Barnum's General Tom Thumb), for example, performed imitations of Napoleon Bonaparte and Revolutionary War soldiers and marched around the stage dressed as a soldier waving a ten-inch sword and performing military drills, though his most famous battle was fought with Queen Victoria's poodle.[19] As the nineteenth century's most famous midget performer, Tom Thumb particularly exemplified the blurring of the categories of adult and child: in the words of Neil Harris, Tom Thumb was the "perfect man-child, the perpetual boy" whose success rested not only on his size but on his "truly childlike benevolence."[20] Similarly, the "little Queen" Lavinia Warren was described in promotional literature as a "woman in miniature": "Her size is that of a child, her language that of an adult." Attempting to conjure Lavinia's image through the medium of print, a "true-life" pamphlet about her and Stratton aims to inspire the reader's "fancy" to evoke an image of the "charming woman" that defies conventional categorization, being neither child nor adult but rather both at once: "The reader may choose from his lady acquaintances a sparkling woman, with dark hair and black eyes, symmetrical figure and soft voice, and, in his imagination, reduce her to the dimensions above named. . . . Or he may reverse the picture, and select a child of perfect mold, with a finely-arched brow, dimpled cheeks, large, lustrous eyes, a nicely chiseled mouth, a rich harvest of hair, and somehow endow her with all the [intellectual and moral] attributes of womanhood."[21] This interplay of categories suggests why the "Tom Thumb Wedding" (uniting Charles Stratton and Lavinia Warren, held in February 1863 in New York City's Grace Church) became a ritual performance among children; W. H. Baker published *The Tom Thumb Wedding* in 1898 as part of the series Baker's Entertainments for Children.[22]

What Bogdan terms the aggrandized mode of presenting "little people" such as Tom Thumb structured Shirley Temple's performances (informing, in particular, the penchant for dressing her in uniforms). In both these spectacles, cuteness derived from the merger of two different representational modes (and their corollary emotional structures): the mock heroic, in which the pretensions of the "low" were satirically mocked; and the sentimental, in which the powerless were sympathized with and pitied. The continuum from prodigious midget to cute child was registered in an industry rumor, reported in a story by Graham Greene, that Shirley was a thirty-year-old midget, married to a dwarf, with a seven-year-old child of her own. (Greene was subsequently sued by Fox and Shirley's parents.)[23] Greene's ironic charge was not entirely without basis: baby impersonators, a staple of vaudeville acts, were quickly absorbed into cinema, from the midget crook in infant drag (played by Harry Earles) in Tod Browning's *The Secret Three*, to Franz Ebert, a midget whose picture was used for years on baby foods and baby powder. Implicitly registering this affiliation between child star and freak, the Academy chose Shirley to present a special Oscar and seven "dwarf" Oscars to Walt Disney for his first feature-length animation, *Snow White and the Seven Dwarfs*, at the Academy Awards ceremony in 1938. The citations for her own special Oscar, awarded in 1935, similarly played upon her diminutive size: "There was one great towering figure in the cinema game in 1934, one artiste among artists, one giant among troupers." More recently, a biographer, Robert Windeler, has described her as "a kind of midget folk heroine."[24]

There was indeed something "freakish" about Shirley Temple's prodigious capacity to absorb, apparently without effort, what her roles required. As *Time* recorded the popular Temple mythology, reiterated in numerous magazine articles between 1934 and 1939, "Her work entails no effort. She plays at acting as other small girls play at dolls. Her training began so long ago that she now absorbs instruction almost subconsciously. While her director explains how he wants a scene played, Shirley looks at her feet, apparently thinking of more important matters. When the take starts, she not only knows her own function but frequently that of the other actors." There were other popular legends: that since birth Shirley had never awakened at night; that she refused to take a bottle and had to be fed with a spoon at three months; that she spoke at six months and walked at thirteen; that she was a genius with an IQ of 155. These legends recall the rhetoric surrounding Tom Thumb: one promotional pamphlet, for example, stated that his full-sized parents had three other ordinary-sized children, and that "there is nothing in his history . . . which furnishes the slightest clue to the astonishing phenomena" of his "miniature features and frame."[25] Similarly, Shirley Temple testimonials—on the order, as one critic notes, of evangelical "witnessings"—imbued the child star with an aura of the miraculous. Adolphe Menjou, registering the uncanny quality of Shirley's prodigious talent, reportedly testified, "That Temple kid scares me. She knows all the tricks. . . . She's an Ethel Barrymore at four." And from photographer Tony Ugrin, who made her still pictures: "I wanted to reach out and touch her as she went by. I could hardly believe she was real."[26] Testimonials such as these return us to the original definition of the term "prodigy": monster, freak.

"Cuteness" as Feminine Spectacle: The Tom Thumb Wedding

The structure of maternal sentiment activated by the cute child performer also organized the exhibition of midgets. Leslie Fiedler invokes the process whereby "little people" were divested of their ancient aura of the sacred and magical during the nineteenth century and domesticated, converted into objects of compassion and pity: There was "something sacred and otherworldly about dwarfs and midgets" in ancient civilizations such as Egypt, where gods like Ptah and Bes were "portrayed in the form of dwarfs. . . . Even after they had become buffoons and court pets in the Middle Ages and Renaissance there still clung to them an aura of the magical." According to Fiedler, the Victorian era "complete[d] the process of demythification by converting them into public exhibits, subjects for medical study, and occasions for pity—like orphans, abused animals, or the deserving poor." Although they, like all "freaks," were known as "curiosities," the curiosity engendered by midgets was tempered by sympathy. As Neil Harris has noted, unlike other freakish spectacles in Barnum's museum, the audience's sympathies were (partially) *with* the exhibited "little people": "Crowds identified with [them], rather than against [them]."[27] Like the cute child's body, the bodies of little people have been the site of a particular kind of erotic investiture, engendering in their viewers the dynamic play between similitude and difference, identification and appropriative desire.

The structure of empathy undergirding the midget's exhibition is quite evident in promotional and journalistic literature about Tom Thumb and Lavinia Warren. One pamphlet on the "charming little woman" Queen Lavinia notes, "While we look upon giants with awe, perhaps admiration, we approach this *petite* piece of humanity with love, and make a pet of her in spite of ourselves."[28] Indeed, the best-known example of the domestication of the midget to which Fiedler refers is the 1863 Tom Thumb Wedding, a public ritual that absorbed the magic traditionally associated with little people by securing them within conventional social structures (fig. 13.1). Literature surrounding the wedding emphasized the expressly *feminine* appeal of the ceremony and its participants: the fact that the marriage was "of

13.1. "The Fairy Wedding Group" by Mathew Brady. Courtesy of Historical Collections, Bridgeport Public Library.

peculiar and touching interest," one account notes, was evident from "the snatches of feminine gossip, in which small sized adjectives and diminutive ejaculations were profusely employed." Similarly, the *New York Times*—which ran a full-page article on the event—describes a "*furore* of excitement . . . an intensity of interest in the feminine world of New York and its neighborhood" generated by "the loves of our Lilliputians." The *Times* estimates that there were "twenty thousand women in this City yesterday morning up and dressed an hour and a half before their usual time, solely and simply because of the approaching nuptials of Mr. Stratton and Miss Warren. . . . Fathers were flattered, husbands were hectored, brothers were bullied and cousins were cozened into buying, begging, borrowing, in some way or other *getting* tickets of admission to the grand affair."[29]

Barnum's official pamphlet of the event, *A Sketch of the Life, Personal Appearance, Character and Manners of Charles S. Stratton*, reinforced the *Times*'s view of the union of "the Loving Lilliputians" as a feminine spectacle and amusement, one that marked out a cultural space for a feminine audience and challenged the strictures surrounding feminine public spectatorship: "ladies stood on tip-toe, some daring ones of small stature actually mounting the seats, so eager in their pleasurable excitement to see, that they overlooked the possibility of being seen."[30] In an era when most commercial amusements were designated for men, and when "respectable" women were relegated to public invisibility, the Tom Thumb Wedding—perhaps capitalizing on the categorical instability of the event as both wedding and commercial exhibit—presented the possibility of an explicitly feminine style of commercial entertainment. Building on ideologies of women's "natural" sympathy for children, the exhibition of "Loving

Lilliputians" configured sympathy as the basis for feminine extradomestic consumption. Carving out a space for feminine mass spectatorship, the Tom Thumb Wedding helped organize cuteness as a mass cultural style.

Like the singular performances of General Tom Thumb, the Tom Thumb Wedding delighted its viewers because it *looked like children imitating adults,* thus assimilating the "freak" into a familial and familiar structure of domination and hierarchy. This sense of child-play informed the audience's response to the Tom Thumb Wedding: describing the Strattons as a "mimic miniature of Adam and Eve," the *Sketch* notes the audience's amusement when the minister addressed the couple during the exchange of vows, "you take this *woman,*" "you take this *man.*"[31] Cuteness devolves from such ritualized mimicry when an audience's sympathies are *with* the actors: staging the "low" imitating the "high" in a controlled, nonthreatening way, the cute transforms transgressive subjects into beloved objects.

Like the appeal of the Tom Thumb Wedding, Shirley Temple's cuteness derives from a combination of precocity and powerlessness. The cute Shirley is marked as derivative, a miniature reproduction of the adult whose mimicry extends biology into behavior. Spouting the hard-boiled dialogue ("Aw, lay off me") of her gambling cohorts in *Little Miss Marker,* performing imitations of Eddie Cantor and Al Jolson in *Stowaway,* and, especially, copying her dance steps from teacher/partner Bill Robinson ("Bojangles"), Shirley enacts the fundamental *ambivalence* of mimicry: her precocity both instates her resemblance to adults and her crucial difference from them. The cute transmutes the radical Otherness of the child—the difference of "unsocialized" child from "socialized" adult—into a matter of scale. That Otherness is thus both acknowledged and repressed. In the cute's structure of mimicry, the negation of difference is displaced from the spectator to the performer: the desire for sameness is here performed as *Shirley's* desire.[32] In her performances, Shirley enacts her dependence on adults, both representationally (insofar as the adult is the "original" she imitates) and literally (insofar as her performance calls attention to the physical limits, especially the smallness, of her body). Her size is crucial in defining her acts as cute: her diminutive physical stature literalizes her subordinate status. In her movies she mainly appears with adults, especially during performance sequences, in order to visually emphasize scale. The domestication of the "miniature" begun by the Tom Thumb Wedding was completed by Shirley Temple, whose films, in narrative and spectacle, ritualize the (re)containment of the cute within familial structures.

This process of domestication is evident in the cute spectacle's preoccupation with the law. The Tom Thumb Wedding, for example, counters the "freak's" transgression of biological law with the imposition of cultural law. Focusing on the marriage ceremony, the primary site in middle-class culture where the body is inscribed by law and situated within a nexus of social and property relations, the Tom Thumb Wedding enacts the translation of the physical body into the social body. Similarly, Shirley Temple's cuteness is linked with the transgression and benevolent recuperation of patriarchal law. This preoccupation with the law is signaled in her films by her frequent association with the military within the narrative and in her dance numbers, where she is often costumed in military garb. All Shirley's films are about transgression: in *Curly Top,* for example, she breaks all the orphanage rules (including the rule against bringing her pet horse and duck into the house); in *Rebecca of Sunnybrook Farm,* she defies her strict aunt in order to perform in a popular radio show; in *The Littlest Rebel,* she displays her Confederate loyalties by taking aim at one Yankee officer with her slingshot and knocking another out of his chair. She is always saved from severe punishment, however, by a chastened and benevolent—because utterly charmed—patriarchal authority. Shirley is perhaps never cuter than when she matches tempers with her curmudgeonly grandfather (played by Lionel Barrymore) in *The Little Colonel,* or when, with her legendary pout, she wags her finger and commands him to behave himself. These films simultaneously emphasize the female child's vulnerability and powerlessness before the law and establish the benevolence of legal authority. Shirley's association with a reconstructed, sentimentalized "law" is apparent in her founding, in the mid-1930s, of the Shirley Temple Police Force; visitors to her film sets, such as Eleanor Roosevelt, left wearing a Shirley Temple Police Force badge. J. Edgar Hoover reciprocated by making Shirley the "first woman G-man" of the FBI.[33]

Domesticating the Otherness of little people entailed a curtailment of desire, especially sexual desire. This was apparent in literature from the Tom Thumb Wedding: the couple were described as "smiling twins," as siblings rather than mates, though fascination with the sexuality of "little people" resurfaced in the titillating speculation about whether or not the couple would have children.[34] Similarly, Shirley Temple's construction as "innocent" required not so much the absence of sexuality as its active disavowal. Shirley Temple films are in fact replete with sexual references. In particular, these films flirt with illicit sexuality, especially pedophilia and (father-daughter) incest: in several films—*Poor Little Rich Girl, Dimples,* and *Curly Top,* to name a few—Shirley's relationship with her father (or father-figure) has overtly incestuous overtones. *Poor Little Rich Girl,* for example, contains a truly remarkable scene in which Shirley lovingly sings to her handsome father (played by Michael Whalen) of her desire to marry him while she caresses him and cuddles in his lap. In keeping with her mission to "melt hearts," Shirley courts her spectator's desire, charming and disarming most adult men in her films: watching these films, the question of how long it would take Shirley to end up on the lap of a particular male actor became a running joke. Staging cuteness as a mini-seduction met not by sexual violence or assault, but by protective care these films reinforce a primary mythology of patriarchal "civilization" in place since the late eighteenth century. That the overtly sexual scenarios and references in Shirley's films did not scandalize 1930s audiences suggests less the fabled "innocence" of those times than the structure of sexual disavowal in which the cute Shirley was embedded.

CUTENESS AND MODERNITY

Constructed by mid-century events such as the Tom Thumb Wedding, the aesthetics of cuteness achieved mass cultural expression in the late nineteenth century. Indeed, the cute— coded as a "feminine" cultural style—appears to have emerged in conjunction with the "feminization" of commercial amusements, especially vaudeville and, later, cinema. Absorbing materials from minstrelsy and the circus, the variety show originated in male spaces, such as saloons and clubs, in the middle of the century. In the late 1880s and the 1890s, the variety show became institutionalized in entertainment halls and reached out (as cinema would later on) for a more "respectable" and *female* clientele. Starting in the late 1880s, vaudeville managers, aiming to expand their audiences, "refined the acts, the audiences, and theatres in order to attract respectable women into hitherto dangerous male environments." "Vulgar" stage language and actions were censored, ethnic humor was toned down, and acts borrowed from the circus and minstrelsy, such as animal acts and blackface, were adapted to meet the standards of "family entertainment." In particular, acts were desexualized: for example, black-face acts were purged of their overt sexual content and sexual play, and African Americans were presented as asexual buffoons. Coinciding with the feminization of vaudeville was a new vogue in child performers, such as the McCoy sisters, the Putnam sisters, Lucie and Vinie Daly, Johnny and Bertha Gleason, the Taylor Twin Sisters, and the blond and "doll-like" Kitty Bingham.[35] Writing of the "public craze" with child stars following ten-year-old Elsie Leslie's 1890 success in "Little Lord Fauntleroy," a writer for *Mumsey's Magazine* described how "little Lord Fauntleroys sprang up on every side, and every new play produced had its child interest. . . . In no country has the child of tender years been permitted to hold so important a place on the stage as in the United States."[36]

In the last decades of the nineteenth century, cuteness as cultural fantasy was engendered through the feminization of vaudeville as well as in other mass cultural sites, such as advertising and popular magazines, especially women's magazines. With the arrival of the screen halftone in the 1890s, advertisements began featuring cute commodity trademarks such as the Gold Dust Twins, the Uneeda Biscuit girl, and the Campbell Soup kid, while middlebrow women's magazines like the *Ladies' Home Journal* and *Harper's Bazaar* ushered in the cute as pictorial style and staple of the feminine vernacular. The widespread use of the term—and perhaps its vogue—was suggested by an article from in the June 2, 1900, issue of *Harper's Bazaar,* "When the Nestlings Come," which opens with the following sentence: "The first word that comes to the mind as we look at photographs of bird babies is 'cute.' " A few issues later, the term appears in an article on "The First Indian Baby Show," a competition for the "cutest" boy and girl organized by a white woman teacher (and judged by other white women) at the Kiowa Mission School. In print as in visual culture, the cute was closely linked with childhood and exemplified the new fascination with childhood and its "charms" featured in popular magazines at the turn of the century. Picking up on these trends, writers and columnists titled the new century "The Century of the Child."[37]

By the mid-1920s, the modern cult of the cute was translated to the cinema, resulting in a wave of film comedies featuring cute children. The epitome of the cute child during this period, Shirley Temple appeared in a number of films notable for foregrounding the fantasies of (maternal) ownership inspired by the cute. (Acknowledging the operability of such fantasies, one critic described Shirley's films as an "assault upon the nation's maternal instinct.")[38] Shirley's films are quite straightforward about the vulnerability of children and their social construction as property; these films are principally concerned with the ease with which children can pass from beloved domestic property to commodities, from the security of domestic ownership to the exigencies of the marketplace. Typically, Shirley's characters start out as orphans or, nearly always, motherless little girls, and the *telos* of her films is directed toward finding good parents and a good home; this at times requires chastening existing fathers, but usually requires finding a brand new (foster) father and mother. She is positioned as a commodity in search of an owner, and her cuteness is her only security in that search; it ensures that she will find a good mother/father, someone who can fully appreciate her. In Shirley Temple movies, as elsewhere, the cute is always shopping for a mother (or maternalized father), and for a properly sympathetic maternal proprietary response. Typically, Shirley circulates among possible parents/owners, often ethnically and class marked individuals, before settling in with a properly warm, and properly rich, white family.

In *Poor Little Rich Girl,* for instance, Shirley's mom has died, and her businessman father neglects her. Pretending to be the fictional orphan Betsy Ware, the heroine of her favorite storybook, Shirley tries out two foster families—she stays briefly with an Italian working-class family, then with a couple of vaudeville performers—before landing back in her properly appreciative familial home (minus her overly stern nanny, a working-class surrogate "mother," who is evidently impervious to the girl's charms). By the film's conclusion, the cute Shirley has managed familial and corporate mergers, apparently affirming the benevolence of patriarchal domesticity and patriarchal capitalism: she facilitates a union between her father and a new wife, and she manages a corporate merger between her father's soap company and his rival's, bringing them together in one big happy family.

Films like *Poor Little Rich Girl* enact, as well as thematize, the property dimension of the cute. Shirley's cuteness is particularly featured in spectacles of tap-dancing and singing, which often disrupt and work against the film narrative. Highlighted in performance sequences, her cuteness is thus directed at spectators both *within* and *without* the film's narrative. This crossing of diegetic or narrative levels is activated by the conventional scenario of maternal absence, a scenario intertextually reinforced through narrative repetition: since within the film's diegesis the space of the mother is empty, the viewer is invited to "occupy" that space.[39] The appeal to the maternal proprietary fantasies of the consumer is especially evident in the scenes in many of her films depicting a sleeping Shirley. Placing the film viewer in the position of parent, voyeuristic shots of Shirley sleeping draw their emotional resonance from the cute child's "innocence" as well as her vulnerability and objectification.

Significantly, it is only after *publicly* displaying her cuteness, usually on stage and/or the radio (though it can also take place in the dining room of the orphanage, as in *Curly Top*), that Shirley's appeal is recognized and fully appreciated. Underlining the essential theatricality of the cute, this narrative structure illuminates the dynamics of cuteness in a mass commodity market. As one writer for her films noted, "Shirley's capacity for love was indiscriminate, extending to pinched misers or to common hobos . . . it was a social, even a political force on a par with the idea of democracy or the constitution." Spreading her power to "melt hearts" through the national market, Shirley Temple exemplified the elevation of cuteness into a national aesthetic.[40]

CUTENESS AS RACIALIZED STYLE: SHIRLEY TEMPLE AND THE CONSTRUCTION OF CUTE (WHITE) GIRLHOOD

Shirley's position as cute child prodigy was anticipated by "little people" such as Tom Thumb and Lavinia Warren, who inspired in their audiences a mixture of fascination and proprietary desire. But the freakish Otherness at the heart of the cute is particularly registered in Shirley's intimate connection with racial Others. Shirley's ties to racial Otherness are featured in several films, particularly those about the Old South, *The Littlest Rebel* and *The Little Colonel*. Indeed, embedded within her song-and-tap-dance numbers are historical traces of Jim Crow performances and resonances of a Sambo-like obsequiousness in her always-ready smile and effort to please. This racial doubling of Shirley's body is rendered explicit in those scenes in which she is paired with Bill Robinson ("Bojangles") as dance partner. References to antebellum "Jim Crow" and the history of slavery complicate the structure of feeling (of maternal cherishing) the cute works to construct, exposing the forms of power and coercion at its core.

Cuteness as a comic theatrical style available to children was intimately bound up with the history of race. The comic child in nineteenth-century America was a racialized construction, a fact evident when one considers the cultural icon, *Uncle Tom's Cabin*—phenomenally popular as novel, play and, later, film. Harriet Beecher Stowe presents the minstrel sprite Topsy as a comic figure and foil for the pious, spiritualized, and deeply serious Little Eva (a role Shirley Temple would adapt in *Dimples*). Mass culture in the late nineteenth century featured an iconography of blackness, derived from plantation humor, that depicted African Americans as comical, inept, and childlike. Some of the first commodity trademarks—such as the Gold Dust Twins and the Pears Soap children—recycled racial stereotypes, featuring black kids with cute features (e.g., large round heads and eyes, chubby limbs). These African-American comic figures, however, usually bore explicit traces of the grotesque or the threatening: in particular, they were often depicted with exaggerated grins or teeth. By the 1930s, blonde, blue-eyed Shirley Temple would purge the cute of its unsettling racial resonances, performing an absorption and domestication of comic styles associated with "blackness" and the black child performer. Shirley's cherubic, dimpled smile mimes, even while it tames, the exaggerated, painted grin of minstrelsy. Even that epitome of cuteness, Shirley's famous "O my goodness!" expression—her face momentarily frozen with wide saucer eyes and pursed lips extruding in an affectionate kiss—should be seen as a racialized style.

Noting the frequency with which Shirley Temple movies included African-American characters, Donald Bogle writes that the child star "occupied a unique position in relation to [African Americans] in films. . . . Blacks appeared so often in her important films that there was an inside industry joke that a Temple picture was incomplete without at least one darky."[41] Shirley Temple films are preoccupied with issues of racial Otherness, and most of her films feature African-American characters. (Notable exceptions include *Stowaway*, in which Shirley plays the daughter of missionaries in China who are killed by bandits, and *Susanna of the Mounties*, in which Shirley plays the only survivor of an Indian massacre.) The trend began when Shirley appeared as a three-year-old in Baby Burlesks, a series of one-reelers that satirized adults and adult movies. In *Kid 'n Africa* (1932), a satire of *Trader Horn* and *Tarzan and His Mate*, Shirley plays Madame Cradlebait, a missionary sent to "civilize" Africans. She is captured by cannibals and put in a large pot to boil until she is rescued by Tarzan (whom she later marries).

But the play with racial Otherness is rendered most explicit in the historical films about the Old South. Like many films from the period, *The Littlest Rebel* and *The Little Colonel* present nostalgic portraits of plantation life. The plot lines of these two films are strikingly similar: in both, Northern males intrude to disrupt the harmonious, interracial world of the Southern plantation; both end with images of national reunion. In *The Littlest Rebel*, Shirley plays Virginia ("Virgie") Cary, motherless daughter of Captain Herbert Cary (John Boles), a Confederate spy who escapes from the Yankees aided by Colonel Morrison, a Yankee whom Shirley has charmed and who has a daughter "just [Virgie's] age." When Cary is recaptured and sentenced to death, Shirley, accompanied by the house slave "Uncle Billy" (Robinson), visits President Lincoln to intervene on her father's behalf. Cary and Morrison receive pardons, and the final scene depicts Shirley being toasted by a group of Yankee and Confederate soldiers, whom she entertains with a rendition of "Polly Wolly Doodle." *The Little Colonel* is set after the Civil War's end (the opening title reads "Kentucky in the 70s"), but the plantation system seems to have survived intact: emancipation evidently has changed nothing, especially for blacks like "Uncle Billy." Here, Shirley is the granddaughter of Colonel Lloyd, a temperamental widower whose Confederate loyalties have led to his estrangement from his daughter, Elizabeth, and her Yankee soldier husband. When Shirley's parents set upon hard times, they return to a cottage on Lloyd's plantation, where Shirley (in the old Colonel's words, "the spitting image of your mother") proceeds to win her grandfather's heart and reunite the divided family.

In both films, the restoration of the (white) family depends upon a reconfiguration of race relations. Familial crisis occasions the parental ministrations of the black servants and Shirley's (re-)positioning in black kinship structures. In *The Littlest Rebel*, Shirley is "adopted" by "Uncle Billy" after her mother's death and her father's imprisonment, while in *The Little Colonel* she is cared for by "Mom Beck" (Hattie McDaniel) and befriended by her grandfather's servant, Walker (Robinson). This racial reconfiguration entails the "blackening" of Shirley, a symbolic process literalized on two occasions. In *The Littlest Rebel*, Shirley— attempting to hide from the Yankees—blackens herself with shoe polish in order to disguise herself among the black children; and after watching a black riverside baptism in *The Little Colonel*, Shirley is literally "blackened" when she performs the ritual with two black playmates in a mud puddle. This racial hybridization is spectacularly evident in Shirley's scenes with Bill Robinson. Certainly, these scenes reinforce racial stereotypes and affirm the racist identification of African Americans with children that dates back to slavery. But by constructing visual equivalences between Shirley and Bojangles, these scenes also problematize Shirley's "whiteness" and underscore the racial ambiguities of the cute child.

As surrogate father, Bojangles is presented in *The Littlest Rebel* and *The Little Colonel* as Shirley's *tutor*; and it is significant that what he teaches Shirley is tap-dancing—a cultural form with African-American roots. This racial lineage is rendered explicit in the finale of *Dimples*, where Shirley, surrounded by a minstrel troupe in blackface playing tambourine and bones, dances the "Juba"—a dance developed during slavery in the Caribbean islands and Southern United States, which evolved into the soft-shoe shuffle and the tap dance. Popularized by a black performer known as "Juba" (William Henry Lane), and adopted by black and white minstrel performers throughout the nineteenth century, the Juba featured shuffling the feet to a chosen rhythm.[42] In Shirley Temple films, the scenes of tutelage with "Bojangles" enact visual symmetries and a process of interracial mirroring and identification—a dynamic captured in the famous staircase dance for *The Little Colonel* (fig. 13.2).

In *The Littlest Rebel* and *The Little Colonel*, the tap-dancing "Poor Little Rich (White) Girl" is shadowed by the presence of black America. The alignment of the cute Shirley with the body of the African-American male evokes the history of slavery and its coercive appropriation of the body—a body forced to work, to reproduce, and, at times, to sing and dance, at the white master's will. By constructing an equivalence between female white child and black male slave, these scenes render ambiguous the fantasies of benevolent ownership and familial assimilation endemic to the cute, disrupting and denaturalizing the identificatory structures in which the cute child is enmeshed. The racial doubling of Shirley's body extended into her political career: as U.S. ambassador to Ghana, Shirley Temple Black was occasionally "mistaken for an actual American black, thanks to her California-based suntan . . . and her [by-then] dark hair and eyes."[43]

13.2. The staircase tap dance with Bill Robinson from *The Little Colonel* (1935). By permission of Shirley Temple Black and Twentieth Century Fox. Courtesy of the Academy of Motion Picture Arts and Sciences.

CUTENESS AND CULTURAL OTHERS

Emphasizing that what is "often referred to as a 'freak of nature'" is actually a "'freak of culture,'" Susan Stewart observes, "We find the freak inextricably tied to the cultural other—the Little Black Man, the Turkish horse, the Siamese twins. . . , the Irish giants." Accounts of pygmies, Stewart notes, can be found in Homer, Hesiod, Herodotus, and Ovid, and thus date back to the West's earliest encounters with other traditions. Nineteenth-century examples of racialized freaks include Admiral Dot, the "North Carolina Twins" Millie and Christine, and Zip the Pin Headed Man—all of whom, like Tom Thumb and Lavinia Warren, were employed by Barnum.[44]

In Shirley Temple films, the essential freakishness of the cute child is expressed by her ties to racial Otherness as fully as by her status as prodigious "little person." Signifying and animating the forms of familial sentiment through which the child is socialized and incorporated within culture, cuteness domesticates Otherness in a double move through which that Otherness is at once affirmed and denied. But the very banality of cuteness—its (mass) production and display in a whole range of commercial contexts—suggests the fragility and tenuousness of the cute's hold on us; it bespeaks the need to compulsively rehearse the most basic social forms to ensure their idealization and transmission. Haunted by its own freakishness, the cute ineluctably points to other possibilities of embodiment, other forms of subjectivity and desire.

NOTES

1. I am grateful to Scott Dykstra, Anne Goldman, Kate McCullough, Susan Jarratt, Victoria Smith, and especially Rosemarie Garland Thomson for their helpful suggestions on this chapter. Thanks, also, to Ann Cvetkovich for chairing the 1994 M.L.A. Conference panel on "Feelings" at which I first presented this work.

2. Bruce McCall, "Ethnicity, Genetics, and Cuteness (Addendum to Recent Fearless Findings)," *New Yorker*, 5 December 1994), 152. I am indebted to Jane Garrity for calling my attention to this article.

3. Toni Morrison, *The Bluest Eye* (New York: Plume, 1993), 20, 19, 22, 62, 73. All further references are to this edition, cited in the text as *BE*. Claudia's identifications are resistant in significant ways: for example, in refusing to mother white baby dolls (and in her and Frieda's symbolic "adoption" of Pecola's child), she rejects the "black mammy" position and stereotype.

4. Richard Brodhead, "Sparing the Rod: Discipline and Fiction in Antebellum America," *Representations* 21 (1988): 67–96.

5. Doris Sommer, "Resistant Texts and Incompetent Readers," *Poetics Today* 15:4 (Winter 1994): 543. For an extended analysis of the complex psychic processes of identification and the highly unstable "identification/desire opposition" in psychoanalytic theory, see Diana Fuss, *Identification Papers* (New York: Routledge, 1995).

6. Mary Ann Doane, *The Desire to Desire* (Bloomington: Indiana University Press, 1989), Carl Naether, *Advertising to Women* (New York: Taylor, 1928).

7. Pierre Bourdieu, *Distinction: A Social Critique of the Judgment of Taste*, trans. Richard Nice (Cambridge: Harvard University Press, 1984).

8. In the late nineteenth century, the popular conception of the child as the "natural property" of the parent appears in narratives of white child slavery (in which children appear as "capital" through which adults satisfy their "horrible cravings"), and in accounts of child abuse published by the newly formed national network of child protection and anticruelty societies. "White Child Slavery," *Arena* 1 (April 1890): 589–603. For a sociological summary of the reconstruction of the child from an "object of use" to an "object of sentiment" between 1870 and 1930, see Viviana A. Zelizer, *Pricing the Priceless Child* (New York: Basic Books, 1985).

9. For an extended analysis of the "negative associations of childhood" with racial Others and an "atavistic savagery" in nineteenth century literature and anthropology, focusing on the British national context, see Cora Kaplan, " 'A Heterogeneous Thing': Female Childhood and the Rise of Racial Thinking in Victorian Britain," in Diana Fuss, ed., *Human, All too Human* (New York: Routledge, 1995), 168–202.

10. Helping to articulate maternal desire within the public sphere, cuteness emerged alongside a Progressive Era political rhetoric that utilized women's domestic identities, especially their identities as mothers, as a means of moral authority enabling their entry into political discourse and the political sphere as such. Paula Baker, "The Domestication of Politics: Women and American Political Society, 1780–1920," *American Historical Review* 89 (June 1984): 620–47.

11. Susan Stewart, *On Longing* (Baltimore: Johns Hopkins University Press, 1987), 123–24.

12. Susan Stewart identifies the constitutive liminality of the freak: "the physiological freak represents the problems of the boundary between self and other (Siamese twins), between male and female (the hermaphrodite), between the body and the world outside the body (the *montsre par excès*), and between the animal and the human (feral and wild men)." Ibid., 109.

13. Robert Bogdan, *Freak Show: Presenting Human Oddities for Amusement and Profit* (Chicago: University of Chicago Press, 1988).

14. Leslie Fiedler, *Freaks: Myths and Images of the Secret Self* (New York: Anchor, 1978), 31.

15. On the politics of these terms, see Joan Ablon, *Little People in America: The Social Dimensions of Dwarfism* (New York: Praeger, 1984).

16. Laurence Hutton, *Curiosities of the American Stage* (New York: Harper and Bros., 1891), 253.

17. Countess M. Lavinia Magri, *The Autobiography of Mrs. Tom Thumb*, ed. A. H. Saxon (Hamden, Conn.: Archon, 1979), 44–45.

18. Bogdan, *Freak Show*, 150.

19. Joseph Boskin, *Sambo* (New York: Oxford University Press, 1986), 108; Bogdan, *Freak Show*, 150–51.

20. Neil Harris, *Humbug: The Art of P. T. Barnum* (Boston: Little, Brown, 1973), 50–51. Tellingly, Barnum characteristically referred to Tom Thumb as "my dwarf."

21. *A Sketch of the Life, Personal Appearance, Character and Manners of Charles S. Stratton* (New York: Samuel Booth, 1874), 8.

22. Stewart, *On Longing*, 119.

23. Robert Windeler, *The Films of Shirley Temple* (New York: Citadel, 1978), 35.

24. Ibid., 27, 13.

25. "Peewee's Progress," *Time*, 27 April 1936, 42; *Sketch*, 4–5.

26. Windeler, *Films of Shirley Temple*, 32. Shirley's "freakishness" was compounded by her racial ambiguity; see below.

27. Fiedler, *Freaks*, 48; Harris, *Humbug*, 49.

28. *Sketch*, 8–9.

29. Ibid., 14; "The Loving Lilliputians," *New York Times*, 11 February 1863, 8.

30. *Sketch*, 15.

31. Ibid., 25, 23.

32. Magazine articles from the period described children's natural propensity (or "instinct") to imitate adults; the *Time* story on Shirley, for example, referred to "a clever child's natural aptitude in imitating her elders." "Peewee's Progress," 42.

33. Windeler, *Films of Shirley Temple*, 13, 38.

34. *Sketch*, 17.

35. Lewis Erenberg, *Steppin' Out: New York Nightlife and the Transformation of American Culture, 1890–1930* (Chicago: University of Chicago Press, 1981), 67–68.

36. Arthur Hornblow, "The Children of the Stage," *Mumsey's Magazine* (October 1894): 33.

37. *Harper's Bazaar*, 25 August 1900, 1037–41; "The Century of the Child," *Harper's Monthly Magazine* 119 (August 1909): 434–38.

38. Frank Nugent, review of *Dimples*, *New York Times*, 10 October 1936, 21.

39. This crossing of diegetic levels was reinforced by the proliferation of commodities bearing the name or image of Shirley Temple, especially the Shirley Temple doll, which gave material shape to audience fantasies of intimate possession. Through the mass reproduction of Shirley's body, the Shirley Temple doll extended the structure of maternal emotion activated by the cute, positioning Shirley as national property. Patricia R. Smith, *Shirley Temple Dolls and Collectibles* (New York: Crown, 1977).

40. Anne Edwards, *Shirley Temple: American Princess* (New York: William Morrow, 1988), 76. During the Depression, the cute was articulated within the dominant ideology of economic reform. In his groundbreaking essay, "Shirley Temple and the House of Rockefeller" (in *American Media and Mass Culture: Left Perspectives*, ed. Donald Lazere [Berkeley: University of California Press, 1987], 164–77), Charles Eckert argues that Shirley Temple's sentimental appeal helped justify the conservative ideology of private charity to meliorate national economic conditions. For Eckert, Shirley Temple is a middle-class incarnation of the small, waif-like charity kids who filled the nation's magazines, and her films enact the Depression's "official ideology of charity" in narrative form. Interestingly, the role of the cute child in publicly recuperating by "maternalizing" capitalists was anticipated by Lia Graf, a "plump, well-proportioned" midget performer in the Ringling Bros. Barnum and Bailey Circus, who in June 1933 was suddenly set onto the lap of J. P. Morgan while he was testifying before the Senate Banking Committee. Reports of the episode stated that the financier seemed, for once, avuncular and quite human. Fiedler, *Freaks*, 85.

41. Donald Bogle, *Toms, Coons, Mulattoes, Mammies, and Bucks: An Interpretive History of Blacks in American Films* (New York: Continuum, 1994), 46.

42. Marian Hannah Winter, "Juba and American Minstrelsy," in *Chronicles of the American Dance from the Shakers to Martha Graham*, ed. Paul Magriel (New York: Da Capo, 1978), 39–63.

43. Windeler, *Films of Shirley Temple*, 104.

44. Stewart, *On Longing*, 109–10.

PART IV

Exhibiting Cultural Freaks

FOURTEEN

Ethnological Show Business: Footlighting the Dark Continent

BERNTH LINDFORS

Ethnological show business—that is, displaying foreign peoples for commercial and/or educational purposes—has a very long history in Europe, and it became an increasingly common form of enterprise after advances in navigational technology half a millennium ago put Europeans in touch with human communities all over the globe. As the world shrank, traffic in all kinds of exotic goods grew. One reads of live Eskimos being exhibited in Bristol as early as 1501, of Brazilian Indians building their own village in Rouen in the 1550s, of "Virginians" on the Thames in 1603, and of numerous other native human specimens from the New World, Africa, Asia, Australia, and the Pacific Islands being conveyed to European cities and towns as biological curiosities in the centuries that followed.[1] In a sense, this trade in odd human bodies was little different from an earlier practice that has continued right up to modern times: the commercial exhibition of *lusus naturae*—human and animal freaks, dead or alive. There appears to be a healthy natural interest in unusual and unnatural beings. Indeed, the stranger the creature, the stronger the draw.

By the end of the nineteenth century ethnological show business had grown into a major form of public entertainment in the Western world. The Wild West shows of Buffalo Bill Cody, the foreign spectacles and sideshows of the Barnum and Bailey Circus, and the national displays at various world's fairs and colonial exhibitions are examples of gigantic international enterprises that catered to this insatiable appetite for savoring the wonderful variety of the human species. The whole wide world was now available for scrutiny—for a small fee. The armchair traveler was in his heyday.

In an interesting essay in a book entitled *Exhibiting Cultures: The Poetics and Politics of Museum Display*, Barbara Kirshenblatt-Gimblett makes the point that

Exhibitions, whether of objects or people, are displays of the artifacts of our disciplines. They are for this reason also exhibits of those who make them, no matter what their ostensible subject. The first order of business is therefore to examine critically the conventions guiding ethnographic display, to explicate how displays constitute subjects and with what implications for those who see and those who are seen. . . . The question is not whether or not an object is of visual interest, but rather how interest of any kind is created. All interest is vested.[2]

It is in this reflexive context that I would like to look at the conventions governing the exhibition of Africans in the British Isles in the nineteenth century, a century that opened with extensive European exploration of the African continent and closed with wholesale European expropriation of that continent. This was the same era that saw the abolition of one system of economic exploitation—the slave trade—and the concurrent institutionalization of another—imperialism. In such a century, how were African peoples represented to the British public? In whose interest was it to see them this way? What subliminal messages lurked beneath the skin of these exhibitions?

Let's start with one of the most notorious figures—namely, Saartjie Baartman, a San woman who was exhibited in London in 1810–11, billed as the "Hottentot Venus" (fig. 14.1). The name was a joke, for in physique she little resembled any European notion of classic beauty. Like many San women, she had steatopygia, a greatly enlarged rump, which appears to have been the single feature of her anatomy sensational enough to bring out crowds to see her. She had been conveyed to England from the Cape by a Boer farmer and a British naval surgeon who had first tried to sell an interest in her to an antiquarian who owned a museum of art and natural history. When this deal fell through, she was put on display in a hall near Piccadilly Circus, which, according to a London *Times* reporter, had

a stage raised about three feet from the floor, with a cage, or enclosed place at the end of it; that the Hottentot was within the cage; that on being ordered by her keeper, she came out, and that her appearance was highly offensive to delicacy. . . . The Hottentot was produced like a wild beast, and ordered to move backwards and forwards, and come out and go into her cage, more like a bear in a chain than a human being. . . . She frequently heaved deep sighs; seemed anxious and uneasy; grew sullen, when she was ordered to play on some rude instrument of music. . . . And one time, when she refused for a moment to come out of her cage, the keeper let down the curtain, went behind, and was seen to hold up his hand to her in a menacing posture; she then came forward at his call, and was perfectly obedient. . . . She is dressed in a colour as nearly resembling her skin as possible. The dress is contrived to exhibit the entire frame of her body, and the spectators are even invited to examine the peculiarities of her form.[3]

Some of the spectators accepted this invitation by touching her rump and searching for evidence of padding or some other artifice beneath her skimpy, skin-colored dress. A woman who saw the show reported that "one pinched her, another walked round her; one gentleman *poked* her with his cane; and one *lady* employed her parasol to ascertain that all was, as she called it, '*nattral.*' This inhuman baiting the poor creature bore with sullen indifference, except upon some great provocation, when she seemed inclined to resent brutality, which even a Hottentot can understand. On these occasions it required all the authority of the keeper to subdue her resentment."[4]

Another spectator told a similar tale of what had transpired on the night he had seen her perform:

14.1. Poster of "Sartjee, the Hottentot Venus."
Courtesy of the British Library.

She was extremely ill, and the man insisted on her dancing, this being one of the tricks which she is forced to display. The poor creature pointed to her throat and to her knees as if she felt pain in both, pleading with tears that he would not force her compliance. He declared that she was sulky, produced a long piece of bamboo, and shook it at her: she saw it, knew its power, and, though ill, delayed no longer. While she was playing on a rude kind of guitar, a gentleman in the room chanced to laugh: the unhappy woman, ignorant of the cause, imagined herself the object of it, and as though the slightest addition to the woes of sickness, servitude, and involuntary banishment from her native land was more than she could bear, her broken spirit was aroused for a moment, and she endeavoured to strike him with the musical instrument which she held: but the sight of the long bamboo, the knowledge of its pain, and the fear of incurring it again, calmed her. The master declared that she was as wild as a beast, and the spectators agreed with him, forgetting that the language of ridicule is the same, and understood alike, in all countries, and that not one of them could bear to be the object of derision without an attempt to revenge the insult.[5]

It is clear from these remarks that not everyone in the audience found this kind of entertainment amusing. Within a few weeks, letters of protest began to appear in the London press complaining not only of the degraded nature of the exhibition but also of the state of servitude in which the woman apparently was being kept.[6] Since slavery had recently been abolished in Britain, why was the keeper of this unhappy woman being allowed to profit from her misery? Such a display was both immoral and illegal.

Members of the African Institution decided to take the matter to court, but the case was dismissed after the Hottentot Venus, interviewed in Low Dutch, testified in behalf of her managers, saying she had freely consented to exhibit her person in England, was earning good money, and wanted the show to go on.[7] There was some doubt that she fully understood the nature of the contract she had entered into, but the presiding magistrate at the Court of the King's Bench felt he had no alternative but to release her into the care of her keeper.

What most impressed ordinary people about this case was not the high conscience of the gentlemen of the African Institution who had brought the action, but the low cupidity of the Hottentot. Her insistence upon her right to make a spectacle of herself, like any profit-minded dwarf or giant in the exhibition trade, became the subject of countless jokes, cartoons, and newspaper doggerel. Here is a sample from a ballad that began to circulate after the court ruled that she could return to the stage:

> *Oh have you been in London towne,*
> *Its rareties to see:*
> *There is, 'mongst ladies of renown,*
> *A most renowned she.*
> *In Piccadillie streete so faire,*
> *A mansion she has got;*
> *On golden letters written there,*
> *"The Venus Hottentot".*
> *But you may ask, and well, I ween,*
> *For why she tarries there;*
> *And what, in her is to be seen,*
> *Than other folks more rare.*
> *A rump she has, (though strange it be,)*
> *Large as a cauldron pot,*
> *And this is why men go to see*
> *This lovely Hottentot.*[8]

Saartjie Baartman's story does not have a happy ending. For the next few years she appears to have continued performing at fairs, festivals, and rented halls throughout the British Isles, and in 1814 she finally wound up in Paris, where she excited the attention of professional zoologists as well as sightseers. When she died there in 1815, her body was dissected by Baron Georges Cuvier, the leading naturalist of his day, who promptly published a scientific paper on the peculiarities of her posterior and private parts.[9] He also arranged for various bits of her body—brain, skeleton, skull, body hair—to be preserved for further scientific scrutiny, and he made waxen molds of her genitalia and plaster casts of her body, one of which stood on display in Case 33 at the Musée de l'Homme until as late as 1982. So Saartjie Baartman has had a career in science as well as in popular culture, having been reified not only as a comic figure of outlandish voluptuousness, but also as a durable set of physiological reference points in biometric discourse. For scientist and lay person alike, she became a somatic cliché, a coarse stereotype of female primitivism. Because she was displayed, treated, and

14.2. "The Bosjesmans going through the war-dance under the direction of Mr. J. S. Tyler." *The Sportsman's Magazine*, 10 May 1847.

conceptualized as little better than an animal, the Hottentot Venus remains even today a potent symbol of Africa's supposed degraded backwardness. Cuvier compared her to a monkey and an orangutan,[10] scientifically dehumanizing her and her kind. It was this sort of biological slur that reinforced European beliefs that Africans were closer to the lower order of brutes than to human beings.

Essentially the same reaction was registered a generation later when a group of five "Bosjesmans" (i.e., San)—two men, two women, and an infant—were exhibited for five years throughout Europe (fig. 14.2). One of the first notices of their arrival in Liverpool in 1846 stated that the Bosjesmans showed "how very nearly sentient beings may sink to, or rather have never risen above, the condition of animals endowed with reason to guide or govern their instinctive propensities. . . . They are supposed to belong to one of the numerous tribes of their benighted country which have not yet emerged from absolute barbarism."[11]

Aside from their diminutive size and odd features (which did not include pronounced steatopygia), what appears to have made the Bosjesmans particularly fascinating to British spectators was their rudimentary life style: they owned very few possessions, used only the simplest tools, built no permanent structures, and wore hardly any clothing. All these traits could have been traced to the fact that they were a hunting and gathering people and therefore had no need for possessions or paraphernalia that would impede their mobility, but the British interpreted a lack of things as a lack of culture and thought less of the Bosjesmans as a result. Commentators tended to agree with the oft-quoted assessment offered by the learned traveler Dr. M. H. C. Lichtenstein that "there is not perhaps any class of savages upon the earth that lead lives so near those of the brutes as the Bosjesmans;—none perhaps who are sunk so low, who are so unimportant in the scale of existence;—whose wants, whose cares, and whose joys, are so low in their nature;—and who are consequently so little capable of cultivation."[12] In short, the Bosjesmans were presumed to be an utterly hopeless lot.

Yet, the very extremity of their "degradation" made them all the more interesting to British audiences, for whenever these visitors deviated even slightly from accepted standards of cultivated behavior, their "foolish" actions were construed not only as further proof of Bosjesman barbarity, but also as clear confirmation of British cultural superiority. The more different the Bosjesmans appeared, the more comfortable the British felt. It was when the "savage" betrayed some sign of common humanity that the "civilized" expressed surprise and a little concern. John Bull did not fancy seeing himself reflected in this monstrously misshapen mirror.

One can find this kind of British cultural prejudice displayed quite openly in statements made by newspaper reporters about the Bosjesmans' most undeniably human characteristic—their language. The Bosjesman phonological system happens to contain a set of implosive consonants, commonly called "clicks," which do not exist in the English phonological system. Since "well over 70 percent of words in Bushman languages begin with a click consonant," [13] this is a very prominent feature in Bosjesman speech. The number and variety of these click consonants, complicated still further by subtle vowel colorings and significant variations in tone, make Bosjesman languages, according to a contemporary authority, "from the phonetic point of view . . . *the world's most complex languages.*" [14] All of this complexity was lost on Victorian British auditors, who heard only the unfamiliar clicking and popping noises and drew their own conclusions.

The greatest temptation was to compare these sounds to those made by nonhuman creatures. The *Liverpool Mail* said that "their language—if the singular sounds by which their conversations are conducted can be termed a language—completely puts our alphabet *hors de combat*. It is not unlike the chirps of birds, and is supposed to consist of about twenty words, whose meanings are varied by the pronunciation." [15] The *Liverpool Chronicle* reported, "It is a perfect novelty to hear them talk, their language resembling more the 'click' of turkeys than the speech of human beings." [16] The *Birmingham Advertiser* described the phenomenon as a "singular compound of inharmonious articulations, copiously interspersed with a kind of chirp or click . . . and bearing no remote analogy to the babel of the smaller birds and animals in a menagerie." [17] Other papers drew comparisons to "the clucking of a hen," [18] "the chucking of fowls or the motion of machinery," [19] or the sound "used by ostlers to urge their horses." [20]

The *Spectator* offered the fullest and most perceptive linguistic description of the clicks, but concluded with an unflattering comparison:

> Three of the consonants, we observed, consisted of these sounds—the noise made by the lips in slightly kissing, as when you kiss your hand; that made by smacking the tip of the tongue against the palate, as you do when tasting a flavour, or as some women do when they express petty vexation; and the clucking noise made with the hinder part of the tongue against the palate to urge a horse or assemble poultry; these three sounds, especially the two former, are consonants of rather frequent occurrence. A vowel sound, often repeated, resembles the French *eu*, but uttered from the chest with the coarse sing-song drawl of a boy driving away birds. The language is as rude and undeveloped, in sound at least, as the physical conformation of the people [who as adults] are undeveloped children, stricken with senility while their forms are still immature. [21]

There was a similar tendency in other papers to associate unusual phonology with a lack of adequate physical, mental, moral, cultural, and/or linguistic development. The *Era* described the Bosjesman language as "wholly incomprehensible, for nobody can interpret it. . . . Their words are made up of coughs and clucks—such as a man uses to his nag—anything more uncivilized can scarcely be conceived." [22] According to the *Manchester Guardian*, this language was "singularly barren, exceedingly harsh and unpleasant to the ear . . . its most remarkable feature [being] some inarticulate clicks and clucks."[23] The *Glasgow Examiner* reported that such language consisted of "a series of *clicks* stuck together in some curious philological way, to represent their few and simple ideas."[24] The *Manchester Express* called it "rude and harsh in the extreme"[25]; the Dublin *Warder* said it was "an unintelligible jargon"[26]; and the *Plymouth Times* found it "so imperfect that its sounds can hardly be rendered in writing by any syllables we can frame."[27] The Bosjesmans obviously were not simply a hopeless lot; their ridiculous language betrayed them as a singularly inarticulate hopeless lot.

Some commentators were unwilling to consider them better than dumb brutes. London's *Morning Post* asserted that "They belong ... to the lowest class of humanity; and the power of speech being excepted, there are many of the inferior animals possessing a greater development of the higher faculties than this savage specimen of human kind." The only example cited to support this dismissive generalization was the beaver, who "possesses the faculty of constructiveness to a very marked extent." The rest of the article was devoted to illustrating the "marked resemblance" between the Bosjesman and the baboon, orangutan, chimpanzee, and monkey.[28] A reporter for the *Cork Southern Reporter* also felt that in their "brutelike indistinctness of language" as well as in a number of other traits, the Bosjesmans "come so near the Monkey tribe, as to make us almost question their humanity."[29]

Of course, a number of journalists were quite prepared to give the Bosjesmans the benefit of the doubt, principally because these grotesque children of nature were able to speak a language, albeit a simple and somewhat beastly tongue. But no reporters of that day believed that a Bosjesman's rudimentary linguistic competence made him the intellectual equal of a European. That would have been carrying liberal ideas much too far. A correspondent for the *Observer* put it this way: "Their distinguishing characteristic . . . as men is the use of language, but besides that they have little in common—either those now on view, or their brethren in the bush—with that race of beings which boasts of a Newton and a Napoleon—of a Fenelon, a Milton, and of Dante."[30] No one would dare to attempt to make monkeys out of such distinguished men.

The arrogant ethnocentrism underlying British responses to the Bosjesmans appears to have been typical of European attitudes toward African peoples during the age of imperialism, but sometimes it is shocking to come across racist remarks made by Victorian gentlemen one might otherwise have assumed to be among the most enlightened observers of the human scene. David Livingstone, for example, speaking specifically of the Bosjesmans, noted that "the specimens brought to Europe have been selected, like costermongers' dogs, on account of their extreme ugliness. That they are, to some extent, like baboons is true, just as these are in some points frightfully human."[31] Charles Dickens, in a humorous essay devoted to debunking the romantic myth of the Noble Savage, had equally uncomplimentary things to say of this troupe of mini-savages:

Think of the Bushmen. Think of the two men and the two women who have been exhibited about England for some years. Are the majority of persons—who remember the horrid little leader of that party in his festering bundle of hides, with his filth and his antipathy to water, and his straddled legs, and his odious eyes shaded by his brutal hand, and his cry of "Qu-u-u-u-aaa!" (Bosjesman for something desperately insulting I have no doubt)—conscious of an affectionate yearning towards that noble savage, or is it idiosyncratic in me to abhor, detest, abominate, and abjure him? I have no reserve on this subject, and will frankly state that, setting aside that stage of the entertainment when he counterfeited the death of some creature he had shot, by laying his head on his hand and shaking his left leg—at which time I think it would have been justifiable homicide to slay him—I have never seen that group sleeping, smoking, and expectorating round their brazier, but I have sincerely desired that something might happen to the charcoal smouldering therein, which would cause the immediate suffocation of the whole of the noble strangers.[32]

Here, in a voice which has come to be regarded as quintessentially Victorian, is one of the first overt suggestions in England of a final solution to the Bosjesman problem. Such genocidal urges, of course, had already been translated into action in the Cape, where British and Boer settlers had felt compelled to deal ruthlessly with such small, ugly, possessionless, monkeylike, clicking, clucking savages. The visceral reactions of Dickens and other spectators to the Bosjesmans were only a confirmation and validation of attitudes that guided British colonial policy.

When ridiculing the notion of the "Noble Savage," Dickens did not confine his remarks to the San. In fact, his principal target was a larger troupe of South African performers who had been transported to London in 1853 by A. T. Caldecott, a prosperous merchant from Natal. These thirteen "Zulu Kaffirs" turned out to be a profitable speculation, for they attracted huge crowds and even won an invitation to appear before Queen Victoria and her children at Buckingham Palace. What helped to make this exhibition more popular than other ethnographic displays was the fact that it was an extremely dramatic performance, not a static sideshow. The performers acted out incidents said to be typical of Zulu life and did so with great fervor. The advertisement placed in the London *Times* on the day the show opened stated that the exhibition would illustrate "in an extensive and unexampled manner this wild and interesting tribe of savages in their domestic habits, their nuptial ceremonies, the charm song, finding the witch, hunting tramp, preparation for war, and territorial conflicts."[33] To explain some of the scenes, Caldecott's son served as an interpreter and master of ceremonies, lecturing briefly on Zulu customs and traditions before they were enacted on the stage.

The earliest review of the "Caffres at Hyde-Park-Corner" (as they came to be called) appeared in the *Times* two days after the premiere. It is worth quoting at length because it is typical of the response of British theater critics to this novel entertainment:

Eleven men, with a woman and a child, are assembled into a company, and instead of performing one or two commonplace feats, may be said to go through the whole drama of Caffre life, while a series of scenes, painted by Mr. Charles Marshall, gives an air of reality to the living pictures. Now the Caffres are at their meal, feeding themselves with enormous spoons, and expressing their satisfaction by a wild chant, under the inspiration of which they bump themselves along without rising in a sort of circular dance. Now the witchfinder commences his operations to discover the culprit whose magic has brought sickness into the tribe, and becomes perfectly rabid through the effect of his own incantations. Now there is a wedding ceremony, now a hunt, now a military expedition, all with characteristic dances; and the whole ends with a general conflict between rival tribes. The songs and dances are, as may be expected, monotonous in the extreme, and without the bill it would be difficult to distinguish the expression of love from the gesture of martial defiance.[34]

In his essay, Dickens elaborated on each of these scenes by emphasizing the Zulus' comically picturesque barbarity. Here, for example, is how he described their preparations for battle:

> When war is afoot among the noble savages—which is always—the chief holds a council to ascertain whether it is the opinion of his brothers and friends in general that the enemy shall be exterminated. On this occasion, after the performance of an Umseb-euza, or war song—which is exactly like all the other songs—the chief makes a speech to his brothers and friends, arranged in a single file. No particular order is observed during the delivery of this address, but every gentleman who finds himself excited by the subject, instead of crying "Hear, Hear!" as is the custom with us, darts from the rank and tramples out the life, or crushes the skull, or mashes the face, or scoops out the eyes, or breaks the limbs, or performs a whirlwind of atrocities on the body, of an imaginary enemy. Several gentlemen becoming thus excited at once, and pounding away without the least regard to the orator, that illustrious person is rather in the position of an orator in an Irish House of Commons. But, several of these scenes of savage life bear a strong generic resemblance to an Irish election, and I think would be extremely well received and understood at Cork.

Dickens followed this up with a paragraph playfully suggesting other parallels between the ceremonies of the noble savage and the practices of civilized man in Europe, but he returned to his main theme in his concluding statement: "My position is, that if we have anything to learn from the Noble Savage, it is what to avoid. His virtues are a fable; his happiness is a delusion; his nobility, nonsense . . . and the world will be all the better when his place knows him no more." Here we are back at the genocidal imperative. Dickens did not explicitly advocate that Zulus, Bosjesmans, and other non-Western peoples be physically exterminated; he may have been too much of a gentleman for that. Instead, he recommended that they be "civilised off the face of the earth"—in other words, subjected to cultural, not literal, genocide. But this may have been only a manner of speaking. Dickens was intent on demolishing a romantic myth of the nobility of uncivilized mankind, and if he employed verbal overkill to accomplish his purpose, he was only behaving as he may have imagined a proper, pragmatic Victorian should to destroy a pernicious illusion. A few laughs at the expense of the Zulus would do his English audience a world of good.

The Zulu Kaffirs of 1853 were only the first in a long procession of Zulu performing groups to appear in the British Isles in the following years. Their novelty value increased during the Anglo-Zulu wars when regiments of Cetewayo's warriors twice massacred British troops in pitched battles. Such proven prowess in combat generated a great deal of curiosity in Europe and the United States about these fierce, courageous, and militaristic people.

Circus entrepreneurs tried to take advantage of this curiosity by recruiting Zulus for their shows. P. T. Barnum even went so far as to offer Queen Victoria's government $100,000 for permission to exhibit the captured Cetewayo for five years, a petition that did not amuse the Queen.[35] A rival showman outdid Barnum by putting on display three of Cetewayo's nieces (whom he billed as the chief's daughters, true "Zulu princesses"),[36] a baby, another Zulu chief, and twenty-three warriors who had surrendered to British authorities in South Africa; it has been reported that "their arrival in London was greeted by over one hundred thousand people on the docks and as far up the street as the eye could reach."[37] Other showmen could not ignore such palpable signs of popularity, and soon spears, shields, feathers, and war paint could be found in abundance in every sideshow and even in circus "specs," or opening pageants.

Needless to say, many of these Zulu performers were frauds. More than one circus veteran has commented on this in his memoirs: "I recollect at the time of the Zulu war how one showman conceived the idea of exhibiting a number of Zulu warriors. There was only one drawback—not a single Zulu was at that moment in the country. But drawbacks do not exist for the born showman and a party of ordinary niggers were easily made up into Cetewayo's savage soldiery."[38] An American showman recalled,

In the side show we had a big negro whom we had fitted up with rings in his nose, a leopard skin, some assegais and a large shield made out of cow's skin. While he was sitting on the stage in the side show, along came two negro women and remarked, "See that nigger over there? He ain't no Zulu, that's Bill Jackson. He worked over here at Camden on the dock. I seen that nigger often." Poor old Bill Jackson was as uneasy as if he was sitting on needles, holding the shield between him and the two negro women. Fortunately for him, about this time the audience was called to another portion of the tent.[39]

But in the years following the war authentic Zulus became more plentiful in both Britain and the United States, and fewer Bill Jacksons had to fill their sandals. The program for Barnum's show at Madison Square Garden in April 1888 advertised "Two Real African Zulus,"[40] and a naturalist writing in 1885 on ethnographic exhibitions at dime museums declared that

The idea that the Dime Museum Zulus were manufactured to order is false. There have been Zulus. These are not, as some of the journalists have wickedly insinuated, Irish immigrants, cunningly painted and made up like savages. They are genuine Zulus; and though we need not believe the lecturer's statement that they fought under Cetewayo at Isandhwalo [sic], and displayed prodigies of valor in order to free their country from British rule ... there is no doubt that they would prove terrible enemies in battle. Looking at their leaps and bounds, and listening to their yells and whistles and the rattling of their assegais against their shields, no one can wonder that English cavalry horses were at first afraid to face them.[41]

Some showmen were afraid to face them, too, and found it more convenient to continue to employ pseudo-Zulus who could be more easily controlled and disciplined. When James Lloyd engaged a dozen bona fide tribesmen for a show that toured Ireland, he found that "their wildness [in performing dances] was disturbingly genuine; this being one of the disadvantages encountered by showmen who, with more honesty than aesthetic perception, prefer Nature to Art. Nature, it has been said, is pulling up on Art; but she has still a long way to go before she produces savages who are equal to the other for show purposes."[42]

That most circus showmen preferred Art to Nature is evident in their use of the term "Zulu," which in American circus jargon gradually expanded its field of reference to include any Negro who participated in the "spec."[43] A black laborer or musician employed by the circus could earn a "Zulu ticket" (a credit slip for more pay) by donning a costume and parading around the hippodrome track in the grand opening pageant. "Zulu" thus became synonymous with artifice and disguise. Pseudo-Zulus proliferated, emerging as a stock character type that eventually entered the standard vocabulary of ethnic imagery projected by such powerful media as Hollywood films.

In the nineteenth century British notions of Africanness acquired a resonance that radiated to other parts of the Western world, where they often became amplified into grotesque caricatures that took on a life of their own, perpetuating themselves as durable stereotypes of barbarism. It may have served British colonial interests to portray subjects in Africa as freaks and savages, but these negative oversimplifications and distortions also served the vested interests of those in the New World who sought to deny basic human rights to black people. It was one thing for Dickens to lampoon what he construed as the eccentric ignobilities of the Zulus. However, the circus entrepreneurs who employed poor old Bill Jackson and others of his kind to "act Zulu" took ethnological show business to a new extreme of theatrical misrepresentation, using a real victim to promote a patently false mythology that to a large extent was responsible for his victimization. The Hottentot Venus, the Bosjesmans, the Zulu Kaffirs, and all the other true and false Africans who literally gave body to such lies were unwitting collaborators in their own exploitation, agents of their own dehumanization. Putting them in the footlights in this fashion was one method of ensuring that in the Western mind, Africa would remain unillumined, an irredeemably Dark Continent.

NOTES

1. Barbara Kirshenblatt-Gimblett, "Objects of Ethnography," in *Exhibiting Cultures: The Poetics and Politics of Museum Display,* ed. Ivan Karp and Steven D. Lavine (Washington, D.C.: Smithsonian Institution Press, 1991), 402.

2. Ibid., 434.

3. London *Times,* 26 November 1810, 3.

4. Mrs. Mathews, *Memoirs of Charles Mathews, Comedian* (London: Richard Bently, 1839), 4:137.

5. A Constant Reader, "The Female Hottentot," *Examiner,* 14 October 1810, 653.

6. See, e.g., *Morning Chronicle,* 12 October 1810, 3, and *Examiner,* 28 October 1810, 681.

7. For an account of these proceedings, see Bernth Lindfors, "Courting the Hottentot Venus," *Africa* (Rome) 40 (1985): 133–48.

8. Broadside reprinted in R. Toole-Stott, *Circus and Allied Arts: A World Bibliography, 1500–1962* (Derby: Harper, 1962), 3:334.

9. *Mémoires du Museum d'Histoire Naturelle* 3 (1817): 259–74.

10. Quoted in Percival R. Kirby, "The Hottentot Venus," *Africana Notes and News* 6 (1949): 60.

11. *Liverpool Mail,* 14 November 1846, 3.

12. Quoted on page 19 of *History of the Bosjesmans, or Bush People; the Aboriginals of Southern Africa* (London: Chapman, Elcoate and Co., 1847), a pamphlet sold at later shows. M. H. C. Lichtenstein's *Reisen im südlichen Afrika in den Jahren 1803, 1804, 1805 and 1806* (Berlin, 1811–1812), first published in English translation in London (1812–1815), was subsequently reissued in English by the Van Riebeeck Society in Cape Town (1928–1930).

13. Anthony Traill, "The Languages of the Bushmen," in *The Bushmen: San Hunters and Herders of Southern Africa*, ed. Phillip V. Tobias (Cape Town and Pretoria: Human and Rousseau, 1978), 138.

14. Ibid., 139, my emphasis.

15. *Liverpool Mail*, 14 November 1846, 3. Cf. *Liverpool Courier*, 18 November 1846, 6; and Dublin's *Saunders's News-Letter*, 16 December 1847, 2.

16. *Liverpool Chronicle*, 5 December 1846, 5.

17. *Birmingham Advertiser*, 6 May 1847, 2.

18. *Midland Counties Herald, Birmingham and General Advertiser*, 22 April 1847, 63.

19. *Glasgow Examiner*, 24 June 1848, 2.

20. *Douglas Jerrold's Weekly Newspaper*, 22 May 1847, 636. Cf. Dublin's *Evening Packet*, 28 December 1847, 3.

21. *Spectator*, 12 June 1847, 564.

22. *Era*, 6 June 1847, 11.

23. *Manchester Guardian*, 10 March 1847, 5.

24. *Glasgow Examiner*, 1 July 1848, 2.

25. *Manchester Express*, 9 March 1847, 3.

26. *Warder*, 22 January 1848, 5.

27. *Plymouth Times*, 3 August 1850, 3.

28. *Morning Post*, 19 May 1847, 6.

29. *Cork Southern Reporter*, 17 February 1848, 2.

30. *Observer*, 21 June 1847, 6.

31. David Livingstone, *A Popular Account of Missionary Travels and Researches in South Africa* (London: John Murray, 1875), 35.

32. Charles Dickens, "The Noble Savage," *Household Words*, 11 June 1853, 197–202. All quotations are from this source.

33. London *Times*, 16 May 1853, 4.

34. London *Times*, 18 May 1853, 8.

35. Irving Wallace, *The Fabulous Showman: the Life and Times of P. T. Barnum* (New York: Knopf, 1959), 111.

36. A poster for W. C. Coup's United Monster Shows at the Great Paris Hippodrome in Chicago in 1881 advertises "Princess Amazulu, King Cetewayo's Daughter and Suite." A newspaper advertisement for the same circus the following year bills "Zulu Princess Amadage, daughter of King Cetewayo, and her maids of honor"; these women were also said to be "the only Female Zulus who ever left Zululand and the only genuine Zulus in America" (Circus World Museum, Baraboo, Wisconsin).

37. William Cameron Coup, *Sawdust and Spangles: Stories and Secrets of the Circus* (Chicago: Stone, 1901), 166.

38. Thomas (Whimsical) Walker, *From Sawdust to Windsor Castle* (London: Paul, 1922), 130.

39. George Middleton, *Circus Memoirs, as Told to and Written by His Wife* (Los Angeles: George Middleton, 1913), 69.

40. Program for P. T. Barnum with Great London Circus, Madison Square Garden, 17 April 1888 (Dyer Reynolds Circus Collection, Memphis State University).

41. J. G. Wood, "Dime Museums as Seen from a Naturalist's Standpoint," *Atlantic Monthly* 55 (June 1885): 760.

42. Samuel McKechnie, *Popular Entertainments through the Ages* (London: Sampson, Low, Marston, n.d.), 210.

43. For this information I am grateful to the late Robert Parkinson, formerly Research Director of the Circus World Museum, Baraboo, Wisconsin. The words are defined in a glossary appended to Esse Forrester O'Brien, *Circus: Cinders to Sawdust* (San Antonio: Naylor, 1959), 260.

FIFTEEN

Ogling Igorots: The Politics and Commerce of Exhibiting Cultural Otherness, 1898–1913

CHRISTOPHER A. VAUGHAN

Of all the distorted images of the Philippines offered for public consumption in the first years of the United States's colonization of the islands, none proved more popular—or more difficult to manage—than that of the Bontoc Igorots. Introduced corporeally to Americans under the auspices of the nascent field of anthropology, the animists from the remote mountains of Northern Luzon quickly achieved prominence far out of proportion to their minority status, drawing huge crowds eager to see the scantily clad "dog-eaters" in the flesh. The Igorots' exotic religious rituals and reputation as fearsome headhunters fed a ravenous public hunger for displays of cultural difference affirming Americans' sense of remove from the spectre of "savagery." As misleading stand-ins for the Christianized (and thus, inconveniently, already "civilized") majority of Filipinos, the Igorots played an important political role in the debate over the United States's embrace of missionary imperialism. As objects of cultural otherness, they exemplified the fluid symbiosis between the cultural project of anthropology and the freakmaking machinery of exhibitionary commerce. As show business sojourners, they achieved fame but not fortune—a bitter bargain given the nature of their notoriety and the hardships many endured.

The Igorots' renown reached its peak at the 1904 World's Fair in St. Louis and was sustained in a series of publicly and privately managed displays at official expositions and carnival sideshows through the following decade. So powerful did the Igorots' image prove that the very government that had put them onstage lost control of the trope and was forced to make extraordinary efforts, including the arrest of former colonial officials, to put the genie back in the bottle. The tale of the Igorot sideshows and the scientists and shady operators who brought them before a receptive public has at its core the tension between education and exploitation, a tension exacerbated by the inconsistent stance of a government playing an obscurantist culture card in the service of a larger imperial game. As an aesthetically arresting culture untouched by Spanish Catholicism and thus eligible for American-style transformation, the Igorots stood outside of the colonial power structure. As anthropological freaks, they were dehumanized, and thus in some important ways depoliticized. They were, in short, perfect subalterns for a colonial power reluctant to acknowledge its baser motives and eager to "discover" fresh frontiers of all kinds.

At St. Louis, the Igorots were presented in the context of the aptly dubbed Philippine Reservation, encompassing a diversity of ethnic groups from across the sprawling archipelago. Though the colorful denizens of the Gran Cordillera were featured prominently in advertisements and fair publications, it was public demand, not government promotion, that placed them at the head of the list of the huge fair's attractions. That demand was fed by newspaper reports and fumbling public relations efforts that called prurient attention to the exhibit. Underlying all the hullabaloo was an enduring American fixation on wildness.

The popular appeal of "wild peoples" at the turn of the century arose amid a discourse of American self-identification influenced by Darwinism, the closing of the continental frontier, concerns about the nation's fast-diversifying ethnic composition, and a national longing for order exemplified in part by the rise of anthropology and ethnology. In the case of the Philippines, the high profile of the "wild peoples" trope owes much to the work of a young ornithologist named Dean C. Worcester. Quick to see the demand for authoritative literature on the newly acquired islands, the ambitious University of Michigan zoology professor converted photographs and field notes from 1887–89 and 1890–92 into *The Philippine Islands and Their People* in 1898. This comprehensive tome, which propelled Worcester into a unique position of power as the only man to serve on the first and second incarnations of the Philippine Commission, laid emphasis on the exotic. Worcester's scholarly focus on fauna and flora predisposed him to train both his camera and his analysis on the natural realm, rather than human affairs. The "non-Christian tribes," who had resisted Spanish colonization for three centuries, fell outside the prevailing definition of "civilization" and thus within Worcester's broad conception of nature. Son of a missionary and a man of keen commercial instincts, Worcester was to trade on images of wildness throughout his long career as a colonial official and traveling Philippines expert.[1]

Worcester was not alone in recognizing the appeal of the "savage" image. The simultaneous rise of photography and anthropology in the last years of the nineteenth century accounts for much of the interest in images of primitivity, but the visual emphasis on physical and cultural difference was widely expressed in popular media as well, often without regard for context. Editorial cartoons routinely depicted Filipinos, along with Cubans, Puerto Ricans, and Hawaiians, as black-skinned, nappy-haired pickaninnies, usually being disciplined by the tall, pale, top-hatted patriarch in the striped pants, Uncle Sam. As an easily differentiated subgrouping of Filipinos whose appearance and primitive weaponry evoked classic American images of Indians, Igorots provided an image imbued with the extra power of photographic "reality." In 1898, New York *Sun* correspondent Oscar King Davis's popular eyewitness account of U.S. soldiers' first contact with the Philippines, *Our Conquests in the Pacific*, made no mention of such peoples, yet the slim selection of photographs accompanying the text were primarily devoted to loincloth-clad tribesmen holding spears or aiming arrows. The Sears catalog for Fall 1900 boasts a drawing of Igorot spearmen in its advertisement for stereoscopic slide packages. Other examples abound in a variety of media almost from the outset of the encounter.[2]

The misrepresentation of the broader Philippine polity inherent in the focus on "savages" served an official agenda. Differentiating Filipinos from Americans as starkly as possible served to bolster claims that "natives" were incapable of self-government and thus required

American supervision. The civilizing mission, a standard justification for establishing control over—and expanding onto the lands of—non-European Others, was the reason cited by President William McKinley when he reluctantly declared U.S. intentions to retain the Philippines following the quick and relatively painless Spanish-American War. Paternalism remained the primary moral stance favoring the colonial project as it came under criticism from a broad coalition of anti-imperialists.

Despite clever public relations and rhetoric designed to appeal to the liberty-loving American people, few Filipino voices found sufficient amplification through popular media to counter the barrage of inaccurate stereotypes. The absence of a voice in the United States was all the more glaring for Filipino ethnic minorities. Aside from the sad, emblematic tale of the bow-and-arrow-shooting Igorots sent to their deaths in the first wave of battle against the Americans on February 4, 1899, the "wild people" largely receded from popular consciousness for the rest of the bloody war.[3]

Interest in Igorots was revived in 1903 with the first publication of what would become a signature feature of *National Geographic:* photographs of bare-breasted women. The shirtless Tagbuana and Negrito women shown in the photos had little connection with the accompanying articles about the eradication of diseases and the discovery of a potential hill station for colonial bureaucrats, but decontextualized images were not at all uncommon as editors adjusted the balance between scientific interest and popular appeal in favor of the latter.[4]

A similar blurring of education and entertainment took place on another front. Growing popular demand for spectacle and display met government desires to commemorate progress in a series of fairs and expositions, each greater than the next as cities vied to assert themselves symbolically as full-grown regional centers. Borrowing a page from international expositions in Paris at which Polynesian and Senegalese villages were re-created, Chicago's Columbian Exposition in 1893 introduced visitors to the world through national theme villages on the Midway of Pleasure. The commercial display of the alien Other may have reached its apotheosis in the shapely form of Fahreda Mahzar, a Syrian belly dancer billed as "Little Egypt, the Darling of the Nile," whose performances created a "hootchy-kootchy" dance show craze foreshadowing the less intentionally erotic appeal of the underdressed Igorots a decade later.

Expressions of interest in displaying Filipinos emerged as early as the 1898 Omaha Exposition, at which a few Filipinos made a brief appearance late in the fair's run, and the 1901 Pan-American Exposition in Buffalo, to which permission for a display of live Filipinos was denied by the solicitor of the treasury. In 1899, France, refusing to acknowledge Filipinos as Americans, denied an application to include Filipinos in the U.S. display at the Paris Exposition.[5]

By 1904, however, U.S. control of the Philippines was established and plans were made for an extensive Philippine Exhibit at the Louisiana Purchase Exposition at St. Louis. Uniting Jefferson's vision of an expanded America with the still controversial embrace of overseas empire represented by the colonization of the Philippines, the exposition was a critical forum for the promulgation of a new imperial agenda. Determined to eclipse the shining example of Chicago's White City, the organizers of the fair staged the grandest event in history. Huge in scale and ambition, it incorporated everything from the Western Hemisphere's first Olympic Games to a Congress of Races. Contending for attention were re-creations of the battles of Manila and Santiago Bay, magnificent art and industry pavilions, a Department of Anthropol-

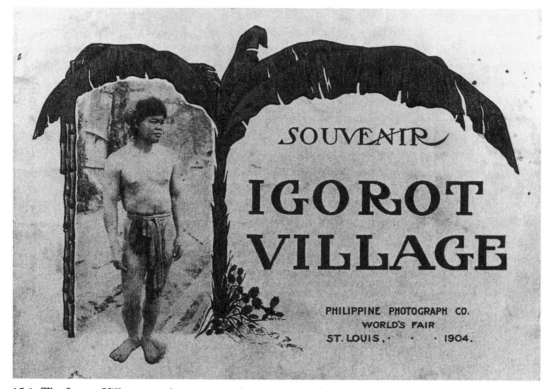

15.1. The Igorot Village was the most popular attraction of the entire 1904 World's Fair in St. Louis. The scanty dress of the Igorots was a principal reason: When an imminent government order to put pants on the Igorots was made public, daily crowds of five thousand at the site immediately doubled as the public rushed to see the "savages" in a "state of nature."

ogy of unprecedented scope, and the rough-and-tumble of the Pike, which was a street of amusements featuring Chinese and Irish villages, Cairo Street, reenactments of battles from the Boer War, and the ever-popular hootchy-kootchy dancers. By all accounts, however, the most popular attraction of the 1904 World's Fair was the Igorot Village (fig. 15.1). Mounted to display the fruits of the United States's recent embrace of colonial empire, the sprawling, forty-acre Philippine Reservation featured separate exhibits for tribes from throughout the archipelago's more than seven thousand islands. The "civilized" Visayans, despite offering hourly theatrical and orchestral performances—concluding with "The Star Spangled Banner," sung in English by the entire village—went relatively ignored in comparison to the Igorots, whose ceremonial dances, near-nakedness, and daily consumption of dog stew captured headlines and the entertainment dollars of fairgoers. Gate receipts at the Igorot concession nearly quadrupled the total for the Visayans and tripled that of the colorful Moros.[6]

The nomadic Negritos, who were held up as even more primitive than the Igorots—and thus bound for extinction—did not generate one-third the revenue or attention paid to the natives of the Mountain Province, in large measure because the Igorots presented image traders with more sensational material. Cigar-smoking women, tattooed members of both sexes, dances celebrating the cooking of dogs—the violation of taboos surrounding diet and the display of the body can be seen as an extension of the hootchy-kootchy dances and cotton

15.2. Fairgoers mingled with the Igorots on display in St. Louis, reveling in what appeared to be an unmediated encounter with humanity's wild nature. The feast dance celebrated the consumption of dog stew—an Igorot delicacy and a source of boundless fascination for Americans titillated by displays of culinary "savagery."

candy of the previous decade and body-piercing and stronger substances today. Known for a tradition of headhunting, the Igorots were unlikely to put such skills on display outside the context of battle, but their public consumption of Man's Best Friend may have raised thoughts of cannibalism (fig. 15.2). Indeed, before they even arrived, newspaper articles heralded their unusual hankering for canine cuisine. The Igorots exacerbated the consternation of conservative readers with their unabashed joy at the prospect of consuming daily what was usually a delicacy reserved for special occasions. The St. Louis Humane Society, citing a local ordinance, condemned the practice but was shouted down by a broad assortment of voices representing both producers and consumers of the most popular show in town. Included among the defenders of dog-eating was the St. Louis *Post-Dispatch*, which wondered, in a tongue-in-cheek front-page headline, whether it was "the beef trust, speaking through the humane society, that would rob the Irrogote [sic] of his cherished dog meat?" The paper's clumsy foray into cultural relativism was undermined by the cartoon above the article, which depicted a bewildered, club-wielding Igorot, thick-lipped and earring-clad, being warned off a prospective meal of poached pooch by a bespectacled, top-hatted Humane Society killjoy. The delicious appeal of what was widely seen as savage dietary perversity helped to build the novelty value of the Igorots to the point where an average of five thousand people a day were visiting the re-created Bontoc village early in the fair's run.[7]

Fair publicity managers were not shy about promoting the dog-eater angle:

> About the time the World's Fair City is waking at early morning, one hundred bare-limbed Igorot often sacrifice and eat a dog on the Philippine reservation. At the same hour, scarcely two hundred yards away, a bugle sounds reveille, and four hundred well-trained soldiers in the blue of the United States Army hustle from their tents. These are the Philippine Scouts. The yells of the dog-dance have scarcely ceased before the blue line is formed for roll call, and the Philippine soldiers stand at attention beneath an American flag, while a Philippine band plays an American air. All of these people live on the same island in the Philippines. The Igorot represent the wildest race of savages, the scouts stand for the results of American rule—extremes of the social order in the islands.[8]

The conscious and exaggerated presentation of difference was in common currency at St. Louis, where fair organizers' anxieties about besting Chicago's commercial success tipped the ethical scales in favor of popular appeal. At the same time, national political leaders pressed for displays projecting an official image Barbara Kirshenblatt-Gimblett has identified as "a utopian national whole that harmoniously integrates regional diversity." The rhetorical linkage of Igorots and proto-American Scouts through geographical proximity served such ends, even if the public relations strategy was inconsistently pursued. Officials charged with presenting the Philippines in the best possible light deflected complaints of sensationalism onto consumers of the alien images. "The advertising departments have avoided official mention of [dog-eating] and have endeavored to call attention to the more worthy characteristics of the natives," went the disingenuous company line. "It is not true that the savages have been unduly exploited at the expense of the more dignified exhibits, but no amount of emphasis on the commercial exhibits, Constabulary drills and Scouts parades has distracted attention from the 'dog-eaters' and 'head-hunters.'"[9]

Generalized concerns about the balance between savagery and civilization in the Philippine exhibit grew specific after complaints about abbreviated Igorot attire reached Washington. Fearing anti-imperialist Democrats would have a field day calling attention to images of half-naked Filipinos in a presidential election year, President Theodore Roosevelt's ordinarily sharp sense of public relations failed him. On June 23, 1904, the War Department's man in charge of Philippine matters, Colonel Clarence Edwards, received a telegram from the office of Secretary of War William Howard Taft, the former governor of the Philippines, stating:

> The President has heard severe criticism of the Igorrotes and wild tribe exhibit on the ground that it verges toward the indecent. He believes either the Igorrotes and wild tribes should be sent home or that they should be more fully clad. He thinks scouts and the constabulary should be given more prominence and that everything possible should be done to avoid any possible impression that the Philippine Government is seeking to

make prominent the savageness and barbarism of the wild tribes either for show purposes or to depreciate the popular estimate of the general civilization of the Islands. I hope you will at once take steps to comply with the President's wishes. You should put more clothing on the Igorrotes and wild tribes and at the gate put signs showing how small a part of the population the Igorrotes and other wild tribes are.[10]

The government's late-dawning concern for proportionality and context gave rise to high-level haberdashery before the day was out. "I think that short trunks would be enough for the man, but that for the Negrito women there ought to be shirts or chemises of some sort," Taft's next telegram suggested. The policy grew firmer the next day: "President still thinks that where the Igorrote has a mere G string that it might be well to add a short trunk to cover the buttocks and the front. . . . Please look into the feasibility of putting short trunks on the Igorrotes." Edwards passed the command to the Igorot Village manager, Dr. Truman K. Hunt, through Philippine Exposition Board member Gustavo Niederlein, adding that promoters should "allow no child to go naked. This will be the best compromise until we see how the matter works out, and fancy the G string can then be restored."[11]

Edwards's prediction that the cover-up would not be sustained was born out, but little could any of the officials have known the magnitude of the reaction the awkward trouser policy would bring. When word got out that the Igorots would soon be wearing Western garb, a flood of protests arrived from prospective fair patrons anxious to visit the exhibit before the change. Whether motivated by prurience or a hunger for authenticity, the voice of the people was loud and clear in favor of more skin. An editorial entitled "Dog-Eaters in Pants" took an aesthetic tack: "The putting of pants on the Igorrote imputes a decided want of culture to the War Department of this, our glorious Empire. It is doubtful art, to say the least. The Igorrote was not half bad, or not much more than half, when we found him. But pants will make him a fright. Draping Venus is as nothing to the crime of creating a scarecrow out of a beautiful live savage. . . . Putting pants on the Igorrote is cruelly incasing him in a capsule to render him less unpalatable."[12]

The contradictory position of the government was evident to all. Courting public approval of the imperial venture through commercial ethnographic display, no matter how scientific the rubric, entailed releasing official control to the forces of the marketplace. St. Louis *Post-Dispatch* editor G. S. Johns put it bluntly: "What do we all go out to the World's Fair for to see? The frank savagery of unaccommodated manhood or the symbol of shamefaced civilization?" In a letter to Philippine exhibit publicity chief Herbert S. Stone, Johns twisted his argument to align science and propriety: "To put pants on them would change a very interesting ethnological exhibit which shocks the modesty of no one into a suggestive sideshow. It would give the public that consciousness of immodesty which is the original sin."[13]

Johns's blithe suggestion that the government would be the promoter of prurience neatly deflected responsibility away from his newspaper, which profited from every controversy it could report or concoct. Within days, under the glare of suddenly aroused national attention, the *Post-Dispatch* was gleefully making journalistic hay from the story. Beneath a large cartoon featuring Taft, trousers in hand, chasing a reluctant Igorot, the top headline proclaimed, "Whoop! How the People Rush to See The Igorrotes Before They Put the Pants On." Subheadings quoted letters from the public—" 'Dear Governor, Please Write and Say What is the Last No-Pant-On Day'"—and asserted that paid admissions at the Igorot Village, spurred by just such concerns, had doubled from five thousand to ten thousand within twenty-four hours. Writer Clark McAdams waxed poetic:

> Blessings on thee, little man, Living on the Eden plan,
> In thy unaffected way, Drawing thousands every day.
> Wild as winds, and free as air, You're a winner at the Fair.
> Ah, is that the monthly draft? No, it is a note from Taft.
> Of what pressing circumstance Does he write? The Igorrotes! They must
>   wear pants!
> The Igorrotes must wear clothes! Impossible! Ten thousand No's!
> Four billion nits! Twelve billion Can'ts! Great Cesar, anything but pants![14]

In seeking to control the image, the government had run smack against the very impulse that drew crowds to walk past two miles of exhibits showing off the latest technological and artistic achievements. A public exposed to a quantum leap in mediated experience over the preceding decade had seized the opportunity to confront directly, in what seemed to most an unmediated encounter, the savage Other. Erecting a thin cloth barrier between admission-paying customers and the image they had come to see was a policy doomed to extinction. By July 14, a barrage of letters from the public—many orchestrated by local newspapers—helped convince Washington that federal interference in local standards of decency was a losing proposition. Citing a face-saving report of nonembarrassment from the fair's Board of Lady Managers, Edwards reported that the president was willing to "abide by their judgment" and allow loincloths to prevail.[15]

"The Philippine Reservation, though two miles from the Lindell entrance, was plainly the Mecca for a majority of the Sunday tourists," one newspaper reported. "Great crowds were seen on the paths leading to the Walled City and the Cuartel, and once the crowds reached the scene of Oriental interest they remained there." Complaints from the less popular Philippine exhibits about the predominance of the Igorots were tempered by the knowledge that most of the crowds in their sector of the fairgrounds had likely come to witness the tattooed bodies and dog-eating of the Igorots, and that some might stay on for, say, a glimpse of the exotic Bagobo or a tune from the refined Visayans.[16]

The Igorots were in competition not only with other Filipino displays, after all, but with the ethnographic exhibits staged by the Department of Anthropology—Patagonian "giants," Japanese aboriginal Ainu, Central African Pygmies, and American Indians, including Geronimo and Chief Joseph—not to mention the elaborate pavilion of ascendant Japan and the centrally located and well-promoted Pike. To have prevailed as the public's favorite, the Igorots had to present something unique. Dog-eating certainly qualified, but it was the perceived overall authenticity of the Igorot Village that elevated the exhibit above the rest: Here, fairgoers decided, was "true" savagery, with all the trimmings.

Set apart from the showmanship of the Pike and the static ethnography of W. J. McGee's Anthropology Department, the Igorot Village was what Kirshenblatt-Gimblett calls an *in situ* exhibition, a site of detailed display in which the "realness" of the ethnographic object allows the observer an active interpretive role. Though accompanied by ample explanatory literature, a hallmark of the contrasting style Kirshenblatt-Gimblett terms *in context* exhibition, the visual, olfactory, and tactile aspects distinguishing the Igorot Village from other exhibits overwhelmed formal elements privileging the perspective of professional presenters. Whether influenced directly by official fair literature or not, however, fairgoers operated within an established frame of reference. The attire, diet, and headhunter image of the Igorot lent themselves perfectly to the trope of savagery. The village's remote location, near the furthest edge of the fairgrounds, may have contributed to the sense of distance from civilization. The backdrop—an "authentic" village inasmuch as it had been constructed by the Igorots themselves—played an important part in completing the mental picture of savagery for which fairgoers apparently sought affirmation.[17]

The St. Louis World's Fair was a self-consciously definitive event for the world's newest colonial power. The presentation of a clear contrast between American civilization and the savagery its new policies purported to eliminate was as crucial to the construction of a new American identity as the technological advances that made the imperial advance possible. The Igorots occupied a space between the Negritos—seen as completely "wild" and thus understood to be doomed in a world with no more place for wildness—and the "civilized" groups whose Anglo-Saxon apogee was being established in the United States. Their freakish predilections, in American eyes, offered an appealing duality. Clearly possessed of dignity and a culture long pre-dating any American traditions, the Igorots posited an alternative existence. Yet their lack of material wealth and "degraded" diet and appearance offered security for fairgoers bent on defining themselves against a dialectical opposite. The Igorot image served to enhance self-identification with "advanced" society by confirming Americans' distance from "backwardness."[18]

While the Louisiana Purchase Exposition represented a mixture of ideological and economic imperatives, the Igorot freak shows emanating from it followed a decidedly commercial path. Citing "the general desire on the part of the people of the United States who did not get to visit the St. Louis World's Fair to see the Igorrotes," the renowned midway impresario Edmund A. Felder proposed a two-year tour that would send the musically inclined Visayans to the best vaudeville houses and the Igorots to Coney Island, state fairs, and the 1905 Lewis and Clark Exposition in Portland. While boasting to Edwards that he had ample capital to stage such an extended display, Felder proposed to divert some of the proceeds from the shows into trail-building and police functions in the Cordillera. Where those diversions would come from was not left entirely to the imagination. "It is the generally expressed opinion," he wrote, "that the Igorot as an individual has no need of money."[19]

That was the operating principle cited by Hunt when he was charged by some Igorots with improperly withholding their wages. The former lieutenant governor of Lepanto-Bontoc disputed the charges and managed to retain control of much of the village's considerable revenues until the end of the year, when Carson Taylor was appointed to take over as banker to the Filipinos. Asked to turn over the funds he was holding, Hunt said there were none. Despite Hunt's financial chicanery, he remained in a strong position to continue promoting the Igorot phenomenon after the fair, in large measure due to the support of Worcester, who asserted that "Dr. Hunt thoroughly understands the handling of such people" and should be allowed to import more Filipinos.[20]

Edwards expressed concerns that shorn of the context provided by their village and the rest of the Philippine Reservation, such a display would create "false public opinion as to the intellectual advancement, social development and political ability of the people of the Philippine Islands generally." Expressing his ambivalence with a telling metaphor, Edwards wrote: "I rather deprecate the idea of taking these people to Coney Island and giving the people of the United States the idea that the majority of the people of the Philippines are similar to the Igorrotes and Negritos, in the same way I would rather deprecate the idea of having Apachee [sic] Indians traveling around to represent Americans." The Colonel then backed away from his concerns, however: "I must admit they have done so, with Buffalo Bill, and it has not hurt us abroad, and possibly might do no harm in the case of the Filipinos."[21]

Ignoring for a moment the absurdity of a direct comparison between the well-established international image of the United States and that of its new, culturally eclectic colony, Edwards's willingness to sanction the jettisoning of the exhibit's context raises a key question: If the purpose of the Philippine Reservation was, as stated, to illustrate the civilizing progress possible under American stewardship by contrasting Igorot and Negrito with Philippine Scouts, what purpose would be served by the unbalanced post-fair presentation of Igorots proposed by Hunt and Felder? The question was to trouble the official guardians of the Filipino image for years, but a hands-off policy with regard to the private exhibition business generally prevailed. Quickly capitalizing on the Igorot craze, Felder, Hunt, and anthropologist Samuel M. McGowan founded the International Anthropological Exhibit Company to stage a national exhibition tour of Filipinos. In the midst of the St. Louis Fair, the company struck a deal with the planners of the 1905 Lewis and Clark Centennial Exposition in Portland, Oregon, for a Philippine Exhibit consisting of Igorot, Visayan, and Negrito displays on the Trail, Portland's version of the Pike.[22]

In addition to foreshadowing the erosion of the barrier between education and entertainment that so tenuously prevailed at St. Louis, the arrangement violated the War Department's plan to return the Filipinos to their homes following the World's Fair. That stricture was already unraveling in the face of strong public demand for more Filipino shows and the willingness of most of the Filipinos to extend their exhibition work. The famed Philippine Constabulary Band booked performances across the country. The Visayans accepted an invitation to the New York Art Exhibition at Madison Square Garden following their St. Louis stint. The Filipino midgets, Juan and Martina de la Cruz, parlayed their status as the world's smallest adult humans from a reasonably successful place on the Pike to an extended stay in the United States as the stars of the traveling Filipino Midget Theater. The Igorots remained the group most coveted by promoters, however, and Hunt had the inside track.[23]

In March 1905, Hunt contracted with fifty Igorots to come to the United States for one year, promising each a fifteen-dollar monthly salary plus all expenses paid. When disputes arose within the partnership, Hunt left the company, offering the Lewis and Clark Centennial an Igorots-only exhibit to replace the initially proposed mix of Filipinos. Felder countered by lining up a new partner, Richard W. Schneidewind, who after being fired from his mail clerk job in Manila for smuggling found work arranging cigar exhibits for Neiderlein at St. Louis. Their Filipino Exhibition Company (FEC) struggled with government reluctance to allow more Igorots to leave the Philippines. Portland's fair managers, mindful that Hunt's Igorots would draw far more crowds than Felder's suddenly uncertain mix, favored Hunt's bid. Hunt, however, pulled out, instead signing a contract with the Benevolent and Protective Order of Elks for a nationwide series of carnival appearances. Faced with the prospect of being unable to deliver the much-advertised Igorot Village, Portland officials appealed to Taft to relax his opposition to allowing a second Igorot troupe into the United States. Taft's approval—a concession to another official body unlikely to have been granted to a private concern—was a boon to the 1905 Lewis and Clark Exposition. The Igorots arrived six weeks before the end of the fair, became a top draw on the Trail, and won several awards.[24]

Though it was placed squarely in the midst of the blatantly commercial operations of the Trail, the Igorot Village was touted officially as an "educative and ethnological" display, even as it clearly bore signs of unscientific cultural tampering. Schneidewind bragged in a letter to Worcester that "at least a dozen of the men and boys can now sing in English about 15 American popular and patriotic songs, and this is an especially well received feature of the exhibit." While diluting the cultural integrity of the exhibit, the promoter laid claim to improved verisimilitude in the area of dog-eating by reducing the incidence of such feasts: "It is believed that they have but a small part in the life of the Igorrotes and that they give a degraded impression of these fine people to the American public." While peddling pious sentiments to the government, Schneidewind was promoting his show at its next venue, Los Angeles' Chutes Park, as "The Call of the Wild." To assure that the call was heard loud and clear by Angelenos, handbills urged readers to visit the "Head-Hunting, Dog-Eating Wild People From the Philippines!" They did so in droves.[25]

Given the only slightly more restrained promotional language employed by the government at St. Louis, such rhetoric probably did not prejudice the government against the FEC. The company's back-channel cultivation of official approval, on the other hand, together with the various awards and commendations sought and received in Portland, may have helped cement its advantage over the renegade operation of Hunt, whose tour had been marred by the deaths of Igorots in New Orleans and Seattle. Such concerns would soon prove vital, for a clash of interests awaited in both operations' next destination, Chicago.[26]

The transition of the Igorot display from government control to private management proved relatively benign in the case of the FEC, though it took a pay raise to convince mutinous Igorots to go to Chicago's Riverview Park instead of home to the Philippines in June 1906. Hunt's road show, however, was fast confirming many of the government's worst fears about losing control of the Igorots. Official concerns were no longer focused so much on the issue of the tarnished Filipino image as on who controlled such images and the consequences for American prestige. When Hunt, who had been importing Igorots without Bureau of Insular Affairs knowledge and staging "dog-eater" exhibitions across the country, turned up across town at the San Souci amusement park in Chicago, Schneidewind and Felder, abhorring head-to-head competition with a "pirated" Igorot troupe, played their trump card: They asked for a federal inspection of the competition, asserting that Hunt's shoddy operation might be "confounded in the public mind" with their own.[27]

Inspections of the competing operations revealed FEC's to be bonded and humane, while Hunt's was found illicit and "atrocious." The Igorots, quartered in tents beneath the loop of the roaring San Souci roller coaster, complained of embezzlement and abuse at the hands of Hunt, who in turn claimed to be holding their money so that they would not lose it. Hunt's myriad maneuvers to evade seizure of his Igorot "property" complicated matters: Rounding up Hunt's troupes for transport back to the Philippines took weeks. Some were pursued to Canada and returned to Chicago, where they were integrated into Schneidewind's operation.[28]

Legal proceedings among Hunt, his partners, various Igorots, and the government extended into 1907, by which point Hunt had been jailed, freed after a mysterious judicial reversal in

Memphis, and hounded as a fugitive. In response to a 1907 inquiry about Hunt's whereabouts from his wife, Else, in New York, Edwards reported the entrepreneur's latest disappearance following his release from jail in Memphis, his potential extradition to New Orleans to face more embezzlement charges, and his correspondence while in the Memphis jail "with his wife in Louisville, Kentucky." Hunt's escapes were said to have been aided by the Elks.[29]

For the U.S. government, Igorot exhibitions had gone from hot product to hot potato in less than two years. In the Philippines, protests over the misrepresentation of Filipinos were constant. At a time when the United States sought to soothe the still-raw wounds of the Philippine-American War, in part by staging the first National Assembly elections in 1907, the Igorot freak shows were an embarrassment and a hindrance to peace and political development.[30]

It was against this backdrop that the Jamestown Tercentennial Exposition was staged in 1907. No Igorots were included, by very conscious choice. "Much of the good impression that should have remained with the thousands of visitors to the Philippine exhibit [at St. Louis] was lost or at least prejudiced by an unfortunate arrangement of the native Filipinos who were a part of the Philippine Reservation," argued the president of the Philippine Exposition Company at Jamestown, William A. Sutherland, who noted the underrepresentation of "the civilized or Christianized races" and the stiff competition from "well-advertised" concessions where the "tom-toms" were "going at all hours, and which made much of the uncouth habits of certain of the tribes. . . . As a consequence, to many the word 'Filipino' became synonymous with 'Igorot, Moro, Tinguiane, Bagobo' and the like." Commercially, the Jamestown fair was far less successful than St. Louis or Portland. Still, Sutherland could not please the Filipinos: In Manila, *La Igualdad* condemned the display of any Filipinos, Igorot or not.[31]

Diplomatic considerations meant little to the promoters of the 1909 Alaska-Yukon-Pacific Exposition in Seattle. Aware of the intense interest the Igorots had created at Portland four years earlier, Schneidewind and Felder ignored the warning of the BIA's Frank McIntyre that "too much prominence should not be given to the Igorots as they are a side show and are not truly representatives of the Filipino people." The profitable Igorot Village was located right at the head of the fair's midway, the South Pay Streak (fig. 15.3). An academic veneer was applied, however, by Cambridge anthropologist Alfred C. Haddon, who used the exhibit to offer a University of Washington summer school course, "The Growth of Cultural Evolution Around the Pacific."[32]

Whether presented as ethnological specimens or freaks, Igorots were turning up across the United States. Writing to a citizen complaining of Igorots in his "respectable" Philadelphia neighborhood, McIntyre lamented that while "the government has discouraged in every legitimate way that it could the bringing of Igorots to the United States," jurisdictional limitations made it impossible to end the popular practice. In 1908, former soldier, teacher, and Philippine Constabulary Captain John R. McRae brought a group of Igorots to Europe, then to the U.S. East Coast. The Philadelphia *North American* treated the Igorots both as creatures of nature—"lithe and graceful as panthers"—and as actors depicting themselves, *in situ:* "The habits and customs of the little brown people from across the Pacific are reproduced with fidelity and accuracy in detail." Dubbing them "head-hunters" (at that point no heads had been taken for years) the newspaper recited the standard elements of the popular trope to stimulate attendance, throwing in a coupon for public school students as extra incentive.[33]

15.3. Ceremonial Igorot dancers occupied a prominent position at the head of the South Pay Streak, the busy midway of the 1909 Alaska-Yukon-Pacific Exposition in Seattle. Promoters ignored government warnings against emphasizing the "savage" spectacle, applying an academic veneer to the exhibit by offering college anthropology courses in "The Growth of Cultural Evolution Around the Pacific." From the private collection of Eric Breitbart.

For all their continued popularity, the public presentation of Igorots by 1908 had become old hat. Their appearance in the private sphere, however, was cause for comment and even alarm. McRae arranged crowded housing for his group of thirty-six in a rooming house described by a local real estate agent as part of a neighborhood filled with "a very refined group of tenants." The appearance of cheroot-puffing old women and children "wearing little else beyond a cheerful smile and a look of contentment" aroused neighbors to cries of "scandalous!" and "simply shocking!" The *Evening Telegraph* fed the fire with its story of the "invasion" of the street by "Uncle Sam's Igorot headhunters." To landlord Edward Potter, however, it was the other way around: Extra curtains had to be hung to avoid the intimidating experience of neighbors gathering around the yard to gawk at the Igorots, whose cultural tradition teaches that it is impolite to stare.[34]

After McRae's troupe ended its summer on Coney Island in 1909, the U.S. government tightened Philippine emigration controls to prevent more exhibits. Even the well-connected Schneidewind had to struggle mightily to gain permission to transport a band of Igorots to Europe in 1911. In 1913, finding no more buyers for his hitherto hot commodity, he abandoned them in Ghent, Belgium. Nine had died, some of starvation. The rest were sent home to obscurity, never again to occupy the profitable, dehumanizing freak show stage.[35]

The powerful act of the gaze functions on many levels, from the invasive stares trained on the shy Igorots in Edward Potter's backyard to the kaleidoscopic spectacle of a dog-stew fest staged for a paying crowd at a World's Fair. Salient throughout America's decade of staring at savages, however, was a process of discovery intimately linking Self and Other. In the face of record-breaking immigration from nontraditional regions that challenged the myth of shared Anglo-Saxon ethnicity, the presence of a markedly differentiated Other made possible the task of defining on cultural grounds a new collective Self. Entering a new epoch of accelerating change in which their own identities would inevitably undergo fundamental alteration, Americans proved eager for the chance to confront a trope they saw as a negative image of themselves—the Other in which so much had been invested in redeeming.

Of course, the Igorot freak shows and anthropological exhibits of the early twentieth century involved more than just the gaze. Human beings and their cultural trappings were collected, like baskets and buttons, or bugs in a jar, for the study and more often the amusement of curious Westerners intoxicated by images of freaks. Under the respectable cover of science, laymen could participate vicariously in an elite activity—ethnology as entertainment. Although some may have straddled the fine line between the two, seeking upward mobility in an age of increasingly stratified cultural hierarchy, for most the corollary benefits of ogling Igorots—breaking loose from Victorian strictures, indulging an informa-tion-age craving for novelty, celebrating American power, sophistication, and whiteness—were more than enough motivation to take a walk on the wild side.[36]

NOTES

1. Dean C. Worcester, *The Philippine Islands and Their People* (New York: Macmillan, 1898).

2. *Sears, Roebuck and Co. Consumer's Guide*, Fall 1900 (Northfield, Ill.: DBI Books, 1971), 218. On the role of photography, see Elizabeth Edwards, ed., *Anthropology and Photography, 1860–1920* (New Haven: Yale University Press, 1992); Oscar King Davis, *Our Conquests in the Pacific* (New York: Frederick A. Stokes, 1899).

3. "The Third Battle of Manila," *Literary Digest* 18 (1899): 180.

4. "Benguet—The Garden of the Philippines," *National Geographic* 14 (May 1903): 203–10.

5. National Archives and Records Administration, Washington, D.C., Record Group 350, File 1157/1; Outlying Possessions Exhibit, Pan-American Exposition, Buffalo, N.Y. (Arts and In-dustry Archives, Smithsonian Institution, Washington, D.C.), Box 52, File 26; NARA RG 350, File 1190.

6. *Report of the Philippine Exposition Board* (Microfilm Reel 159, No. 3, National Museum of American History, Smithsonian Institution, Washington, D.C.), 26–30.

7. St. Louis *Post-Dispatch*, 6 April 1904, 1.

8. *The Philippine Exhibition Souvenir Guide* (St. Louis, 1904).

9. Barbara Kirshenblatt-Gimblett, "Objects of Ethnography," in Ivan Karp and Steven D. Lavine, eds., *Exhibiting Cultures: The Poetics and Politics of Museum Display* (Washington, D.C.: Smithsonian Institution Press, 1991), 389; *Report of the Philippine Exposition Board*, 33.

10. NARA RG 350, File 9640/3.

11. Ibid.

12. St. Louis *Republic*, 28 June 1904; NARA RG 350, File 9640/13.

13. NARA RG 350, File 9640/18.

14. St. Louis *Post-Dispatch*, 3 July 1904; NARA RG 350, Filer 9640/27.

15. NARA RG 350, File 9640/13.

16. NARA RG 350, File 9640/1.

17. Kirshenblatt-Gimblett, "Objects of Ethnography," 388–90.

18. The use of "wildness" in opposition to "civilization" serves to authenticate the cultural self in the same manner as other constructions based on dialectical antithesis (such as heresy:orthodoxy and madness:sanity). See Hayden White, *Tropics of Discourse: Essays in Cultural Criticism* (Baltimore: Johns Hopkins University Press, 1978), 150–52.

19. Edmund A. Felder to Col. Clarence Edwards, 22 December 1904, 24 December 1904, NARA RG 350, File 13431–3.

20. A. L. Lawshe to Col. Clarence Edwards, 15 October 1904, NARA RG 350, Folder 9640/32; Jester to Edwards, File 9640/33; Report of Harry C. Lewis to Edwards, 30 December 1904, RG 350, File 9640/38

21. NARA RG 350, File 10622; Col. Clarence Edwards to Civil Governor, Philippines, 19 January 1905, RG 350, File 13431–3.

22. Robert Rydell, *All the World's a Fair: Visions of Empire at American International Expositions, 1876–1916* (Chicago: University of Chicago Press, 1984), 194.

23. NARA RG 350, File 10000/24, 25,26, 33; RG 350, File 9639/37, 55. Promoted as twenty-seven and twenty-nine inches tall on the letterhead of Evans & Fairley, their Des Moines-based promoters in 1906, the same "midgets of all midgets" were by 1911 being billed on G. W. Fairley's letterhead as twenty-one and twenty-four inches tall. Their appeal, alas, had also shrunk, and Fairley was reduced to beseeching the government on behalf of "the little man," who had been cheated of his savings by a full-sized Filipina in Mobile, Alabama. NARA RG 350, File 10622.

24. NARA RG 350, File 13847/40; Rydell, *All the World's a Fair,* 195–96; RG 350, Files 9957, 2388/3,7; 13431/9.

25. NARA RG 350, File 13431/9; Advertising Brochure in RG 350, File 13431/3.

26. NARA RG 350, File 13431/21.

27. NARA RG 350, File 13431/10; RG 350, File 13431/20.

28. NARA RG 350, Files 13431/24, 25, 47; 13847/9, 11; RG 350, File 13847/11, 12, 22, 23; 37, 39, 52.

29. NARA RG 350, File 13847/4, 37, 40, 52, 61, 138,187; File 9640/45.

30. NARA RG 350, File 13847/9; RG 350, File 15000/3.

31. NARA RG 350, File 15000/1, 2.

32. NARA RG 350, File 16030/20; Rydell, *All the World's a Fair,* 197.

33. NARA RG 350, File 11761/10; *North American,* 13 November 1908, in RG 350, File 11761/9, 14.

34. *Evening Telegraph,* 11 December 1908, in NARA RG 350, File 11761/11.

35. McRae later made a career promoting "The Wild Man of Borneo." NARA RG 350, File 13431/54, 56; Troy *Times,* 7 and 8 November 1913; New York *Sun,* 6 November 1913.

36. On the importance of collection and display as key processes in the formation of Western identity, see James Clifford, "On Collecting Art and Culture," in *The Predicament of Culture* (Cambridge: Harvard University Press, 1988). On the redrawing of cultural boundaries at century's turn, see Lawrence W. Levine, *Highbrow Lowbrow: The Emergence of Cultural Hierarchy in America* (Cambridge: Harvard University Press, 1988).

SIXTEEN

"What an object he would have made of me!": Tattooing and the Racial Freak in Melville's *Typee*

LEONARD CASSUTO

It is not unsurmised, that only when extraordinary stimulus is needed, only when an extra strain is to be got out of them, are these hapless 'Gees ennobled with the human name.

—HERMAN MELVILLE, "THE 'GEES"

A friend of mine who prides himself on being tolerant told me recently about a private embarrassment he had experienced over a few months a couple of years ago. One of his gay male friends had taken to kissing him by way of greeting, and the practice was inwardly repulsing him. My friend took this as a test. He challenged himself to become more open to such intimacies, and essentially forced himself to overcome his upset and distaste at being kissed by another man. By dint of his considerable effort, the experience eventually became familiar to him and his feelings of distress went away. My friend told me this story with a certain amount of pride—which seems justified—but learning such tolerance isn't always as simple as it was for him. Sometimes the beliefs of a whole culture are arrayed against the effort to be open-minded—as they were in pre-civil rights Mississippi, for example, against any white person who might have been inclined to treat African Americans as friends or equals. Racist acculturation in the Jim Crow South put insidious pressure on such well-meaning people to adopt local prejudices and public practices such as wiping one's hand after shaking hands with a black man.[1] When the beliefs and traditions of an entire society dictate against tolerance, even defending it becomes exceedingly difficult, let alone practicing it. In the end, talking the talk is usually easier than walking the walk.

Typee, Herman Melville's 1846 novel of an individual's encounter with a radically different culture and its customs, shows how difficult it is to rise above the beliefs of one's own group, and how elusive the ideal of open-minded human equality can be when those beliefs are challenged. Based closely on Melville's own experience in the Marquesan Islands, *Typee* features a narrator, Tommo, who jumps ship in the Marquesas, eventually finding himself among the Typee tribe.[2] Despite the notorious Typee reputation for cannibalism, Tommo brings the best of intentions to his relations with them. He consciously seeks to understand their customs and appreciate their lives from their perspective, not his own. In particular, he seeks to avoid the Western attitudes toward Polynesians that were prevalent during Melville's time, pointedly rejecting prevailing interpretations of them as subhuman barbarians, cannibals, and heathens. But this noble effort ultimately breaks down, and Tommo flees in a panic over the discovery of what he presumes is cannibalism. The result, Melville shows, is the loss of a moral and epistemological center of gravity for both the narrator and his audience.

Writing at a time when race had become the central issue in American political and social life, Melville seeks the roots of prejudice, the cause and effect of perceived difference among human beings. *Typee* dramatizes the encounter with racial difference through the adventures of a would-be anthropologist who at first appears to be a modern cultural relativist out of place and time, but who eventually shows his true colors—or rather his "true color." When he betrays a fear of blackness, Tommo ultimately shows himself to be more like his nineteenth-century American peers than he prefers to admit.

Melville uses several potent symbols to signal Tommo's position in the web of Western belief and practice, but the most important of these is the facial tattoo. Such Typee adornment—which Tommo dramatically refuses—becomes the literal marker in his mind between "normal" (linked to whiteness and American identity) and "freak," a liminal figure who is foreign and black. *Typee* expresses the multiple connections among the heyday of abolitionism, the glaring and newly exploitable weaknesses in slavery ideology that the movement reflected and fed off of, the proslavery activity that rose in response to abolitionism, and the rise of the freak show—all of which appeared in the United States at about the same time. The freak show entered American society when institutionalized racism became the subject of increased social scrutiny and public debate and the socially constructed barriers separating black from white came under increasing attack. Tattooing in *Typee* embodies this tension, acting as a code for racial difference that visibly links color to freak status.

It was no accident that the freak show was known in the circus trade as a "Nig Show," and Melville crystallizes the significance of that nickname in *Typee*.[3] The freak show—and especially its tattooed members, black and white—brought physical anomaly, the racial other, and the racial freak (a nonwhite "primitive") together under the tent. The existence and continuing popularity of the racial freak suggests that the freak show drew most of its power from the psychic energy generated by a racially divided society. Tommo's fear in *Typee* of becoming a racial freak thus stands as an individual manifestation of an increasing tension that permeated American culture generally in the 1840s, a tension linked to the unraveling of the racial distinctions central to American social organization and the meaning of being "white."

Resisting the Grotesque

Once he finds himself among the Typees, Tommo compares his own customs with theirs in an unusually fair-minded way for his time.[4] Though the study of "exotic" cultures was catching on in the United States when Melville wrote *Typee* in the mid-1840s, anthropology did not enter the social sciences until the next century. In its place evolved a nineteenth-century science called ethnology that claimed the study of alien cultures as its province. By 1850, ethnology was firmly established; its methods were hierarchical, relying on a scale of humanity ranging from "primitive" to "civilized." In contrast to such assumptions, Tommo's egalitarian practice at first resembles that of the twentieth-century ethnographer, somehow practicing an early version of cultural relativism before anthropology was invented.[5] Aware of his natural Western bias, Tommo keeps his bearings and makes adjustments, such as when he realizes that the Typees have their own eating etiquette even if they don't use silverware. He even keeps his composure when he sees men with green skin, remarking simply that they gain that strange cast when their tattoos start to age.

What is crucial here—and also remarkable—is that Tommo resists the urge to react to these phenomena as grotesque. Instead of allowing visceral revulsion to take hold, he deliberately distances himself and examines things rationally. Green men are therefore described to us with nearly the same dispassion as the thatch of the native huts might be. The narration is explicit (scaly skin, folded flesh, bald and puckered heads, etc.) but the narrator himself seems unfazed.

Melville's strategy is to incite the grotesque while showing Tommo's own seeming immunity to it. But Melville shows that for all of his skill and balance, Tommo fails to master his experience. He occasionally reveals his suppressed alarm with seemingly offhand comments. He refers to the green men at one point as "repulsive looking creatures" (12/93),[6] for example, a description that betrays some buried Western value judgments. These suppressed values eventually flare up and overwhelm his generous openness, and as he falls from the pan-cultural heights he betrays all of the judgments he thought he had been avoiding. Two Typee practices in particular combine to push him off his high perch: tattooing and cannibalism. Tattooing will be my primary focus here.

Initially, Tommo seems quite comfortable with the Typee practice of extensive tattooing. He speaks of it as though it were removable decoration, a set of "simple and remarkable . . . ornaments" (11/78). He even calls the tattooing on one warrior "the best specimen of the Fine Arts I had yet seen on Typee" (18/136). But everything changes for Tommo when the tribe's tattoo artist, Karky, wants to tattoo *him*. When the tattooist examines his face, Tommo calls it an "attack." Fear takes over: "When his forefinger swept across my features, in laying out the borders of those parallel bands which were to encircle my countenance, the flesh fairly crawled along my bones. At last, half wild with terror and indignation, I succeeded in breaking away from the three savages" (30/219). From that point forward, says Tommo, continuing demands to tattoo him made life a "burden."

Melville makes clear that Tommo fears his face will be "ruined for ever" (30/220). This judgment shows how alien to him the Typees remain. Tommo's diction suggests that if he were tattooed, his face would not be his own any longer; it would be a "ruined" representation of him. It follows that Tommo still sees himself with Western eyes, as a Westerner—but if he were tattooed, his identity would be materially changed from "American" to "Typee." His early description of his valet Kory-Kory is therefore telling: he compares the native's striped facial tattoos to prison bars (11/83). This simile implies that if Tommo were tattooed in this way, he would become a kind of a prisoner himself, an American captive within Typee society with no choice but to become Typee.

Nor does his fear end there. One remark of his is particularly telling; it gives this essay its title, and will become the fulcrum for much of the argument that follows. It is a direct admission of the source of Tommo's terror: "What an object he [Karky] would have made of me!" (30/219). This observation—made after his escape and return to the United States—shows that Tommo is concerned not simply with crossing the border separating American from Typee, but also with slipping over the one separating human being from thing. He feels that if he had been marked as a Typee, he would cease to be a person at all in his own (American) eyes.

Tommo's reaction to the threatened tattooing suggests that deep down, he has always seen the Typees as "objects." But he also sees them and interacts with them as fellow humans. By embedding this unarticulated, unconscious contradiction within Tommo's mind, Melville shows just how human objectification works—and fails. Tommo has divided Typees and Westerners into distinct categories and ranked the Typee category below his own, as a race of "objects." On the other hand, Tommo wants human company, and he readily embraces the society of the Typees. As he shows in his relationships with Kory-Kory, Fayaway, and others, the Typee are people whom he can respect, even love. (The true test of "belonging" to a culture may be the ability to fall in love with one of its members.) The Typee thus become freaks in Tommo's eyes: now objects, now humans, in constant transit between the two categories.

Tommo's exclamation is most obviously an expression of rage, but it is also an intimate confession. Tommo is declaring who he is by reviling against who—or what—he is not. His dramatic refusal to be tattooed is the first of a series of contextual links to the American culture of his day, marking a trail that leads to one of nineteenth-century America's fastest growing public attractions: the freak show.

Tommo fears becoming a freak in part because he fears becoming a physical oddity, but also because that he knows what happens to such anomalies: they are displayed before the eager eyes of others.[7] Indeed, the freak show was—and is, in the few that still exist—a carefully bounded form of human display that purported to spotlight the edges of humanity itself. These edges were populated by human anomalies that included people with odd bodies, but also people from odd—that is, non-Western—cultures.

But Tommo is already an anomaly with an odd body who is displayed before the populace. As an untattooed adult man, he appears as a kind of freak to the Typees. If facial tattoos would make him look like a freak in his own eyes, they serve precisely the opposite function for the Typees themselves. To the Typees, Tommo would appear less like a foreign "object" if he wore tattoos than if he did not. Without tattoos, Tommo is a "non-Typee," a freak of sorts in the eyes of the group. With them, he would embody normality—for them. Tommo's fear of losing his status as a "normal" American contrasts with his fear of becoming a "normal" Typee. These multilayered Melvillean ironies inform the author's deeply nuanced evocation of one of antebellum America's fastest emerging cultural institutions, and the complicated motivations behind it.

Freaks and freak shows are the visible artifacts of an attempt to cast a group of humans outside of the human category, but the fetishistic attention that they received serves alone as ample evidence of the failure of that attempt: if freaks were truly nonhuman, after all, they would have been held in zoos, not displayed on special stages that served as liminal "freak spaces." And they would not have been displayed in ways that consciously evoked the reminder of the humanity that they possessed all along ("armless wonders," for example, performed everyday human tasks such as writing or sewing for their audiences).[8] As Leslie Fiedler eloquently puts it, "The true Freak . . . stirs both supernatural terror and human sympathy, since, unlike the fabulous monsters, he is one of us, the human child of human parents, however altered by forces we do not quite understand into something mythic and mysterious, as no mere cripple ever is."[9] The simultaneous attraction (or curiosity) and repulsion (or fear) of freaks results from the combination of both of these psychic vectors. Freaks are pushed out of the realm of humanity and held within it by the same exhibit.

This dynamic instability underlay Americans' fascination with the freak show, even as the same tension between human and nonhuman was undermining the ideology of American slavery (which held people to be property). Tommo's panic draws its force from all of these oppositions. In depicting Tommo's fear in these terms, Melville provides an indirect and typically prescient analysis of the racial tensions of 1840s America, and he shows that these tensions feed on the ambivalence created by the freak.

THE TATTOOED FREAK

Melville wrote about freak displays in a short 1847 parody of P. T. Barnum contained in a series of sketches about Zachary Taylor, "Authentic Anecdotes of 'Old Zack.'"[10] This brief spoof shows Melville's full awareness of the attraction of human curiosities and the consequent popularity of early museum culture. Tattooed sailors, as Melville certainly knew, were sidewalk exhibits whose popularity can be dated back to the early nineteenth century.[11] When the freak show came to public prominence during the decades leading up to the Civil War, tattooed people quickly emerged as a popular exhibit that shortly became a freak show staple. Demand for them grew throughout the nineteenth century and into the twentieth (when the market became glutted after the World War II). All freaks are elaborate social constructions, as Robert Bogdan has shown, and tattooed people were no exception. The typical exhibit featured the decorated person on display, with the tattoos serving as the basis for a wild story, usually concocted by the promoter and written up in a pamphlet offered for sale, containing a detailed account of how he became a marked man.

Tattooed men (tattooed women were not exhibited until after the Civil War) generally told fantastic tales of kidnap and captivity in which their tattoos were forced upon them as torture or punishment by barbaric savages. The English sailor John Rutherford was the first to ply his trade as a tattooed man. First displaying himself in 1828, he told an outlandish story of capture by primitives, six years of captivity, compulsory marriage to the chief's young daughter, and forcible tattooing of his body by tribespeople. Eventual exposure of the true story (a much more pedestrian affair) would ruin much of his appeal, but his invented tale gained long life in a different way: it became a narrative paradigm for those who followed him.[12] Such stories of tattooing branched from the broader category of "survival literature," which was itself a branch of travel writing. Survival literature first appeared during the eighteenth century; its dominant themes, as Mary Louise Pratt notes, were sex and slavery.[13] The tattoo narrative exploited the conventions of survival literature, with the actual tattoo acting as a symbolic conflation of these two main themes.

The first tattooed man exhibited in the United States was James O'Connell (fig. 16.1), who made his circus debut in the mid-1830s. O'Connell sold a book (written in 1836 by a ghostwriter) and a pamphlet (later adapted from the book) that told a hair-raising story of adventures aboard ship and in exotic lands, which featured—as Rutherford's story did—his forced tattooing. O'Connell claimed that he was made to submit to tattooing by Micronesian island maidens, with custom dictating that the final tattooist become his wife. O'Connell's story, and especially the pictures on his body that went with it, made him a financial success

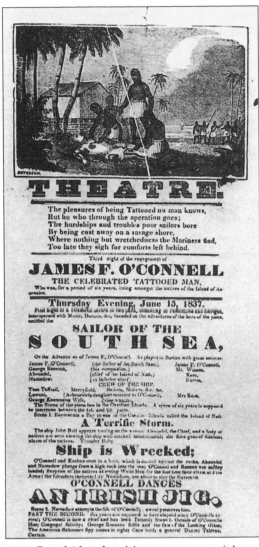

16.1. Broadside advertising appearance of James F. O'Connell, "The Celebrated Tattooed Man, Who was, for a period of six years, living amongst the natives of the Island of Ascension." Courtesy of the Buffalo and Erie County Public Library Rare Books Room.

at the time of *Typee*.[14] His entrepreneurial acumen inspired many imitators, and the tattooed man became a freak show institution.

Neither Rutherford nor O'Connell were tattooed on their faces, unlike the Polynesian natives who were also on exhibit in freak shows at the time. By showing Tommo's dread of facial tattooing, Melville equates white tattooed freaks with such native exhibits, and so raises the stakes of the cultural game—even as he anticipated the evolution of the tattooed freak. The next famous tattooed exhibit, from the 1870s onwards, was "Captain Costentenus," whose face *was* tattooed (along with his entire body). Not surprisingly, Costentenus also told a fantastic, fabricated story of coercion, with his tattoos allegedly being a three-month torture and punishment at the hands of either Chinese or Burmese barbarians, depending on which version of the story one consults (fig 1.4). Many more tattooed freak show acts followed the popular example of Costentenus, mostly variations on the standard story of capture and forced tattooing, until the popularity of the tattooed woman widened the story possibilities beginning in the 1880s.[15]

Typee appeared just at the time when the tattooed man was becoming a familiar freak show sight and his story a conventional tale of suspense, adventure, and unique torture. Melville imparts full awareness of this to Tommo, and with it a notable ironic ambivalence. Tommo's own story feints toward coercion, effectively threatening to become the kind of account of forced tattooing that was told by countless tattooed freaks. In fact, Tommo's story—which, unlike his face, he chooses to display publicly—could even be read as a tattooing narrative, minus the tattooing. Even though Tommo recoils from the tattooing itself, *Typee* embraces the stories that surround the American display of the practice. In writing and selling his story of near-tattooing, Melville flirts, through Tommo, with the role of tattooed freak, suggesting that part of Tommo is attracted to it, just as he is partly attracted to being a Typee.[16] But Tommo finally forbids himself such equivocation when he realizes what he risks by it: national membership, class membership, racial membership, and as a result, human membership as he understands it.

Indeed, the generic story of captivity and forcible tattooing reflected on the teller in two important ways that would have terrified Tommo. First, it portrayed the tattooed freak as someone without will, as one who had been unable to prevent his body—his most personal space—from becoming indelibly marked. Tattooing thus stands as an immediately visible reminder of a failure of will. Ironically, tattooing was actually one of the few ways that an able-bodied person could voluntarily become a freak, yet the conventional exhibition of such people invariably made this decision appear involuntary. Such paradox further suggests the crucial importance of volition to the construction of the tattooed freak. The role of women in the standard narrative also underscores this theme. Women are closely implicated with the coercive aspects of the standard tattooing narrative, with forced marriage frequently accompanying forced tattooing. (In O'Connell's case, the two are conflated, with the female tattooist literally marking him—against his will—as her husband.) This reversal of gendered power relations figures the tattooed man as a woman, and the bodily violation of tattooing as a figurative form of rape. At a time when the gendered spheres of American society were moving apart, the tattooed freak—as well as the fear of becoming one that Tommo shows in *Typee*—taps into a deep well of anxiety over male power and sexual integrity.[17]

Second, tattoos mark their bearer as someone without social mobility. Tattooed people are freaks, and because the tattoos are permanent, so is the class status of the person marked with them. Thus, if an unmarked man can normally live anywhere he likes, facial tattoos would turn him into a tattooed freak with a single vocation and a single location, with the freak show merging the two. Tattooing thereby knocks the rungs out of the American ladder to success, the climbing of which ostensibly translates hard work into socioeconomic improvement.

These unpleasant possibilities underlie Tommo's fear of being tattooed because they threaten to erase the primary coordinates by which he locates his sense of self. First, they violate his own expectations of himself as an American citizen, a free man who can, in theory, enact his own desires and rise as high as his initiative might take him.[18] As a tattooed man, Tommo's horizons would be necessarily limited. He sees this as a threatened loss of his nationality itself: "I should be disfigured in a manner as never more to have the *face* to return to my countrymen" (30/219). Second, the possible loss of will and social mobility threaten Tommo's self-image as quasi-modern anthropologist. If marked as a Typee, he would permanently become a Typee—no longer able to pass in and out of cultures as he now does. In effect, Tommo fears being imprisoned inside the narrative of a freak show exhibit pamphlet. He fears being catalogued and characterized by scientists of his day (whose judgments were prominently featured in such pamphlets), and he fears being permanently slotted in a space where he feels he does not, and cannot, belong.[19]

Tommo's fear of losing control points to the freak's passivity before the spiel of the carnival talker, who guides the spectator's gaze and therefore controls the terms of the display. The carnival talker creates the human oddity as a grotesque freak by instructing the audience on how to look at the exhibit. Mercy Lavinia Warren, the thirty-two inch wife of the famous midget General Tom Thumb, declared, "I belong to the public"[20]—a thought that would be particularly upsetting to Tommo, who wants so badly to believe he belongs to himself alone that he creates an illusion of himself as a pan-cultural man, a temporary member of whatever group suits his fancy. In doing so, he represses his American cultural membership, his desire to be a Typee, and his curiosity about what it might be like to be a tattooed man.

The spectacle of the tattooed freak clearly embodies great and disturbing fears for Tommo, but even this is not what frightens him most. His greatest fear arises from comparison with another group of tattooed people who were displayed at freak shows: the racial freaks. More than anything, Tommo fears becoming one of them.

THE RACIAL FREAK

Virtually all freak shows displayed non-Westerners in full native regalia, with South Sea Islanders as frequent subjects of this treatment, along with Africans (The first Polynesian viewed in the United States was a tattooed man, whose 1774 exhibit antedated the institutionalized freak show.)[21] The continuing popularity of such displays reflected an American fascination with the other side of the world at a time when it could not easily be reached. It was standard practice to exhibit non-Westerners in freak shows as primitive humans or "missing links," with diorama displays of rudimentary foreign or jungle backdrops.[22] Such racial freaks were among the most popular acts in freak show history.

Racial freaks were not physically anomalous within the context of their own culture—that is, there was nothing "odd" about their bodies in the eyes of their own peers. Instead, it was their simple presence in the United States, among people who lived differently, that served as the basis for their display. Allegations of cannibalism usually provided the rhetorical leverage to place them in this liminal space. Cannibalism was a hot issue in the nineteenth-century United States as it was in *Typee*, a source of national fear and fascination and one of the most important American symbols of un-civilization. In connection with scientific discourses of the day, it was the key to turning "exotic" into "primitive" and "atavistic." Though some South Sea Islanders practiced cannibalism, the truth was less sensational than such labels would imply. Cannibalism has always and only been ritual (as Peggy R. Sanday says, it is never "just about eating"), and only certain members of certain South Sea Islands societies practiced it.

But these facts mattered little to Americans unaccustomed to distinguishing among groups of dark-skinned people, and not at all to freak show promoters, who had no particular use for facts when a salacious story could be invented instead. As a result, all South Sea Islanders were labeled as cannibals, and loose allegations of cannibalism became the means of relegating them to a lower position on the chain of being. Not surprisingly, Barnum was the first to bring these "cannibals" to the freak show.[23]

Tattooing was the visible symbol of cannibalism and all of the beliefs that went with it at that time. Tattooed tribes were considered to be cannibalistic tribes, and tattooing itself was seen as a sign of atavism and a physical marker for the presence of cannibalism. Naturalists (the early equivalent of biologists) and ethnologists saw tattooing as the "ultimate sign of primitiveness," and the notorious Cesare Lombroso would cite tattoos—along with dark skin—as signs of criminality a few decades later.[24] Such beliefs helped to make tattooed islanders among the most marginal of all freaks—and the anticipation of being grouped with them is a major source of Tommo's terror at having his face marked.

For Tommo, this amounts to a fear of being black. The possibility of labeling and displaying non-Westerners as barbaric, subhuman creatures—as freak show promoters did—lay in their color as well as their habits; their dark skin made it possible to exile them to the edges of the human category as it was defined in America. The importance of color to the creation of racial freaks rests on the confluence of ethnological analysis of racial freaks with the various pseudoscientific results of both pre- and post-Darwinian racial science. The ethnological scrutiny of native peoples and cultures took place in the larger context of numerous intertwining nineteenth-century scientific debates over the species and origins of the "races of man." Together, these early studies amounted to a concerted scientific enterprise dedicated to demarcating immutable racial categories and demonstrating the innate inferiority of non-whites. Early scientists buttressed their racialist conclusions with evidence from fields like phrenology (which compared the skulls of "lower races" with those of higher animals), the related field of craniometry, and naturalism (which combined taxonomy with biblical study to produce the doctrine of "polygenesis," which held that there had been a separate creation of different Adams and Eves of different races, who had developed separately and at different rates). Evolutionary thought before and after Charles Darwin trafficked heavily in throwback imagery, with "inferior races" being presented in both freak shows and scientific publications as unevolved humans or "missing links." Reginald Horsman documents the exhaustive and highly convoluted attempts to construct racial difference for social ends by an early scientific establishment that built its reputation for empirical rigor on the foundation of racialist analysis of freaks (both racial freaks and human oddities), blacks, and Native Americans.[25]

Racial "science" and freak show pamphlets grow from the same root, with one emphasizing the narrative of pathology (a rational account of "how it got that way") and the other the narrative of wonder (an emotional response to a spectacle of compromised humanity).[26] The early study of the cultures of native peoples was part and parcel of the discourse of racial inferiority, and the goal of nineteenth-century science was the same as that of the freak show: to construct and scrutinize the edges of humanity. Thus, the discussion of tattooing and cannibalism in Tommo's time was part of a larger discussion about race—and Tommo's fear of being tattooed is essentially a fear of losing his color. Tommo hints at this fear at different points in *Typee*. Consider, for example, his telling aversion to having "my white skin" marked (30/219). Of course, being black in antebellum America usually meant being a slave. Tommo relates his own experience to slavery on a number of occasions. First, the lack of will inherent in the generic tattooing narrative—where the author has his tattoos "forced" upon him—implies an actual slavery that was indeed written into most of the narratives. Second, descriptions of Tommo as a kind of slave frame *Typee:* he renders the sailor's lot as a kind of slavery and his own final escape from the Typees as the thwarted sale of a captive.[27]

Melville manipulates these descriptions to evoke the genre of the slave narrative. The allusions would have been topical; Melville wrote and published *Typee* during the height of popularity of fugitive slave narratives. Further, Melville incorporates many of the conventions of the fugitive slave's discourse both to underscore Tommo's portrait of himself as a slave and to shorten the distance between the faraway Marquesan Islands and the United States of America. In the first case, Tommo recounts how he had "made up my mind to 'run away' " from a life in which his "tyrannical" captain/master neglects the sick and starves the healthy, meeting any protests with "the butt-end of a handspike" (4/20–21). This passage encapsulates the fugitive slave narrator's conventional description of his cruel treatment in slavery. In both cases, the account of mistreatment is meant to justify the decision to escape. When Tommo prepares to jump ship, he takes precautions to avoid being captured—the "ignominious" fate of a runaway slave (5/30). While he waits to get away from the Typees at the book's end, he witnesses a bargaining session for himself, in which his life is valued in terms of cotton cloth, gunpowder, and a musket, articles of "extravagant value" (34/249–50). This scene matches another conventionalized passage in the slave narrative, in which the slave describes his own sale, underscoring the incongruity of exchanging a human being for money.

Freak shows also depended on such dealings in human flesh—but instead of selling differentiated bodies, freak shows sold the privilege of gazing upon them. Broadly speaking, these spectacles helped Americans establish the coordinates of who "we" were by showing what "they" were—thereby establishing what "we" were not.[28] Many cultural tensions have been offered as causes of the growth of the freak show, including urbanization, industrialization, immigration, and the early pressure to define national identity in post-Revolutionary America. But color was arguably the primary determinant of the dominant "we" of nineteenth-century America (as it may still be today). It follows that the American freak show rose in response to racial tension, and that its most important purpose was the deflection of racial anxiety onto a class whose difference was (to the viewer) apparently undeniable and literally spectacular.

Racial difference was less reliable than the odd body as a measure of such difference. The long (and ongoing) history of racial science—and its proliferation during the decades before the Civil War—reflects the fact that racial otherness is a construction that requires constant maintenance, remaining difficult and slippery. For proponents of such inequality, this was a source of constant concern. Freak shows reflect this anxiety—on both sides of the Mason-Dixon Line—in a reified form.[29] Though they did not spotlight race directly, freak shows refracted it through the prism of physical anomaly, supported by an underlying premise of human inequality. Little wonder, then, that the popularity of freak shows exploded immediately after the Civil War, when racial anxiety and ideologies of inequality persisted even though slavery did not. Freak shows did not truly dwindle in America until the 1940s. Though various reasons have been offered for the decline (increased communication, the popularity of socialistic thinking which sought to minimize differences among people, the medicalization of human anomaly), it is, I think, no coincidence that the civil rights movement started to make itself felt around that time, with its social and legal successes making naked attempts at human objectification harder to sustain in mainstream society.[30]

Freaks were a more secure receptacle than race for American "not-me" for three main reasons. First, exposure to them was temporary, so that freaks (unlike blacks) always stayed unfamiliar. Second, the viewing of freaks was highly structured in a way that was possible precisely because it was temporary. This structured viewing experience could be manipulated to underscore the ideology of difference, while racial encounters (which could happen anytime) could not be so regulated. The freak show was consistently and primarily mediated by an enormous show business emphasis on difference, an emphasis that, in the small performative doses in which it was presented, overwhelmed the truth of the situation: that these were simply people displaying themselves before other people. Third, freaks, unlike blacks, represented no threat—sexual, economic, or otherwise—to dominant white culture. Their display took place at a socially marked physical distance from "us" as a safe spectacle, with the freak being a socially designated receptacle for the desire for recognized dominance from the designated other.

Tommo fears the distorting hyperexotic presentation of the exotic that is typified by the freak show, but his irrational, deeply felt fear of being tattooed similarly reflects the racial ideology that makes the freak show possible. Tommo's reaction to the Typees as "object[s]" shows Melville's awareness that ethnologic thinking is not underpinned by "logic" at all, but rather by deep fear, motivated in racialism, that "they" are the same as "us." Though he argues throughout his narrative that the Typees are essentially the same as Westerners, Tommo's panic proves that he never really believed it.

Freak shows filled a gap that they did not create. This space, between the desire for absolute racial difference and the fact that none exists, was wide and deep in a culture that relied on such difference for its very organizing principles. The gap was occupied by fetishizing practices like blackface minstrelsy, displacing strategies like plantation fiction and Sambo stereotyping, empirically driven attempts at denial like racial pseudoscience—and also by freak shows. The freak show thus stands as both a cultural symptom and a cultural tool. It was a symptom of a need (for hierarchy, for difference, for a feeling of superiority) and a tool deployed—unsuccessfully—to meet that need. Freak shows were a performance of one kind of imaginary difference in an effort to assert another.

Given that the United States has always been a racially obsessed society, why did freak shows arise precisely when they did? If their primary function was to deflect racial anxiety, then what was raising that anxiety to levels that would create a need for freak shows in the United States more than a decade before the Civil War? The answer, as Melville suggests in *Typee,* is that the 1840s was a key decade in the history of American race relations, a time when American society was dividing along racial issues that would, in less than a generation, turn into battle lines. In just a decade or so, abolitionism had grown from a tiny group of agitators into a national social and political movement of transformative power. This antislavery force, aided by the recalcitrance of the Southern opposition, quickly matured into a juggernaut of popular opinion and political activity, leading directly up to the Civil War.

It was this racially divided American society of the 1840s that nurtured the freak show, which quickly took root and thrived in its troubled soil. Like blackface minstrelsy, the freak show expressed "contradictory impulses" that made it an "index of racial feeling" in both the North and the South. In other words, the freak show expressed what Eric Lott calls "the racial unconscious," implicating cross-cutting desires for difference and superiority—but it also expressed a desire for sameness by identifying freaks as fellow humans. These opposing desires fuel the attraction-repulsion complex that the freak show evokes.[31] By linking tattooing and blackness, and blackness and freak shows, Melville forges a signifying chain in *Typee* that leads revealingly back into the racial unconscious. Following it, we may understand the dark origins of the American freak show, and an important source of its powerful, inarticulate effect. When Melville published *Typee* in 1846, his book appeared before a reading public inflamed by racial conflict—and frequently amused by human oddities. In his first novel Melville shows that, for Northern and Southern readers alike, the two were deeply and intimately related.

NOTES

Many of the ideas in this essay received their first airing as part of a panel at the 1993 American Studies Association Conference. I would like to thank Lawrence Buell, the panel's respondent, for his useful suggestions for revision.

1. For a striking example of this malignant acculturation, see David Halberstam, *October 1964* (New York: Random House, 1994), 221–22.

2. Charles R. Anderson was the first to expose *Typee* as a fiction rather than a factual travel narrative, the latter being a label that Melville actually encouraged (*Melville in the South Seas* [New York: Dover Publications, 1966]).

3. Bernth Lindfors, "Circus Africans," *Journal of American Culture* 6, no. 2 (1983): 10. Robert Bogdan argues that the presentation of racial freaks served to justify slavery and helped to sustain inequality after the war (*Freak Show: Presenting Human Oddities for Fun and Profit* [Chicago: University of Chicago Press, 1988], 187, 197). This is true as far as it goes, but, as I will suggest, it also rather simplifies the cultural work of the freak show. The freak show, like the minstrel show, is a site of racial conflict, not of resolution. It represented fears and anxieties at a time when the ideology of inequality tried to sustain itself against powerful social and political forces that threatened to erode it.

4. Tommo's openness has attracted a lot of critical attention over the years. See especially T. Walter Herbert's *Marquesan Encounters: Melville and the Meaning of Civilization* (Cambridge: Harvard University Press, 1980), in which he describes Tommo's perspective as that of a "beachcomber," one who seeks to enter different cultures at will.

5. Ethnology filled a social need for inequality that cultural anthropology does not. The social and legal institutions of the antebellum United States were racially and hierarchically organized, and the study of native cultures naturally followed suit. The nineteenth-century study of "exotic" cultures thus supported the assumptions of the Western culture that sponsored it. Not until the early twentieth century were the essentialist explanations of mid-nineteenth-century ethnology finally demolished, paving the way for cultural relativism to enter and make anthropology recognizable to the modern eye. See Carl N. Degler, *In Search of Human Nature: The Decline and Revival of Darwinism in American Social Thought* (New York: Oxford University Press, 1991), 59–211.

Though current scholarship rightly questions the detachment of the cultural anthropologist and calls the practice of cultural relativism into question, the modern anthropologist has more self-awareness and clearly tries harder to examine native cultures on their own terms than her nineteenth-century counterpart did. For recent self-analysis of anthropological and ethnographic practice, see, e.g., the work of James Clifford, Renato Rosaldo, and Clifford Geertz. As an implicit critic of his narrator, Melville himself occupies this ambivalent perspective in the structure of the novel. It is yet another aspect of Melville's extraordinary prescience that *Typee* can be said to predict both the rise of modern cultural anthropology and its practitioners' subsequent criticism of their own practice.

6. Herman Melville, *Typee* (1846). Ed. Harrison Hayford, Herschel Parker, and G. Thomas Tanselle (Evanston, Ill.: Northwestern University Press; Chicago: Newberry Library, 1968), chapter 12, 93. Future citations will be given parenthetically within the text by chapter and page.

7. John Evelev precedes me to this point in his interesting biographical reading of *Typee*, " 'Made in the Marquesas': *Typee*, Tattooing, and Melville's Critique of the Literary Marketplace," *Arizona Quarterly* 48, no. 4 (1992): 21. His focus on Tommo's threatened tattooing and potential freak status centers on the "conflict between Melville's romantic rejection of an objectifying mode of literary representation"—represented in the novel by Tommo's refusal to be written on by Karky—and Melville's "desire to find a place and succeed within that same system," as illustrated by his real-life willingness to make various changes necessary to sell his book and make a name for himself.

8. Racial freaks, whom I discuss below, were exhibited the same way, but what was "normal" for them (clothing, food, cultural practices) was not seen that way by their audience—which was, of course, the point.

9. Leslie Fiedler, *Freaks: Myths and Images of the Secret Self* (New York: Simon and Schuster, 1978), 24.

10. Herman Melville, "Authentic Anecdotes of 'Old Zack,' " in *The Piazza Tales and Other Prose Pieces, 1839–1860*, ed. Harrison Hayford, Alma A. MacDougall, G. Thomas Tanselle et al. (Evanston, Ill.: Northwestern University Press; Chicago: Newberry Library, 1987), 215, 218–19, 225. Melville mocks Taylor's heroic reputation by imagining Barnum making entreaties to display in his museum a tack from the general's saddle, his pants, and finally Taylor himself. Barnum promises that Taylor would enjoy treatment commensurate with that accorded Tom Thumb.

11. Bogdan, *Freak Show*, 241.

12. Ibid., 242.

13. Mary Louise Pratt, *Imperial Eyes: Travel Writing and Transculturation* (London: Routledge, 1992), 86.

14. O'Connell exhibited himself at circuses and museums (including Barnum's) from at least the mid-1830s until his death (probably in the mid-1850s). Saul H. Riesenberg carefully documents O'Connell's life in "The Tattooed Irishman," *Smithsonian Journal of History* 3 (1968): 1–17, an examination that exposes many inconsistencies in O'Connell's own account, and from which my own summary is largely drawn. For a brief overview of O'Connell's career, see Bogdan, *Freak Show*, 242–43.

15. Bogdan, *Freak Show*, 243–46, 250–51.

16. In noting this ambivalence, Evelev places it within the context of Melville's conflicted view of fame, financial success, and the capitalist market system that defined and housed these goals ("Made in the Marquesas," 26, 35).

17. The popularity of tattooed women effectively drove tattooed men out of the freak show business (Bogdan, *Freak Show*, 251–52), and Carol J. Clover's gender-based analysis of horror movies, *Men, Women, and Chain Saws: Gender and the Modern Horror Film* (Princeton: Princeton University Press, 1992), chap. 2, offers a clue to why. Clover argues that the protagonist of slasher horror films is invariably female—Clover calls her the "Final Girl"—because her gender enables the (predominantly male) audience for such movies to identify with her fear and anxiety through a socially acceptable (i.e., female) receptacle for those emotions. In other words, the Final Girl refracts male fear through a female character because it is considered "acceptable" for women to scream and cry. It is more than possible that the tattooed woman deflected male fears (and desires?) in the same way.

18. I am indebted to Rosemarie Garland Thomson's description of the way the freak generally embodies a lack of will in *Extraordinary Bodies: Figuring Physical Disability in American Literature and Culture* (New York: Columbia University Press, 1996).

19. For the narrative conventions of a freak show pamphlet, see Bogdan, *Freak Show*, 19.

20. Ibid., 161.

21. Ibid., 178.

22. Ibid., 106. The scenery got more involved as the practice became more popular over time.

23. Peggy Reeves Sanday, *Divine Hunger: Cannibalism as a Cultural System* (Cambridge: Cambridge University Press, 1986), 3. For a discussion of the sensational aspects of South Seas cannibalism in nineteenth-century America, see Gavan Daws, *A Dream of Islands: Voyages of Self-Discovery in the South*

Seas (New York: W. W. Norton, 1980), 18–19. For a brief account of Barnum's exploitation of "cannibals," see Bogdan, *Freak Show*, 178–79.

24. See Bogdan, *Freak Show*, 241–43; and Stephen Jay Gould, *The Mismeasure of Man* (New York: W. W. Norton, 1981), 123–43, esp. 129.

25. See Reginald Horsman, *Race and Manifest Destiny: The Origins of American Racial Anglo-Saxonism* (Cambridge: Harvard University Press, 1981), esp. chaps. 7 and 8; and Gould, *The Mismeasure of Man*, chap. 2. Though Darwin did not publish *The Origin of Species* until 1859, evolutionary thought was familiar and popular during the decades before the dramatic introduction of his theory of natural selection, and these ideas, frequently intertwined with religious dogma, informed much early racial science. (Because natural selection, with its lack of teleology, did not meet with universal acceptance, racial science continued more or less unabated after Darwin, albeit with some new vocabulary.) Horsman focuses on phrenology and Gould on craniometry as roots of polygenesis; these early "sciences" overlapped conceptually with "teratology," or the study of monsters, an early approach to the taxonomy of freaks documented by Bogdan.

26. This dichotomy is drawn from Thomson's analysis of the freak show in her forthcoming *Aberrant Bodies*. Stephen Greenblatt compares this experience of wonder to "ravishment, . . . an overpowering intensity of response [to] . . . something amazing" (*Marvelous Possessions: The Wonder of the New World* [Chicago: University of Chicago Press, 1991], 16).

27. Robert S. Levine has noted the analogy that Melville makes between the sailor and the slave. See *Conspiracy and Romance: Studies in Brockden Brown, Cooper, Hawthorne, and Melville* (Cambridge: Cambridge University Press, 1989), chap. 4.

28. For a brief discussion of some of these possible causes, see Bogdan, *Freak Show*, 10. I am mainly drawing on a more sustained discussion in Thomson, *Extraordinary Bodies*.

29. Eric Lott has recently shown how blackface minstrelsy reflects the racial anxieties of the Northern working class before the Civil War (*Love and Theft: Blackface Minstrelsy and the American Working Class* [New York: Oxford University Press, 1995]). My argument is similar, focusing on a different cultural practice.

30. For speculation on the decline of freak shows, see Bogdan, *Freak Show*, 62–68 and passim; and Fiedler, *Freaks*, 16.

31. Lott, *Love and Theft*, 4, 5. Not surprisingly, minstrelsy enjoyed its greatest popularity during the period 1846–54 (ibid., 9), coeval with the heyday of abolitionism and Southern plantation fiction—and with *Typee*. "For a time in the late 1840s," says Lott, "minstrelsy came to seem the most representative national art" (ibid., 8).

SEVENTEEN

The Circassian Beauty and the Circassian Slave: Gender, Imperialism, and American Popular Entertainment

LINDA FROST

By early 1856, P. T. Barnum had gone bankrupt; the year before, he had sold his collections at the American Museum to John Greenwood, Jr., his former manager, who also traveled for Barnum to procure the "oddities and amusements" for which Barnum was by this time famous.[1] (On March 24, 1860, Barnum would buy these properties back and, as A. H. Saxon puts it, announce "his solvency from the stage of the Museum.")[2] In a letter written during this time to the Massachusetts legislator and dentist Dr. David K. Hitchcock, Barnum first alludes to his financial frustrations, and then proceeds to talk about one of the Museum's latest endeavors:[3]

> Greenwood in getting up the "Congress of Nations" wants two beautiful Circassian slaves. I have written Mr. Brown, our consul in Constantinople, about it, but it struck me that you could perhaps manage it through your young dental Turk [Hitchcock's student]. . . . He wants to *hire* 2 beautiful Circassian girls & their mother or father or some other protector for 1 to 2 years. I suppose they would have to be bought, then give them their freedom and hire them, making contract through U.S. consul. Will you tell me whether it is feasible to get them & do what you can to aid Greenwood in the matter?
>
> For my own part, I have renounced business & care forever.[4]

Nothing apparently came of this request, just as nothing came of Barnum's claim to have "renounced business" forever. In May of 1864, Barnum wrote of the matter again to Greenwood, who was then in Cyprus. This time, Barnum clarified the value of the figure he sought:

> I still have faith in a beautiful Circassian girl if you can get one very beautiful. But if they ask $4000 each, probably one would be better than two, for $8000 in gold is worth about $14,500 in U.S. currency. . . . You can also buy a beautiful Circassian woman for $200 [$2000?], do so if you think best; or if you can hire one or two at reasonable prices,

do so if you think they are pretty and will pass for Circassian slaves. But in any event have one or two of the most beautiful girls you can find, even if they cost $4000 or $5000 in gold. . . . If you don't find one that is beautiful & possesses a striking kind of beauty, why of course she won't draw and you must give it up as a bad job. . . . If she is beautiful, then she may take in Paris or in London or probably both. But look out that in Paris they don't try the law and set her free. It must be understood that she is free.[5]

Barnum's instructions tell us several things. The legendary beauty of the Circassian woman or girl bought in the slave markets of Constantinople supposedly constituted the primary appeal for American audiences of the freak more commonly known as the "Circassian Beauty"; Barnum notes this when he advises Greenwood to be sure to obtain a girl or woman who will "draw." Barnum is likewise quite prepared to engage in slave trafficking in order to win such an entertaining prize, a practice he supposedly opposed in his own country at this time; "look out that in Paris they don't try the law and set her free," Barnum warns Greenwood after clarifying the amount Greenwood should spend on the "Beauty"—as much as four or five thousand dollars in gold.[6] The fact of the Circassian Beauty's slave status was represented somewhat differently once she appeared on the American Museum's stage, but it remained a constitutive part of her performative identity as a freak exhibit. And it is precisely this performativity that Barnum's message further reveals; he tells Greenwood to go ahead and hire one or two women if he can't actually buy any, but only if he thinks "they are pretty and will pass for Circassian slaves." The Circassian Beauty was in fact a complex and contradictory figure in nineteenth-century American popular culture, a woman who represented far more to the consumers of that culture than just the "striking kind of beauty" with which Barnum seems most concerned here.[7]

In response to Barnum's requests, a Circassian Beauty was finally procured for the museum and put on exhibit sometime in 1864. But the woman's regional origin and the circumstances by which she was obtained are a matter of some historical dispute. Zalumma Agra, alleged daughter of a Circassian prince and fugitive from a country caught in the land struggles of the Crimean War, had, as the story goes, never actually been sold into the slavery of the Turkish harems, but was rather *about* to be sold when Greenwood arrived on the scene to "rescue" her. He then went on to "rescue" Zalumma from savagery by overseeing her education and assuming the role of both guardian and tutor. So goes the Barnum tale; according to Robert Bogdan, there is an alternative story:

> According to an unpublished version by John Dingess, a contemporary of Barnum, Greenwood returned from his trip empty handed. A few weeks after his return a young woman came to the museum looking for work. She had bushy hair but nothing remark-able enough to make her a museum attraction. Disappointed by Greenwood's lack of success, but still bent on getting a Circassian, Barnum saw in her the possibility of creating his own Circassian, and he hired her. A Turk, residing in New York, was consulted as to appropriate dress and name, and in a short time the girl appeared at the museum in her silks as a full-fledged Circassian.[8]

Bogdan claims that Barnum's presentation of the Circassian Beauty "launched the prototype of a self-made freak," what he calls "a creation that wove the history of science together with tales of erotic intrigue from Asia Minor, current events, and a good portion of showman hype."[9] Circassian Beauties sprang up at dime museums and sideshows following Barnum's presentation of Zalumma, and they were to continue as a freak mainstay until the beginning of the twentieth century.

Bogdan places the Circassian Beauty within the "exotic mode" of freak performance, highlighting the way in which the Circassian, like such freak exhibits as the "Wild Men of Borneo," were touted as examples of the primitive, inaccessible, and preferably dangerous lives lived either geographically or chronologically far away from white middle-class America. Particular aspects of the popularly circulated story of the Circassian Beauty were likewise emphasized in her performance; she was not only beautiful, but also a kind of cultural ambassador for a humble, mountain farming people at the mercy of the tyrannical Russians, with whom the Circassians were at war, and the "primitive" Turks, who dealt in the trade of their women. The Caucasus region in which Circassia was located also had a special significance to pseudoscientific, anthropologically minded Americans. The German anatomist Johann Friedrich Blumenbach introduced the term *Caucasian* when he argued, based on his measurements of skulls obtained from Caucasus, that Caucasus was the "origin not only of Europeans, the Caucasian type, but of all humans." Given that such monogenist thought held that humans supposedly "degenerated in appearance" as they dispersed throughout the world, Blumenbach and his followers believed that "the purest and most beautiful whites were the Circassians, one tribe of the Caucasian region of Russia, a mountainous area on the Black Sea close to Turkey, then the Ottoman Empire."[10] Racial superiority to some degree concretized the Circassian Beauty's beauty, making her the whitest, racially "purest" specimen of a human woman to be found on earth.[11]

Part of the contradiction of the Circassian Beauty resides in her not-quite-but-almost slave status. The celebrated fact of the Circassian slave's racial purity is sustained in spite of the evil and dark Turk who desires her. On one hand, the image of the Turk echoes a primitivity that the Northern popular press attributed to an array of opposing forces at home: the Confederate who not only maintained the slavery of a colonized and oppressed people, but also "barbarically" killed and maimed Union soldiers in the Civil War then being fought; and the African-American whose free movement in white, Euro-American culture not only threatened white dominance of resources and their use, but the hegemonic definition of what it actually meant to be an American. The unsullied purity of the Circassian Beauty therefore seems in part to represent a Northern anxiety about racial mixing, particularly in regard to the anticipated effects of emancipation. In her role as a symbol of endangered-yet-rescued whiteness, the Circassian slave mirrored Northern whites' representations of the white American woman herself, potentially endangered by the "dark" and savage forces suddenly "unleashed" in the South. Miscegenation as a concept and as a term came into being in the nineteenth century and was ubiquitous in popular texts of the time. Furthermore, the question of who actually physically portrayed and embodied the Circassian Beauty complicates this issue of representation so that the Circassian Beauty becomes an overdetermined signifier of the dominant cultural concerns of Victorian America, embodying notions of colonial ambition and Orientalism, the superiority of the United States and Manifest Destiny, the position of women within Victorian America and the cult of True Womanhood, the purity of the white race and the sexualization of the African-American woman.

The story Barnum tells in the autobiographical *Struggles and Triumphs; or, Forty Years'*

Recollections of P. T. Barnum of Greenwood's attempt to obtain a Circassian woman for show at the museum highlights the otherness of Eastern and specifically Turkish culture that undergirded the Circassian Beauty as an exotic and compelling figure. The steamer on which Greenwood sailed to Constantinople also carried the harem of a Turkish pasha; one day while sitting on deck, Greenwood made the mistake of offering his hand to help one of the women step over a fence erected to separate the harem's members from the rest of the travelers. He was "immediately seized by two of the Pasha's attendants, violently shaken, and taken to task in Turkish for daring to offer to touch the hand of one of his Excellency's women."[12] Saved by an English- and Arabic-speaking Greek acquaintance, Greenwood was, according to Barnum, lucky not to have been "bastinadoed, or even bowstrung."[13] This incident even merits an engraving in Barnum's text, an image that seems to resonate with the next and final episode of Greenwood's search for the Circassian Beauty. In the illustration, a veiled woman in flowing robes stands on a partition above the other travelers as if put on display like a slave in the marketplace. Greenwood is held by two of the pasha's thugs while the harem's lord stands in the background, his mouth an elongated "o." The helpful Greek stands to the left, hands open in a supplicating manner.[14]

Having narrowly escaped this difficulty, Greenwood puts himself in further danger by "posing" as a slave-buyer and touring the slave markets of Constantinople. As Barnum tells it, Greenwood dressed in Turkish costume and learned a few Turkish words in order to gain access to the marketplace. Nevertheless, he "ran a risk of detection many times every day," although he did manage to see "a large number of Circassian girls and women, some of them the most beautiful beings he had ever seen."[15] Barnum here plays up the exoticism of the environment from which his Circassian Beauties originated by highlighting the danger posed to Greenwood by his own naturalized cultural practices, behaviors as simple and mundane to the American reader as helping a woman step over a fence. Moreover, the danger that surrounds Greenwood masquerading as a Turk—something evidently terribly difficult for him to do despite the fact that he is there to engage in the same slave-buying practice as the other Turks—further heightens the sense of intrigue surrounding the Circassian women themselves as they move, mysteriously veiled, through a society largely invisible to the Western male eye. Throughout his description of this incident, Barnum plays up the qualities of Orientalism that Edward Said argues were in fact distilled in Western thought during the nineteenth century: the Orient's "sensuality, its tendency to despotism, its aberrant mentality, its habits of inaccuracy, its backwardness."[16] It is significant that even while Greenwood does not here apparently win the prize he practically risks his life to obtain, he is able to *see* "a large number of Circassian girls and women," an experience of victorious cultural penetration given the protected and isolated nature of the harem. Greenwood's gaze is passed on to the audience via the freak exhibit itself, and it is this transaction that the freak performance depends upon.

Of course, it was the controlled viewing of this figure that made money for Barnum and other showpeople during this time. And that viewing was controlled not only by the money it cost to see the Beauty herself, but also by the showman/manager who cast the audience's viewing of the freak within a particular context. Barnum published a freak history of one of his Circassian Beauties in 1880 called *Zoe Meleke: Biographical Sketch of the Circassian Girl.* The freak history was a chapbook—in this case, just sixteen pages long—in which the freak's identity, place of origin, capabilities, and manner of procurement were all discussed in relative detail, and it probably reflects much of what the showman actually said during the freak's time on stage. Designed to complement the showman's presentation and introduction of the freak to audiences, freak histories and freak portraits were sold at exhibitions, and proceeds from their sale in part went to the freak performers. The pamphlet provides biographical information on Zoe Meleke, a historical context of sorts detailing Circassia's political difficulties to which Zoe falls victim, and an explanation of her loss of Arabic and gain of excellent English skills (something perhaps better explained by Zoe's probable American, not Circassian, background), as well as the writer's personal beliefs on women's education and social status.[17] It is an intriguing and confusing document. Clearly intended to arouse the patriotic spirit of the reader, *Zoe Meleke* indicates more of the politicized tensions that undergird the signification of the Circassian Beauty.

Zoe is presented to the American people as an entity—spiritual perhaps, but certainly delectable—to be consumed: "Among the most charming attractions offered to the American people of the present day, as a most chaste and delicate curiosity, is a young and beautiful native of Circassia."[18] Almost all freaks were performative, not simply in their construction as, say, "missing links" when they were actually microcephalic, but because they also performed various acts of skill or amusement; "armless wonders" would cut paper dolls out in front of their audience with their toes, and Tom Thumb and the "giants" in Barnum's employ would stage David and Goliath battles. Zoe's particular talents are not so clearly defined in her "history," but it is stressed that she is proficient in those "charms" that amplify "female beauty and intellect"; she writes articles for publication, is "affable and pleasing in conversation," and is not only "naturally of a high order of intellect," but "thoroughly refined by education and classical culture" (2, 4). What begins to make Zoe stand out seems not so much to be her recent affiliation to a life of enticing if immoral sensuality and power, but rather her rapid assimilation into American culture and Western civilization. "She expresses her preference for America over Europe," Barnum's anonymous writer informs us, "and thinks the people of the United States are the most prosperous and free in the world" (3). Freedom here is defined in terms of American prosperity and how "far in advance of all the other nations of the world in modern improvements" America is, particularly "in the application of steam to ships—to railroad cars, and to all kinds of machinery; in the invention of works of art, of the telegraph, and the great progress in agriculture" (3).

America is "free" not only because of its technological improvements, but also because of its attitude toward women. While "it was long before the intellectual rights of women were acknowledged" and "frivolity and other feminine faults were favorite themes for satire with the writers of the age of Charles the Second," Barnum's author assures us that this is no longer the case: "The flippant invectives on the sex, of which the writers of a former age indulge, would no longer be tolerated in society. . . . To no class is mental culture of more importance than to woman" (5). The writing becomes more and more rhetorically heartfelt and dogmatic as it progresses in this vein, the (presumably male) author carefully qualifying that while women should be educated to protect them from the "horrors of melancholy," he does not "mean that women should be eminent linguists and mathematicians. The education I wish them to receive would be confined to the bestowing upon them powers of thought, and treasures for thought" (6). By the end of this passage, not only has he made a case for the selective education women should receive and why, but he has also illustrated the benefits Zoe has undoubtedly gained by leaving her uncivilized Circassia behind and accepting America into her heart—and head: " 'The face that is the index to no mental excellence will lose its power, and the eyes brightened by no ray of genius, its luster.' What more can be said in the behalf of this lovely Circassian girl?" (6).

The history continues to expound not only on Zoe, but on Circassia and how "its women are as beautiful as houris," and how "the slave markets of Turkey have long been an emporium for the sale of these lovely but unfortunate creatures, to supply the seraglios and harems of the Sultans and his subjects" (8). Practically invisible to the people of the West, Circassia is, the author assures us, merely a diamond in the rough: "The steady onward march of civilization will probably reveal . . . amid the spurs and slopes and glades of the mountains of Circassia, another Golconda, another Potosi, another California, or all combined; and argosies, bearing untold wealth, the product of her womb, may, even within the present century, be plowing the waters of every clime" (9). Much of the Circassian Beauty's attraction seems to lie in the potential for gain locked within Circassia's as yet uncolonized (at least by Western forces) territories—the "product of her womb." But the Circassian Beauty herself is described as the most promising of the as yet largely unrealized natural resources Circassia has to offer: "the Circassian Girl, who is now a refined, intelligent and Christian woman, might have been enrolled upon the scroll of humanity, in company with the great mass of her countrywomen, as the beautiful but ignorant *habitat* of a Pagan's harem" (11–12). When Mr. Long, Zoe's Western rescuer and guardian and Barnum's Circassian connection, is exalted for his redeeming work with her and the author notes that "visitors have come by the scores to see this Circassian beauty," one wonders to what this beauty actually refers (14). Is it the beauty of the Circassian woman or the beauty of the barbarian "civilized" into Christianity and Western culture that fascinates her numerous fans and onlookers? What, if anything, is the difference?

Although America had not yet entered the global colonizing movement in which Britain, Spain, France, Holland, and other European countries were vigorously active (and would not do so until the turn of the century), the dominant Euro-American force was involved in several such battles within its own boundaries: the move to obliterate and exterminate the Native American tribes throughout the country, the struggle to maintain power over the newly freed African-Americans, and the fight to maintain economic and political dominance over the growing immigrant population. All of these struggles invariably invoked the rhetoric of colonization, of Manifest Destiny and the racial superiority of a "civilized" white American populace. This rhetoric was (and is) gendered, which complicates our understanding of it. While the Circassian Beauty superficially appears to highlight some kind of celebration of emancipation, of release from a bondage both sexual and spiritual in nature, her immediate alignment with a powerfully colonialist, paternalistic force—a Greenwood who would buy such a girl if possible, a Long who would civilize and cultivate her to an agreeably American taste, or a Barnum who would exhibit her as a consumable entertainment commodity— effectively reinscribes the colonial force from which she has supposedly been rescued. The Circassian Beauty as a freak is rescued from first Russian and then Turkish oppression only to be realigned with a new American colonizer; she, in fact, chooses this colonizer, welcoming her own "refinement" and reshaping herself into an acceptable mate for him. Not only does Zoe's story, told as it is by this Barnum author, discount the possibility of the Circassian Beauty as some kind of celebration of liberation, it in fact recasts her cage in the form of American Victorian womanhood; rather than an exotic, sensuous harem dweller, Zoe is now—thankfully, we are assumed to understand—"a most chaste and delicate curiosity."

Slavery and colonial activity are at the heart of a story written by "Lieutenant Murray"

(Maturin Murray Ballou) called *The Circassian Slave: or, The Sultan's Favorite: A Story of Constantinople and the Caucasus,* which was first published serially in the Boston periodical *Gleason's Pictorial Drawing Room Companion* in 1851. *The Circassian Slave* was republished as a dime novel by Gleason's firm, for which Murray wrote and of which he later assumed leadership.[19] Widely traveled himself, Murray specialized in tales of exotic, faraway lands and stories of the sea. *The Circassian Slave* is in part such a tale, but it is also a document that promotes an American ethic of naturalized individualism within an exotic context. Prefaced by a statement of authenticity of the character of the lands and peoples described, Murray's story opens on a "hot, sultry summer" afternoon at the slave markets in Constantinople: "here are Egyptians, Bulgarians, Persians and even Africans; but we will pass them by and cross to the main stand, where are exposed for sale some score of Georgians and Circassians."[20] After describing the "motley crowd" that throngs the marketplace, Murray notes how bursts of laughter broke "from an enclosed division of the place where were confined a whole bevy of Nubian damsels, flat-nostriled and curly-headed, but as slight and fine-limbed as blocks of polished ebony" (10). These African women lie "negligently about, in postures that would have taken a painter's eye" but, as Murray assures us, "we have naught to do with them at this time" (10). Indeed we don't, for Murray proceeds to the sale of the Circassians, who are described as "fair and rosy-cheeked" and exposed "only so far as delicacy would sanction, yet leaving enough visible to develope *[sic]* charms that fired the spirits of the Turkish crowd" (10).

Murray's story will not be about slavery as Americans know and practice it, although his characterization of the "Nubian damsels" in the slave market is grounded in the American stereotype of African women's promiscuity; that of the Circassians, exposed "only so far as delicacy would sanction," likewise supports the notion of white women's "modesty" and sexual propriety. In fact, the story focuses on one Circassian woman in particular—Komel Gymroc, or "Lalla" as she is known in the Sultan's harem to which she is sold—who is simply not slave material. *The Circassian Slave* promotes an ideology of slavery that suggests that those who can remain and survive in it are probably best suited for that life. The Circassian society Murray describes raises its daughters to anticipate—happily, for the most part—a life of luxury and wealth in the Turkish harems. But Komel, whom the Sultan realizes to be of "the better class of her own nation," does not deserve the life of a harem slave (14). Slavery is not depicted as necessarily negative, but rather as a realistic choice for a suitable class of people. And while Murray indeed leaves the "Nubian damsels" behind, the brief but telling image of them as sexualized and "negligently lying about" serves as another indication of whom slavery may in fact suit.

Komel, we learn, is a sixteen-year-old Circassian who has been taken into bondage against her will by a jealous lover. She is bound by her affections to a childhood companion, Aphiz Adegah, and they are depicted as pastorally united and blissful prior to Komel's abduction: "They had grown up together from very childhood, played together, worked together, sharing each other's burthens, and mutually aiding each other; now quietly watching the sheep and goats upon the hillsides, and now working side by side in the fields, content and happy, so they were always together" (22). Circassia is a land in tumult, described in much the same way as Barnum's author described it: "Circassia, the land of beauty and oppression, whose noble valleys produce such miracles of female loveliness, and whose level plains are the vivid scenes of such terrible struggles; where a brave, unconquerable peasantry have, for a very long period, defied the combined powers of the whole of Russia, and whose daughters, though the children of such brave sires, are yet taught and reared from childhood to look forward to a life of slavery in a Turkish harem as the height of their ambition" (21).

The beauty of Circassia's women is an act of compensation on the part of Providence because, according to Murray, they are "unendowed with mental culture" and in "want of intellectual brilliancy" (21). "No wonder, then," he explains, "educated, or rather uneducated as they are, that the visions of their childhood, the dreams of their girlish days, and even the aspirations of their riper years, should be in the anticipations of a life of independence, luxury and love, in those fairy-like homes that skirt the Bosphorus at Constantinople" (21). In this capacity, these women have attained positions, if not of power, at least of prestige: Circassia's "daughters have been the mothers of the highest dignitaries of the courts, and Sultan Mahomet himself was born of a Circassian mother" (21). Murray does not clearly condemn or condone the slavery he depicts; rather, it seems to be the best for which many of these less-than-bright women can hope. And this slavery has not prevented their attainment of esteem; they are, after all, mothers to many powerful men. Murray here seems to use the plight of the Circassians to reflect problematic notions of white American womanhood, highlighting the role of the mother as one of potential grandeur in a society in which white women are economically and socially, if not literally, enslaved; if not openly disconcerted, Murray at least sounds wistful that such a situation exists.

The slavery of the harem itself is described as a luxurious and mindless one. Komel walks into a "gilded cage" when she enters the harem of the Sultan to which she has been sold: "the costly and graceful lounges, the heavy and downy carpets, the rich velvet and silken hangings about the walls, the picturesque and lovely groups of female slaves that laughed and toyed with each other, mingling in pleasant games, the rich though scanty dress of these favorites of the Sultan, all were confusing and dazzling to her untutored eye" (13). And while "days and weeks passed on in the same routine of fairy-like scenes, and the Sultan's slaves counted not the time that brought to them but a never varying dull monotony of indolent luxuriance," Komel's "natural" intellect suffers in such a sweet but stifling atmosphere (40).

The quality of laziness that Said emphasizes as constitutive of the Orient in Western discourse of Orientalism is sharply juxtaposed with Komel and her loved ones. And, of course, it is just this quality of intellect and restlessness that further heightens her attractiveness for the Sultan. Described as "a noble specimen of his race, tall, commanding, and with a spirit of firmness breathing from his expressive face," the Sultan is himself the son of a Circassian (11). While he does not seem to be intellectually deficient in any way, he does exhibit "a doomed darkness of expression" that causes Komel to tremble before him (11). The Sultan is the symbol of Eastern tyranny, the representation of Turkish cruelty and oppression: "Stern and imperious by nature, it was not usual for him to evince such feeling as had exercised him towards [Lalla/Komel], and it was plain that his heart was moved by feelings that were novel there" (12). Komel is the essence of American Victorian womanhood, "trapped" in an Eastern body: "She possessed all that soft delicacy of appearance that reminds the sterner sex how frail and dependent is woman, while she bore in her face that sweet and winning expression of intellect, that, in other climes more favored by civilization, and where cultivation adds so much to the charms of her sex, would alone have marked her as beautiful" (15–16).

Troubled by the emotional intensity that accompanies his new acquisition, the Sultan calls a slave to bring him his pipe, and he is "soon lost in the dreamy narcotic of the tobacco" (12).

The Sultan does not know precisely how to handle his new feelings given that he has been taught to "look upon the gentler sex as toys, merely, of his own," and when it comes to the question of possession of Komel, he remains the savage (29). When Komel's lover, Aphiz, comes to the palace in search of her, having earned a favor from the Sultan by coincidentally saving his life from Bedouin thieves, the Sultan immediately imprisons and attempts to execute him (he does not, of course, succeed). When Komel begs him to free Aphiz, her pleas are "received by the Sultan in that cold, irascible spirit that seems to form so large a share of the Turkish character" (34). The Sultan's memory is unfortunately short, and because he doesn't remember "how unlike her people she had already proved herself" and doesn't realize "that his high station, his wealth, his pomp and elegance" are thought of by Komel "only as the flowers that adorn the victim of a sacrifice," he does not anticipate what we readers do— her escape (46). Komel returns to her homeland with Aphiz, who has also escaped from the Sultan's clutches. Despite the years that pass, the "Brother of the Sun . . . does not forget [the woman] who had so entranced his heart, so enslaved his affections, and then so mysteriously escaped from his gilded cage" (67).

Joanna De Groot argues that the nineteenth-century discourse of Orientalism was a means by which men explored "*their own* identity and place in the world as sexual beings, as artists and intellectuals, as imperial rulers, and as wielders of knowledge, skill, and power."[21] For De Groot, "the concepts of 'sex' and 'race' which came into use in European culture, elite and popular, did not just make the control of women or natives easier, but also expressed the conflicts, desires and anxieties which were part of the lived relationships between sexes and races, the *realities* of sexuality and imperial power."[22] The Circassian slave of both Barnum and Murray is a woman of controlled possibility. She has been pulled from a state of debauchery and tyranny realized in the fictionalized harems described in these documents, but that state has less to do with the institution of slavery than with Western descriptions of the weaknesses and evils of the Orient.[23] The Circassian Beauty becomes the idealized colonial subject, she who is primed for "civilization" and exhibits the naturalized individualism and intellect of Western and particularly American culture, traits that allow her to attract without effort. Lalla, Murray's Circassian slave, is particularly evocative to the Sultan, who purchases her not only because she is beautiful and intellectually and emotionally sensitive, but because she is deaf and mute (she is struck so when she witnesses the murder of a defender and friend on the night of her capture into slavery; she regains her hearing and speech after seeing Aphiz in the Sultan's palace). For Murray, the worth of Lalla/Komel as a subject with the potential to be civilized is apparent on sight. The same is true of Barnum's Circassian Beauty, whose primary achievement seems to be her ability to see America as the bastion of civilization and progress that it claims to be.

Carte de visites or postcards taken of the Circassian Beauties and sold and circulated in the latter part of the nineteenth century represent these women in a variety of settings and poses.[24] One Beauty, fully clothed in a long white gown with a high neck and encircled by a large wreath made of branches, looks more like a Western bride than a harem slave. This interpretation of the Circassian Beauty seems to realize visually much of what the texts discussed above say about her, that she is charming, delicate, intellectual, and chaste—the perfect model of Victorian American womanhood. What is interesting is how contradictory to this conception of womanhood most of the surviving visual images of the Circassian Beauty seem to be. Rather than highlighting their modesty and chastity, their propriety and intellectual capability, these photographs emphasize the exoticism and eroticism of the Circassian Beauty. Some display their stockinged legs in reclining postures; one woman, photographed by the Obermuller and Son studio on Cooper Square in New York, reclines on an ornately carved wooden bench, her silky tunic provocatively sheering at her waist while her legs stretch to her side. The setting for the photograph is primitivist—palms frame the Beauty as she leans on an animal skin draped over the bench. Another Obermuller portrait features a Beauty reclining on a roughly carved rock in the parlor of a house, stairs rising off to the left. She too boasts long, stockinged legs and a loose leotard, her ankles crossed demurely at the bottom of the rock. Another, photographed by the Henshel studio in Chicago—"Miss Fatima" according to the writing on the back of the print—wears a white camisole with short pantaloons, long white gloves, and a long velvet ribbon tied in a large bow around her neck (fig. 17.1). Her shoulders bare, she leans against a column while cupids dance on the building's border below her in bas relief. One stockinged leg is daringly drawn up to allow her knee to rest on the building's edge and the other extends before her; elbow bent, she rests her head in the cup of her palm. She is almost smiling.

Other images emphasize the exotic dress of the Orient—a woman with ropes of huge pearls around her neck, over and under her bosom and down the length of her arms, another with a tightly fitted silk gown, "stars of the East" embroidered along its hem, an ornately bordered cape over her shoulders. Often the studios incorporated tropical plants and animal skins into the background of the photograph. All of these women exude the slight sense of mystery necessary for the exotic flavor of the performance. Most are tantalizingly attired. But there is really only one thing all of the Circassian Beauties have in common: their huge, bushy hair.

According to Bogdan, the women performing as Circassians soaked their hair in beer and teased it to make it frizz and stand up.[25] In fact, the hairstyle of the American-made Circassian Beauty probably had nothing to do with actual images of the harem woman from Turkey; in the engraving that accompanies Murray's story in *Gleason's Pictorial Drawing Room Companion*, Lalla/Komel is veiled, her long, straight black hair shimmering beneath the veil. She is carefully covered, dressed in traditionally puffy pants and layers of shifts, shawls, and scarves. But the American freak show Circassian Beauty always sported large, Afro-like hair and, as these images show, usually less rather than more clothing. These women look more like nineteenth-century pin-ups than they do harem dwellers, which brings yet another facet of the Circassian Beauty's signification in American culture to light: while, textually, Barnum's writer describes Zoe Meleke as the very model of Victorian womanhood—modest, intelligent, and pure, racially as well as sexually—visually, the Beauty is something quite different, a sexualized figure intended to entice. She may well represent the reason why Victorian patriarchal culture constructed such a controlling domestic ideology; the Circassian Beauty embodies sensual pleasure and, more importantly, a tremendous sexual power that is resolutely female.

While somewhat confusing, the signature hairstyle of these women is clearly vital to our understanding of the Circassian Beauty's signification in American culture. If we go by John Dingess's story of the procurement of Zalumma Agra for the American Museum in 1864, the fact that the woman hired to perform the role of the first American Circassian Beauty had bushy hair may be the reason why it became the freak's trademark. The freak "original" quickly became that figure's prototype for all similar performances; as Dingess comments,

17.1. *Miss Fatima, age 20*. Harvard Theatre Collection. The Houghton Library.

17.2. *Zumigo the Egyptian, age 20, born in Cairo.* Harvard Theatre Collection. The Houghton Library.

thirty years after Zalumma's first appearance, freak lecturers other than Barnum would still announce that their Zalumma (who was not even old enough for the story to be true) "was brought to this country by John Greenwood for Barnum's American Museum."[26] But the Circassian's bushy hairstyle certainly echoes other Barnum exhibits, especially his display of "Fiji Cannibals" and other so-called "primitive" groups.[27] One variation of the Circassian Beauty captured by the "freak photographer" Charles Eisenmann in New York shows a woman in a tightly fitted fringed bodice and shorts, her bosom and hips amply displayed (fig. 17.2). She wears stockings and is photographed against the typical leafy set. According to the writing on the back of the photo, this woman is "Zumigo the Egyptian, age 20, born in Cairo." Albeit not a true "Circassian Beauty," Zumigo is cast within that framework; her hair stands a triumphant almost two feet out from her head. The presentation of Zumigo illustrates how the trademark Circassian Beauty's hair would have resonated for contemporary audiences with the images of African and tribal women circulating in the culture. Perhaps it is no accident that the two primary characteristics of these Circassian Beauties are their bushy hair and their evocative postures; just like the "Nubian damsels, flat-nostriled and curly-headed" lying "negligently about" in Murray's story, the images of the African-American woman's hair and promiscuous sexuality were mythic cultural stereotypes that nineteenth-century audiences would have swiftly put together.[28]

De Groot believes that the Oriental women portrayed by European painters and artists were "socially marginal, sexually powerless, and vulnerable, and regarded by westerners and Middle Eastern societies as inferior, morally suspect, even virtual prostitutes."[29] Further, she points out that these women " 'become' whoever artists want them to be, yet they were actually flesh-and-blood women whose lives were no less real for being hidden from history."[30] Just as the "real" Circassians are lost in the artistic Orientalism of male European art, the "real" performers of the American Circassian Beauty are likewise lost, nameless or renamed women hidden behind the photographed performance of the freak show. While these women were probably not "real" Circassians, they were commodified within the market of American popular entertainment as were their Eastern sisters within the slave markets of Constantinople.

Who these women actually were has been suggested by circus press agent Dexter Fellows, and his suggestion illustrates how the disempowering, "enslaving" representation of women in American culture continues, with one culture's slavery merely revamped and grafted onto another. Given that the lighter the skin of the Circassian Beauty, the more likely she was to impress upon the audience her racial purity, Fellows explains that "whenever a showman encountered an unpigmented Irish or Norwegian female, he forthwith engaged her, at a salary far in advance of what she was capable of earning at the washtub, as 'Zuleika, the Circassian Sultana, Favorite of the Harem.' Such, at least, was the history of the Circassian lady from Jersey City."[31] Just like the "lucky" Circassian girl who got out of the workhorse world of her countrywomen by entering the slavery of the Turkish harems, the immigrant girl in New York could also leave the drudgery of the "washtub" behind to join the market of commodified bodies in the American freak show.

What the image of the Circassian Beauty may finally show us is how the signification of women in nineteenth-century American culture—the representations of her sexuality, her intellectual capability and freedom, her body and its control, as well as her position as a commodity in capitalism—not only depended upon the popular representations of women from other cultures, but in fact duplicated those meanings. The Circassian Beauty, then, depicts a harem slave who is reenslaved into Victorian American domesticity, only again to be enslaved as a sexualized immigrant commodity of public entertainment, a force that likes its women and cultural others beautifully caged.

NOTES

1. Thanks go to a number of people who have helped in various ways with this project: Leonor Delazega and Robert O'Connor of the Hertzberg Circus Collection, Michael Dumas of the Harvard Theatre Collection, the library staff of the American Antiquarian Society, and Marilyn Grush and Eddie Luster of the Mervyn Sterne Library at the University of Alabama at Birmingham, all for their help in locating and making available indispensable research materials; Rebecca Bach for her invaluable editorial advice; Scott Sandage for his historical expertise and intellectual comradery; and Rosemarie Thomson for her interest in the first place. Parts of this project were supported by a Faculty Research Grant from the University of Alabama at Birmingham.

2. A. H. Saxon, introduction to *Selected Letters of P. T. Barnum* (New York: Columbia University Press, 1983), xxx.

3. A. H. Saxon, *P. T. Barnum: The Legend and the Man* (New York: Columbia University Press, 1989), 361.

4. Barnum, *Selected Letters*, 91–92.

5. Ibid., 125–27.

6. Saxon discusses Barnum's contradictory attitudes and actions regarding slavery and African-Americans in *P. T. Barnum;* although Barnum publicly championed the cause of the North and abolition, he also allegedly bought and sold several slaves himself while touring in the antebellum South. Saxon sums up the discussion by saying: "Let us be candid about the matter and have done with it: Barnum's opinion of blacks during the pre–Civil War era was no higher than that of most of his countrymen, whether Southerners or Northerners. They were chattels, things to be bought and sold, like any other commodity" (85). See Saxon, *P. T. Barnum,* 82–85.

7. My concern in this chapter is with the way in which the harem dweller is represented within the image of the Circassian Beauty; for more on the harem itself, see Malek Alloula, *The Colonial Harem,* trans. Myrna Godzich and Wlad Godzich (Minneapolis: University of Minnesota Press, 1986); Alev Lytle Croutier, *Harem: The World Behind the Veil* (New York: Abbeville Press, 1989); N. M. Penzer, *The Harem: An Account of the Institution as It Existed in the Palace of the Turkish Sultans with a History of the Grand Seraglio from Its Foundation to Modern Times* (London: Spring Books, 1936); and Leslie P. Peirce, *The Imperial Harem: Women and Sovereignty in the Ottoman Empire* (New York: Oxford University Press, 1993).

8. Robert Bogdan, *Freak Show: Presenting Human Oddities for Amusement and Profit* (Chicago: University of Chicago Press, 1988), 238.

9. Ibid., 239, 237.

10. Ibid., 237.

11 Circus press agent Dexter Fellows says the same, highlighting the role of skin color in the Circassian's presentation: "The theory that Caucasians were the purest and most primitive stock of the white, or European, race gave rise to the mistaken notion that they must of necessity be either albinos or people whose extreme blondness ran to pink eyes and white hair" (Dexter Fellows and Andrew A. Freeman, *This Way to the Big Show: The Life of Dexter Fellows* [New York: Halcyon House, 1936], 292). This possibly explains how Circassians came to be represented by albinos as the freak show progressed throughout the nineteenth century.

12. P. T. Barnum, *Struggles and Triumphs; or, Forty Years' Recollections of P. T. Barnum, Written by Himself* (Buffalo: Courier, 1875), 580.

13. Ibid., 581.

14. Ibid., 580–81.

15. Ibid., 581.

16. Edward Said, *Orientalism* (New York: Vintage, 1978), 205.

17. This is Bogdan's explanation of Zoe's odd linguistic skills; see Bogdan, *Freak Show,* 239.

18. *Zoe Meleke: Biographical Sketch of the Circassian Girl* (New York: P. T. Barnum's Greatest Show on Earth, 1880), 1. Further references to this pamphlet will be cited parenthetically in the text.

19. For more on Murray, see Peter Benson, "Maturin Murray Ballou," in *Publishers for Mass Entertainment in Nineteenth-Century America,* ed. Madeleine B. Stern (Boston: G. K. Hall, 1980), 27–34.

20. Murray, Lieutenant. *The Circassian Slave: or, The Sultan's Favorite: A Story of Constantinople and the Caucasus* (Boston: F. Gleason, 1851), 9. Further references to this novel will be cited parenthetically in the text.

21. Joanna De Groot, " 'Sex' and 'Race': The Construction of Language and Image in the Nineteenth Century," in *Sexuality and Subordination,* ed. Susan Mendus and Jane Rendall (New York: Routledge, 1989), 100.

22. Ibid.

23. Said notes that one of the primary features of Orientalism is that it reflects the relationship between European (and Euro-American, by extension) and Oriental powers as one between the strong and the weak, a point that supports Said's argument that Orientalism always has at its center the political control of the East (*Orientalism,* 40).

24. The photographs I discuss below can be found in the Harvard Theatre Collection. Only some have identifying titles or captions which I have included when possible.

25. Bogdan, *Freak Show,* 239.

26. Quoted in ibid., 240.

27. Ibid., 184.

28. At least one writer of the period depicted life in the Turkish harems as something more resembling America's slavery system than what writers like Murray show. *Thirty Years in the Harem; or, the Autobiography of Melek-Hanum, Wife of H. H. Kibrizli-Mehemet-Pasha* (New York: Harper and Bros., 1872) describes the life of a harem slave—and particularly that of the Circassian slave—as a miserable one. Melek-Hanum's account echoes African-American slave narratives such as Harriet Jacobs' *Incidents in the Life of Slave Girl* in that the same central elements of danger appear—the violent, raping master, the jealous, murderous mistress and the ever-present possibility of sale into an even worse situation.

29. De Groot, " 'Sex' and 'Race,' " 120.

30. Ibid., 121.

31. Fellows and Freeman, *This Way to the Big Show*, 292–93.

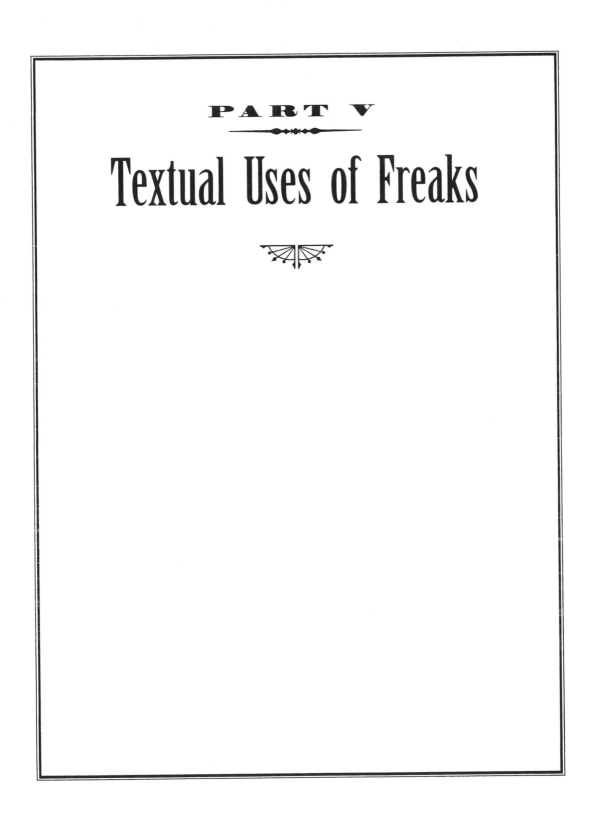

PART V

Textual Uses of Freaks

EIGHTEEN

"One of Us": Tod Browning's *Freaks*

JOAN HAWKINS

Tod Browning's 1932 production, *Freaks,* certainly stands as a classic in studies of freakishness and freakmaking. Removed from distribution by Metro-Goldwyn-Mayer (MGM) shortly after its release and banned outright in Great Britain, the film—as *The Encyclopedia of Horror Movies* points out—immediately "acquired an unsavoury reputation which lingers on even though denied by the film itself."[1]

Freaks tells the story of a circus midget's impossible love for a "big woman,"[2] the circus trapeze artist, Cleopatra. When she becomes aware of Hans the midget's love for her, Cleopatra contrives to marry him for his money (Hans, we learn, has a fortune). Shortly after the wedding, she and her strongman lover begin administering poison to Hans. The other freaks in the circus become suspicious, however. Following the "code of the freaks," they kill the strongman and mutilate Cleopatra, turning her into a chicken-woman, the star of the Freak Show.

Critical reception was mixed.[3] Confusion over the film seems to have stemmed largely from the use of real freaks to play the parts.[4] Critics worried that the film merely replicated the most unsavory aspects of the freak show. The *New York Times* reviewer talks about "the underlying sense of horror . . . that fills the circus sideshows."[5] *Variety* faults the film for its "too fantastic romance," claiming that "it is impossible for the normal man or woman to sympathize with the aspiring midget."[6] And *Time* refuses to evaluate the picture at all, detailing instead all "the misfits of humanity" it numbers among its cast: "A man without legs walks on his hands. A woman without hands eats with her feet. A Negro with no limbs at all lights a cigaret [sic] with his teeth. Siamese twins have courtships."[7]

Certainly, publicity for the film points up *Freaks'* relationship to the carney culture it so poignantly depicts. "Unlike anything you've ever seen," the Rialto Theater's 1932 ad for the film proclaims. "The *strange* and *startling* love-drama of a *midget,* a lovely *siren,* and a *giant!*" In addition to Leila Hyams, Baclanova, Wallace Ford, and Rosco Ates, the ad lists "a horde of caricatures of creation—not actors in make-up—but *living, breathing* creatures as they are and as they were born!" The base of the ad carries a warning: "Children will not be permitted to see this picture! Adults not in normal health are urged not to!"[8]

18.1. Poster for Tod Browning's 1932 film, *Freaks*. Courtesy of the Ron Becker Collection, Syracuse University Library, Department of Special Collections.

Although both critical reaction and box office success appear to have been mixed, mass public reaction was not. A few favorable statements buried in otherwise ambivalent reviews were not enough to counter the negative reviews that appeared in the local press. Despite the fact that the film had shown good box office receipts in some areas, theater owners—particularly those in rural areas—refused to handle the film. At the same time, parent-teacher associations and what Leslie Fiedler calls "other organizations specializing in moral indignation" lobbied against the movie. Even some of the freaks who had played in the film, Fiedler notes, "most notably the Bearded Lady, were convinced in retrospect that Browning had vilified their kind and said so in public."[9] It was in the face of so much opposition that MGM withdrew the film from circulation shortly after its release. While the film could be seen, without the MGM logo, on the exploitation film circuit, it remained unavailable for mainstream viewing in the United States from 1932 (when MGM shelved it) until its revival in 1962.

Watching *Freaks* today is an unnerving experience, although not for the reasons implied by the 1932 reviews of the film. It is not seeing the freaks lead normal lives ("Siamese twins have courtships") that is unsettling. On the contrary, the film's apparent thesis—namely, that "freakishness is only skin deep, and that differently formed people have all the feelings, intelligence and humor of 'normal' folks"[10]—is one that most contemporary audiences find appealing. "What keeps *Freaks* 'freakish,' " as the Pacific Film Archive notes for the film point out, "is rather the duality of Browning's own intentions. Despite being one of the few films that, *mutatis mutandi*, treats the Other as 'one of us'; and despite purporting in the original prologue to be an exposé of the exploitation of 'nature's mutants,' *Freaks* is guilty of the crime it denounces." Through "its bizarre revenge plot" and its periodic insistence on the "code of the freaks," the film "traps its characters in a horror mode."[11] It reinscribes physical difference as a thing to be feared.

The first half of the film goes to great lengths to "normalize" the freaks. We see differently formed people going about the everyday business of life. Frances, the armless woman, eats; Randian, the "living torso," rolls and lights a cigarette; Frieda, a midget, hangs out the laundry. And while it is tempting to read these actions—as the *Time* review of the film does—as a series of sideshow acts, the presence of sympathetic "big people" in nearly all these scenes helps to mitigate the performative aspect. Randian is in the middle of a conversation with one of the Rollo brothers—the circus acrobats—when he lights his cigarette. Similarly, Frances, the armless woman, is listening to one of the Rollos brag as she eats her evening meal. Frieda, as she hangs out her laundry, exchanges confidences with Venus, the circus seal trainer. The film clearly brackets these exchanges as everyday conversation ("You're not singing this morning, Frieda," Venus observes, as she sits on her wagon step to sew and chat). It also uses the "big people" as audience stand-ins: much like the screaming victims in traditional horror films, they "cue" us to the appropriate audience response.

Furthermore, there seems to be something odd about most of the "normal" people in the film. The Rollo brothers' excessive bragging appears here as far more quirky than Randian's dignified cigarette routine. Rosco, the man who works with Hercules, stutters. The sword-swallower and the fire-eater are lumped with the freaks in the circus attractions. And Phroso the clown, the most sympathetic "big man" in the film, refers ominously to his "operation" and appears a little slow in his dealings with the street-smart Venus.

Even Cleopatra, the "Queen of the trapeze" and the "most beautiful big woman" Hans has ever seen, appears here as somehow too large. Seen in Hans's wagon after her marriage to him, Cleopatra must hunch over in order to move around. And Venus, Phroso's sympathetic, conventionally formed lover, calls Cleo a "big horse" when she learns from Frieda about the trapeze performer's designs on the midget. But it is Cleo's perverse nature that most establishes her as the "living monstrosity" of the circus. Initially flirting with Hans as a nasty joke, Cleo turns deadly serious when she learns he has money. "Midgets are not strong," she tells her lover Hercules. "He could get sick. . . . It could be done." And the hunched position she must assume in order to give Hans his poisoned medicine once he does, in fact, become ill, is simply the visible sign of the predatory nature Cleo has nurtured all along. "In this extraordinary film," Ivan Butler writes, "Browning has turned the popular convention of horror topsy-turvy. It is the ordinary, the apparently normal, the beautiful which horrify—the monstrous and distorted which compel our respect, our sympathy, ultimately our affection. The visible beauty conceals the unseen evil, the visible horror is the real goodness."[12]

Just in case the audience somehow fails to get the point that it is the "freaks" in this film who deserve our allegiance and sympathy, Browning includes at least two scenes that make the film's thesis quite explicit. When Hans falls ill, Venus confronts Hercules and makes it clear that she does not regard herself as one of his "kind." "You better get Cleo to tell the doctor what she put in the wine last night," Venus tells Hercules, "or I'll tell the coppers."

"So," he replies, "you'd tell on your own people." "My people," Venus says, pulling herself up, "are decent circus folks, not dirty rats what would kill a freak to get his money."

A more telling scene, however, occurs early in the film. The setting here shifts away from the cloistered world of the circus to the surrounding countryside. We see a gentleman walking with his groundsperson, Jean, who is struggling to describe the horrors he has just seen. "Horrible, twisted things," he says, "crawling and gliding." The gentleman assures the distraught man that he'll clear his grounds of any "things" or persons who do not belong. We then see—in long shot—Madame Tetralini, the owner of the circus, and a group of circus freaks that she has brought out for exercise. The human skeleton is lying on his back, playing a reed pipe. The pinheads, Schlitze, Elvira, and Jennie Lee, and some of the midgets are dancing in a circle, singing and giggling. Nearby this strange pastorale, Madame Tetralini sits, reading. As the disgruntled Jean moves in to chase the strange band away, the camera comes in for a medium to medium-close shot. Madame Tetralini rises; Schlitze and Elvira run to her for protection. The other freaks gather closely around. Clinging to her skirts, they—especially Schlitze and Elvira—look like frightened children. And children, Madame Tetralini explains, is exactly what they are. "These are children from my circus. . . . When I get the chance I like to take them into the sunshine and let them play like—children. That is what most of them are—children." When the gentleman gives them permission to stay and calls the still-sputtering Jean away, Madame Tetralini scolds her charges for being frightened. "Shame. . . . How many times have I told you not to be frightened. Have I not told you that God looks after *all* His children."

Madame Tetralini's speech, like Venus's, is clearly meant to remind the audience that physical difference is an accident of birth. Her gentle insistence that we are *all* God's children functions here as a reproach to any Philistines in the audience who might believe—as Jean and Hercules clearly do—that differently formed people are "little apes" or "monsters." But Madame Tetralini's speech points to one of the subtler aspects of the film: While it is certainly true that the freaks are all God's children (i.e., God's offspring), it is not so clear that all the freaks—or even "most of them"—are literally "children" (i.e., innocent and helpless beings), as Madame Tetralini claims.

Although some of the freaks—most notably the pinheads—*are* portrayed as childlike throughout most of the film, the male freaks included in the pastoral scene are all explicitly linked to the adult world. The human skeleton playing the reed pipe appears in a later sequence as the proud father of the bearded lady's baby. Randian, the "living torso," has a mature, weather-lined face and sports several tattoos. And the midget who leads the band in thanking the gentleman for allowing them to stay is obviously mature. It is he who proposes and leads the "one of us" toast at the wedding banquet, who seems to organize and orchestrate the surveillance of Cleo when Hans gets sick, and who first calls the audience's attention back to the freaks' "code." Enjoying a glass of wine with Frances, the armless lady, he angrily predicts that Cleo will have problems if she tries "doing *anything* to one of us."

If it is wrong to judge people as "monsters" simply because they are differently formed, it is equally wrong (and potentially dangerous)—the film seems to be saying—to attribute childlike qualities (like helplessness and innocence) to adult people who happen to be diminutive in size. And this is a mistake that many of the "normal" people in the circus make. Even Cleo, who plays on Hans's adult sexual feelings throughout the first half of the film, periodically confounds his appearance and behavior with that of a child. She laughs at his courtly manners behind his back and teases him when he shows signs of jealousy. At the wedding banquet she accuses him of acting like "a baby" when he does not join in her outburst; and she further humiliates him by taking him on a piggyback ride around the deserted table. Even in her gentle moments, Cleo tends to infantilize Hans. She calls him "my little," in a vain attempt to convince him of her affection, and tells his friends to go home so that she can tuck him in for the night. But Hans is not "a baby"; he is, as he tells her early in the film, "a man" who has the same feelings "big people" have. And these feelings turn quite nasty when he begins to suspect that Cleo is trying to poison him.

It is Hans's and, by extension, *all* the freaks' revenge against Cleo that helps to establish *Freaks* as a true horror film. Certainly, the revenge sequence is terrifying in a way that suspense can never be. But if the freaks' revenge inscribes the film as part of the horror genre, it also reinscribes the freaks as monsters within that genre. In fact, the entire revenge sequence can be read as a systematic reversal of the earlier pastoral scene, which attempted to establish the freaks as harmless children. Whereas the pastoral takes place in a contained, sunlit space, the revenge sequence unfolds at night during a rainstorm; its overt sense of menace derives precisely from the fact that the freaks can *not* be contained. Anywhere that Cleo runs, she is vulnerable. Furthermore, whereas the pastoral sequence expounds antifreak prejudice (in the form of Jean's tirade to his employer) in order that Madame Tetralini might refute it, here Jean's anxieties about the freaks are given literal expression. Pursuing Cleo through the mud and rain, the freaks here *do* crawl and glide; and given the fact that it is night, they *do* resemble "horrible twisted things," rather than differently formed people. Finally, while the pastoral scene attempts (somewhat unsuccessfully, as I argue above) to represent the freaks as "children," the revenge sequence shows clearly that the most childlike freaks can be quite vicious. Even Schlitze—perhaps the most childlike pinhead—appears monstrous here, as she gambols through the mud clutching a knife.

If the pastoral scene shows a group of vulnerable freaks who cling to a big woman, Madame Tetralini, for protection, the revenge sequence depicts a big woman who desperately needs protection from a band of marauding freaks. It is clear that Cleo occupies the star-victim position here. From the moment she runs screaming into the night with the band of vengeful freaks behind her, Cleo begins attracting audience sympathy. And it is this very shift in audience sympathy—*away* from the freaks and *toward* their intended victim—that tends to undermine what Robin Wood would call the earlier "progressive" nature of the film.[13]

Furthermore, there are indications that the freaks have done this sort of thing before. The barker's ominous references to the "code of the freaks," as well as the prologue's invocation of such a code, sensitizes the viewer from the very beginning to the possibility of freak violence. Even the "progressive" sequences of the film—those which show the freaks behaving "normally" at home—hint at a dark side of freak culture. Relaxing over a glass of wine, Frances, the armless woman, and her friend, the midget who played a leadership role in the earlier pastoral scene, gossip about the budding romance between Cleo and Hans:

SHE: Cleopatra ain't one of us. Why, we're just filthy *things* to her. She'd *spit* on Hans if he wasn't giving her presents.
HE: Let her try it. Let her try doing *anything* to one of us.
SHE: You're right. She don't *know* us; but she'll find out.

Frances's observation that Cleo doesn't really "know" the freaks serves in part to remind us that the freaks are a marginalized, maltreated group. Like any such group, they have been forced to adopt an inscrutable, "unknowable" public demeanor in order to survive. But the reminder comes at a very odd moment in the film. Just when the film appears to be downplaying difference (by showing that the freaks' domestic lives are not very different from those of "big people"), it explicitly connects the idea of difference to an implicit threat ("She don't know us; but she'll find out"). This threat is, of course, realized in the revenge scene.

While there is a certain poetic justice to Cleo's final transformation, her emergence as a chicken-woman further complicates the depiction of physical difference in *Freaks*. For Cleo is constructed, not born, as a freak. And this construction seems to have two implications for the film. On the one hand, it works as a nice metaphor for the way that freaks are shown as "social constructs" throughout the film (i.e., the film shows that there is nothing inherently freakish about differently formed people and that in the freaks' world, it is "big people" who seem abnormal and odd). On the other hand, however, it directly contradicts the argument for tolerance that we are given at the beginning of the film. Having been initially reminded by the barker that physical difference is an "accident of birth," not the visible sign of some inner monstrosity, we are ultimately presented with a woman who has been turned into a freak as punishment for her immorality and greed (i.e., a woman whose physical difference is the tangible sign of her inner monstrosity). The fact that Cleo—the true "living monstrosity" in the circus—is transformed into a physical "monstrosity" raises the possibility that physical difference can be the tangible sign of inner depravity, which serves to partially blunt the progressive edge of *Freaks*.

The film itself seems to acknowledge the fact that it comes perilously close to completely undermining audience sympathy for the freaks. Although Cleo's appearance as a chicken-woman seems to be the logical conclusion to the film,[14] *Freaks* has a brief coda whose only purpose seems to be the recuperation of audience sympathy for Hans. In the coda, Phroso and Venus bring Frieda to see Hans. Hans, who has been a recluse since leaving the circus, does not wish to see his old friends; but Phroso and Venus contrive to enter and to leave Frieda with him. "Please go away," Hans tells them, "I can see no one." "But Hans," Frieda tells the now-sobbing midget, "You tried to stop them. It was only the poison you wanted. It wasn't your fault."

Besides providing a romantic ending (Hans and Frieda are together again) to an otherwise grim film, the coda serves to remove responsibility for Cleo's condition from Hans. But it also serves to establish Hans as another victim of the freaks' revenge. Completely broken by the events he seems to have unleashed, Hans now can bring himself to see no one. Hidden away, he is even more isolated from the "normal" world than he was in the circus. And it is hard not to see this all as somehow Cleo's fault. She is the one, after all, who encouraged his attentions, who gave him "ideas"—first to send her gifts and later to marry her; and she's the one who tried to poison him.

In fact, the film's ending can be read as the logical conclusion to Hans's relationship with Cleo. For, in true horror-victim fashion, Hans seems to be completely feminized in this scene. While Phroso and Venus's tiptoed exit—complete with pokes in the side and broad winks to one another—leads the audience to expect to see the midgets in a passionate embrace, the final shot of the film shows a completely unmanned Hans sobbing in Frieda's arms. And it is the unmanning of Hans—the divestment of both his money and his sexual pride—that Cleo apparently has in mind all along. From the beginning of their relationship, Cleo seems to have mounted a campaign of sexual humiliation against Hans. "Are you laughing at me?" Hans asks Cleo when she first attracts his attention. And it is Hans's sexual humiliation that Frieda tries to prevent when she goes to see Cleo in her wagon. "Everybody's laughing," she tells Cleo, "because he's in love mit you. . . . I know you just make fun, but Hans, he does not know this. If he finds out, never again will he be happy."

Despite Frieda's attempts to comfort Hans with the thought that Cleo's tragedy was not his fault, one has the impression that the *real* cause of Hans's depression at the end of the film is the collapse of the marriage itself. For Hans finally did find out that Cleo was just making fun. "I don't blame you, Cleo," he tells her on their wedding night, "I should have known you would only laugh at me." And having found out, Hans—as Frieda predicted—can never again be happy.

The coda, then, attempts to undo some of the revenge sequence's impact. Having been forced—almost against its desire—to see the freaks as monsters, the audience can return at the end to its earlier vision of Hans as Cleo's victim. It is significant, though, that such a return can be effected only through the complete feminization and infantilization of Hans. As the camera rests on Frieda and Hans at the film's end, Cleo's earlier taunt (that Hans was a "baby," not a man) seems to have been realized. Having failed in his efforts "to be a man" (i.e., to win Cleo's respect and to control her punishment), Hans is recast at the end as Frieda's "baby." Sobbing in his fiancée's arms, he seems to be destined for maternal rather than sexual love.

Freaks remains a troubling film to watch largely because of its own internal demonization of the freaks and because of the demands it makes on the audience (first we sympathize with the freaks, then with their victims, then with the freaks again). But equally troubling are the misogyny and gynophobia that run throughout the film. From the opening barker's speech— "Friends, she was once a beautiful woman"—to the revelation of the chicken-woman, the film's real topic seems to be "dames" who "squeal when [they] . . . get what's coming to [them]."[15] And it is the punishment of one such "dame," Cleopatra, that I wish to reconsider here.

On one level, there is an element of poetic justice in Cleo's final transformation. Having previously refused to become "one of us" symbolically during the wedding banquet scene, Cleo is literally transformed into a freak as punishment for her arrogance and for her betrayal of one of the freaks. But there is also a strong sexual component here. Not only did Cleo plot to kill her husband, she sexually humiliated him in front of all his friends. Kissing Hercules passionately at the wedding banquet, insulting the wedding guests, and, finally, symbolically unmanning Hans (with the piggyback ride around the table), Cleo emerges here as the quintessential transgressive woman, and her mutilation appears as an atavistic enactment of the punitive scarring visited upon adulteresses in certain preindustrial tribes. The goal is to ruin her looks so that she cannot attract other men. As in any ritual designed to bring female sexuality under control, the rape imagery in the revenge sequence is strong. When Hans demands in the wagon that Cleo turn over her little black bottle of poison, one of his friends dramatically opens a switchblade. In the hands of the midget, the knife looks enormous; the spring action of the weapon combined with its piercing, penetrating function seem perhaps too obvious a phallic symbol for Hans's assumption of authority over his wife. Later, in the chase scene, everyone—even the pinheads—is armed with some kind of phallic weapon.

Interestingly, Cleo alone is mutilated in *Freaks*. As J. Hoberman and Jonathan Rosenbaum point out, the story's original ending called for the castration of Hercules, as well as for Cleopatra's mutilation.[16] Originally, both of the lovers were to be treated with sexual brutality—essentially, to be "neutered." The transformation of Hercules' punishment from castration to swift capital punishment (one of the midgets throws a knife into Hercules' back) is just one of the elements that is troubling here. For it is not really certain that Hercules is being "punished" at all. When the midget throws his knife into the strongman's back, Hercules is in the process of strangling Phroso. The knife attack is, then, as much an expedient means of saving Phroso's life as it is punishment for the crimes that Hercules committed against the freaks.

If—as the original ending for *Freaks* would suggest—mutilation and castration are the appropriate penalties for sexual transgression, then Cleo takes the punishment for both herself and Hercules. Her mutilation stands in for *two* violent and disfiguring acts: her own symbolic rape and Hercules' castration as well. In that way, Cleo may be said to serve the same symbolic function that Carol J. Clover maintains the female victim in contemporary slasher films always serves. As her body symbolically becomes the site for Hercules' punishment as well as her own, Cleo becomes the figure onto which the male experience of castration may be quite literally displaced.[17]

But Cleo's punishment symbolizes a kind of female castration as well. For if Cleo is, as I argued earlier, a monstrous figure, much of her monstrosity derives from her assumption of male prerogatives and roles. It is Cleo who takes the sexual initiative with both Hans and Hercules ("So that's how it is," she tells the strongman after she calls him to her wagon, "You have to be called.") It is Cleo who devises the plan to kill Hans and avail herself of his money. And it is Cleo who takes responsibility for carrying the plan out. Physically stronger than anyone in the circus except Hercules,[18] Cleo's very physiognomy establishes her as an androgynous creature. As Ivan Butler describes her, she is "tall, blonde, almost aggressively vital.... One critic described her performance as 'voracious,' and there is indeed at times a nasty feeling that at the back of her mind is an obscene desire to sink her teeth into the midget and gobble him up."[19] Certainly, she physically dominates Hans. Carrying him piggyback around the banquet table, she asserts her physical strength and humiliates him in front of his friends. Carrying him to his own wagon when he is ill, she reinforces his position as feminized victim.

Cleo's sexual criminality is compounded, then, by the masculine codes she so readily assumes. Not only does she betray Hans in standard femme fatale fashion, she also overtly usurps his position of physical and emotional dominance. Demonstrating that she is a better man than Hans will ever be, Cleo becomes what Susan Lurie would designate a "phallic woman."[20] And, as such, she must literally be "cut down to size" by her husband and his friends.

Cleo's mutilation—her punishment for transgressing certain sexual and gender limits—is the culminating event in a film obsessed with the meaning of physical difference. In fact, its presence here serves to highlight the degree to which *Freaks'* obsession with physical difference can also be read as an obsession with gender difference. The film repeatedly raises gender issues and questions the basis of gender assignment and identity. The silence that falls over the performers whenever the half-woman, half-man Josephine/Joseph walks by, the accouchement of the bearded lady, and Hans's struggle to be recognized as a "man" are all indications of the way in which "freakishness" in this film seems inevitably to involve gender duality or confusion. Even the performers associated with the freaks are often cast in sexually ambiguous roles. Rosco, the stutterer who performs with Hercules, dresses as a Roman lady for his act. And Phroso the clown refers to an unspecified "operation" in one of his early conversations with Venus.[21]

But if Cleo's mutilation is the culminating event in a film obsessed with gender confusion and duality, it is also the culminating event in a film haunted by misogyny. Punished for betraying Hans and for transgressing her gender/sexual role, Cleo emerges as the "*most amazing*, the *most* astounding living monstrosity of all time." She emerges as the quintessential example of what Phroso designates as essential femininity: At the hands of the freaks she becomes one of those "dames" who "squeal when [they] . . . get what's coming to [them]."

I realize I have raised more questions about the function of gender in *Freaks* than I have been able to answer here. But identifying provocative patterns and raising questions about latent material may be the only possible way to analyze a horror film that, as Raymond Durgnat maintains, "at every turn evokes the name of Buñuel."[22] Despite its apparently tidy structure—framing device plus story plus framing device plus coda—*Freaks* resists the kind of analysis that most horror films invite. The film, as I have tried to show, does not really establish itself as a horror film until the freaks begin stalking Cleo—almost two-thirds of the way through the movie. And playing with our very notions of what constitutes freakishness and monstrosity, the film demands a complicated viewer response that, as Durgnat argues, fits our expectations of avant-garde cinema more than it does our expectations of horror.

It is in its treatment of sexuality and gender, however, that the film becomes most difficult to pin down. Cleo functions both as an essentialized female who fills the role that Phroso assigns to *all* women near the beginning of the film (dames who squeal when they get what's coming to them), and as an androgynous character who looks like a woman and performs like a man. Furthermore, even her sexual motivation appears to be fluid here. For all of her femme fatale dealings with both Hans and Hercules, Cleo gives strong indications that at least her *initial* advances towards Hans may be motivated more by her antagonism toward Frieda than by the joke she wishes to play on Frieda's fiancé. It is Frieda's eye she catches when she makes her first pass at Hans. And, immediately after flirting with him, she approaches the diminutive woman seated on horseback and fluffs up her ballet skirt. "Nice, nice," she says. ("Don't, don't," Frieda replies). Later she torments Frieda by thanking Hans for the gifts he has sent her. "By me, she has no shame," Frieda tells Venus. "*Always when I can hear it* she says to him, 'thanks, my darling, for this and thanks, my darling, for that' " [emphasis mine]. Finally, Cleo only decides to marry Hans after Frieda comes to her wagon and begs her to stop toying with his affections.

There are, then, two erotic triangles at play in *Freaks*. There is the Cleo-Hans-Hercules configuration, the triangle that explodes into open conflict at Hans and Cleo's wedding banquet. But there is also the less obvious triangle of Cleo-Hans-Frieda, a triangle that is just as fraught with psychological turmoil and intensity. What interests me here is the power model implied by the Cleo-Hans-Frieda triad. As René Girard argues in his book *Deceit, Desire, and the Novel*,[23] there are always two active members of an erotic triangle (the rivals), and it is their relationship that structures the dynamics of power within the threesome. As Eve Kosofsky Sedgwick points out, this observation has enormous implications for the sexual dynamics that take place within the ménage. "What is most interesting in his [Girard's] study," she writes "is its insistence that, in any erotic rivalry, the bond that links the two rivals is as intense and potent as the bond that links either of the rivals to the beloved: that the bonds of 'rivalry' and 'love,' differently as they are experienced, are equally powerful and in many senses equivalent."[24] Sedgwick uses this observation to analyze the ways in which depictions of the traditional erotic triangle (two men and one woman) introduce the notion of male homosocial desire into Western literature. What she does not consider—and what *Freaks* only hints at—is the degree to which female *gynosocial* desire (in this case Cleo's bond with Frieda) may be viewed as profoundly threatening and disruptive to a system in which, as Sedgwick points out, "sexuality functions as a signifier for power relations."[25]

Claude Lévi-Strauss once postulated that the exchange of women (through marriage and sexual liaisons) forms the basis of patriarchal sexual economy and, by extension, of patriarchal society itself. "The total relationship of exchange which constitutes marriage is not established between a man and a woman," he writes, "but between two groups of men [the woman's kin and the kin of her prospective husband], and the woman figures only as one of the objects in the exchange, not as one of the partners."[26] The point of such an exchange is to cement liaisons between different kinship units; the woman, in this model, becomes the conduit for an alliance between men. Girard, of course, draws heavily on Lévi-Strauss's cultural paradigm to bolster his argument about the nature of adulterous liaisons. And, as Sedgwick demonstrates, the classic Girardian threesome—two men vying for one woman—does nothing to alter Lévi-Strauss's model. If anything, it reinforces the basis of the sexual economy, as the circulation of the woman causes the men—in both Sedgwick's and Girard's view—to forge a powerful relationship to one another. But when a man becomes the object of rivalry between two women and, hence, is designated as a commodity of sexual exchange, the male basis for power becomes seriously compromised. Here, the important relationship, the *active* relationship, is the one that obtains between the two women rivals. The man is merely the " 'conduit of a relationship' in which the true *partner*" is a woman.[27]

In the microcosmic world of the circus, then, Cleo functions as a disruptive force on two counts. Not only does she refuse to keep the social place assigned to her by the dominant sexual economy, but she also builds relationships that seem to threaten the very existence of the patriarchal sexual economy itself. To put it another way, Cleo is not merely struggling for position in a world order whose legitimacy she recognizes. She is behaving in a way that usurps the very basis of male power.[28] And it is for the role she plays in compromising the foundation of male dominance that Cleo ultimately must be reduced to a hen.

Oddly, it is the freaks in the film—those most associated with mixed and confused gender identities—who become, in this context at least, the enforcers of a patriarchal social order that has spurned and marginalized them. Chasing Cleo through the woods and mutilating her, they seem unwittingly to become the instruments of the dominant society's revenge as well as the enforcers of the "code of the freaks." That is perhaps the most troubling dimension of a film that continually defies the very viewer expectations it works so hard to elicit. But in ultimately identifying the freaks' revenge with the enforcement of patriarchal sexual hegemony, *Freaks* also introduces a theme that Wood has identified as standard in horror: It illustrates the basic connection that always exists between the monster and the "normal" world (s)he menaces.[29] For it is precisely when the freaks turn monstrous—when they seem to step outside the bounds of normal social constraints—that they become enforcers of patriarchal convention. It is when they become monstrous that they most clearly function—within the dominant society—as one of us.

NOTES

I would like to thank William Nestrick, who first suggested that I write on *Freaks,* and whose help and suggestions were crucial to the development of this chapter. I would also like to thank Carol J. Clover, Michael Lucey, Skip Hawkins, and Richard Hutson for their valuable critiques of an earlier version of this chapter, and for their encouragement.

1. Phil Hardy, Tom Milne, and Paul Willemen, *The Encyclopedia of Horror Movies* (New York: Harper and Row, 1986), 51.

2. This is the term that Hans uses throughout the film to describe Cleopatra. "She is the most beautiful big woman I ever saw," he tells his fiancée Frieda at the beginning of the film.

3. See, e.g., "Not for Children," *New Yorker,* 16 July 1932, 45; and "The Circus Side Show," *New York Times,* 9 July 1932, 7.

4. I have decided to use the word "freaks" despite—or perhaps because of—its derogatory connotations. Whether or not physically challenged people are "freaks" is, after all, one of the crucial questions posed by the film; and it is, I believe, the central issue involved in the film's suppression.

5. "The Circus Side Show," 7.

6. The reviewer's discomfort with the use of real freaks in the film is obvious here. One year after *Freaks* was made, *King Kong*—surely the most fantastic love story of all time—was released to rave reviews. See *Variety,* 12 July 1932, n.p.

7. "Freaks," *Time,* 18 April 1932, 17.

8. The ad appeared in *New York Times,* 9 July 1932, 7.

9. Leslie Fiedler, *Freaks: Myths and Images of the Secret Self* (New York: Simon and Schuster, 1978), 296.

10. Program note in the Pacific Film Archive series Received Images: A Reading of Disability in Cinema, University Art Museum and Pacific Film Archive *Calendar,* July 1990, University of California at Berkeley, © Regents of the University of California.

11. Ibid.

12. Ivan Butler, *Horror in the Cinema,* 2d rev. ed. (London: A. S. Zwemmer; New York: A. S. Barnes, 1970), 65.

13. For Wood, horror films "are progressive precisely to the degree that they refuse to be satisfied with . . . [the] simple designation of the monster as evil." See Robin Wood, *Hollywood from Vietnam to Reagan* (New York: Columbia University Press, 1986), 192.

14. In terms of both structure and plot, the shot of the chicken-woman seems like an appropriate place to end. Structurally, it parallels the barker's speech that opens the film and completes the opening sequence's missing shot. Thematically, it unveils the monster that the audience has been waiting to see.

15. Early in the film, Venus leaves the strongman, Hercules, with whom she had been living. As she carries her things back to her own wagon, she sees Phroso taking off his makeup. Realizing that he has heard the entirety of her argument with Hercules, Venus lashes out at Phroso. "Women are funny, ain't they?" she says sarcastically. Phroso follows Venus back to her wagon, where he replies, "You dames are all alike . . . how you squeal when you get what's coming to you."

16. J. Hoberman and Jonathan Rosenbaum, *Midnight Movies* (New York: Da Capo, 1983), 297.

17. See Carol J. Clover, *Men, Women and Chainsaws: Gender in the Modern Horror Film* (Princeton: Princeton University Press, 1992), 50–53.

18. In fact, Cleo's preference for men who can physically dominate her is one of the few traditional female codes she follows.

19. Butler, *Horror in the Cinema,* 66.

20. See Susan Lurie, "Pornography and the Dread of Woman," in *Take Back the Night,* ed. Susan Lederer (New York: William Morrow, 1980); and Barbara Creed, *The Monstrous Feminine: Film, Feminism and Psychoanalysis* (London: Routledge, 1993).

21. At the end of his argument with Venus, Phroso advises her not to start drinking. "Say, you're a pretty good kid," she tells him. "You're darn right I am," he replies. "You should have caught me before my operation." Given the sexual tenor of the scene, the audience is led to see the operation as somehow sexual—an old war injury, like the one suffered by the narrator of *The Sun Also Rises,* perhaps?

22. Raymond Durgnat, "Freaks," *Films and Filming* 9, no. 1 (August 1963): 23.

23. René Girard, *Deceit, Desire, and the Novel: Self and Other in Literary Structure*, trans. Yvonne Freccero (Baltimore: Johns Hopkins University Press, 1972).

24. Eve Kosofsky Sedgwick, *Between Men: English Literature and Male Homosocial Desire* (New York: Columbia University Press, 1985), 21.

25. Ibid., 7.

26. Claude Lévi-Strauss, *The Elementary Structures of Kinship* (Boston: Beacon Press, 1969), 115; quoted in Sedgwick, *Between Men*, 26.

27. Sedgwick, *Between Men*, 26

28. This is very complicated because Cleo also functions as an object of sexual exchange between Hercules and Hans.

29. See Robin Wood, "Return of the Repressed," *Film Comment*, July-August 1978, 26.

NINETEEN

An American Tail: Freaks, Gender, and the Incorporation of History in Katherine Dunn's *Geek Love*

RACHEL ADAMS

One is not born, but rather becomes, a woman.
—SIMONE DE BEAUVOIR, *The Second Sex*, 1952[1]

Organisms are not born, but they are made.
—DONNA HARAWAY, "The Promises of Monsters," 1992[2]

A true freak cannot be made. A true freak must be born.
—KATHERINE DUNN, *Geek Love*, 1989[3]

These epigraphs reflect an ongoing preoccupation within feminist theory with how best to explain women's difference. Simone de Beauvoir's once-revolutionary statement acknowledges that gender is not inherently connected to biology, but rather is assumed through the repetition of a complex and arbitrary system of practices. Expanding Beauvoir's claim, Donna Haraway asserts not only that gender is a discourse mapped onto the body, but that our experience of the body itself materializes only through the various social interactions that define its boundaries. In each critic's constructivist understanding, femininity emerges as an oppressive discourse that must be understood and rescripted.

In contrast, Olympia Binewski, the narrator and protagonist of Katherine Dunn's 1989 novel *Geek Love*, emphasizes essential bodily difference as a determining factor in her social identity: one does not become a freak, but rather is born one. Within the context of the novel, which chronicles the downfall of a family of carnival freaks deliberately created by Lillian and Al Binewski through exposure to radiation and the massive ingestion of drugs, Olympia's essentialism is "false"; the "masterpiece" of her differently shaped body is not natural but the product of her parents' careful and intentional experimentation. However, within the context of the scene, in which the unfortunate dwarf is lifted onstage at a strip club as the men in the audience laugh and jeer, her insistence on the value of authentic bodily difference is a legitimate defense against humiliation. Although Olympia's assertion seems to counteract the constructivist ideology of the novel, this inconsistency ultimately indicates that claims about identity are always context-specific. As Diana Fuss has argued, the charge of essentialism so frequently leveled against theories of identity needs to be tempered by an understanding of the context and consequences of that essentialism: "The question we should be asking is not 'is this text essentialist (and therefore "bad")?' but rather, 'if this text is essentialist, *what motivates its deployment?*' "[4] Countering poststructuralism's blanket critique of identity politics, Fuss advocates a consideration of "the political investments of the subject's complex positioning in a particular social field."[5] At various moments *Geek Love* invokes both essentialist and constructivist models of identity, creating a tension that, on the one hand, demonstrates that prejudices against bodily difference are culturally produced, and on the other, recognizes the materiality of the body as it experiences pain or becomes the subject of violence or ridicule. I read the novel's vacillation between essentialist and constructivist understandings of the body not as a logistical inconsistency, but as paradigmatic of how Americans attempt to manage the problem of bodily difference that has persistently troubled the nation's social and legal structure.

This problem is generated by the inability of constitutional law—which guarantees the abstract equality of all citizens—to protect the rights of those who *look different*. Political and social theorists have repeatedly demonstrated the failure of the American legal system to recognize difference in cases involving affirmative action, fetal rights, and sexual harassment where the blindness of the law to race and gender obstructs the rights of the injured party.[6] In such cases concepts crucial to American national identity, such as individual merit, blind justice, and abstract standards, ignore the historical conditions that have shaped the identities of marginalized people or, as Patricia Williams puts it in her discussion of affirmative action, "a refusal to talk about the past disguises a refusal to talk about the present."[7] Williams posits historical understanding as a remedy to institutional blindness by addressing the past experiences of inequality that have shaped the current interests, abilities, and beliefs of marginalized groups. *Geek Love* is a text that explores the necessity of situating the problem of difference and equality within history. Focusing relentlessly on the physical body as a site of oppression, the novel illustrates what Michel Foucault has called the "microphysics of power," which situate domination deep in the ritualized practices of everyday life,[8] but it also posits the body firmly anchored within history as a site for the reclamation of agency.

The relationship between history and the body becomes increasingly fraught as technology develops unprecedented capabilities for altering the physical form that call into question the limits of knowledge and the boundaries of the human body. *Geek Love* critiques institutions that endorse bodily transformation as a means of escaping from history and suggests instead that this new plasticity of the body must be informed by a knowledge of one's personal past and its position within local and national history. In *Geek Love*, however, history, like bodies, is malleable, and its significance shifts depending on the context of its retelling. Faced with potentially limitless possibilities, the novel manifests an anxiety—shared by many critics of postmodernism—about boundaries and limitations. Without recourse to the natural, who is to say when science should stop trying to change the body's shape and genetic makeup? And without master narratives that signal the Truth, how can we maintain a sense of the significance of past events?

In *Geek Love*, the freak show becomes the locus for this anxiety about the malleability of bodies and history. The freak's partial identity, her inability to fit into fixed categories of definition, is what designates her as a human oddity worthy of display for profit. In the past, individuals born with bodily differences, such as Siamese twins, dwarfs and midgets, or the human torso, would premise their sideshow exhibits on displays of their normality, which demonstrated their ability to accomplish everyday tasks with ease, to think intelligently, and to engage in respectable relationships with others.[9] Exhibits focused on the performer's healthy relationship with a spouse, ability to bear children, and acceptance into polite society as part of her freakishness. For example, the human torso Prince Randian was celebrated for his ability to roll a cigarette and light it with his mouth, and the marriage of the Siamese twins Chang and Eng to two normal sisters was widely publicized as proof of their remarkable condition. In contrast, those performers who were not born true freaks, such as the snake charmer, the savage, the strongman, or the tattooed person, emphasized their *difference* from the average person. In either case, the exhibit was premised on the deviance of the freak's body; its titillating transgression of boundaries—savage/human, child/adult, man/woman, self/other—called into question the audience's preconceived notions of the possibilities and limitations of the human body.

In unsettling the stable boundaries of the human body, the freak show also throws into crisis fixed ideas about genealogy and history. The "true life" pamphlets that frequently accompanied exhibits provided a biographical description of the subject, his or her physical oddities, "official" endorsements of authenticity by doctors and scientists, and, in more exotic cases, descriptions of the geography and native people of the freak's country of origin, which were often grossly exaggerated or patently untrue. According to Robert Bogdan, "Some pamphlets were forty and more pages long, going on in elaborate, fraudulent detail about the trek through the jungle that resulted in finding the lost tribe of which the exhibit was a member—when in fact the person was born and raised in New Jersey."[10] The very identity of the freak is thus premised on the invention of a history that will draw maximum crowds and profit. If some biographies embellished the freak's identity by inventing exotic, faraway origins, others displayed an anxiety about genealogy, insisting on the normality of the freak's parents and offspring. Such pamphlets emphasized the freak's ability to produce normal, healthy offspring, as if to insure the audience of the isolated deviance of the freak's body against an anxiety about the generation of a race of similarly freakish progeny. Both those biographies that claimed affiliation with exotic tribes and those that described their subjects as isolated anomalies reflect an anxiety about the freak's place in history and work to situate her outside of, or as a bizarre and impotent anomaly in, mainstream American life.

Although the freak show has all but vanished from American culture, the questions it raises about the significance and definition of the human body have multiplied as science develops unprecedented capabilities for understanding, penetrating, and restructuring the inner and outer spaces of the body. As *Geek Love* so brilliantly demonstrates, both the freak show and new surgical technologies converge in their obsession with sexuality, production, and reproduction. The novel critiques those institutions that focus on the body with the ostensible goal of bettering human life, but ultimately offer only fetishized models of beauty and perfection that endorse bodily transformation as a means of escaping from history. Medical technology, which promises improved health and longevity, becomes instead a means of normalizing the body, of producing replicants of a single, idealized model. The ability to replicate bodies and body parts—now possible through cosmetic surgery, with more sophisticated processes such as cloning projected in the near future—combined with new reproductive technologies that allow sex without reproduction, in vitro fertilization, fertility treatments, and surrogate pregnancy focus the crisis of definition most prominently on the female body.[11]

In *Geek Love* the tension between production and reproduction, procreation and replication, is most tellingly illustrated in the conflict over whether Olympia's estranged daughter Miranda will choose to keep her tail or have it surgically removed. The conflict over Miranda's tail is the central structuring device of the narrative (the tale), the occasion for repeated movement between accounts of the present and memories of or documented information about the past. A vestigial remnant that recalls the human body's articulation with the natural and animal worlds, as well as Miranda's connection to her own bizarre familial past, the tail thematizes the necessity of thinking about bodily difference within the context of personal and collective history.

AN AMERICAN TAIL

Early in the novel, Miranda must choose whether to keep her tail, which she displays for profit by dancing naked at the Glass House, or to take the large sum of money the wealthy heiress Mary Lick offers her to have it removed. By leaving Miranda the story of her past, Olympia provides a third choice: to keep her tail but to understand it as the product of a family history rather than simply as a fetishized object of male desire. This choice is paradigmatic of the novel's insistence on the historical nature of embodied identity. Knowing your own history becomes a means of negotiating between institutions that attempt to impose an official version of identity and those that seek to erase the past altogether. For Michel de Certeau, the retelling of officially sanctioned histories in "ordinary language" allows for the insertion of "the insignificant detail" that "makes the commonplace produce other effects."[12] The retelling of stories, which enables the ordinary person to make meaning out of official narratives, may become an empowering tactic for asserting agency and staking a claim in the workings of large and often impersonal cultural institutions. In the face of institutions that seek to classify them as disabled, monstrous, or perverse, the freaks in *Geek Love* recount their past as a means of affirming their unique form of embodiment and situating their family history within the context of American national identity.

The novel's intervention in American historiography focuses on the freak show, a form of entertainment distinctly associated with the low, the spectacular, and the mass culture audience, as it traces the freaks' experiences and subjectivities as they move through the small towns, highways, shopping malls, and supermarkets that make up the American landscape. Significantly, the Binewski children's origins are connected to a date of national victory; they derive ceaseless delight from the story of how their parents met on a Fourth of July weekend when Lillian Hinchcliff, "a water-cool aristocrat from the fastidious side of Boston's Beacon Hill," gets the handsome Aloysius Binewski out of a pinch by agreeing to geek for him, an outrageous and profane juxtaposition of blue-blooded Americana with the low and spectacular that is characteristic of the novel. Aloysius, the Binewski patriarch, "was a standard-issue Yankee, set on self-determination and independence." A self-made man who brings the carnival success through the Franklinesque virtues of thrift and ingenuity, Aloysius conceives of the ingenuous plan of breeding his own freak show because, as Lillian often remarks, "What greater gift could you offer your children than an inherent ability to earn a living just by being themselves?" (7). Recognizing the significant relationship between the body and the ability to generate income, the Binewskis are excellent interpreters of the capitalist system that constructs the body as a commodity.

The Binewskis solidify their children's sense of identity through the retelling of family history, which cements their connection to one another through a shared extraordinary past reflected in their extraordinary bodies. But in spite of their affirmation of familial bonds and indisputable American patriotism, the Binewskis are unable to maintain their sense of place within a larger national context that would provide them with a historical understanding of the freakish body. Significantly, even the youthful Lil is unable to connect her own local experience to historical events; she clearly remembers July 3rd as the date when she saved Al, yet she muses, "it was during a war, darlings ... I forget which one precisely" (4). This forgetting of national events presages Lil's eventual drug-induced oblivion, which causes her to believe she is completely alone in the house where she lives with both her daughter and granddaughter. Unable to accept her "failures," the freakish offspring who died in utero or soon after birth, Lil keeps them stored in jars of formaldehyde that she visits each day. Refusing to mourn their deaths, she engages in the melancholic practice of obsessively polishing their jars. The end of *Geek Love,* which reveals the novel as an extended act of mourning through the retelling of history, will provide an alternative to Lil's willed ignorance of the past.[13]

Similarly, Arty, the eldest Binewski son, has a strong sense of interpersonal relationships but little understanding of context. As Norval Sanderson, a journalist who keeps records of the carnival's proceedings, writes: "National and international politics are outside [Arty's] experience and reading. Municipal power relationships, however, are familiar tools to him. He has no real grasp of history—seems to have picked up drifts from his reading—but he is a gifted analyst of personality and motivation" (190). Devoid of any conception of the larger operations of power or history, Arty is a skilled manipulator of the local and specific, a quality that brings him temporary success but eventually causes his downfall, a question to which I return in my discussion of the Arturan cult.

Of course, this disregard for national politics and history may have to do with the minimal role that marginalized people have been accorded in the making of such structures. As feminists and scholars of color have long pointed out, the creation of history has always been the prerogative of the privileged white male, while women and other marginalized groups are persistently associated with the low, the bodily, and the everyday. In its recuperation of the other in American culture, the novel focuses incessantly on bodily difference in explicit and magnificent detail to demonstrate that an alternative American history would necessarily examine the way that official narratives work to occlude the subjection of deviant bodies. *Geek Love* delineates the way that freaks are able to manipulate their excess embodiment for the purposes of profit and personal empowerment. While outside the carnival gates bodily difference is confronted with stares of pity and disgust, the freaks create a space where they voluntarily display their bodies as spectacles for the viewing pleasure of "norms," who they condescendingly describe as "assembly-line items" (282), "engulfed by a terror of their own ordinariness" (223). This pride comes from the kind of essentialism expressed in Olympia's statement: "A true freak cannot be made. A true freak must be born." However, with Arty's rise to power the freaks become unable to situate their claims to authenticity within history and instead focus on turning their unique bodies into commodities. This kind of bodily authenticity, which involves replication rather than reproduction, increasingly serves the ends of men while proving harmful and disempowering to the female freak.

"it's the Era of Freakiness!": The Cult of the Body

While a history of marginalized people would need to focus on the body in pain and as the subject of violence, disembodiment has typically been a privilege accorded to those who are wealthy and powerful enough literally to "forget" their fleshly origins. Lauren Berlant argues that within a liberal democracy, disembodiment is the prerogative of certain privileged citizens: "The white, male body is the relay to legitimation, but even more than that, the power to suppress that body, to cover its tracks and traces, is the sign of real authority, according to Constitutional fashion." Those who do not embody this normative ideal because of race or gender experience a "surplus corporeality" where the "body is not abstract, but hyper-embodied, an obstacle and not a vehicle to public pleasure and power." [14] This ideal of disembodiment materializes in the cult that evolves around Arty, born with flippers instead of arms and legs, who capitalizes on the success of his sideshow act by inducing his followers to give up all of their money and work for the privilege of gradually having their arms and legs amputated in his image. Historically, religious cults in America have encouraged extreme bodily deprivation in order to break down the will and reach spiritual insight. The Arturan cult, however, like the contemporary "cult of the body," has new technologies at hand that go beyond simple deprivation in their ability to penetrate and reconfigure both the interior and exterior of the body itself. Ironically, while the cult claims to offer the privilege of *disembodiment* through literal means—the amputation of limbs—it actually approximates numerous contemporary cultural institutions that *fetishize the body,* such as cosmetic surgery, bodybuilding, and the diet industry. The partnership of the skilled surgeon Doc Phyllis and the psychic Fortunato—who can enter the patient's brain to eliminate pain and trauma—which enables the bodily mutilations of the Arturans, taps into an anxiety about the ability of advanced medical technologies to alter the contours of the body in unprecedented ways. These invasive technologies combine with the language of self-help, which provides instruction on how to "become happy with your inner self," to create a contradictory discourse about the body that asserts, on the one hand, the capacity for change and perfection, and on the other, its insignificance to personal satisfaction.

Not surprisingly, Arty's first acolyte is Alma Witherspoon, an obese, working-class woman whom he addresses directly during one of his shows: "Can you be happy with the movies and the ads and the clothes in the stores and the doctors and the eyes as you walk down the street all telling you there is something *wrong* with you?" His question recognizes that idealized images of femininity make women feel constant dissatisfaction with their appearance as it is perceived by others. Using the rhetoric of pop psychology, Arty consoles Alma by asserting that these are culturally produced ideals that wrongly conflate virtue and intelligence with physical beauty. He assures her that what she really wants "to know is that you're *all right!* That's what can give you peace!" (178). But in this case, the signifier for being "all right" is remaking oneself in Arty's image: promising a refuge from a world filled with "terrorist attacks, mass murders, disease, divorce, crooked politicians, pollution, war and rumors of war" (231), the cult offers its members a personal means of escape rather than considering the source of their disillusionment in collective or historical structures, hence its motto, "Peace,

Isolation, Purity" (227). While Arty seduces Alma Witherspoon by promising her freedom from a culture where judgments of personal value are made on the basis of physical appearance, he introduces her into a strikingly similar world, where virtue is determined by how closely the initiate approximates yet another bodily ideal. Adopting the rhetoric of advertising, Arty boasts that his cult is a desirable "choice" available to those who can afford the admission fee, but the pretense of free will conceals a constrained situation that offers only the choice of escape, not a means of coping with or changing the world itself.

This form of escapism, which focuses on the body at the expense of more collective, historically informed strategies for change, approximates contemporary "health" industries such as bodybuilding for competition, which offer individual satisfaction through bodily change and endorse an ideology that combines self-help and physical enhancement. Bodybuilding for competition is distinguished from most other forms of strength-enhancing fitness in that, while it gives the individual an appearance of well-being and massive strength, it is in fact dangerously unhealthy and can be fatal. Like the Arturan cult, bodybuilders reject dominant beauty ideals, deliberately making the body a spectacle by taking the culturally valued attributes of strength, fatlessness, tan, and muscle to grotesque excess. Significantly, competitive bodybuilding self-consciously appropriates the discourse of the sideshow: as a recent letter to *Muscular Development* enthused, "It's the era of freakiness! (. . . and there's nothing wrong with freakiness . . . it's the name of the game!)"[15] Likewise, Sam Fussell writes: "It's the Greatest Show on Earth. The bodybuilder comes complete with everything but a velvet restraining rope and castors. To this day, 'freaky' is the highest compliment one bodybuilder can pay another."[16]

Geek Love draws a striking parallel between the fictional cult with its genesis in the sideshow and contemporary institutions such as bodybuilding that are obsessed with defying biology and history to alter the human form beyond the possibilities provided by "nature." Both the bodybuilder and the Arturan believe in the infinite malleability of the human physique. Emphasizing excess, the language of bodybuilding boasts of the ability to create a body larger and more muscular than could occur in the natural world. Bodybuilders and Arturans share a nonessentialist view of the boundaries of the body in which drugs and surgery are necessary products in its recreation.[17] Unlike feminist understandings of an inessential body, which envision an increased acceptance of difference, these cults of the body work toward an idealized final referent. If they signal a radical redefinition of bodily appearance, it is not toward a new acceptance of physical difference and variety, but rather toward replicating a single fetishized ideal. The freakishness of bodybuilders challenges dominant beauty ideals but does not undermine the existence of an idealized shape and size. Likewise, the Arturans can have their limbs removed in an *approximation* of their leader, but Arty remains the true freak, authentic because he was born with bodily difference rather than having to work for it. Because he "has no real grasp of history," Arty seeks to remove bodies from their sociopolitical contexts and fashion new identities for them. However, this solution works only temporarily for a woman like Alma Witherspoon, whose immobile torso is soon "retired" to be replaced by a series of identical acolytes. Like the movies, ads, and medical practitioners he criticizes, Arty's authentic freakishness calls for replication of an idealized model rather than new ways to think about difference.

PRODUCTION, REPRODUCTION, AND THE FEMALE FREAK

Arty's ability to turn his peculiarly formed body into an ideal demonstrates his talent as a manipulator of the local and specific. But if the cult works through the creation of replicants in the image of one, idealized form, then the female body, with its ability to create originals through reproduction, poses a threat to Arty's absolute power.[18] Although the "truth" of the freak may be determined through biological birth, the novel imagines radical forms of sex, conception, and pregnancy that shift received notions of what it means to be a woman and the boundaries of the human body itself. Lil and Al's breeding experiments, the twins' desire for an abortion, and Olympia's artificial insemination all suggest an inessential understanding of the female body and its capacity and desire for reproduction. Because the ability to reproduce freaks, creating difference rather than similarity, calls Arty's regime into crisis, he must maintain complete dominion over the sexual and reproductive activities of each of his sisters.

The Siamese twins, Electra and Iphegenia, threaten Arty because they are able to draw such large audiences, and as they mature, they begin to capitalize on their appeal both onstage and off. Realizing the erotic suggestion of their joined bodies, which play directly into male fantasies of multiple orifices and partners, Elly states matter-of-factly: "You know what the norms really want to ask . . . How do we fuck? That and who, or maybe what. Most guys wonder what it would be like to fuck us. So, I figure, why not capitalize on that curiosity?" (207).[19] While initially Iphy has doubts about relinquishing her virginity—the twins' disagreement suggesting the mixed messages that women receive about sex—after their first experience they willingly offer themselves to those who are able to pay their exorbitant prices, making a profit off of their already objectified condition Their story suggests that if women both inside and outside the carnival gates are treated as sexualized objects, subjected daily to desiring male gazes they cannot avoid, then there is little difference between the twins' performing onstage and off, and their prostitution offers them a means of controlling the uses to which their bodies will be put. As Anne McClintock has argued, depending on the circumstances, prostitution can be an empowering choice for women who otherwise would have little control over their bodies, sexuality, or working conditions.[20]

Precisely because the twins' prostitution guarantees them a degree of autonomy, the enraged Arty unceremoniously "gives" them to the Bag Man "just to fuck" (245). By "giving" his sisters away, Arty reaffirms their status as objects of exchange. After forcefully preventing them from aborting the resulting pregnancy, he has Elly, the more dominant and aggressive twin, lobotomized, leaving Iphy to care for both the fetus and the limp torso of her sister. Norval Sanderson describes "the pale Iphy in her painful progress down the row toward the Chute with her swollen belly pulling her forward while she struggles to balance the flabby monster that sprouts from her waist" (272–73). Her pathetic attempts to support the senseless torso of her sister call attention to the parasitic nature of unwanted pregnancy: like the passive and drooling Elly, the fetus is another alien "monster" dependent upon the body of the mother. In contrast with the "choice" offered by the Arturan cult, in this sequence the novel makes its most explicit endorsement for the protection of women's right to make decisions about sex, pregnancy, and reproduction. Rather than simply affirming the necessity of "choice"—which disturbingly participates in the logic of the Arturans—Geek Love shifts the grounds of the abortion debate to reveal the larger questions obscured by the rhetoric of pro-life/pro-choice. Elly's lobotomy and unwanted pregnancy vividly illustrate the ways in which legal intervention in questions of reproduction, motherhood, and fetal rights can deny the subjectivity and bodily integrity of pregnant women.[21] The final conflict between the twins represents the only possible outcome for the persistent denial of bodily integrity: the body that turns on itself as the two subjectivities violently enact their divided loyalties.

Because of their beauty and exotic body the twins experience in extreme form many of the same obstacles as "norm" women. Olympia's extreme ugliness, however, excludes her from the patriarchal system of exchange at work within the novel. As Luce Irigaray has described it in "Women on the Market," women living under patriarchal capitalism become like commodities, objects of exchange by and for men. As such, women have no inherent value; their worth is determined solely through their appeal to men: "in order for a product—a woman?—to have value, two men, at least, have to invest (in) her."[22] If this is the case with the twins, who so accurately mirror male fantasies and spend their lives moving from one site of domination to another, then what becomes of the woman who is so ugly that she is desired by no one?

Olympia's extreme ugliness renders her, in effect, a worthless commodity. She is the only woman in the novel who remains unattached to any partner, a position that grants her an agency unavailable to other women, but also causes her profound isolation and loneliness. As Alma Witherspoon would attest, a culture obsessed with images of beauty leaves little room for the empowerment of ugly women. Eve Kosofsky Sedgwick makes a similar argument about the fat woman in a clothing store who has the economic means to make a purchase but receives a message that "your money is not negotiable in this place." Although she has money to spend, she experiences the "precipitation of [her] very body as a kind of cul-de-sac, blockage or clot in the circulation of economic value."[23] Similar to the fat woman, the dwarf is an obstacle in the exchange of commodities and bodies, and Olympia, like Alma, seeks refuge in disembodiment. Yet unlike the Arturans, who seek disembodiment through the amputation of limbs, Olympia assumes a prosthetic identity as a radio personality fittingly called "the Story Lady," which allows her a form of escape from a body that on the street, is met either by pitying stares or averted glances that seek to render her invisible.

Her one positive bodily experience is pregnancy, which she achieves without physical penetration or other intimate human contact. Asking Chick to use his telekinetic powers to move Arty's sperm, "the little wiggly things," into her body, Olympia undergoes a fantastic form of artificial insemination that parallels recent scientific advances that allow for impregnation without intercourse. Like a sperm bank donor, Arty never knows he is the father of the child, and his crass economic pragmatism forces Olympia to give Miranda up when they discover that her only asset is a curly, pink tail, an unmarketable spectacle.

In the case of both the twins and Olympia, pregnancy and reproduction—which signal the ability to generate life, to produce more freaks—threaten Arty's coercive system of replication. If the cult establishes his absolute autonomy through the subjection of others, female freaks hold the possibility of making other freaks that might challenge his authority. As I have argued, the making of freaks is, of course, also the making of history. While Arty attempts to obstruct Olympia's attempts to start a new family, after the carnival comes to a fiery end she works to reestablish a connection to her daughter and to leave her with the story of her own past, a knowledge that can inform the decisions that Miranda makes about her body. Olympia's plea that she keep her tail is less a resort to authentic bodily integrity than a recognition that familiarity with her past might complicate or change what otherwise appear to be endless and inconsequential options.

POSTMODERN PLASTICITY AND THE TECHNO-FREAK

The freaks in *Geek Love*, who simultaneously proclaim their own authenticity and use various technologies to manipulate the body, provide an interesting limit case for questions that arise in an age when science and theory are engaged in a radical redefinition of what it means to be human.[24] Cybernetics, the information superhighway, artificial organs, gene splicing, and other newly developing technologies raise the stakes for ontological and epistemological debates that were once purely speculative. Feminists have focused on the effects these developing technologies, at once promising and extremely dangerous, might have on the female body: fantasies of the infinite malleability of the human form, reproduction without sex, and consumption without labor are potentially liberating or dangerous, depending on their context and consequences. *Geek Love* imagines one nightmare scenario in which the combination of technology and feminism becomes profoundly destructive.

Inspired by the practices of the Arturan cult, Mary Lick takes what Susan Bordo has called "postmodern plasticity" to horrifying extremes by offering disembodiment as a solution to a life where beauty and sexuality are distractions from more important callings. For Bordo, the problem with "postmodern plasticity"—the sense of limitless freedom to alter and correct the contours of the body—is that it embraces normalizing standards of beauty premised on a willful ignorance of the historical inequalities that have been connected to various forms of bodily difference. She writes: "Gradually and surely, a technology that was first aimed at the replacement of malfunctioning parts has generated an industry and an ideology fueled by fantasies of rearranging, transforming, and correcting, an ideology of limitless improvement and change, defying the historicity, the mortality, and indeed, the very materiality of the body."[25] Although "the ideology of limitless improvement" is primarily geared toward the replication of a slender, white, beauty ideal, Mary Lick uses medical science to subvert these normalizing impulses. If patriarchal culture objectifies women by judging their value on the basis of physical appearance, Mary's brand of feminism sees the eradication of the "femaleness" of the female body—by removing breasts and hair, sewing shut the vagina, clitorectomy, and other types of mutilation—as the only solution to gender inequalities. Olympia's discovery that Mary has offered her daughter a large sum of money to have her tail removed, thus beginning a gradual process of disfigurement, necessitates her violent intervention to preserve both tale and tail.

Mary's scopic addiction to "changing people" involves sponsoring surgical mutilations of the female body so that she can watch them taking place and capture them on film for later. A horrifying antidote to the beauty myth, "Mary Lick's purpose is to liberate women who are liable to be exploited by male hungers. These exploitable women are, in Miss Lick's view, the pretty ones. She feels great pity for them" (162). Using her vast wealth, Mary pays promising young women to have their bodies altered so that they are no longer beautiful, thus "liberating" them to pursue advanced professional careers. Imposing her own asexuality onto other women, she dreams of manufacturing a race of professional superwomen who would live alone, caring only for themselves and the furthering of their high-powered careers. In her version of feminism, the body is always a dangerous detraction from more important concerns. By using technology to mar its beauty, she fantasizes that she is liberating women from the distractions of physicality in order to achieve more important goals.

Yet her interventions are not limited to eradicating beauty and the attributes of femininity. Significantly, her first operation is on Carina, "Half black. Half Italian. Poor as shit. A dropout but she tested high in aptitudes" (159). After using acid to mar her beauty, Mary funds Carina's college education and helps her to get a job as a translator. Carina's operation literally burns the skin from her face, erasing the physical markings of her racial identity, while her "education" removes her from her "shit poor" class affiliation. Although it may be problematic to associate race with physical characteristics, the destruction of those features seems a particularly violent and perverse solution to racial inequality, for if Carina's ethnic hybridity and extreme poverty are inscribed upon her body, their erasure signals the intentional obliteration of her history in the service of what one wealthy, white woman perceives as a more rewarding existence. The danger of Mary Lick is not her rejection of an essential, unchanging bodily identity, but rather her need to remake the bodies of underprivileged women in the image of her own desires.

The fatal confrontation between Olympia and Mary Lick occurs in the locker room of a health club, the site of Americans' compensatory search for the perfect body in the face of disillusionment with other, more collective forms of embodiment, such as religious, political, and national identity. Caught in the deadly cloud of sterilizing chemicals Olympia has prepared for her, Mary Lick dies and takes the dwarf along with her. At the end of the novel, a newspaper clipping describing the two women's deaths and a letter from Olympia reveal that the narrative is her way of posthumously bequeathing the Binewski family history to its final descendant. Unlike Lil's melancholic attachment to her dead babies, Olympia's letter accomplishes the work of mourning by working through the trauma of her family's violent death and the loss of her only love, her brother Arty.

Miranda, who has always had an aesthetic attraction to individuals with various bodily deformities as the objects of her medical illustrations, now possesses the history of her own difference. If the men who leer at her and "want to pump her full of baby juice" (18) when she dances nude onstage invest her tail with one set of meanings, her family history provides an alternative. By leaving Miranda's future unresolved, the novel does not attempt to reconcile or evaluate these meanings. This refusal to make evaluative judgments or offer a way out of its relentless horrors may be one reason some reviewers felt dissatisfied with *Geek Love*, dismissing it as pure spectacle overcome by its own perversions. Mary Lick remarks soon before her death, "It's amazing that you and I are so much alike, isn't it?" and Olympia agrees: "She's right. We each appear totally alone in our lives. . . . We choose to seem barren, loveless orphans. We each have a secret family. Miss Lick has her darlings and I have mine. All we've really lacked is someone to tell" (340).

The act of telling is a way for Olympia to memorialize her own death and to commemorate the lives of a family that would not be recognized by mainstream history. In her letter, she bestows a sense of collective identity that Miranda did not previously have: "I can't be sure what the trunk will mean to you, or the news that you aren't alone, that you are one of us" (348). This sentence echoes the climactic "wedding feast" of Tod Browning's 1932 film *Freaks*, in which the tall, beautiful Cleopatra is threatened by a throng of angry freaks who chant that she is "one of us." And indeed, by the end of the film the opportunistic Cleopatra is punished for marrying Hans the midget for his money: inexplicably, through the freaks' violent collective intervention, she becomes "one of us," a squawking, half-woman encased behind bars at the freak show. Like *Geek Love*, the spectacle of her grotesque body, which is suggested at the film's opening but not revealed until the end, becomes the occasion for storytelling that will invest her difference with meaning. As an audience stares open-mouthed at Cleopatra's cage, the barker launches into the film's narrative, which reveals the origins of her misshapen form as a just punishment for her avarice and cruelty. As Mary Russo has argued, the image of Cleopatra's body "remarginalizes the sideshow freaks as commercial oddities who, perhaps, should not be blamed for their inhuman behavior."[26]

Do the film and the novel leave the freak's body—and, significantly, in both cases it is a female freak—invested with purely negative meanings? In *Freaks*, becoming "one of us" is a punishment, while *Geek Love*, although more ambiguous, nonetheless connects Miranda to a history of violence and pain. Both texts move to normalize the freak's shocking body, as the film's epilogue finds Hans and Frieda enjoying a placid bourgeois retirement, and Olympia makes herself invisible by adopting a prosthetic identity. However, her death implies that American culture has not yet made room for an acceptance of physical difference, and the novel's power lies precisely in its refusal to suggest a utopian community that would relieve its readers of an overwhelming sensation of oppression and constraint: if "norms" view freaks as the stuff of nightmares, *Geek Love* seems intent on producing precisely that effect.[27] Both novel and film insist upon the necessity of the past in defining who we are and how we will live in the present. And although Olympia resists an outright condemnation of Mary Lick's behavior, the novel does problematize the use of economic and emotional coercion to induce individuals to undergo physical alteration as a solution to social inequalities. As we develop the technology to effect increasingly radical transformations of the body and more sophisticated forms of prosthetic identity that promise its transcendence, *Geek Love* suggests that history will become more—and not less—important. If we no longer have recourse to nature or essence to make ethical claims about the body, the continual retelling of tales and tails becomes our only means of working through the past to invest our bodies with the weight of history and memory.

NOTES

I am grateful to Maurizia Boscagli for her careful reading and comments on an earlier version of this chapter; to Rosemarie Thomson for her encouragement of many drafts of the present chapter; and to Parker Douglas, Jon Hegglund, Amy Rabbino, Chris Schedler, Kim Stone, and especially to Jon Connolly for their generous and insightful suggestions.

1. Simone de Beauvoir, *The Second Sex*, trans. and ed. H. M. Parshley (New York: Alfred A. Knopf, 1952), 301.

2. Donna Haraway, "The Promises of Monsters: A Regenerative Politics for Inappropriate/d Others," in *Cultural Studies*, ed. Lawrence Grossberg, Cary Nelson, and Paula Treichler (New York: Routledge, 1992), 295–337.

3. Katherine Dunn, *Geek Love* (New York: Warner, 1989), 20. All subsequent references are cited parenthetically in the text.

4. Diana Fuss, *Essentially Speaking* (New York: Routledge, 1989), ix.

5. Ibid., 20.

6. See Patricia J. Williams, *Alchemy of Race and Rights: Diary of a Law Professor* (Cambridge: Harvard University Press, 1991); Lauren Berlant, "America, 'Fat,' the Fetus," *Boundary 2* 21, no. 3 (Fall 1994): 144–95; Susan Bordo, "Are Mothers Persons? Reproductive Rights and the Politics of Subjectivity," in *Unbearable Weight: Women, Western Culture, and the Body* (Berkeley: University of California

Press, 1993), 71–98; Linda Singer, "Reproductive Regulations in the Age of Sexual Epidemic," in *Erotic Welfare: Sexual Theory and Politics in an Age of Epidemic* (New York: Routledge, 1993), 88–99; Iris Young, *Justice and the Politics of Difference* (Princeton: Princeton University Press, 1990).

7. Williams, *Alchemy of Race and Rights*, 104.

8. Michel Foucault, *Discipline and Punish*, trans. Alan Sheridan (New York: Vintage, 1977), 26.

9. Most historical information on sideshows cited here is indebted to Robert Bogdan's *Freak Show: Presenting Human Oddities for Amusement and Profit* (Chicago: University of Chicago Press, 1988).

10. Ibid., 20.

11. Feminist critics attuned to the dangers of new reproductive technologies have argued that opportunities for increased reproductive capacity are typically marketed toward wealthy, white families, while poor and minority women are encouraged to use birth control or permanent sterilization. See, e.g., Bordo, "Are Mothers Persons?"; Linda Singer, "Bodies-Pleasures-Powers," *Erotic Welfare: Sexual Theory and Politics in an Age of Epidemic* (New York: Routledge, 1993), 113–30.

12. Michel de Certeau, *The Practice of Everyday Life*, trans. Steven Rendall (Berkeley: University of California Press, 1984), 89.

13. See Sigmund Freud, "Mourning and Melancholia" (1917), *Standard Edition*, ed. James Strachey (London: Hogarth, 1957), 14:237–58. This concept has more recently been taken up by critics interested in the relationship between mourning and history, individual and collective trauma, such as Carl Gutiérrez-Jones, *Rethinking the Borderlands between Chicano Culture and Legal Discourse* (Berkeley: University of California Press, 1995); Dominic LaCapra, *Representing the Holocaust: History, Theory, Trauma* (Ithaca: Cornell University Press, 1994); Constance Penley, "Spaced Out: Remembering Christa McAuliff," *Camera Obscura* 29 (May 1992): 179–214.

14. Lauren Berlant, "National Brands/National Bodies," in *Comparative American Identities*, ed. Hortense Spillers (New York: Routledge, 1991), 113–14.

15. Don Ross, "Chizevski Bashing Unwarranted," *Muscular Development*, February 1994, 189. This article participates in the ongoing debate over whether the ideal for female bodybuilders should be large size or a more stereotypically feminine shape. As bodybuilding is a sport designed to enhance particularly masculine traits, the standards for female competitors continue to be hotly contested.

16. Sam Fussell, "Bodybuilder Americanus," *Michigan Quarterly* 32, no. 4 (Fall 1993): 578.

17. Describing the process the bodybuilder undergoes to become "a self-willed grotesque," Fussell offers yet another trope on Beauvoir's famous quote: "Bodybuilders are made, not born, and they are years in the making" (ibid., 583).

18. N. Katherine Hayles has read the novel's recurrent focus on reproduction as thematizing postmodern anxiety about the potential of advanced genetic science to alter human DNA codes. Although her analysis highlights the novel's concern with the uneasy relationship between technology and the human body, it surprisingly neglects to connect the anxiety about reproduction with domination of and violence against the female body. "Postmodern Parataxis: Embodied Texts, Weightless Information," *American Literary History* 2, no. 3 (Fall 1990): 394–421.

19 Leslie Fiedler's salacious account of the universal appeal of Siamese twins affirms this male fantasy: "In all ages, joined twins have evoked erotic fantasies in their audience, since they suggest inevitably the possibility of multiple-fornication—or at least the impossibility of sexual privacy." *Freaks: Myths and Images of the Secret Self* (New York: Simon and Schuster, 1978), 206.

20. Anne McClintock, "Screwing the System: Sexwork, Race, and the Law," *Boundary 2* 19, no. 2 (Summer 1992): 94.

21. For more on the problematic focus on "choice" within debates over reproductive politics, see Bordo, "Are Mothers Persons?" 93.

22. Luce Irigaray, "Women on the Market," in *This Sex Which Is Not One*, trans. Catherine Porter (Ithaca: Cornell University Press, 1985), 181.

23. Eve Kosofsky Sedgwick and Michael Moon, "Divinity: A Dossier, a Performance Piece, a Little Understood Emotion," in *Tendencies* (Durham: Duke University Press, 1993), 217.

24. See, e.g., Rosi Braidotti, "Organs without Bodies," *Differences* 1 (Winter 1989): 147–61; Donna Haraway, *Simians, Cyborgs, and Women: The Reinvention of Nature* (New York: Routledge, 1991); Hayles, "Postmodern Parataxis."

25. Susan Bordo, " 'Material Girl': The Effacements of Postmodern Culture," in *Unbearable Weight: Women, Western Culture, and the Body* (Berkeley: University of California Press, 1993), 245.

26. Mary Russo, *The Female Grotesque: Risk, Excess, and Modernity* (New York: Routledge, 1995), 93.

27. Contrast this with the 1995 Academy Award-winning film, *Forrest Gump,* and the way that its freaks—Lieutenant Dan, Bubba, Jenny, and Forrest himself—are ultimately normalized, written back into a bland story about America that takes the most charged moments in recent history and rewrites them to erase their political content.

TWENTY

Freaking Feminism: *The Life and Loves of a She-Devil* and *Nights at the Circus* as Narrative Freak Shows

SHIRLEY PETERSON

Let the priests tremble, we're going to show them our sexts.
—HÉLÈNE CIXOUS

Freaks, as Leslie Fiedler observes, fascinate the rest of us because they seem to represent otherness—an otherness that, but for a twist of fate, might include us. Ultimately, he concludes, this otherness is illusion, and since antiquity, freaks in various forms have actually embodied our cultures' fears about ourselves—our "secret selves."[1] Fiedler's point here echoes Freud's assessment of the uncanny as "that class of the frightening which leads back to what is known of old and long familiar."[2] The freak, in other words, is the projection of what culture fears most about itself.

While Fiedler amply illustrates how these fears have taken a variety of gendered forms, feminist cultural critics might make more than he does of the peculiar way the illusion of "otherness" commonly links freaks to women within the "us" of patriarchal culture. In *The Second Sex*, of course, Simone de Beauvoir emphasizes the otherness of the female in patriarchy, which identifies woman as the primordial freak of nature, that figure of deviance from normative humanity. She is

> what man decrees; thus she is called "the sex", by which is meant that she appears essentially to the male as a sexual being. For him she is sex—absolute sex, no less. She is defined and differentiated with reference to man and not he with reference to her; she is the incidental, the inessential as opposed to the essential. He is the Subject, he is the Absolute—she is the Other.[3]

The arts have long represented woman's otherness to man, lending validity to the notion of female freakishness, particularly as it relates female sexuality to the uncanny.[4] This chapter explores the way that two novels, Fay Weldon's *The Life and Loves of a She-Devil* (1983) and Angela Carter's *Nights at the Circus* (1984), enlist freakishness for a feminist agenda by foregrounding what Mary Russo calls the "grotto-esque": that which is "hidden, earthly, dark, material, immanent [and] visceral."[5] As narrative freak shows, these works also constitute what Hélène Cixous calls "sexts"—"female-sexed texts" that convert patriarchal fear of the feminine into female empowerment and force a confrontation with the illusion that underlies female otherness.[6] They imply that this illusion, while reassuring some in their normality, also invests the other with a good deal of power that, if unleashed, could undermine the very foundations of culture. Beyond this critique of patriarchy, however, Weldon and Carter expose the "other" woman within feminist culture as well, thereby questioning the boundaries of feminist ideology in the 1980s.

Weldon's and Carter's novels partake of a long, albeit uneasy, association of feminism with freakishness. At the turn of the century, the women's suffrage movement was considered by some a freak show of its own. It succeeded partially by making a spectacle of female otherness, and critics consequently condemned its proponents as a band of "unsexed" creatures, both physically and psychologically deformed.[7] In British novels, for example, Mrs. Humphry Ward (leader of the anti-suffrage movement) and H. G. Wells, (advocate and practitioner of "free love") respond in ironically similar fashion to female political aspirations by depicting feminist activists as physically and psychically deformed viragoes, deserving the punishment their authors impose on them.[8] Both novelists inscribe the visual images of decrepit and dangerous suffragists promoted in anti-suffrage political cartoons and posters of the time.[9] Even Virginia Woolf, the celebrated mother of modern feminism, and Rebecca West, one of the most notorious feminist writers of her day, depict female political activists in ambivalent terms.[10] These writers indicate the uneasy alliance between the early feminist agenda rooted in nineteenth-century femininity and the politically transgressive power of the "unsexed" being. To be unsexed, of course, is to inhabit the realm of the freak who challenges "the conventional boundaries between male and female, sexed and sexless, animal and human, large and small, self and other, and consequently between reality and illusion, experience and fantasy, fact and myth."[11] The protagonists of Carter's and Weldon's novels, Sophie Fevvers and Ruth Patchett, reject feminine reservations about transgressing these boundaries and in the process turn a veritable no-man's land into a source of female power.

It is precisely the power of this position that both Weldon and Carter find vital for a postfeminist age. Carter's bird-woman, Sophie (or Fevvers), and Weldon's "uneasy giantess," Ruth, are "extra-ordinary" in an age in which image is everything for women. As the celebrated winged aerialist of turn-of-the-century London, Sophie depends on the spectacle of abnormality for her livelihood. She flaunts her plumage like a "Brazilian cockatoo" (*Nights*, 15). Her six-foot wing span carries her between trapezes to the tune of—"what else—'The Ride of the Valkyries'" (*Nights*, 16). Yet it is the limitations of her act that intrigue Jack Walser, crack reporter. In the parlance of the sideshow, Walser believes Sophie is a "gaff," or a fraud. Nevertheless, he notes the paradox that "in a secular age, an authentic miracle must purport to be a hoax, in order to gain credit in the world" (*Nights*, 17). Does she, in fact, inspire awe by sheer artifice? Sophie, whose career began in the freak show, knows the value of illusion to women. Despite her authenticity, she relishes the uncertainty in spectators. Within the sideshow code of ethics, of course, amplification of the truth is not only standard procedure but part of the attraction.[12]

Weldon's two-hundred-pound Ruth embodies such clichés as the woman scorned, the fury of whom men have long been warned in literature. One of society's female outcasts, she has gratefully married, hoping to normalize her excessive being, only to have her freakishness reinforced by her husband, the aptly named Bobbo. But Bobbo denies Ruth's feminine identity even at the most degraded level: "I don't think Ruth is a natural rape victim, somehow. Are you darling!" (*She-Devil*, 37). Ruth's response to Bobbo's cruelty illustrates the narrative project of both writers. Her transformation from downtrodden suburban "angel in the house" into an avenging she-devil has its narrative equivalent in these novels which embrace the freakish image in the interest of reconstructing form. Condemned by husband Bobbo as a "she-devil" for refusing to accept their lie of a marriage, Ruth undergoes a strange evolution. As her mind immediately clears, she liberates desire from the restraining manacles encoded in the Litany of the Good Wife (*She-Devil*, 26). Inasmuch as she has been robbed of her legitimate wifely role by the love goddess of romance fiction, Mary Fisher, she finds the inversion of the love goddess particularly suitable to herself: "Peel away the wife, the mother, find the woman, and there the she-devil is" (*She-Devil*, 49). As writers, Weldon and Carter offer readers a parallel transformative experience. By undermining the conventions of romantic myth, particularly the fairy tale's enshrinement of marriage as the happy ending, they reconstitute myth as a narrative exploration of female desire freed of patriarchal authority. Just as Ruth rejects the static command, "we are as God made us," for an empowering new motto, "we are here in this world to improve upon his original idea" (*She-Devil*, 131), Weldon and Carter share a disregard for the literary/cultural authorities of the past who define normative femininity. To be unsexed, these writers imply, can be a liberating experience.

Challenging patriarchy, however, is only part of Weldon's and Carter's project. While both writers acknowledge feminism as a force in their lives and in their writing,[13] their works engage feminism with a boldness and directness that, in the popular vernacular of the postmodern counterculture, "freaks out" feminism. In other words, if within patriarchal culture, the female "other" represents a repressed version of the patriarchal self, then within feminist culture, the "other" woman is the lesbian, the prostitute, the hag, and the fury— those dimensions of the feminine that the politics of equality during the 1960s and 1970s repressed in order to validate feminine experience and expression. As Maggie Humm explains it, "Feminist theory has changed from the 1970s when it minimized differences between women to celebrating in the 1990s the electric charge of racial and sexual 'difference' and women-centered perspectives."[14] The operative word here is "difference" and the way in which discourses of difference have evolved to confront some key feminist principles, particularly those regarding normative femininity.[15] Perhaps Carter's response to the popular feminist novel *The Women's Room* (1977) helps illuminate the shift that she and Weldon represent: "I wouldn't see the point of writing that novel; I thought the premises of her idea of emancipation were pretty ropey. I don't think it's good art, good fiction or good propaganda—if propaganda is what you want."[16]

By placing these novels in the historical context of what Susan Faludi calls the anti-feminist "backlash" of the 1980s, we begin to see how they are both a response to patriarchal authority and to feminism.[17] The term itself, "freaking feminism," articulates a hysterical patriarchy's condemnation of feminism (i.e., "Those freaking feminists!"). Moreover, the term suggests a reexamination of feminism as an established institution of social change with its own notions of normative femininity (i.e., to "freak out" or, perhaps more to the point, to "out the freak" within feminism). This dual agenda gives the novels a surprising boldness that, from a 1990s perspective, seems to coincide with a subtle, yet important, reconception of the feminist agenda.

By way of vexing patriarchy, the novels employ some similar strategies. Both feature women who radically defy the stereotype of normative femininity. Ruth bears a six-foot-two-inch frame ("fine for a man but not for a woman"), dark hair, jutting jaw, sunken eyes, hairy moles, hooked nose, broad back and shoulders, muscular legs, and comically truncated arms. She is the anti-Barbie, an embodied disjunction: Her "nature and looks do not agree" (*She-Devil*, 5). If Ruth is the consummate loathly lady, Sophie Fevvers's vulgar, yet splendid, form explodes such archetypes. With her winged humpback, she resembles less an angel than a dray mare. Her gaudy multicolored feathers, she concedes, are only illusion insofar as they are dyed (her natural color being blond, like "that on my private ahem parts") (*Nights*, 25). Sophie matches Ruth's six-foot-two stature, surpassing her current love interest, Walser. To Walser, she is both freakish and disturbingly alluring: "Her face, in its Brobdingnagian symmetry, might have been hacked from wood and brightly painted up by those artists who build carnival ladies for fairgrounds or figureheads for sailing ships. It flickered through his mind: Is she really a man?" (*Nights*, 35).

In their physical deviations from normative femininity, both Ruth and Sophie challenge the aesthetic standards and male/female polarization in which patriarchal culture is heavily invested. But, as Robert Bogdan maintains, being a freak is not primarily a physiological condition: "Freak is a frame of mind, a set of practices, a way of thinking about and presenting people. It is the enactment of a tradition, the performance of a stylized presentation."[18] Thus, Ruth's and Sophie's freakishness is historically and culturally specific and entirely performative within a burlesque tradition that elaborates and frames their corporeality. Like such sideshow attractions as bearded ladies and hermaphrodites, they function as sites of contradiction, challenging notions of stable identity and pointing to cultural dissonance.[19]

One of the ways that femininity is modeled and contained within patriarchy has been through myth and folklore, genres populated with freaks, monsters, and human mutants that act as warnings against deviance. A translator of Charles Perrault's fairy stories and an editor of fairy and folk tales, Carter nevertheless claims to be "in the demythologising business," and she is drawn to myths in the first place "because they *are* extraordinary lies designed to make people unfree."[20] Carter's Sophie evokes and undercuts numerous myths. She's billed as the "Cockney Venus," a blend of the vulgar and divine, recalling common carnival attractions such as The Bald Venus and The Bearded Venus, and perhaps alluding to the notorious Hottentot Venus.[21] Privately, Sophie thinks of herself as "Helen of the High Wire," which comically links her to the classical femme fatale and evokes the category of freak in which hybrids are common. Like Helen, offspring of Leda and Zeus, Sophie was hatched and takes after her "putative father, the swan, around the shoulder parts" (*Nights*, 7). At Ma Nelson's brothel, where Sophie grows up and where her freakishness and youth make her a natural Cupid, a painting of "Leda and the Swan" adorns the parlor. Sophie fondly recalls this rendering of "what might have been my own primal scene, my own conception, the heavenly bird in a white majesty of feathers descending with imperious desire upon the half-stunned and yet herself impassioned girl" (*Nights*, 28). Readers of Carter's other reworkings of myth will recognize the "impassioned" victim here as a challenge to more conventional readings that denigrate female eroticism as sexual deviance. And readers of W. B. Yeats's famous "Leda and the Swan" might find in Sophie an amusing answer to his perplexing question: "Did she put on his knowledge with his power?" Apparently more than that.[22]

If Sophie's mythical and mysterious birth gives her the power to soar above the common lot of humanity rather than making her "unfree" as myths tend to do, Carter also reminds us that such flights of fancy can be dangerous for women. While Sophie relishes the role of spectacle, in Madame Schreck's museum of woman monsters (an inextricable dark underside to the brothel) she illustrates Fiedler's observation that "freak shows always implicitly suggest . . . that we only make believe that horror is make-believe."²³ At first, her role seems innocuous enough, even somewhat comic, in the peep show housed in the bowels of Schreck's museum and known as The Abyss. Among such "prodigies of nature" as Fanny Four Eyes, Sleeping Beauty, the Wiltshire Wonder (three feet high), Albert/Albertina ("half and half and neither of either"), Cobwebs, and Madame Schreck herself (who began her career in side-shows as a Living Skeleton), Sophie performs in *tableaux vivants* for the viewing pleasure of the truly horrifying, who bring their terror with them: "The Sleeping Beauty lay stark naked on a marble slab and I stood at her head, full spread. I am the tombstone angel, I am the Angel of Death" (*Nights*, 70). Madame Schreck's museum makes explicit the voyeuristic impulse that links the freak show to the pornographic display. Both exhibitions operate out of a consumer culture that creates its taboos only to turn them into viable commodities. The violence of such an economy ensures the management of otherness safely within the limits of dominant culture.

The museum also recalls fantasies of the Marquis de Sade, and the arrival of Christian Rosencreutz completes the Sadeian model.²⁴ Much as Sade's virtuous Justine can only escape into further degradation, Sophie escapes from Madame Schreck's only to find herself in an even more sinister environment. In Rosencreutz's Gothic mansion, Sophie discovers that she is to be the sacrificial offering designed to provide Rosencreutz with eternal youth, a perversion of her function as Angel of Death. Rosencreutz constitutes a pornographic nightmare. He is obsessed with "the female part, or absence, or atrocious hole, or dreadful chasm, the Abyss, Down Below, the vortex that sucks everything dreadfully down, down, down where Terror rules" (*Nights*, 77). Like the pornographer, his horror of the feminine is really a horror of his own mortality²⁵—a horror "we only make believe . . . is make believe." As both freak and female, Sophie is "the reconciler of the grand opposites of death and life" (*Nights*, 81) who mediates an impossible position that offers escape from what Rosencreutz fears most— the annihilation of the self. If Sophie emerges victorious from this encounter, it is only thanks to Ma Nelson's phallic sword and to her recognition that in the grandiose myths that direct Rosencreutz's schemes, she might be invested with the power of *"elixum vitae"* (*Nights*, 83), but that kind of power is an illusion in itself used on women to ensure their cooperation in the status quo.

Weldon's novel also invokes only to debunk a number of myths, beginning with the irony of Ruth's biblical name, which implies compassion and pity. If initially deserving the name, she becomes Ruth-less, both figuratively and literally, in her campaign to equalize an unjust world. She is born a Cinderella, without the redeeming beauty, but with a neglectful mother, favored sisters, and no fairy godmother; consequently, she grows freakishly "lumpish and brutish" in an attempt to protect the nerve endings she wore outside, rather than inside, her skin (*She-Devil*, 8). The eroticized romantic myths that Mary Fisher peddles like valium to bored middle-class housewives are not written for Ruth, whose marriage quickly dispels any romantic illusions she may harbor. Conversely, Ruth's story recalls the terror of *Frankenstein*, as earthquakes and electrical storms accompany the final surgical phase of Ruth's self-reconstruction. Warned of God's anger, she responds: "Of course he's angry. . . . I am remaking myself" (*She-Devil*, 269). As both monster and monster-maker, she usurps the role of agent denied to her before her "fall" from grace. Like Lucifer, she "take[s] up arms against God Himself" (*She-Devil*, 94). Since Lucifer was male, Ruth thinks she just might do better. Yet the outcome of her surgery reinforces Kathy Davis's conclusion that women who have had cosmetic surgery seek to "be ordinary rather than beautiful."[26] As Ruth's doctor surmises, "If you have been extraordinary all your life, . . . just to be ordinary must be wonderful" (*She-Devil*, 253). If myths involve wish-fulfillment, this is the wish of the freak to be normalized. On the other hand, it also expresses the wish of the normal to expel the imagined freak in themselves. If myths have coercive power, Ruth's reconstruction witnesses the cultural pressure to conform that has propelled cosmetic and reconstructive surgery into a multimillion-dollar industry.

The most provocative myth, however, behind Ruth's transformation is that of Hans Christian Andersen's *The Little Mermaid:* "Hans Andersen's little mermaid wanted legs instead of a tail, so that she could be properly loved by her Prince. She was given legs, and by inference the gap where they join at the top, and after that every step she took was like stepping on knives. Well, what did she expect? That was the penalty. And, like her, I welcome it. I don't complain" (*She-Devil*, 173). Later, when Ruth has completed her transformation into beautiful seductress, she dances with her doctor, now hopelessly in love with her, but "with every step it was as if she trod on knives" (*She-Devil*, 275). This parable of the virtues of female suffering is reinterpreted from Weldon's feminist standpoint as a story about the mutilating influence of cultural myths, especially on women. Like the mermaid, Ruth inhabits the space reserved for freaks of nature, those who defy conventional categories. The mermaid's freak appeal lies in her combined state as human/beast, and in the more threatening form of the Siren she embodies a particular kind of sexuality that promises more than the usual fare. Acquired normalization, however, has its price. For instance, the normalization of the mermaid requires an abdication of sexual power (even though from a male perspective legs are more accommodating than tailfins) along with conformity. Ruth pays with a great deal of pain and degradation, eventually gaining only a pyrrhic victory. She models herself on Mary Fisher, a combined mermaid (seductress) and siren (temptress) in her High Tower beckoning unwary sailors to the rocks below. By now, all Sailor Bobbo (in prison) can remember of Mary is "the bit where the legs split off from the body." But he can't recall her face, so regular and perfect: "She is all women because she is no woman" (*She-Devil*, 186). Mary/Mermaid/Siren reminds us of the impossibility of a real woman in the romantic myth (including its pornographic versions), which depends on anonymity and conformity to impossibly idealized models.

Whereas Mary's Christian name also ironically implicates her as the virgin servant to male deity, Ruth's revision of Mary eschews her virginal dimension. In fact, one of the ways Weldon and Carter might be said to "freak out" feminism is by joining the vestal virgin with the whore in a feminist-driven erotics that subverts what seem to be mutually exclusive categories. Both novels ironically make reference to Vesta, virgin goddess of hearth and home. In Carter's novel, Ma Nelson's brothel features a virtual temple to Vesta in its drawing room, in which "buxom, smiling goddesses supported [the] mantelpiece on the flats of their upraised palms, much as we women do uphold the whole world" (*Nights*, 26). Each afternoon, ex-prostitute Lizzie burns "sweet-scented woods" and "burning perfumes" like a priestess of pagan ritual. In *She-Devil*, Ruth takes the alias Vesta Rose, "a name that in her childhood she had always longed to have" (*She-Devil*, 126). And later, with the financial backing of fellow freak and lesbian lover Nurse Hopkins, she starts the Vesta Rose Employment Agency, designed in part to find secretarial work for women coming into the labor force after years of domestic slavery. Providing job training, day care, shopping, and delivery services, it becomes a model of successful female enterprise, extolled by the corporate world as "an example to the weak-willed and complaining of what women could do if they really tried, if they hadn't been fortunate enough to marry well" (*She-Devil*, 139). This smug statement takes on an ironic meaning in Ruth's case, however, who demonstrates the feminist implications of "agency" by using Vesta Rose to avenge herself on her husband and his mistress.[27] The agency is ultimately Ruth's means of infiltrating Bobbo's workplace and sabotaging his future. Consequently, we might be reminded more of the mythical Bacchantes, the intoxicated females of Bacchanalian ritual who tear creatures to shreds and devour them. The final irony of the Vesta motif in both works is that, as they embark on the next phases of their lives, both Sophie and Ruth burn house, home, and brothel to the ground in response to the tyrannies of patriarchy.

If neither Ruth nor Sophie are whores in the conventional sense, they certainly brandish the whore's erotic threat as a means to a feminist goal. Ruth's sexual encounter with Carver, the unsavory caretaker of her suburban paradise, Eden Grove, underscores their commonality as oddities in this suburban sideshow. Carver understands the sexual allure of the freak, described here by Fiedler: "All Freaks are perceived to one degree or another as erotic. Indeed, abnormality arouses in some 'normal' beholders a temptation to go beyond looking to *knowing* in the full carnal sense the ultimate other. The desire is itself felt as freaky, however, since it implies not only a longing for degradation but a dream of breaching the last taboo against miscegenation.[28] Carver has experienced something of this before as the troll-like ogre of Eden Grove: "Good, suburban wives, neatly dressed and properly washed, seeking something beyond degradation so that it approached mysticism, trit-trotting into his shed" (*She-Devil*, 59). But his faith in himself is shaken before Ruth. Impotent and quivering before this strange goddess, he is reduced to a writhing body on the floor.

Sophie's upbringing in Ma Nelson's brothel and Lizzie's dismissal of marriage as "prostitution to one man instead of many" (*Nights*, 21) undercut the virgin/whore dichotomy upon which patriarchal culture evaluates women. Within this community of fallen women, whom Sophie regards as mothers, she has surprisingly learned to regard her body not as a sex object but as "the abode of limitless freedom": she can fly (*Nights*, 41). Walser's condescending remark that he had "known some pretty decent whores . . . whom any man might have been proud to marry" (*Nights*, 21) seems especially fatuous in the face of Sophie, whose primal "fall," in her inaugural flight, takes on biblical proportions: "Like Lucifer, I fell. Down, down, down. . . . I was not yet ready to bear on my back the great burden of my unnaturalness" (*Nights*, 30). Sophie's fall, though literal, is symbolic of all women incapable of bearing the "unnatural" bifurcation of the virgin/whore.

Like his counterpart Carver, Walser succumbs to the erotic appeal of his female freak of nature to the extent that he is reduced first to a whore-like clown in a circus in order to be near her and finally to a babbling idiot in an outpost of Siberia before being restored his (hu)manhood. Sophie's physicality, although often grotesque, is nevertheless intoxicating to the reporter/inquisitor. Initially desiring to expose her falseness, he is consistently subdued by her sensual, if unusual, charms: "Walser, confronted by stubbled, thickly powdered armpits, felt faint; God! she could easily crush him to death in her huge arms, although he was a big man with the strength of Californian sunshine distilled in his limbs. A seismic erotic disturbance convulsed him—unless it was their damn' champagne" (*Nights*, 52). Later, in the circus where Walser plays a clown he discovers firsthand how whoredom performs a scapegoat function in the interest of dominant culture's protection against its own freakishness (he's presumably already been initiated, having been buggered in Damascus). In this parody of Christianity with chief clown Buffo the Great as Christ figure presiding over his apostles, and the saints reduced to mere "spectacle[s] from any freak show" (*Nights*, 120), we see the burlesqued equivalent to Madame Schreck's horror chamber in which Sophie plays the analogous role of whore/entertainer. Clowns are the "whores of mirth, for, like the whore, we know what we are . . . mere hirelings hard at work and yet those who hire us see us as beings perpetually at play" (*Nights*, 119). As Captain Kearney predicts, Walser's fate is to make a fool of himself in this debased carnival atmosphere; however, the circus experience is finally transformative and cathartic for Walser. As a reporter, Walser has managed to extend his skepticism "even unto his own being." In his world travels, he had never found himself, "since it was not his *self* which he sought" (*Nights*, 10). Through his own "enfreakment,"[29] then, Walser confronts the horror of the other only to find himself.

This "circus as life" metaphor explicitly links Carter's work to Mikhail Bakhtin's theory of the carnivalesque. Furthermore, both novels' freakish characters and the excessiveness of their protagonists fit Bakhtin's notion of the Rabelaisian grotesque: "The essence of the grotesque is precisely to present a contradictory and double-faced fullness of life. Negation and destruction (death of the old) are included as an essential phase, inseparable from affirmation, from the birth of something new and better. The very material bodily lower stratum of the grotesque image (food, wine, the genital force, the organs of the body) bears a deeply positive character. This principle is victorious, for the final result is always abundance, increase."[30] Ruth's and Sophie's "gargantuan" qualities include not only their size but also the authors' emphasis on the female body as the site of desire. In this respect, Sophie's appetite and lewdness make her an even more Rabelaisian character than Ruth, whose desires seem firmly rooted in hatred, committed to revenge, and consequently less celebratory and life-affirming. Consequently, Ruth's surgical reconstruction of herself, while in one sense regenerative, is self-defeating. As Marlene Hunter, the "impossible male fantasy made flesh," she concedes that "in the end [Mary] wins" (*She-Devil*, 259, 266). While tapping the power of the grotesque, Weldon's tale maintains some ambivalence about the transformation of Ruth into she-devil. If Davis's reading of this "fairy tale" overstates Ruth's victory through cosmetic surgery, she rightly notes the novel's challenge to orthodox feminism: "Weldon's novel offers a scathing portrayal of the feminine beauty norms without reducing women to the position of deluded victim. Her protagonist is a 'she-devil' and, if we might wish her a better life, the matter of her agency cannot be ignored."[31] We might wonder, though, if the "negation and destruction" of the old Ruth yields a "better" woman as well as a more autonomous and powerful one.

Although these modern versions of the medieval virago of carnival allow us to witness "certain essential aspects of the world . . . accessible only to laughter,"[32] Mary Russo notes the "dangers for women . . . within carnival" partially arising from the nature of spectacle.[33] In what sense and to what degree, she asks, can women make spectacles of themselves with impunity? In the psychological dynamics of voyeurism, the spectacle is by nature in a masochistic position: "In other words, in the everyday . . . world, women and their bodies, certain bodies, in certain public framings, in certain public spaces, are always already trans-gressive—dangerous, and in danger."[34] Certainly Sophie's experience in Madame Schreck's museum and later with Rosencreutz underlines this point, turning her otherwise profitable freakishness into a danger to herself. Furthermore, Russo maintains that Bakhtin's emphasis on the grotesque body as female, represented in Kerch terra-cotta figurines of senile pregnant hags, is problematic for feminist readers who find the image "loaded with all of the connotations of fear and loathing associated with the biological process of reproduction and of aging."[35]

Finally, female freakishness is complicated by the idea promoted in recent gender theory that all femininity constitutes masquerade to some extent:[36] "Deliberately assumed and foregrounded, femininity as mask, for a man, is a take-it-or leave-it proposition; for a woman, a similar flaunting of the feminine is a take-it-*and* leave-it *possibility*. To put on femininity with a vengeance suggests the power of taking it off."[37] Putting on femininity with a vengeance is exactly what Ruth and Sophie do, and in so doing they spotlight the performative function of both freaks and females within patriarchy.[38]

In conclusion, it is worth noting that both of these novels appeared in the middle of the Thatcher era, a contextual irony that perhaps fulfills Rebecca West's prediction to feminists in 1918 as they celebrated their achievement of the vote: "The arguments of oppression are not less dangerous from the lips of women than they are from men. . . . Without doubt women will be able to represent snobbery, prejudice, the desire to gain a simulacrum of true power by the cheap means of persecuting weak and unhappy classes or peoples, just as well as men have done."[39] If feminists in 1918 could have conjured a future feminine freak, she might well have resembled the Iron Lady of the 1980s, who as prime minister ironically embodied feminism's promise. And West's caution to feminists not to assume moral superiority is well taken. Set beside this image, then, is that of Ruth, "a lady of six foot two, who had tucks taken in her legs. A comic turn, turned serious" (*She-Devil*, 278). Ruth reminds us, as West did earlier, how it's all about power in the end, about who defines the borders between normal and freak, center and margin.

If Weldon's novel concludes on a bittersweet note with Ruth's and Bobbo's roles simply inverted, *fin-de-siècle* optimism characterizes the conclusion to Carter's novel. On the brink of the twentieth century, Sophie marries a much-changed Walser. Yes, he has fought tigresses, but he has also posed as a chicken. Now initiated in "the higher form of the confidence trick" by a Siberian shaman, he is worthy of Sophie Fevvers, the new woman for a new century.

Nights at the Circus also offers a refreshing contrast to Tod Browning's film *Freaks* (1932).[40] In that film the aerialist Cleopatra is transformed from a "normal" into a freak as punishment for her sexual betrayal of a midget. Subsequently, she horrifies spectators (in both the sideshow and the theater) during the film's final moments by displaying her "fowl" body. Not so with Sophie Fevvers. In bed with Walser, now grown to know himself and "smothered in feathers and pleasure" (*Nights*, 294), Sophie howls with delight at having once again mastered the illusion, this time the illusion that she had been a virgin. The Rabelaisian laughter with which Carter ends her novel is cosmic, celebratory, and transcendent while reminding us that in the best freak shows the joke is really on the audience: " 'To think I really fooled you!' [Sophie] marvelled. 'It just goes to show there's nothing like confidence' " (*Nights*, 295). By controlling the illusions about women, Sophie Fevvers, a woman of "confidence" and female freak extraordinaire, redefines the borders between normal and transgressive femininity and consequently gets the last laugh.

NOTES

1. Leslie Fiedler, *Freaks: Myths and Images of the Secret Self* (New York: Simon and Schuster, 1978), 314.

2. Sigmund Freud, "The 'Uncanny,'" in *Standard Edition,* ed. James Strachey (London: Hogarth, 1957), 14:220.

3. Simone de Beauvoir, *The Second Sex,* trans. and ed. H. M. Parshley (New York: Knopf, 1993), xl.

4. See Terry Castle, *The Female Thermometer* (New York: Oxford University Press, 1995), 21–43.

5. Fay Weldon, *The Life and Loves of a She-Devil* (New York: Ballantine, 1985); Angela Carter, *Nights at the Circus* (New York: Penguin, 1986); all further references will be abbreviated as *She-Devil* and *Nights* and cited in the text; Mary Russo, *The Female Grotesque: Risk, Excess, and Modernity* (New York: Routledge, 1994), 1.

6. Hélène Cixous, "The Laugh of the Medusa," *Signs* (summer 1976): 877.

7. See Sandra Gilbert and Susan Gubar, *No Man's Land: The Place of the Woman Writer in the Twentieth Century,* vol. 1, *The War of the Words* (New Haven: Yale University Press, 1987), 65–121; Susan Kingsley Kent, *Sex and Suffrage in Britain: 1860–1914* (Princeton: Princeton University Press, 1987).

8. Mrs. Humphry Ward, *Delia Blanchflower* (New York: Hearst's International Library, 1914); H. G. Wells, *Ann Veronica* (1909; reprint, London: J. M. Dent, 1966).

9. See Lisa Tickner, *The Spectacle of Women: Imagery of the Suffrage Campaign 1907–14* (Chicago: University of Chicago Press, 1988).

10. See Virginia Woolf, *Night and Day* (1919; reprint, New York: Harcourt, 1937), *Mrs. Dalloway* (New York: Harcourt, 1925), and *The Years* (New York: Harcourt, 1937); Rebecca West, *The Judge* (1922; reprint, London: Virago, 1980), and *The Young Rebecca: Writings of Rebecca West 1911–1917,* ed. Jane Marcus (New York: Viking, 1982), 109, 202–6, 243–63, 365–70.

11. Fiedler, *Freaks,* 24.

12. Robert Bogdan, *Freak Show: Presenting Human Oddities for Amusement and Profit* (Chicago: University of Chicago Press, 1988), 108–13; see also Sally Robinson, *Engendering the Subject: Gender and Self-Representation in Contemporary Women's Fiction* (Albany: State University of New York Press, 1991), who argues that "a 'genuine' woman, in order to take an active subject position, must pretend to be 'artificial'—a woman masquerading as an idea of a woman" (123).

13. See interviews with both writers in Michelene Wandor, ed., *On Gender and Writing* (London: Pandora, 1983), 69–77, 160–65.

14. Maggie Humm, ed., *Modern Feminisms: Political, Literary, Cultural* (New York: Columbia University Press, 1992), 54.

15. See, e.g., Kathy Davis, *Reshaping the Female Body: The Dilemma of Cosmetic Surgery* (New York: Routledge, 1995). Davis's fresh insight into a topic of traditional disdain to feminists reflects the dynamics of feminist theory over the past twenty-five years.

16. See John Haffenden, *Novelists in Interview* (London: Methuen, 1985), 94.

17. Susan Faludi, *Backlash: The Undeclared War against American Women* (Crown: New York, 1991).

18. Bogdan, *Freak Show,* 3.

19. Marjorie Garber calls such a phenomenon "category crisis" in her discussion of transvestism in heterosexual culture. *Vested Interests: Cross-Dressing and Cultural Anxiety* (New York: Routledge, 1992), 16–17.

20. Wandor, *On Gender,* 71.

21. See Fiedler, *Freaks,* 143. For discussion of the celebrated nineteenth-century Hottentot Venus, see Angela Carter's "Black Venus," in *Black Venus* (London: Chatto and Windus, 1985), 9–24; Jill Matus, "Blonde, Black and Hottentot Venus: Context and Critique in Angela Carter's 'Black Venus,'" *Studies in Short Fiction* 28, no. 4 (fall 1991): 467–76; Sander Gilman, *Difference and Pathology: Stereotypes of Sexuality, Race and Madness* (Ithaca: Cornell University Press, 1985), 76–108.

22. See, e.g., "The Bloody Chamber" and "The Company of Wolves" in Angela Carter's *The Bloody Chamber* (New York: Penguin, 1981); W. B. Yeats, *The Poems of W. B. Yeats,* ed. Richard J. Finneran (New York: Macmillan, 1983). For further discussion of the Yeats link, see Linda Hutcheon, *The Politics of Postmodernism* (New York: Routledge, 1989), 98; see also Elaine Jordan, "The Dangers

of Angela Carter," in *New Feminist Discourses,* ed. Isobel Armstrong (New York: Routledge, 1992), 129.

23. Fiedler, *Freaks,* 290.

24. Carter argues that Sade "creates a museum of woman-monsters [in which] he cuts up the bodies of women and reassembles them in the shapes of his own delirium." Angela Carter, *The Sadeian Woman and the Ideology of Pornography* (New York: Pantheon, 1978), 25–26.

25. See Susan Griffin, *Pornography and Silence: Culture's Revenge against Nature* (New York: Harper, 1981), for an elaboration of this point.

26. Davis, *Reshaping the Female Body,* 12; see also pp. 90–91.

27. Davis ponders the paradox of agency for women in a culture that makes cosmetic surgery seem like a choice: "Women's willingness to calculate the risks of surgery against its benefits can only make sense in a context where a person is able to view her body as a commodity, as a possible object for intervention—a business venture of sorts." *Reshaping the Female Body,* 157.

28. Fiedler, *Freaks,* 137.

29. See David Hevey, *The Creatures Time Forgot: Photography and Disability Imagery* (London: Routledge, 1992), 58.

30. Mikhail Bakhtin, *Rabelais and His World,* trans. Helene Iswolsky (Bloomington: Indiana University Press, 1984), 62. See also Rory P. B. Turner, "Subjects and Symbols: Transformations of Identity in *Nights at the Circus,*" *Folklore Forum* 20, nos. 1–2 (1987): 39–60.

31. Davis, *Reshaping the Female Body,* 66

32. Bakhtin, *Rabelais,* 66.

33. Mary Russo, "Female Grotesques: Carnival and Theory," in *Feminist Studies/Critical Studies,* ed. Teresa de Lauretis (Bloomington: Indiana University Press, 1986), 214.

34. Russo, "Female Grotesques," 217. See also Laura Mulvey, "Visual Pleasure and Narrative Cinema," *Screen* 16, no. 3 (autumn 1975): 6–18; Mary Ann Doane, *The Desire to Desire* (Bloomington: Indiana University Press, 1987).

35. Russo, "Female Grotesques," 219.

36. See, e.g., Judith Butler, *Gender Trouble: Feminism and the Subversion of Identity* (New York: Routledge, 1990), 43–57; Joan Riviere, "Womanliness and Masquerade," in *Formations of Fantasy,* ed. Victor Burgin, James Donald, and Cora Kaplan (New York: Methuen, 1986); Mary Ann Doane, "Film and the Masquerade: Theorizing the Female Spectator," *Screen* 23, nos. 3–4 (September-October 1982): 74–88.

37. Russo, "Female Grotesques," 224.

38. See Robinson, *Engendering the Subject;* Carter's masquerader also turns an active gaze on the male spectator and in the process causes quite a bit of discomfort. It is in this sense that the female subject in this text is both spectacle and spectator" (122).

39. Rebecca West, "Women as Brainworkers," in *Women and the Labor Party,* ed. Marion Philips (New York: B. W. Huebsch, 1918), 58.

40. Tod Browning, *Freaks* (Los Angeles: Metro-Goldwyn-Mayer, 1932).

TWENTY-ONE

Teaching Freaks

BRIAN ROSENBERG

All who profess to an academic interest in freaks would do well to ponder the words of Ward Hall, a freak show manager for over four decades, who observed, without rancor, that the chief difference between exploitative scholars and reporters (like myself) and exploitative entrepreneurs (like himself) is that "we paid these people."[1] Or, consider the more desperate words of Robert Wadlow, the tallest human being on record, who confessed that he "was more concerned about how physicians would present him than he was by his treatment at the hands of any showman."[2] For me these comments have formed part of a larger, ongoing process of self-examination that began when I decided not long ago to teach "Freaks" to a group of college sophomores. I've wondered whether the decision was simply one manifestation of the restlessness that overcame me as I approached the age of forty—a safer, less expensive alternative to buying a used Harley-Davidson; whether it was an attempt by one who typically teaches safe, conservative British literature courses, where an act of political extremism means substituting Joanna Baillie for Percy Shelley on a syllabus, to walk on the pedagogical wild side; whether, worst of all, it was an attempt to pander to the darker aspects of popular taste little different, as Hall suggests, from the strategies of any carnival huckster. If this last was my intention, the evidence suggests that I succeeded: on the sole basis of the unexplained but arresting title, nearly sixty students attempted to preregister for a course with a limit of eighteen. That's never happened for my seminars on Charles Dickens.

Although there may be an element of truth in each of these self-accusations, I've come to believe that my urge to teach "Freaks" was more than merely a desire a fill classrooms or to test the limits of acceptability more radically than my colleagues who teach alternative traditions or queer theory—or, at least, that whatever my motives at the start, my decision to teach the course proved in the end to be a wise one. Certainly one might argue that reading *Great Expectations* should be higher on any student's list of priorities than pondering representations of phocomelics and Siamese twins, and I would by no means advocate substituting the latter activity for the former. But one measurement of the appropriateness of the material in any course must be the extent to which it encourages complex modes of thought and highlights issues of broad significance, and by this standard the subject-matter in "Freaks" succeeded admirably. More than any "Introduction to Poetry" I have taught, this course underscored the importance of word choice; more than any survey of Romanticism, it foregrounded the interdependence of subject and object; more than any widely focused core course, it cast into relief the defining assumptions of various humanistic and scientific disciplines. It was a course—possibly the first I've taught—in which issues of theory and ideology seemed to the students naturally to emerge from contemplation of the material and not to be imposed from without.

My chief goal when I began planning "Freaks" was less ambitious but nonetheless important to an extent obvious to anyone who's ever stepped to the front of a classroom: I wanted students to talk, often and with animation, and I wanted to select a subject that would encourage them to do so. During the previous semester I'd taught a seminar on "Fictional Autobiography" that began conventionally enough (*Great Expectations, Villette, A Portrait of the Artist as a Young Man,* etc.) but that ended with Günter Grass's *The Tin Drum* and Katherine Dunn's *Geek Love*—two novels that adapt and subvert the traditional *Bildungsroman* and that happen to be narrated by dwarfs. These dwarfs, moreover, embrace rather than bemoan their condition, seizing it as an opportunity to escape the restrictions imposed by "normal" social and personal interactions. Whether I consciously paired two dwarf novels I cannot in all honesty recall—surely I must have known what I was doing—but the result, serendipitous or not, was inspired. The sessions on the two novels were the most lively of the semester and, indeed, among the best I've been lucky enough to teach. Students seemed captivated in particular by issues relating to the freakishness of the protagonists, spending whole class periods arguing about Oskar Matzerath's decision to stop growing at the age of three, "towered over by grownups but superior to all grownups,"[3] or about Arturo Binewski's reflections on the "horror of normalcy."[4] Other periods were spent pondering the allure of the freak show and considering the connotations of the word "freak" and how they differed from those of "disabled person" or "cripple." Among the more useful (though chastening) things I discovered was that my lack of knowledge and formal training on these various subjects mattered little to the quality of the discussion.

Thus inspired, I sought an opportunity to continue and broaden the study of "freaks" and found one in a course required at the liberal arts college where I teach. In place of the traditional freshman composition class, our institution offers a sophomore writing class, on the principle that sophomores have more to write *about* than do entering freshmen and will therefore take writing instruction more effectively. (Generally, I think, this has proven to be true.) Sections of the course are taught by faculty from all departments, each of whom is expected to design a topic around which readings, writing assignments, and class discussion will center. Because students in each section are likely to represent a diverse range of academic interests and competencies, instructors are encouraged to think in more interdisciplinary terms than they might ordinarily and to select topics that are relatively accessible. Here, more than in any English class, seemed to be a context in which I might appropriately draw upon high and popular culture and a variety of disciplines and media to teach "Freaks," and in which I might use the compelling nature of the material to good effect. One doesn't have to be Peter Elbow to recognize that most students will be more interested in writing about "bizarre accounts of normal humans turned into freaks" (to quote one particularly lurid dust jacket)[5] than in writing about the state of contemporary letters. The *Weekly World News* beats the *New York Review of Books* at the check-out counter every time.

How complicated it would be to teach this material became apparent before I had decided upon a single text, writing assignment, or discussion topic when, prodded by the registrar, I was forced to submit a course title. "Freak" is, of course, a word that in the wrong context can become as inflammatory and offensive as any racial or ethnic slur, and it was in precisely this context that I intended to use it: for the purposes of my course, "freaks" were not members of the sixties counterculture, fans of the Grateful Dead, or aberrations of a general kind, but human beings whose physical abnormalities or deformities were the defining features of their lives. I prefer to consider myself the sort of person who would not consciously inflict pain on these individuals or, indeed, use any language in a hateful or harmful way. But like others who have studied the topic (and others who have stood before a sideshow?), I found the use of the word "freak" alluring and next to unavoidable, and I was quite willing to adopt the apologias of my predecessors as my own. I decided at the same time to make the title of the course its initial topic of discussion, and to ask students to weigh the merits of the blunt "common sense" of Daniel P. Mannix—"I don't know of any word that expresses the concept of a dramatic physical deviation from the ordinary as well as 'freak.' So I'll use it"[6]—the reportorial accuracy of Robert Bogdan—"The word *freak* offends most people. Disability rights activists find words such as *midget, giant,* and *pinhead* degrading. I use them here because individuals in the business used them"[7]—and the appeal to myth and memory of Leslie Fiedler:

> Perhaps the very word "Freak" is as obsolescent as the Freak show itself, and I should be searching for some other term, less tarnished and offensive. God knows, there are plenty: oddities, malformations, abnormalities, anomalies, mutants, mistakes of nature, monsters, monstrosities, sports, "strange people," "very special people," and *phenomenes.* . . . For me, however, such euphemisms lack the resonance necessary to represent the sense of quasi-religious awe which we experience first and most strongly as children: face to face with fellow human beings more marginal than the poorest sharecroppers or black convicts in a Mississippi chain gang.[8]

Naturally, I was also influenced by the drawing power of "Freaks" as a course title, just as Bogdan and Fiedler must have recognized that book titles such as *Freak Show* and *Freaks,* however historically and psychically accurate, would attract more buyers than tamer alternatives. But, like them, I hoped to problematize the word by turning its implications and, more broadly, the very impulses that attracted students to the course, into one subject of the course itself: to entice them into the freak show and then to ask them *why* they were there.

Once I began seriously to investigate potential material for the course, my preliminary fear that there might not be enough turned quickly into the realization that there was far more than I could possibly include. My aim was to begin the semester with the consideration of such general issues as the definition of "freak," the meaning of "normalcy," and the lure and legitimacy of the freak show, supplementing the discussion with relevant historical, critical, or theoretical readings, and then to examine creative treatments of these issues in works drawn from a variety of art forms and media. What I found, as I expected, was a relatively limited selection of useful background material, but, to an extent I had not expected, a vast amount of interesting creative depictions widely varied in form and quality. Eliminating obviously mythic or fantastic variants—I had no desire to study the Cyclops or the Seven Dwarfs—there remained a rich tradition of artistic representations of the freakish. If "human oddities" were not quite up there with young-men-coming-of-age and fallen women as recurrent figures in art, they were at least a persistent presence. One could in fact construct a high culture version of a "Freaks" course made up entirely of respectable stuff: Velázquez (*Las Meninas*) and Montaigne ("Of a Monstrous Child"), Edgar Allan Poe ("Hop-Frog") and Mark Twain (*Pudd'nhead Wilson*), Vladimir Nabokov ("Scenes from the Life of a Double Monster") and Pär Lagerkvist (*The Dwarf*). An admittedly peculiar Victorian-Edwardian version of the course might center around Dickens, Victor Hugo, Lewis Carroll, and Walter de la Mare (author of the little-read *Memoirs of a Midget*). At another extreme, a pornographic-scatological version might include the Siamese-twin fiction of John Barth ("Petition") and Donald Newlove (*Leo and Theodore*) and the comic-book art of Robert Crumb and Bill Griffith.

My decision was to assemble a mix of material that came out somewhere between the extremes of the Harvard Classics and head comics, that is, that neither anesthetized students against the shock of the subject-matter nor disguised its ultimate seriousness. Given my sense of the purposes of the course and the likely student constituency, I chose to combine verbal and visual texts and to rely heavily, if not exclusively, on those designed to be accessible to a large though reasonably literate audience (in other words, not the *Weekly World News*). I chose too to concentrate on European and especially American works produced during the past century, since one of my goals was to establish the place of freaks in the culture students knew best. The cinema therefore became a valuable resource for me, since there the representation of freaks has already reached either its apogee or its nadir, depending upon one's sense of the appropriate. What I finally presented to students was a collection of films and photographs, novels and essays, stories and poems that might begin to suggest the significance of freaks to modern society and the modern imagination.

Initially, however, we needed to define our subject, and to that end we began by reading excerpts from the two most important scholarly treatments of freaks in recent years, Leslie Fiedler's *Freaks: Myths and Images of the Secret Self* (1978) and Robert Bogdan's *Freak Show: Presenting Human Oddities for Amusement and Profit* (1988), and by considering (with merciful brevity) a few case studies from medical journals. What became clear only as discussion unfolded was that the competing definitions of the "freak" offered in these works presented to the class, in a schematized but telling form, the general divisions among disciplines—natural science, social science, humanities—with which students in most American colleges and universities are familiar. From the journals emerged a definition of the freak—or "monster," to use a "term frequently appearing in the older literature to designate a grossly malformed fetus"[9]—devoid of ethical or social considerations, based wholly on the detailed, detached observation of physiology. Photographs more gruesome than anything seen in a B-grade horror film were offered to the reader for clinical rather than aesthetic or emotional consideration, as if the object pictured were not a human being but a specimen. Even the faces of the individuals in the photographs seemed drained of affect and identity. The entire procedure conformed closely to the students' naive sense of the "objective" work typically performed by the biologist or chemist.

Fiedler and Bogdan seemed to students to exemplify a basic distinction between the humanist and the social scientist. For Fiedler the nature of the freak is defined largely in aesthetic, psychological, and mythic terms: "The true Freak . . . stirs both supernatural terror and natural sympathy, since, unlike the fabulous monsters, he is one of us, the human child of human parents, however altered by forces we do not quite understand into something mythic and mysterious, as no mere cripple ever is. . . . Only the true Freak challenges the conventional boundaries between male and female, sexed and sexless, animal and human, large and small, self and other, and consequently between reality and illusion, experience and fantasy, fact and myth."[10] This is very nearly the freak as art-object, described in terms usually reserved for painting and poems. Freakishness—like the beauty of the Sistine Chapel or the brilliance of *Hamlet?*—is a quality *inherent* in particular objects and is finally irreducible to a simple definition or explanation. Bogdan will have none of this. For him freakishness is not inherent but *constructed,* the freak, however deformed, not born but made: " 'Freak' is not a quality that belongs to the person on display. It is something that we created: a perspective, a set of practices—a social construction." Fiedler's approach, in Bogdan's view, "reifies 'freak' by taking 'it' as a constant and inevitable outpouring of basic human nature" and, rather than "penetrating the socially constructed dimension of the freak show, . . . merely mystifies it."[11]

These simple distinctions among disciplinary approaches were eventually and beneficially blurred. Students came fairly easily to see that the "objectivity" of the scientist or physician was a position constructed as carefully as any and more subtly than most; that in Fiedler's quest for the mythic, prototypical freak, he perhaps too quickly dismissed the differences among cultures and historical periods; and that Bogdan, beneath the dispassion of the social scientist, was beguiled by the inexplicable mystery of the freak nearly as powerfully as Fiedler. Thus the lesson was two-fold: that the same subject is likely to be understood in different ways by individuals in different fields, and that each field has its own preferred evasions and sleights-of-hand.

As we worked through the creative material I'd chosen for the syllabus, it became clear that most modern representations of the freakish might be divided into distinct categories, or tended at least to develop a set of recurrent responses. In Poe's "Hop-Frog," about a diminutive court jester who responds to an act of cruelty by roasting the king and his ministers, H. G. Wells's *The Island of Dr. Moreau,* in which surgically manufactured man-beasts destroy their creator, or any of countless horror films and stories I might have used, the freak becomes an embodiment of our darkest nightmares, something alien not to be disturbed or challenged. In Thomas Mann's "Little Herr Freidemann," Nabokov's "Scenes from the Life . . . ," and David Lynch's film version of *The Elephant Man,* the hunchbacked dwarf, Siamese twins, and grotesquely malformed man, respectively, are sentimentalized into objects of intense pathos, becoming stand-ins for the modern, sensitive-thus-alienated individual. Freaks in such works tend to enjoy music, gardens, and building miniature cathedrals. The darkly comic potential of freaks is explored in a vein of Southern Gothic that runs through Eudora Welty ("Petrified Man"), Flannery O'Connor ("Parker's Back"), and Ann Beattie ("Dwarf House") and in the postmodern fiction of Barth and Elizabeth McCracken ("It's Bad Luck to Die").[12] The point in these stories is generally to ask whether the literal freaks are actually so peculiar as the physically normal but internally stunted individuals by whom they are surrounded. Though the distinction is difficult to draw, one might argue that all the aforementioned works are not so much about freaks as about normal reactions to freaks or the hidden qualities in normals to which freaks give perceptible form. Thus the attractiveness of the subject: in a century where the response to perceived difference has been such a devastating historical force and where the alienated anti-hero has been so popular a figure in literature, the freak, so flamboyantly different and unavoidably alienated, becomes emblematically useful. Significantly, all of the works I've mentioned, with the possible exception of *The Elephant Man,* are products of artists who draw upon freakish subjects at most occasionally and who seem to feel no desire to explore the subject of freakishness in great depth—that is, whose interest in the freakish is relatively "normal."

The most provocative works studied in the course turned out to be ones in which the attitude toward freaks was more ambiguous, uncertain, or conflicted, and in which the freak was not easily reduced to an object of pity, horror, or comedy. I have in mind particularly Tod Browning's 1932 film *Freaks,* the posthumously published collection of Diane Arbus's photographs, and Dunn's novel *Geek Love,* which together, in my view, comprise the most interesting—if not always the most polished or accomplished—imaginative representations of freaks in modern American art. For all three artists, the freak appears to be not a casual or occasional subject, but one to which they are drawn by some compulsion or necessity: after an early career as a contortionist and sideshow barker, Browning made a string of bizarre silent films populated by genuine or counterfeit freaks (typically played by Lon Chaney); Arbus was lured away from fashion photography in part by her fascination with freak shows and carnivals; and Dunn, who remembers herself as "an ugly kid [with] a deep, huge voice" and the nickname of "Toad," calls her freak novel the repository of "all I had tried to learn."[13] The work of each re-creates in the viewer or reader something of the ambivalence of the patron of an actual freak show and holds that ambivalence up for consideration; there is no safe distance from the freaks or from one's own discomforting responses.

Elsewhere in this book is a fuller discussion of the plot, virtues, and inadequacies of the film *Freaks* than I can provide in this context. I'll simply note, for what it is worth, that Browning must be acknowledged as the father of freak studies in this century: Arbus's repeated viewing of the film in a revival house is described by David Skal as "a distinct epiphany" in her artistic development;[14] Fiedler calls his book "a belated tribute to that great director and his truly astonishing film";[15] and Bogdan identifies the same film as his "invitation to journey into the world of freak shows."[16] In my course, *Freaks* was viewed early and became the work to which students most often turned for examples and comparisons. Many of them claimed not to "like" it (I'm not sure I *like* it), but most seemed interested in talking about their responses to it. What chiefly fascinated them, of course, was Browning's casting of such actual sideshow greats as Johnny Eck the Half-Man and Prince Randian the Human Torso as characters in the film, a decision that raises a host of compelling ethical and aesthetic issues; but they were also taken by what Martin Norden calls the film's "chilling, contradictory quality,"[17] that is, its delicate balance (or confused indecision) between sympathy for and revulsion at its misshapen subjects. Characters who are one moment described as "God's children" are the next crawling through the slime prepared to murder and mutilate, so that one can't quite tell whether Browning wants to embrace or obliterate them. If we see his freaks engaged in the "normal" activities of playing, eating, and giving birth, we also hear them chanting in some alien tongue "Gooble, gobble, one of us," which severs them from the "normal" world. Surely this mix of reactions approximates the confusion of the gawker before the sideshow giant, who can be seen to sweat and tremble but who seems, at the same time, other than human.

Arbus was the surprise of the course. If Browning's attitude toward his freakish subjects is ambivalent, hers is inscrutable, and I had feared that students might be frustrated by the mystery. Instead, they were attracted and tried mightily to make sense of "Mexican dwarf in his hotel room in N.Y.C. 1970," "Tattooed man at a carnival, Md. 1970," and, my favorite, "A Jewish giant at home with his parents in the Bronx, N.Y. 1970," and of Arbus's commentary (decidedly Fiedleresque) on her own interests:

> Freaks was a thing I photographed a lot. It was one of the first things I photographed and it had a terrific kind of excitement for me. I just used to adore them. I still do adore some of them. I don't quite mean they're my best friends but they made me feel a mixture of shame and awe. There's a quality of legend about freaks. Like a person in a fairy tale who stops you and demands that you answer a riddle. Most people go through life dreading they'll have a traumatic experience. Freaks were born with their trauma. They've already passed their test in life. They're aristocrats.[18]

Arbus is among the very few artists who seem to foreground the freaks' view of themselves, and this is, as Susan Sontag has observed, "a large part of the mystery of [her] photographs. . . . Do [her subjects] see themselves, the viewer wonders, like *that?* Do they know how grotesque they are? It seems as if they don't."[19] The pride or complacency on the faces of Arbus's freaks, indeed their very acquiescence in being so frankly posed and photographed, interferes with the compassionate, horrified, or amused response customarily elicited by freak-art, comparably, again, to the way the willingness of the sideshow exhibition to *be* exhibited complicates the reaction of the viewer. As a number of commentators have observed, and as many students quickly recognized, Arbus also manages to transform every individual she photographs into an apparent "freak," blurring the line between the monstrous and the normal. Her children and married couples typically appear more distraught and inspire more unease than her midgets and transvestites.

Teaching *Geek Love* was, as I noted, one of my original sources of inspiration for the course and turned out again to be an engrossing experience. Not surprising, given that Dunn's novel managed on the one hand to be castigated by reviewers as "an orgy of sadism and violence" and "a snuff film made legitimate by a reputable publishing house,"[20] and on the other to be nominated for the 1989 National Book Award. The book is both gruesome and good, which is a nearly sure-fire combination in a class of college students. It is also a radical attempt to re-imagine traditional ideas of normalcy and acceptability. More disturbing to readers than Dunn's collection of Siamese twins, dwarfs, phocomelics, telekinetics, and psychotics who murder, mutilate, and crassly manipulate seems to be her valorization of freakishness in its most extreme forms: with the help of liberally ingested "drugs, insecticides, and eventually radioisotopes," Lil and Al Binewski create a family of freaks, proud of having bestowed upon their children "an inherent ability to earn a living by just being themselves." Their daughter Olympia, the bald-albino-hunchbacked-dwarf who narrates the novel, considers it her "curse" that she is "a freak but not *much* of a freak," and their armless/legless son Arturo glimpses the "norms" in the sideshow audience and sees beings "engulfed by a terror of their own ordinariness. They would do anything to be unique."[21] While most works in this genre present, for obvious reasons, a "normal" view of freaks, allowing the reader to observe from a position of relative security, *Geek Love* seems to approach something like a freakish view of normals, leaving the reader considerably more exposed. And that view seems to have some basis in truth. Bearded woman Percilla Bejano, when asked the obvious question—Why not shave?—replied, "If I did, I'd be down in the tip with the rest of you instead of standing here on the platform making a good living." [22]

I've spent a good deal of time trying to gauge and make sense of student response to the general subject and specific contents of the freaks course, since in some ways I consider that response the central subject of the course itself. As I wrote in my syllabus, "One cannot talk about freaks without talking about the *viewing* of freaks, so, in a sense, the course is about us"—about why we've chosen to sit in a room and talk with passion about human beings whose chief claim on our attention is some gross physical deformity. Simply by virtue of getting into a course from which forty of their classmates were excluded, the students began with a sense of privilege or exclusivity. When asked *why* they had enrolled, they provided predictable answers: curiosity, an interest in horror developed through fiction or films, a sense of adventure. Many of the students claimed to "see themselves" as freaks—I had three with nose studs and two with iridescent hair, and this on a conservative campus—and to view the course as self-exploratory. A few others defined themselves, with what I suspect was more honesty, as "normal," and their interest in the freakish as voyeuristic. All in all, the responses were comparable to, though more freely volunteered than, what one might expect to elicit from patrons lining up to enter the "freaks" tent at a county fair.

I cannot overestimate the extent to which the apparently unrespectable nature of the material in the course inspired student enthusiasm. Probably the most crudely manipulative portion of my syllabus was the following unsubtle note: "One final, quite serious warning: this course is not for the squeamish. No sane person could be exposed to all this stuff without at times feeling horrified, revolted, even outraged. But if you believe that your revulsion and outrage are likely to interfere with your ability to study and discuss the material, you should enroll in a different class. I'd prefer not to listen to objections from you (or your relatives) later in the semester." Of course this had them salivating. There is no surer way of sparking enthusiasm in undergraduates than by convincing them that they are engaging in an illicit activity. In this case, moreover, the engagement was risk-free: not only was there no punishment looming as the price of participation, there was actually a reward promised for participating well. Again like the freak show, the course provided a temporary, controlled opportunity for minor transgression, only here the transgressors were not being duped out of money (unless one considers paying tuition for a course on freaks being duped), but were being paid in As, Bs, and credits toward graduation. It was the sanitized version of a peep show.

I like to think that the students lured into this particular tent were treated to more than an exhibition of grotesquery. The one thing the viewer at a freak show, strip club, or perhaps even beauty pageant does *not* want to do is think too deeply about his motives for attending or about the humanity of the individuals being observed. This is precisely what I asked the class to do, repeatedly and at length, and in the end is what distinguishes the viewing of an Arbus photo or the reading of Dunn's novel from a simple act of voyeurism. These works are, in effect, freaks or strippers who stare back, who make us aware of our role in the act of exhibition, and who sensitize us to the somewhat unsavory motives and impulses that under ordinary circumstances we are inclined to overlook. As one reviewer says of *Geek Love*, "one hand beckons us to gape at [the] assembled monstrosities, while the other wags a finger at our queasy fascination." [23] In my course, wagging a finger meant not chastising students for their interest—I was surely in no position to do so—but asking them to reflect upon it. The aim was not to arrive ultimately at any convincing explanation, but to raise questions similar to those discussed by Fiedler and Bogdan: Is the freak born or constructed? What role does language play in the creation of the freak? Does the existence of the freak blur distinctions we usually take for granted? Is normalcy definable?

As I hope is already apparent, many of the basic questions raised in the freaks class would be equally relevant to the discussions of race and gender that very commonly arise in today's literature and history classrooms. It's a small and natural step to move from considering the power of the word "freak" to considering that of the word "nigger," or from examining the social construction of freakishness to examining that of gender; thinking about exclusion on the basis of physiological difference leads almost inevitably to thinking about exclusion on other bases as well. What distinguished the discussions of these issues in the freaks class from those I had had in other contexts was the relative absence of the skepticism and resistance I typically encountered in my students—mostly white, conservative, upper-middle class—and the presence of more intellectual enthusiasm. The same sophomores who rolled their eyes at a feminist reading of a Shakespeare sonnet and, for that matter, participated actively in the fraternity culture on campus, were willing in this case to accept without hesitation the argument that language, social practice, and stereotypes all *matter* and all contribute to the creation of the freak. Perhaps this is simply because the situation of the freak is so extreme as to cast these issues into bold relief, rendering obvious and explicit what might be subtle and implicit in other cases. There were, additionally, no divisions within the group comparable to the racial, gender, and socioeconomic divisions that sometimes heighten tensions and enforce silence during classroom discussions of politically weighted issues. For the purposes of this course, everyone in the room was the same, a "norm," and the subjects under discussion safely distant and alien—not immediately present and not regularly encountered during ordinary activities. (I've imagined often how different the class would have been had a student with some extreme physical difference been enrolled, or had someone had a "freak" in the family.) Fiedler's claim that the politics of "physiologically deviant humans . . . remains a politics without a program"[24] may be less true today than twenty years ago, given the rise of disability-rights movements, but still such movements have no history of provoking, and not much current power to provoke, the anger and resentment often inspired by racial, ethnic, and sexual agendas. Students were prepared to accept with perfect equanimity the argument that norms had made and mistreated freaks and even to include themselves in the indictment, manifesting little of the defensiveness usually inspired by charges of racism or sexism.

Ironically, then, this course on a topic ostensibly shocking and offensive turned out finally to be more comfortable for students than courses on topics more familiar. And this is both its chief limitation and, I am hoping, its most enduring value. Because "freaks" are so tiny and invisible a minority—particularly on a campus such as mine, where individuals with even minor physical disabilities are virtually absent—their study can never have for most students the importance or relevance of the study of race or gender, and a course in freaks can never substitute for courses on these more broadly significant subjects. Students talk easily about freaks because in the end the topic doesn't matter to them very much, and because their own secure sense of being "normal" insulates them from feeling the pain of deformity. By the standards of Olympia Binewski, even the most socially inept or unattractive student in the group doesn't begin to approach the margins of normality. However polite or "politically correct" the society, moreover, and despite the best efforts of disability-rights activists, there continues to be no stigma attached to the abhorrence of freaks comparable to the stigma attached to racism or ethnic separatism, and there is a sense that such abhorrence is somehow natural. On the other hand, this feeling of insulation, of safety, brings the benefit of enabling students to talk about subjects they shy away from in other, more uncomfortable contexts and, maybe, of carrying over and sensitizing them in those contexts. Lessons about the complex interactions between subject and object or insider and outsider learned in this setting will perhaps not be quickly forgotten. It is my guess and certainly my hope that the encounter with "the alien, the other ... preeminently represented by the Freak"[25] will encourage students to think more carefully about the ways they construct and understand "aliens" and "others" closer to home—that if the line between "us" and "them" is blurred in this case, it will be more readily blurred in others. Perhaps, too, it will reveal to them the limited extent to which any categorizations based wholly on physical difference are "natural." In any event, holding on to such a hope seems preferable to the alternative, which is to concede that Ward Hall is fundamentally correct and that freak show manager and freak scholar (or teacher) are colleagues, engaged in different but finally comparable forms of exploitation.

NOTES

1. Quoted in Robert Bogdan, *Freak Show: Presenting Human Oddities for Amusement and Profit* (Chicago: University of Chicago Press, 1988), 268.

2. Quoted in ibid., 275.

3. Günter Grass, *The Tin Drum*, trans. Ralph Manheim (New York: Random House, 1961), 60.

4. Katherine Dunn, *Geek Love* (New York: Warner, 1989), 223.

5. Quoted from the back cover of Daniel P. Mannix, *Freaks: We Who Are Not as Others* (New York: Pocket Books, 1976; reprint, San Francisco: Re/Search Publications, 1990).

6. Ibid., 8.

7. Bogdan, *Freak Show*, xi.

8. Leslie Fiedler, *Freaks: Myths and Images of the Secret Self* (New York: Simon and Schuster, 1978), 16–17.

9. *Stedman's Medical Dictionary*, 1976 ed., s.v. "Monster."

10. Fiedler, *Freaks*, 24.

11. Bogdan, *Freak Show*, xi, 7.

12. No wonder that Jeanne Schinto refers to freaks as "an American short story staple." Jeanne Schinto, "Freaks, Etcetera," *Belles Lettres: A Review of Books by Women* 9 (winter 1993–94): 28.

13. Katherine Dunn, "Katherine Dunn in Her Own Words," in *Geek Love*, 352, 354.

14. David J. Skal, *The Monster Show: A Cultural History of Horror* (New York: Norton, 1993), 17.

15. Fiedler, *Freaks*, 18.

16. Bogdan, *Freak Show*, viii.

17. Martin F. Norden, *The Cinema of Isolation: A History of Physical Disability in the Movies* (New Brunswick: Rutgers University Press, 1994), 116.

18. Diane Arbus, *Diane Arbus: An Aperture Monograph* (New York: Aperture Foundation, 1972), 3.

19. Susan Sontag, *On Photography* (New York: Farrar, Straus and Giroux, 1977), 35–36.

20. Dinitia Smith, review of *Geek Love*, by Katherine Dunn, *Nation*, 15 May 1989, 673–74.

21. Dunn, *Geek Love*, 7, 103, 223.

22. Quoted in Mannix, *Freaks: We Who Are Not as Others*, 95.

23. Matthew Giunti, review of *Geek Love*, by Katherine Dunn, *Christian Century*, 5 July 1989, 664–65.

24. Fiedler, *Freaks*, 13.

25. Ibid., 54.

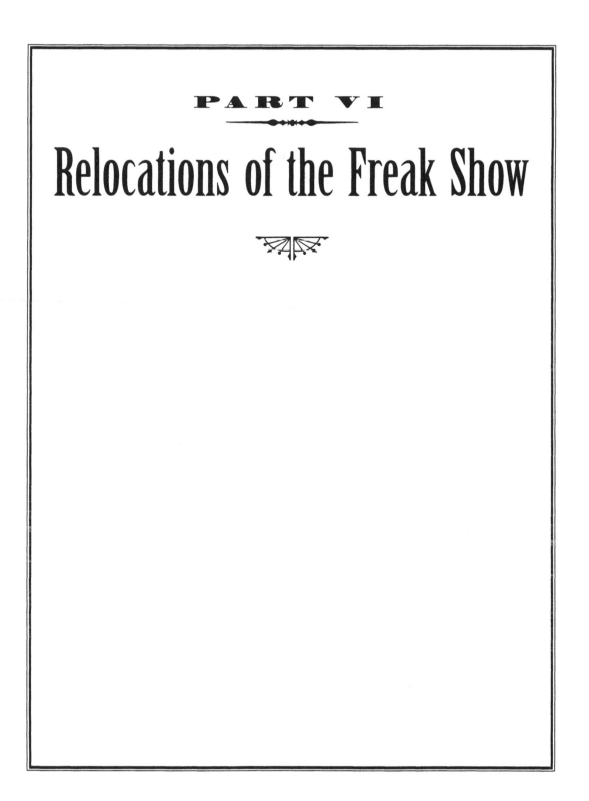

PART VI

Relocations of the Freak Show

TWENTY TWO

The Dime Museum Freak Show Reconfigured as Talk Show

ANDREA STULMAN DENNETT

Freaks are what you make them. Take any peculiar looking person whose familiarity to those around him makes for acceptance, play up that peculiarity and add a good spiel, and you have a good attraction.
—CLYDE INGALLS

The dime museum—a distinctly American form of popular entertainment—flourished in the late nineteenth century. As an entertainment venue it peaked between the years 1880 and 1900 and was in decline by the following decade. For a low, one-time admission charge, the dime museum dazzled men, women, and children with its dioramas, panoramas, georamas, cosmoramas, paintings, relics, freaks, stuffed animals, menageries, waxworks, and theatrical performances. Nothing quite like it had existed before.[1] No previous amusement had ever appealed to such a diversified audience or integrated so many diversions under one roof.

One feature that distinguished most dime museums from genuine historical or art museums was live performance. In addition to providing melodramas, strolling musicians, and lecturers, most museums exhibited an array of freaks, who were displayed on platforms, either together or throughout the various curio halls. To be considered fit for exhibition as a museum oddity, a person did not have to be taller or shorter than average, or fatter or thinner, or even deformed. Many other criteria came into play.

Five classes of human anomalies were displayed in dime museums: natural freaks, those who were born with physical or mental anomalies, such as midgets and "pinheads"; self-made freaks, those who cultivated freakdom, such as tattooed people; novelty artists, those who were freaks because of their "freakish" performances, among them snake charmers, mesmerists, hypnotists, and fire-eaters; non-Western freaks, those who could be promoted as exotic curiosities such as "savages" and "cannibals," usually billed as being from Africa; and finally the fake freaks, or "gaffed freaks," those who faked freakishness, such as "Siamese Twins" who were not attached, or the "Armless Wonder" whose arms were hidden under his costume.[2]

Before the emergence of dime museums in the mid-nineteenth century, the majority of human oddities in the United States were itinerant performers, their careers handled (or mishandled) by managers, who usually booked them into taverns, rented storefronts, or concert and lecture halls. With the advent of dime museums, the luckier freaks became at least somewhat more stable participants in the popular entertainment industry. Performing in an organized freak show was a relatively respectable way to earn a living, and many performers—the tattooed people, sword swallowers, and snake charmers—turned themselves into freaks to become part of the industry.

The dime museum freak show, or "platform entertainment," as it was known, was a huge crowd pleaser and a solid moneymaker, giving proprietors a powerful incentive to treat their freaks well. Successful museum managers such as George Huber and Phineas T. Barnum understood this point and cherished their freaks as they would any other profitable investment. Both Huber and Barnum provided lodgings for many of their freaks on the top floors of their museums. Although the accommodations were far from glamorous, they were cheap, and there was always plenty of food, heat, and companionship. Out-of-town actors often shared lodgings with these platform entertainers. As young performers, for example, the famous vaudevillians Weber and Fields worked at many museums on the East Coast. While at Keith & Batcheller's Dime Museum in Boston during the early 1880s, they slept in the attic along with other museum employees, paying six dollars a week to "Mom Keith" for room and board. According to their biographer, Felix Isman, the large attic room was divided into individual cubicles: "Eight-by-ten partitions in which the actors both dressed and slept lined the walls and opened upon the dining-room, occupying the center of the attic floor."[3]

Although the dime museum business provided a certain opportunity for otherwise impoverished and lonely freaks, the conditions endured by most were far from glamorous. Many were abused by small-time museum operators, kept to grueling schedules, and given only a small percentage of their total earnings. Individual exhibits were hired for one to six weeks by the proprietors of dime museums; the average freak performed in ten to fifteen shows a day and was shuttled back and forth week after week from one museum to another. Some, however, like "George, the Turtle Boy" (who was displayed at Huber's Museum three years running), had long-term contracts.[4]

Many freaks were lucky and gifted enough to earn a good livelihood through exhibitions, and some became celebrities, commanding high salaries and earning far more than acrobats, novelty performers, and actors. The salaries of dime museum freaks usually varied from twenty-five to five hundred dollars a week, substantially more than lecture-room variety performers were paid; they received twenty-five to thirty-five dollars for a so-called single act and fifty to seventy-five dollars for a double.[5] By contrast, late-nineteenth-century stage actors were paid only thirty-five to eighty dollars a week.[6]

Charles Stratton, "General Tom Thumb," probably the most famous freak of all time, eventually split his weekly profits with Barnum. Stratton owned a house in Bridgeport, Connecticut, several pedigreed horses, and a yacht. And he was not unique. A number of freaks were able to afford real estate and to retire comfortably; Chang and Eng, the original Siamese twins, owned a farm, a business, and several slaves in North Carolina; Millie-Christine, conjoined singers, earned five hundred dollars a week and owned a plantation in North Carolina; Zip, Barnum's "What is It?" exhibit, owned property in New Jersey and lived in an elegant house in Connecticut, a gift from Barnum; diminutive Admiral Dot owned and operated a small hotel in White Plains, New York. Commodore Nutt, a mid-century midget, was heralded as the thirty-thousand-dollar Nutt because he had a three-year contract worth that sum, an extraordinary amount of money at the time.[7]

Although many freaks were paid handsomely, museum managers were often insensitive about performance schedules; profit margins were their main concern. This was especially true with their top attractions, since the more shows these freaks performed, the more tickets were sold. When Theodor Jeftichew, "Jo-Jo, the Dog-Faced Boy," appeared at the Globe Museum in New York, his managers arranged to have him perform twenty-three shows during a twelve-to-fourteen-hour day.[8]

In fact, a freak was simply a commodity packaged by museum operators and showmen in such a way as to bring in business. Novelty, variety, and humbugging, the trademarks of the successful museum, all figured in the exhibiting of human oddities. The display of phony freaks occurred regularly, especially among the smaller dime museums, which needed the drawing power of fabulous attractions to lure customers away from the larger establishments. Not only did managers manufacture freaks, they also lied to the public about the exhibition of celebrity attractions. For example, once in the 1880s when Jo-Jo was performing in Europe, his name appeared on the bill of a Jersey City museum. A fellow performer, believing the New Jersey Jo-Jo an impostor, attempted to discredit the animal imitator by trying to make him laugh or fight during his performance (Jo-Jo usually only growled on stage). After a week of such antics, the Jersey City Jo-Jo pulled his wig off to reveal that he was indeed a fake.[9]

Showmen also fabricated the biographies of freaks to make their oddities more fascinating. For example, when Barnum first exhibited Charles Stratton as "General Tom Thumb" in 1843, he told the public the prodigy was eleven years old instead of five, fearing some would think Tom Thumb an unusually short child instead of an anomaly. In addition to giving Stratton a new name, Barnum provided him with British ancestry, believing it added class.

Inches were added to the height of giants and subtracted from that of midgets; Fat Ladies gained pounds and Skeletal Men lost them. Superlatives abounded, and every display was billed as the tallest, smallest, fattest, ugliest, or hairiest—and of course the most extraordinary or original. Vivid and provocative epithets often followed the names of performers. Lizzie Harris, who weighed 676 pounds, was heralded as the "Largest Mountain of Flesh Ever Seen." Captain and Mrs. Bates were billed as "Extraordinary Specimens of Magnified Humanity." The captain was 7 feet 11 1/2 inches tall and weighed 478 pounds. His wife was the same height and weighed only sixty-five pounds less.[10] Midgets were given exotic new names usually with titles. There was General Mite, Baron Littlefingers, Prince Ludwig, Duchess Leona, and Baroness Simone. They appeared with normal-sized people or sometimes with giants to emphasize their tiny stature. Several freaks had routine partners or alter egos: the diminutive Admiral Dot often shared a platform with the seven-foot giant Anna Swann, and Mrs. Tom Thumb stood in the spotlight with Noah Orr, who was just over seven feet tall and tipped the scales at 516 pounds.[11]

Although physical anomaly was the only real drawing power of most natural freaks, some were truly talented. General Tom Thumb sang and danced his way into the hearts of Americans and Europeans alike. The general's repertoire included several "Negro songs," as well as dances such as the polka and a so-called "Highland Jig." He also did impersonations of Napoleon Bonaparte and Frederick the Great. In addition to performing on platforms in the curio halls, Stratton acted in plays and afterpieces presented in museum lecture rooms. He made his acting debut December 4, 1848, when he was nine years old, in a play called *Hop O' My Thumb*, about a miniature—and precocious—child who outwitted a giant that had been terrorizing the kingdom of Old King Cole. It was the perfect vehicle to illustrate the comic skills of Stratton, who was seen running under the legs of adults, being dragged in a shoe, and getting served up in a pie.

One premise of the dime museum freak show was that most people have an innate desire to behold the misfortunes of others. The historian George C. D. Odell, after years of chronicling dime museum entertainments, came to believe that "the freaks of the dime museum served the purpose of raising dull persons from the throes of their inferiority complexes." He thought pleasure seekers could not look at such "monstrosities" without convincing themselves that, after all, their normal selves were "pretty good, if not beautiful."[12] Watching freak performers, Odell believed, built self-esteem; people left freak shows feeling more at ease with their lot in life. Freaks were created by others out of fear. Modern medicine was still in its infancy, and the average person was afraid of being incurably different, unalterably abnormal. But the definition of "normal" was narrow, and this very narrowness, a product of ignorance, was in its way comforting.

Most dime museums routinely closed for the summer. Many freaks found work during these months with circuses or with independent traveling museums. "Barnum's Great Asiatic Museum and Menagerie," organized in 1851 by Barnum, Seth B. Howes, and Tom Thumb's father, Sherwood Stratton, toured the country for four years complete with a 110-foot tent. Barnum's "Great Traveling World's Fair, Museum, Menagerie, Polytechnic Institute and International Zoological Garden," as well as many other well-known traveling museums, such as Colonel Wood's Museum, toured up and down the Mississippi in the late 1850s. Some set up in vacant storefronts or on the boardwalks of resort areas. The larger ones—consisting of a few wax effigies, some animals, and a carload of freaks—attached themselves to circuses or equestrian shows.

Most traveling museums did not operate on a very grand scale. The majority were small and somewhat decrepit, cropping up on carnival midways and at other types of outdoor fairs. By the 1880s most were limiting their displays to human oddities, and gradually, around the turn of the century, the word "sideshow" replaced "museum."[13] It was with the advent of the sideshow that the display of human oddities for profit began to turn seedy. Sideshows were part of the outdoor amusement industry; the image (and the reality) was of crude platforms on floors of grass and straw under tents. The smells and noises of circuses and carnivals came to be associated with the exhibition of freaks. Ironically, this was the antithesis of the atmosphere at a freak show in an elegant dime museum.

The days of the glorified freak show were gone by the turn of the century. By 1910, there was no longer an abundance of dime museums, with their organized freak displays, as there had been in the 1880s and 1890s. In the twentieth century, the exploitation of freaks for profit began to be frowned upon. In part because of the world wars and their devastating effects on the bodies of survivors, there came a gradual awareness of society's responsibility toward people with disabilities. Prostheses were devised for those who lacked limbs, modern medicine demystified many of nature's mutations, and hormone therapy began to be administered to people with growth problems.

With the demise of the dime museum, freak performers became largely itinerants. Anomalies who still wanted to exhibit themselves for money could find work at world's fairs, amusement parks, carnivals, and the circus. But as the decades passed, it became more and more difficult for freaks to find legitimate jobs.[14] Even when freaks could find work, the salaries they earned were rather meager.

Coney Island, a permanent midway, represented a new form of commercialized entertainment for an urban, industrial society that had come of age. The Brooklyn beachfront resort, along with its three amusement parks and independent entertainments, symbolized changes in American manners and morals. Once known as a scandalous and unsavory place, during the years 1897 to 1904 Coney Island was transformed into a technologically sophisticated center of mass entertainment that attracted patrons from all socioeconomic levels.[15] Coney Island's attractions included Steeplechase Park (1897–1965), Luna Park (1903–46), and Dreamland (1904–11).

Located in the heart of Dreamland, Lilliputia was a municipality of three hundred midgets organized by Samuel W. Gumpertz, a longtime showman. Everything in the city, from the bathrooms and bedroom furniture to the fire department, was constructed precisely at half-scale. The town also had its own government and operated as did any small city. Spectators entered Lilliputia and walked like Gulliver among the midgets who might be shopping, cleaning, or doing any other ordinary tasks. After fire destroyed Dreamland on May 27, 1911, Gumpertz put up a tent outside the ruins and opened his "congress of freaks."[16] While the embers still smoldered, Gumpertz turned Dreamland into a popular sideshow attraction, displaying a collection of "living wonders" from all over the world and turning Coney Island into the "world's capital of the eccentric and the bizarre."[17] For well over thirty years, Gumpertz's Dreamland Circus Sideshow attracted scores of freaks who were tempted by the community life of the seaside resort; Gumpertz became the twentieth-century czar of the freak show world.

Live freak shows long remained part of the American carnival and circus traditions. Most legitimate non-circus-related sideshows, however, were associated with the "Ripley's Believe It or Not!" tour created by Robert Ripley in 1933 for the Chicago World's Fair. Following the fair, Ripley traveled with a company of twenty-five living oddities and some three hundred inanimate objects.[18] Some of his more famous freaks were "Grace McDaniels, the Mule Faced Woman," "Roy Bard, the Ossified Man," "Laurello, the Man with the Revolving Head," "Leo Congee, the Human Pin Cushion," and Paul Whitaker, a black man from Georgia who could pop his right eye out a full inch beyond its socket. "Paul Desmule, the Armless Man," used his toes to hurl knives with ten-inch blades at a human target.[19]

Today the era of P. T. Barnum and the freak show is long past. Such shows are thought to be dehumanizing and have been outlawed in many states. Ironically, however, freak shows provided more independence to some disabled people of the past century than do today's affirmative action programs. Freaks had marketable attributes, and those who were exhibited had an opportunity to become celebrities, to obtain fame and fortune. In support of this idea, in 1972 the Florida Supreme Court struck down a 1921 law banning freak shows, ruling that the state had no business preventing anyone from earning an honest living.[20]

The concept of the freak show is not dead; there are many modern versions of these nineteenth-century spectacles, reconfigured for contemporary society. However, in the new format the position of the born freak has been, for the most part, filled by the novelty performer and the self-made freak. For example, Dick Zigun, a young man from Barnum's hometown of Bridgeport, Connecticut, since 1980 has devoted his energy to preserving popular forms of entertainment. Zigun, a playwright and graduate of the Yale Drama School, founded Coney Island, USA, a museum and theatre company dedicated to reviving the parades, sideshows, and other performance elements typical of Coney Island at the turn of the century. There are no born freaks at this show, since it is "performance-oriented, rather than gawker-oriented."[21] Without real human anomalies, only a cast of self-made freaks such as "Electra, the Electric Girl" and the "Illustrated Man," this show is no more than a magic show. It does not affect its audience on a deeply visceral level.

This type of freak show is less effective in part because self-made freaks fail to amaze the modern spectator. In our late-twentieth-century culture, the self-made freaks on the platform are not very different from the people we see at the downtown mall or on the subway. Our culture has developed a very vocal subculture that believes the body is a personal canvas to be redesigned as the owner sees fit. Body jewelry and the piercing of cheeks, nose, lips, navel, and nipple, which have never been associated with Western notions of beauty, have become very popular in the 1990s. While the piercing of genitalia still seems outrageously freakish to most of us, ear, nose, navel, and nipple piercing is now mainstream; the Gauntlet, a piercing parlor, advertises in the Manhattan Yellow Pages. Tattooing, now frowned upon because of health risks, is nevertheless a booming industry. Tattoos are no longer seen as the mark of the criminal or as the macho insignia of soldiers and sailors, but as living art. Celebrities such as Cher, Whoopi Goldberg, and Prince all sport tattoos. According to *Glamour* magazine, body engravings are more than acceptable, they are hip.[22]

During the 1960s and 1970s, Americans witnessed a cultural and aesthetic revolution in which many artists created ephemeral projects that contested the perception of the human body and its function. Numerous performance artists, from Vito Acconci to Karen Finley, transformed their bodies, turning themselves into self-made freaks in order to shatter cultural taboos about bodily functions and human sexuality. Modern body artists, using their own tissues as the medium of expression, challenge twentieth-century social concepts of sex and individuality. Similarly, certain nineteenth-century freaks suggested ambiguous types of sexuality and aroused the erotic fantasies of a sexually repressed audience. In an interesting echo of the old freak shows, performance artists Linda Montano and Tehching Hsieh attached themselves to each other with an eight-foot rope tied at the waist in 1983–84. Their project, titled *Rope*, called for them to remain joined for an entire year. In essence their contrived life style of enforced intimacy mirrored the interdependency of natural Siamese twins. Montano and Hsieh each explored how a state of perpetual attachment would affect them as people and as artists. Seeing a man and a woman joined together evokes taboo topics and erotic images. While observing any part of *Rope*, spectators might ask such questions as: How do they go to the bathroom, shower, or even sleep? Just as Chang and Eng, the original Siamese twins, had conflicting personalities, Montano and Hsieh disagreed about the intent of their project: she was more spiritual and he was more formal.[23]

From body piercing to body art, many Americans are symbolically illustrating that they are in control of their lives as well as negating the importance of the body in mass culture. Thus, in a world where body modification is accepted and body piercing and tattooing are commonplace, the man who hammers nails into his tongue or drives spikes up his nose is no longer outrageously freakish. No one can make big money exhibiting such people these days; nor can a would-be Barnum exploit our continuing fascination with the born freak. The problem for a modern promoter, therefore, is how to reconfigure the nineteenth-century freak show for a late-twentieth-century audience. What kind of exhibition would be grotesquely fascinating, politically correct, and a sure draw?

The most obvious modern form of the freak show is the television talk show, an environment in which dysfunctional human beings parade themselves in front of an audience. If, as Odell claimed, the old-time freak show made spectators feel at ease with their lot in life, so too does the daytime talk show, where the inner monologue of the viewer is, "I'm so glad that's not me!"

As the dime museum freak show transforms itself into the TV talk show, attention shifts from physical to psychological freakishness. Although today's talk shows promote themselves as "discussion programs" and do indeed occasionally address a politically important issue, their basic appeal is pure voyeurism (whether it be a celebrity interview or a debate about interracial dating). People in bizarre situations more or less beyond their control, either psychologically or physically, hold themselves up for public scrutiny. These shows are both alluring and revolting, but indisputably successful. Taboo subjects, ranging from homosexuality among teenagers to sexual relations between unmarried relatives, are aired daily from 9 A.M. to 5 P.M. With just a press of a button audiences can tune in to Oprah Winfrey, Phil Donahue, Geraldo Rivera, Sally Jessy Raphaël, Montel Williams, Jerry Springer, Maury Povich, Charles Perez, Jenny Jones, Richard Bey, or Ricki Lake. Recent issues of *TV Guide* list seventeen talk shows, not including the prime-time magazine shows, which incorporate similar devices.

Talk shows recycle many of the conventions of the earlier freak shows. For example, television hosts closely resemble the lecturers of the dime museums. Typically, there were no seats in the curio halls of dime museums; patrons were ushered from platform to platform by a lecturer, whose role was that of master of ceremonies. During his performance, the lecturer, usually given the pretentious title of "Professor," held the audience's attention by describing the freaks displayed on the various platforms. In addition to a carrying voice, the lecturer needed to have both magnetism and eloquence. His elocutionary style usually was patterned on the traditional hyperbolic spiel of carnival barkers, and his recitations were filled with classical and biblical allusions.

Talk show hosts also guide their audiences from exhibit to exhibit, explaining the tragic plight of each person in turn. Unless there is a celebrity guest on the show, what viewers usually see is a lineup of three to ten people who have similar bizarre problems. This format, which involves introducing one guest, one freak, at a time, also echoes the dime museum arrangement. Television hosts, like the museum lecturers before them, keep the show moving and structure the performance to fill the allotted time. A host must be pleasant-looking and have an ease not only with the guests and the studio audience but with the home audience as well. Many times his or her own confession, or spiel, is as interesting as the problem of the freaks on stage: the death of Raphaël's daughter, and the fact that Raphaël is an adoptive mom; Oprah's being abused as a child, her weight battles, and her recent admission on the air to having used cocaine. James B. Twitchell believes that Oprah, an extremely wealthy and powerful black woman, is fascinating to watch for her "ability to reverse color-line expectations." She is a "twentieth century wishful resolution to P. T. Barnum's questioning title of liberated blackness in our culture," the "What is It?"[24]

As with the freak shows of the dime museums, the sensational aspects of the TV talk shows are played down and the educational aspects heightened to legitimize these spectacles. Sometimes midgets or other anomalous or disabled persons appear on talk shows, but mostly these appearances are promoted as enlightening and informative. Like the medical testimonials provided by "doctors" at museum freak shows, psychologists and other behavioral "experts" are often featured to help the audience understand a particular problem and to validate a show's subject. For example, on a *Geraldo* program called "He/Shes Who Sleep with Straight Men," aired April 26, 1995, a psychologist, introduced halfway through the program, participated minimally by answering only two questions. Clearly the show was not about understanding the deviant behavior, it was about voyeurism; it was a freak show.

Although talk shows are marketed as informative, producers heighten the shock value of segments in many ways. One involves deceiving the guests. On a February 1995 *Jenny Jones Show* program about May-December relationships, the producers arranged for a nineteen-year-old black woman go on a date with a forty-six-year-old white man so as to stretch the boundaries of the topic to include interracial dating. The infamous *Jenny Jones Show* program, "Secret Crushes," led to a murder when a male guest found out his secret admirer was a man, not a woman. Jon Schmitz, who was so excited about appearing on the *Jenny Jones Show* that he bought three hundred dollars' worth of clothing to impress his secret admirer, killed the man who claimed to have a crush on him three days after the show was taped in March 1995.[25] The producers insisted their guests were aware the admirers might be of either sex and claimed this was not an "ambush" show.[26] The program was never aired.

This kind of manipulation of the personal lives of freak performers is not a new concept. For example, while on display at Worth's Museum in May 1888, J. W. Coffey, the elegant skeleton man who carried a walking stick and wore a high hat, morning coat, wing collar, and bow tie, advertised in the *New York Herald* for a wife. Coffey, who was five feet six inches tall and weighed a mere seventy pounds, was looking for a "plump and pleasing person" to be his life's companion. He received numerous responses and selected a wife from among the applicants. Worth managed to make a profit from the publicity by exhibiting Coffey and his new wife through the end of the 1888 season.

Marriages were often arranged between incongruous freaks, and most of these unions were exploited for profit. It is not known whether Mr. and Mrs. Atherton, a Skeletal Man paired with a Fat Lady, were really married. The "Original Aztec Children," Maximo and Bartola, who were publicized as brother and sister, in fact were married on January 1, 1867, while on tour in London.[27] Probably no one will ever know whether they were actually siblings and their marriage a publicity stunt, or whether they were only marketed as brother and sister and their marriage a true legal love match. Some marriages between freaks, of course, were undoubtedly genuine, bringing fame and fortune to the couples. Chauncey Morlan and Annie Bell were married November 30, 1892, at Huber's Museum. The newlyweds were exhibited for six weeks to a capacity crowd; everyone wanted to see the "heaviest couple alive," whose combined weight was more than fourteen hundred pounds. Anna Swann, the "Nova Scotia Giantess," married another giant, Martin Van Buren Bates, billed as the "Kentucky Giant," in London on June 17, 1871. The day after their wedding, a reception was held in their honor, with such guests as the Prince of Wales and other British dignitaries.[28]

The Siamese twins Chang and Eng provided an even more titillating look at freak marriages. By the age of twenty-eight, these twins had accumulated a small fortune, become American citizens, and changed their surname to Bunker. In 1843 they married sisters in a double wedding ceremony; Eng married Sara Ann Yates and Chang married Adelaide Yates, and between them they fathered twenty-two children. They came out of retirement in 1850 and began appearing in public with their wives and children.[29]

Siamese twins posing with their normal spouses and offspring not only prompted questions about everyday privacy, but also raised issues of sexual privacy. Sex was a powerful component of the performance text of the freak show; spectators imagined sexual intercourse between incongruous partners—the fat woman and the thin man, the bearded woman (who may not after all, be a woman) and her husband—and among couples like Chang and Eng and their wives. Such performances readily inspired images of transgressive sex, ambiguous sex, homosexuality, bisexuality, and group sex, challenging the conventional boundaries between male and female, self and other. Tattooed women, fat women, and skeletal women were costumed in short, sleeveless dresses to better verify their freakishness. Snake charmers wore minimal clothing, exaggerating their wildness and exoticism. Sometimes patrons were allowed to touch the limbs of Fat Ladies or pull the whiskers of Bearded Ladies. It was deeply arousing to Victorians to touch a strange woman in a legitimate, respectable setting, and it was a tantalizing and disturbing sight for the other spectators, especially adolescents. A wondrously titillating dialectic emerged, in which performers were alluring as well as repulsive.

Transgressive sex and incongruous couples are central themes of many TV talk shows as well. The following is a sample of the programs aired from October to November 1994: "Infidelity and Pregnancy," "Contrasting Styles of Female Behavior," "Acting Like a Member of a Different Race," "Teens and Chastity," "Mates with Dissimilar Sex Drives," "Twins with Different Sexual Preferences," "Homosexual Marriages," and "Bigamy."[30] Interracial, swinging, May-December, and other incongruous couples inspire images that push the envelope of traditional sexuality. One February 1995 *Jenny Jones* program, for example, featured a married couple with an extreme age difference: the woman was twenty-seven and the man seventy-eight.

Homosexuality and transvestism, also popular program topics, are twentieth-century manifestations of the incongruous couple theme and the sexual-ambiguity motif. On *Geraldo's* "He/Shes Who Sleep with Straight Men" program, beautifully coiffed "women," with ample bosoms, in skin-tight outfits, coolly told the audience they were transvestites, biologically males. The host referred to them as "ladies." Their male sexual partners, for the most part, knew they were men. The feelings of shock and confusion stirred in the audience at the moment of discovering the true sex of these beauties must have been similar to those felt by nineteenth-century audiences who came face to face with the sexual riddle of a Bearded Lady.

Being a public spectacle in a dime museum or talk show is not without its consequences: marriages break up, family members and friends stop talking to one another, and, as in the Schmitz case, some have even died. In 1892, Henry Stratton won a fasting contest at Huber's Museum; however, he died as a result of his forty-five-day feat.[31] The dime museum patron, like the talk show spectator, not only enjoyed watching human anomalies, but received a thrill from occasionally playing "freak for a day." There were a host of museum-sponsored public contests, from beauty pageants, baby shows, and boxing matches to unique forms of competition such as gum-chewing, quail-eating, and having the smallest feet.[32] Talk shows mirror these spectacles with programs like *Richard Bey's* "Bikini Contest," and *Geraldo's* "Hunk of the Year Contest."[33]

Society has begun to accept the physical differences between people and to integrate what were once called "nature's mistakes." The Americans With Disabilities Act protects people from discrimination. Despite this contested assumption, there remains one true physical freak in modern culture: the obese person (see fig. 22.1). The Fat Lady still evokes horror. Being fat is so stigmatized in American culture that fat people are often perceived as having mental, emotional, and even moral impairments.[34] The fat person is perpetually rejected by society, which disregards his or her needs: buses accommodate wheelchairs; most buildings have ramps; but in public vehicles and buildings, no larger chairs exist for the larger person. Seats are actually getting smaller, so that restaurants, buses, airplanes, and movie theaters can enlarge their seating capacities. Airplanes do offer seat-belt extenders for those with a larger

22.1. One freak figure that has endured from the dime museum through to the contemporary talk show is the fat person, shown here in a dime museum cabinet photograph. Courtesy of Robert Gould Shaw. Harvard Theatre Collection, The Houghton Library.

girth, but it must be humiliating to ask for one. In almost every aspect of daily living the fat person is positioned outside the norm.[35]

The meaning of fat has changed over the past century. Fat used to be a description; today it is a moral indictment. It has become more stigmatized than it was in the dime museum freak show. A dime museum lecturer, Professor Bumpus, once described Cherrie Burnham, a 610-pound woman, as "fat," "beautiful," and "magnificent," with "cheeks like the sun-kissed melon!" He compared her to Queen Victoria, Boadicea, and Delilah.[36] Contrastingly, *Mirabella* magazine recently featured an article in which the author wrote that her bright and witty friend, a woman who weighed more than three hundred pounds, had only one identity: fat.[37]

Although fat is not solely a feminist issue, fat women signify differently from fat men, and the nineteenth-century freak show did not exhibit many fat men. Most large men were either billed as Giants or as the "Heaviest Human Alive." "Fat" was a term primarily associated with women or young boys, as with "R. J. James, the Fat Boy," or "Chauncey Morlan, the Fat Boy."[38] Robert Bogdan observed that Fat Ladies were exhibited in a comical fashion.[39] Obese women had such titles as "Dolly Dimples" or "Baby Ruth." They wore little-girl outfits and acted in a self-mocking, coquettish manner. Never was a fat man paired with a skeletal woman; it was always the other way around. In the hierarchy of the freak world, the Fat Lady had little status. While many freaks earned hundreds of dollars a week, fat women were hired for only twenty-five to fifty dollars a week.[40]

Talk show programs with titles like "You're Too Fat to Wear That," "Mom I Don't Want to Be Fat Like You," and "You're Too Fat for the Beach" continue the freak show tradition of ridiculing fat women.[41] Rarely do overweight women appear on talk shows by themselves; usually they are paired with a slim relative who serves to emphasize their fatness. After being publicly humiliated, these women customarily cry, yearning for acceptance from their family as well as the audience. The obese person is not looked on with sympathy, as a born freak might be, but is viewed as a type of the self-made freak, someone responsible for his or her own condition. Society has not truly accepted some of the latest medical explanations of certain types of obesity, which involve genetics and glandular and hormonal problems; the fat person is believed simply to lack willpower and self-control.[42] The problem, wrote Kim Chernin, is not in our bodies but in our "attitudes toward the body."[43] Being slim is highly valued in our society, and fat people seem to be flouting an unwritten law and thwarting our mutual expectations of sane, reasonable behavior.[44]

The television talk show is undeniably a late-twentieth-century freak show that uses many of the conventions established more than a hundred and fifty years ago by the dime museums. The freak show was—and is—about spectacle: it is a place where human deviance is enhanced, dressed, coiffed, and propped up for the entertainment of a paying audience. The freak show is about relationships: *us* versus *them*, the normal versus the freaks. It is about culture, which determines what is freakish and what is not. It is about the human body and society's perception of normal and abnormal. It is about psychology and deviant behavior. But most importantly, it is about people on display and the public examination of what are essentially private affairs.

NOTES

1. Brooks McNamara, " 'A Congress of Wonders!' The Rise and Fall of the Dime Museum," *Emerson Society Quarterly* 20, no. 3 (1974): 219.

2. Robert Bogdan, *Freak Show: Presenting Human Oddities for Amusement and Profit* (Chicago: University of Chicago Press, 1988), 9.

3. Felix Isman, *Weber and Fields* (New York: Boni and Liveright, 1924), 50.

4. "Huber's Museum in the Discard," *New York Telegraph*, 17 July 1910.

5. Barry Gray, "Freaks and What I Know about Them," *Cincinnati Billboard*, 20 March 1920.

6. Weldon B. Durham, *American Theatre Companies* (Westport, Conn.: Greenwood, 1986), 69.

7. Robert Toll, *On with the Show* (New York: Oxford University Press, 1976), 279; Walter Bodin and Burnet Hershey, *It's a Small World* (New York: Coward-McCann, 1934), 240; William G. Fitzgerald, "Side-Show III," *Strand Magazine*, June 1897, 521.

8. Isman, *Weber and Fields*, 42.

9. Ibid., 44.

10. "Barnum and Brady, Pictures from the Collection of Frederick Hill Meserve," clipping file, New York Public Library, Lincoln Center; George C. D. Odell, *Annals of the New York Stage* (New York: Columbia University Press, 1927–1949), 7:503.

11. See Odell, *Annals of the New York Stage*, vols. 12–16.

12. Ibid., 15:455.

13. Don Wilmeth, *American and English Popular Entertainment* (Detroit: Book Tower, 1980), 241.

14. Oliver Pilat and Jo Ranson, *Sodom by the Sea* (Garden City, N.Y.: Doubleday, Doran, 1941), 179.

15. John Kasson, *Amusing the Million: Coney Island at the Turn of the Century* (New York: Hill and

Wang, 1978), 3, 8; Andrea Stulman Dennett and Nina Warnke, "Disaster Spectacles at the Turn of the Century," *Film History* 4 (1990): 101.

16. Alva Johnston, "Profiles: Boss of the Circus," *New Yorker,* 6 April 1933.

17. Edo McCullough, *Good Old Coney Island* (New York: Charles Scribner's Sons, 1957), 258, 265.

18. "Ripley Gleans Curious Facts on Every Hand," *New York Times,* 27 December 1934.

19. "Ripley's Show Boasts 25 Wonders," *New York Times,* 26 December 1934; "5,000 Enjoy Ripley's Odditorium at Opening of Show Here," *Washington Times,* 5 January 1934.

20. Frederick Drimmer, *Very Special People* (New York: Amjon, 1973), 15.

21. Janice Paran, "Home Is Where Their Art Is," *American Theater,* October 1992, 34; Douglas Martin, "The Rebirth of a Sideshow at Coney Island," *New York Times,* 4 September 1992.

22. "Dos & Don'ts," *Glamour,* January 1995, 112.

23. Linda Frye Burnham, "*High Performance,* Performance Art, and Me," *Village Voice,* 24 June 1986.

24. James B. Twitchell, *Carnival Culture* (New York: Columbia University Press, 1992), 202.

25. Michelle Green, "Fatal Attraction," *People,* 27 March 1995, 40–43.

26. Ibid., 42.

27. Bogdan, *Freak Show,* 131.

28. Ibid., 207.

29. Leslie Fiedler, *Freaks: Myths and Images of the Secret Self* (New York: Simon and Schuster, 1978), 214–18.

30. *TV Guide,* October-December 1994.

31. Odell, *Annals of the New York Stage,* 15:150.

32. Ibid., vols. 14 and 15.

33. *Richard Bey,* "Bikini Contest," 1 July 1995; *Geraldo,* "Hunk of the Year Contest," 20 March 1995.

34. Natalie Allon, "The Stigma of Overweight in Everyday Life," in *The Psychological Aspects of Obesity,* ed. Benjamin B. Wolman (New York: Van Nostrand Reinhold, 1982), 131.

35. Ibid., 132.

36. Rollin Lynde Hartt, *The People at Play* (Boston: Arno, 1974), 94.

37. Barbara Grizzuti Harrison, "Flesh, Food and Fashion," *Mirabella,* January 1995, 21.

38. "The Fat Man and His Friends," *American Heritage* 17, no. 4 (June 1966): 35; Gahan Wilson, "Freaks," 25 April 1966, 30–32, Clipping file, New York Public Library, Lincoln Center; Bogdan, *Freak Show,* 13.

39. Bogdan, *Freak Show,* 114.

40. George Middleton, *Circus Memoirs* (Los Angeles: George Rice, 1913), 72. Of course, there were exceptions such as "Big Winny," whom he paid three hundred dollars a week.

41. *Sally Jessy Raphaël,* 24 April 1995; *Ricki Lake,* 27 April 1995; *Richard Bey,* 10 July 1995.

42. Allon, "The Stigma of Overweight in Everyday Life," 131.

43. Kim Chernin, *The Obsession: Reflections on the Tyranny of Slenderness* (New York: Harper and Row, 1981), 30.

44. Marcia Millman, *Such a Pretty Face: Being Fat in America* (New York: W. W. Norton, 1980), 71.

TWENTY THREE

Freaks in Space: "Extraterrestrialism" and "Deep-Space Multiculturalism"

JEFFREY A. WEINSTOCK

BOUNDARY BREAKERS

Freaks are those human beings who exist outside the structure of binary oppositions which govern our basic concepts and modes of self-definition. They occupy the impossible middle ground between binary pairs.

—ELIZABETH GROSZ[1]

The alien ... always positions itself somewhere between pure familiarity and pure otherness. ... Taking its place on the border between identity and difference, it marks that border, articulating it while at the same time disarticulating and confusing the distinctions the border stands for.

—MICHAEL BEEHLER[2]

A mixed category, the monster resists any classification built on hierarchy or a merely binary opposition, demanding instead a "system" allowing polyphony, mixed response ... and resistance to integration. . .

—JEFFREY JEROME COHEN[3]

It is no accident that Elizabeth Grosz, Michael Beehler, and Jeffrey Jerome Cohen figure freaks, aliens, and monsters in nearly identical terms: the three categories are merely three branches of the same amorphous and disturbing family of "boundary breakers." All three, in their relationship with and proximity to the "human" and the "normal," raise and problematize the discreteness of opposing categories such as Self/Other, Difference/Sameness, Human/Nonhuman, Normal/Abnormal. All three transgress schemes of cultural categorization. All three simultaneously fascinate and horrify.

Yet, in a late-twentieth-century American context, the three are not the same. If I can extrapolate from my own refusal to equate freak show freaks with monsters, I suggest that the terms "freak" and "monster" resonate differently in contemporary American culture. To locate the site of the extraterrestrial alien in the contemporary Science Fiction (SF) text, we first need to differentiate between the concepts of the modern freak and the monster.

To the extent that it is possible and desirable to draw distinctions between the two, I suggest certain contingent and contestable differences. As opposed to the monster, I propose that the freak is, as Fiedler notes, "one of us."[4] Though corporeally or behaviorally different in some disturbing way, the freak remains identifiably *human*.[5] The monster, as Cohen has remarked, exists at more of a remove: there is something irreducibly superhuman or nonhuman about it; having a human body differently configured, the monstrous body exists *beyond* the human.[6] Thus, on a continuum stretching from human to nonhuman, from a mythical conception of a unified, bounded self to an equally mythical notion of an absolute other, the freak remains contiguous with the human, while the monster exists at a farther remove, at a point approaching the unknowable. A gap exists between the monster and the human, a gap problematically occupied by the freak.

A second distinction between the freak and the monster is the aspect of physical threat. One component of Noël Carroll's definition of the monster, as articulated in *The Philosophy of Horror*, is the ability of the monster to cause bodily and/or psychic harm to those it encounters.[7] If we are willing to adopt Carroll's definition in this context, then another distinction that can be drawn between the freak and the monster is threat potential. The encounter with the freak does not imperil the immediate health or physical well-being of the observer. This is not to say that the freak is not dangerous in its own way, but the threat of the freak exists at the level of psychological dis-ease; the corporeal freak induces anxiety via the stimulation of repressed fears concerning bodily integrity and social individuation. Although the proximity of the freak to the "normal" may be disconcerting and produce anxiety, the freak generally does not endanger those it encounters.

Although never "human," the extraterrestrial can fall anywhere on the continuum between human and monster: the alien can be unproblematically monstrous (e.g., the ever-popular, disgusting, dangerous, and emphatically nonhuman Blob), or as close to human as possible without actually being human (e.g., *Star Trek*'s Spock).[8] Most aliens fall somewhere in between monster and human: into the freak zone.

Perhaps it is not coincidental that 1940, the date Robert Bogdan defines as the swan song of the American freak show, is also the same date noted as the beginning of what has been dubbed by SF critics and aficionados as the "Golden Age of Science Fiction." The American SF scene in the 1940s witnessed an explosion of popularity and creative talent. Authors such as John Campbell, Lester del Rey, Robert Heinlein, Theodore Sturgeon, Isaac Asimov, Clifford D. Simak, and Ray Bradbury opted to write in and transformed the SF genre, fashioning a bevy of unfamiliar worlds and exotic aliens in the process.

To what can we attribute the attraction of speculative formats in the 1940s? Perhaps with the freak show's waning hold on American culture, along with society's moral reevaluation of exhibiting real-world non-Western or disabled people for amusement, a psychic *need* for freaks found expression in SF fiction and film. Although the freak show may be all but extinct in contemporary America, it remains alive and kicking on the big screen, where Wookies, Draks, Klingons, Ewoks, and a host of other aliens spanning the alphabet from the lovable E.T. to the mischievous Q to the imperialistic V enthrall and disturb viewers with a vast array of somatic forms and divergent cultures. The freak show, the exhibition of difference for amusement, the apex of terrestrial "political incorrectness," is alive and well in space.

This chapter will concentrate on two SF series, both of which have enjoyed immense popularity in America and worldwide: the George Lucas *Star Wars* trilogy, *Star Wars* (1977),

The Empire Strikes Back (1980), and *The Return of the Jedi* (1984); and the recent television series *Star Trek: The Next Generation (STNG),* aired from 1987 to 1994. These two SF series present alien races in two distinct manners: whereas the *Star Wars* movies exoticize and emphasize the alien as freakish and essentially inferior in a manner that I will refer to as "Extraterrestrialism," the more "progressive" *STNG* attempts to assert (not unproblematically) an ethic of cultural relativism that I will call "Deep-Space Multiculturalism." Before I explore this difference, however, it is worth noting in brief the ways in which the American freak show, from its earliest inceptions, has always been "science fictional."

SCIENCE/FREAK/FICTION

The work of Bogdan makes evident that the freak emerged from the conjunction of science *and* fiction. As he staunchly maintains, the "freak" is not an essential ontological category, but a construct produced at the crossroads of multiple discourses, including the medical, anthropological, and economic. Always problematically articulated in opposition to varying conceptions of "normalcy," the freak "is not a quality that belongs to an individual. . . . [It] is a frame of mind, a set of practices, a way of thinking about and presenting people."[9] In this sense, freaks are always already fictional—not born, but made. And the text that is the freakish body can be read to reveal the ideologies and attitudes of the cultural context that scripted it.

Bogdan observes that scientific and medical discourses have been heavily implicated in constructing and modifying the changing story of the freak. Nineteenth-century American scientists and physicians, intent upon establishing "scientific" classifications for "freaks of nature," achieved heightened visibility by serving as "experts" in cases of "human curiosities," and the fact that "reputable scientists" were interested in such things legitimated the public's voyeuristic interest in freak exhibits. In addition to the interest displayed in freaks by physicians and scientists, the "educational" and "scientific" value of the freak show was further legitimated both by the association of freak displays with museums, which frequently incorporated exhibits of "human curiosities," and by the continuing exploration of the globe. Bogdan notes that non-Western people brought back to the United States and exhibited as freaks "stimulated the popular imagination and kindled belief in races of tailed people, dwarfs, giants, and even people with double heads that paralleled creatures of ancient mythology."[10] The "freak" thus became a locus defined by the convergence of nineteenth-century scientific and anthropological discourse, as well as folklore and mythology.

Added to the stories told by science and the freak-tales already prevalent in the culture were those told by the showmen. Bogdan writes that showmen "embellish[ed] their exhibits with presentations that were in some cases half-truths and in others out-and-out lies. . . . Mid-nineteenth century America provided the ideal venue for humbug to be institutionalized as a fine art and as a basic and lasting part of the freak show."[11] Drawing from nineteenth- and early-twentieth-century scientific reports and travelogues, freak show promoters, exploiting and feeding the public's interest in the "exotic" and the "primitive," claimed to have gathered their exhibits from various mysterious parts of the world. Bogdan even details a few (precocious) instances in which the exhibit's origin was claimed as extraterrestrial.[12] Together, the showmen and the prevalent scientific discourses collaborated to script the popular conception of the freak.

If science, as Donna Haraway maintains, is "our myth," a story about knowledge and power, a "contestable text,"[13] then the exhibition of the freak show freak was always a double fiction, the showman's story layered upon the scientific story. Contemporary SF follows this same recipe in building its aliens: juxtaposing and enmeshing the scientific with the fantastic and sensational, SF merely relocates the terrestrial freak into orbit. Inasmuch as SF aliens frequently function as thinly veiled metaphors for real-world racial, ethnic, religious, somatic, and political groups, the presentation of exotic extraterrestrials often functions prejudicially and imperialistically, much as the actual incorporation of non-Western peoples into the freak show did in the nineteenth and early twentieth centuries.

Extraterrestrialism

Science Fiction provides a rich source of generic metaphors for the depiction of otherness, and the "alien" is one of the most familiar: it enables difference to be constructed in terms of binary oppositions which reinforce relations of dominance and subordination.
—JENNY WOLMARK [14]

If "Orientalism," as famously proposed by Edward Said, is the manner in which ideas of the "Orient" and the "Oriental" were constructed and existed for the West as "a topic of learning, discovery, practice" on the one hand, and a site of "dreams, images, fantasies, myths, obsessions and requirements"[15] on the other, then it seems appropriate to refer to constructions of exoticized space aliens in SF texts as "Extraterrestrialism." The ostensible difference between Orientalism and Extraterrestrialism is, of course, that the former has affected and continues to affect millions of real-world inhabitants. Orientalism, as a system of discursive practices involving the stereotyping of the "Oriental" as biologically inferior and serving to justify imperialism, has functioned as a powerful real-world force.

In contrast, Extraterrestrialism refers to purely fictitious creations. However, the alien is never innocent, never totally divorced from real-world politics. As numerous SF critics have observed, "one cannot depict the totally alien."[16] Extraterrestrials, particularly because they do *not* exist in the real world outside of the texts and tabloids that give them life, readily become metaphors for terrestrial groups and situations, thereby constructing and reinforcing specific ideological positions. Leighton Brett Cooke explains, "Fictional aliens are shaped to satisfy the fantasy needs of human readers; there is little else they could be expected to do."[17] Cooke adds, "By now, the potential of science fiction for the expression of xenophobic, even racist sentiments is well acknowledged."[18] As with the stereotypical "Oriental," underlying the imagining of aliens are specific configurations of power. As we shall see with the *Star Wars* movies, for example, Extraterrestrialism, by drawing from repertoires of real-world stereotypes, can function as an unproblematic extension of Orientalism. Depictions of aliens in SF texts can tell us a great deal about the extent to which a given culture values and fears human difference and diversity.

Star Wars and the Deviant Alien

The American freak show has not disappeared, it simply has been relocated to "a galaxy far, far away." Presented as fairy tales, dislocated in time and space, the *Star Wars* movies wear their ideological affiliations on their sleeves. As John Fieder notes, "The rebels are clean, white Americans who befriend life-like machines. The Empire's vaguely Prussian militarists are machine-like men. The odd extraterrestrial stands in for ethnic variation in traditional American style, either dangerous scum . . . or as the inarticulate sidekick, Chewbacca."[19] Chewbacca is Big-Foot in space, the freak show hirsute man in orbit, the missing link between man and animal. However, if we cast *Star Wars* in the mode of the traditional American romance, a tradition structured, as Fiedler notes, by the homosocial pairing of the white hero and his nonwhite companion, (Huck and Jim, Ishmael and Quee-Queg, etc.),[20] then the depiction of Han Solo's furry sidekick as an "inarticulate," ape-like brute incorporates some well-known and particularly nasty racist stereotypes of black men. Chewbacca as both missing link and subordinate nonwhite companion reifies the position of white male as top of the evolutionary ladder. Perhaps Chewbacca's hulking presence serves as substitute for the displaced black body of James Earl Jones, present only as the authoritative voice of the black-garbed Darth Vader.

Particularly interesting in *The Return of the Jedi* is the ease with which the "good" Annakin Skywalker is separated from the "dark" side of the "force" and recuperated as Luke's father once he sheds Darth Vader's black exterior (and the voice of James Earl Jones). Conveniently forgotten in the drive towards reunification of the family that occurs at the end of *Jedi* (a Disneyesque reunification in which the role of the mother, as it is throughout the trilogy, is excluded entirely) is Annakin-as-Vader's complicity not only in a multitude of individual deaths, but in the destruction of an entire *planet*. The *Star Wars* trilogy exhibits a Manichean pattern of black-and-white morality in which the metaphors of "light" as good and "dark" as evil are realized not only in the "dark" and (presumably) light sides of the "the force," but also in the corporeal divisions of "clean white" rebels and nonwhite alien scum.[21] The clearest illustrations of this operative Extraterrestrialism, the exhibition and exoticization of freakish aliens implicitly presented as inferior, occur in the memorable cantina sequence of *Star Wars* and in the stronghold of Jabba the Hut sequence in *Jedi*.

Lucas provides this description of Luke's descent into the cantina: "The murky, moldy den is filled with a startling array of weird and exotic alien creatures and monsters at the long metallic bar. At first the sight is horrifying. One-eyed, thousand-eyed, slimy, furry, scaly, tentacled, and clawed creatures huddle over drinks."[22] As Luke enters the cantina, the camera lovingly lingers on one freakish form after another as the alien denizens cavort and mingle, banter in strange dialects, consume dangerous-looking concoctions, and nonchalantly take draughts from hookahs. A conjunction of the freak show and the opium den, the outlandish inhabitants bear witness through their physical representations to Ben Kenobi's characterization of the Mos Eisley spaceport as "a wretched hive of scum and villainy."[23] Here deviation from the white human norm represented by Luke and Ben unproblematically correlates with moral degeneracy, for this carnivalesque atmosphere is a mercenary world without law or compassion.

As Ben separates from the young, wide-eyed Luke to look for off-world transport, Luke is accosted by a drunken alien, referred to in the script as a "hideous *freak*,"[24] and his facially disfigured human companion. A fight ensues, during which Ben severs the arm of one of Luke's assailants with his light-saber. The cantina patrons, momentarily distracted by this eruption of violence, return to their activities at the end of the skirmish unfazed and unexcited; we are to understand that such displays of aggression are common in this establishment. Confirming this assumption is Han Solo's execution of the unsubtly named "Greedo," the "slimy green-faced alien"[25] bounty hunter who has just expressed his delight at an opportunity to kill the cornered Solo. As before, the freakish cantina clientele barely acknowledge the killing. For his part, an unconcerned Solo tosses a few coins on the bar on the way out, mumbling, "Sorry about the mess." Within the *Star Wars* universe, the killing of an alien is of little importance.

The cantina sequence is a freak show pure and simple. It is structured as a world of difference and deviance, and the camera's isolation of monstrous form after monstrous form for the audience's amusement turns this spectacle into an extraterrestrial exhibition. The unquestioned correlation of external difference and disfigurement with moral degeneracy works to essentialize the freakish alien as inferior. This is the first test of Luke's *bildungsroman* development and serves as a powerful lesson: beware the freak. In contradiction to the familiar maxim, books *can* be read by their covers: external ugliness is symptomatic of internal moral degeneracy. (I shall address the correlation of *cuteness* with innocuousness and naiveté presently). And it is appropriate that a limb is severed in this sequence, prefiguring both Luke and Vader's loss of right hands in *Empire* and *Jedi*, respectively, as well as C3PO's numerous dismemberments and Luke's decapitation of the fantasy Vader in *Empire*. Luke, and the *Star Wars* movies more generally, display a preoccupation with issues of bodily integrity and bodily limitations. Perhaps one function of the somatic freak is to excite anxiety in the viewer by triggering repressed memories of the pre-Oedipal body-image.[26] The morphological alien stimulates uneasiness about the integrity of one's own body, an uneasiness articulated in the cantina sequence by Luke's juxtaposition of freakish alien bodies with a severed arm.

The moral degeneracy of the unwholesome alien is corroborated by the court of Jabba the Hut in *Jedi*. Jabba himself is the most monstrous creation of the *Star Wars* series and is described enthusiastically in James Kahn's novelization of the movie as follows:

> His head was three times human size, perhaps four. His eyes were yellow, reptilian—his skin was like a snake's . . . covered with a fine layer of grease. He had no neck, but only a series of chins that expanded finally into a great bloated body. . . . Stunted, almost useless arms sprouted from his upper torso, the sticky fingers of his left hand languidly wrapped around the smoking-end of his water-pipe. He had no hair—it had fallen out from a combination of diseases. He had no legs—his trunk simply tapered gradually to a long, plump snake-tail that stretched along the length of the platform like a tube of yeasty dough. His lipless mouth was wide, almost ear to ear, and he drooled continuously.[27]

Greasy, diseased, bloated, misshapen, incomplete—Jabba is a freak show unto himself, suggesting simultaneously the fat man, the legless wonder, a misshapen fetus, and the enlarged head of an achondroplastic dwarf. And, of course, to confirm Jabba's alien degeneracy, as with the Cantina denizens, he does not speak English. Like the cantina, his stronghold, populated by an array of evil-looking aliens, is a bastion of debauchery. From his position on the platform, Jabba surveys his domain and ogles his scantily clad slave dancer, before gleefully feeding her to his pet monster to the delight of his court. The water-pipe (present also in the cantina), as well as Jabba's sultan-like reclining position on the dais and the haremesque slave dancer, make the link between Orientalism and Extraterrestrialism obvious. Jabba's engorged size and repulsive appearance correlate directly with his unrestrained appetite for wealth and power. In opposition to Jabba's excess, the white, human heroes demonstrate the (American) virtues of self-government, control, and discipline. Jabba's degeneracy is the unrestrained appetite of the "Oriental despot" and, to the extent that the viewer consciously or unconsciously makes this connection, Extraterrestrialism functions as a futuristic extension of Orientalism.

Of course, not all aliens in the *Star Wars* movies are evil monsters, and the audience easily can identify which aliens are safe and friendly: as a rule, ugly aliens are bad, cute aliens are good (albeit still inferior). The latter is the role of the ever-lovable Ewoks, those funny, furry, diminutive second cousins to the Wookie whose presence dominates much of *Jedi* and for many is its most memorable aspect. We know that these walking teddy bears are innocuous because they are cute; within the world of *Star Wars*, this is assurance enough. Tribal forest dwellers, the Ewoks are also figured as being too "primitive" to be sneaky or double-dealing; they live in trees, ornament themselves with crude bone necklaces, and believe in magic. If Chewbacca fills in as the nonwhite companion of the American romance, then the Ewoks play on an equally stereotypical construction of the "primitive" African pygmy tribe living in the jungle, astounded by the white man's technological "magic" and too simple to be devious. Through Chewbacca and the Ewoks, the *Star Wars* movies evoke both the threatening and trivialized stereotypes of Africans. In each case, the intellectual superiority of the white male is reconfirmed by comparison.

A powerful discourse of Extraterrestrialism thus operates in the *Star Wars* movies: the intrinsic difference of the alien often translates into inferiority and moral bankruptcy, while simultaneously affirming the valor and superiority of the white male heroes. The essentialized alien others and the fear of difference operative in the *Star Wars* features reveal that the impulse to exhibit freakishness has been relocated from the terrestrial freak show into SF cinema. In fact, most of the extraterrestrials in the *Star Wars* movies suggest a freak show parallel: as noted, Chewbacca is a missing link or hirsute man and Jabba is both fat man and a legless wonder. The Ewoks suggest the "cute" freak show midget. Further, by suggesting that Chewbacca is black, Jabba is the "Oriental despot," and the Ewoks are "primitive" tribal members, the racist, hegemonic resonances of alien representations find grounding in real-world discourse. It matters little whether the audience recognizes specific racist overtones behind the representation of any individual alien species, because the general equation of the *Star Wars* movies is unmistakable: difference equals danger. The white male Jedi, fighting to maintain his position of authority in a universe of freaks and evil others, is the top of the evolutionary ladder. The audience views an array of alien others at which to gawk and laugh, but the serious job of saving the universe lies with the "normal" white male humans.[28]

DEEP-SPACE MULTICULTURALISM?

In contrast to the *Star Wars* movies' imperialist view of difference, the question of how to deal with alien races and cultures in nonprejudicial and nonimperialistic ways is a persistent theme of the *Star Trek: The Next Generation* series. In its ostensible sensitivity to the value of diversity, its resistance to judgments based on appearance and degree of deviance from a humanoid norm, and its incorporation of both nonwhite and alien others into the crew of the *Enterprise, STNG* apparently demonstrates an ethic of what I will refer to as "deep-space multiculturalism." The back cover to *The Star Trek: The Next Generation Companion* describes the program as follows: "Led by Captain Jean-Luc Picard . . . , the *U.S.S. Enterprise* blazed a trail of understanding across an unfamiliar galaxy. . . . [It] brought to vivid life a future where cooperation and mutual understanding proved the key to solving humanity's problems—and enabled galactic civilization to flourish."[29] To its credit, the series indeed does take major steps toward dismantling unfounded conjunctions of physical difference with intellectual inferiority and/or moral degeneracy. However, in contradiction to this utopian universe of the future suggested in the quotation above, the world of *STNG* is not a perfect galaxy of peace, love, and understanding. Although the bridge of the *Enterprise*, under the moderate and controlled command of Captain Picard, is a locus of "enlightened understanding," the rest of the universe always has something to learn about being "human." And inasmuch as its alien representations slip with greater or lesser degrees of ease into identifiable metaphors for real-world groups, racist and imperialist ideologies again reassert themselves, even beneath the deep-space multicultural façade of the *Enterprise* bridge.

Several "alien" races are represented on the bridge of the *Enterprise:* there is Worf, the black Klingon, chief security officer (the brawn); Data, the android (the brains); and the half-Betazoid ship's counselor, Deanna Troi (the sensitive female/sex object). All three of these characters, however, fail in different ways to measure up to the level of human white male; each is in some way, either literally or metaphorically, "alien."

The fact that Worf was raised by human foster parents means that there is not a "full-blooded" alien on the bridge of the *Enterprise*. Indeed, Worf can be integrated into the crew precisely because his savage Klingon instincts have been "tempered" by his lifelong association with humans. In spite of this, Worf is still depicted constantly fighting to pass as human, to suppress his Klingon instincts—nature and nurture are in constant conflict. Klingons in *STNG*, though more trustworthy than Romulans because they rigorously adhere to an honor code, are warriors one step away from barbarians. In the episode entitled "Birthright,"[30] Worf teaches certain isolated Klingon youth the art and glory of the hunt. In the forest, armed with a spear, Worf literally can smell the scent of his prey. The bloodlust of the Klingon warrior, not surprisingly, translates into equally aggressive and animalistic sexual practices: aroused Klingons growl at each other and Klingon foreplay is very violent. The racist stereotype of the primitive animal savagery of the black man requires little elaboration. As with Chewbacca, the black Klingon finds its freak show parallel in the missing link or wild man. Worf's human masquerade frequently slips to reveal his essential otherness—a "primitive" savagery that removes the black man from the circle of "enlightened humanity" back to the freak show stage, again reconfirming the superiority of the controlled, "evolved" white male.[31]

In contrast to the hypermasculine Worf, Deanna Troi, the half-Betazoid "empath" (the *Enterprise*'s exotic Circassian beauty), assumes the typical feminine role of sensitive nurturer. For the first several seasons, Counselor Troi had the dubious distinction of being the only bridge member to wear a skirt. Several costume changes later, Troi was still the only officer to don a cleavage-accentuating scoop-neck. Only half-Betazoid, Troi's telepathic abilities are not keen enough to actually read thoughts—she is restricted to sensing emotional states. Although she assumes more authority as the series progresses, in Cassandra-like fashion, the bridge crew typically acknowledge her assessment of a given situation and then continue with whatever plan they were already considering. Troi's primary role on board the *Enterprise* is as psychologist for the crew and love interest for, first Riker, and then Worf. (Her involvement with the aggressive Worf at the end of the series' run seems to confirm the sexist assumption that all women *want* to be dominated). Mary Jo Deegan's analysis of the role of women in the original *Star Trek* series seems equally applicable to *STNG:* "Since all men vie for power, human and alien males have a common bond. In their lust for power even male Klingons behave more like men than human women do."[32] In Deegan's evaluation, women in *Star Trek* are always "aliens," secondary figures who either "provide romance or reveal that any woman's desire for power is 'abnormal.'"[33]

Data, the android, although not an "alien" in the biological sense, most clearly exemplifies the extraterrestrial position as articulated by *STNG*. Data *wants* to be human and is constantly learning what it means *to be* human. Deprived of emotions and coolly logical, Data is *STNG*'s Spock substitute. The series chronicles Data's development and his convergence with "humanity," which within *STNG* is the evolutionary apex—the position occupied by the white male. Synonymous with goodness, decency, integrity, ingenuity, and compassion, "human" serves not simply as a biological designation, but as a moral marker. Alien races are assessed by the extent to which they can understand and approximate the human. It is taken as self-evident that all alien cultures, if they do not already, will understand and recognize the obvious superiority of human parameters such as beliefs in the ideas of individual responsibility and equity, and the experiences of guilt and compassion.

In general, alien races in *STNG* can be divided into two categories: those races (generally depicted as "primitive") that need to learn emotional restraint (e.g., races such as the Klingons that need to be taught moderation), and those (generally technologically advanced) races that need to "loosen up" (e.g., Vulcans and androids). Through this universe of inadequate alien others travels the remarkably controlled and duty-bound Captain Picard, exemplifying the virtues of the Aristotelian mean and, Christ-like, teaching both the barbaric primitive races and the logical, emotionally frigid races he encounters the value of *mercy*.[34] Physical diversity is tolerated to the extent that the alien's *values* coincide with the "human."

Although *STNG* staunchly maintains the universal superiority of the "human," it has taken a major step forward from the alien depictions found in the *Star Wars* movies; physical deviation from a humanoid norm is no longer automatically equated with moral degeneracy.[35] The shift is somewhat comparable to the rejection of the permissible exhibition of non-Western others as freaks in favor of a more tolerant ethic of cultural relativism. The continuing *Star Trek* series *(Deep-Space 9* and *Star Trek Voyager)* now find themselves facing the same conundrum confronting contemporary ethnography: how to survey/study/write about other cultures without objectifying and "dehumanizing" the other. *STNG*'s progressive thinking never reached the level of questioning its own authority or realizing the collaborative production of ethnographic knowledge. How far the spin-off series will go in this direction remains to be seen.

HORRIBLE OTHERS, HORRIBLE SELVES

This essay started with three quotations, each suggesting how freaks, aliens, or monsters function as categorical boundary breakers, entities that transgress cultural schemes of classification and violate hierarchical structures of binary opposition. The construction of the alien is always a complex play of disavowal and identification. The extraterrestrial alien, as a fictional creation, must function as a site of tension between self and other. As a projection of otherness generated from within the self, the figure of the alien articulates what a given culture perceives as different, aberrant, strange, freakish. Extraterrestrialism, the process of "othering" that essentializes alien difference as inferiority, acts to reify and reinforce the "human" as superior. Inasmuch as the freakish SF alien frequently draws from real-world racial stereotypes, the "human" frequently narrows to white, American, and male.

Yet, the alien is a site of ambiguity, anxiety, and contestation. The vehemence with which the alien, the freak, and the other are renounced, degraded, and disavowed by a culture, be it on the freak show stage or in the SF feature, suggests a commensurate level of anxiety in the collective distancing psyche. Constructed as a freak, a curiosity to be exhibited and gawked at, the alien calls the human into question. To live with the alien, the freak, and the monster is to come to terms with ourselves.

NOTES
I offer my thanks to Jeffrey Cohen, Noreen O'Connor, and Jill Angelino for their advice and insight.

1. Elizabeth Grosz, "Freaks," *Social Semiotics* 1, no. 2 (1991): 25.

2. Michael Beehler, "Border Patrols," in *Aliens: The Anthropology of Science Fiction*, ed. George E. Slusser and Eric S. Rabkin (Carbondale and Edwardsville: Southern Illinois University Press, 1987), 32.

3. Jeffrey Jerome Cohen, "Monster Culture (Seven Theses)," introduction to *Monster Theory: Reading Culture*, ed. Jeffrey Jerome Cohen (Minneapolis: University of Minnesota Press, forthcoming), 6.

4. Leslie Fiedler, *Freaks: Myths and Images of the Secret Self* (New York: Doubleday, 1978), 24.

5. This distinction results, at least in part, from modern medicine's recuperation of the freak as pathological. As Robert Bogdan observes, during its heyday the freak show was a form of amusement incommensurate with pity. It did not force spectators to confront their own racism, imperialism, and handicapism; rather, it confirmed prejudices and beliefs in inherent racial inferiority and the undisputed superiority of the West. See Robert Bogdan, *Freak Show: Presenting Human Oddities for Amusement and Profit* (Chicago: University of Chicago Press, 1988), 111, 197, 267, 277. I suggest that from a nineteenth-century perspective, the freak and the monster, if not identical, were much closer in proximity that they are in contemporary American culture. As medical science increasingly became able to identify the biological basis of many physical abnormalities, and in some cases provide treatments, the notion of freak as ontological other was destabilized and the physically deviant freak was relocated from the realm of the monster to that of the human.

6. Jeffrey Jerome Cohen, personal communication, June 1995.

7. Noël Carroll, *The Philosophy of Horror* (New York: Routledge, 1990), chap. 1.

8. In fact, inasmuch as "human" serves not just as a biological category but a moral marker, the alien, by desiring to be human, establishes certain criteria for defining the human, and often ends up being *more* human than human. The alien in this context not only recognizes its fundamental *lack*—its "want-of-being," as Lacan would say—but strives to realize a definition of "human" that few humans demonstrate. See the "Deep-Space Multiculturalism?" section of this chapter.

9. Bogdan, *Freak Show*, x, 3.

10. Ibid., 6.

11. Ibid., 31.

12. "In the 1920s and 1930s, Eko and Iko, brothers with albinism and dreadlocks, were presented as ambassadors from Mars discovered near the remains of their spaceship in the Mojave Desert." Bogdan, *Freak Show*, 105.

13. Donna Haraway, *Simians, Cyborgs, and Women: The Reinvention of Nature* (New York: Routledge, 1991), 185.

14. Jenny Wolmark, *Aliens and Others: Science Fiction, Feminism and Postmodernism* (Iowa City: University of Iowa Press, 1994), 2.

15. Homi K. Bhabha, *The Location of Culture* (New York: Routledge, 1994), 71.

16. Gregory Benford, "Effing the Ineffable," in Slusser and Rabkin, *Aliens*, 14.

17. Leighton Brett Cooke, "The Human Alien: In-Groups and Outbreeding in *Enemy Mine*," in Slusser and Rabkin, *Aliens*, 183.

18. Ibid., 181.

19. John Fieder, "Embracing the Alien: Science Fiction in Mass Culture," *Science-Fiction Studies* 9 (1982): 33–34.

20. See Leslie Fiedler, *Love and Death in the American Novel* (New York: Doubleday, 1960).

21. Billy Dee Williams's character Lando Calrissian in *Empire* and *Jedi* only slightly complicates this assessment. Women (Leia) and animals (Chewbacca), those who feel rather than think within Lucas's universe, instantly distrust him, as does the audience. Although he turns out okay in the end, we never entirely get over our initial negative reaction to the character.

22. George Lucas, script to *Star Wars*, in *The Art of Star Wars*, ed. Carol Titelman (New York: Ballantine, 1979), 58–59.

23. Ibid., 53.

24. Ibid., 59, emphasis mine.

25. Ibid., 70.

26. According to Jacques Lacan, prior to the mirror stage the infant is incapable of controlling the movements of its body and is dependent upon the care of others. The child's recognition of the mirror image as its own and joyous assumption of a spatial identity are undercut by the gap between the unity of the image and the continuing fragmentary character of the infant's existence. This discrepancy occasions a kind of primal paranoia—the self is alienated from itself, and this discordance lies at the foundation of the Lacanian notion of human identity. According to Lacan, fantasies about the dissolution of bodily unity and control stem from repressed memories of the lived bodily experience of the infant prior to the mirror stage. I am proposing that the somatic freak can excite such pre-Oedipal memories in the viewer. See Jacques Lacan, *Écrits*, trans. Alan Sheridan (New York: W. W. Norton, 1977), 1–7; and Elizabeth Grosz, *Jacques Lacan: A Feminist Introduction* (New York: Routledge, 1990), 45.

27. James Kahn, *The Return of the Jedi* (New York: Ballantine, 1983), 336.

28. At the end of *Star Wars*, Luke and Han receive medals while Chewbacca stands by and is excluded. Perhaps his loud growl, upsetting the solemnity of the ceremony, is one of frustration rather than joy!

29. Larry Nemecek, *The Star Trek: The Next Generation Companion* (New York: Simon and Schuster, 1995), back cover.

30. This episode first aired February 22, 1993.

31. If Worf incarnates one stereotype of the black man as feral, then the other black male character on the show, Geordi La Forge, incarnates the opposite stereotype of the subservient black man.

32. Mary Jo Deegan, "Sexism in Space: The Freudian Formula in 'Star Trek,'" in *Eros in the Mind's Eye*, ed. Donald Palumbo (Westport, Conn.: Greenwood, 1986), 221.

33. Ibid., 209.

34. It is intriguing that the captain of the *Enterprise* should be a Frenchman, John-Luc Picard, portrayed by the commanding British Shakespearean actor, Patrick Stewart. Presumably, Captain Picard unites the stereotypes of British reserve and duty with French *joie de vivre*, although the former quality seems to be much more in evidence.

35. It should be noted that only rarely is the open-mindedness of the *Enterprise*'s crew to physical "abnormality" pushed to the limit. A salient aspect of *STNG* is the improbably high occurrence of anthropomorphic alien races. Klingons, Romulans, Vulcans, Betazoids, Ferengi, Bajorans, and so on are all differentiated from humans solely by minor facial and cranial deviations. "The Chase," a sixth-season episode first aired April 26, 1993, explains the biological similarity of so many divergent races through recourse to a common ancestor that "seeded" similar DNA codes on a variety of worlds.

TWENTY-FOUR

Being Humaned: Medical Documentaries and the Hyperrealization of Conjoined Twins

DAVID L. CLARK AND CATHERINE MYSER

Nor was it without some reason that I believed that that body which, by a special right, I call mine, belonged to me.

—DESCARTES, *Meditations*

[I]f a foot, or an arm, or any other part, is separated from my body, it is certain that, on that account, nothing has been taken away from my mind.

—DESCARTES, *Meditations*

If anomalously embodied subjects are no longer exhibited in freak shows, as they were for centuries, they remain today the peculiar object of public fascination in which it is very difficult, perhaps impossible, to distinguish simple or even morbid curiosity from outright voyeurism, with all the force of surveillance, objectification, fetishization, and hyperrealization that such forms of looking entail. That extraordinary bodies continue to be the stuff of spectacle is perhaps no more obvious than in the case of conjoined twins, whose birth and surgical separation consistently excite fierce media interest, including the production of full-length documentaries, one example of which is the focus of our attention here. Documentaries about conjoined twins have a mixed inheritance that reflects the complex work they must perform in the subjection of the extraordinary body. These antecedents include the wonder book, which makes specialized knowledge of human oddities available for the polite conversation of lay people; the anatomy lesson, in which the visibility of the flesh, or at least of a deracinated version of it, is inversely proportionate to the visibility of the lived body; the clinical report or case history, whose explanatory narrative transforms the subject into the "patient"; the freak show, with its carefully managed combination of pathos, hyperbole, and prurient amazement; and the television hospital melodrama centered upon the benevolent work of heroic physicians. These elements are woven into the earnestly instructive framework of the documentary genre, whose naturalistic strategies conceal the degree to which the film stages the spectacle it purports to describe. Notwithstanding significant shifts in the cultural construction and reception of the humanly "monstrous," contemporary representations of the extraordinary body in documentaries therefore provide a uniquely illuminating instance of what Neil Harris said of P. T. Barnum's career, namely "the involvement of the politics of entertainment with the politics of life."[1] Our chief interest here is "the politics of life," or, more precisely, the political history of the body, both ordinary and extraordinary, that documentaries about conjoined twins inherit, reiterate, and displace in spectacular fashion. What roles do the twins and their physicians play in this theater of surgery performed internationally before a potential audience of millions? What does it mean to watch the televised representation of these fused and exotic bodies, at once maximally visible and coolly distant, while they undergo the most radical forms of morphological transformation at the hands of the surgeons?

By way of addressing these admittedly large questions, this chapter examines *Siamese Twins*, a documentary written, produced, and directed by Jonathan Palfreman for the PBS television series *Nova*.[2] First broadcast in the United States in 1995, *Siamese Twins* is about Dao and Duan (their full names are never provided), nearly three-year-old conjoined twins born in Thailand and living in what is vaguely identified as "a Bangkok orphanage." The film follows the twins for about eighteen months, after they have been brought to the United States by an international adoption agency for the purpose of separation. The narrative falls roughly into three unevenly divided sections: the first section begins with the twins' arrival in America and includes scenes of family life with their caregivers, Barbara and David Headley, punctuated by various tests in Children's Hospital of Philadelphia to determine the viability of separation surgery (summer 1993); in the second segment, we witness the preparations for surgery, as well as the preseparation and separation surgeries themselves, under the direction of Dr. James O'Neill, head of pediatric surgery (September to December 1993); the concluding section focuses briefly on postoperative life, including rehabilitation therapy (May 1994), a fourth-birthday party (June 1994), and the twins attending preschool (January 1995).

In its most affecting moments, and there are many of these, *Siamese Twins* powerfully conveys the spirited endurance of Dao and Duan, who are subjected to a series of stark dislocations, both physical and psychical: their transportation from their home in Bangkok to an alien culture in Philadelphia, a series of invasive tests and painful preoperative procedures, the dangerous separation surgery itself, and the subsequent shock of their radically altered bodies. Any alleviation of the pain of this extended trauma comes from Dao's and Duan's foster caregivers, whose presence in the film forms a familial alternative to the clinical setting of Children's Hospital of Philadelphia. At their adopted home, the children receive respite from their subjection merely as "patients" and as anomalous bodies in need of repair, even if it is here that we also witness, inevitably, the shaping effects of other discursive regimes. But it is the medical environment where the film's greatest emphasis lies: unlike *Katie and Eilish* (a British documentary about a set of Irish conjoined twins in which the details of the separation surgery are deliberately underplayed so as to allow the camera to linger over the twins' family life),[3] Palfreman's film is arguably not "about" the children at all, except as a means by which to represent the sophisticated medical technology available at Children's Hospital, and the extraordinary medical expertise—pediatric surgeons, urologists, radiologists, plastic surgeons, neurosurgeons—concentrated there. Although Dao and Duan are rarely absent from any frame, it is the doctors who form the consistent focal point of the documentary, making it the postmodern expression of a mise en scène that could be said to have begun with Rembrandt's *The Anatomy Lesson of Dr. Nicolaas Tulp*.[4] In other words, Palfreman's documentary realizes a certain technologized medical gaze, a gaze whose view is insistently actualized in frames filled with images of Dao's and Duan's exposed flesh. Under this close surveillance, the twins are paradoxically both present and absent, because they are reduced to something closer to malformed skin and bones, a "surgical field" in which the new masters of the body will carry out their good, though dangerous, work.

Fully a third of Palfreman's film concerns the graphic details of the fourteen-hour surgery itself, and another third is taken up with the physicians puzzling and triumphing over various bodily "obstacles" to the separation. At no point is the question of *whether* the surgery should take place seriously considered, a startling omission to which we will return; neither are the profound "psychological" implications of the separation addressed, except in passing, and then only *after* the operation has occurred. The suggestion is that in this surgical theater, the physical condition of the twins is so intolerable, and their reconstruction as separate individuals so imperative, that these other considerations are without consequence, or, significantly, of interest mostly to the foster parents. The questions faced by the physicians and caregivers alike prior to separation are represented as mostly surgical in nature, never truly ethical, epistemological, or phenomenological, notwithstanding the fact that Dao and Duan resistantly *embody* these questions, and do so in such a palpably obvious way, simply by being who they are. In short, the documentary proves the point of Leslie Fiedler's observation that conjoined twins "have become supernumeraries" in a spectacle "starring the doctors who make normal human beings out of monsters."[5] True to the psychoanalytic framework of his study, Fiedler's term for this spectacle is "psychodrama," and it is there where our work has a different emphasis. For *Siamese Twins* stages something closer to a theater of medical *regimes*, not personalities; the "monsters" that the "doctors" humanize are not those that dwell within, but, as it were, those that live "without," if by that term we mean the disciplined social body whose normative ideals Palfreman's physicians reiterate.

We wish to concentrate on the film's strategies in *normalizing* Dao and Duan, especially on the ways that the twins' morphological construction or interpellation—to use Althusser's term[6]—parallels and is reciprocally implicated in their cultural interpellation. By the end of the story, being happily integrated into American society and being "carved" into separately embodied individuals (this is a verb to which one of the surgeons resorts) amount almost to the same thing. The film makes this process of interpellation possible by almost completely erasing any evidence of the twins' life in Thailand prior to coming to Philadelphia. At one point Barbara Headley inadvertently articulates this cultural effacement and its exclusionary premises: "When they first asked us to find a home for these children, they were just children, like strangers," she says: "They didn't have a personality, they didn't have anything." There is a curious slide here between two forms of poverty, one real—for the twins, in the narrowest sense, "have" nothing when they are brought to the United States—the other, clearly hallucinated. What Headley intimates in an offhand and no doubt well-meaning remark, *Siamese Twins* pursues as its working assumption. With their life in Thailand deleted, it becomes much easier to pretend that Dao and Duan are blank slates, when in fact they are slates whose profound cultural inscriptions have been simply been rubbed out in and by the film. Of course, Dao and Duan *do* possess personalities before coming to America, and so "have" a great deal, but of that abundance we see and hear almost nothing. For a fleeting instant, and then only as a flashback, we glimpse the twins sitting on the bare floor of their home in a "Bangkok orphanage." As the only visual image of the twins' Thai life in the film, it comes freighted with significance. Filmed not at eye level but from above so as to emphasize the twins' helplessness and isolation, these images also simultaneously reassure us that Dao and Duan nevertheless remain within the benevolently elevated sight of America, whose subject position we as audience members are assumed automatically to occupy as viewers of this documentary. Watching these brief scenes, it is hard not to wonder if the documentary is here also playing on the media image of a "Third World" orphanage—familiar to television viewers from various overseas relief campaigns—as a place of physical deprivation in need of "First World" support and intervention. It seems important to the film's logic that Dao and Duan are orphans, which is to say disconnected from "home" even while at home, and therefore all the more easily figured as "rescuable" and "rescued" from a place that is in any case apparently incapable of offering them either a "true" family or adequate medical care. In the absence of any other details, "Thailand" and "Bangkok" are figures that attract almost exclusively negative connotations, especially concerning children: "Siam" is the prototypical birthplace of malformed infants, and now the site of an AIDS epidemic of almost unimaginable proportions; "Bangkok" is the Asian city of appalling and prurient opportunities, where impoverished rural families sell their children into sex slavery. Compared to Thailand, America can only mean health, prosperity, technological prowess, robust individuality, and familial integrity.

When the film opens, Dao and Duan have already made the long journey to Philadelphia. Their arrival is deemed more important than their departure and all that led up to it, implying that they have come from a place so distant and so foreign that it has dropped out of sight and out of mind before the film has begun. And so their arrival is in effect a nativity scene, in which the twins are born again, borne across the Pacific and delivered safely to America. It is telling that Dao and Duan are first greeted by a flurry of photographers' flashguns, since this celebrity scene anticipates the ways in which their *images* and *imaging* will become crucially important in the documentary. The narrator solemnly tells us that the twins now "begin a new life in a strange land," underlining the fantastic cultural logic of the film, which asserts that lives can stop and start anew with a plane ride. It is not so small a world after all, or rather, it is a world whose geographical imaginary conveniently shrinks and expands according to the ideological uses that this geography serves. Moreover, the suggestion is that an orphaned, Thai life has such a tenuous hold on its infant subjects that mere weeks in America is all it takes to be evaporated, as if it had never happened at all. Throughout the film, Dao's and Duan's indelibly Asian faces and Thai speech form a persistent countermemory to the film's colonialist amnesia. Against the film's dominant logic, these sights and sounds remind us that the elided place where the twins first learned to speak, and love, and learn— generalized as "Thailand"—is not *this* place and will *never be this place*. Barbara and David Headley remark that Dao and Duan know only a few English words, inadvertently calling attention to the fact that, with one brief exception in the opening seconds of the film, no one in the documentary speaks Thai—even of the most elementary kind—to the children in order to help alleviate their isolation. When we are told that the twins nevertheless converse with each other in their native language, the documentary provides us with an image of the children sustaining a tiny island of their "former" lives in a sea of American middle-class culture. When the children are not enduring medical procedures, they are repeatedly shown to be happily embracing this culture, whether eating fast food or watching television: by "culture," the documentary clearly means a culture of consumption.[7] That acculturation is successfully taking place seems mostly important to those who are observing the twins. One of the first things said in the film is Barbara Headley's revealingly anxious allegation that within one day Dao and Duan "feel very comfortable." The narrator confirms this expectation of ease when he tells us that "only six weeks after arriving in Philadelphia, . . . [the twins] are getting the hang of American life"—which is to say, a certain bourgeois version of that life, complete with Barney, Coca Cola, McDonald's hamburgers, birthday cake, frilly dresses, and a large, white house in the fashionable suburbs of Philadelphia.

Insofar as Dao and Duan are given a historical context at all, it comes in the specious form of comparisons to the life of Chang and Eng Bunker, the prototypical and stereotypical instance of concorporate embodiment whose freak show name also forms the title of the documentary. Although brief, the account of the Bunker twins says a great deal about the documentary's assumptions concerning corporeality, both ordinary and extraordinary, and so it is worth pausing to consider in some detail. As the image of the twins in their Bangkok orphanage dissolves into a photograph of their morphological namesake and precursors, Dao and Duan are identified as "in a sense, true Siamese twins." What constitutes this "truth" remains unexplained, presumably because it is so thoroughly caught up in a web of falsehoods, beginning with the racism that underwrites the identification of a "pathology" with an othered cultural group (as in the case of "mongolism," a term still too often used to name subjects with Down's syndrome). How, then, are Dao and Duan "true Siamese twins"? "True" like Chang and Eng, who were in fact Chinese, not Siamese, and whose conjoined morphology was quite unlike that of Dao and Duan? "True" as Siamese, when "Siam" is itself a kind of lie, a nineteenth-century colonialist projection of the West upon the East that is revived in this film in a way that is at once quaint and patronizing, while at the same time registering a certain exoticism that will soon be tamed by Barney and by surgery? While the identities of Dao and Duan are flattened out to fit the generality of "true Siamese twins," the particularities of their life as *Thai* children are once again effaced, spirited away to a time that the narrator vaguely associates, in the shape of the Bunker twins, with "the last century." Chang and Eng, we are told, "travelled to America, where they found work as entertainers." Of course, this is a hallucination of the Bunker's life, for they did not "travel" to America, but, like slaves, were purchased and transported there by two Yankee merchant skippers. The narrator similarly passes over the freakish nature of their labor, peremptorily translating its voyeuristic exploitation into mere "entertainment," which is to say a form of popular diversion not entirely unlike the television documentary itself.

Lest this mirroring connection between the two "shows" go undeveloped, the camera cuts from the faces of Chang and Eng to a flyer advertising their "work" in similarly normalizing terms, "respectfully" informing the "Ladies and Gentlemen of Boston" when and where they will "receive Visitors." Seeing a handbill entitled "Siamese Twins" within a film entitled *Siamese Twins* inadvertently comes close to producing what literary criticism calls a *mise en abyme*, the point at which a text vertiginously becomes the object of its own representation. Given the ways in which the film draws parallels between the two sets of twins, it is almost impossible not to read this advertisement without also considering whether or to what degree contemporary documentaries contain traces of the freak show from which they try to distance themselves. There is a forthrightness about reproducing this advertisement, for it puts to us that for all of its earnestness, the film is, after all, circulated in a medium that is massively committed to the task of recreation. In *Siamese Twins*, "the two great streams of appeal— amusement and instruction"—that Robert Altick describes as finding separate media late in the nineteenth century would appear to be complexly reunited on television late in the twentieth.[8] Does the virtualized universe of television make what was once an obviously exploitative spectacle into something safe, that is, as hygienic and enlightened as the theater of surgery? Fiedler, for example, has written evocatively of what it means to observe conjoined twins: "the beholder sees them looking not only at each other, but—both at once—at him," a moment that Fiedler says breaks the distinctions that normally hold between "audience and exhibit, we and them, normal and Freak."[9] What, then, does it mean to look at conjoined twins *on television*, where this (uneven) two-way visual communication is short-circuited, thereby providing the viewer with a perfectly panoptic vantage point, freeing him and her to look at will without feeling the ambiguous *anagnorisis*—or re-cognition—that might come of a returned gaze?

At the very least, our gaze as viewers repeats from without what occurs within, for Dao and Duan are caught up in an extraordinarily *spectacularized* environment of redoubled images and imaging. In this thoroughly representational economy, the twins are dematerialized in several ways, even as their material form is maximally displayed. For example, the extreme close-ups of the various surgeries so shrinks the distance separating viewer and object that the body simply dissolves into the meaty and unfamiliar recesses of its own viscera. The twins are subjected to an array of imaging technologies (from crude hand-drawn diagrams and over-heads, to CAT scans, MRI, and x-rays) that bring the innermost reaches of their bodies into hypervisibility. Each of these images has its attendant medical observers and interpreters *within* the documentary, making the representation of the twins the object of the film's representation; in other words, at these moments we are watching others watch Dao and Duan. Sophisticated, rotating three-dimensional computer graphics supplement the narrator's visualization of the twins' morphology, momentarily giving their body a ghostly transparency and our eyes a penetrating power that mimics the imaging technologies that the film showcases. If Dao and Duan are captured *in* images, they are also captured *by* images, the most vivid instance being the scenes depicting them listlessly watching Barney on television during a three-month period while they are immobilized in a body cast. This is an experiment in cultural conditioning—Barney, we could say, is the very image of monstrous difference suppressed and domesticated—that even the narrator concedes will be trying. Finally, the narrative includes scenes in which the documentary maker films other photographers in the process of making their own images. The most curious example of this latter form of redoubled spectacularization—of making a spectacle out of a spectacle—occurs during the filming of a large preoperative conference, in which the attending Thai doctors are depicted not as actively participating but as passively videotaping the proceedings. This image comes uncomfortably close to the racist cliché of the camera-touting Asian tourist. Under these theatricalized conditions, the naturalistic distinction between representation and its object wavers and threatens to dissolve into layers of spectacles within spectacles.

Nested within the documentary, ostensibly as medical historical background to Dao's and Duan's condition, the story of the Bunker brothers is in fact two conjoined stories: one of desire fulfilled and the other of desire thwarted. Each story informs our reception of Dao's and Duan's experience in America. In the first instance, Chang and Eng function typologically as "Siamese" twins who escaped a primitive and presumably penurious "Siam" to make their fortune in a more civilized and wealthy America, thereby setting the example that Dao and Duan are destined to repeat. "Chang and Eng Bunker prospered," the narrator assures us, "bought land in North Carolina, married two sisters, and between them fathered twenty-two children." The accompanying family photograph holds out the promise of a happy, middle-class domestic life that Dao and Duan too can expect. In case we have missed this parallelism, the narrator reminds us in the film's closing moments that "like the Bunker twins before them, Dao and Duan have found a future in America." The fact that the prosperity of the Bunkers was irrevocably linked to the display of their anomalous bodies for the amusement and titillation of America, and that twenty years after buying that land in North Carolina their "prosperous" financial circumstances were unstable enough that they were compelled in their old age to display these bodies once again, goes neatly unspoken.[10] Instead, the Bunker brothers are broadly assimilated to the fertile, heterosexual normality whose middle-class values the documentary unwaveringly shares, here by measuring their success in America by the number of their possessions and the size of their families.

The Bunkers have everything that Dao and Duan are assumed to want—everything, that is, but the most personal and the most valuable of "personal property," the very condition of the possibility of democratic self-sufficiency: namely, individual agency.[11] "For all their success, the Bunker twins wanted more than anything to be separated," the narrator baldly states, even though the biographical evidence is, at the very least, that Chang's and Eng's thoughts and feelings about separation changed over the course of their long lives.[12] The syntax of the narrator's apparently neutral description inscribes a narrative of frustrated desire onto Chang's and Eng's biographical history. According to this narrative, the accumulation of ever more precious forms of chattel—land, wives, children—could not take the place of what the twins really wanted, namely discrete corporeality. Embodiment here comes close to being defined as a property relation, exactly as it is in Descartes's *Meditations*;[13] in a documentary that reduces embodiment to malleable flesh, figuring corporeality in this way comes to have its own perversely rational logic. Did the Bunkers want "*more than anything* to be separated" (emphasis ours), or is it the case that the narrator—again, speaking on behalf of an audience that is presumed to hold self-sufficiency, both economic and corporeal, as a virtue above all others—imposes this desire upon the Bunkers? We cannot know for sure, since we do not hear from Chang and Eng: the grainy black and white stills of their "inscrutable" faces so easily become a mute surface upon which almost anything can be projected. About the matter of separation we do not hear from Dao and Duan either. But precisely because Dao and Duan are unable to voice their own desires, Chang and Eng in effect speak for them in the film, the assumption being that the prototypical "Siamese" twins can in fact speak for all others. This ventriloquization is in fact doubled in nature, since Chang and Eng are also mouthpieces, here of the documentary's fundamental assumption that nothing could be more desirous than a singular body, nothing more essential to the intelligibility of human beings—not to mention Western, democratic, capitalistic culture—than individual agency. Nevertheless, if this is what the film wants more than anything else, it is a natural virtue and a principle of normality that is not so natural that it does not need to be reiterated through this extraordinary double simulation. In other words, the simple fact that this staged and stagy reiteration of the norm is necessary at all suggests, albeit faintly, that there is nothing natural or given about it.

Although Chang and Eng did not find a surgeon able to divide their bodies, the narrator states that "today," in "the age of high-tech medicine," Dr. O'Neill "would have little difficulty separating them." The surgeon goes on to describe how he would perform the procedure (using, for example, "a thick ligature"). As if working in a virtual surgical reality, he conducts the separation of the Bunker twins in advance of the real operation on Dao and Duan, suggesting that the prowess of this "high-tech medicine" is so great that it can reach back into "last century" and repair its malformed bodies after the fact. Dr. O'Neill will today fix in our minds what yesterday could not be remedied in the flesh. Moreover, through Dr. O'Neill's intervention, what remained only the abiding object of the Bunker's desire is now about to become a reality for Dao and Duan, so that one pair of "Siamese twins" fulfills the dreams of another. Like Chang and Eng, Dao and Duan share in the prosperity of America; unlike the Bunkers, however, they can own their own bodies as well.

Dr. O'Neill's return in the documentary signals its shift to the technical spectacle of the surgeries themselves. With that shift comes a panoply of scenes that increasingly disembody the twins, re-creating them as fantastically malleable surfaces to be molded and reconstructed at will by each of the medical specialties in turn. There are scenes displaying their grossly swollen skin ("expanded" by the plastic surgeon to make up for the "lack" of skin that the surgery produces); scenes in which their body becomes a kind of fleshly whiteboard upon which different surgeons trace their incision lines with a black felt pen; scenes in which the pediatric surgeon describes the initial stage of the operation as "opening the pages of a book," as if the interior volume of the twins' body were in fact made up of a layered series of discrete surfaces or leaves; and scenes in which the narrator mimics and confirms the perspective of the physicians by describing the twins as "the surgical field." While from the point of view of the doctors these sorts of details may be unexceptional, within the context of the documentary they serve to emphasize both the two-dimensional plasticity and the compartmentalization of Dao's and Duan's body, and thus to flatten its extraordinary features, rendering them banally vulnerable to the most radical change. As a depthless surface, the disembodied body is infinitely compliant and hollow, a docile ensemble awaiting not only its reconfiguration but also its reanimation by the physicians' touch.

But Dao and Duan do *not* constitute a "surgical field" whose planar coordinates can simply be rearranged. Their body sticks, and overlaps, and melds in extraordinary ways that resist both straightforward separation and the medicalized assumptions about embodiment that underlie it. There is a conceptual and physiological thickness to the twins that resists the cutting force of the surgical regime. This is nowhere more problematically apparent than over the question of how the various "shared" organs, systems, and limbs are to be divided between the children. That these organs cannot simply be halved means that a number of critical decisions must be made about the overall nature of each child's corporeality: the question is no longer *how* the bodies shall be separated, but *who* will receive which organ. Faced with this problem, the physicians are compelled to think of Dao and Duan not only as a body made up of parts and surfaces, but also as persons for whom "quality of life" is in some unspecified way significant. The narrator broaches the issue twice, but both times in a manner that is at once simplistic and defensive: "Dividing conjoined twins is not about equality and fairness. O'Neill and his team have given Duan the third leg, the common rectum, and the largest part of the bladder, because the blood and nerves that serve these organs are principally under Duan's control." And again: "Although it might seem unfair that Duan, who will also get the third leg, also gets the most of the bladder, these decisions are made purely on medical grounds. The point is not to simply divide the shared organs equally, but to give the organ to the twin in whom it has the best chance of surviving and growing. This depends most critically on the nerve and blood supplies."

What do these directions by the narrator accomplish? By informing us that separation is not about "equality and fairness," the narrator reduces a complex ethical question to a matter of literal, physiological "equality," that is, of the symmetrical distribution of body parts. A charged point at which the documentary might reflect more carefully upon the assumptions guiding the surgical regimen is thus allowed to slip away. Instead, Palfreman handily capitulates to that regimen by appealing to "grounds" whose "purity" is a euphemism for being free from the taint of complication, almost as if they were the conceptual equivalent of the sterile "surgical field" that the physicians labor to protect from biological contamination (and that we observe from the safe distance of our televisions). Several questions arise: Why would anyone want to make such radically life-altering "decisions" based on only *one* narrowly prescribed set of "grounds"? Why are "medical grounds" assumed to be wholly divorced from the question of "fairness," and from many other ethical questions that could here be fruitfully evoked?[14] Is the renunciation of "fairness" as a treatment criterion not itself a profoundly ethical decision, if only in a negative mode? Speaking on behalf of the doctors, our narrator is not the one to pose these questions, since they would only compromise the putatively disinterested position of the attending surgeons. In terms of the narrative of the documentary, when the issue of separating the twins' organs is raised, we are already deep inside the technicalized environment of Children's Hospital, long past what the narrator calls "the point of no return." Thus it is all the more difficult to imagine other sets of criteria, other interests that could inform the decision-making. Here Palfreman's physicians risk committing what Robert Veatch calls "the technical criteria fallacy."[15] By arbitrarily narrowing the means by which treatment decisions are made to "technical measures of prognosis," these decisions are deemed to be solely "the *doctors'* responsibility." This "fallacious generalizing of the physicians' expertise to matters of moral and other value choices"[16] obscures the fact that *no* treatment decision is or can be made "on purely medical grounds." Value judgments with ethical motivations and implications are always already present even if they are unacknowledged or only partly examined. Palfreman in fact concedes this point when, slightly earlier in the film, he states that the choices made by Dao's and Duan's doctors "not only determine the success or failure of the operation, but also the quality of each twin's life." In the medical ethics literature, "quality of life" is a notoriously difficult term to define, precisely because so many interests are involved in determining what it means and to whom. For this reason, it exceeds the competence of those who proceed "on purely medical grounds"; yet this is precisely the competence that the documentary assumes the doctors possess. As it is represented in the documentary, the "medical" criterion used by Dr. O'Neill and his team to judge which twin ought to get the third, "shared" leg or the major part of the bladder or colon is the "technical" determination of which of the two twins has "control" of these body parts, and of the blood and nerves "supplying" them. In this way, the doctors believe they can decide in which twin the organ or limb in question "has the best chance of surviving and growing." But we should remember that we are speaking here not only of single organs or limbs "surviving and growing," but also of persons whose postoperative existence directly depends upon the viability of these body parts. If the subject who thrives is the one who will most decisively take her "place in society and be productive" (to cite Dr. O'Neill's concluding characterization of the proper object of separation surgery), then the "purely" technical criteria behind the surgical decisions turn out to be "impurely" *utilitarian* in nature.

The fact that having "control" over the relevant organs and limbs is the metaphor that is most consistently used to rationalize these surgical-ethical decisions is revealing in a film for which individual agency, which is to say complete self-control, is masterfully important: under these conditions, one useful, able agent is assumed to be "better" than two "disabled" agents. And the documentary prepares us for that functional logic by consistently differentiating between the twins on the basis of their relative self-control and ability. Dao and Duan are equal, each deserving of the same care and the same medical expertise, to be sure. Yet from a utilitarian perspective one is more equal than the other. Dao is "more fragile," "weaker," less in "control" of the shared organs and limbs; she is smaller, and, as the narrator tells us early in the film, "Wherever Duan wants to go, Dao must follow." David Headley refers to the children as "the big one" and "the little one," before self-consciously reminding himself that they should be called by their proper names; Barbara Headley asks Duan after the separation to point to "where [Dao] . . . was on you," unintentionally characterizing the smaller sister as a kind of parasitic appendage. Fragility, weakness, littleness, and dependency are all evocatively normative terms whose meanings spill messily over the boundary that is imagined to divide the technical from nontechnical accounts of the twins' bodies. Physical differences between conjoined twins are not uncommon; what interests us here is the way in which these details form not only a morphological background to the evaluative criteria, but also, more important, an *alibi* for their operation. Because she does not have "the best chance of surviving and growing" (the questionable assumption here being that "she" is the sum of her body parts), Dao functions as a kind of living organ donor to Duan; hers is the embodiment—we do not say *body*—that will be more severely sacrificed for the benefit of her bigger, more viable sister.

The resolutely nontechnical starkness of that evaluation tends to be palliated in the documentary, surfacing only after the surgery is over, when, confronted with the image of Dao's wholly altered life, it seems more difficult than ever to continue speaking of decisions being based on "purely medical grounds." With the long surgery completed, we glimpse the full extent of Dao's incompleteness: she "now has only one leg, a partial bladder, and half a pelvis." The narrator appears to realize that this is a fundamentally inopportune time to argue that "dividing conjoined twins is not about equality and fairness," but then makes a supplemental claim whose defensiveness inadvertently brings out how dissatisfying that argument may always have been: "She will require extensive reconstructive surgery to her bladder and colon, but today's procedure will leave her with a complete set of reproductive organs. If she survives, like Duan, she will be able to have children when she grows up." According to this utilitarian calculus, social productivity and re-productivity are interchangeable values. That we have twice been told that "equality" is not a principle that can be applied to separation surgery does not prevent Palfreman from resorting rhetorically to it, here in the curious form of imagining some sort of organ exchange: Dao's intact ovaries and uterus are figured forth as recompense for her absent leg and incomplete bladder. This substitution, moreover, will make her "like" Duan, underlining once again Dao's differentially determined existence. What would motivate this compensatory gesture, except the naive belief—identified by Michel Foucault as the sign of modernity itself—that sex "harbours what is most true in ourselves"?[17] Secure in possessing her sex, the logic of this gesture suggests, Dao remains at the most fundamental level whole, notwithstanding the insults that her extraordinary body has withstood at the hands of her surgeons. Even if her surgery has only allowed her morphology to approximate the norm, she can look forward to the deeper completeness that will come—and the narrator (speaking for whom? On what authority?) says it *will* come—when she, like her sister, is interpellated into compulsory maternality. Palfreman's remark recalls his earlier references to Chang and Eng Bunker, whose abnormal corporeality is partly redressed by the domestic normality that came of having all those children. We are also reminded that, next to the sex life of conjoined twins, nothing seems to attract more prurient interest than their reproductive capacities. Perhaps the freak show fascination with the one is only a displaced expression of the other.

More astonishingly still, Palfreman's account of Dao's future is framed by the grim suggestion that she in fact may not have a future: *"If she lives,"* the narrator says. Palfreman's qualification cuts in several directions. To begin with, it starkly puts to the audience what was obscured under the rubric of "purely medical grounds." It means that Duan has been deemed as the *salvageable* sister, and the possible consequences of that decision include the death of Dao. But a television documentary, like a nineteenth-century freak show, is meant to entertain as well as teach, and it is telling that Palfreman's qualification serves both interests simultaneously. For the phrase, brief as it is, also powerfully theatricalizes the postoperative scene. Dao *does* in fact live and thrive. Since this is not a real-time live broadcast the *prospect* of her death can only be exploited to create suspense and extract the maximum pathos from the situation. In turn, this pathos contains and palliates whatever concerns we might have about the "equality and fairness" of the separation by suggesting that such concerns are immaterial when Dao's life hangs in the balance.

"I like that. Yeah, I like that," pronounces Dr. O'Neill, as he looks down upon his completed work, giving it a muted blessing. As Palfreman's documentary moves toward its conclusion, the narrator observes that after "ten days . . . both twins are doing well physically, but psychologically, they're having trouble adjusting. . . . Dao and Duan are among the oldest conjoined twins to be separated, no one's sure how two sisters joined for three and a half years will cope with being physically separate individuals." Thus it is not until after the surgery is over, narratively speaking, that the "psychological" consequences of the separation are explicitly addressed. Having assumed that conjoined existence is intolerable, and that the prospect of the twins living separately outweighs the risks of undergoing life-threatening, near-experimental surgery, Palfreman has from the start narrowed the terms by which he might consider these consequences. In a documentary that is crowded with every manner of medical specialist, the absence of a child psychiatrist is revealing, for it points to, among other things, a hierarchical exclusion of nonsurgical concerns even *within* the discipline of medicine. Whatever mental trauma the children suffer is instead left in the hands of the female caregiver, Barbara Headley, thereby safely exiling this "trouble" to a quasidomestic space removed from the hygienic surgical field. There is perhaps no better indication that we are gazing upon a mostly "depassioned" world of the Cartesian body[18] than when we hear the narrator coolly characterize the postoperative recovery in terms of "adjustment" and "coping," as if the twins were adapting to a new school rather than *living* a radically altered form of embodiment. We are encouraged to believe that the problem is one of Dao and Duan positively "adapting" to their new status, when in fact it is more likely negatively a question of mourning the loss of the old body, or, more precisely, of negotiating between the body image that each child possesses as the fundamental matrix of her twinned embodiment and the physical morphology that the surgeons have bequeathed her. Even to describe this complex situation as "psychological"—as opposed to "physical"—is grossly to underestimate its nature, since whatever the twins are as embodied beings, both before and after surgery, handily exceeds this sort of deracinating and decorporealizing dualism, even if it is the dualism that made their bodies susceptible to division in the first place.

Unlike bacteriological infection, the "psychological" effects of the surgery cannot be one postoperative complication among many, because these effects go to the heart of Dao's and Duan's existence as joined incarnate lives. As Elizabeth Grosz suggests, the "corporeal link" that is forged between conjoined twins may not be something that can simply be "effaced."[19] Even the narrator must admit this fact, conceding as he does that "no one's sure" what it means for twins to be surgically separated at the relatively advanced age of "three and a half years." "No one's sure": in the wake of that rare concession of the limits of medical expertise, we are left to imagine the depths and extraordinary complexity of the twins' intertwined embodiment, the corporeal jointures and subtle knots that resist the scalpel as they do our understanding. Of course, their age is also a measure of the risk that the surgeons are willing to assume, a sign of their pushing the surgical envelope. But we might also see it as an upper limit for candidacy for separation surgery, beyond which, presumably, the "psychological" consequences actually *do* begin to impinge upon the decision to perform the surgery. Other questions arise: If age three and a half, why not two, or one? How does one determine the degree or maturity of corporeal—rather than "physical" or "psychological"—linkage in conjoined twins? What is clear is that at three and a half the surgeons are working at an experimental horizon beyond which little is known, but that this ignorance and the dangers springing from it will not stop them from proceeding.

Although there is no doubting the resilience of the twins, the idea that they have "come to terms" with their resected bodies in "ten days" is surely pure wish fulfillment, and it reminds us that this is the accelerated hyperreality of television, in which medical crises are by convention resolved within a miraculously compressed temporality that both soothes the soul and satisfies the sponsors. Unlike *Katie and Eilish*, in which one of the twins dies in the initial days after surgery, l'affccman's documentary ends happily; the hint of "psychological" problems about which "no one knows" dissolves amid the closing images of Dao and Duan celebrating their fourth birthday and attending preschool "like millions of their peers." The pressure for the twins to assimilate to a state of sameness organizes the film's conclusion, notwithstanding the fact that their significant differences go down to their sinews. Where before the separation Dao's lack of "control" over certain organs and limbs was the criteria that favored Duan in their surgical distribution, after the separation the surgery itself is credited with the twins coming into a morphological symmetry. For example, Dao's progress is largely measured by how rapidly she becomes more "like Duan" in "height, weight, and appearance." Although prior to the operation "equality and fairness" were deliberately excluded from decisions regarding the quality of postoperative life, they are treated as signs of the twins' health as individuals once the surgery is completed. In this way, "equality and fairness" are smuggled back into the documentary's narrative as working virtues, since they literalize and embody a democratic vision of free and equitable personhood—the very condition of taking one's "place in society and be[ing] productive," as Dr. O'Neill says. About what it means to occupy that useful place, of course, Dao and Duan say nothing. But that silence is itself telling, for it brings out the paucity of firsthand accounts of the lives of conjoined twins, separated or not. In the absence of these undoubtedly extraordinary stories, others—including ourselves—are always willing to speak.

> And this also means that we never know, and never have known, how to *cut up* a subject.
> —JACQUES DERRIDA, " 'EATING WELL,' OR THE CALCULATION OF THE SUBJECT"

What provisional conclusions can we draw from Palfreman's documentary, and what suggestions can we sketch out in the way of a theoretical framework for future research into media representations of the medical treatment of conjoined twins? Media accounts conventionally emphasize that the separation of conjoined twins tests the limits of medical knowledge and surgical expertise, as if anomalous bodies were in a form of contest with the medical regime. Beyond the benevolent desire to help the twins, "winning" this contest has important implications for the prestige and wealth of the hospital (and the surrounding community) in which the surgery is conducted. But the medicalized staging of conjoined twins as primarily a technical challenge conceals the deeper epistemological and phenomenological hazard that they embody: namely, the threat that they pose to normative conceptions of corporeality.

Conjoined twins have always raised disturbing questions about the nature of the "relation" between body and self.[20] It is not so much their fused bodies that prove troublesome as the implications that their concorporate existence have for conventional expectations about embodiment. Are they two different subjects within one body? Or, more radically, are they two differently embodied subjects? That embodiment is properly a singular condition would appear to be a given, indeed, *the* given of human existence: I alone possess the body that I am. But what seems to be given or "natural" about the materiality of the body is inevitably caught up in a network of culturally and historically variable assumptions—what Foucault calls "regulatory ideal[s]"[21]—that function in prescriptive ways to differentiate between "normal" and "abnormal" forms of corporeality. From the point of view of Palfreman's documentary, the notion of singular embodiment—one person to one body—operates as one of these ideals and in a way that recalls the regulatory principles by which gendered bodies are constructed and policed. As Judith Butler has argued, characterizing a body as gendered is never merely a description of a preexisting condition, but "is itself a *legislation* and a *production* of bodies, a discursive demand, as it were, that bodies become produced according to principles of heterosexualizing coherence and integrity."[22] In other words, the mutually reinforcing notions that one must have "a" sex and only one sex, and that there is in fact "a" distinct sex to be "had," operate as normative ideals that produce, shape, constrain, and simplify the irreducibly complex condition of gendered embodiment.

The notion of singular embodiment functions in a similar prescriptive and idealizing fashion. What, after all, does it mean to "have" or "possess" a body? Having "a" body, like having "a" sex, is at best an abstraction that obscures the fact that there is no single "sex" or form of "embodiment" as such, much less a single way to "have" or to "be" these things. Yet the compulsion to assume a properly singular corporeality—again, like singular sexuality—has a tremendous, even killing force in our culture. This constraint is perhaps no more apparent than in the case of conjoined twins, whose surgical separation marks the extent to which the medical regime is willing to go to (re)construct the body so that it more closely approximates what is posited as ideal and reiterated as normal. It is important to emphasize that both conjoined and singular bodies can only *approximate* this ideal condition. The notion of a discrete subject inhabiting the self-contained body that it *is* is exactly that: a powerful (yet paradoxically disembodied) *notion* that real, lived bodies of all shapes and sizes are nevertheless compelled to mimic, and against which their normality or abnormality is measured. As Butler points out, the very fact that bodies are repeatedly and forcefully made to answer to these ideals means "that bodies never quite comply with the norms by which their materialization is impelled."[23]

In the case of the media representation of conjoined twins, this distance between the regulatory ideal and its fleshly approximation is spectacularly evident because the surgical reconstruction of their bodies only approximates morphologically what is imagined to be the case phenomenologically. Here the striking visual image of bodies in the process of being refashioned into a physical condition of separateness must *stand for* or simulate the creation of singularly embodied life. But the division of a concorporate body no more bequeaths "individuality" to each twin than the surgical creation of sex organs makes a body "gendered." In both instances, bodies are compelled to comply with normative ideals or "phantasms"[24] that make these bodies knowable and pliable—"docile," as Foucault would say.[25] From both Foucault and Butler we know that this forced compliance is a phenomenon as wide and as deep as the social body itself. The media representation of conjoined twins simply reiterates its normative work in a remarkably condensed and vivid fashion. Perhaps this is what makes the medical documentary so compelling, since it gives *both* the force of subjection and the impossibility of a body ever being fully subjected the most lurid display. The documentary does not simply document a surgical triumph; *as* a representation, as the site in which images are trafficked, it is a spectacular expression of the "discursive demand" that bodies become produced according to certain regulatory ideals. Representations of separation surgeries are thus "performances" of subjection insofar as they stage, theatricalize, and cite the *assujettissement*—that is, the simultaneous creation and constraint—of the "human" as singularly embodied. Singular embodiment functions as an ideal to be mimicked because it can only be an imagining of what it might mean to "have" "a" body; it is a figure that simplifies, unifies, and stabilizes the irreducibly excessive condition of embodiment—or more precisely, *embodiments*, since there is no single manner of being incarnate. As such, singular corporeality can be usefully compared to the category of "sex," since it operates as "a principle of intelligibility for human beings, which is to say that no human being can be taken to be human, can be recognized *as* human unless that human being is fully and coherently"[26] in possession of its "own" body. (Re)producing this ideal, reiterating it as the law of human intelligibility, media representations of conjoined twins either underplay or ignore altogether the question of whether they *should* be separated and dwell almost exclusively on the technical conundrum of *how* that separation is to take place; the former question is largely ruled out of bounds because it is assumed that conjoined life, precisely because of its imagined phenomenological *un*intelligibility, must be intolerable. Dividing out the phenomenological and ethical questions from the "medical" difficulties thereby becomes one of the enabling conditions of the division of the bodies themselves.

Nevertheless, as spectacularly anomalous bodies, conjoined twins remain ambiguously resistant bodies, corporeal instances whose strangeness and difference act to throw into sharp relief the exclusionary forces that (re)produce them *as* anomalous. Recalling "the etymological roots of both *mirabila* and *monstrum*," Stephen Pender notes that monstrous bodies "are always in some way about seeing."[27] But when we observe the separation of conjoined twins in a documentary, for example, at what are we in fact looking? The question is not as easily answered as it might seem, for in at least three related ways media representations of conjoined twins are an example of what Jean Baudrillard calls the "simulacra" or the "hyperreal."[28] In each case, the collective act of looking at the twins is also, in a sense, a looking *away*—a failure, due partly to their capture by images and imaging technology, to see that the twins are who they are *because*, not in spite of, the bodies they "have."

1. Katharine Park and Lorraine Daston have cogently shown how, with the advent of modernity, the reception of anomalous bodies shifted from viewing "monsters as prodigies to monsters as examples of medical pathology."[29] While we cannot disagree with the overall shape of their argument, it seems worth asking how, in the postmodern milieu of media images and simulations, this line of development from the freak as sign or augury to the freak as sickness is complicated, perhaps even folded back upon itself. Contemporary representations of conjoined twins pathologize them, to be sure; yet deviant corporeality remains uncannily portentous, even if what it provides comes in the form of a profoundly secular revelation: through it, we witness the advent of a world of fully instrumentalized bodies, a "high-tech" place of "postmodern plasticity"[30] where there will be no morphology, no matter how malformed, that cannot be altered and normalized. Under these spectacularized conditions, we are not so much looking at conjoined twins as peering in awe at the expensive expertise that will transform us by transforming them.

2. In order to be anatomized and resected, the twins must be disembodied. That is to say, their always exorbitant existence as incarnate beings evaporates amid the clinical hypervisibility of their interior and exterior morphology. This narrowing of human life is what makes bodies available to medical knowledge and susceptible to the kind of radical division that Descartes imagines in one of the epigraphs to this chapter. Documentary representations of separation surgery would appear to be the epitome of what Francis Barker calls "the abstracting gaze of science [that] seeks a decorporealized body of and for knowledge." We see this "Cartesian body . . . subordinated to a hygienic and surgical science"[31] not only in the deliberate reduction of amorphous "individuality" to physical morphology, but also in the assumption that the twins are somehow freestanding entities that are more or less *already* separated within the anomalous body that "disables" or "enslaves" them. ("Free at Last" is the revealing title of an Australian magazine article on a recent separation surgery in New York.)[32] But we have known since Sigmund Freud that "the ego is first and foremost a bodily ego,"[33] inextricably woven into bodily functions, mappings, perceptions, and desires. Embodiment is not reducible to the body, because "the thought of the body" is also "the thought that *is* the body".[34] Notwithstanding the objectifying and deracinating demands of the medical regime, *embodiment* remains an unstable nexus of discursive forces that explodes the distinction between mental and bodily realms. Because it is the site of histories without boundaries or focal points, and of ongoing negotiations and adaptations of flesh and world, corporeality is messy, not hygienic. Conjoined corporeality is, as it were, messier still. It may even be the case, as Elizabeth Grosz points out, that "those who have shared organs, a common blood circulation and every minute detail of everyday life" possess a uniquely complex corporeal connection that cannot simply be dissected out.[35] To the extent that medical surveillance fails

to see that surgical separation tears much deeper than the flesh, conjoined twins are *over-looked:* they are unseen, paradoxically, because they are seen too much.

3. As Mark Poster characterizes it, Baudrillard's "simulation is different from a fiction or lie in that it not only presents an absence as a presence, the imaginary as real, it also undermines any contrast to the real, absorbing the real within itself."[36] For Baudrillard, the exemplary instance of this hyperreality is Disneyland, in which the difference between the play-world of the theme park and the surrounding work world is the lie that covers up the fact that American society is so saturated with media images that it is unreal through and through: the "real" world is the fiction that the "unreal" world produces as its own outside, thereby collapsing the difference between what is "true" and what is "imaginary." A roughly analogous phenomenon characterizes Palfreman's documentary in two ways. First, in emphasizing the extraordinary concentration of medical expertise marshaled around the twins, the film reiterates the stark difference between two worlds: the theater of surgery at Children's Hospital of Philadelphia (whose grimly appropriate acronym is C.H.O.P.) as the very special place where bodies are transformed; and the world of the viewer, who is momentarily given the unusual privilege of seeing this transformation in the way that the doctors and nurses usually do. But this distinction between the site of radical surgical intervention and spectators who view it from the safe distance of their living rooms masks the ways in which the medical regime everywhere acts to demarcate and discipline bodies, and everywhere compels bodies to assume the regulatory ideals that determine what is intelligible and what is unintelligible, what bodies matter and what bodies do not.

Second, the spectacular difference between the blurred and aberrantly fused flesh of the twins and their distinct, more or less intact bodies after separation surgery is the fiction that belies the fact that bodies are never wholly distinct entities to those who live them, as it were, from within. Media images of conjoined twins show their bodies as both "fixed" and "fixable": that is, as something that can be both repaired *and* apprehended, or perhaps apprehended *through* being repaired. (We might recall that conjoined twins are differentially diagnosed and renamed according to where they are "fixed" to each other.) The silhouette of their liberated bodies is as "real," surely, as the surgical incisions that divide one twin from the other, and the suture lines that seal each body up into itself. But in the realm of representation, this too is hyperreal, a reality that passes over into something much less determinate, since the *image* of fleshly closure masks the irreducibly nonclosural and unfixed condition of embodiment. In this way, media representations of surgical separations constitute a kind of Lacanian *stade du miroir* in which the subject is misrecognized (but also fixed and celebrated) as unitary because it appears morphologically intact and distinct. But the difference between the properly proportioned body and the monstrous body is always undercut by the generally improper and ill-proportioned nature of corporeality—neither inside nor outside, subject or object, flesh or spirit, but the site of what Maurice Merleau-Ponty evocatively calls the "chiasmic crossing" of these and other terms.[37] Hence Gayatri Chakravorty Spivak's point: "If one really thinks about the body as such, there is no possible outline of the body as such. There are thinkings of the systematicity of the body, there are value codings of the body. The body, as such, cannot be thought, and I certainly cannot approach it."[38] We can therefore say, after Baudrillard, that although we appear to be looking at the division of conjoined twins, *"separation" has not taken place.*[39]

NOTES

1. Neil Harris, *Humbug: The Art of P. T. Barnum* (Boston: Little, Brown, 1973), 292.

2. It is crucially important to emphasize from the start that our analysis of Palfreman's documentary addresses the filmic *representation* of the life of Dao and Duan, which includes the representation of the words, actions, and motives of their caregivers and physicians. In other words, our interest is in how the twins are subjected within and through the narrative of the documentary, and in how this subjection plays out for a television audience. An investigation of, for example, medical regimen at work in Children's Hospital of Philadelphia *as such* would require a separate and somewhat different form of analysis.

3. Space does not permit us to discuss in any detail *Katie and Eilish: Siamese Twins* and *Life without Katie,* both produced by Mark Galloway for the BBC's *First Tuesday* documentary series. It is interesting to note, though, how the postoperative death of one of the twins in *Katie and Eilish* casts a pall over the film; it is the terribly saddening excess that the documentary's ambivalent allegiance to the medical regime cannot quite contain. *Life without Katie,* the curious short film made after *Katie and Eilish,* plays a complexly supplemental role in the midst of these ambiguities: it is at once an attempt to rationalize the death, a work of mourning, and the filmic equivalent of a phantom limb. Although there are significant differences between these documentaries and Palfreman's film, the subjection of concorporate embodiment remains strikingly similar. In complex ways that still need careful analysis, both documentaries demonstrate Elizabeth Grosz's point that "in spite of the state of health of siamese twins, there seems a medical imperative for surgical intervention, even if surgery may actually endanger lives that may otherwise remain healthy and well." See Grosz, "Freaks," *Social Semiotics* 1, no. 2 (1991): 34–35.

4. For an illuminating analysis of how Rembrandt's painting "point[s] forward to a modern, surgical regime of the body," see Francis Barker, *The Tremulous Private Body: Essays on Subjection* (London: Methuen, 1984), 73–112.

5. Leslie Fiedler, *Freaks: Myths and Images of the Secret Self* (New York: Anchor, 1993), 199.

6. See Louis Althusser, "Ideology and Ideological State Apparatuses," *Lenin and Philosophy,* trans. Ben Brewster (London: Monthly Review, 1971).

7. The documentary is itself hardly immune to the logic of late capitalism. Television images and plush-toy versions of "Barney" figure so prominently in the narrative that Palfreman is obliged to acknowledge who holds copyright in the credits, lest he be accused of "consuming" or marketing this image without acknowledging whose property it is.

8. Robert Altick, *The Shows of London* (Cambridge: Harvard University Press, 1978), 509.

9. Fiedler, *Freaks,* 36.

10. See ibid., 214.

11. For an evocative discussion of the complex ways in which the Bunker twins served these and other social interests in nineteenth-century America, see Allison Pingree, "America's 'United Siamese Brothers': Chang and Eng and Nineteenth-Century Ideologies of Democracy and Domesticity," in *Monster Theory: Reading Culture,* ed. Jeffrey Jerome Cohen (Minneapolis: University of Minnesota Press, 1996).

12. Kay Hunter points out that the Bunker twins came closest to requesting that they be separated just prior to their marriages, but that their fiancées successfully convinced them "to give up on their idea of being cut asunder." See Hunter, *Duet for a Lifetime: The Story of the Original Siamese Twins* (New York: Coward-McCann, 1964), 86–87.

13. Barker makes this point about Descartes in *The Tremulous Private Body,* 98.

14. For a discussion of some of these questions, see Catherine Myser, "A Philosophical Critique of the 'Best Interests' Criterion and An Exploration of Clinical Ethical Strategies for Balancing the Interests of Infants or Fetuses, Family Members, and Society in the United States, India, and Sweden" (Ph.D. diss., Georgetown University, 1994).

15. Robert M. Veatch, "The Technical Criteria Fallacy," *Hastings Center Report* 7, no. 4 (August 1977): 15.

16. Ibid., 16.

17. Michel Foucault, *Herculine Barbin: Being the Recently Discovered Memoirs of a Nineteenth-Century Hermaphrodite,* trans. Richard McDougall (New York: Pantheon, 1980), ix.

18. Barker, *The Tremulous Private Body*, 97.

19. Grosz, "Freaks," 35.

20. In this context, it seems important to put the word "relation" in quotation marks, since it begs the question of whether we can speak intelligently of the self apart from its embodiment.

21. See, e.g., the final chapter of Michel Foucault's *The History of Sexuality: Volume I, An Introduction*, trans. Robert Hurley (New York: Vintage, 1980), 135–59.

22. Judith Butler, "Sexual Inversions," in *Discourses of Sexuality: From Aristotle to AIDS*, ed. Domna C. Stanton (Ann Arbor: University of Michigan Press, 1992), 351.

23. Judith Butler, *Bodies That Matter: On the Discursive Limits of "Sex"* (New York: Routledge, 1993), 2.

24. Butler usefully distinguishes between "fantasy" and "phantasmatic." The latter term, she argues, is "to be understood not as an activity of an already formed subject, but of the staging and dispersion of the subject into a variety of identificatory positions." "Phantasmatic identification" is the process by which the subject imagines "the possibility of approximating" a "sexed position marked out within the symbolic domain." By mimicking this symbolic image or ideal the subject is compelled into "the assumption of sex." See *Bodies That Matter*, 267n. 7, 96–97.

25. See Michel Foucault, *Discipline and Punish: The Birth of the Prison*, trans. Alan Sheridan (Vintage: New York, 1979), 135–69.

26. Butler, "Sexual Inversions," 352. Here we partly reproduce Butler's account of the category of "sex" in Foucault's work. Elsewhere Butler argues that "It is not enough to claim that human subjects are constructed, for the construction of the human is a differential operation that produces the more and the less 'human', the inhuman, and the humanly unthinkable". Our argument is that concorporate embodiment is the "less 'human'" against which the fully human ideal of singular corporeality secures its authority. See *Bodies That Matter*, 8.

27. Stephen Pender, " 'No Monsters at the Resurrection': Inside Some Conjoined Twins," in *Monster Theory: Reading Culture*, ed. Jeffrey Jerome Cohen (Minneapolis: University of Minnesota Press, 1996).

28. Jean Baudrillard, *Simulacra and Simulations*, trans. Paul Foss, Paul Patton, and Philip Beitchman (New York: Sémiotext[e], 1983).

29. Katharine Park and Lorraine Daston, "Unnatural Conceptions: The Study of Monsters in Sixteenth- and Seventeenth-Century France and England," *Past & Present* 92 (1981): 23.

30. Susan Bordo, *Unbearable Weight: Feminism, Western Culture, and the Body* (Berkeley: University of California Press, 1993), 245–46.

31. Barker, *The Tremulous Private Body*, 96, 97.

32. Janice Hopkins Tanne, "Free at Last," *Australian Magazine*, 5 February 1994, 14.

33. Sigmund Freud, "The Ego and the Id," in *The Standard Edition of the Complete Psychological Works of Sigmund Freud*, ed. James Strachey (London: Hogarth, 1961), 19:26.

34. We are grateful to Will McConnell for this phrasing and this insight.

35. Grosz, "Freaks," 35.

36. Mark Poster, introduction to *Jean Baudrillard: Selected Writings*, ed. Mark Poster (Stanford: Stanford University Press, 1988), 6.

37. Maurice Merleau-Ponty, *The Visible and the Invisible*, trans. Alphonso Lingis (Evanston: Northwestern University Press, 1968).

38. Gayatri Chakravorty Spivak, "In a Word: Interview," *differences* 1, no. 2 (1989): 131.

39. Here we recall Baudrillard's strategically hyperbolic position that "the Gulf War did not take place." See "The Reality Gulf," *Guardian*, 11 January 1991; and *"La guerre du Golfe n'a pas eu lieu,"* *Liberation*, 29 March 1991. If we know that the twins have been surgically divided, this does not necessarily mean that we know what, precisely, "separation" and "separateness" mean.

TWENTY-FIVE

Bodybuilding: A Postmodern Freak Show

CECILE LINDSAY

The Freak show itself has not died.
—LESLIE FIEDLER

Published in 1978, Leslie Fiedler's *Freaks: Myths and Images of the Secret Self* remains a benchmark for the study of cultural constructions of an "other" that reflect the subterranean fears, dreams, and myths of selfhood and society.[1] For Fiedler, the true freak (as opposed to the accidental one) stirs us to terror and sympathy because "he is one of us, the human child of human parents, however altered by forces we do not quite understand into something mythic and mysterious" (24). Fiedler identifies the source of the true freak's capacity to arouse sympathy and fear as the effacement of those fundamental categories by which we order our existence: "Only the true Freak challenges the conventional boundaries between male and female, sexed and sexless, animal and human, large and small, between self and other, and consequently between reality and illusion, experience and fantasy, fact and myth" (24).

This definition of the true freak in many ways also describes the contemporary bodybuilder. Bodybuilders seek to maximize the visible muscularity of their physiques through a combination of progressive weight training, a diet and aerobic exercise regime aimed at minimizing subcutaneous body fat, and a physical presentation that displays the extreme degree of muscular definition and vascularity achieved by this regimen. The episodic culmination of a bodybuilder's practice is a "show," a competitive event at which he or she is judged on body symmetry, muscularity, and artistic display of the physique in a choreographed routine performed to music. Through these practices, bodybuilders defy normative assumptions about human bodies and the categories that delimit and define them: male versus female, natural versus unnatural, normal versus abnormal. Like Fiedler's freak, the bodybuilder confounds illusion and reality: the impression of monstrous scale is most often the result of extreme muscular definition highlighted by oil and muscles flexed to a maximal degree—an illusion evident when a competitor who looked like a giant on stage sits down beside you after his or her routine and turns out to be of diminutive height and normal weight. Fact and myth are also blurred in popular reaction to bodybuilders. For instance, it is widely believed that big muscles "turn to fat" upon cessation of weight training, while in fact muscles shrink when training stops. And myths about the inflexibility of "muscle-bound" athletes are belied by posing routines that feature gymnastic feats and by the increasing number of men's and women's sports that make use of weight training. Finally, the bodybuilder's visible difference, especially when on display, arouses both fascination and repulsion—both terror and sympathy—in observers and spectators.

Fiedler's definition of the true freak as a transgressor of categories thus has uncanny parallels with today's bodybuilder. In fact, the bodybuilder finds new categories to blur—for example, that opposing humans to machines, as technological innovations supply prosthetic implants, surgical alterations, and chemical and nutritional enhancements to muscular development. And yet, while the bodybuilder is born the "human child of human parents," and is genetically predisposed to success or failure in building his or her body, it is through personal choice and action that he or she becomes a Freak. It is perhaps in this erosion even of the category of "true" or "produced" Freak that contemporary bodybuilding provides a postmodern context for the continued interrogation of the Freak as cultural "other," and for the continued interrogation of the body as a site of contestation over essential versus constructed attributes. Indeed, we need only look back to the circuses, vaudeville acts, and carnival side shows of the late nineteenth century to confirm a continuum between that fin-de-siècle's terrors and sympathies and those of our own. In this chapter, I examine how today's bodybuilder transgresses and reconfigures modern categories, provoking both affirmation and condemnation, and thereby constituting a locus for challenges to and enforcement of cultural norms grounded in the body. In this way, I endeavor to show how bodybuilding in late twentieth-century culture illuminates some of the paradoxes and potentialities of the postmodern condition.

A History of Freaks: Nineteenth-Century Strong Men and Women

Individuals of extraordinary dimensions and/or physical strength have been displayed or have performed since antiquity. In the eighteenth century, strong men and women like the Englishman Tom Topham and an Italian woman with the stage name "Sansona" performed feats of strength in public performance.[2] By the latter half of the nineteenth century, popular interest in challenges to the limits of human strength arguably reached an all-time high. A French physical culture enthusiast, Edmond Desbonnet, published an exhaustive account, amply illustrated, of "the Kings of Strength." Subtitled "A History of All the Strong Men from Antiquity to Our Days" and published in 1911, Desbonnet's book captures the era's excitement about displays of strength and physique and remains even today the definitive work on early strong men and women.[3] In the final decades of the nineteenth century, with the advent of what Robert Bogdan terms the "developing popular amusement industry,"[4] the circus, vaudeville, and carnival came to provide a venue for strength and physique performers. The imagination of fin-de-siècle Europeans and Americans was fired by ponderous and powerful men and women, whose acts were designed to both astonish and entertain. One such performer was billed as Apollon, "the Demigod of Strength." A Frenchman born in 1862, he stood well over six feet, with a muscular and well-shaped physique. In his music hall act, sandwiched between the risqué numbers of Paris's *Folies Bergères,* he dressed in revealing costumes and impersonated an escaping prisoner by bending real iron bars.[5] Audiences also appreciated a Miss Darnett, the "singing strong lady" who sang while lying face up, her hands and feet extended below her, and supporting on her chest and thighs a platform holding a piano and accompanist.[6] That these performers are recognized as precursors by contemporary bodybuilding culture is evidenced by a regular column in *Ironman* magazine entitled "Gallery of Ironmen," which features late nineteenth- and early twentieth-century strong men and women. Here one can read about the life, looks, and performances of bodybuilding predecessors such as Apollon, Louis Cyr, Horace Barré, Eugen Sandow, and Lionel Strongfort or, occasionally, strong women such as Kate Sandwina, Madame Minerva, Madame Montagna, or the Great Vulcana. Two of these figures were especially successful in their time and pioneered the beginnings of bodybuilding as it is known today: Eugen Sandow and Kate Sandwina (who, born Kate Brumbach, adapted Sandow's stage name for her own strength and balancing act).

Eugen Sandow (fig. 25.1) was the greatest exhibitor of the twenty-year "Golden Age" of professional strong men beginning in the 1890s. Born in 1867 in Königsberg as Frederick Mueller, Sandow changed the direction of strength performance by combining his physical beauty and artistry with showmanship and feats of strength. In their monumental *Anomalies and Curiosities of Medicine,* published in 1896, physicians George Gould and Walter Pyle discuss Sandow and other "Modern Hercules" under the category of "Physiologic and Functional Anomalies," a chapter that also treats athletic feats such as endurance running and swimming as well as contortionism. Here, Sandow is described as possessing "remarkable strength and control over his muscles" (466) and as a clever gymnast who used light and posing to highlight certain body parts: "and in a brilliant light [he] demonstrated his extraordinary power over his muscles, contracting muscles ordinarily involuntary in time with music, a feat really more remarkable than his exhibition of strength" (467). Described as a wondrous freak, Sandow thus marks a transition to muscle display as an aesthetic and entertainment activity; Gould and Pyle go on to signal "the beautiful muscular development of this remarkable man" (467). Indeed, the physicians included photographs of Sandow to illustrate the anomalous condition of "extreme muscular development." In 1890, Sandow appeared in one of Thomas Edison's early experiments with moving pictures, inaugurating cinema as a venue for masculine muscle display, paving the way for the Italian dockworker "Maciste" who starred in twenty-nine films beginning in 1914, the "B-movie" star Joe Bonomo of the 1920s, and on to Victor Mature and Johnny Weismuller in the 1950s—long before Arnold Schwarzenegger and Lou Ferrigno filled the large and small screen of late twentieth-century popular entertainment.

Kate Sandwina likewise combined extravagant size, strength, beauty, and star quality in the context of circus performance. Born in Germany in 1864, she was the daughter of strength performers; her lesser-known sisters also had a strength and athleticism act. Sandwina's size was by all accounts spectacular: circus posters tout her height as six feet one inch and her weight as 220 pounds at age twenty-three. More modest accounts put her at five feet eleven inches and 209 pounds at the same age.[7] What is generally agreed is that the Barnum and Bailey Circus publicity describing her as "The Most Beautiful . . . The Most Skillful . . . The Strongest of the World's Women" was an accurate characterization of her reception by the American circus audience.[8] Billed as "Germany's Herculean Venus," Sandwina attracted large audiences with her mythical proportions, androgynous persona (at once superhuman male hero and supernatural female beauty), strength, and glamour. Like Sandow, her combination of revealing costumes and showmanship most likely overshadowed her remarkable physical abilities.

25.1. Fin-de-siècle strong man Eugen Sandow. Bequest of Evert Jansen Wendell. Harvard Theatre Collection. The Houghton Library.

Exhibitors such as Sandow and Sandwina caught the fancy of the same fin-de-siècle crowds that flocked to see human freaks, oddities, prodigies, and curiosities. Of more interest than a typology of these displays of human difference, as Bogdan argues, is how the institution of popular entertainment came in the latter half of the nineteenth century to organize formal exhibitions of anomalous persons for the purpose of amusement and profit. Why did the nineteenth century become so fascinated with human differences, particularly the visible, physical ones that became the staple of freak shows?

One approach to that question lies in science. The nineteenth century was an era so dominated by science that it has been called the "Age of Science,"[9] and its principal focus was what we now call biology. Although for much of the eighteenth century the old belief endured that all existence was divinely organized into a great chain of being, this conviction succumbed to the evidence of extinct fauna, whose discovery belied the notion of a permanent, stable, and perfect creation. New information and hypotheses about the nature and place of organisms sparked debates about evolution and the postulation of the possibility of new species. Nineteenth-century biology was driven by the impulse to establish categories, make distinctions, and determine the laws of nature; debate focused on inherited categories such as mind and body, human and animal, male and female, living and nonliving. The unprecedented popularization of science spawned books of taxonomies and texts on natural history, making it possible for amateurs of zoology to collect and classify segments of the natural order. This classificatory impulse paradoxically held within it a fascination with the anomalous and the exception—hence Gould and Pyle's exhaustive 1896 catalogue (nearly a thousand pages with 295 illustrations) of the "Anomalies and Curiosities" of human medicine. I propose that it was a parallel enthusiasm for the delineation of normative classifications *and* for their exceptions that accounts for the spectacular success of freak shows in the period between 1840 and 1940, identified by Bogdan as the heyday of this form of entertainment.[10]

Although a number of important studies have demonstrated the establishment of restrictive cultural norms (particularly those of gender role and appearance) at about this time,[11] it also seems clear that the era of the freak show was in some ways more receptive to the transgression of such classificatory categories than twentieth-century culture has become. For although Gould and Pyle considered Eugen Sandow's muscular development to be anomalous enough to merit photographic plates in their work, they also praise his beauty and grace. And while Kate Sandwina in no way conformed to the frail, consumptive model of Victorian femininity, she was considered highly attractive and was married to a handsome acrobat whose height she exceeded by at least half a foot; perhaps the pressure to display gender dimorphism that makes contemporary couples select mates of a culturally approved height was not as pervasive in fin-de-siècle America and Europe as it is today.[12] At a time when the conventional distinctions and categories by which we have come to order existence were crystallizing, a measure of "play" still existed within and between classes of beings. As we shall see, bodybuilders of the late twentieth century perhaps face more restrictive enforcement of conventional categories of corporal existence than their precursors, even as they surpass bodily limits unimaginable a century ago.

TERROR AND SYMPATHY: CULTURAL REACTIONS TO BODYBUILDERS

From his vantage point at the end of the hippie era, Fiedler noted in 1978 that the term "freak" had become an honorific for socially dissident young people at the same time as it increasingly became socially inappropriate to apply the term to those groups it had traditionally designated. Today, bodybuilders compliment each other with the term "freak"; it is an expression of awe and respect for those who push their physical development beyond current limits. "Freakiness" is what is to be achieved, what the "pros" possess, what is most often acquired through drug use in addition to intense workouts. It is also, however, at least in part, what one is born with: a genetic predisposition for fabulous muscularity. Freakiness as an affirmation of physiological dissidence stirs both fascination and repulsion, both emulation and rejection in non-bodybuilders and even within bodybuilding culture and industry.

Bodybuilding never fails to elicit strong reactions, be it from mainstream culture or from the scholarly elite of contemporary society. Although Americans have become accustomed, via cable sports channels, to witnessing high-level bodybuilding competitions, many still find the bodies on display there unappealing or even repellent. The English professor mother of a gangly Oxford graduate turned amateur bodybuilder reports that a female friend to whom she showed pictures of her son over lunch responded: "Oh God, not while I'm eating!"[13] This might be chalked up to the mid-life intellectual's lack of stomach for things bodily, but college student surveyed about their reactions to photographs of a professional female bodybuilder also reacted negatively, using terms like "disgusting, too big, beastly, looks like a man, intimidating, unfeminine."[14] Mainstream culture's reaction to the bodybuilder adds a valence of disapprobation, perhaps tinged with intimidation, to the recoil one might also exhibit before a freak show.

Within bodybuilding culture, "freakiness" is much more acclaimed in males than in females. Since the early 1980s debate has raged within the pages of bodybuilding publications over acceptable levels of muscularity for women. A typical title on the cover of a bodybuilding magazine reads "Femininity: Do Female Bodybuilders Have It?" (*Muscle and Fitness*, November 1989). What is at stake in this question is a cultural definition of somatic sexual difference. Female bodybuilding is disputed even within bodybuilding culture because it challenges a deeply held cultural assumption: the equation of muscularity with masculinity. Although male and female bodies have virtually identical musculature and exhibit similar responses to strength training (wider shoulder and back, narrower waist and hips, flaring thighs and increased muscular size and definition overall), perceptible muscularity continues to signal masculinity. The consumer industry of bodybuilding presents at once the social preconstruction of muscularity as masculinity and the questioning of that categorical equation by radically muscular women. For instance, the major monthly bodybuilding magazine, *Muscle and Fitness*, has been criticized since the mid-1980s for consistently displaying on its cover very muscular, well-known male bodybuilders with anonymous female models possessing no perceptible muscular development. Typically, these models have very smooth, thin limbs and very large breasts; they are generally posed as clinging to or supported by the muscular male star. Such a presentation encodes feminine powerlessness, dependency, and submissiveness overlaid with a display of exaggerated secondary sex characteristics that signals reproductive capacity and sexual receptivity. Over the years, female readers have complained in letters to the magazine editors about what they see as a double standard: articles and regular columns inside the magazine feature female contests and contestants, but the consumer target of the cover and the advertisements remains the male.[15] While seeking mainstream commercial success, these magazines and the industry they represent nevertheless constitute the site of conflictual impulses: between covers that hyperbolize traditional definitions of gender dimorphism, there are displays of female muscularity that much of the population finds shocking.

Bodybuilding as a commercial enterprise and would-be entertainment industry finds itself negotiating rival pressures. One the one hand, gym owners, magazine publishers, and product vendors seek the widest possible participation in and observation of the sport. Thus female competitors and contests comprise a market opportunity. On the other hand, the industry recognizes that negative popular sentiment toward highly muscular women must be palliated and the female competitors' physical appearance made palatable if the sport is to receive mainstream consumer acceptance. One strategy for marketing female bodybuilding has been to control how competitors look by adopting certain unstated standards for judging competitions. Because the criteria of muscularity, symmetry, and posing style cannot be quantitatively measured, judging in bodybuilding competitions is fairly subjective. Female competitors complain that criteria change from one contest to the next: full-blown muscularity, hardness, and mass may prevail in one contest; the next week the very same competitors will receive widely divergent placings because a smaller, softer, more conventionally feminine look is being enforced. Increasingly, elite female bodybuilders acknowledge the pressure to refrain from achieving extreme muscularity and to market themselves as conventionally attractive through breast implants and other cosmetic enhancements, including facial surgery. Lenda Murray, the current top-ranked female professional, stated after one of her Ms. Olympia victories: "People need to stop and think. The IFBB [International Federation of Body Building, the major promotor of competitive exhibitions] wants us to lose some size and muscle. I had to diet longer to be a slightly smaller version of what I could really be."[16] While Murray's tone is mildly rebellious toward the limits she was forced to respect in order to win, another victorious competitor, Sue Price, is more plaintive than angry as she recalls a contest in which the audience urged her to transgress the boundaries of female muscle decorum: "I don't know if the judges want to see it all, after what happened to me at the 1992 Nationals (when she placed fifth). It's like playing with matches. I don't want to burn the house down. I only showed the cross-striations after people in the audience started yelling for me to hit my legs. I said to myself 'I hope the judges forgive me if they don't really want to see that.' I only contracted for a second but I could really grind on that thigh if I wanted to. I'm just afraid."[17] The competitor's fear of the judges' distaste is echoed in "Power and Sizzle," a recent column introduced in *Flex* magazine to calm the fears aroused by the heightened muscularity of top-level female competitors and, perhaps, to market a new erotic standard linking muscular female bodies to traditional sexual display. This column regularly features a collection of photographs of female competitors, either nude or in costume, posed in conventionally erotic or provocative postures. The self-declared aim of this regular feature, repeated with each issue, is to defuse negative or fearful reactions to female bodybuilders:

> Women bodybuilders are many things, among them symmetrical, strong, sensuous, and stunning. When photographed in competition shape, ripping and grimacing or squeezing out shots, they appear shredded, vascular, and hard, and they can be perceived as threatening. Off season they carry more body fat, presenting themselves in a much more naturally attractive condition. To exhibit the real, natural side of women bodybuilders, *Flex* has been presenting pictorials of female competitors in softer condition. We hope this dispels the myth of female bodybuilding and masculinity and proves what role models they truly are.[18]

Like many competitors, the women quoted earlier go to great lengths to encode conventional femininity in their grooming, posing, and sexy photo layouts published in bodybuilding magazines and books (see fig. 25.2). Although their careers depend on marketing themselves as attractive, nonthreatening women, they nevertheless long to fully develop the muscular potential that some of their spectators find wondrous.

The challenge to conventions of somatic gender difference posed by transgressive female physiques led in 1986 to mandatory drug testing for female competitors. When women protested that men's contests were not drug tested, Ms. Olympia promoter Wayne DeMilia responded that testing females was necessary because "their gender is changing faster. Some of the women are not totally female."[19] At about the same time, however, a Mr. Slate wrote in his letter to the editors of *Modern Bodybuilding:* "Of course the debate will rage about what a woman is supposed to look like. But I thought the sport was bodybuilding."[20] In respect to female bodybuilding, bodybuilding culture itself is clearly caught up in conflictual discourses pitting essentialist views of sexual difference and physical appearance against a bodybuilding

25.2. Contemporary bodybuilding competitor Sue Gafner. Reprinted from Bill Dobbins, *The Women: Photographs of the Top Female Bodybuilders*. New York: Artisan, 1994.

ethic of undifferentiated, transcendent muscularity. Audiences sympathetic to maximal muscularity are at odds with an entertainment industry seeking to display a calculated, profitable level of "freakiness."

In recent years bodybuilding has captured the attention of scholars in a number of fields, from anthropology and sociology to philosophy. To date, most of this research has dealt with female bodybuilding and the vexed question of resistance versus compliance to cultural norms of femininity. Feminist analysts of female bodybuilding have found in it a counterpractice that is "traumatically unsettling" to mainstream culture's systems of gender differentiation.[21] Many see in female bodybuilding a mode of personal and political resistance to an "ideological complex of patriarchy, heterosexuality, and homophobia that equates muscularity with masculinity" in a network of hierarchical categories disadvantageous to women.[22] Despite its potential for challenging and redesigning constructed attributes of femininity in a more empowering manner, most scholars still find female bodybuilding to be co-opted by societal and market pressures to comply with mainstream definitions of femininity and female beauty.[23]

Recognizing that for female competitors bodybuilding is "saturated with contradictions," some feminist analysts still see there at least a potential for personal self-shaping and political resistance.[24] Analysts of male bodybuilding, however, are critical of a practice they see as symptomatic of what ails contemporary society. For instance, sociologist Alan Klein uses a classic Marxian analysis to conclude that male bodybuilders are alienated and objectified, seeking to overcome, through maximized physiques, psychological problems and insecurities stemming from poor self-image, failed family relationships, and the inability to relate to others. For Klein, bodybuilding is "a sport subculture built on a neurotic core."[25] Sam Fussell, the Oxford graduate turned obsessive amateur bodybuilder mentioned earlier, makes a similar point in his bodybuilding autobiography, using his own fears and self-loathing as evidence. While Fussell talks about "hating to be human" as his motivation for bodybuilding, Klein deplores how bodybuilding, like much of contemporary popular culture, idealizes the body as a machine.[26] Here we find again the language of Fiedler's definition: the bodybuilder as freak transcends and disrupts categories of existence unquestioned even in the analytical discourses of Marxism, contemporary sociology and psychology, and confessional autobiography.

A telling example of such category disruption and the terrors it stirs is Klein's discussion of the mind-body opposition fundamental to Western culture. For Klein, no other "subculture" splits self and body as much as bodybuilding; the bodybuilder is objectified and alienated in the mirrors that line the walls of his gym and in his view of his own body as "an externalized object or machine." In place of this reified body Klein advocates instead a body that is "utilitarian, functioning on our behalf and as an extension of ourselves."[27] Klein's language eloquently translates his own sense of distance between "ourselves" and our body as tool—a useful prosthetic "extension" or robot "functioning" to accomplish the volition of the immaterial mind that for Klein seems to *be* the self. Klein's analysis enforces the very category distinctions for which he indicts the bodybuilder. It could be argued, however, that bodybuilding, like all sports, is a complex interaction of mind and body. Focus, concentration, mental imagery, and feedback help the weight trainer to accomplish a challenging lift or feel the training effect. The interaction of muscle work and brain chemicals generates a sense of mental and physical well-being. In one sense, moreover, bodybuilding is among those sports in which mentality and physicality are most thoroughly merged; in the diet phase of competition preparation, rationality and mental control play as large a role in the final competitive outcome as lifting weights and posing.[28] Klein's critique of male bodybuilders fails to recognize their potential for disruption of cultural categories and constructs them as freaks through a discourse of psychological and social pathology perhaps more revelatory of Klein's own cultural and intellectual fears than generalizable as a description of contemporary bodybuilders. As Bogdan notes, "How we view people who are different has less to do with what they are physiologically than with who we are culturally."[29]

The Bodybuilder as Postmodern Freak

While most scholarly treatments of bodybuilding analyze either males or females, Anne Bolin's article "Flex Appeal, Food, and Fat: Competitive Bodybuilding, Gender, and Diet" explores what makes male and female bodybuilders more alike than different. An amateur bodybuilding competitor and anthropologist, Bolin finds that in the liminal phase of precontest dieting male and female bodybuilders come to resemble each other closely in their goals, strategies, and appearance. While muscularity is culturally linked to masculinity, femininity is traditionally associated with a propensity for body fat. Diet, as Bolin points out, has been read as the enforcement of patriarchal norms equating femininity with frailty, thinness, and neoteny. When male bodybuilders pursue an exacting diet aimed at stripping off subcutaneous fat, they cross over into a culturally feminine domain. Yet neither male nor female bodybuilders diet to be "thin"; both prize maximal muscularity, thereby placing themselves in a culturally masculine domain.

Elsewhere Bolin has noted that while muscles traditionally encode the agonic power of masculine strength, women's power has resided in the hedonic realm of display and beauty. Since Eugen Sandow, strong male physiques have participated in the hedonic code. Other cross-over qualities establish male and female bodybuilders as "beings of the same category":[30] vascularity, hairlessness, loss of breast tissue in females and occasional enlargement of nipples in males due to steroid use, and an ideal body type for both consisting of wide shoulders and back, narrow hips, and flaring thighs.[31] Indeed, bodybuilders seem to transcend the category of the human in the discourse of the gym and the muscle magazine; recently a victorious competitor was praised in the pages of a bodybuilding magazine for her "coconut delts, cobra lats, bellowing thighs" in a cascade of metaphors mixing the vegetal and animal kingdoms to characterize the woman's otherness.[32]

Contemporary bodybuilders are constructed as freaks—either affirmatively by sympathetic practitioners and fans or negatively by general or scholarly opinion and skittish entrepreneurs—primarily on the basis of their violation of widely held cultural categories such as those opposing masculine and feminine qualities, or those contrasting virtuous intellectuality with narcissistic corporality. Yet other, more subterranean classifications are transgressed by the contemporary bodybuilder in ways that make him or her an exemplar of postmodernity. In 1949, Simone de Beauvoir explained in *The Second Sex* the difference between transcendence and immanence: a human subject who carries out a project, who acts upon the world to alter it, is transcendent; one who fails to act upon external reality, who merely exists as an object in the world, is immanent. Beauvoir's existentialist categories were enunciated in respect to women's lives under patriarchy early in what many describe as "postmodernity": the epoch following World War II, in which modern assumptions about traditional categories describing being, society, and the human subject came under scrutiny and philosophical attack. By 1962, J. L. Austin had provided an example of the postmodern blurring and coalescence of categories when he demonstrated that speech is sometimes action: in *How To Do Things with Words*, Austin termed "performatives" those special speech acts that perform the action to which they refer. Postmodern bodybuilders perform themselves; they *are* their own acts; they incarnate their own projects and embody their own achievements. Complicating the residual categories of modernity, bodybuilders are at once active, (self)transformative agents and the object of others' spectatorial, evaluative, or erotic gaze.

For postmodern theorists such as Donna Haraway, our epoch is not only postgender, it is witness to the breakdown of modernity's other boundaries, those between the human and the animal, between the animal-human and the machine, and between the physical and the nonphysical. The cyborg world Haraway describes is characterized by "transgressed boundaries, potent fusions, and dangerous possibilities which progressive people might explore as one part of needed political work."[33] A micropolitics of multiplicity and respect for the myriad of singularities, of the "little stories" that make up human existence, also figures in the writings of Jean-François Lyotard on what he calls the postmodern condition. Elsewhere I have argued that Lyotard's formulation of a postmodern ethics intersects in significant ways with his characterizations of the postmodern body as traversed by masculine and feminine qualities, as pure surface without interiority or exteriority.[34] For Lyotard, modernity was "work on the limits of what was thought to be established, in thought as well as in the arts, sciences, technologies, and politics."[35] Surpassing the established limits of the past, the postmodern bodybuilder even blurs the lines between the domains Lyotard cites: his or her practice participates in the realm of sport, art, dance, beef- or cheesecake, and science. For Haraway, as for the sympathetic spectator of bodybuilding shows, this freaky subject is a wondrous being, a hybrid blurring the lines between true and produced freak: "By the late twentieth century, our time, a mythic time, we are all chimeras."[36]

While Haraway argues for the pleasures of confused boundaries, the confusion operated by today's bodybuilders and other category transgressors such as homosexuals, transsexuals, in vitro parents, pregnant women who seek to abort, or white middle-class youth who sport nose rings and tattoos is threatening, even sacrilegious to a society in the grip of cultural conservatism and resurgent religious fundamentalism. In the waning millennium, bodybuilding is at once an arena of ever-expanding corporal potentialities and a domain where a panicked politics of bodily control seek to limit corporal experimentations through the construction of the postmodern freak as pathological other. Bogdan is right in correcting Fiedler's fascinated drift in focus from "us" to "them"; our culture's "sympathy and terror" before today's freak is the measure of our own vexed postmodernity.

NOTES

1. Leslie Fiedler, *Freaks: Myths and Images of the Secret Self* (New York: Simon and Schuster, 1978).

2. David Willoughby, *The Super-Athletes* (New York: A. S. Barnes, 1970), 53; and Fiedler, *Freaks*, 124.

3. Edmond Desbonnet, *Les Rois de la force* (Paris: Librairie Berger-Levrault, 1911).

4. Robert Bogdan, *Freak Show: Presenting Human Oddities for Amusement and Profit* (Chicago: University of Chicago Press, 1988), 10.

5. David Chapman, "Gallery of Ironmen: Apollon," *Ironman*, November 1990, 123.

6. George M. Gould, M.D. and Walter L. Pyle, M.D., *Anomalies and Curiosities of Medicine* (New York: Bell, 1896).

7. David Chapman, "Gallery of Ironmen: Kate Sandwina," *Ironman*, June 1990, 70; Armand Tanny and Leo Gandreau, "Iron Ladies," *Muscle and Fitness*, March 1985, 104–6, 210.

8. Chapman, "Gallery of Ironmen: Kate Sandwina," 90.

9. David Knight, *The Age of Science: The Scientific World View in the Nineteenth Century* (New York: Basil Blackwell, 1986).

10. Bogdan, *Freak Show*, ix.

11. See, e.g., Anne Bolin, "Vandalized Vanity: Feminine Physiques Portrayed and Betrayed," in *Tattoo, Torture, Mutilation, and Adornment*, ed. Frances E. Mascia-Lees and Patricia Sharpe (Albany: State University of New York Press, 1992), 79–99; Susan Bordo, "Reading the Slender Body," in *Body/*

Politics: Women and the Discourses of Science, ed. Mary Jacobus, Evelyn Fox Keller, and Sally Shuttleworth (New York: Routledge, 1990), 83–112; and Ellen L. Bassuk, "The Rest Cure: Repetition or Resolution of Victorian Women's Conflicts?" in *The Female Body in Western Culture*, ed. Susan Rubin Suleiman (Cambridge: Harvard University Press, 1985), 139–51.

12. In *Physical Appearance and Gender* (Albany: State University of New York Press, 1992), 182, Linda A. Jackson reports that a random pairing of males and females would produce a female taller than the male once out of every twenty-nine pairings. In reality, a recent study of 720 married couples produced only one such couple. Contemporary Americans appear to select spouses who conform to dimorphic standards.

13. Betty Fussell, "My Son the Bodybuilder," *Lear's*, November 1989, 79.

14. Bolin, "Vandalized Vanity," 91.

15. In *Little Big Men* (New York: State University of New York Press, 1993), 87, Alan Klein links these magazine covers to a conscious strategy on the part of bodybuilding's major entrepreneur, Joe Wieder, to combat the popular stereotype associating bodybuilding with homosexuality.

16. Lenda Murray, interview with Reg Bradford, *Muscular Development*, March 1993, 90.

17. Sue Price, quoted in *Muscular Development*, January 1995, 86.

18. "Power and Sizzle: Sue Price, A Core of Confidence," *Flex*, January 1995, 124.

19. Teagan Clive, "Ladies First," *Ironman*, April 1989, 157.

20. *Modern Bodybuilding*, February 1990, 13.

21. Janet Gaines, introduction to *Fabrications: Costume and the Female Body*, ed. Janet Gaines and Charlotte Herzog (New York: Routledge, 1990), 26.

22. Laurie Schulze, "On the Muscle," in *Fabrications*, 74.

23. See Schulze, "On the Muscle"; Bolin, "Vandalized Vanity"; Anne Balsamo, "Feminist Bodybuilding," *Women, Sport, and Culture*, ed. Susan Birrell and Cheryl L. Cole (Champaign, Ill.: Human Kinetics, 1994), 341–52; Christine Anne Holmlund, "Visible Difference and Flex Appeal: The Body, Sex, Sexuality, and Race in the *Pumping Iron* films," in *Women, Sport, and Culture*, 299–314; Sharon R. Guthrie and Shirley Castelnuevo, "Elite Women Bodybuilders: Models of Resistance or Compliance?" *Play and Culture*, vol. 5 no. 4 (November 1992): 401–8.

24. Bolin, "Vandalized Vanity," 90.

25. Alan Klein, "Man Makes Himself," *Play and Culture*, vol. 5, no. 4 (1992): 329–37 (quote on p. 329); see also Klein, *Little Big Men*.

26. Sam Fussell, *Muscle: Confessions of an Unlikely Bodybuilder* (New York: Poseidon, 1991), 173; Klein, "Man Makes Himself."

27. Klein, "Man Makes Himself," 330, 331.

28. "Bodybuilding is one of several sports in which diet is accorded such a high status in training and preparing for a contest. When bodybuilders were asked to rank the diet in terms of its relative importance for competition, it was not uncommon for them to assign 90 to 98% of the precontest preparation, 3 to 4 months before the competition, to a strict eating program." Anne Bolin, "Flex Appeal, Food, and Fat: Competitive Bodybuilding, Gender, and Diet," *Play and Culture*, vol. 5, no. 4 (November 1992): 381–82.

29. Bogdan, *Freak Show*, 10.

30. Bolin, "Flex Appeal," 34.

31. In his groundbreaking work *Making Sex: Body and Gender from the Greeks to Freud* (Cambridge: Harvard University Press, 1990), historian Thomas Laqueur posits that the one-sex model of fundamental resemblance and continuum between males and females held from classical times through the Renaissance, but gave way, in the late eighteenth century, to the dichotomous two-sex model that still dominates our social and natural sciences today.

32. *Muscular Development*, January 1995, 87.

33. Donna Haraway, *Simians, Cyborgs, and Women: The Reinvention of Nature* (New York: Routledge, 1990), 150.

34. Cecile Lindsay, "Lyotard and the Postmodern Body," *L'Esprit créateur*, vol. 31, no. 1 (Spring 1991): 33–47.

35. Jean-François Lyotard, *Tombeau de l'intellectuel* (Paris: Galilée, 1984), 73.

36. Haraway, *Simians, Cyborgs, and Women*, 150.

TWENTY-SIX

The Celebrity Freak: Michael Jackson's "Grotesque Glory"

DAVID D. YUAN

The freak show is virtually extinct in the West.[1] One might even be tempted to say that the freak no longer exists; perhaps the term "freak" will soon become as archaic as "savage" or "darky." Why is it, then, that Americans are as fixated on freaks and freakishness today, in the late twentieth century, as they were in P. T. Barnum's time? The tabloid press, which today includes television programs and on-line computer sites as well as newspapers, has more than a faint whiff of the old ten-in-one about it. Outlandish stories of three-hundred-pound babies, alien abductions, and Siamese twins frequently appear, but it is what we might call tales of celebrity freakishness that today occupy the main stage. The celebrity is already set apart from normal society: enlarged by fame and the adoration of fans, he or she socializes with other celebrities and lives a life whose richness and splendor are not beyond the fan's imagination, but utterly beyond the fan's experience. But the celebrity freak tests the boundaries of acceptable, or even comprehensible, behavior. The celebrity freak at his weirdest is comparable in the tabloid pantheon only to the extraterrestrials who compete with him for tabloid space.

Michael Jackson, the self-designated King of Pop, is willingly or unwillingly the definitive celebrity freak of our times. At least since the mid-1980s, Jackson has been more famous for his freakishness than for his talent as a singer, songwriter, and dancer. This might not be so startling except for the fact that Jackson's contributions to American music have been genuinely important. The central achievement of Jackson's career is his 1982 album *Thriller*, the best-selling music album of all time, with world sales of close to 44 million. *Thriller*, which dominated popular music in the mid-1980s, was a rare commodity: a work that was genuinely innovative and transgressive—in the sense that it broke through both artistic and social barriers—but that was also so close to being universally accessible that it became one of the greatest popular art successes in history. As critic Dave Marsh wrote prophetically just after the release of *Thriller*, "Jackson . . . has become a necessity . . . for those who pretend to know about American music."[2] Another reviewer proclaims that Jackson "practically invented a new genre of mass entertainment, and made himself into the most popular performer in the history of American music."[3]

For many African Americans, including those who do not particularly like Jackson's music, his achievement retains a special significance. While Jackson was preceded by many vastly talented African-American musicians and entertainers, his achievement in shattering the sales records for an album in *any* music category was a long-awaited moment for African Americans. Jackson was told that there was a ceiling for black stars in America—the biggest black star still could not surpass the biggest white star. When Jackson, irked by the fact that "They call Elvis [Presley] the King," asked "Why don't they call *me* that?" he was advised to curb his ambition because " 'the white man will never let you be bigger than Elvis."[4] When Jackson actually surpassed Presley in record sales, it was a signal event in American cultural history, comparable to the now well-analyzed breakthroughs of Joe Louis in boxing and Jackie Robinson in baseball.

And yet even after Jackson's highly publicized achievement, Elvis remained the King of Rock 'n' Roll. Jackson countered with a campaign to cement his own sobriquet, "The King of Pop," in America's cultural consciousness. He also married Elvis Presley's daughter, Lisa Marie Presley, prompting journalist Margo Jefferson to ask: Where else would Lisa Marie Presley, who spent her childhood in "the shadow of Graceland," go "now that she is grown" but to Jackson's Neverland?[5] Jefferson adds: "[w]ho but Michael Jackson could come close to equaling [Elvis Presley's] power and his ultimately grotesque glory?"[6]

The dilemma for Jackson is that the more loudly he has proclaimed his greatness as an entertainer and artist, the less the critics and the public have been interested in his multidimensional artistry, and the more they have been interested in the bizarre stories and allegations that swirl around him. The association between Jackson and freakishness now has a long history. For a perplexed public, it is above all what Jackson has done to himself (the cosmetic surgery, white makeup, hairdos, and costumes) and what he may have done to others that make him freakish; he is viewed as the agent of his own "enfreakment," to use David Hevey's term.[7] The "Elephant Man" (Joseph Merrick), the celebrated freak of the nineteenth century whom Jackson has admitted reminds him of himself, nevertheless conveys the opposite sense of enfreakment. With Merrick it is assumed that his freakishness is purely an accident of nature, completely beyond his control or his encouragement. As Peter Graham and Fritz Oehlschlaeger argue in *Articulating the Elephant Man*, any notion that a modern public may entertain about Merrick is necessarily mediated by the ideologies of the physicians, anthropologists, playwrights, and filmmakers who have rendered his "life" for us.[8] But the stark evidence of Merrick's dramatically deformed bones, the photographs and plaster casts of his misshapen flesh, are silently but powerfully convincing; a man like Merrick would have had no choice about enfreakment.

From the public's perspective, Jackson's enfreakment did not occur until after he became an adult, when his behavior seemed to become progressively more bizarre and disturbing. The parade of weird tales about "Wacko Jacko" (the moniker the tabloid press prefers) began with stories about Jackson sleeping in a hyperbaric chamber to prevent aging. The next big tabloid story about Jackson (which was quickly picked up, however, by the "legitimate" press) was that he had offered the London Hospital half a million dollars to buy the Elephant Man's skeleton. It was (and continues to be) reported that Jackson has altered his face through a series of plastic surgeries in an effort to appear, to "be," more Caucasian and less African American. Jackson himself has said that he has vitiligo, a skin disorder that causes a patchy depigmentation, and that he uses light makeup to even out the blotches. Moreover, it was rumored that Jackson is homosexual and is contemplating a sex-change operation, that he has been castrated, or that he takes special drugs to preserve his high, boyish voice; it was also reported that Jackson is obsessed with the actress Elizabeth Taylor, has built a shrine to her in his home, and has invited her to sleep with him in his hyperbaric chamber. Less facetiously, Jackson, the man who would be a savior to all the world's children, was accused of sexually molesting a young boy who was a guest at his estate. A criminal investigation was launched, but both criminal and civil cases against Jackson were dismissed after Jackson settled the civil case out of court—a move that ensured that rumors and doubts about his conduct would continue.

While I was in the midst of tracing the history of Jackson's enfreakment and thinking about its implications for American culture, Jackson, now thirty-seven, released his album *HIStory: Past, Present and Future Book 1,* in which he attempts to do the same. The double album divides neatly into "Past" and "Present" sections: disc 1 is a review of his old hits; disc 2 introduces fifteen new songs, in which Jackson reviews his recent and not so recent personal history. "Tabloid Junkie" looks back at the early Jackson myths (the hyperbaric chamber, etc.); "Scream" and other songs seem to examine the more recent child-abuse scandal and the "press abuse" that Jackson claims he has suffered. The "future" the album's title alludes to is vaguer and more elusive than Jackson's past or present, perhaps because Jackson's future as a professional entertainer is largely to be decided by his audience's reaction to this massive retrospective/prospective work. As its title suggests, the album and booklet sum up all the showmanship, humbug, and artistic brilliance that Jackson has been perfecting in his thirty years of performing.

It is impossible to examine here all of the fascinating details of Jackson's life and art that are relevant to his freakish image: his childhood; the network of references to monsters, animals, and freaks in his albums and music videos; his penchant for fantastic disguises; the symbolic richness of the cinematic and circus memorabilia that decorate his Neverland estate, and so on. Therefore, I have largely restricted my analysis to two classic publicity stunts conceived by Jackson himself—the hyperbaric chamber photograph and the Elephant Man skeleton hoax—and to the physical examination Jackson was forced to undergo during the police department's investigation into the child-molestation charges. I will also situate my analysis of these events against the "narrative" of Jackson's body suggested by his frequent bodily alterations. My assumption throughout is that Jackson defines freakishness differently than does his audience. Thus we need to understand both how Jackson manipulates his own enfreakment (his efforts to encourage or subvert enfreakment) and how the audience and its culture participate in the construction of the freak.

Both Jackson and his audience perceive freakishness as a type of theatricalized transgression. Like the classic freak show with its hermaphrodite, its African albino, and the like, Jackson's public persona challenges boundaries of gender, sexuality, and race. In fact, this violation of or blurring of boundaries is integral to Jackson's rise to superstar status. The freakish transgression draws attention to the fact that a cultural value has been constructed around a particular physical characteristic: skin color and texture, having identifiably male or female sexual characteristics, the presence or absence of hair on certain body sites, having fewer or more limbs than is "normal," the size and shape of the head, and so on. Whether the freakish attribute challenges or ratifies the reigning ideology of the body is a complex issue, involving not only the performer, but how the performer is presented and what the audience's assumptions are. It is here that Jackson and his audience appear to diverge. Initially, the audience receives a vicarious thrill from Jackson's acting out of corporeal transgression(s). But eventually the audience's desire that the celebrity fulfill a particular identity (racial pioneer, sexless children's entertainer, heterosexual or homosexual erotic hero) overwhelms their tolerance for Jackson as a mercurial figure "morphing" effortlessly from role to role. The plasticity of Jackson's persona becomes a strategy for eluding the audience.

I propose two categories, "static enfreakment" and "plastic freakishness," to distinguish between how the audience perceives Jackson, and the enfreakment that Jackson fears the audience is trying to impose upon him.[9] The human curiosity at the dime museum or the circus sideshow epitomizes static enfreakment: he or she is a silent, unmoving object of the audience's gaze, to be looked at while the showman runs through his spiel. The Elephant Man began his life as such a spectacle, and after he died his skeleton became the ultimate in static curiosities when it was put on display in a glass case at the London Hospital, which had been his home. If the static curiosity is that which has been fixed, frozen, stuffed, or pickled, the "plastic freak" by contrast is free to move and moves to remain free. The plastic freak seeks to elude fixity and definition; his "true" identity remains hidden as he weaves images and stories around himself to arouse curiosity.[10] As Jackson himself once put it: "the bottom line is they don't *know* and everyone is going to continue searching to find out whether I'm gay, straight, or whatever. . . . And the longer it takes to discover this, the more famous I will be."[11]

Jackson's goal is to be freakish enough to arouse a restless public's interest, but not so freakish that fans are shocked or repulsed by him. But Jackson feels he must avoid static enfreakment above all; he must always be moving, evolving, transforming himself. In the world of pop entertainment, stasis means a weakening of one's grip on the public; entertainers not on the cutting edge soon become irrelevant. Stasis means allowing the mystery that is vital to celebrity to be dissolved under the fixed gaze of a public intent on knowing all there is to know. The theme running through Jackson's music videos, for example, is escape and metamorphosis: Jackson metamorphoses from man to zombie, from man to animal, from man to cyborg in an attempt to escape fans, reporters, or cartoon-like villains.

Stasis is the common theme running through the hyperbaric chamber and Elephant Man hoaxes, as well as Jackson's examination ordeal. The Elephant Man's skeleton in its glass cabinet and the memorably eerie photograph of Jackson "asleep" in the hyperbaric chamber evoke a sense of a life arrested, a living being once capable of responding to its environment has been reduced to a static curiosity that will remain conveniently silent while it is gawked at by spectators. The police department's examination of his body constitutes for Jackson the most threatening and abject example of static enfreakment. (It is not appropriate to debate here whether such an examination was warranted, or speculate about Jackson's sexual conduct. Whether Jackson is guilty or innocent of child molestation, the relation of his examination to a history of institutionalized racial humiliation and abjection and to the classic freak show remain issues relevant to this discussion.)

In 1983, Fred Astaire, impressed by Jackson's galvanizing performance during a Motown television special, telephoned to congratulate him, praising him for being "an angry dancer" and "a *hell* of a mover."[12] Astaire summed up the essence of Jackson's public persona in a word: "mover." Jackson's art exists in the combination of his hyperkinetic, explosive yet subtle dance "moves" with the lyrics and music of his songs; this is why Jackson has always insisted that his videos are the real measure of his achievements. Jackson is doing something more encompassing than "dancing." Not just specific dance steps, but every gesture, every facial expression, and every detail of his costume signify during Jackson's best performances.

What is Jackson's famous "moonwalk" if not a theatricalization of the admonition in Ralph Ellison's *Invisible Man* to "move without moving?"[13] To "move without moving" suggests an even more difficult project: to transgress without transgressing. The pop star must be able to break rules and boundaries while somehow holding on to his wholesome image. Elvis Presley, whose success pushed at class and racial barriers in the postwar United States, was also a transgressive "mover" and, to many, a freakish figure. Presley's critics were outraged before the unforgivable spectacle of a sexy, young white man who had learned to sing and move like a black entertainer (e.g., Presley's famous pelvic gyrations). As his fame reached national proportions, Presley too had to tackle the tricky problem of "moving without moving," vis-à-vis his breakthrough performance on television's *Ed Sullivan Show*. The network crudely solved the "problem" by simply refusing to show the lower half of Presley's body. If Presley's moving and singing like a black man seemed freakish and grotesque to white mainstream society, it also defined his contribution to American culture. On the other hand, NBC's transformation of Presley into a cathode-tube "half man" or "legless wonder" on the *Ed Sullivan Show* rendered him a genuinely abject spectacle, even as Presley's appearance on the show vastly expanded his fame.[14]

In the most general sense, Jackson, like Presley, could not avoid freakishness. The very achievement that makes a Jackson a popular culture innovator must be riskily won by the performance of a transgressive act. Indeed, Jackson is potentially much more transgressive and threatening than the typical sideshow freak; Jackson is not ensconced in a socially marginal context (the *side*show) that is only seasonally accessible to mainstream society. The transgressive acts performed by a mass media star like Jackson are much more likely to "contaminate" the public as his records and videos circulate worldwide.

The history of American entertainment (and Jackson's own place in that history) is never far from Jackson's mind.[15] He has made it clear that he believes African-American music should not be relegated to "sideshow" status in American cultural history. Jackson (who once performed a pseudo-minstrel number with Paul McCartney) would surely wish to challenge the ideological basis of classic blackface minstrelsy, in which African Americans are allowed to be present to American culture only by being literally absent (from the stage).[16] The story of Jackson's own professional evolution has him developing from a helpless and unaware *naif* (an eight-year-old star manipulated by his powerful father) to become an immensely powerful captain of his own destiny and the destinies of many others who are dependent on him in one way or another, including the press. It is important to recognize how the oft-told history of Michael Jackson's rise to stardom resembles the institutional history of African-American entertainment—and the institutional history of the freak show.[17]

After Michael left the Jackson 5 to develop himself as a solo star, he was finally able to exercise complete control over his career. He swiftly began to reshape his musical approach, but he also eagerly began to participate in the broader task of promoting and marketing himself. Having left the Jehovah's Witnesses, Jackson gave his manager a copy of a book about P. T. Barnum's "theories and philosophies," telling him "[t]his is going to be my bible and I want it to be yours" and adding "I want my whole career to be the greatest show on earth."[18] Jackson would undoubtedly have been aware of Barnum's famous hoaxes (Joice

Heth, the Feejee Mermaid, the Cardiff Giant, etc.) when he concocted his own hoaxes (the hyperbaric chamber and Elephant Man skeleton myths). Furthermore, Jackson would seem to subscribe to Barnum's line of justification for humbug: any publicity is good publicity, and a good hoax serves the public good by sharpening the wits of the citizenry.[19] It is intriguing that many of Barnum's hoaxes played with a similar dialectic between static and plastic freakishness: the Cardiff Giant was supposed to be the calcified remains of a genuine giant; the Feejee Mermaid was actually a monkey torso grafted onto a fish's body and tail; and Barnum encouraged speculation that Joice Heth might not even be human, but rather a fiendishly realistic robot. These hoaxes played with the distinction between the animate and the inanimate, the organic and the inorganic, much as Jackson's music videos and hoaxes do.

For all that the press has done to cement Jackson's reputation as the ultimate celebrity freak, Jackson himself initiated the tabloid sensationalism in the mid-1980s, when he conceived of the hyperbaric chamber and the Elephant Man skeleton hoaxes. The hyperbaric chamber story appeared first. After Jackson was burned during the filming of a Pepsi commercial, in January 1984, he inspected an oxygen (hyperbaric) chamber used to heal serious burn victims, even though his burns were not extensive enough to require hyperbaric treatment. Reportedly, when Jackson's plastic surgeon theorized that the hyperbaric chamber might be used to prolong life, Jackson thought of buying one. After his manager, Frank Dileo, talked him out of it, Jackson developed the notion of using the hyperbaric chamber as a publicity stunt, concocting the story that he wanted to sleep in the chamber every night so that he could live to be a hundred and fifty years old. Jackson instructed Dileo to manage the publicity. Dileo made a deal with the *National Enquirer:* he gave the paper the photo of Jackson in the hyperbaric chamber in exchange for the guarantee of "a cover feature."[20] Later, Dileo planted the hoax-story in the "legitimate" press by convincing a publicist who did not work for Jackson to testify that the entertainer was indeed sleeping in the special chamber.

The resulting photograph (fig. 26.1) is one of the most compellingly eerie of all the exhibits in the tabloids' "Wacko Jacko" collection. The coffin-like hyperbaric chamber has a glass shell that allows a head-to-foot view of Jackson, dressed in striped shirt and dark trousers but shoeless, eyes closed; below Jackson's chin, a beam of light bounces off the glass, adding a magical dazzle to the portrait. Dials, buttons, and something that looks like a radio receiver are visible below the glass shell, on the machine's massive base. The photograph is richly evocative, both in terms of Jackson's private imaginings and the public myths of popular American culture. Many of Jackson's videos are in a science fiction vein: "Smooth Criminal" features Jackson transforming himself into an enormous cyborg (a rocket-powered man/machine hybrid) as he defends the world's children from an evil drug-pusher; "Dancing Machine" features a gyrating "female" robot; "Ben" contrasts Michael's sweet singing with scary scenes of an ecological disaster—a world overrun by rats. A common image in the videos is Jackson fleeing, often from fans, in rocket-ships or other futuristic, jet-powered machines—jet cars or jet motorcycles, for example. If Jackson's videos typically act out fantasies of escape and metamorphosis, the hyperbaric chamber image seems to celebrate the stasis he so assiduously avoids. The contrast between the eerily still Jackson in this photograph and Jackson the consummate "mover" onstage or Jackson the protean superhero in his cartoon-like videos is stunning. The hyperbaric chamber image suggests death even as it tantalizes us with the promise of eternal life—surely it is no coincidence that his waxy pallor makes him look like a cadaver or a vampire in its coffin. If this is eternal life, there is

26.1. Michael Jackson in the hyperbaric chamber. Courtesy of AP/Wide World Photos.

something distinctly sinister about it. (Note the photograph's gothic flourishes: how the long fingers of Jackson's left hand extend spider-like on the white sheet he lies on.)

Why should Jackson display himself in this bizarre way? What did he think he would gain by disseminating this image and the strange legend that accompanied it? First, there is no doubt that Jackson succeeded in attracting vast publicity without singing a note or dancing a step. As a piece of showmanship, the hyperbaric chamber hoax represented a kind of experiment in audience control. Jackson may have surmised that if the public believed this outlandish tale, then they would believe anything—and a gullible audience is readily manipulated to the showman's advantage. Beyond this show business utility, the hoax carefully reflected Jackson's ambivalence about celebrity. The hyperbaric chamber seems to offer up an utterly motionless, helpless Michael to his eager fans. And yet Jackson hermetically sealed in his glass chamber is, while absolutely visible, also absolutely untouchable. This tableau is an acute summary of the celebrity's existence: the celebrity is forever being observed, but real intimacy with him is impossible. At this level, the hyperbaric chamber image reflects Jackson's fantasies of the all-consuming audience: his autobiography, *Moonwalk*, presents Jackson as constantly in danger of being consumed by his admirers, literally picked apart for souvenirs—a swath of his shirt, a clump of hair and scalp.

By contrast, fans interviewed about Jackson stress his almost perfect inaccessibility, his squadrons of bodyguards and retainers, the hired police who accompany him to the tall gates of his walled estate. For Jackson, the hyperbaric chamber might represent a hopeless fantasy about protecting himself from damage or "contamination" by the public (Jackson, after all, wears a surgical mask when he goes out in public). For all his elaborate protections, Jackson has confessed that he is still afraid of people and what they might do to him. For the public, the hyperbaric chamber and the accompanying story might be taken as fact, and Jackson's rather self-parodic fantasy of purity and untouchability accepted without irony. Conversely, the photograph's evocation of contamination brings to mind Jackson's role as a cultural transgressor: a marginal figure in terms of race and class who nevertheless realized the Promethean feat of becoming the world's most popular entertainer. Jackson has often portrayed himself as the messianic superstar who is feared even as he saves the world.[21]

Jackson, approaching middle age, has increasingly been compelled to build monuments to himself (like the gray Jackson statue featured on the cover of his latest album and in the accompanying video). Even the hyperbaric chamber image can be viewed as a kind of monument to an immortal celebrity whose grip over the future is as secure as his grip over the past. During the Soviet reign, Lenin, icily preserved in a glass display coffin, was one of the most popular spectacles in the world, viewed by millions of worshipful fans every year. The telling contradiction for Jackson is that he finds the idea of himself as the object of this sort of personality cult attractive, even as it provokes the very stasis he has been running from for so long.

Jackson's "success" with the hyperbaric chamber photograph prompted another hoax: the tale of his pursuit of the Elephant Man's skeleton. The parallel between Jackson in his hyperbaric chamber and the Elephant Man in his glass cabinet is clear: both present a static curiosity to be gawked at by spectators. Jackson's interest in the Elephant Man was piqued by the 1980 film *The Elephant Man* directed by David Lynch. Reportedly, Jackson watched the film fifteen times in his private screening room, crying all the way through it.[22] J. Randy Taraborrelli writes that Jackson, like Merrick, was "an outsider . . . searching endlessly for love and acceptance."[23] Jackson's interest deepened after he read medical books on the Elephant Man's condition, culminating in a visit to the London Hospital Medical College, where he inspected the Elephant Man's skeleton. In May 1987 after his visit, Jackson concocted the scheme to make an offer for the skeleton as a publicity stunt. Jackson's manager was asked to handle the publicity from there, and Dileo announced that Jackson, impressed by "the ethical, medical, and historical significance of the Elephant Man," had offered the London Hospital Medical College half a million dollars for his skeleton. In fact, Jackson had made no such offer to the Medical College at the time.[24] UPI and the Associated Press, however, quickly picked up on the story and spread it throughout the world. Reporters subsequently thought to contact the London Hospital to corroborate the story and were told that no offer had been made for the skeleton; moreover, the skeleton was not for sale. Dileo allegedly urged Jackson to make a genuine offer to buy the skeleton, which Jackson agreed to. After Dileo offered one million dollars for the skeleton on Jackson's behalf (the higher amount creating the appearance of a tense bidding war for the remains), a London Hospital spokeswoman curtly informed the press: "If indeed [Jackson] has offered to buy it, it would be for publicity and I find it very unlikely that the medical college would be willing to sell it for cheap publicity reasons."[25] Jackson, apparently, never did acquire the skeleton, although rumors persist that he did (as late as 1993, Jackson was still being asked about it).[26]

It is intriguing to imagine Jackson, having watched Lynch's *Elephant Man* over and over again, being compelled to visit the London Hospital and see the archaeological evidence of Merrick's predicament for himself, rather than depending solely on the movie's version of Merrick's life. Bones are primary evidence, or at least we like to think so. If there is an overarching reason for the relentless press interest in Jackson, it is that the press never seems to penetrate down to Jackson's "bones," down to the "real" man. Jackson, who has very deliberately avoided static enfreakment, has so far proved too mercurial, too elusive to be categorically "known." The enigmas continue to multiply: Is Jackson a child molester or a child savior? Does he suffer from vitiligo, discoid lupus, or some as yet unnamed skin disorder? Was his marriage to Lisa Marie Presley a loveless corporate merger, or a genuine love affair?

Whether or not Jackson was ever serious about owning the skeleton, his interest in the Elephant Man does not appear to have faded when the London Hospital Medical College dismissed his offer. In his music video "They Don't Care About Us" Jackson even dances with an animator's fantastic rendition of the Elephant Man's bones: a skeletal human figure on which is superimposed a genuine elephant's massive skull and tusks. No textual reference to the Elephant Man appears in Jackson's autobiography, but an arresting black-and-white photograph of Jackson dressed in dancing regalia (fedora and glove) does appear to be a reference to the Elephant Man. Graham and Oehlschlaeger describe the parallels: "His hat, curls, and contorted profile with puffed-out upper lip suggest Merrick's large, lumpy head. The twist of the torso and partial bend to the legs give an impression of spinal curvature and hip misalignment. . . . [One] hand has a blurred, flipperlike quality."[27] However, they view Jackson's evocation of the Elephant Man's deformities somewhat skeptically: "Dandiacal self-deformity is as piquant a sauce for Jackson as high-life fantasies were for Merrick."[28] But the more one examines Jackson's life, the less frivolous his affinity for Merrick seems. One can criticize Jackson's excessive self-pity, but I believe his identification with the Elephant Man is sincere—albeit still "dandiacal," or theatrical, in part. A capacity for taking his dandyism seriously is something that Merrick would have shared with Jackson.

For many, the Elephant Man epitomizes primary, "natural" freakishness. But as *Articulating the Elephant Man* argues, even Merrick's freakishness cannot be understood without interrogating the culture in which he lived. Graham and Oehlschlaeger view Jackson and Merrick as "protean" figures who are "partly innate, partly made, and partly reflected"; both became public spectacles and both sought to achieve "the triumph of grace over awkwardness."[29] Impressed by these parallels between Jackson and Merrick, they are compelled to ask if Jackson should be seen as "a fellow sufferer existing between celebrity and freak—gazed at, appropriated, and reduced to the role he plays, colonized by the dominant values of his culture? Might an enormously successful black entertainer consider the Elephant Man his Victorian counterpart?"[30]

Has Jackson been "reduced" to a prepared role, and "colonized" by his culture? In my view, Jackson would not have been so feverishly popular, nor would he have aroused such a variety of intense responses (curiosity, reverence, skepticism, devotion, disgust, etc.), if he had never escaped from a prepared role in American culture. But this is not to say that the question of colonization is irrelevant to Jackson's enfreakment. We see Jackson's dilemma most clearly in his effort to shatter prepared roles and to transgress, but to do so without offending. Jackson must move without moving; to transgress too boldly means the censure of angry parents, newspaper columnists, and pressure groups (Jackson's most recent controversy is over the alleged anti-Semitism of his song "They Don't Care About Us"). If Jackson has been assigned a role, it is the unenviable one of being a G-rated controversial artist. But if this is a role that his record company and others would like him to accept, it is still Jackson who has decided to accept it.

If Graham and Oehlschlaeger argue too one-sidedly for Jackson's victimization by a dominant culture, other critics err in insisting that Jackson alone is implicated in his enfreakment. For example, his claims that there are medical reasons for some of the body alterations he has initiated have often been dismissed or ignored. Jackson's claims must be examined critically, but many of his critics appear to make the same mistake that Barnum claimed his critics made: they carry skepticism so far that they "will sometimes deceive themselves by being too incredulous."[31] In other words, we can acknowledge Jackson's manipulation of enfreakment while also acknowledging the plausibility of some of his claims. If Jackson does have vitiligo (and the police department's examination in 1993 indicates that he does have either vitiligo or a symptomatically related disorder), that alone supplies a surprisingly rich ground for an "affinity" with Merrick. The traditional diagnosis of Merrick's disorder was that he had a severe form of neurofibromatosis. This diagnosis has very recently been corrected, but the medical books Jackson would have consulted about the Elephant Man in the mid-1980s would have offered the neurofibromatosis diagnosis—and since this disease affects skin pigmentation, medical textbooks typically discuss it together with vitiligo, partial albinism, and other dermatological disorders.[32] Thus it is possible, even probable, that while Jackson perused a medical book for information on the Elephant Man's disease, he stumbled on a discussion of his own disorder—or vice-versa. The empathy Jackson might already have been feeling for the Elephant Man would have been ratified by the manner in which medical classification had associated the two disorders.

Moreover, Jackson's alleged vitiligo suggests another dimension to his complex self-image. There is a long history in the United States and Europe of blacks with curiously mottled skin being exhibited in dime museums, circuses, and carnivals as well as at medical colleges and academies of science (see fig. 26.2). Jackson may very well have learned about this aspect of

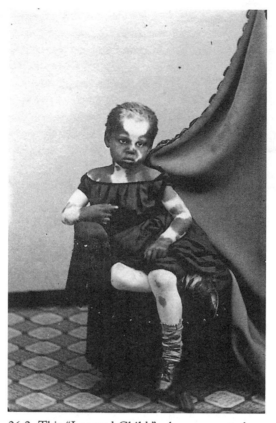

26.2. This "Leopard Child," who appears to have vitiligo, was exhibited by P. T. Barnum at the American Museum. Photograph by Mathew Brady. The Meserve Collection at the National Portrait Gallery, Smithsonian Institution.

the sideshow, given his keen interest in theater history, Barnum, and freaks. Whatever the extent of Jackson's awareness of "Human Leopards" and "Spotted Families," he has admitted to feeling extremely self-conscious about performing while suffering from vitiligo, even though the evidence of his disorder is hidden.

Against the intertwined historical background of blacks as physical curiosities and blacks as entertainers, Jackson's body remains enigmatic, but at least we are now able to situate the enigma itself in a meaningful historical context. If the Leopard Child represents the static enfreakment of a human curiosity, Jackson's goal is obviously to defy this fate. If his role as a boundary-breaking pop entertainer necessarily entails a degree of enfreakment, Jackson means to use enfreakment itself to excite and manipulate his audience, while always trying to remain at least one step ahead of us.[33] The Leopard Child would likely have performed in silence while a professional talker "presented" the condition that made him a curiosity; like the Elephant Man in the Lynch movie's grim sideshow scenes, the Leopard Child might well have been obliged to strip entirely at the climax of his performance, or at least come as close to total nudity as possible. Physical exposure is fundamental to Jackson's performance as well.

One of his stage maneuvers is a measured sort of striptease: while performing a series of complicated dance moves, he slips his jacket and shirt from around his shoulders, revealing his naked torso; he turns to face the audience and freezes for just an instant—and then he covers himself and is once again in fluid, rapid motion. The point is that Jackson's "exposure" is extraordinarily brief, measured, and utterly within the performer's control. Moreover, as the most recent interviews with Jackson suggest, even instances of blatant "exposure" such as his onstage striptease may not be what they seem; cunning makeup and even plastic surgeries might be mediating between the audience and the object of its desire. And yet if this piece of stagecraft is successful, Jackson will have succeeded in titillating his audience with what appears to be a bold gesture: a celebrity relinquishing his bodily privacy, literally giving himself to us.[34]

Jackson's face has become the site for much of the debate over his freakishness. Many critics (including Michael's brother Jermaine) complain that the purpose of his nose surgeries and his white makeup is to retreat from his African-American heritage; Michael explains that he uses makeup because he wants to cover up his vitiligo blotches. But neither the accusations nor Jackson's explanations are fully satisfying. If Jackson had merely wanted to look Caucasian, he could have done so without taking his cosmetic reconstruction nearly as far as he has. And if disguising vitiligo blotches was his sole object, Jackson might have used dark makeup to cover them rather than the clown-like white makeup he uses. Taraborrelli points to evidence that the real meaning behind the facial alterations is Jackson's wish to look as little like his father as possible.[35] But Jackson's mask-like public face is too outré to be explained in these rather pedestrian ways. Jackson has constructed for himself a mask that calls attention to the fact that it is a mask; one does not have to do that if the goal is simply to look white, or to erase the family resemblance.

The most reasonable explanation for Jackson's cosmetic remodeling is that he is pursuing all of the aforementioned goals at once—and reaching beyond them. His former wife Lisa Marie Presley offers a more revealing analysis of Jackson: "He's an artist . . . if he sees an imperfection, he changes it, he's constantly remodifying something, reconstructing himself, resculpting himself."[36] Presley's analysis brings the controversy over Jackson's body back to the issue of plasticity. Thus Jackson's bodily reconstruction becomes the most spectacular demonstration of his power over "natural history": he refuses to be limited by inherited traits. Does Jackson defy natural history out of a hatred for his father? Does he defy inherited racial characteristics because he is ashamed to be black? Persistently queried about the racial issue, Jackson has always replied, predictably, that he is proud to be black.[37] His face, the site of so much controversy and interpretation, reveals that his cosmetic project is more inclusive than his critics maintain. The point is not to so much to exclude blackness or his paternity, but to include all the things Jackson is *not* supposed to be. The effect of Jackson's alterations is to make him look androgynous rather than feminine, multiracial rather than "black" or "white." Jackson, long fascinated by his Asian fans, has given himself eyes that look more Asian than Caucasian. Color photographs of Jackson show that he varies his facial skin tone a great deal: often it is extremely white, but sometimes it is much darker, closer to bronze. It is as if Jackson, who has long aimed at entertaining all the world's peoples despite profound differences of language, culture, and race, has tried to make himself *look* the part of the universal entertainer. The modification of his face allows him to appear utterly unique, and in appearing unique he becomes accessible to everyone. Jackson in his public makeup and costume looks like nothing so much as a meticulously indeterminate cartoon character in a Disney movie: the hybrid, not-quite-Indian Pocahontas or the not-quite-Semitic Aladdin. Jackson has made his face into a "grotesque" in the sense that it has become a complex amalgam of signifying characteristics that together prevent Jackson from being "read" or typed in conventional ways: the boundaries of race, gender, and age do not seem to apply to Jackson.

And yet the spectacle of Jackson's "whiteface" mask often astonishes and offends because its strangeness compels us to examine how culture constructs meanings around bodily differences—and the fact that such constructed meanings are often irrational. Thus Jackson's putatively comforting explanation that he uses cosmetics only to disguise his vitiligo lesions serves not so much to settle the matter as to provoke a deeper question: Why do we call vitiligo a "disease" if its only "symptoms" are cosmetic? Is the anxiety and discomfort, the disease, of our neighbors enough to constitute "sickness"? For other critics, Jackson's face may be seen as a kind of brutal caricature of the more subtle efforts many undergo every day to lighten themselves and reap the social and economic rewards believed to be bestowed on the lighter-skinned in our society.[38] Is Jackson's face offensive because it compels us to examine the role of *complexion* (not simply "race") in constructing a social hierarchy?

Hopefully this chapter has already indicated why the physical inspection Jackson underwent in 1993 (the inspection and filming of his body and its vitiligo lesions) was a realization of his worst fears. The parallel between Jackson's inspection ordeal and the freak show is clear, although the involuntary condition of the inspection made it a more genuinely abject situation. Jackson, devotee of Lynch's *Elephant Man,* might well have had that movie's grim sideshow scenes or perhaps the later scenes at the medical theater in mind as he anticipated his own inspection.

According to biographer Christopher Andersen, the inspection was performed early in the Justice Department's investigation (December 1993) because police were concerned that Jackson had already begun to alter the markings on and around his genitals and torso, markings that prosecutors would use to corroborate the alleged victim's claim that he "had an intimate knowledge of Michael's body."[39] When Jackson's attempts to avoid the inspection failed, he was duly examined at his Neverland estate by a team of two police officers, one police department physician, one still photographer, and one videographer. A distraught Jackson pleaded, "Please, do I have to go through with this?" but to no avail. Reportedly, the police were specifically trying to verify the plaintiff's description of Jackson as being "half black and half white," and having black rings around his thighs and buttocks and "pink-white vitiligo blotches around his genitals."[40] The photographer and videographer "circled him slowly, making a painstaking visual record" of Jackson's lower body for about five minutes, after which Jackson cried "Make them stop!" The men stopped photographing him, but then Jackson was examined by the physician, "who spent another fifteen minutes scribbling down detailed notes about the distinguishing characteristics of Michael's buttocks and genitalia." Allegedly, the Santa Barbara District Attorney had wanted the physician to "measure the size of Jackson's genitals and the dimensions of the skin discolorations . . . but Cochran [Johnnie Cochran, Jackson's attorney at the time] successfully fought that request."[41]

The accuracy of the details included in this account may never be fully verified; Andersen has not named his sources.[42] Both the criminal and civil court cases against Jackson were dismissed after he settled the civil case. The police records are obviously confidential. My reason for repeating Andersen's version of the event is that his account (and related versions) has been most widely disseminated, and it is the public's impression of the event that is important to this analysis. At any rate, the essentials of the story were verified by Jackson himself in a press conference he held two days after he was examined. If the most immediate threat to Jackson was prosecution, he was nevertheless equally concerned about the threat to his public image. It turned out to be the latter threat that sustained itself; the threat of prosecution was quickly scuttled by a settlement rumored to be in the millions of dollars. Ultimately, what counted in the Jackson sex scandal was the classic struggle he had been waging virtually his entire life: the struggle to control his image, avoid static enfreakment, and maintain his aura of mystery. Jackson rightly perceived the examination as an effort to strip away his public persona and discover the "intimate" facts about him. Such an effort, however legal, was viewed by Jackson as having ramifications that went well beyond the specific allegations he faced. For Jackson, the examination was an assault not only on his right to "privacy" (which even the noncelebrity enjoys) but on his right to preserve the mysteriousness of his *public* persona. Moreover, the molestation scandal threatened to explode the oxymoronic role that Jackson had tried to live out for so long: the role of harmless transgressor. Jackson's once playful sexual ambiguity seemed to be hardening into a tangibly abhorrent perversion. The physical examination, which sought to interpret vitiligo markings as if they were hieroglyphs, and the FBI's anthropometric "proof" that Jackson fit the profile of the child molester were from this perspective attempts to "fix" Jackson, classify his body and his character, and dispel all ambiguities.[43]

Jackson understood, then, that the press conference he held to offer his version of the examination's meaning would be crucial—even if his court cases were dismissed. His appeal was written carefully with help from his advisors. The four-minute press conference was first broadcast live worldwide on CNN and then again on the network evening news. In his statement Jackson proclaimed his innocence and called for a "speedy end to this horrifying, horrifying experience." He demanded: "Don't treat me like a criminal, because I am innocent." The focus of his statement, however, was on the "dehumanizing and humiliating" physical inspection: "They served a search warrant on me which allowed them to view and photograph my body, including my penis, my buttocks, my lower torso, thighs, and any other areas that they wanted. . . . It was the most humiliating ordeal of my life. . . . But if this is what I have to endure to prove my innocence, so be it."[44]

Whatever Jackson's innocence or guilt, his speech was riveting and powerful. He not only firmly denied any wrongdoing, he allowed the viewer to imagine how degrading it would be for an innocent man to be examined in such a way by the authorities. Jackson's statement evokes both recent and historical encounters between blacks and the law: the Rodney King beating, Clarence Thomas's self-described "high-tech lynching," the studied persecution and humiliation of blacks by police during and preceding the civil rights movement. One of the tragedies endemic to a nation with a history of legalized racial injustice is that an event like the examination of Jackson's body carries with it racist overtones, whatever the specific legal necessity invoked by authorities, and whether Jackson is guilty or innocent of the charges.

However, it does not seem that Jackson has been entirely successful in reversing the damage the molestation scandal wrought. The press still keeps a watchful eye on Jackson whenever he is around children. Jackson's ability to manipulate the press and reinvent his public image is still formidable, but his assumption that he can completely master the audience was always false; the apparent failure of the *HIStory* album to reach the lofty sales goals set for it despite a vast promotion campaign is the most recent evidence of that. Jackson's contrived "controversies" have a way of getting out of his control, and unplanned controversies have a way of upstaging his best-laid plans.

On the other hand, Jackson's public still cannot claim to have an "intimate knowledge" of the pop star either; they still have not penetrated his mystery. After his December 1993 press conference, "lie detection" experts pounced on the tape of his testimony: one consultant declared, "The stress in Jackson's voice shows that he's lying."[45] But the would-be anthropometrists who claim to have discovered the incontrovertible truth about Jackson have never been convincing. Jackson, for his part, has failed to accept that his deliberate indeterminacy will always allow the audience to imagine its own version of his character, his longings, and his motives. If Jackson's fans and critics are denied the final knowledge that they are feverishly pursuing and are instead forced to invent it, his bid to control his audience is equally fruitless.

NOTES

1. Robert Bogdan, *Freak Show: Presenting Human Oddities for Amusement and Profit* (Chicago: University of Chicago Press, 1988), 2.

2. Dave Marsh and John Swenson, eds., *The New Rolling Stone Record Guide*, rev. ed. (New York: Random House, 1983), 248.

3. Excerpt from a review published in *The New Yorker*. Quoted in J. Randy Taraborrelli, *Michael Jackson: The Magic and the Madness* (New York: Ballantine, 1992), i.

4. Don King, quoted in Taraborrelli, *Michael Jackson*, 445.

5. The Neverland ranch is Jackson's estate in California. Margot [sic] Jefferson, "Michael, Lisa, Diane and a Greek Chorus." *New York Times @times top news online*, America Online, 25 June 1995.

6. Ibid. In 1996, after this chapter was submitted for publication, Jackon and Lisa Marie divorced.

7. David Hevey, *The Creature Time Forgot: Photography and Disability Imagery* (New York: Routledge, 1992), 53.

8. Peter W. Graham and Fritz H. Oehlschlaeger, *Articulating the Elephant Man: Joseph Merrick and His Interpreters* (Baltimore: Johns Hopkins University Press, 1992), 10–11.

9. For my use of the term "static enfreakment" I gratefully acknowledge David Hevey, who coined the basic term "enfreakment."

10. In this chapter, the pronoun "he" refers to either gender in those sentences where avoiding a gendered pronoun would be awkward; since the principle referent in this essay is Michael Jackson, I feel that this use of "he" is appropriate.

11. Taraborrelli, *Michael Jackson*, 388.

12. Michael Jackson, *Moonwalk* (New York: Doubleday, 1988), 213.

13. The "moonwalk" is the name Jackson uses for a dance move that has come to be closely associated with him (although he did not invent it). To "moonwalk" is to glide backwards while your feet appear to be moving forwards.

14. Legless sideshow performers are called "half men" or "legless wonders" in carnival parlance.

15. See, e.g., *Moonwalk*, 213–15; and note 17 below.

16. See Eric Lott, *Love and Theft: Blackface Minstrelsy and the American Working Class* (New York: Oxford University Press, 1993), for an excellent discussion of the ideology of blackface minstrelsy.

17. The earliest black entertainers in America, of course, were slaves managed by white owners. Later black stars (singers, dancers, musicians) were usually tightly controlled by white managers. The black entertainer was typically viewed as gifted with a splendid natural talent (for singing, dancing, etc.) but lacking in the intellectual power to manage, or even to fully understand, his talent. Eventually, black managers and label owners began to appear (Motown's Berry Gordy being the most famous), but like their predecessors, they continued to exercise complete control over the performers; still later, black pop singers such as Stevie Wonder and Marvin Gaye became powerful enough to insist on a greater measure of autonomy. Jackson was keenly aware of these developments, and he was the only member of

the Jackson 5 to actually confront Berry Gordy and demand that the group have more control over the "product" (Taraborrelli, *Michael Jackson*, 426). For more on Jackson's early career, see Jackson, *Moonwalk*; and Taraborrelli, *Michael Jackson*.

18. Quoted in Taraborrelli, *Michael Jackson*, 426.

19. P. T. Barnum, *Struggles and Triumphs*, ed. Carl Bode (New York: Penguin, 1981), 120.

20. Taraborrelli, *Michael Jackson*, 426.

21. In the climax to Jackson's *Smooth Criminal* film, his cyborg identity is finally revealed to his adoring band of child-fans, but significantly this revelation terrifies the children even as cyborg-Jackson rescues them from the sadistic drug-pushing villain. Jackson as planetary messiah, firing nuclear missiles from his steel knuckles before flying off to a distant star, is awful in the biblical sense, and thus intimacy with him, like intimacy with Yahweh, is charged with danger even for the faithful. At Madame Tussaud's Wax Museum in London—a favorite sightseeing destination for Jackson—the wax figure of Adolf Hitler, unlike any of the other figures, is housed in its own glass cabinet. I was told that without the glass cabinet the despised Hitler's figure would doubtless be vandalized; in fact, dried spittle was visible on the outer glass. Tussaud's "Hitler" needs to be protected from the public, but his isolation in a glass cage (like a poisonous reptile at the zoo) suggests the notion that the public still needs to be protected from him, too. Jackson himself is also represented at Tussaud's museum, where he enjoys posing next to his wax double for publicity photos.

22. Christopher Andersen, *Michael Jackson: Unauthorized* (New York: Simon and Schuster, 1994), 79.

23. Taraborrelli, *Michael Jackson*, 431.

24. Ibid., 431.

25. Ibid., 432.

26. Jackson told Oprah Winfrey that it was just "Another stupid story. Where am I gonna put some bones, and why would I want them?" (Michael Jackson, interview with Oprah Winfrey, ABC, 10 February 1993).

27. Graham and Oehlschlaeger, *Articulating the Elephant Man*, 188.

28. Ibid., 188.

29. Ibid., 190.

30. Ibid.

31. Barnum, *Struggles and Triumphs*, 281.

32. See, e.g., Jean Paul Ortonne, David B. Mosher, and Thomas B. Fitzpatrick, *Vitiligo and Other Hypomelanoses of Hair and Skin* (New York: Plenum, 1983).

33. During his recent interview with Diane Sawyer, Jackson, asked to respond to the critics' negative reaction to his controversial promotional video, cryptically replied: "That's what I wanted. They've fallen into my trap" (interview with Diane Sawyer, *PrimeTime Live*, 14 June 1995).

34. Jackson's soft-focus nude scene with Lisa Marie Presley in a recent video may be viewed in a similar way: the "exposure" is highly contrived, and while it raises our expectations, it fails to solve the mystery of Jackson's sexuality.

35. Taraborrelli, *Michael Jackson*, 253.

36. Lisa Marie Presley, interview with Diane Sawyer, *PrimeTime Live*, 14 June 1995.

37. For example, during the interview with Diane Sawyer, Jackson stated: "I love black."

38. For a discussion of skin color bias among African Americans, see Kathy Wilson, Midge Wilson, and Ronald Hall, *The Color Complex: The Politics of Skin Color among African Americans* (New York: Anchor Doubleday, 1993).

39. Andersen, *Michael Jackson: Unauthorized*, 332.

40. Ibid., 332.

41. Ibid., 333.

42. Nor have I repeated here all the details included in Andersen's treatment of the incident in *Michael Jackson: Unauthorized*; I have included the details that have been corroborated. For Andersen's complete account, see 332–40.

43. Andersen summarizes the FBI's comparison of Jackson with their "profile of a career pedophile": *"excessive interest in children; refers to children as 'pure,' 'innocent,' etc.; age and gender preference; identifies*

with children more than adults." Finally, the FBI noted: "The homes of some pedophiles have been described as shrines to children or miniature amusement parks" (ibid., 339). Hopefully it is possible to be skeptical toward the FBI's disturbingly simplistic "profile" while remaining neutral about Jackson's guilt or innocence. But if the FBI's profile describes the classic pedophile, it would also serve as a good description of Walt Disney or Bozo the Clown.

44. Quoted in ibid., 334.

45. Charles R. McQuiston, quoted in ibid., 334.

CONTRIBUTORS

RACHEL ADAMS is a doctoral candidate in English at the University of California, Santa Barbara. She is currently writing her dissertation on representations of bodily difference in twentieth-century American culture.

ROBERT BOGDAN has been teaching courses since 1971 in research methods and the sociology of disability at Syracuse University, where he directs the interdisciplinary doctoral program in social sciences.

LEONARD CASSUTO is an associate professor of English at Fordham University, and was recently a Fulbright Lecturer in Tanzania. His chapter in this volume is adapted from his forthcoming book, *The Inhuman Race: The Racial Grotesque in American Literature and Culture.*

DAVID L. CLARK is an associate professor of English at McMaster University, where he is also director of projects and programming for Plurality and Alterity: Discourses and Practices, an interdisciplinary research group. He has coedited and contributed to *Intersections: Nineteenth-Century Philosophy and Contemporary Theory* and *New Romanticisms: Theory and Critical Practice.*

JAMES W. COOK, JR., is currently finishing his Ph.D. in U.S. history at the University of California, Berkeley, where he is at work on his dissertation, entitled "Masters of Illusionism: A History of Victorian America and Its Puzzling Visual Culture."

ANDREA STULMAN DENNETT recently completed her doctoral dissertation, "The Origin and Development of the Dime Museum in America, at New York University. She has published several essays on popular entertainment including "Disaster Spectacles at the Turn of the Century" and "A Postmodern Look at EPCOT's American Adventure."

LESLIE FIEDLER is Samuel Clemens Professor of English and State University of New York Distinguished Professor at SUNY, Buffalo. The author of more than twenty-five books, he has earned numerous awards and prizes for his criticism and fiction and has lectured all over the world.

ERIC FRETZ is an assistant professor of English at Loras College in Dubuque, Iowa. He has published articles on Hawthorne and Fitzgerald.

LINDA FROST is an assistant professor of English at the University of Alabama at Birmingham. She is currently working on a book-length study of spectatorship, national identity, and nineteenth-century American popular and print cultures.

DAVID A. GERBER is a professor of American history at the State University of New York at Buffalo. His major projects as a scholar have been in the field of social history, in which he has written about racial minorities and immigrants as well as people with disabilities.

ELLEN HICKEY GRAYSON teaches the history of ideas at the Maryland Institute College of Art in Baltimore. As a Smithsonian fellow at the National Museum of American Art, she recently completed her dissertation, "Art, Audiences, and the Aesthetics of Social Order in Antebellum America: Rembrandt Peale's *Court of Death*."

ELIZABETH GROSZ teaches philosophy, women's studies, and critical theory at Monash University in Australia. She is the author of *Space, Time and Perversion: A Politics of Bodies* and the coeditor, with Elspeth Probyn, of *Sexy Bodies: The Strange Carnalities of Feminism*.

JOAN HAWKINS is an assistant professor at Indiana University, Bloomington. She is currently working on a book on the postcolonial depiction of race and racism in American horror films.

BERNTH LINDFORS is a professor of English and African literatures at the University of Texas, Austin. The founding editor of *Research in African Literatures,* he is the author and editor of numerous books, most recently *Black African Literature in English, 1987–1991* and *Long Drums and Canons: Teaching and Researching African Literatures.*

CECILE LINDSAY is a professor of French and acting dean of the Graduate School at the California State University, Chico. A serious recreational bodybuilder for eleven years, she has published a book on Claude Ollier as well as articles on fin-de-siècle and twentieth-century French literature, postmodern theory, and French feminist thought.

LORI MERISH is an assistant professor of English at Miami University, Oxford. Her work has appeared in *Novel American Quarterly* and *American Literary History.*

CATHERINE MYSER is an assistant professor in the Center for Medical Ethics, Law, and the Humanities at the University of Florida College of Medicine. A former research fellow in the Center for Biomedical Ethics at Stanford University, she has worked as a medical educator and clinical ethical consultant in medical schools and hospitals in Sweden, India, Australia, and South Africa.

RONALD E. OSTMAN is a professor of communication at Cornell University. Formerly a professional journalist, he has authored or edited four books and continues to contribute to the popular press.

SHIRLEY PETERSON teaches in the English Department of Daemen College in Amherst, New York. She is currently coediting a collection of essays on feminism and modernism.

ALLISON PINGREE is a preceptor of expository writing at Harvard University. Her research focuses on constructions of personal identity in American literature and culture. She is completing a manuscript on "figures of replication": characters, gestures, images, and language in late nineteenth- and early twentieth-century American fiction that critique dominant cultural values not through direct opposition, but through literalization.

BRIAN ROSENBERG, chair of the English Department at Allegheny College, is the author of *Little Dorrit's Shadows: Character and Contradiction in Dickens*, and *Mary Lee Settle's Beulah Quintet: The Price of Freedom*.

NIGEL ROTHFELS received his Ph.D. in history from Harvard University in 1994 and is associate editor and a research associate at the Center for Twentieth Century Studies, University of Wisconsin-Milwaukee. He is currently working on a book entitled "Bring 'Em Back Alive," an examination of the exotic animal and people trades in nineteenth-century Germany.

EDWARD L. SCHWARZSCHILD teaches American literature and culture for the Honors Program and Department of English at Sweet Briar College in Virginia. He is currently at work on a book entitled *Imagining Some United States: Photography, Nation-Making, and the American Writer*.

PAUL SEMONIN who received his Ph.D. from the University of Oregon, is a historian currently at work on a manuscript on the discovery of mastodon bones in eighteenth-century America.

ROSEMARIE GARLAND THOMSON is an assistant professor of English at Howard University. Her essays on disability in literature and culture have appeared in *American Literature, Feminist Studies*, and *Radical Teacher*. She is the author of *Extraordinary Bodies: Figuring Physical Disability in American Literature and Culture*.

CHRISTOPHER A. VAUGHAN, a journalist with extensive experience in Asia and Latin America, is an assistant professor of journalism and mass media at Rutgers University. His current project addresses issues of national and ethnic identity formation in the context of a changing communications environment.

JEFFREY A. WEINSTOCK, a university fellow in the Program in the Human Sciences at George Washington University, also lectures in the English Department. Currently at work on his dissertation on American ghost stories, he is coediting a collection entitled *Imaginary Geographies* with Jeffrey Jerome Cohen.

DAVID D. YUAN, has recently completed a dissertation in English and American literature at Stanford University, entitled "Curious Bodies: The Body as Spectacle and the American Body Politic, 1840–1898."

INDEX